ML

A HISTORY OF

CAN.

ARCI

VOLUME 1

Research was assisted by
a generous grant from

THE SOCIAL SCIENCES AND HUMANITIES
RESEARCH COUNCIL OF CANADA

Published with the assistance of

THE GETTY GRANT PROGRAM

Harold Kalman

A History of
Canadian
Architecture

Volume 1

Oxford University Press

TORONTO   NEW YORK   OXFORD

Oxford University Press
70 Wynford Drive Don Mills Ontario M3C 1J9

Oxford New York
Athens Auckland Bangkok Bombay
Calcutta Cape Town Dar es Salaam Delhi
Florence Hong Kong Istanbul Karachi
Kuala Lumpur Madras Madrid Melbourne
Mexico City Nairobi Paris Singapore
Taipei Tokyo Toronto

and associated companies in
Berlin Ibadan

Oxford is a trademark of Oxford University Press

Canadian Cataloguing in Publication Data

Kalman, Harold, 1943–
A history of Canadian architecture

Includes bibliographical references and index.
ISBN 0-19-541159-5 (v. 1 : pbk.)
ISBN 0-19-541160-9 (v. 2 : pbk.)

1. Architecture – Canada – History. I. Title.

NA740.K35 1995   720'.971   C94-931102-2

Copyright © Oxford University Press 1994

Design: Jeffrey Tabberner
Cover photograph: Owen Fitzgerald

1 2 3 4—98 97 96 95

This book is printed on permanent (acid-free) paper. ∞

Printed in Canada

CONTENTS

Abbreviations in Captions

ANQ	Archives nationales du Québec
BCARS	British Columbia Archives and Records Service
CIHB	Canadian Inventory of Historic Building
HWS	Hellmut W. Schade—Scholastic Slide Service
IBC	Inventaire des biens culturelles/Ministère de la culture et des communications du Québec
MMCH	McCord Museum of Canadian History
MTRL	Metropolitan Toronto Reference Library
NAC	National Archives of Canada
NFB	National Film Board
NMC	National Map Collection, National Archives of Canada
NSM	Nova Scotia Museum
PAM	Provincial Archives of Manitoba
PANB	Provincial Archives of New Brunswick
PANL	Provincial Archives of Newfoundland and Labrador
PANS	Public Archives of Nova Scotia
PC	Parks Canada
SAB	Saskatchewan Archives Board

PREFACE

THIS is a book about Canadian architecture—a simple enough statement, although one that may be queried by some readers, who will want to know what is meant by 'Canadian', and by 'architecture'.

The word 'architecture', for me, includes just about everything that people have built: places where they have lived and worked, utilitarian structures, monumental public buildings, engineering, landscapes, neighbourhoods, and cities. A useful term for all these things is the 'built environment'. Some writers make a distinction between 'architecture'—by which they mean 'high' architecture, structures that have been consciously designed with specific models or ideals in mind—and 'building', meaning vernacular structures that do not embody wilful design decisions. This distinction, and the traditional preference for the former, reflects the élitist values held by an earlier generation.

Times have changed. Historians in all disciplines have shown an ever-growing interest in the ways of life and accomplishments of 'ordinary people' from all cultures, along with those of the political and other leaders of the dominant societies. Taking a cue from geographers and ethnographers, architectural historians have recently turned their attention to vernacular building—dwellings, farms, and factories of working people and ethnic minorities. 'Architecture' and 'building' are not really different species at all, and they now share centre stage. This book maintains the new enthusiasm for the commonplace—without losing any passion for the impressive, fashioned monuments that assert the status of the powerful. Canada is made up of people in all walks of life, and our history can be told only by appreciating everybody's architecture.

By 'Canadian' I mean the architecture of the many cultural groups that have lived within the geographical boundaries of Canada ('...from Bonavista to Vancouver Island/From the Arctic Islands to the Great Lakes waters/This land was made for you and me.'), as well as architecture that is characteristically Canadian. Some curmudgeons have wrongly argued that the latter does not exist. It is true that much that was built in Canada was derivative, closely related to sources in Europe and the United States. But that did not prevent the development of a uniquely Canadian character. Early houses in the St Lawrence valley differ from those that preceded them in France; Georgian houses in Nova Scotia and Ontario are not the same as British or New England Georgian (nor were they like each other); the buildings of Ukrainian-Canadians in the Prairies were inspired by those in the Old Country, but are unique to their new land; Prairie modernism is distinct from modernism elsewhere; and British Columbia's aboriginal peoples built marvellous dwellings that resemble nothing found anywhere else. These differences are *Canadian*. Architecture, after all, is no more or less than an expression of the values of the people who built it. And just as Canada has a unique social and political history, so too does it have a unique architectural history.

This work, then, is not just a history of Canadian architecture; it is also a summary history of Canada and Canadians as seen in their most permanent creations: buildings and communities. Architecture is both the design and the expression of a culture, and these two themes are interwoven from start to finish. Another recurrent theme is the interaction of people with their environment, to produce shelter and buildings for their activities. All these perspectives, seen together, will help the reader to understand why people built the way they did.

Much has been published about Canadian architecture, but most writers have tended to focus rather narrowly on a particular region, period, architect, style, building-type, or cultural group. Few have ventured to look at the country as a whole. The principal exception was Alan Gowans, who did so in his *Looking at Architecture in Canada* of 1958, which was expanded in 1966 as *Building Canada: An Architectural History of Canadian Life*. (Interestingly, these two books were produced by the same editor and publisher—William Toye and Oxford University Press Canada—as the present history, and Gowans and I both studied under the same mentor, the late Donald Drew Egbert at Princeton University.) Alan Gowans' landmark publications, and the Canadian Centennial of 1967, were two factors that inspired increasingly sophisticated architectural scholarship, which in turn led to many fine books and articles on specific aspects of Canadian architecture. But while the recent works superseded much of Gowans' pioneering research, they tended to lose sight of the big picture he painted.

This *History of Canadian Architecture* is the first comprehensive study to incorporate the superb research of the last quarter-century. The first volume begins with aboriginal structures in the East and ends with both native and European-Canadian buildings in the West; the second volume moves from the effect of the transcontinental railway on the opening up of the country, and proceeds—with stops to look at town-planning and at building in the Far North—to examine modern and post-modern architecture. The two volumes together encompass buildings and communities throughout the land, discussing those of all its peoples, including First Nations, the French and British who founded the present political system, and many among the Europeans and Asians who chose to make Canada their home. The primary objective has been to make available a vast cache of material to a wide audience in a clearly organized and readable manner. Because of the wealth of recent published and unpublished research, secondary sources have provided the main fund of information. They are identified in the endnotes, where the reader will find an extensive bibliography pertaining to the entire scope of this history of Canadian architecture.

The organization follows no rigorous framework, but rather flows in a way that I thought best suits each period and architectural event under discussion. Some chapters are organized around historical periods or geographical regions, while others treat certain architectural styles or building-types. While the work embraces all built phenomena, its main focus is on *buildings*. It is not a history of interior design, construction, engineering, landscape architecture, urban planning, or heritage conservation—although it addresses aspects of all those important disciplines. Because of the breadth of Canadian architecture, the text has had to be selective—some buildings are discussed in detail, others are passed over quickly, and many important buildings have regrettably been omitted. Planning is a recurrent theme—Chapter 12 is devoted to it, and many other chapters feature discussions of individual cities whose development epitomizes the themes of those chapters. But these ventures into planning are only sidebars, and are not to be taken as comprehensive urban histories.

A few words about technical details. Measures are given in both imperial and metric format (but when the dimension comes from a historical text, its original form is retained). Translations from French that are not otherwise credited are by the author. Birth and death dates, where known, are given for architects (and many engineers, artisans, and builders), but not for people in other walks of life. Buildings and places that are illustrated are initially cited in **bold-face** type. The text (in the use of the past or present tense) indicates whether a building has been demolished. Dates given for buildings are usually those of the construction of the primary portion, as closely as can be determined. In order to show as many buildings as possible, the illustrations are primarily exterior 'portraits', with consequently a limited number of plans and interiors (and no details). Secondary views are often available in the works cited in the endnotes.

While many individuals and institutions (as well as countless works of scholarship) have contributed to this study, it is in some ways the co-operative product of the community of architectural historians. The Social Sciences and Humanities Research Council of Canada contributed generously to research; and the Getty Grant Program contributed generously to publication. My own firm, Commonwealth Historic Resource Management Limited—and in particular John J. Stewart, my co-principal—allowed me the time to write this book. Linda Kalman, my wife, gracefully accepted its incursions into our home life. William Toye, C.M., has edited the manuscript tirelessly, while improving the text immeasurably with some of his own sensitive observations of architecture and history. I am also grateful to Sally Livingston for preparing the detailed indexes for both volumes.

The book has benefited from suggestions and criticisms offered by its Board of Advisers, who include Canada's best architectural historians. One adviser was exceptionally helpful in a second role: Robert Hill shared his immense research on Canadian architects, which is to be published as *A Biographical Dictionary of Architects in Canada: 1800-1950*.

Many people assisted with research: Carolyn Young, Meg Stanley, Fern Graham, Edgar Tumak, Ian Doull, Diane Kalman, Judy Oberlander, and Larry Turner. Meg Stanley and Patricia Buckley procured the illustrations. Kirtlye Woodruff and Janice Sonnen assisted with administrative tasks. David Byrnes executed the drawings, using AutoCAD and a personal computer. Hellmut W. Schade and Brian Merrett, two of the many architectural photographers represented, took numerous pictures on request. Architectural historian William Dendy, some of whose photographs are included, intended to provide more, but his death in May 1993 prevented this.

In addition, countless people across the country were contacted for specific information or illustrations. Their help is acknowledged in the endnotes, and my warm thanks go out to them all.

HAROLD KALMAN

BOARD OF ADVISERS

CHAPTER 1

THE FIRST BUILDINGS

MOST ARCHAEOLOGISTS agree that the first humans arrived in North America at the end of the last ice age, about 12,000 BC (expressed by archaeologists as 14,000 BP—before present). They came from Asia by way of the land-bridge across the Bering Sea, and settled in unglaciated portions of Alaska and the Yukon. Around 12,000 BP their descendants migrated southeastward, between the Laurentian and Cordilleran ice sheets—the glaciers that covered today's Rocky Mountains and Laurentian Shield—populating large portions of the continent by 10,000 BP.[1]

In each of Canada's geographical regions, aboriginal people—Canada's First Nations—developed appropriate architectural forms, responding to environmental challenges with the materials that were readily available. Trees provided saplings, boughs, and bark; the earth yielded rocks, sod, and snow; and the hunt supplied skins and bones. Tools were fashioned from a variety of materials. A strong sense of design, and sophisticated methods of joining materials, produced an impressively broad range of buildings for a variety of dwellings and ritual uses. Many cultures developed a different type of dwelling for each season, and for each activity. The winter required a well-insulated structure that would withstand the cold and the snow, while summer dwellings had to provide ventilation. Portable dwellings served the hunt, whereas permanent ones were better suited for agriculture and fishing. Once a building-form had developed and proved its value, it persisted as long as the people retained their ways.

Initial contact with Europeans forms the watershed around which the native past is divided into two periods: the prehistoric, or pre-contact, era, which lasted for many millennia; and the historic, or post-contact, age, whose duration has been less than five hundred years.

Our knowledge of the earliest peoples and their shelters is scanty. A few caves that show signs of human occupation for 10,000 years or more have been discovered in the northwest part of the continent. The Bluefish Caves in northern Yukon, where humans butchered large mammals somewhere between 10,000 and 13,000 BP (or possibly earlier), may be the oldest. The Charlie Lake Cave, near Fort St John, British Columbia, contains cultural deposits—tools, a bead, and bison bones—that go back to about 10,500 BP. But there is no evidence to show that it was used as a shelter. It is thought that the early Peace River Bison Hunters who occupied it may have lived in skin tents.[2]

More is known about the dwellings of later cultures, particularly those that flourished during the last two millennia. Sources of information on prehistoric architecture are nevertheless elusive and incomplete. The descriptions and drawings made by the earliest explorers and missionaries reveal the nature of buildings at the time of initial contact and, by extension, the buildings of the late prehistoric period. For an understanding of the structures of earlier eras, we must rely on archaeological investigation.

Architectural historians in Canada have shown little interest in native buildings. The relevant literature is almost exclusively the work of anthropologists, archaeologists, and social historians, whose interest in native architecture is motivated far more by what it may reveal about the customs of the people who built and occupied the constructions than by their nature. Although architectural history is concerned with the social and economic reasons for buildings' being what they are, its primary interest is in the built artifacts themselves. The following discussion of aboriginal building, therefore, translates the observations of one set of disciplines into the language and framework of another.

This chapter looks selectively at the architecture of native peoples who lived in the eastern part of Canada: in the cultural area that is known as the Eastern Woodlands, as well as in the eastern part of the immense Subarctic region. It also examines the buildings of the first Europeans who made contact with the aboriginal people. The architecture of the Plains Indians is discussed in Chapter 7; that of the Northwest Coast and Plateau Indians in Chapter 8; and the dwellings of the aboriginal peoples in the Arctic are introduced in Chapter 13.

Aboriginal Peoples in the East

The Eastern Woodlands Indians

The natives who lived in the hardwood and coniferous forests of today's eastern Canada—from the Maritimes to the Great Lakes, as well as in much of the northeastern United States—were made up of two unrelated linguistic groups: Iroquoian and Algonquian. At contact, the Iroquoian groups lived in the St Lawrence Valley and southern Ontario. The Algonquian groups were located east, north, and west of them: in the Atlantic provinces, the Ottawa River Valley, north of Lake Huron, and the Lake Superior region. Both subsisted on hunting, fishing, and gathering, and the Iroquoian groups also depended on agriculture—on growing corn, squash, and beans. The trapping of fur-bearing animals, particularly beaver, became essential to the native economy in the historic period, once the Europeans came to North America to trade for furs.

The primary dwelling of both groups was built with a frame of branches or saplings and covered by bark or mats. Details varied between groups, and among tribes or regions. The Iroquoian dwelling, known as the longhouse, was long and narrow, and was home to many related families. The Algonquian dwelling, the wigwam, was usually circular or oblong in plan, and either conical or domed in form, and was generally occupied by only one or two families.

The Iroquoian longhouse The peoples who spoke the Iroquoian languages included the Huron, who lived east of Georgian Bay; the Petun, southeast of Georgian Bay; the Neutrals, centred in the Hamilton-Niagara area and near present-day Brantford; and the St Lawrence Iroquoians, who lived along that river. The traditional home of the Five Nations

Iroquois (the Mohawk, Oneida, Onondaga, Cayuga, and Seneca) was in the Finger Lakes region of today's New York State, until many of them came to Canada as United Empire Loyalists after the American Revolution. Although the Five Nations more or less annihilated both the Hurons and the Neutrals in the seventeenth century, all of the Iroquoian groups had similar lifeways and shelters. With an economy that was to a considerable extent agriculturally based, they created stable settlements with semi-permanent structures, and would remain in one place as long as the land they cultivated was productive—often a few decades.

The basic Iroquoian dwelling was the **longhouse** [1.1], an oblong bark-covered structure that was inhabited by a number of families related matrilineally (through the mother's side). The 'elevation of the cabins of the savages' has been reproduced from a map of Fort Frontenac, near today's Kingston, Ontario, and was drawn *c*. 1720. The longhouse varied greatly in size. The typical Huron longhouse was about 80 by 28 feet (24 by 8 m) and had three hearths down the centre (two families usually shared a hearth), although the length might be between 30 and 180 feet (9 and 55 m), and there might be as many as twelve fires. The village consisted of a group of longhouses, often surrounded by a palisade. Most villages were located on defensible sites near water, wood, and arable land. The siting of houses became increasingly uniform over time, and eventually many houses were oriented northwest-southeast, so that the end faced the prevailing winter winds. Although the distance between houses varied, 10 feet (3 m) may be taken as the norm.[3]

Archaeologists have identified the remains of oval (and probably communal) houses on sites dating to the end of the first millenium AD at Princess Point (near today's Hamilton) and on Kipp Island (in the Seneca River, NY), and the origins of the longhouse may well go back several thousand years earlier. A twelfth-century Pickering culture village—called the Miller site, east of Toronto—contained at least six longhouses between 38 feet (11.6 m) and 60 feet (18.3 m) long, with parallel walls, rounded ends, and as many as five hearths in each. A defensive palisade of poles surrounded the village. During the next few centuries, longhouses and villages grew in size.

The **Nodwell site [1.2]** near Southampton on Lake Huron, inhabited around 1340, had twelve longhouses of varying sizes, the largest being 139 feet (42.4 m) long. (The traces of one house lay

1.1 Longhouse near Fort Frontenac (Kingston, Ontario). Detail from a map of Fort Frontenac, *c*. 1720. Edward E. Ayer Collection, The Newberry Library, Chicago. From a photograph held by the NAC.

although the size of the individual longhouse appears to have diminished. At the **Draper site [1.3]**, a Huron village northeast of Toronto, four phases of village growth over the period of only a few decades can be identified, culminating in a 15-acre (6-hectare) settlement with 38 longhouses surrounded by a triple palisade; it was likely home to more than 2,000 people.[5] A century later, in 1615, Champlain wrote that the Huron village of Cahiagué, east of Georgian Bay, had 'two hundred fairly large lodges', although he may have been exaggerating—and the site appears as well to have been two separate villages. The average Huron village in the early seventeenth century accommodated some 1,200 people.

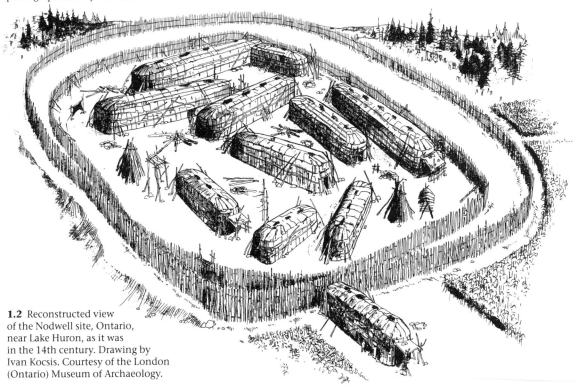

1.2 Reconstructed view of the Nodwell site, Ontario, near Lake Huron, as it was in the 14th century. Drawing by Ivan Kocsis. Courtesy of the London (Ontario) Museum of Archaeology.

beneath two others; hence the illustration shows only eleven.) The houses varied in size and interior arrangement, suggesting that they were expanded as needs changed. A double palisade surrounded this village, where an estimated five hundred people lived for at least twenty years.[4]

Around AD 1500, shortly before contact with Europeans, the Iroquoian world mushroomed in size, reaching an estimated population of 60,000 by the beginning of the seventeenth century. Villages grew rapidly and were more heavily fortified,

The Iroquois villages and longhouses south of Lake Ontario were even larger. A late-fourteenth-century structure some 334 feet (102 m) long and 23 feet (7 m) wide was found at Hodwell Hill near Syracuse, New York, and one 400 feet (122 m) long was identified at the nearby Schoff site (1410). These villages rarely exceeded one hundred longhouses. One of the largest in Ontario was at the Moyer site, in the southwestern part of the province near the Forks of the Grand River, which measured 306 feet (93.3 m) by 28 feet (8.4 m).

1.3 Reconstructed view of the Draper Site, east of Toronto, Ontario, as it was in the 16th century. Drawing by Ivan Kocsis. Courtesy of the London (Ontario) Museum of Archaeology.

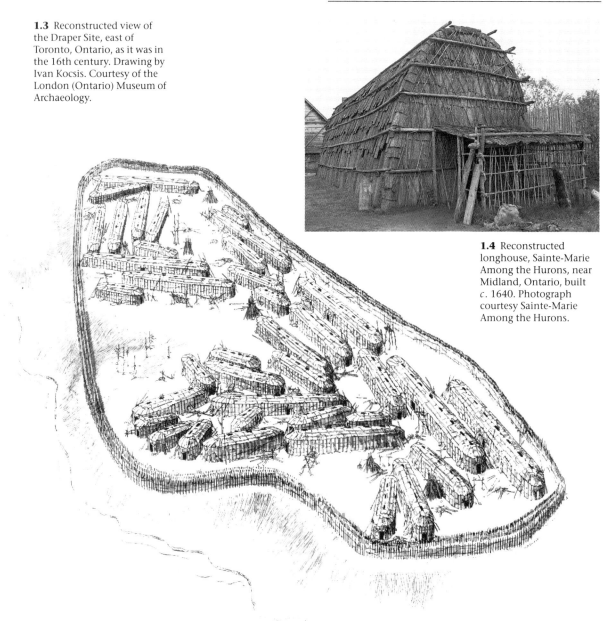

1.4 Reconstructed longhouse, Sainte-Marie Among the Hurons, near Midland, Ontario, built *c.* 1640. Photograph courtesy Sainte-Marie Among the Hurons.

The exterior walls of the longhouse were constructed by driving into the ground a double row of saplings 2 to 4 inches (5 to 10 cm) in diameter and eighteen inches (45 cm) apart. The poles of the opposite walls were bent towards each other and tied at the top to form a tensile barrel-vaulted frame. Sheets of bark—the Huron preferred cedar, but also used elm and other woods—were fastened between the poles, and additional saplings were attached horizontally on the outside for reinforcement and to hold the bark in place.

Father Joseph-François Lafitau, a Jesuit missionary who was posted near today's Montreal in the early eighteenth century, sketched a five-fire longhouse and described its exterior covering. He noted that the bark slabs were around 6 feet by 1 foot, and continued:

These pieces of bark lap one over the other like slate. They are secured outside with fresh poles similar to those which form the frame roof underneath, and are still further strengthened by long pieces of saplings split in two, and are fastened to

4

the extremities of the roof, on the sides, or on the wings, by pieces of wood cut with hooked ends, which are regularly spaced for this purpose.[6]

Posts placed down the centre provided additional support for the roof. Holes were cut in the roof to allow smoke to escape, and these provided the only light. A door was usually located at or near each end.

Sleeping platforms were arranged along both long walls, leaving a corridor about 10 or 12 feet (3 to 3.7 m) wide down the middle. The hearths were located some 20 feet (6 m) apart along this central passage. Two families shared a hearth, one family on either side. A vestibule at either end of the longhouse provided storage space for corn and firewood, and additional storage was available beneath the beds. If it is assumed that a typical family had about eight members, and that a hearth served two families, then the number of occupants of a particular longhouse would have been about sixteen times its number of hearths.

Each longhouse was probably home to a defined social group, likely an extended 'matrilocal' family. Life within the longhouse was communal, with all economic and social needs shared. In this respect the longhouse was a microcosm of Iroquoian society. The natives recognized this, and used architectural terminology—indeed, the longhouse itself—

1.5 Drawing of the interior of a longhouse, Sainte-Marie Among the Hurons, by Carole Richards. Courtesy Sainte-Marie Among the Hurons.

as a metaphor for life. The League of Five (later Six) Nations—the confederacy of Iroquois tribes in northern New York State—called themselves the 'people of the longhouse'. The westernmost tribe, the Seneca, were called the 'keepers of the western door', and the Mohawks, who lived in the east by the Hudson River, were the 'keepers of the eastern door'. The Onondaga in the centre were the 'keepers of the fire'.

Since longhouses were made of perishable materials, our knowledge of them is based on early descriptions, the drawings of European observers, and archaeological investigation. A more tangible notion of their appearance can be appreciated at **Sainte-Marie Among the Hurons [1.4]**, the reconstructed Jesuit mission near Midland, Ontario, where replicas of a longhouse, a second longhouse frame, and an Algonquian wigwam have been built, along with a dozen-and-a-half timber buildings that were originally erected by the priests and their helpers. Missionaries had worked among the people of Huronia since 1615. In 1639 the Jesuits began to build a permanent establishment, believing that it might provide the natives with an example of civilized Christian life. Ten years later the mission was burned by its occupants to prevent it from falling into the hands of an attacking party of Iroquois. (In this year, 1649, Fathers Jean de Brébeuf and Gabriel Lalemant were tortured and burned at the stake.) The construction of replicas of 22 buildings at the mission was undertaken in the 1960s under the direction of Dr Wilfrid Jury of the University of Western Ontario's Museum of Indian Archaeology, after years of painstaking archaeological and documentary research by Kenneth Kidd of the Royal Ontario Museum and by Jury. The new construction focused on the buildings in the European compound, but also included a four-hearth longhouse from the Indians' enclosure, which had originally been built in the Huron fashion by French labourers under the direction of Father Isaac Jogues.[7] Other longhouses have been reconstructed elsewhere in Ontario, in Midland and at the Lawson site near London.

No reconstruction can capture the smoke, dust, gloom, smells, sounds, insects, and mice that permeated the original longhouses [1.5]. While longhouse life was surely comfortable for the natives, Europeans found it intolerable. In the series of reports sent from Quebec to the Provincial Father of the Society of Jesus in Paris, known as the *Jesuit Relations*, Father Jérôme Lalemant describes his own jaded response to the Hurons' domestic life:

If you go to visit them in their cabins—and you must go there oftener than once a day, if you would perform your duty as you ought,—you will find there a miniature picture of Hell,—seeing nothing ordinarily but fire and smoke, and on every side naked bodies, black and half roasted, mingled pell-mell with the dogs, which are held as dear as the children of the house, and share the beds, plates and food of their masters. Everything is in a cloud of dust, and, if you go within, you will not reach the end of the cabin before you are completely befouled with soot, filth and dirt.[8]

The Ontario Iroquois, particularly the Hurons, were dispersed and nearly destroyed by the Five Nations Iroquois. Those who survived war and disease were absorbed into the dominant New York tribes. The social system changed, formal village life disintegrated, traditional building techniques were lost, and the Ontario Iroquoian languages became extinct. Despite the massive changes, the Iroquois of today in southern and eastern Ontario and southwestern Quebec still respect the tradition of the longhouse. Many continue to build it as a sacred meeting-hall, although the contemporary longhouse has log or stud walls and gabled roofs.

1.6 Longhouse, Sour Springs, Six Nations Reserve, near Brantford, Ontario, c. 1870s. Photographed in 1943. Peabody and Essex Museum/Peabody Museum Collection/neg. A3255 (E.S. Dodge).

The **Seneca longhouse at the Six Nations Reserve** [1.6] near Brantford, Ontario, is a log building that was erected in this manner in the 1870s. About one-fifth of the community on the reserve consider themselves to be 'followers of the longhouse'.[9]

The Algonquian wigwam The people who spoke the Algonquian languages included the Beothuk, a now-extinct group who lived in today's Newfoundland; the Micmac, who lived in the coastal areas of the present-day Maritime Provinces and the Gaspé peninsula; the Algonquin, in the Ottawa River Valley; the Ottawa, located further west; the Ojibwa, who occupied the land between Georgian Bay and Lake Superior; and the Cree, who were distributed from northern Quebec to the Alberta plains. Since many built their traditional dwellings well into historic times, their buildings are known more through the records of anthropologists and artists than from archaeological investigation.

The Algonquian groups had a more mobile way of life than the Iroquoians, as they were not dependent on agriculture. Their annual cycle might take them to a summer site to fish and forage for berries, to a family hunting ground, and to one or more winter homes. Consequently they developed a transportable building-type known as the wigwam. Although it differed in form among tribes and re-

6

1.7 Micmac wigwam—probably in Dartmouth, Nova Scotia—photographed in 1860. National Anthropological Archives, Smithsonian Institution/Photo No. 47728.

gions, the wigwam was generally a one- or two-family house with a round or oblong floor plan about 12 to 15 feet (3.5 to 4.5 m) in diameter and built of a frame of saplings or pliable poles that were inserted into the ground and lashed together at the top. A series of light horizontal members (stringers) was tied to the frame to strengthen it, and to support the outer covering of sheets of bark or mats of reeds. When the natives moved from one place to another, they would remove the exterior covering and carry it with them. The poles would usually be left standing, to be re-used on some later occasion either by themselves or by others. (This is a tradition that survives today among canoe-trippers in the Temagami Lakes and other parts of northern Ontario: wooden tent poles are left behind at familiar camp sites to be re-used by other travellers.)

The principal differences among wigwams are related to whether they were conical or domed in shape. The cone-shaped wigwam was used more often by Algonquian tribes in today's Canada, whereas the dome was found more frequently among those in the present northern United States. Other variations concern structural details, the nature of the cladding material, the floor plan, and patterns of use.

The Micmac in the Atlantic region built cone-shaped wigwams with circular or elliptical floor plans. Typically, four poles about 14 feet (4 m) long were lashed together at the top and the other ends would be inserted into the ground. Additional poles were then inserted between the principal ones, coming together at the top. One or more rings of horizontal stringers reinforced the cone. The outer covering was usually sheets of birchbark sewn together, but skins, woven mats, or evergreen boughs were also used. An insulating layer of grass was sometimes inserted beneath the bark. The **conical Micmac wigwam [1.7]** at Dartmouth, Nova Scotia, photographed in 1860, was covered in bark. (A twentieth-century wigwam at North Sydney on Cape Breton Island, photographed in 1916 by Frank Speck, was covered with tar paper, cloth, and bark.) Additional poles were then laid on top of the cladding to hold down the bark. A smoke hole was left open at the apex.[10]

The interior of the wigwam was a single space divided into several functional areas. The hearth occupied the centre, and cooking equipment hung

1.8 The Mamateek (Beothuk winter wigwam), drawn by Shawnadithit, 1820s. These drawings first appeared in James P. Howley's *The Beothuks or Red Indians: The Aboriginal Inhabitants of Newfoundland* (1915).

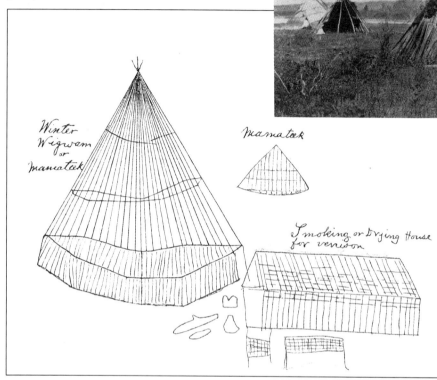

1.9 (*above*) Ojibway tents on the Red River, Manitoba. Photograph by Humphrey Lloyd Hime, 1858. PAM/N12566.

from a rack below the smoke hole. The floor was covered with interlaced scented fir boughs, and furs were placed on top of these for sleeping. Possessions were stored around the perimeter in a very space-efficient manner. As historian Duncan Campbell reported after he visited Micmac wigwams in Nova Scotia in 1873:

> There is a place for everything and everything in its place. Every post, every bar, every fastening, every tier of bark, and every appendage, whether for ornament or use, in this curious structure, has a name, and every section of the limited space has its appropriate designation and use. Perhaps it would be impossible to plan a hut of equal dimensions in which the comfort and convenience of inmates could be so effectively secured.[11]

The winter camp of the Micmac consisted of one or more wigwams in the occupants' family hunting or trapping territory; they did not grow crops before contact. Palisaded settlements existed on Cape Breton Island and at Richibuctou, on the east coast of New Brunswick. Summer settlements were arranged less formally and likely extended along a section of coast or river bank.[12]

Conical wigwams of a similar type were found among the Algonquian peoples from Newfoundland to the Great Lakes. In Newfoundland, the **Beothuk winter wigwam** [1.8] (*mamateek*) was six- or eight-sided, constructed of thin poles covered with overlapping sheets of birchbark that were held in place by additional poles that leaned against the exterior surface. The conical roof was supported on low upright walls, which were also covered with birchbark and had earth piled against them to provide additional protection from the weather. The summer *mamateek* was smaller and lacked the vertical foundation walls. The Beothuk also erected rectangular buildings, with gabled or

8

conical roofs and walls of caribou skins, for storage and for preserving meats. An important source for our knowledge of the buildings and customs of this culture is (Nancy) Shawnadithit (c. 1801-29), the last Beothuk, who recorded information and produced sketches for explorer and anthropologist William Eppes Cormack shortly before her death from tuberculosis in St John's.[13]

Father Chrestien Le Clerq described the wigwam of the Micmac who lived on the Gaspé peninsula, and marvelled at its portability:

> Their wigwams are built of nothing but poles, which are covered with some pieces of bark of the birch, sewed one to another; and they are ornamented, as a rule, with a thousand different pictures of birds, moose, otters and beavers, which the women sketch there themselves with their paints. These wigwams are of a circular form, and capable of lodging fifteen to twenty persons; but they are, however, so made that with seven or eight barks a single one is constructed, in which from three to four fires are built. They are so light and portable, that our Indians roll them up like a piece of paper, and carry them thus upon their backs wheresoever it pleases them, very much like the tortoises which carry their own houses.[14]

Far to the west, the Ojibwa who lived between Lake Huron and the eastern prairie also built conical wigwams. Humphrey Lloyd Hime photographed a group of **Ojibwa tents [1.9]** on the shore of the Red River in Manitoba in 1858, while he was

surveyor on the government expedition led by Henry Youle Hind. Three bark-covered wigwams are seen, one of them with the covering on only one side. Bundles of sticks leaning against the bottom of the dwelling in the foreground helped to keep the bark in place.

The Ojibwa also built circular and oblong domed wigwams, usually as winter dwellings. They were constructed by setting cut saplings upright into the ground at intervals of about 2 feet (60 cm) and then bending two opposite poles towards the centre and tying the ends together with strips of basswood or oak. When all the poles were so tied, horizontal members were added to strengthen the frame. A row of mats woven from cattails or bullrushes was often placed along the circumference as high as the first horizontal stringer, and the remainder of the wall and roof was covered with sheets of bark. A smoke-hole was left in the centre and the door was covered with bark, hide, or a blanket. The Irish-born author Anna Jameson sketched a pair of **domed wigwams [1.10]** at Sault Ste-Marie in the 1830s. This domical form was more common among Algonquian groups in the US than Canada, including those Ojibwa who migrated south of Lake Superior into today's Wisconsin and Minnesota (where they are known as Southwestern Chippewa). Wigwams of this kind were observed in the

1.10 Wayish-ky's Lodge, Sault Ste-Marie, Ontario. A sketch by Anna Jameson made on 31 July 1837. MTRL. By permission of J.D. Bain.

1.11 The frame of a Midewiwin lodge, Rainy River, Ontario. Photograph by T.L. Tanton, 1934. Canadian Museum of Civilization/77894.

present New England states by Giovanni da Verrazano in 1524, sketched by Champlain in 1605-6, and encountered—and imitated in their own dwellings—by the new Americans who arrived in 1620 on the *Mayflower*.[15]

The Ojibwa (and Chippewa) sometimes elongated the wigwam into forms whose plans resembled Iroquoian longhouses: the conical form was made longitudinal with the insertion of a long ridge pole. This kind of dwelling was shared by several families and called a 'long tent'. The domical wigwam was elongated for sacred use by the Midewiwin, or Grand Medicine Society, a secret-ritual society that developed among the Ojibwa and the Lake Winnipeg Saulteaux in the early eighteenth century and involved training in the medical arts. Midewiwin (*mite'wika'n*) lodges 100 feet (30 m) or more long were built of bowed saplings tied together at the top to form an arch, and the lower portion of the frame (up to about one's waist) was often covered with brush, skins, or cloth. Such a lodge—used by the Mide priests for initiation and instructional ceremonies—was sometimes known as the 'blue house', perhaps referring to the blue of Lake Superior. The **Midewiwin lodge [1.11]** at Rainy River, Ontario, is one of several such buildings that were photographed while they still stood.[16]

The Ojibwa, Saulteaux, and other Algonquian groups utilized additional ritual dwellings as well. These included the sweatlodge, a small conical tent in which water was thrown on hot stones to

1.12 A Chippewa shaman standing beside the frame of his Shaking Tent. Milwaukee Public Museum/neg. no. 50113.

make steam; the menstrual hut, a small wigwam used by women during their menses; and the smallest yet most alluring of the lot, the shaking tent.

The shaking tent (or conjuring lodge) was used by a shaman to help find lost objects or people, or to identify good hunting grounds, foresee the future, cure illness, and combat sorcery—in short, to do many of the same kinds of things that are expected of a spiritualist's séance. The tent was a circular, open-topped structure, perhaps 4 feet (1.2 m) in diameter, shaped much like a large barrel and usually covered with rawhide. Rattles were fastened to the frame. In the photograph a Chippewa shaman is seen standing next to the frame of his **shaking tent [1.12]**. After dark he would enter the tent and begin to sing and drum to summon his spirit helpers. When the supernatural assistants arrived—generally in the form of a turtle or some other animal—people would watch the tent sway wildly, see unusual lights, and hear strange animal sounds. The Lake Winnipeg Saulteaux continued this practice until the 1950s, and the Cree community at Norway House performed the shaking-tent ritual as recently as 1974.[17]

The wigwam may be encountering a contemporary revival, on both sides of the international border, because of the renewed interest among natives in the ritual of the sweatlodge.

European Visitors

Popular history credits Christopher Columbus with having 'discovered' the Americas in 1492, and names John Cabot as the first European to visit Canada, five years later. But European fishermen had already been aware for centuries of the continent across the Atlantic Ocean. Their principal point of early contact was the Strait of Belle Isle, the narrow passage that separates today's Newfoundland from Labrador. Adventurers from Scandinavia created temporary settlements in this region about a thousand years ago, and Basque whalers and fishermen from northwestern Spain worked the waters in the sixteenth century. Both made contact with natives. But the most lasting contact was made with the arrival of French settlers and explorers in the sixteenth and seventeenth centuries—which disrupted and threatened the traditional lifeways of the Indians.

1.13 Site plan of Norse settlement at L'Anse aux Meadows, Newfoundland, *c*. 1000. PC.

The remainder of this chapter considers the buildings of the early Norse and Basque visitors, and of the first French settlers. Our knowledge of the buildings erected by the first two groups has been gained primarily through archaeology carried out in recent decades, supported by documentary evidence. The architectural accomplishments of the first French settlers have been described in vivid accounts by explorers and colonizers; only recently have efforts been made to supplement these records with archaeological investigation.

The visitors and settlers of all three cultures developed ways of building (originating with the architectural traditions of their homelands) that required significant adaptations to the rigorous Canadian environment. A harsh climate, available materials, and responses to hostile natives led to the development of new and rather primitive building forms that had not previously existed in either Europe or America. Such initial experiments in building on the new continent set precedents for future compromises between retaining traditional architectural forms and devising innovative ways of coping with unfamiliar surroundings. This spirit of compromise continued, during the period of

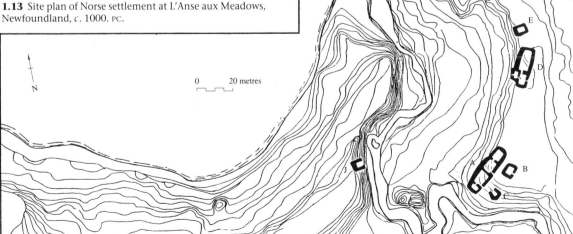

more intense architectural activity in the seventeenth and eighteenth centuries, and will be examined in later chapters.

Norse settlement

The Icelandic sagas describe a number of Norse voyages made around the year AD 1000 to lands south and west of Greenland, the most celebrated of which was Leif Eiriksson's exploration of Vinland ('wine land'), named for the wild grapes he found growing there. Many dismissed this as legend, but not so Helge Ingstad, a Norwegian explorer and writer. In 1960 he searched the coasts of New England and the Atlantic provinces for geographical features or old ruins that might resemble the Vinland of the sagas. He may have found them near **L'Anse aux Meadows [1.13]**, a small outport at the northern tip of Newfoundland. A group of grass-covered mounds shown to him by a resident looked as if they might be the remains of houses. (As early as 1914, Newfoundlander William Munn suggested that this was a Norse site.) Ingstad, and his archaeologist wife Anne Stine Ingstad, spent the next eight years directing excavations at the site, and their findings confirmed that these were indeed the remains of a Norse settlement.[18]

The mounds turned out to be the lower walls of buildings that resemble Norse houses that have been excavated in Greenland and Iceland. Proof that they were built around the year 1000 was provided by a few unquestionably Norse artifacts found on the site—small in size and few in number, but sufficient as evidence. The most exciting find was a spindle whorl of soapstone—a small disk with a hole in it used for spinning wool, a device unknown to North American natives. Since spinning was women's work in Norse society, the find suggested that women as well as men were living at L'Anse aux Meadows. That this is a Norse site—and a locale of the earliest European attempt to live in North America—is undisputed. What remains controversial is whether it is Leif Eiriksson's Vinland (his descriptions of wild grapes and a frost-free winter do not fit Newfoundland) or a different Norse community. One alternative suggestion is that L'Anse aux Meadows reveals the attempt at colonization made in c. 1004 by the Icelander Thorfinnr Karlsefni, who led a flotilla of four ships out of Greenland containing 160 people, cattle, and other domestic animals. Among the places they landed were those they named Helluland ('rocky land'), often identified with the south coast

of Labrador, and Markland ('wooded land'), thought to be the forested central and northern Labrador coast. They established a camp at Straumfiord—likely the Strait of Belle Isle—on the southern shore of which is L'Anse aux Meadows.

Evidence of eight buildings was found here, strung out in a line parallel to the shore about 650 feet (200 m) inland. All had sod walls and roofs placed over a wood frame. Three of the structures (identified as A, D, and F on the plan) were long, narrow dwellings, each capable of accommodating perhaps twenty people. The largest (building A) was 87 feet (26.6 m) long and contained four rooms in a row; the others were also divided into a number of rooms. Stone hearths used for heating and cooking had slate ember pits similar to those found in Iceland and Greenland—and at Brattahlid, Greenland, the home of Eirik the Red and his son Leif Eiriksson. Wall construction was apparently based on a traditional Icelandic-Greenland technique, and the shape of the dwellings was consistent with Icelandic and mainland Scandinavian pit buildings of the late tenth and early eleventh centuries.[19]

The other five buildings were much smaller. Buildings E and G were artisans' workshops, B was a combined dwelling and workshop, C may have been used for storage, and J (by itself, closer to the shore) was a blacksmith's workshop. In the smithy, archaeologists found a stone anvil and a crude forge, as well as deposits of charcoal, slag, and iron ore. Radiocarbon dating techniques have corroborated that they were formed in the eleventh century, making this the locale of the first-known iron smelting in North America. The ore was extracted from peat bogs, a technique used by the tenth-century Norse.

The site could have accommodated as many as 85 people. The buildings were substantial enough to suggest that they were intended for year-round use. Since there are no remains of farm buildings, the community likely comprised a trading-post and ship-repairing depot that could have served as a base for the Vinland explorers.

In 1968 the Canadian government declared L'Anse aux Meadows a National Historic Site, and in 1977 a 20,000-acre (8,000-hectare) National Historic Park—further honouring it the next year by nominating L'Anse aux Meadows as the first place in Canada to be named to UNESCO's prestigious list of World Heritage Sites (the inauguration was held in July 1980). An agreement was reached with the government of Newfoundland and Labrador whereby control of the site would be transferred to

Parks Canada. The federal agency carried out its own archaeological dig between 1973 and 1976, under the direction first of Bengt Schonback and then of Birgitta Wallace, who re-excavated the Ingstads' work and extended the site. More than 2,000 additional artifacts and bits of debris were found, including a wood floorboard from a Norse boat. The excavated site was subsequently filled again with earth and sod to protect it from deterioration and vandalism.[20]

Parks Canada has reconstructed three of the buildings [1.14]. The foundations were made of modern concrete for durability. Above them, Norse construction methods were simulated as closely as they could be determined. A wood frame was assembled from peeled logs, its notched joints held together by wood nails called 'treenails' or 'trunnels'. Smaller branches were lashed together with roots, twigs, or leather thongs made from sealskin and other animal hides. The walls and roofs were constructed of strips and blocks of sod (providing good insulation) cut from the ground; some walls are more than 6 feet (2 m) thick. The houses represent a good use of locally available materials to withstand the cold, windy winters—and presumably experience gained in building Greenland settlements.

The replicated houses are filled with household implements and tools. Fires burn on the stone hearths, the smoke escaping through openings in the sod roof. Visitors can smell the smoke, feel the damp dirt floor, and muse about what it would have been like to sleep on the earth platforms.

This and the other Norse settlements in North America (none of which have yet been identified) were short-lived. The Norse instigated an unfortu-nate encounter with curious Inuit at the site that Karlsefni called Hop—possibly located near St Paul's Bay on the west coast of Newfoundland—and several settlers were killed. Thorvaldr Eiriksson, Leif's brother, was himself killed by Inuit on the Labrador coast, and Karlsefni fought with a group of Indians. Whether as a result of these incidents, or simply because there was nothing to be gained by continuing the Vinland venture, the Norse decided—around the year 1006, according to the sagas—to abandon the settlements on the new continent. They returned to Greenland and Iceland. This abandonment is consistent with the archaeological evidence: the small amount of accumulated garbage (middens) suggests a short period of occupation.[21]

Basque whaling stations

Ships from the Basque country—the land along the Bay of Biscay, in northern Spain and southwestern France—began frequenting present-day Canadian waters in the first half of the sixteenth century. They came to the Strait of Belle Isle, which they knew as the Gran Baya (Grand Bay) of Terranova (subsequently translated as Newfoundland), to hunt whales, and also to the Grand Banks off the shore of Newfoundland to fish for cod (which had been observed in vast numbers by John Cabot in 1497). From the early 1540s until about 1620, a fleet of as many as twenty or thirty galleons would depart the Basque ports of Spain in the late spring,

1.14 Reconstructed Norse house at L'Anse aux Meadows, Newfoundland, as it appeared *c*. 1000. Photograph by Wayne Sturge, 1991. Industry Trade and Technology, Newfoundland and Labrador.

headed for semi-permanent whaling stations located along a 150-mile-long (250 km) strip of the present Labrador coast. They would arrive just as the Arctic pack ice was breaking up and migrating whales began to appear. The centre of activity was the fine harbour at Red Bay (about 70 miles, or 110 km, across the Strait from L'Anse aux Meadows), which was known in the sixteenth century as Butus or Buteres. During the peak years of Basque whaling, which lasted from about 1545 to 1585, more than 1,000 Basques—mostly men between their early twenties and early forties—would be based each season at Red Bay; there were another 500 or so up the coast in the Chateau Bay area (today's Henley Harbour) and fewer in other coves. The whalers would return to Europe around the middle of January, but on two occasions in the 1570s the severe weather forced them to winter in the Strait of Belle Isle. They encountered natives, mostly Micmac, with whom they established peaceful relations.[22]

Information on the activities and the buildings of the Basque whalers has been coming to light only since the 1970s. Historical geographer Selma Barkham's persistent research among documents in Basque archives led to the discovery of shore facilities in Labrador by archaeologists from Memorial University of Newfoundland, under the direction of Dr James Tuck, and of Basque shipwrecks by divers from Parks Canada. Although much remains to be learned about the construction and appearance of the whalers' buildings, enough is already known to provide a preliminary picture of their Labrador communities.

The Basque whaling stations were complex industrial communities set up to process whale by-products and ship them to European markets. Unlike the Inuit, who used all parts of the whale, Europeans were wasteful, and discarded the carcass after extracting the portions they wanted. The basic product was whale oil, which was extracted by trying (rendering) the blubber. It was used for lamps and lubricants, in the cloth and leather industries, as additives to drugs, and for other purposes. Whale oil was very valuable: one cargo, sent out from Labrador in 1571, was worth 10,000 ducats, the cost of two large galleons. After 1580 the stations also produced baleen (also called whalebone), taken from the mouth of the whale—a flexible precursor of plastics—that was used for a variety of products, from corset stays to buggy whips. The northern right whale was the principal prey.

Red Bay alone had more than a dozen shore

1.15 Excavation of a Basque tryworks at Red Bay, Labrador, showing the base of a stone wall. Second half of the 16th century. The Basque Project, Archaeology Unit, Memorial University of Newfoundland.

stations in sheltered locations. The remains of a number of different kinds of structures have been found. Along the water's edge were stages or wharves, constructed of carefully mortised timbers fastened with wooden dowels (tenons) and weighted down with rock ballast. Here the blubber was flensed or cut into strips.

1.16 A reconstructed 16th-century Basque tryworks at the Canadian Museum of Civilization, Hull, Quebec. Fabricated by Taylor Manufacturing Industries, Special Projects Group. Photograph courtesy Taylor Manufacturing Industries.

The blubber was then hauled up a timber ramp to the **tryworks** [1.15], where it was minced into smaller pieces and rendered in copper cauldrons suspended over circular stone ovens about 4 feet (1.3 m) in diameter. A tryworks contained between one and six ovens arranged in a line parallel to the shore. The largest of the excavated tryworks was almost 32 by 30 feet (10 by 9 m). The oven area was separated from the work area (on the landward side) by a low stone wall about 3 feet (1 m) high, made of a rubble stone core and larger, well-fitted facing stones (brought over as ballast) held together by mortar of grey clay impregnated with whale oil to achieve a hard, cement-like consistency. The same clay lined the ovens' fireboxes.

Around the perimeter of the structure a series of timber posts, fastened with hand-forged nails, supported a roof covered with clay tiles—the curved, overlapping red roof tiles that we know as Spanish tile, and which, along with the clay, nails, and axes, were brought from the Basque country. The ovens do not seem to have had chimneys, so smoke must have escaped either through holes in the roof or out the open sides of the structure. Although all of the tryworks have long collapsed and can be interpreted only by archaeologists, a **reconstructed tryworks** [1.16] at the Canadian Museum of Civilization in Hull, Quebec, gives a good idea of its likely appearance, particularly as original tiles were used. The beaches and gardens of Red Bay remain littered with fragments of tile, which generations of Labrador children have used as chalk and as pigments for painting model boats.[23]

The remains of cooperages and whalers' dwellings have also been found at Red Bay. The former, where coopers lived and constructed the barrels that were essential for storing and shipping the whale oil (a large galleon might hold between one and two thousand barrels of oil), reveal that cooperages were built of fieldstone walls and a tile roof, with wood used for framing and support. One cooperage, about 45 feet (14 m) long and 26 feet (8 m) wide, had no need for a rear wall because it was built against a vertical outcrop of bedrock. Incorporating natural features into man-made structures is characteristic of Basque building in Spain.

More than a dozen small whalers' dwellings—far less substantial than the cooperages—have been found on two islands at Red Bay. Those crew members who lived ashore occupied simple structures whose light wood frames were covered with baleen and perhaps cloth. Most used small crevices in rock outcrops as hearths. Many men must have remained on the ships, since a reference written in 1584 at Puerto Breton in Terranova (now Carrol Cove, west of Red Bay; the name is a likely indication that sailors from Brittany called at the Labrador coast) mentions 'the men sleeping aboard ship' and 'half the men still boiling whale oil on shore at midnight.'[24]

The Basque whaling industry in Terranova was reduced significantly towards the end of the sixteenth century. The principal causes seem to have been the depletion of the whale stocks, the weakened Spanish economy after the defeat of the Armada, rising commercial competition from England and the Netherlands, and France's increasing sovereignty over the land. The Basques had come solely to exploit natural resources, anticipating the motives of many subsequent entrepreneurs. When the industry was no longer profitable, they left. By the 1620s the Basques had abandoned the Strait of Belle Isle entirely and moved their whaling activities to the Norwegian Arctic islands of Spitsbergen.

Champlain and His Settlements

France also showed an interest in the new land across the ocean. In 1534 François I commissioned Jacques Cartier, a veteran Breton navigator from Saint-Malo, to go to the New World in search of gold and a passage to China. The destination of his first voyage was Baie des Châteaux—the Strait of Belle Isle—and he sailed there directly, so he must have already been familiar with it.[25]

Cartier made three voyages to Canada. In 1534 he raised a cross on the Gaspé shore and took possession of the land for France. On his second journey, in 1535-6, he discovered the St Lawrence River (which he called the Rivière du Canada), sailed upriver to the Lachine Rapids at Hochelaga (Montreal), and wintered at Stadacona (Quebec). The Iroquois also called the village 'Canada' and used the name as well for the territory that it controlled. Cartier's third voyage had colonization as its objective. He brought five ships carrying convict settlers and animals, establishing a settlement called Charlesbourg-Royal, some 9 miles (14 km) upriver from Stadacona. He built two small forts, but native harassment contributed to making the short-lived colony a total failure. His explorations, however, were a success, even if he did not reach the Pacific, found no metals more precious than iron pyrites and quartz, and left no settlers. Cartier's achievement was ascertaining that the St Lawrence River—which he called 'by far the mightiest river we have ever seen'[26]—and its tributaries had fertile shores and led deep into the interior of the continent, and that the natives were eager to trade for furs. This encouraging information eventually led to France's domination of much of North America for more than a century.

The first successful effort at establishing a colony in today's Canada was made by Samuel de Champlain (*c*. 1570-1635), a native of Brouage, a port on the west coast of France. Between 1603 and 1615 Champlain undertook seven voyages to Canada, making early contact with Basque sailors and benefiting from their familiarity with the Strait of Belle Isle. Beginning his Canadian career as a geographer, he ended it in Quebec as the governor of the new colony and as the generally acknowledged father of New France.[27]

The habitations

Île Sainte-Croix In 1603 Pierre du Gua de Monts (1558?-1628) received royal patents that gave him a monopoly on trade and colonization in Acadia, the land along the eastern shores of today's Atlantic provinces and New England states. De Monts set out for Acadia in 1604 with two ships carrying between 120 and 150 men, including several of high social rank; his compatriot Champlain accompanied him as his geographer. Economic exploitation was the primary motive for this expedition, which led to the establishment of the first successful European colony north of the Gulf of Mexico.

After exploring the Nova Scotia coast and the Bay of Fundy, the men sailed into Passamaquoddy Bay and decided to establish the settlement on a small island that they named Île Sainte-Croix because of the cross-like branching of the river just above the island (the Sainte-Croix River, which separates Canada and the US). The island subsequently became known as Dochet Island, and is situated just within the state of Maine; it is recognized as an international historic site. De Monts and Champlain chose the island largely for defensive purposes and because it was a good place to trade with the natives; they also believed that it had fertile soil (the gardens did not, however, do well) and recognized the ready availability of building materials.

Directed by de Monts, the colonists began fortifying the site by constructing a 'barricade' at the south end of the island, commanding any traffic coming up the river, that served as a platform for their cannon. They then turned their attention to building the settlement, which they called their *habitation*. Champlain described it in his *Voyages*:

> Sieur de Monts proceeded to employ the workmen in building houses for our abode, and allowed me to determine the arrangement of our settlement. After Sieur de Monts had determined the place for the store-house,...he adopted the plan for his own house, which he had promptly built by our good workmen, and he assigned to each one his location....[The workmen] all set to work to clear up the island, to go to the woods, to make the framework [*charpenter*], to carry earth and other things necessary for the building[s]....
>
> Meanwhile, work on the houses went on vigorously and without cessation; the carpenters engaged on the storehouse and dwelling of Sieur de Monts, and the others each on his own house, as I was on mine, which I built with the assistance of some servants belonging to Sieur d'Orville and myself....An oven was also made, and a hand-mill for grinding our wheat, the working of which involved much trouble and labour to the most of us, since it was a toilsome operation. Some gardens were afterwards laid out on the mainland as well as on the island ....[28]

Champlain's keyed map [1.17] of the settlement (titled *habitation de l'île ste croix*)[29] gives a good idea of its layout and a sketchy impression of the construction and appearance of the buildings. In the upper right (the northeast) a palisade fence (O) surrounds the storehouse or magazine (C) and de Monts's house (A), as well as the 'public building wherein we spent our time when it rained' (B); and it seems (although the location of the palisade here is not clear) that the fence also encloses several houses, including Champlain's (R on the map—just below A and B—although erroneously shown as P in Champlain's legend). The houses of de Monts and the other notables are covered with steep hipped (*pavillon*) roofs, a form popular in France for the castles and palaces of people of quality, and de Monts's house has a dormer window. The roofs of the storehouse—which has small windows for security—and the public building have a less noble (and easier-to-construct) gabled form, typical of the European dwellings of the lower classes. Even in these tentative North American beginnings, architecture was a vehicle for expressing social values.

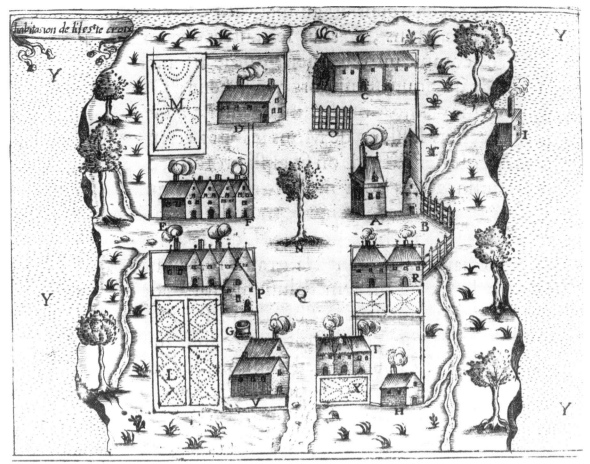

1.17 The *habitation* at Île Sainte-Croix, 1604, from Champlain's *Voyages* (1613), p. 38. Rare Book Collection, National Library of Canada/neg. 15306.

The remainder of the buildings stood outside the defensible palisade. Swiss mercenaries lived in a 1½-storey gable-roof dwelling with two chimneys and a large garden behind it (D). To the south are two rows of tall and narrow gable-roof townhouses that were the dwellings and shops of the artisans (E, F, P). South of the well (G) are the dwellings of the Sieur Boulay and other workmen (Q, which is printed too high) and the priest (V). To the southeast are more houses (T), with their gardens and the bakery (H). Along the eastern shore was the cookhouse (I), cantilevered over the river to make water collection and garbage disposal more convenient.

The construction of some buildings was described by Marc Lescarbot—a Paris lawyer who was resident in Acadia two years later (1606-7)—in his *Histoire de la Nouvelle-France* (1609):

> M. de Monts worked away at his fort, which he had placed at the [north end] of the island...And outside the said fort was the barracks for the Swiss, large and spacious, and other small build-ings like a suburb [*un faux-bourg*]. Some had built log-huts [*quelques-uns s'étoient cabannés*] on the mainland near the stream. But inside the fort was the dwelling of the said M. de Monts, built of fair sawn timber [*fait d'une belle & artificielle charpenterie*], with the banner of France overhead. Elsewhere within the fort was the magazine, wherein lay the safety and the life of each, built likewise of fair timber, and covered with shingles.[30]

The buildings that were built of sawn lumber must have been cut in France and brought out by boat, since the settlement had no sawmill.

Southwest of the *habitation* (outside Champlain's picture) was the chapel, which Lescarbot described as being 'the little chapel built after the Indian fashion' (*batie à la Sauvage*)—the first of

17

many small missionary chapels built in the new colony. De Monts and many of the party were Huguenots, and so they brought a Protestant minister as well as a Catholic priest, and it may be presumed that they held their Protestant services in the public building.[31] A water mill was begun, to ease the chore of grinding wheat, but it was never completed.[32]

No indication is given about the construction of the other buildings. Historian W.F. Ganong believed that 'all the other buildings were evidently log-huts',[33] but there are no grounds for assuming log construction either in the texts or in the building experiences of the settlers. We know that there were a number of carpenters in the party, that Lescarbot implied that many trees were felled, and that Champlain described the workmen undertaking *charpente* (which usually suggests a frame, not a feature of 'log-huts') in the woods, and hauling earth. Furthermore, it may be assumed that the workers would have used a familiar building technique. It is therefore reasonable to conjecture that the ordinary buildings were constructed of *colombage bousillé*, a technique in which a frame is made of closely spaced timbers and the interstices are filled with a mixture of clay (which Champlain noted was found on the island) and mud, and a binder of straw or pebbles. This technique subsequently became predominant in Acadia and was used as well in the St Lawrence region. The bake oven would have been built of brick or stone. The chimneys might have been either masonry or wood covered with clay; the latter method was later used in Acadia.

In the centre of the *habitation*'s four quadrants is 'the public square (*la place*) with a tree in the middle of it' (N); a roadway leading in each direction from the square produces a cruciform plan. Even in as hastily built a village as this, symmetry and formal geometry were important town-planning features, since they helped to remind the inhabitants that their civilized values would dominate nature and the natives.

The community at Île Sainte-Croix feared the natives more than nature, but it was nature that did them in. The winter of 1604-5 was a disaster. The first snow fell on 6 October, and the cold became increasingly intense—far colder than the settlers had ever experienced. With so many trees cut down, there was no protection against the wind or the heavily drifting snow, which remained on the ground until April. Ice-floes cut the people off from shore, and from their supply of fresh water, fire-

wood, and game. Even the liquor froze. Forced to rely on a diet of salt meat and a meagre supply of frozen vegetables, many succumbed to scurvy. Of the 79 men who wintered on the island, 35 died and 20 more became gravely ill. Champlain may have been the first to write of Canada: 'There are six months of winter in this country.'[34]

Port Royal When spring finally arrived, the survivors abandoned Île Sainte-Croix and relocated their settlement across the Bay of Fundy at Port Royal, an elevated site (near today's Annapolis Royal on the Nova Scotia shore) whose harbour Champlain had admired a year earlier. As Champlain explained:

> ...we fitted out two pinnaces (*barques*) which we loaded with the woodwork of the houses at Ste Croix, to transport it to Port Royal twenty-five leagues distant, where we judged the climate to be much more agreeable and temperate.[35]

The men cleared the heavily forested site and began to erect houses. De Monts and some others returned to France before winter, and so the reduced population required fewer buildings than at Sainte-Croix. Champlain remained, and François Pont-Gravé (or Gravé Du Pont) took command in de Monts's place.

Lescarbot again fills in some details about the buildings:

> It was decided to make their plantation at Port Royal until it was possible to carry out further explorations. So now there was a great to-do, with every one busily packing up. The buildings, which had cost a thousand labours, were pulled down, except the store-house, which was too large to transport. To finish all this took several voyages. When everything had reached Port Royal, further toil awaited them....M. du Pont... with great diligence, as is his nature, set to work to prepare and to perfect what was required to house himself and his men, which was all that could be done during that year in such a country.[36]

They completed the buildings before the onset of winter. The second winter was much easier than the first; the French traded with the Indians for furs of beaver, otter, and moose, and for fresh meat. Champlain describes the **habitation at Port Royal** [1.18]:

> The plan of the settlement was ten fathoms in length and eight in breadth, which makes thirty-

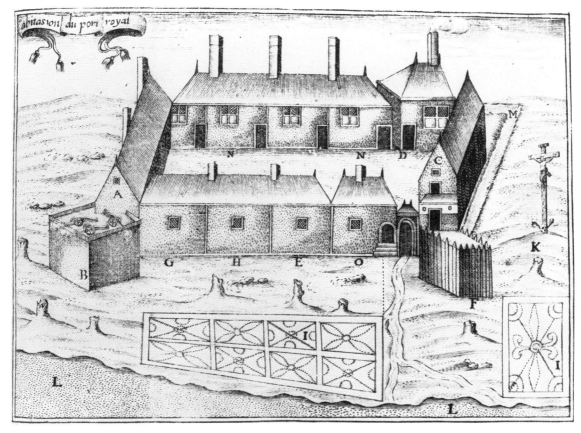

abitasion du port royal

1.18 The *habitation* at Port Royal, Nova Scotia, 1605, from Champlain's *Voyages* (1613), p. 99. Rare Book Collection, National Library of Canada/neg. 8760.

six in circumference. On the eastern side is a storehouse of the full width, with a very fine cellar some five to six feet high. On the north side is the Sieur de Monts' dwelling, constructed of fairly good wood-work. Around the courtyard are the quarters of the workmen. At one corner on the western side is a platform whereon were placed four pieces of cannon; and at the other corner, towards the east, is a palisade fashioned like a platform, as can be seen in the following picture.[37]

His view of the *habitation* is carefully drawn, but some elements contradict his description and details in a second illustration, perhaps the fault of the engraver.

The Port Royal settlement consisted of a single range of buildings, linked around a central courtyard to form a continuous perimeter wall, eliminating the need for an external defensive palisade. The cannon platform is visible in Champlain's view on a bastion at the southwest corner (B), and the small palisade at the right stands as a second bastion (F)

beside the entrance gate. The four sides of the quadrangle, going counter-clockwise from the gate, contain the storehouse (C), the only building to have a cellar; de Monts's dwelling (D), in which Pont-Gravé and Champlain presumably resided, and the residences of the gentlemen and officers (N); the dwelling of the workmen (A); and a service wing, comprising the bakery (G), the kitchen (H), the blacksmith's shop (E), and a building used for storing rigging (O). The roofs again indicate social hierarchies, the gentlemen's houses having hipped roofs and the workmen's houses being covered with a gable roof. Tall chimneys project through roofs of both kinds. The windows on the perimeter wall are smaller than those that open on the courtyard, for defensive reasons.

The only component that resembles its counterpart at Sainte-Croix is de Monts's house, and it may well have been disassembled and re-erected (it was, after all, prefabricated in France in the first place).

19

For the other buildings, the timber—which both Champlain and Lescarbot said was floated across from Île Sainte-Croix—was likely re-used, though no attempt was made to recreate their previous appearance.

Outside the *habitation* are seen the gardens (I, the geometric patterns at the bottom and right) and the cemetery (K). The drainage ditch on the right (M) was dug in the second year at the instigation of Lescarbot, who complained that 'the water from the surrounding soil ran beneath their cellars, which was very prejudicial to their health.' Champlain's map of the area (not illustrated here) shows a field for growing grain (now part of the town of Annapolis Royal) and a water-powered gristmill, which allowed the men to abandon the difficult labour of hand-milling. The community abounded in technical skills for this and other endeavours, since the artisans included 'numerous joiners, carpenters, masons, stone-cutters, locksmiths, workers in iron, tailors, wood-sawyers, sailors, &c.'[38]

Port Royal was the first European settlement of any permanence in America north of St Augustine, Florida, which had been founded by the Spanish in 1565. The *habitation* was built in the summer and fall of 1605—two years before the English colony at Jamestown, Virginia, and fifteen years earlier than the arrival of the *Mayflower* at Plymouth, Massachusetts.

The measure of permanence is, however, a relative assessment. The winter of 1605-6 took its toll, but this time sickness claimed only six men. The following winter Champlain created the *Ordre de bon temps*—the Order of Good Cheer—as a social club to help pass the time, and Lescarbot organized *Le Théâtre de Neptune en la Nouvelle-France*, the first theatrical event in the new land. Champlain himself took up gardening and experimented with fish-farming during the summer. But prosperity seemed remote, and when de Monts's fur-trading monopoly was revoked in 1607, the *habitation* was temporarily abandoned. Jean de Biencourt de Poutrincourt, one of the original settlers, received a land grant at Port Royal and returned in 1610 to resuscitate the colony. Even this was short-lived: three years later, on 1 November 1613, the English privateer Samuel Argall sailed out of Virginia and looted the settlement, stole anything of value that he could find—even carpenters' work and nails—and set fire to all that remained. A few dogged settlers remained with Poutrincourt's son Charles. Although a Scottish colony was briefly established there, the land was returned to France in 1632 and

a new Port Royal, located a short distance up the Annapolis River at today's Annapolis Royal, became the nucleus of the colony of Acadia.

Nothing remained of de Monts's and Champlain's *habitation* but a farmer's field. Early in the twentieth century, as Canadians started to develop a historical consciousness, and preservation sentiments began to be tweaked, there was a groundswell of support first for commemorating, and then for reconstructing, the historic buildings. W.F. Ganong located the site of Port Royal in 1911 through a careful examination of the land, together with an analysis of Champlain's map and descriptions. The site was marked by the federal government in 1924 with a cairn and a bronze plaque on the recommendation of the Historic Sites and Monuments Board of Canada, which had been formed five years earlier.

Some people wanted more. Harriette Taber Richardson, a resident of Cambridge, Massachusetts, who spent the summers and falls at Annapolis Royal to seek relief from her allergies, became fascinated with Champlain and the early settlement, reading the descriptions, transcribing the maps, and even translating Lescarbot's play into English. Then, as she later wrote:

> In the autumn I had been working on the garden site. I remember a quick shower and the beauty of the rainbow whose arch seemed to rise from the garden of Lescarbot. The night was full moon and as I was awaiting sleep, a shock almost electric sprang all unexpectedly—a new idea. The thought was why should it not be possible to rebuild the *habitation* as a gift and a token of the friendliness on our side of the border?[39]

Richardson gained support for her reconstruction scheme from a number of influential people, including L.M. Fortier, the honorary curator of nearby Fort Anne National Park and president of the Historical Association of Annapolis Royal; historian J. Clarence Webster, a member of the Historic Sites and Monuments Board of Canada; and Frank Gilman Allen, the governor of Massachusetts. In 1928 Harriette Richardson organized the Associates of Port Royal as a fund-raising group. She and Fortier began to lobby the federal government, while the Historical Association acquired title to area properties. Technical assistance, as well as inspiration, came from the professionals who were involved in the celebrated reconstruction of Colonial Williamsburg in Virginia, including architect C. Coatsworth Pinckney of Boston, and from historical illustrator Charles W. Jefferys of Toronto.[40]

Their initiative met resistance first on philosophical grounds, because the Dominion Parks Branch (predecessor of Parks Canada) and many members of Webster's board opposed the restoration and reconstruction of destroyed sites as being artificial, favouring instead the preservation and enhancement of what remained from the past. But political pressure prevailed, and after a delay caused by the Great Depression, the federal government announced in 1938 that it would allocate $30,000 to the development of Port Royal.

Archaeological excavations carried out in that year uncovered rubble-stone foundations for most of the walls, hearths, and chimneys at an average depth of 21 inches (53 cm) below the present surface of the ground, identified the cellar of the storehouse, and located a well in the middle of the courtyard—not shown on Champlain's drawing. (Subsequent investigation, in the 1960s, questioned the accuracy of the first dig.) It was concluded that Champlain's dimensions of 10 by 8 *toises* (about 64 by 51 feet, or 20 by 16 m) referred to the interior courtyard and not to the entire *habitation*. The planning team, noting that Champlain did not describe the method of construction, assumed that the skilled artisans identified by Lescarbot would have used the traditional means of construction they knew from their homeland. (A writer describes what is new and unusual, rarely

discussing what is familiar and taken for granted.) After consultation among architects and antiquarians in France and Quebec, including architect Ramsay Traquair and anthropologist Marius Barbeau, they concluded, probably correctly, that the wall construction would have used the technique of *colombage*. They also decided, likely wrongly, that the timber framing would have been covered externally with horizontal siding (a feature of New England buildings) and internally with plaster or wood panelling.[41]

In 1939 the reconstruction of Port Royal [**1.19**] was undertaken in this manner under the direction of architect K.D. Harris, of the surveys and mapping branch of the Department of Mines and Resources, which was then responsible for historic sites. The 'new' buildings are now more than a half-century old. Accurate or not, they—like the original Port Royal *habitation* destroyed more than three centuries earlier—have become an integral part of the historic fabric of the Fundy basin.

Quebec Although de Monts never returned to North America after the terrible winter at Île Sainte-Croix, he retained an active interest in colonizing the new land as a means of controlling the fur trade and finding the elusive route to China. He decided that the 'Rivière du Canada' charted by Cartier would provide better opportunities, and so in 1608 he commissioned Champlain—who had spent the winter of 1607-8 in France—to lead a new expedition across the Atlantic. This time the destination was the St Lawrence River and the former Indian village of Stadacona. It was now controlled by an Algonquian-speaking group, the Algonquins (the Iroquois—Cartier's allies, who had left the river and moved south—were now the enemy), and the native inhabitants called it Kebec. Champlain recounts (in translation) the founding of the colony in this way:

> From the island of Orléans to Québec is one league, and I arrived there on July the third. On arrival I looked for a place suitable for our settlement, but I could not find any more suitable or better situated than the point of Québec, so called by the natives, which was covered with nut-trees. I at once employed a part of our workmen in cutting them down to make a site for our settlement, another part in sawing planks, another in digging the cellar and making ditches, and another in going to Tadoussac [at the mouth of the Saguenay] with the pinnace to fetch our

1.19 Reconstruction of the *habitation* at Port Royal, Nova Scotia. Nova Scotia Supply and Services, Visual Communications/20909.

ABITATION. DE QVEBECQ

1.20 The *habitation* at Quebec, Quebec, 1608, from Champlain's *Voyages* (1613), p. 187. Rare Book Collection, National Library of Canada/neg. 8759.

1.21 (*below*) C.W. Jefferys' interpretation of Champlain's *habitation* at Quebec. From H.P. Biggar ed., *The Works of Samuel de Champlain*, volume 2 (1925). Used with the permission of the Champlain Society.

effects. The first thing we made was the store-house, to put our supplies under cover, and it was promptly finished by the diligence of everyone and the care I took in the matter.[42]

This time Champlain was in charge. During the first weeks his elevated position nearly cost him his life, when a small group of disgruntled workmen plotted (unsuccessfully) to kill him. Once the leader was hanged and the other conspirators had been sent off to France in irons, construction resumed:

I continued the construction of our quarters [**1.20**], which contained three main buildings of two stories. Each one was three fathoms long and two and a half wide. The storehouse was six long and three wide, with a fine cellar six feet high. All the way round our buildings I had a gallery made, outside the second story, which was a very convenient thing. There were also ditches fifteen feet wide and six deep, and outside these I made several salients which enclosed a part of the buildings, and there we put our cannon. In front of the building there is an open space four fathoms wide and six or seven long, which abuts upon the river's bank. Round about the buildings

C.W. JEFFE

22

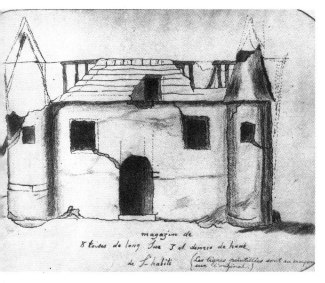

1.22 A drawing, made in 1680, of the second *habitation* at Quebec ('le magasin du Roi'), 1624-6. ANQ, Collection initiale/N 1173-98.

are very good gardens, and an open place on the north side of a hundred, or a hundred and twenty, yards long and fifty or sixty wide.[43]

In a twentieth-century interpretation of the first **habitation** at Quebec [1.21]—by C.W. Jefferys, based on Champlain's own drawing and description—it can be seen that the entrance from the river was made through a palisade and across a drawbridge, which spanned a moat that went the whole way round the complex. Cannon emplacements are seen at either side of the drawbridge and at the far right. The building complex looks very much like a fortress. To the left of the entry is the storehouse; to its right is a two-storey building with a steep gable roof containing Champlain's quarters (on the ground floor near the door), lodgings for workmen, and the blacksmith's workplace. The two-storey building behind it accommodates additional workmen and provides storage for weapons. The tower to the left of centre is a dovecote. The projecting gallery above the ground floor—which would become an important feature of Quebec architecture—extends around the entire complex. A steep escarpment rises behind the little settlement.

Twenty-four men prepared to spend the first winter at Quebec. Once again scurvy took its devastating toll. By spring, sixteen had died. Although the next few years were difficult ones for the little colony, Champlain undertook an important pro-

gram of exploring the interior and making valuable alliances with the native peoples along the St Lawrence and Ottawa Rivers, and in the Great Lakes basin. He spent the winter of 1615-16 in Huronia, some 700 miles (1100 km) inland from Quebec—a remarkable achievement.

Champlain was rewarded for his work in 1620 by being formally appointed Governor of New France. Continuing to improve the colony, he built a fort on top of the escarpment (the site of the future Château Saint-Louis), which was pulled down and rebuilt in 1629, and he rebuilt the *habitation* of 1608—which was 'falling to pieces'. The appearance of the **second *habitation*** [1.22] (1624-6), which subsequently became known as the *Magasin du Roi* (the King's storehouse), is known from plans made in the 1630s and a sketch of 1680 (two years

1.23 Excavation of the north-west tower of the second *habitation* at Quebec, 1624-6, seen from the west looking north. IBC/1976-R.12.9

before it was destroyed by fire), at which time it was already in ruins. The north façade looked very castle-like, with a planar central portion flanked by two circular towers and covered by a steep roof. Its composition was not unlike that of a medieval château on the Loire, a traditional building-type with which Champlain and his builders would likely have been familiar. The design symbolized feudal control (as had de Monts's houses at Île Sainte-Coix and Port Royal), transferring the traditional French castle/palace form to the infant colony.

The foundations [1.23] of the second *habitation*—which has been called the first stone building in Canada—were unearthed by archaeologists during excavations undertaken between 1976 and 1980. They confirmed that the walls were made of stone (mostly local schist, but with some limestone and granite); the floor structure was wood and covered with red, pink, and yellow tiles; and the roof was slate. Bricks found on the site may have been among the 10,000 bricks ordered from France in 1618.[44]

In 1627 Champlain's hopes for the success of his settlement rose when the Compagnie des Cent-Associés (also called the Compagnie de la Nouvelle-France) was granted a royal charter, with a mandate to develop a strong French colony in the New World. In the following year, just as the settlement seemed about to prosper, Quebec was challenged and besieged by the English adventurer Sir David Kirke (subsequently the governor of Newfoundland) and his four brothers. In July 1629 Champlain and his 75 colonists surrendered, and Champlain was taken to England; but he was back in France before the end of the year. The country was restored to France in 1632. By now in his sixties, Champlain returned to Quebec in May 1633 with a new contingent of colonists, and found the second *habitation* in ruins. He supervised its repair.

As he wrote to Cardinal Richelieu in 1634:

> . . . I have rebuilt the ruins of Quebec, enlarged the fortifications, increased the number of buildings, erected two new *habitations*, one of which is 15 leagues above Quebec and commands the entire river, so that it is not possible for a ship to sail up or down it without being stopped by a fortress I have built on an islet that duty obliged me to name for you. . . . The other [Trois-Rivières] is placed in one of the best parts of the country. . . .[45]

A year later Champlain suffered a paralysis. He died in his beloved Quebec on Christmas Day, 1635. The great explorer had laid the infrastructure for colonization and for the fur trade—although the merchants in France, to whom he was responsible for most of his career, were interested only in the latter.

Mission chapels

Religion was not a high priority for Champlain, and there was no chapel in his *habitation* at Quebec. But the religious communities in France—who saw the settlement of the New World as an unprecedented opportunity to convert the '*sauvages*' to Christianity—flocked to the new colony. The Récollets, a French branch of the Franciscan Order, came to New France in 1615; Jesuits arrived in 1625; and other orders appeared somewhat later. Immediately upon the arrival of the Récollets, Champlain had a small chapel built for them, a short distance northwest of the *habitation*. Père Jean Dolbeau celebrated the first Mass there on 25 June 1615, a month after his arrival.[46]

The Récollets, and their black-robed Jesuit rivals, subsequently built a chapel at virtually every post, fort, or any other place where the Indians were known to congregate—simple, primitive structures built hastily from light materials. In 1624 Récollet Père Sagard described the first type of chapel used by the missionaries as a 'bark hut' (*cabane d'écorce*).[47] Additional information on their appearance is available in the *Jesuit Relations*. A chapel built at Trois-Rivières, in 1634, was described by Père Paul Le Jeune as follows:

> Our house in this first stage was no more than several pieces of wood joined one against the other (*quelques busches de bois jointes les unes auprès des autres*), coated around the openings with a little earth, and covered with grass; we only have twelve feet square in all for the chapel and for our dwelling, as we wait for a building of dressed wood to be completed.

Two other accounts corroborate that the natives built the chapels, and that expediency provided the architectural solution:

> The Christians [converted Indians] built a church, which was in a state in which to recite the Holy Mass, in less than two hours. They are skilful at sticking poles into the ground [*planter des perches*] to make a hut [*une cabane*], either round or square.

Also:

> Sunday was approaching, [and so] the chief ordered his people to make a fine large cabin which would be used only for prayer: the young men went to get bark, and the women and the girls to get fir branches, which are very attractive and still green; having built the church, the old men directed their people to cover themselves as richly as they could to honour the prayer.[48]

It would be expected that the natives would build the mission chapels in the manner to which they were accustomed, just as the European settlers did. The early chapels were similar in construction technique to a domed Algonquian wigwam. Small trunks, or medium-sized branches of trees (*pieux*), were sharpened at the end and driven side-by-side

into the ground to form walls, with the cracks between them filled with mud or clay. This form of construction is generally known as *pieux en terre*, *en pieux*, or *piquets de bouts*. The roof of pliable branches, bent to form a vault, was covered with bark to keep out the rain. Architectural historian Alan Gowans, who sketched a plausible **reconstruction of an early mission chapel** [**1.24**], has suggested that the door might have consisted of a sheet of bark or cloth; and that a table covered with a white sheet, and supporting a few candles, could have served for the altar.[49] One is reminded of the chapel, built at Île Sainte-Croix in 1604, that Lescarbot described in his *Histoire* as being 'the little chapel built after the Indian fashion' (*'batie à la Sauvage'*).

Some visual evidence of the appearance of these chapels—albeit formalized, dressed up in allegory, and produced at a distance from the frontier of New France—is seen in the painting *La France apportant la foi aux Hurons de la Nouvelle-France* [**1.25**]

1.24 (*above*) A reconstruction drawing by Alan Gowans of an early 17th-century mission chapel in New France. From Gowans, *Church Architecture in New France* (1955), p. 15.

1.25 *La France apportant la foi aux Hurons de la Nouvelle-France*, *c*. 1670, attributed to Frère Luc. Monastère des Ursulines, Quebec.

(France Bringing the Faith to the Hurons of New France), which hangs in the Ursuline Convent in Quebec. Painted around 1670 by an unknown artist, although sometimes attributed to the renowned Frère Luc, it shows a native (who has covered himself richly) kneeling before the figure of France, who holds a painting of the Trinity with the Holy Family, and points to the Holy Family in the heavens above. The scene is set along a river, presumably the St Lawrence, and a ship is anchored at the right. To the left are two mission chapels, and small square cabins that seem to be constructed with a light wood frame (and perhaps a pliable infill material).

The large canvas was likely painted in France—perhaps in Nantes; and possibly because the Hurons at Quebec, in 1666, wished to commemorate their conversion to Christianity with a painting. One would therefore not expect the architectural details of the chapels to be accurate; but their scale, and their apparently temporary nature, fit the documentary sources.[50]

The religious needs of the first Europeans who came to New France were inevitably met by members of Roman Catholic orders. But once Quebec, Montreal, and Trois-Rivières developed into towns, and farms and villages appeared in the St Lawrence valley, the people were served by an influx of clergy, and by a bishop. The churches that were then built (some of which are discussed in the next chapter) assumed paramount importance in the life of New France.

NEW FRANCE

NEW FRANCE (as a large portion of our continent was called before Britain acquired the territory through military action) was a possession of the French Crown. Its young society was forced to reconcile the ways of the motherland—including its ideas of establishing an impressive governmental and religious presence in the colony—with the realities of a naïve society, an immature economy, and a harsh and threatening environment. Social structures and buildings alike reflect this difficult process.

In 1627 the Compagnie des Cent-Associés had been granted a charter to develop a French colony. Its directors, however, showed more interest in the fur trade than in stimulating settlement, and their work was impeded by the ongoing Iroquois wars. A mere 2,500 Europeans were living in the St Lawrence valley in 1660, most of them in or near the towns of Quebec, Trois-Rivières, and Montreal. As a consequence of the company's failure, the young Louis XIV revoked its charter in 1663 and made New France a royal colony. Two years later he appointed Jean Talon as the first intendant (chief administrator) 'of Canada, Acadia and Newfoundland' and charged the forty-year-old civil servant with making the colony into a populated and prosperous place.[1]

With the full support of the King's minister, Jean-Baptiste Colbert, the energetic Talon was largely successful in his entrepreneurial initiatives. In order to increase numbers, he offered free passage and cheap land to settlers, brought over *les filles du roi*—hundreds of young women who became wives of members of the predominantly male community—and imposed laws rewarding those who married early and fining those who did not. His industrial programs included the encouragement of commercial farming, fishing, shipbuilding, crafts, and trade in goods other than furs. By the time of Talon's departure for France, in 1672, the population had doubled and industry was dramatically on the increase.

Even after peace with the Iroquois was achieved in 1701, the development of New France was hampered by wars between France and her European neighbours, which led to frequent skirmishes on American soil. During the period of relative peace that followed the Treaty of Utrecht in 1713 the colony prospered. There was a considerable amount of construction in both urban and rural areas, and the fortress town of Louisbourg was built on Île Royal.

Tensions between France and England over both their American and European interests led to an outbreak of fighting in 1755, and a year later this escalated into what came to be called the Seven Years' War. The French fortifications at Louisbourg fell to the British in 1758. A year later British troops, under the command of General James Wolfe, surprised the French garrison at Quebec by climbing up an undefended cliff, and despite a valiant counter-attack by the Marquis de Montcalm on the Plains of Abraham, Quebec fell. France surrendered its Canadian colony, and in 1760 New France became a part of British North America.

Although the French colony lost its political autonomy, the residents were allowed to maintain their language, French civil law, and seigneurial system. Architecture, too, developed along traditional lines that were established in the seventeenth century. Rural building continued much as if nothing had happened, and only the cities of Montreal and Quebec revealed the impact of British rule.

Settlement

Towns

Quebec was the original political, commercial, and religious centre of the colony, and it remained the largest town in the colony until it was surpassed in size and commercial importance by Montreal at the end of the eighteenth century. (Some early Montreal buildings are introduced later in this chapter, and the city is discussed in Chapter 5.) Trois-Rivières, located between the two and named after the three arms of the St Maurice River, which empties into the St Lawrence at this point, appeared as if it might develop into a significant city; but it could not compete with Montreal or Quebec and had only 586 inhabitants at the time of the Conquest. The fortress town of Louisbourg was built on Cape Breton Island in the early eighteenth century and was briefly an urban outpost of the fragile French empire.

Quebec The earliest settlement at Quebec, Samuel de Champlain's *habitation* (1608), was introduced in Chapter 1. Champlain worked hard to build a colony, but with only indifferent results. His replacement as governor, Charles Huault de Montmagny, arrived in 1636—the year after Champlain's death—determined to make the post into a town and to impose a sense of order on its growth. Under his direction Jean Bourdon, the colony's first engineer and surveyor, produced a map in 1640 that indicated (for the first time) a regular street alignment and confirmed that Quebec would develop into a town with two distinct areas divided by a formidable natural escarpment. The Lower Town, a confined area between the cliff and the river, grew up around Champlain's *habitation* and became the residential and commercial district, characterized by narrow streets and small lots; while the Upper Town grew around the fortifications (Fort Saint-Louis) and became the military, administrative, religious, and agricultural centre with wide streets and ample properties, including land grants to religious communities.[2]

The dominant building in early Quebec was Fort Saint-Louis, which had initially been built by Champlain in 1620 on the bluff high above his trading post and which he rebuilt nine years later. Governor de Montmagny strengthened the fortification and within it he built a one-storey château as his own residence in 1647. The Château Saint-Louis was frequently repaired and enlarged, most notably by Governor Frontenac, who rebuilt it with two storeys in 1692-1700. The architect was François de Lajoüe (*c*. 1656-*c*. 1719), a stone-cutter from Paris who was summoned to Quebec about 1688 to work on the churches of the town, and who quickly became a leading contractor and architect. After being given a third storey in 1808-11, the Château Saint-Louis was destroyed by fire in 1834.[3]

An official residence was also required for the intendant, when this office was created by Louis XIV in 1663. On his arrival Jean Talon first lived in the Sénéchaussée, where the governing Council met (it was demolished in the early eighteenth century), and later moved into his own house. In 1688 his successor, Jacques DeMeulles, acquired a brewery on the St Charles River, a tributary of the St Lawrence just north of Champlain's *habitation*—the brewery was one of the industries that had been established by Talon—and transformed it into a palace. A new and grander Intendant's Palace was built in 1715; it survived the British seige of 1759, but was damaged by the American seige in 1775 and fell into ruin.[4]

The religious orders, like the temporal leaders, erected imposing institutional buildings. The Récollets built their residence of Notre-Dame-des-Anges on the St Charles River in 1620, but they left Canada nine years later when Quebec was captured for Britain by the privateering Kirke brothers (it was restored to France in 1632). On their return in 1670 the Récollets found the buildings in ruins and immediately began to rebuild; one wing was erected by Governor Frontenac, who reserved an apartment for himself (the wing was demolished in the eighteenth century).

In 1692 Bishop Saint-Vallier purchased the Récollet monastery and converted it into a public hospital, the **Hôpital-Général**. Much of the work—some of it alterations and some new construction—was done in 1710-12 under the direction of the Quebec-born master mason and architect Jean-Baptiste Maillou *dit* Desmoulins (1668-1753). One of the portions likely built by Jean Maillou, as he is known, is the Infirmary Wing [2.1], seen here in an early-twentieth-century photograph, with the raised-bed gardens tended by the Augustine sisters in the foreground. The wing has three full storeys and an attic floor within the gable roof illuminated by dormer windows. The austere walls are constructed of rubble stone with flat lintels over the doors and windows (the seventeenth-century openings had low segmental-arched heads). The roofs are covered with tin tiles

2.1 Hôpital-Général, Quebec, Quebec. Infirmary Wing, *c*. 1710-12. Photograph by Ramsay Traquair, 1928. Ramsay Traquair Archive, no. 105791. MU.

(*ferblanc*, actually tin-plated iron), and the fragments of wall that protrude through the roof at intervals are fire-breaks, intended to arrest the spread of fire. The steeple (called a *clocher*, because it contains a bell or *cloche*) marks the entrance to the chapel and the nuns' choir, whose walls (seen at the right) are those of the early Récollet church of Notre-Dames-des-Anges. Another survival from the Récollets is the wood-panelled refectory, claimed as one of the oldest continually inhabited rooms in North America.[5]

The design approach seen in the Hôpital-Général—featuring large, plain rubble-stone buildings organized around one or more courtyards—was characteristic of the many institutional buildings in the colony. It appears as well, for example, at the Séminaire (founded in 1663),[6] the Jesuit College, and the Ursuline Convent, all of which developed large building complexes erected over extended periods.

Little is known about the dwellings of the first settlers, other than that they were generally small—often about 20 feet (6 m) square—and not very comfortable, and were built in a variety of materials that are discussed below with domestic architecture. Mère Marie de l'Incarnation described the house of Jean Juchereau de Maur in the Lower Town: 'The small house is so poorly built that through the planks we can see the stars at night, and one can hardly keep a candle lighted because of the wind.'[7]

Louis de Buade, Comte de Frontenac, came to Quebec in 1672 as the new governor and, like de Montmagny nearly forty years earlier, determined to impose order on the urban form as well as the inhabitants. On his arrival he described his impressions to Colbert:

Nothing appears to me so beautiful and magnificent as the situation of the city of Quebec, which could not be better sited to become some day the capital of a great empire; but I find that so far people have made what seems to me to be a very great error in allowing houses to be built to the whim of individuals, and without any order, because in settlements such as these which might one day become quite considerable, we should, I believe, consider not only the present situation, but also those things that might be attained.[8]

A year later he commented on the limited space available for expansion:

It is necessary, if we want [the city] to be enlarged and embellished, that we take greater care than has been done until now with the alignment of houses that are built...because if no regulations are enacted and if we do not constrain those who have lands within the boundaries that are to be determined...from now until five hundred years from now, there will be no more houses in Quebec than there are at present, and there will not be an inch of land to give to the many people who ask me for some on which to build new houses.[9]

In order to address these issues, Frontenac brought in a series of regulations that were the first planning controls in the colony—and in today's Canada. Construction was forbidden in Quebec unless it followed the alignment of projected streets and received the governor's approval. In addition, the first of many building standards intended to lessen the risk of fire were introduced.[10]

Fire was a very real hazard, and on the night of 4 August 1682 a dreaded blaze broke out:

A house in Lower Town caught fire and as all the houses were very inflammable, being built only of wood and the season being very dry, the fire spread so quickly that in a short time the whole town was reduced to ashes....We awoke to terrible cries coming from the neighbourhood and we were very alarmed to see that it was as light as day outside. The flames were so fierce and high that they caused great fear. Nothing could be saved of fine and beautiful merchandise which was stocked in the shops and more was lost that sad night than the whole of Canada possesses at present.[11]

Fifty-five houses—two-thirds of the Lower Town—were destroyed. Reconstruction began immediately, funded to a large measure by the generosity of the wealthy merchant Charles Aubert de la Chesnaye, whose grand stone mansion was spared by the flames. Intendant DeMeulles and hydrographer Jean-Baptiste-Louis Franquelin seized the opportunity to enlarge the houses, regularize the street plan, and create a unified market square—the Place du Marché—with about twenty houses, mostly built of stone, set around it. The square was completed in 1688 with the construction of the church of Notre-Dame des Victoires. Two years earlier DeMuelles's successor, Intendant Champigny, had erected a bronze bust of Louis XIV in the square, and from that date it was known as **Place-Royale [2.2]**.[12]

The buildings of Place-Royale were badly damaged during the bombardment of Quebec in 1760—more than 40,000 cannonballs and 10,000 bombs fell on the city during the two-month British attack—and during the next two centuries many more changes occurred. In the 1960s the Government of Quebec set aside funds to restore those buildings that had survived from the French regime and reconstruct the ones that had been replaced. Several post-Conquest buildings were recklessly demolished in the process. (This nationalistic policy was discontinued in the 1980s.) The Place-Royale of today—zealously, if somewhat

2.2 Place-Royale, with the Church of Notre-Dame des Victoires, Quebec, Quebec. Photograph by Luc Noppen.

2.3 An inset view of Quebec, Quebec, from a map by Jean-Baptiste-Louis Franquelin, 1688. ANQ/no.E-6-7 /nn 6830051.

inaccurately, recreated—gives the visitor to Quebec an excellent idea of the character of the square at the end of the French regime. The photograph shows the Church of Notre-Dame-des-Victoires. The two-storey house to the left was the residence of Jean-Louis Fornel, a wealthy merchant with interests in the Labrador fishery. It was entirely reconstructed in 1964 to its present appearance, believed to have been the way it looked at the end of the eighteenth century, although documents since discovered show that it had three, and not two, storeys before the bombardment. In the foreground is the larger house of Marie-Anne Barbel, Fornel's widow, who carried on his business after his death in 1745. Master mason Joseph Routier (1708-59) built this house for Barbel in 1754-5. It has been restored according to its description in the building contract between Barbel and Routier. The third house along this east side of Place-Royale, in the shadow of Notre-Dame-des-Victoires, is known as La Gorgendière.[13]

The appearance of **Quebec in 1688** [2.3] is seen in a detailed view by Franquelin that was included as an inset in his large map of North America. The spectacular natural setting that so impressed Governor Frontenac is evident. The Lower Town is shown as a compact agglomeration of buildings, but a keen eye can pick out Place-Royale near the centre (with the bust of the King), the cannon emplacement on the waterfront to the left, and to the right the mansion of Charles Aubert de la Chesnaye (almost directly below the three tall spires). Houses are strung out at a lower density along the river to the left (south) and right. Rue de la Montagne, lined with buildings, leads up the hill to the Upper Town, where the large institutions are all located: from left to right, the principal ones are the Château Saint-Louis (the broad, fortified building with two rows of dormer windows in the roof); the Ursuline convent (with a small cupola over one

31

of its two tall wings); the Jesuit church (with the two tallest spires, exaggerated in the illustration); in front of it, the broad, incomplete tower of the Cathedral of Notre-Dame, at this time under construction to expand the small church of Notre-Dame-de-la-Paix, which can be seen to its right; and, finally, the broad expanse of the Séminaire. The complex at the far right is the original Récollet monastery, soon to become the Hôpital-Général, on the shore of the St Charles River. (Those buildings that have not already been discussed will be introduced later in this chapter.)

The threat of enemy attack was constantly present, whether from the restless Iroquois or from France's belligerent European neighbours, the British. The wooden palisade seen above the Lower Town represents the beginning of an *enceinte* (enclosure) around the city, but it provided poor protection. Engineer Robert de Villeneuve (*c*. 1645-d. after 1692) was sent to Quebec in May 1685 by Louis XIV's military architect Sébastien le Prestre de Vauban (1633-1707), Europe's leading expert on fortifications, in order to direct the construction of better defences. Villeneuve proposed extending the *enceinte* around the entire city. When Port Royal fell to Admiral William Phips and the British in May 1690, and with the Iroquois massacre at

Lachine in 1689 still fresh in the colony's memory, the Town Major, François Provost, built a palisade along the western boundary in only six weeks. It consisted of eleven masonry redoubts—independent armed outworks—connected by wooden palisades that were constructed by inserting stakes into the ground. This was reinforced by engineer Josué Dubois Berthelot de Beaucours (*c*. 1662-1750) in 1693 with earthworks and bastions (diamond-shaped structures that provided good firing angles on two faces, and that followed the techniques of Vauban); additional improvements were undertaken by Beaucours and his successors in the following decades.[14]

The most important of these successors, in terms of his contribution to the architecture of New France, was Gaspard-Joseph Chaussegros de Léry (1682-1756). He was born in Toulon and, like his father and brother (and, after him, his son and son-in-law), was a military engineer. He served for ten years with the French armed forces, during which time he wrote a long 'Traité de fortification' (completed in 1714 but not published). He was posted to New France in 1716 to improve the defences of Quebec and was subsequently appointed chief military engineer for the colony, responsible for designing and building fortifications, town plan-

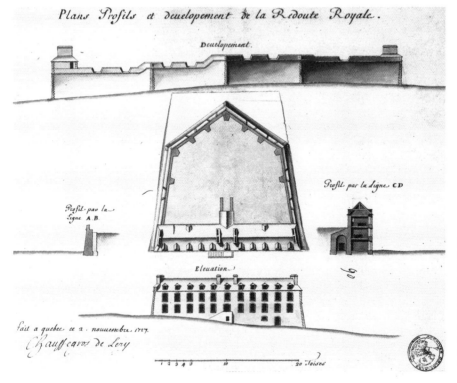

2.4 La Redoute Royale, Quebec, Quebec. Elevations, plan, and section by Gaspard-Joseph Chaussegros de Léry, 1727. From *Atlas Moreau de Saint-Rémy*/F3 290.90. Archives nationales (France), Centre des Archives d'Outre-Mer, Aix-en-Provence.

2.5 Hope Street (rue Sainte-Famille), with a funeral procession, Quebec, Quebec. Watercolour and pen-and-ink drawing by James Pattison Cockburn, 1830. Royal Ontario Museum/951x205.18.

ning, and public buildings. Chaussegros was a versatile and imaginative leader whose list of achievements is impressive. They included designing the forts at Chambly and Niagara, alterations to the Château Saint-Louis, a new Intendant's Palace after a fire in 1726, and much more—although he seems to have been only an indifferent engineer who failed to gain a coveted appointment to the military engineer corps. He remained in Quebec until his death.[15]

Chaussegros continued to improve the *enceinte* and its fortifications, helping to make the city of Quebec a walled fortress. The many components on which he worked included the construction of the new barracks (*nouvelles casernes*) at Parc de l'Artillerie (1749-52), which were about 600 feet (200 m) long, the longest in North America; and completing the **Redoute Royale [2.4]**, located behind the Ursuline Convent, a pentagonal stone structure with a battlemented gun platform and a three-storey wing that served for a time as a military prison. Begun by Beaucours in 1712, the redoubt was completed in 1745.[16] Chaussegros also pro-

posed expanding the redoubts on Cap-Diamant, the high plateau just southwest of the Upper Town (on the left in the Franquelin view), to create a large citadel as an independent defensive work that would both support the *enceinte* and command all shipping on the St Lawrence. France, however, balked at the cost of the citadel project, just as it had skimped over the years on all of the defences at Quebec. It was left to the British conquerers to complete the fortifications (see pages 221-9).

Quebec grew considerably during the eighteenth and early nineteenth centuries, under both French and British rule. The population increased from 2,000 in about 1710, to 5,000 on the eve of the Conquest, to 20,000 in 1820. The Lower Town was expanded slightly by landfill, but most of the new development occurred in the Upper Town. A watercolour view drawn in 1830 by James Pattison Cockburn, one of many scenes of Quebec by that talented officer-artist, shows a funeral procession

2.6 Château Saint-Louis, Louisbourg, Nova Scotia. Built *c*. 1730 and reconstructed in the 1960s. Photograph by Ted Grant, 1972. Courtesy of the Canadian Museum of Contemporary Photography, NFB Collection/72-1706.

proceeding along **rue Sainte-Famille** [**2.5**] towards Notre-Dame Cathedral, a tower of which is visible on the left, beyond the gable end of the Seminary chapel. The one-storey houses with large dormer windows are typical of those built in the early seventeenth century. The two-storey houses were built both before and after the Conquest; the one in the left foreground sports a classical doorway and a bowed window characteristic of British classicism, whereas the steeper roofs of the two houses facing the end of the street suggest that they were built during the French regime. The house half-way up the left, with the ladder on its roof, was built by Chaussegros for himself, and in 1830 it was occupied by two descendants, the Honourable Chaussegros de Léry and the notary public William de Léry. The steeple on the axis of the street (competing with that of the Catholic Cathedral on the left) is part of the Anglican Cathedral [**4.51**]. The newer buildings respect their predecessors in massing, scale, and character, revealing a consistency and a strong local flavour that were oblivious to political change.[17]

Louisbourg As part of the terms of the Treaty of Utrecht (1713) France ceded to Britain its claims to Newfoundland and Acadia. In order to provide itself with an economic and military foothold on the Atlantic coast of North America, France retained Île Royale (Cape Breton Island) and Île Saint-Jean (Prince Edward Island). The town of Louisbourg (named after the King) was established on the former. Some 160 people arrived in Louisbourg in 1713, most of them fishermen (but there were also some carpenters) from Placentia in Newfoundland, and within two years the population had grown to about 750. There was little security in the early years, because it was uncertain whether or not Louisbourg would become the island's principal town, and this was reflected in the temporary nature of the first buildings.

The earliest houses were built by the newly arrived Newfoundlanders in the manner of that earlier colony: with closely spaced, upright poles driven into the ground, covered with roofs of boards or bark (see page 89). The technique was known in French as *piquets de bout*, *pieux en terre*, or *en pieux*—the English-speaking Newfoundlanders later called it studded construction—and the houses were known to the settlers as *piquets*.[18]

Louisbourg was made the capital of Île Royale in 1719, partly because of its excellent all-weather harbour. The French government provided the funding to build a permanent fortified administrative and military centre with a resident governor. Although Louisbourg was technically responsible to New France, it functioned much as an independent colony. The fortress town was constructed in the 1720s and 1730s, and it became home to as many as 4,000 civilians and to a garrison of be tween 1,000 and 4,000 soldiers. All construction materials, tools, and beasts of burden had to be brought out from France or imported from New England. Even house frames were shipped from New England. Once built, Louisbourg became a centre of military and commercial activity and ranked as the third-busiest seaport on the continent, after Boston and Philadelphia. The town was reasonably self-sufficient, trading cod for food and supplies and serving as an important base for France's large fishing industry.[19]

The townsite occupied nearly 60 acres (24 hectares) and was laid out according to European planning ideals on a rectangular grid of about thirty blocks. A total of forty-five blocks were numbered, but not all were complete or buildable, in part because some influential citizens refused to accept the new boundaries—a kind of 'citizens' revolt' against abstract planning! (Some suburbs developed outside the fortified townsite.) To the north and east lay the harbour and the Atlantic Ocean, defended by three batteries: one on a small island; the Royal Battery, facing the harbour and the town; and a third one in the town. A bastion and a demi-bastion (a bastion with only a single flank) were later added to the seaward defences. To the west and south lay open land, and here the town was defended—poorly, as it turned out—by a 'curtain' (a wall) reinforced with two bastions and two demi-bastions, each named after a member of the royal family.

Once Louisbourg was designated the capital, a number of large public buildings were erected, mostly in masonry. Military engineer Jean-François de Verville (c. 1670/5-1729) began to build the defences; he was replaced by Étienne Verrier (1683-1747), who in two decades as the town's chief engineer was responsible for its layout, designed most of the public buildings, and completed the fortifications.[20]

The largest structure in Louisbourg—and also the largest in New France, and possibly in all of North America—was the citadel, located along the southwestern perimeter wall. It was made up of the **Château Saint-Louis [2.6]**, a structure nearly 365 feet (111 m) long, completed in the early 1730s, that contained wings for the governor and the civil administrator (the latter, known as the *commissaire-ordonnateur*, preferred, however, to live in the town), as well as officers' quarters, barracks, and a chapel; and the King's Bastion, a principal component of the landward defences. The façade of the Château Saint-Louis, facing Place d'Armes (the mil-

itary parade) and the town, gave the appearance of a broad, two-storey building with projecting wings at the end, a medium-pitched roof pierced by many large chimneys and small dormer windows, and a central clock-tower and spire. The walls were rubble stone, with vertical pilaster strips of brick inserted between every pair of shuttered windows. The only exceptions to this treatment were the entrance pavilion, capped by a small roof, and the four tall windows of the chapel to its left. Other public buildings, including a large hospital, were similar in appearance. A number of imposing gates gave the town an air of formality.[21] (The tall lighthouse is illustrated in **5.1**.)

The constant humidity, the frequent freeze-thaw cycles, and the speed with which the buildings were erected made maintenance an ongoing and serious problem. The rapidly deteriorating stone walls were stabilized first with mortar and then with wooden planks fastened with nails and iron clamps. Despite these efforts, it was said that during Louisbourg's two sieges the bastions suffered more from the concussion of the French forces' own cannon than by shots fired by the enemy.[22]

A considerable amount of private construction occurred as well [2.7], and the many buildings included houses, shops, taverns, storehouses, stables, and other service structures. Masonry, *colombage* (wood frame with masonry infill), wood frame with vertical board siding, and upright logs (*piquets*) were among the materials used. The sidewalks were cobbled and the streets unpaved. The town had more than one hundred gardens—most of them private vegetable and herb gardens—and maintained a lively marketplace.[23]

2.7 Rue Toulouse, Louisbourg, Nova Scotia, looking towards Port Frédéric. Reconstructed in the 1960s. The Fortress of Louisbourg, National Historic Site/Slide 05 R04607.

The life of Louisbourg was short, because the site was overlooked by hills and therefore poorly defended. The town was besieged by the British navy and New England land forces in 1745. Cannon fire from the hills to the west breached the walls, and the garrison surrendered before an assault was launched. All was for naught, however, since in 1749 Île Royale was returned to France by treaty and the fortifications were strengthened. A second siege was undertaken in 1758 by a force of 15,000 British soldiers, supported by more than 150 ships, led by Generals Amherst and Wolfe. The same vulnerable positions were again battered—François Bigot, the financial commissary of Île Royale from 1739 to 1745, described the Dauphin Gate as being no stronger than a country house[24]—and once more the town was forced to surrender. The residents were repatriated to France, and because the British had no need for Louisbourg—Halifax, founded in 1749, would suffice as a maritime port—and feared that it might again be returned to France, they systematically demolished the fortifications. With the signing of the Treaty of Paris in 1763, France lost all her possessions in North America, with the exception of unfortified fishing stations on the islands of Saint Pierre and Miquelon.

Although the buildings and fortifications of Louisbourg were destroyed by the British, the ruins acquired a significance that was romanticized in the 1880s by historian Francis Parkman:

> Here stood Louisbourg; and not all the efforts of its conquerors, nor all the havoc of succeeding times, have availed to efface it. Men in hundreds toiled for months with lever, spade, and gunpowder in the work of destruction, and for more than a century it has served as a stone quarry; but the remains of its vast defences still tell their tale of human valor and human woe.[25]

Retired naval officer D.J. Kennelly purchased a part of the Louisbourg property in 1903 and developed the ruins as a privately operated historic attraction. Support for the development of the site as a national historic park led to planner Thomas Adams's being sent to Louisbourg in 1923. In his report to James Harkin, National Parks Commissioner, Adams (see Chapter 12) recommended minimal intervention in the site:

> The site of the Fort is an impressive one, apart from its exceptional historic interest. There is a certain grandeur and wildness about the harbour of Louisbourg and the surrounding hills, as seen from the site, that makes one feel in a mood to enjoy its romantic character and visualize the historic events that were witnessed from it.... [I] enjoyed witnessing everything on the site—whether in ruins or changed by nature—that belonged to the distant past, and disliked the structures or improvements that had been carried on in recent years.[26]

As at Port Royal, local historians disagreed with this approach and wanted the site actively developed. The property was acquired by the Department of the Interior in 1928 and some of the ruins were stabilized. A museum was built in 1935 (designed by W.D. Cromarty [1884-1960] of the Department of Public Works) and in 1940 the site was formally established as a National Historic Park. In the following years activity picked up. Nineteenth- and twentieth-century houses were removed and a campaign of serious archaeological investigation was begun in 1961. This led to the painstaking—and expensive—reconstruction of several blocks of private houses and commercial buildings, the town quay, the citadel, and part of the fortifications. Work continued over a period of more than two decades, and was made possible by the survival of some 500 maps, plans, and views drawn by French engineers. Louisbourg is now a popular tourist attraction, immersing visitors in the vividly animated re-creation of the life of the fortress town as it might have been in the early 1740s, at the peak of its prosperity.

The seigneurial system

The Compagnie des Cent-Associés, which was permitted by its charter to allocate the land in New France as it saw fit, chose to grant large parcels to the most influential colonists, who in turn subdivided the land to tenants. The grants were called seigneuries, and they were given to landlords called seigneurs; the tenants were known as *censitaires* or *habitants*. The first seigneuries were located along the St Lawrence River between Quebec and Montreal, and they later spread along the Richelieu and Ottawa Rivers and the more remote reaches of the St Lawrence.[27]

The seigneuries varied in size, with many of the early grants being particularly large. When the seigneuries were subdivided for the tenants, the property lines were usually drawn perpendicular to the river—although the boundaries might be influenced by other natural features, such as hills—creating individual properties (*rotures*) that were narrow and deep, each with frontage on the river

2.8 *A View of Château-Richer, Cap Torment and Lower End of the Isle of Orleans near Quebec 1787*. Watercolour by Thomas Davies. National Gallery of Canada/Acc. no. 6275.

(at first the sole means of transportation) and going back far enough to provide land for cultivation, pasture, and firewood. Many lots were sliced yet again, when an *habitant* left his property to more than one son, and with each subdivision the slices became narrower and narrower. As a measure of control, an ordinance of 1745 prohibited the erection of buildings on rural lots that were narrower than $1\frac{1}{2}$ arpents (just under 300 feet).[28]

This system of land division created river lots, and was based on the experience in Normandy, whence many of the settlers had come. The *habitants* usually chose to build their houses at the front of the property, close to the river and the houses of neighbours. So consistent was this development that a traveller in the 1700s could see almost all the houses in Canada while canoeing along the St Lawrence and Richelieu Rivers.

The eighteenth-century rural landscape is illustrated well in Thomas Davies' watercolour, *View of Château-Richer* (*c.* 1787), which looks northward from the Côte de Beaupré on the St Lawrence, a short distance below Quebec [2.8]. The Île d'Orléans is seen at the right, and the promontories of the Canadian Shield are seen in the centre dis-

tance. Eel traps have been constructed on the tidal marshes of the river. The stone farmhouse in the centre foreground is surrounded by wood barns, smaller outbuildings, and a kitchen garden. Houses and barns of a similar appearance, some with thatched roofs, extend along the shore, the picket fences indicating the boundaries of the narrow properties.[29] (River lots of this kind became the characteristic survey system adopted by French-speaking Canadians as they migrated west, and are found along the Red and Assiniboine Rivers in Manitoba, and along portions of the North and South Saskatchewan Rivers in Saskatchewan and Alberta; see Chapter 7.)

The row of river lots was referred to as a *rang*, which is sometimes translated as 'range'. As the lots became so narrow that further subdivision across their width was futile, a second row was created at the rear of the first *rang*. The earliest of these *second rangs* was formed in 1722 at Saint-André-de-Tilly, and *troisième rangs* appeared near Trois-Rivières in the 1760s.[30]

2.9 *Rang du second ruisseau* (second creek road), Calixa-Lavallée, Quebec. IBC/75.657.28A(35).

Since the *second rangs* had no river frontage, they required land access. Roads were built between the first and second *rang*, and the houses on the second *rang* were usually placed close to the road. *Rangs doubles* developed in time, with houses facing each other on either side of the road. The first through road, known as the *Chemin royal* (Royal highway), linked Quebec with Montreal in 1734.[31]

Natural landscape features influenced the division of land. At Calixa-Lavallée (formerly the parish of Sainte-Théodosie, but renamed in 1974 to honour the composer of *O Canada*, a local son)—a portion of the former seigneury of Verchères east of Montreal—each of the roads that separate the three *rangs* follows one of three creeks, providing the properties with access to fresh water. Generally (with, of course, exceptions) the roads run east-west, but the lot lines, and most of the houses, are oriented precisely north-south. This creates a deviation between the alignment of the houses and that of the roads, which can be seen clearly in an aerial view of the *rang du second ruisseau*, the second creek [**2.9**].[32]

The seigneur retained a *domain* near the centre of the seigneury, a property that was wider than those of the *censitaires* and that also fronted on the river. A part of the *domain* was used as a common by the *habitants*, and sometimes land was provided by the seigneur for a church and presbytery.

The seigneur and the *censitaire* held certain mutual obligations. The seigneur was required to retain an inhabited manor on the *domain,* although it was not necessary that he himself live there, and he had to build and operate a communal mill. He was also expected to contribute to the building and operation of the church and the presbytery. The *censitaire*, for his part, had to clear his land and live on it, and to pay annual rent (*rentes* or *cens*) at the manor, usually on St Martin's Day (11 November). He was also required to do necessary work on roads and bridges. The seigneur sometimes demanded labour (*corvée*) as well as rent from his *habitants*, but this was discouraged by the authorities.

The seigneurial system had much in common with the feudal system in France, in which serfs were strictly dependent on their lords. It was introduced in New France, however, more likely as an effective method of settling the colony rather than to extend an archaic and repressive social system. Early commentators emphasized the impact of the seigneurial system on the environment—its land division, landscape, and architecture. It has been argued, however, that the seigneury was not a

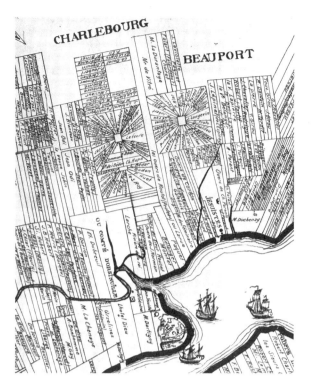

2.10 Plans of Charlesbourg and Bourg-Royal, Quebec. Detail from *Carte du gouvernement de Quebec levée en l'année 1709 par S. Catalogne...et dressé par Jean Bt. Decouagné.* Original in the Dépôt Général des Cartes, Plans et Journaux de la Marine. PF 127-2-2. Bibliothèque nationale, Paris. This print—from a 1921 transcript by A.E. Courchesne—is held by the NAC/C-15703.

cohesive social unit, and that the seigneur rarely was seen as a leader by his *habitants*. 'The social structure of the colony', writes Cole Harris, 'would not have been markedly different if all *rotures* [properties] had been held directly from the king, and the Canadian *seigneur* eliminated.'[33]

The residents of nineteenth-century Quebec increasingly resented the seigneurial system. It was viewed as favouring the privileged classes and interfering with economic development. The seigneuries were abolished in 1854, when *censitaires* were permitted to claim ownership of their land.

2.11 Aerial view of Charlesbourg, 1937. Photograph by W.B. Edwards. Archives de la Société historique de Charlesbourg.

Villages

In 1665 Louis XIV advised Talon that the settlers should be regrouped to live in villages to provide a measure of defence against Iroquois attack, as well as to allow more efficient administration and better access to common lands and facilities. Talon began to lay out several villages, but for the most part early attempts at creating nuclear settlements received little co-operation from the *habitants* and were unsuccessful. Beyond the half-dozen sites set aside by Talon, the land-division pattern would have required a seigneur (or the Crown) to acquire several *rotures*, or to subdivide the domain in order to provide a plot for a village. Perhaps the most important reason for the failure of villages was the *habitants'* resistance. As an anonymous report of around 1689 explained: 'There is no doubt that... the people of this country, neither docile nor easy to govern, are very difficult to constrain, for they like freedom and no domination at all.'[34]

Despite these difficulties, there were six villages (as well as some smaller hamlets) in New France at the end of the French regime. Each was the centre of a parish, and each had a prominent church. **Charlesbourg** [2.10], near Quebec, was the only one laid out by Talon that was still in existence a century later. Established on land owned by the Jesuits, the town was one of four—the others were called Bourg-Royal, Bourg-la-Reine, and Bourg-Talon—intended to be laid out on a formal plan, with a central common from which wedge-shaped properties radiated. (Only Charlesbourg [2.11] and Bourg-Royal were actually developed in this manner.) The residents were supposed to live on their farms at the perimeter of the central area. Such an ideal plan was rooted in French seventeenth-century formal landscape and urban design, but it was somewhat out of place—and hence short-lived—in New France. Over time the central common was subdivided into small lots and new streets were added: the original intentions were obscured only in the 1950s.[35]

Other villages were located close to Montreal. Boucherville, on the south shore of the St Lawrence River, was founded in the early 1670s by Pierre Boucher on land he had set aside for this purpose. The villagers lived on small plots on a grid of streets, and the farmers' fields were located at a distance from their residences. The largest house in the village was the seigneur's manor (see page 40). Boucherville, like the other villages, developed into a service centre for the surrounding agricultural region. In 1723 it boasted five bakeries, a general store, a store that sold wheat, four storage sheds for grain, and a forge, and may well have had other commercial facilities in addition to its thirty-five houses.[36]

More common than nuclear villages were the lines of farmhouses, each at the front of its own narrow slice of land, that straggled along a road—often running past more than one seigneury—and gave the appearance of being an organized village. The road might run either along the river or between two *rangs*. A parish church, a presbytery, and a manor eventually appeared among the houses, along with some service facilities. This linear (or 'strip') development, with one or two streets perpendicular to the highway giving access to properties on a more remote *rang*, remains characteristic of many present-day French-Canadian communities.[37]

Domestic Architecture

The dwelling of the rural *habitant* is the most familiar architectural image from early Quebec. Simple, rectangular, and compact, with a steep roof embellished with heavy chimney and perhaps also curved 'bellcast' eaves (so-called because they are shaped like the flare of a bell) extending over a raised porch, it is one of the most recognizable of Canadian built forms. The appearance of the Quebec house was determined by a number of factors, including the settlers' European experience, their social and economic situation, the climate, the available materials, and even the Iroquois wars. In spite of an overall consistency, however, numerous differences are found in construction, plan, and detail.

The variety in materials was already evident early in the French regime. Pierre Boucher—a soldier, governor of Trois-Rivières, and the first seigneur of Boucherville—noted this in 1663:

What are the houses built of? Some are built entirely of stone [*toutes de pierres*] and covered with boards or planks of pine: others are built of wooden framework or uprights, with masonry between [*de collombages ou charpente et massonnées entre les deux*]; others are built wholly of wood [*tout à fait de bois*]; but all the houses are covered [*couvertes*], as I have said, with boards.[38]

Ramsay Traquair (1874-1952), a respected architect and teacher at McGill University, and one of the first distinguished students of Quebec architecture, concluded that the first houses in New France were built of wood.[39] Some scholars have agreed that wood was the earliest and most common material in seventeenth-century New France, while others have suggested that stone and wood, with clay or stone infill—materials known in the old country—were first used. Although the question of the earliest materials remains unsolved—to a large extent because little that was built of wood during the French regime remains standing—it is now certain that the vast majority of rural houses after 1660 were built of wood, with and without masonry infill (see page 48).

The individual construction types provide a convenient means of classification. Stone houses are discussed first, because of their far-higher survival rate and our consequent familiarity with them.

Stone houses

One of the oldest houses to survive to the present day is the Cléophas **Girardin house** [2.12] in Beauport, near Quebec. Probably built between the 1650s and 1670s, and possibly not achieving the appearance in the illustration until the 1730s, it has since been altered by its present owners, the Sisters of the Congregation of Notre-Dame; but its earlier appearance is known from a photograph published by Pierre-Georges Roy in 1927. The importance of the house lies in its providing evidence of the source of a type of Canadian house in Normandy. Geographer Georges Gauthier-Larouche has demonstrated its resemblance to **La Mulotière** [2.13], a sixteenth-century house near Tourouvre, in the Perche district of Normandy. This Norman house was acquired in 1598 by Mathurin Maudit—whose cousin, Robert Giffard, was in New France briefly in 1627 and returned in 1634 as the first

2.12 Girardin house, Beauport, Quebec, *c.* 1650s-70s. Photographed in the 1920s, before the 'restoration'. ANQ, Collection initiale/P600/GH 370-149.

2.13 La Mulotière, near Tourouvre, Normandy, France, 16th century. From Mme Pierre Montagne, *Tourouvre et les Juchereau* (1965).

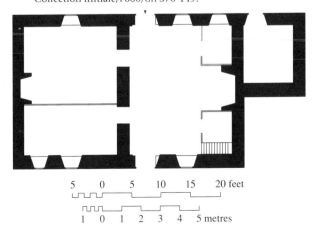

2.14 (*left*) Plan of the Girardin house, Beauport, Quebec, 1650s-70s. Drawing by David Byrnes.

seigneur of Beauport. Built by Cléophas Girardin within a generation or two of settlement, it was located inside the palisade erected by Giffard. Many features of the two stone houses are very similar, including their proportions, the steep gabled roof (with a slope of about 60°), the eaves that curve outwards slightly at the bottom and project a few inches from the wall, the end gables with chimneys, and the form and placement of the dormer windows. Even the relationship of the attached dependency—probably a dairy—is remarkably close.[40]

5   0   5   10   15   20 feet

1   0   1   2   3   4   5 metres

The ground floor [2.14] consisted of two rooms of approximately equal size, separated by a stone bearing-wall penetrated by two doors. Each room was located by a large fireplace in the exterior end wall. The second storey, an attic within the slope of the roof, also contained two rooms. In the seventeenth century uses were not differentiated by separate rooms, as they are today. Some houses of the period had only a single multi-purpose room on the ground floor—a survival of the *chambre* of medieval France—that was used for eating, receiving guests, sleeping, and various domestic activities. Many houses, like the Girardin house, had two rooms. The larger one combined the functions of kitchen and livingroom and during the cold winter months was also used for sleeping; the smaller one was a formal parlour reserved for special occasions, and may not have been used at all during the winter. One or two small spaces might have been partitioned off one of the rooms to be used as a bedroom(s) by the parents or grandparents (corresponding to the *cabinet(s)* of France). The attic, usually (as here) reached by a steep staircase, provided additional sleeping quarters, as well as storage for grain and perhaps other commodities. The plank floors might well have been painted yellow and covered with carpets or hooked rugs. Chests of drawers, and armoires placed against the walls, would have provided storage, and there might have been a *cabane*, or alcove bed, that provided a space-efficient sleeping area.[41]

The Girardin house illustrates the transfer of a traditional medieval house-form from Normandy to the St Lawrence valley and is 'vernacular' or 'folk' architecture. An unassuming, unstudied building erected by artisans according to local custom, it is not the product of conscious decisions about style or design, but incorporates the forms and materials that were most familiar to the new settlers. Houses of this kind were found by the hundreds or thousands in northern and central France—La Mulotière is convenient to cite simply because of the Giffard connection.[42]

In some respects, however, the Norman house was not well suited to the environmental conditions the immigrants found in their new homeland. The exterior walls and foundation were constructed of fieldstone (also called rubble masonry or random fieldstone)—stones of varying sizes and shapes that were collected while clearing the rock-littered fields of the Canadian Shield. Stone is strong and relatively permanent, but it offers little in the way of insulation. Stone buildings were

2.15 Gérard Morisset house, Cap Santé, Quebec, probably 1696. IBC/8161-D--2.

therefore very cold in winter. Mère Françoise Juchereau de Saint-Ignace complained about the cold in the Hôtel-Dieu in Quebec: 'In these stone buildings, there is an accumulation of frost on the walls which causes an unhealthy chill.'[43]

In order to help retain some warmth during the cold winters, and also to protect the mortared joints from deteriorating (the frequent freeze-thaw cycles were particularly damaging), stone walls were usually covered with a stucco-like layer of lime plaster known as *crépi*. The white coating—seen in the photograph of the Girardin house—was one of the ways in which the European prototype was made more appropriate to the climate, the land, and the way of life of New France.

The **Morisset house** [2.15] at Cap-Santé, about 30 miles (50 km) upriver from Quebec, is of particular interest because it was the home of architect and architectural historian Gérard Morisset (1898-1970), who restored the house in 1948. Morisset abandoned his notarial practice in 1929 to study architecture and art history in France. On his return to Canada he dedicated himself to researching and photographing the historic buildings of Quebec: in 1937 he was placed in charge of the Inventaire des Oeuvres d'Art (now the Inventaire des biens culturelles du Québec). He subsequently served as the first secretary of the Commission des Monuments Historiques du Québec, and as conservator at the Musée du Québec. The house—also known as the Chevalier house, after early-twentieth-century owner Joseph Chevalier—was likely built in 1696, and is therefore another rare survivor from the seventeenth century. Like the Girardin house, the Morisset house is representative of many modestly scaled farmhouses in the Quebec City region.[44]

It faces the southern sunshine and the St Lawrence River. Its symmetrical façade has two large casement windows on either side of a central door, which is protected by a small porch, and the main floor receives additional illumination from windows on the sides and rear. Two smaller windows on each side provide light for the attic, as does a modern dormer over the entrance. The roof is framed with a simple king-post truss—a horizontal tie-beam bridges each pair of rafters on opposite slopes, and is connected to the ridge by a vertical post (called a king post)—and a second tie-beam (or collar) is located lower down. The connections were all mortised and made without metal fasteners.

The plan is a simple rectangle, 41 feet (12.5 m) wide by $25\frac{1}{2}$ feet (7.8 m) deep. The principal storey was originally divided into two rooms; the room on the east was entered directly from the central door, and was therefore slightly wider than the other. Each room has a fireplace (and a chimney) along the side wall. The gable roof is very steep—its slope is 52°—and the height above the foundations is $31\frac{1}{2}$ feet (9.6 m).

The outbuildings have all disappeared, leaving the house standing in isolation. Outbuildings required to operate a farm were usually grouped with the house around a courtyard. For example, an other farm of the period, the Charles Belanger property at Château-Richer, had—in addition to the house, which was also used as a granary—a wood barn 46 by 24 French feet (slightly larger than an English foot—about 14 by 7.4 m) thatched in straw (thatched roofs were common in eighteenth-century Québec);[45] a log stable (écurie) 40 by 12 feet (12.3 by 3.7 m); a wood cow-barn (étable) 40 by 28 feet (12.3 by 8.6 m), also thatched; a chicken house; and a bake house, built of vertical posts with a stone chimney, 16 by 10 feet (4.9 x 3.1 m).[46] (Farm buildings of this kind, although on another property, can be seen in Thomas Davies' watercolour view of Château-Richer, 2.8.) In some cases the house and barn were combined in a single building, but this kind of maison-bloc was rare.[47]

Numerous variants of this type of house were built in New France, all of them having a familiar vertical massing. The **Villeneuve house** [2.16] at Charlesbourg differs from the Morisset house in its hipped (rather than gabled) roof and central chimney. Owner Louis Villeneuve established in 1908 that his ancestors (then named Auclair) had lived on the same land since 1684—he received an 'old families' medal as a tribute—and this has traditionally been accepted as the date of construction. However, it has recently been suggested that the substantial size of the house, and the documents, point rather to a date in the beginning—or perhaps even the middle—of the eighteenth century. The

2.16 Villeneuve house, Charlesbourg, Quebec, probably early 18th century. IBC/8865(A-13).

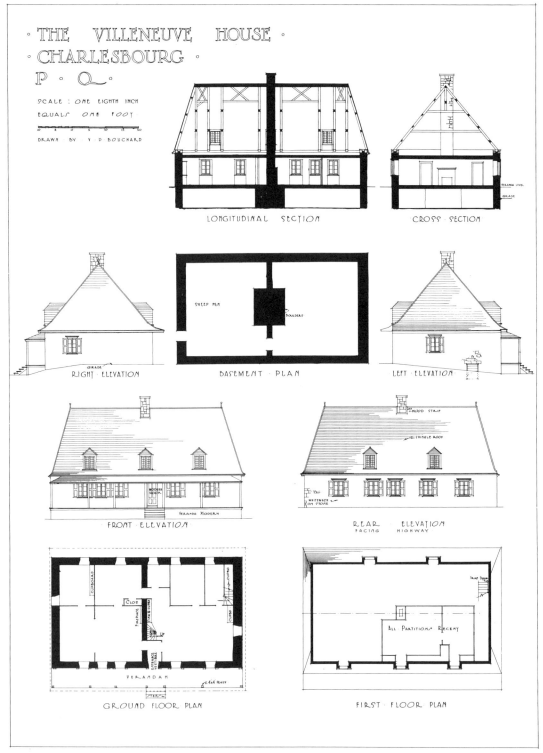

2.17 Plans, sections and elevations of the Villeneuve house, Charlesbourg, Quebec, probably early 18th century. Drawing by V.D. Bouchard. Ramsay Traquair Archive, no. 45.01/004 009/3, MU.

builder may have been François de Lajoüe, the architect of the second Château Saint-Louis; documents show that he sold a farm-lot and buildings in St-Bernard (the original name of the area) to Pierre Auclair in 1701. The Villeneuve and Girardin houses may both have been erected in more than one phase—as indeed many Quebec houses were.[48]

The steep hipped roof is certainly the dominant feature of the Villeneuve house. Its height, from the eaves to the ridge, is about 20 feet (6.2 m), or twice the height of the squat stone walls, and the chimney increases its verticality yet more. The hipped form (a *pavillon* roof), which appears on many farm houses in Quebec, was not characteristic of peasants' houses in France, where it was often seen on larger country houses and châteaux—the dwellings of the ruling class. Its use on farm houses in Quebec must therefore have been a new-world adaptation, perhaps to heavy loads of snow, or to a memory of Champlain's *habitations* at Île Sainte-Croix and Port Royal—or an imitation, naïvely purged of class distinctions, of the Château Saint-Louis at Quebec.[49] The eaves of the Villeneuve house are flared ever so slightly, foreshadowing the curved bellcast eaves that became common in the early nineteenth century. The ladder affixed to the roof provides access to the chimney in case of fire or the need for repair. The roof was very well constructed. As in the Morisset house, upper tie-beams are reinforced with king posts and backed-up by a second row of collars, and these are supplemented here by trusses in the form of an 'x'—called a Croix de Saint-André, after the x-shaped cross of St Andrew—that provide longitudinal wind-bracing. The carpentry and joinery generally show a high level of craftsmanship.

The principal façade, which has a porch (or *galerie*) of relatively recent construction, is oriented south towards the farmland of the St Lawrence valley, while the north front (seen in the photograph) faces the Laurentians. The walls are built of stone and covered with *crépi*, and the northeast end (exposed to the prevailing wind) has an additional external layer of wood siding to protect the masonry. This was a common practice, although clapboards were often removed as heating systems improved. While Pierre Boucher commented that 'all the houses are covered…with boards', he was referring not to the walls (as many writers have erroneously maintained) but to the roofs' (then called *couvertures*) being covered ('*couvertes*', Boucher's word) with boards.[50]

The area of the Villeneuve house is nearly twice that of the Morisset house—56 feet (17.1 m) wide and 32 feet (9.7 m) deep. The spacious plan [2.17] is again divided into two principal units, here about equal in size and separated by a stone wall that provides support for the chimney; the entrance leads directly into one of them. A series of partitions that are not original forms a second range of small rooms within the two main rooms, and creates what British architectural historians call a 'double-pile' plan. The smaller rooms indicate the tendency over time to subdivide spaces for more specialized activities, probably as bedrooms and pantries. A staircase leads to an attic, which likely provided space for sleeping and storage. The windows have panelled shutters.

Although both gabled and hipped roofs were common among houses in the Quebec region, casual analysis has suggested that most of those in the Montreal region had gabled roofs with a large chimney in each end wall. The **Hector Brossard house [2.18]** at Laprairie, on the south shore of the St Lawrence across from Montreal, likely built in the late seventeenth century, is similar in size and proportions to the Morisset house, although its roof pitch is much lower.[51] Other houses in this region, such as the Joseph Chaput house at Varennes and the Cherrier house at Repentigny,[52] have steeper roofs than the Brossard house, but all have squarer plans and consequently a lower, blockier, chunkier massing than the typical houses near Quebec.

2.18 Hector Brossard house, Laprairie, Quebec, late 17th century. IBC/5342 A-3.

2.19 Ferme Saint-Gabriel, Pointe Saint-Charles (Montreal), Quebec, begun 1698. Ramsay Traquair Archive, no. 101983, MU.

An early—and, historically, very significant—house that displays many of these features (although it is larger and was built for a special purpose) is the **Ferme Saint-Gabriel** [2.19] at Pointe Saint-Charles, now a part of Montreal. It is closely associated with Marguerite Bourgeoys, the most important woman in Ville-Marie and the first Canadian woman to be canonized (in 1982). She arrived from France in 1653 and organized the Congrégation de Notre-Dame de Montréal, a non-cloistered religious order that provided teachers and schools for the young colony (and is the present owner of the Girardin house at Beauport). She also served as a chaperone for the *filles du roi*. In 1668 Soeur Bourgeoys bought a farm, containing a wooden farmhouse, at Pointe Saint-Charles. This house was destroyed by fire in 1694 and was replaced by the present stone house in 1698. It has been used continuously since that time as the 'home farm' of the Sisters of the Congregation. The house stands somewhat incongruously in an industrial area near the Lachine Canal and is open to visitors.[53]

The original, central portion of the house is rectangular, 52 feet (15.9 m) wide and 20 feet (6 m) deep, and is built of rubble stone walls two feet (60 cm) thick. The larger of the two rooms on the ground floor (separated by a stone wall) is used as a common room [2.20], and the smaller as a kitchen. The house has a full upper storey that is used as a chapel and a dormitory. Its floor is constructed of $1\frac{1}{2}$-inch (38-mm) boards laid directly on top of 7″ x 10″ (18 x 25 cm) beams, without joists. The floor assembly is exposed to view from the ground floor. There is also an attic floor that is illuminated by dormer windows whose sills are set directly onto the plate at the top of the stone wall, a French method of construction that contrasts with the English manner of placing the dormers higher and entirely within the roof. At each end is a massive hearth and chimney. The house was enlarged by the addition of a low wing at either end (in 1726 and 1728), and a cupola has been placed atop the roof, over the second-storey chapel.

Differences among rural farmhouses built during the French regime in the Quebec and Montreal regions were noted a half-century ago by a number of scholars, who attributed them to the overseas origins of the settlers as well as to the conditions present in their new land. Morisset characterized the houses from the Quebec region as being wide and shallow, covered with ochre *crépi* or lime whitewash, having large windows with painted shutters, and covered by a steep, shingled roof with as many as three or four chimneys. He related them to the houses of Normandy, particularly those of Seine-Inférieure. In contrast, he suggested, the Montreal region's houses were short, massive, as deep as they were wide, flanked by robust chimneys and built of dark, heavy stones in thick white mortar, pierced by narrow windows, and often with dormer windows—the house 'seeming to rise from the ground like a domestic fortress.' He saw this style as coming from Brittany, particularly Basse-Bretagne, Anjou, and Maine.[54] Other scholars, following this lead, continued to assert the link between Quebec and Normandy, and between Montreal and Brittany, noting that these regions provided most of the settlers in New France. (Early writers, however, rarely attempted to identify specific buildings in those parts of France as sources.) The heaviness of the Montreal house has been attributed as well to the threat of Indian attack— which was so prevalent that carpenters demanded

armed protection while on the job—whereas this was less of a risk in the Quebec area because of the presence of the garrison.[55]

A new generation of scholars has questioned the contrasts between the Quebec and Montreal regions, suggesting that Morisset's conclusions were premature. Luc Noppen acknowledges the differences, but attributes them not to French sources but to the fact that the Montreal houses were later and based on urban models. Yves Laframboise notes that 'a careful examination confirms that all of our rural houses are far from conforming to these two types and to the characteristics that have been attributed to them.'[56] In an inventory of the houses of Neuville (a village not far from Cap Santé, in the Quebec region), which he directed in 1974-5, Laframboise discerned a regional type of house that differs, if only subtly, from the Quebec-region house described by Morisset. It may be anticipated that new definitions of regional types will emerge as research continues.

2.20 Common room, Ferme Saint-Gabriel, Pointe Saint-Charles, Quebec. Ramsay Traquair Archive, MU.

Wood houses

The vast majority of rural houses built in the French regime were constructed of wood, or a combination of wood and masonry. Wood was readily available as a waste product of clearing the land, and its insulating properties were soon appreciated. Recent work by Georges-Pierre Léonidoff, based on an exhaustive search of notarial documents that provide specific information on the construction of houses, has demonstrated the overwhelming predominance of wood after 1660.[57] Since few early wood houses—and, it seems, none from the seventeenth century—have survived, they are far less familiar than those of stone. The plans, massing, and exterior design of houses built of wood were comparable to those built of stone, and so the main interest in a discussion of wood houses lies in their construction techniques. Countless terms have been used to describe the various methods; those in most common usage are introduced here.

Heavy-timber frame This was a technique that was brought from France to New France with the earliest settlers. The principal structural members were vertical posts (*poteaux*) made of squared timbers, usually set onto a horizontal wood sill (in which case they are called *poteaux sur sole*, although sometimes they were placed directly on the ground and are known as *poteaux en terre*), and spaced as far apart as eight feet or as close together as a few inches. The interstices between the timbers were filled with masonry, wood, or a combination of materials. The joints between the timbers were mortised and tenoned: a tongue (or tenon) in the post fit into a slot (or mortise) in the sill, and the assembly was held together with a wooden pin (or dowel). A horizontal member, called a plate, rested on top of the posts and supported the roof. Diagonal bracing was often used at the corners for stability.

Documentary sources abound in references to this kind of construction. De Monts's house at Île Ste-Croix, erected in 1604, was described by Lescarbot as being of 'fair sawn timber' (also translated as 'fair and well-constructed timber-framing'), although the nature of the infill is not cited, and we have seen that the buildings there and at Port Royal were likely built of timber frames.[58] Within a decade or two, the medieval European technique of infilling the timber frame with stone and clay, called *colombage* (half-timbering), had become commonplace. The Récollet Order's house of Notre-Dame-des-Anges, constructed on the St Charles River at Quebec in 1620, was 'built of good strong framing and between the heavy timbers is walling 8 or 9 inches thick up to the roof—of good stone.'[59] Six years later Champlain directed the building of the colony's principal farm at Cap Tourmente, below Quebec, which included three houses 'of wood and clay in the manner of those that are built in the villages of Normandy'[60]—showing that Champlain himself was aware of the source of this medieval construction technique. And in 1644 Mère Marie de l'Incarnation reported in a letter to her son that, although many of the public and institutional buildings in Quebec were stone, the houses 'of the habitants are of framework filled with stone, two or three being also entirely of stone.'[61]

Colombage pierroté—infill of rubble stone, held together by a mortar made from a mixture of lime, clay, or mud (often with a binder of straw or pebbles)—was certainly the most common kind of infill in early New France. If the infill is brick, it is known as *colombage briqueté*; if it consists of a mortar-like material with little or no stone or brick, the construction is termed *colombage bousillé*. The exterior surface of the completed wall was often covered with wood siding or else rendered with a mortar-like mix. (The process of covering the wall with this mixture is called *bousillage*; in common usage the word connotes a botched job! See the Acadian and Métis houses described on pages 81 and 352-5.) When the walls are half timber and half infill, this method of construction is called 'half-timbering'.

Colombage pierroté was widely used in Normandy, including the region around Rouen, from which many early settlers came.[62] Although the new Canadians built frequently in that manner at first, they soon abandoned it because it was unsuited to the harsh climate, which quickly eroded the infill.[63] (New England builders encountered the same problem and responded by covering the frame and infill with horizontal clapboard.) Consequently, few examples of the technique survive in Quebec. One survivor is the much-altered Pichet house at Sainte-Famille on the Île d'Orléans, which was built some time between 1688 and 1772 (and is believed to be *c.* 1760). The wood sill is set on a stone foundation. The narrowly spaced posts and the stone-and-mortar infill were covered on the exterior with vertical boards—which protected the mortar from the weather, although they may not have been original—and more recently with imita-

2.21 Lamontagne house, Rimouski, Quebec, mid-18th century. Ministère de la Culture, Direction du Bas-Saint-Laurent.

2.22 Barn, Petit-Saguenay, near Saint-Siméon, Quebec, mid-19th century. Photograph by C.M. Barbeau, 1948. Canadian Museum of Civilization/J-3188.

tion brick siding, leaving the wall construction visible only in the attic, between the floor and the wall plate. The house was originally heated by a single central fireplace and consisted of a single room 47 feet (14.3 m) by 26 feet (7.9 m), with a small dairy at the end. The steep roofs had no dormer windows. Another survivor is the **Lamontagne house [2.21]** in Rimouski-Est, built in the middle of the eighteenth century, extensively restored by the Ministère des affaires culturelles in 1980-1, and now open to the public. The vertical timbers are spaced between 6 and 9 inches (15-23 cm) apart. The exterior was covered with vertical boards on the outside and with *crépi* inside.[64]

Colombage was common at Louisbourg, and the technique can be examined there in carefully reconstructed form. The method gradually disap-

peared in New France during the eighteenth century, but it survived well into the nineteenth in buildings on the Prairies erected by the French-Canadian carpenters of the Hudson's Bay Company.

The infill often consisted of wood rather than masonry. Squared logs were stacked horizontally (or vertically) in the spaces between the posts; horizontal infill logs were secured by tenons (or tongues) that fit into vertical grooves in the sides of the framing posts. (The connections were a larger-scaled version of the tongue-and-groove joint of today.) The posts were typically about 6 to 8 feet (2 to 2.5 m) apart, probably because it was convenient to make the horizontal infill logs this length. This technique, called *poteaux en coulisse* (grooved-post or post-and-groove), was an adaptation of the European *colombage* to the Canadian environment. The term *poteaux sur sole* (posts on sill) is sometimes used for this technique, but leads to confusion since it describes both *colombage* and *poteaux en coulisse*, both of which have structural posts resting on sills. It is therefore clearer to use a term that describes not the structure but the infill: *colombage* refers to masonry infill, and *poteaux en coulisse* to log infill.

As with the other kinds of wood construction, *poteaux en coulisse* was once common but is now quite rare in Quebec. Many of the survivors are barns and secondary structures, and it is easy to 'read' the construction in these farm buildings because, in contrast to houses, they were rarely if ever covered with exterior siding. A **barn at Petit-Saguenay [2.22]**, north of Saint-Siméon, probably built in the middle of the nineteenth century, illustrates the technique well. The long walls are divided by the posts into four structural bays, whereas the end walls consist of a single length of timber.[65]

This wall system is of particular interest because of its offspring. Thick sawn planks—3 to 4 inches (7.5-10 cm) thick or more, and laid on their edges—were sometimes inserted between the posts instead of hewn logs, in which case the term *madriers en coulisse* is used. Nineteenth- and twentieth-century carpenters continued to use horizontal planks and vertical posts set at intervals, substituting nails for the tenons and grooves. Plankwall construction, as the method has come to be known, was commonly used by Quebec builders as recently as the 1970s.[66] *Poteaux en coulisse* had an important progeny outside Quebec as well: it became the principal technique adopted by the builders for the western fur trade, and will be re-introduced in Chapter 7.

Log construction Houses might be constructed with load-bearing walls of logs, making the frame and the infill one and the same. In the most common method, logs were squared (with a broadaxe, adze, or saw), laid horizontally, one on top of the other, and connected at the corners with a splayed interlocking joint, learned from cabinet-making, called a 'dovetail'—or, in French, a *queue d'aronde* (swallow's tail)—because of the resemblance of the joint to the fan-like shape of the bird's tail. (In the seventeenth century the technique was known as *tête de chien* or dog's head!) If one surface of the key is splayed and one horizontal—simpler to craft but less rigid—the joint is called a 'half-dovetail'. This system of building with horizontal logs is therefore called *pièce sur pièce à queue d'aronde* [2.23]. (The expression *pièce sur pièce* is a generic term used to describe any method of laying squared timbers—*pièces*—on top of each other, whether *en coulisse* or *à queue d'aronde*.) The house in the photograph displays this technique (its corner joints have remained secure in spite of advanced deterioration).[67]

Although usually squared, the logs might be left rounded and connected with less-sophisticated notched corner joints (*pièce sur pièce en boulins* in French, and 'saddle-notched' in English), or the two might be combined [2.24]. An inventory of the possessions of Montrealer Louis Prud'homme,

compiled in 1673, describes 'an old house built of *pièce sur pièce*, partly squared and partly rounded, threatening to collapse.'[68] The wood was usually protected with either lime whitewash or *crépi*.

This technique, of course, is what the English-speaking world calls log-cabin construction. Horizontal logs were not known to English settlers in North America until the eighteenth century. Their first use in the US—as well as the source of the dovetail joint—is widely accepted to have been in the buildings of the Swedes and Germans who

2.23 (*above*) Log house in the Montreal region, constructed with the technique known as *pièce sur pièce à queue d'aronde*. Photograph by François Varin.

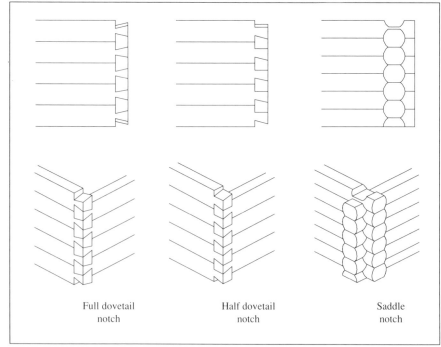

| Full dovetail notch | Half dovetail notch | Saddle notch |

2.24 Methods of log construction. Drawing by David Byrnes.

settled in the eastern US in the seventeenth century. However, it may have been the French who introduced horizontal log construction. Henri Joutel, who was with La Salle in Texas in 1685, clearly implied, in the following description of two Texas buildings, that dovetailing was by then already considered to be a Canadian technique:

> The first one was built *in the manner of Canada*, and the other almost in the same way...since the pieces of the latter were very straight and thick, they fit better; all of the pieces were fastened in a dovetail (*en queue d'aronde*) at the corners.[69]

Horizontal log construction was certainly in common use in Quebec by the middle of the seventeenth century—particularly in the Montreal region, where it was used for more than three-quarters of houses built between 1660 and 1726[70]—and by the late eighteenth century it had become the predominant technique in every region of Quebec. Whether French-speaking builders in North America developed the form independently, or adopted it from the buildings of the other European-American cultural groups, remains a matter for debate, as does the question of whether wood or stone was used first in New France. (See also the discussion of Acadian houses below.)

Another form of building in wood, *pieux en terre*, or palisade construction—a row of poles or logs (*pieux*) set in the ground to form a solid wall—was seen in the early mission chapels of New France. This form of construction emerged throughout Canadian building; it will reappear in the French and English 'tilts' of Newfoundland [3.2].

The rural house after the Conquest

At the end of the French regime, and in the early years of the nineteenth century, the house evolved into a more spacious building in which regional differences mostly disappeared, particularly in the more prosperous areas of rural Quebec. What emerged was the *'maison canadienne'*, as Morisset called it, or the *'tradition québécoise'*, in the words of architectural historian Yves Laframboise. The new type reflected both the increased stability of the province and the growing English influence after the Seven Years' War and the British Conquest.

The **Beauchemin house** (*c*. 1770) at Varennes, on rich agricultural land along the south shore of the St Lawrence a short distance downriver from Boucherville, is a handsome fieldstone dwelling from the beginning of this later stage in development [2.25]. (The adjacent Beauchamp house, built at the same time, is nearly identical.) It is deeper

2.25 Beauchemin house, Varennes, Quebec, *c*. 1770. Photograph by Yves Laframboise, 1972.

2.26 C.-X. Larue house, Neuville, Quebec, 1854. IBC/75.189.14A(35).

and taller than most of the houses we have seen before, having a second storey, illuminated by dormer windows, that is set within the high slope of the roof and contains an attic above it. Being larger than most of its predecessors, the house required more heat, and so each of the gabled end walls contains a pair of chimneys. (The four chimneys probably indicated affluence and social status.) The centre of the gable wall in the photograph is pierced between the chimneys on the second-floor by a door (which originally had a block and pulley over it) that was used to bring in grain and other commodities that were stored on the upper floors of the house.[71]

The steep roofs are covered in tin. Available only as an import from France—and hence expensive—tin, like slate, was reserved for churches and other important buildings. But when tin came down in price, its durability and fireproof qualities made it very popular for ordinary Quebec houses. The rural landscape of Quebec is still dominated by shiny roofs of this material.[72]

The roof slope of the Beauchemin house ends in deep bellcast eaves. These project sufficiently to protect from icicles, rain, and summer sun the raised porch, or veranda (*galerie* in French, and often called 'gallery' in English-speaking Quebec), that runs the length of each façade. The eaves, which were likely extended some time after the house was built, are supported by posts that rest on the floor of the porches. One porch is cantilevered out from the wall and raised high enough to be accessible even with an accumulation of snow on the ground. The deep curved eave and raised gallery, which began to appear in tandem around the beginning of the nineteenth century, would become the most recognizable feature of the French-Canadian house.

Various sources in France, and in American colonial buildings, can be identified for the eaves and galleries. Shallow curved eaves are found in Normandy (as at La Mulotière), and deeper bellcast eaves (without galleries) are seen further up the coast in French and Belgian Flanders.[73] Houses (and public buildings) with porches, and with deep eaves supported by posts, appeared (apparently earlier than in Quebec) in the French-speaking communities of the Mississippi valley in the middle of the eighteenth century. Several houses at Ste Geneviève, Missouri, for example, have porches of this kind on the front and back, and in some cases on all four sides; one contract made in 1770 for a house in that community specifies that the house shall have a porch $4\frac{1}{2}$ feet wide all around it.[74]

Porches supporting curved eaves are also characteristic of the seventeenth- and eighteenth-century Dutch Colonial architecture of New York and the other central Atlantic states, particularly in houses built by Dutch settlers of Flemish descent.[75] Whether the deep eaves and galleries of the Quebec house were adapted from French or Dutch buildings to the south (and linked by trade routes up the Mississippi and Hudson-Richelieu river systems), or whether they represent an independent and parallel development, has not been determined.

In Quebec the covered veranda—which appeared in tropical architecture from the East to the West Indies, offering protection against the sun—protected a house from the winter snow as well as the summer sun. It was one of the many ways in which the house-form evolved to respond to its environment.

Other adaptations to the climate include covering the stone walls with *crépi* and boards; raising the ground floor high, above snow level; insulating the floors; using double window sashes and doors (although at first windows were covered with paper and not glass); installing shutters; and experimenting with types of central heating (the stove and stove-pipe emerged as a reasonably effective solution).[76] Building with wood, which insulates against cold better than stone, may also have been a response to the winter climate—but, as was noted above, there is still no certainty about whether stone or wood was used first.

The general form of the Quebec house continued well into the nineteenth century. While the roof slope gradually became less extreme, the bellcast eaves, galleries, and dormer windows remained characteristic. Plans became larger and were divided into more rooms. The exterior façade was often symmetrical, five bays wide with a central doorway, and simplified classical ornament appeared around the windows and doors—both features showing the influence of the English Georgian house. Stone, wood, and occasionally brick were used as construction materials. The **C.-X. Larue house** (1854) at Neuville is a handsome nineteenth-century example in stone [2.26].[77]

In the middle of the nineteenth century, house-types characteristic of other regions of the country began to replace the traditional French-Canadian form. But (though it was altered in the 1950s) the Joseph Gagnon house (1890) at Château-Richer,[78] and many others like it, demonstrate that the old form persisted to the end of the nineteenth century in some regions of the province. In the 1960s the traditional house-form was revived as an expression of Quebec nationalism, and it has been enjoying a strong renaissance ever since.

Manor houses

The seigneur was obliged to build a manor (as well as a mill), but he did not have to live in it. Many seigneurs remained in France and left their manors to be inhabited by their agents or tenant farmers; and other manors belonged to religious orders. Those manor houses that were actually built by seigneurs for their own use give us some insight into the social order and values of the day.

The manors followed the same building patterns as the dwellings of their farmer tenants. Many were grander, with more and larger (and better furnished) rooms, while others were no larger than a *censitaire*'s house. The **manor house at Boucherville [2.27]**, built by Pierre Boucher in the 1660s,

2.27 Manoir Boucher, Boucherville, Quebec. Photograph by Edgar Gariépy. ANQ, Collection initiale/P600-6/GH 971-52.

was in the latter category. Originally called Fort Saint-Louis—and later known as Château Sabrevois and Villa de la Broquerie (after the names of the families into which Boucher women married)—Boucher's manor was a stone house only three bays wide with a pair of chimneys.[79] It was destroyed by fire in 1971.

Boucher's Fort Saint-Louis was a fort in name only, but a few manors were fortified for protection against Iroquois attack. One was the manor of Charles Le Moyne, the Baron de Longueuil, which was also situated across the St Lawrence from Montreal. It had four towers and high walls—very much in the spirit of a medieval castle. Inside the walls was a large courtyard with a well, stables, and other facilities that made it a self-sufficient, defensible

2.28 Manoir Mauvide-Genest, Saint-Jean, Île d'Orléans, Quebec, 1734. IBC/75-293A(22).

facility. The British and American armies recognized this, and each occupied it in turn in the late eighteenth century. It was destroyed by fire at the end of the century.[80]

The surviving manor that provides the best impression of the social status of a substantial resident seigneur during the French regime is the **Manoir Mauvide-Genest** [2.28] at Saint-Jean de l'Île d'Orléans. This beautiful and historic island, a short distance downriver from Quebec City, has maintained its agricultural character and its relative isolation in a large measure because for many years it avoided being linked to the mainland by a bridge—built in 1935—and has been protected by planning and heritage controls since that time. The island was granted in 1636 by the Compagnie des Cent-Associés to another company headed by Jacques Castillon of Paris. The seigneury subsequently changed hands a number of times. Guillaume Gaillard, councillor in the Conseil Supérieur, purchased it in 1712; and in 1734 (or shortly afterwards) he built the present manor, which takes its name from seigneur Jean Mauvide, who lived here between 1752 and 1764.[81]

Like the dwelling of an *habitant*, the Manoir Mauvide-Genest is a compact rectangular block; but it is much larger than a farmhouse, evidently accommodating a grander lifestyle and indicating the seigneur's wealth and power. The house is a full two storeys high (plus an attic) and nine bays wide. Its walls are built of rubble stone with cut-stone dressings around the windows and doors, all covered with *crépi*. The composition terminates in a tall hipped *(pavillon)* roof, broken by dormer windows and two chimneys and extending to bellcast eaves. The plan is divided into two unequal sections, as were farmhouses, but in the manor each part contains several rooms and is entered by a separate door. The smaller right-hand portion was used for a kitchen. The manor was rescued from near collapse by the Pouliot family—descended from the Genest family, as was Mauvide—who purchased and restored it in 1926, and added a lower chapel wing at the extreme right in the 1970s. Today the house (partly in private use) contains a restaurant and small museum. It has been classified as a historic site by the Quebec goverment.

The same architectural traditions were followed in the presbyteries—the residences of the parish priests—that were usually built next to the parish church. The Presbytery at Batiscan, possibly built as early as 1696 (and subjected to many subsequent repairs and restorations), is nearly 60 feet (19 m) wide, slightly larger in its floor-plan than the Ferme Saint-Gabriel, although smaller than the Manoir Mauvide. Its scale implies that the social position of the priest was considerably higher than that of the *habitant*, but not quite so elevated as the seigneur's.[82]

The urban house

Seventeenth- and eighteenth-century houses in the urban centres of Quebec, Trois-Rivières, Montreal, and—during its short period of growth—Louisbourg resembled rural farmhouses in many respects, although their design responded to the more restricted sites. The materials and construction techniques used in rural buildings—especially stone, *colombage*, and *poteaux en coulisse*—were commonplace, although once again it is mostly the stone houses that have survived.

The **Jacquet house** [2.29] at 34 rue Saint-Louis in Quebec's Upper Town, was built about 1675 and is the only intact seventeenth-century dwelling in the city. The original owner was François Jacquet *dit* Langevin, a slate-roofer whose nickname indicates that he came from Anjou, a leading slate-producing region of France. The house was built for Jacquet by Pierre Ménage (1645-1715), a native of Poitiers who came to Quebec about 1669 and was involved as a master carpenter in most of the city's important building projects during the next thirty years. A single storey high (like most other early houses in Quebec), the Jacquet house is built of stone and covered with *crépi*. It presents a compact three-bay façade to rue Saint-Louis, and its front door is flanked by a pair of casement windows.[83]

Ménage's daughter, Marie-Anne, married architect François de Lajoüe in 1689, and shortly afterwards Lajoüe acquired and enlarged the Jacquet house. He developed the attic into a second storey, illuminating it with hooded dormer windows at the front. The extremely steep pitch of the roof, and its slight change in slope halfway up (barely perceptible in the photograph), probably resulted from Lajoüe's work. At the rear the house had a covered gallery with an external wood staircase that opened onto a courtyard and stables. (Balconies that projected over the street were prohibited from 1686 onwards, but were permitted in private courtyards.[84]) Despite what appears today to be its diminutive size, the house was considered to be one of the largest on the street, which was inhabited by many artisans and craftsmen. This reveals the small scale of the city and its buildings in the seventeenth century, and also indicates Lajoüe's growing affluence and status—which were derived from his important (if brief) career in Quebec as a land surveyor, master mason, building contractor, architect, military engineer, and business entrepreneur. As was mentioned above, Lajoüe may have built the Villeneuve house at Charlesbourg, which is also distinguished by its very steep roof.

The Jacquet house has had an interesting history. It used to be called the Montcalm Hotel because of the popular, but erroneous, belief that General Montcalm died there in 1759 after the Battle of the Plains of Abraham. Subsequent verified occupants include Gaspard-Joseph Chaussegros de Léry, *fils*

2.29 Jacquet house, Quebec, Quebec, *c.* 1675. IBC/77-398(45).

2.30 Estèbe house, 92 rue Saint-Pierre, Quebec, Quebec, 1752. CIHB, Historical Photo File/05102008200000092.

2.31 Upstairs hall, Estèbe house, Quebec. Photograph by Ramsay Traquair, 1925. Ramsay Traquair Archive, MU.

(1721-96), like his distinguished father a military engineer; and Philippe Aubert de Gaspé, author of *Les anciens canadiens* (1863), which inspired the name of the restaurant (*Aux anciens canadiens*) that now occupies the house. The adjacent two-storey house on rue Saint-Louis, and the wing that now extends down rue Desjardins—both of them parts of the present-day-restaurant—are nineteenth-century structures.

Some French-regime houses were much larger. An impressive extant example is the **Estèbe house** [**2.30**] at 92 rue Saint-Pierre, built in 1752. The Lower Town was so crowded that the only way to expand was up, and so Guillaume Estèbe, a wealthy merchant and a member of the Governor's Council, built a house with two full storeys, a high attic, numerous tall chimneys, a vaulted basement, and rubble-stone walls nearly three feet (1 m) thick. Cut-stone string courses between the storeys and corbels supporting the end parapets provide rare exterior ornament and express Estèbe's ambition. The builders were three well-known master masons: Nicolas DaSilva *dit* Portugais, Pierre Delestre *dit* Beaujour, and René Paquet, one of whom likely also provided the designs. The house was entered by a door in the centre of the basement level, which brought the visitor up a run of stairs into a large central hall, in the middle of which was originally a second, open, staircase leading to the upper floor. At the rear, a gallery led down to warehouses and a wharf on the river.[85]

The symmetry and formality of this plan—unusual for a residence in New France—could be found only in the dwellings of the very rich and powerful. Many of the rooms have fine wood panelling [**2.31**], which was photographed and drawn by Ramsay Traquair. Delicate mouldings define the curved heads of the rectangular panels, which are set in tall, narrow strips that extend from a low panelled dado to the cornice. The panelling was probably installed for a later owner—possibly Swiss merchant Benjamin Comte, or his former clerk, Pierre Fargues—some time after the bombardment of Quebec in 1759, which damaged or destroyed nearly every house in the Lower Town.

Swedish botanist Peter Kalm, who travelled in New France in 1749-50 and published his observations, described Quebec residences at length:

Most of the houses in Quebec are built of stone, and in the upper city they are generally but one story high, the public buildings excepted. I saw a few wooden houses in the town, but these may not be rebuilt when decayed. The houses and churches in the city are not built of bricks, but of the black 'lime-slate' [or calcareous schist] of which the mountain consists and whereon Quebec stands....

The private houses have roofs of boards which are laid parallel to the spars, and sometimes to the eaves, or sometimes obliquely. The corners of houses are made of a gray small-grained limestone...and the windows are generally encased with it....The outsides of the houses are generally whitewashed. The windows are placed on the inner side of the walls; for they sometimes have double windows in winter....The rooms are warmed in winter by small iron stoves, which are removed in summer. There were no dampers anywhere. The floors are very dirty in every house and have all the appearance of being cleaned but once every year.[86]

Kalm arrived in Quebec after visiting Montreal. Of the dwellings there he wrote:

Some of the houses in the town are built of stone, but most of them are of timber, though very neatly built. Each of the better sort of houses has a door towards the street, with a seat on each side of it, for amusement and recreation in the morning and evening.[87]

Montreal houses were often blockier and heavier-looking than those in Quebec, with chimneys in the gable ends, rather like the farmhouses in the Montreal region (which may have imitated the urban form). Most were built of the hard, dark-grey limestone that has come to be known as Montreal greystone. The Château de Ramezay on rue Notre-Dame, the city's best-known survivor from the French regime, exhibits these squat proportions. This much-altered building has had a long and illustrious history. It was built in 1705 by 'master mason and architect' Pierre Couturier (*c.* 1665-1715) for Claude de Ramezay, governor of Montreal; enlarged and partially rebuilt in 1755 by 'master mason and contractor' Paul Tessier *dit* Lavigne (1701-73) for the India Company; and was then put to a variety of uses—as an annex to the Legislative Buildings, a courthouse, a school, and now a museum.[88]

The **Maison du Calvet** [**2.32**], on rue Saint-Paul at rue Bonsecours, is characteristic of later eighteenth-century houses in Montreal. It was probably built about 1770 for Pierre du Calvet, a Huguenot merchant and fur-trader who was jailed for providing information and supplies to the

American general, Richard Montgomery, in 1775 and was subsequently banished for treason after writing letters to George Washington. Built a full three storeys high to provide the high density appropriate to urban real estate, the house has a gabled roof with a lower pitch (about 45°) than that of the Jacquet house or of farmhouses of earlier years—which reflects an ongoing trend towards gentler slopes. The five bays facing rue Saint-Paul are irregularly spaced, responding to the room sizes rather than to rules of symmetry. The window openings diminish in size from floor to floor, with the higher ground floor having the largest.[89]

The materials, and some of the construction details, respond in part to a series of ordinances (today we would call them building codes) that were passed from the late seventeenth century onward in order to reduce the ever-present risk of fire in cities and towns. Building practice in New France was based on French civil law, the *Coûtume de Paris*, as modified by the Intendant. When Claude-Thomas Dupuy was appointed Intendant in 1725, he found Quebec 'ungraceful and appalling'. After his own palace burned down a year later, he did more than just complain. He introduced an 'Ordinance with regulations for the construction of houses in incombustible materials in the cities of the colony' (1727). This, and subsequent ordinances, forbade frame houses and recommended stone construction, banned external wood trim, regulated roof materials, prohibited roofs with excessive internal wood structural members (such as mansard roofs), provided minimum dimensions for chimney flues, required fireproof attic floors, and recommended that stone walls be continued up above the roof to make it harder for fire to spread from one house to another. Despite these laws, many wood houses continued to be built in the three cities, particularly in Trois-Rivières, indicating that the choice of stone (which was more expensive than wood) was much more a factor of prosperity than of regulations.[90]

The 'fire-breaks' stipulated by the ordinances are seen in the two thick gables that terminate a few feet above the line of the roof of the Maison du Calvet; these raised parapets—and the chimneys embedded in them, joined by a horizontal parapet—became a significant feature of urban houses. Two adjacent houses often shared a common wall on the property line (the Maison du Calvet and its neighbour, however, do not); this 'party wall' was known as a *pignon mitoyen*, a term that remains in use to this day.

2.32 Maison du Calvet, Montreal, Quebec, *c*. 1770. Photograph by Harold Kalman, 1990.

The oblong plan of the Calvet house is more nearly square than the plans of farmhouses of the day, and its slightly oblique left-hand (west) wall follows the alignment of rue Bonsecours. The mason who built the house was Jean Mars.[91] He may well have been the designer as well, since the houses of artisans and lesser merchants, like those of Jacquet and du Calvet, were rarely the work of architects. They were urban variants of the vernacular rural houses of New France, built according to custom and folk tradition rather than formal design.

This urban house-type persisted into the nineteenth century. English artisans and construction techniques began to have an impact around 1810-20, and classical decoration began to be seen in the following decade. Brick was introduced around 1840, particularly in Montreal, and change came rapidly thereafter.[92] (Nineteenth-century housing in Montreal is discussed on pages 251-3.)

Rich merchants, and government and church leaders, erected houses on a much more ostentatious scale, often consciously modelled on architect-designed, palace-like prototypes in France. The wealthy Quebec merchant Charles Aubert de la Chesnaye, with trading interests from Hudson Bay to the Mississippi, built a house in 1678, next to Place Royale, that emulated the scale of the great *hôtels* of Paris. Three storeys high and about 125 feet (40 m) long, it comprised a main block and two projecting wings (*pavillons*) grouped around a courtyard that was enclosed by a wall along the street and was entered through a formal gate. The top storey and an attic were contained within a double-sloped mansard roof—Quebec's first instance of a roof-form that was popular in Paris—with two tiers of dormer windows. The house survived the great fire of 1682, but its appearance is known only from a crude image on the Franquelin map of 1688 [**2.3**]. Its imposing scale is nevertheless obvious.[93]

Philippe de Rigaud, Marquis de Vaudreuil, who served terms both as governor of Montreal and as governor general of New France, built himself a fine residence in Montreal that was worthy of his position. Like the house of Aubert de la Chesnaye, the **Château de Vaudreuil** (1723-6) on rue Saint-Paul contrasted sharply with the vernacular houses of the towns and countryside of New France—and also with the previous governor's house, the Château de Ramezay. It was the work of Gaspard-Joseph Chaussegros de Léry, the military engineer who was also a professional building-designer. He consciously followed precedents and principles of 'high' architecture—the buildings of polite urban society—to make a social, as well as an architectural, statement [**2.33**]. It was in his capacity as chief military engineer that Chaussegros was instructed to prepare plans for the governor's residence.[94]

Vaudreuil died before his house was completed. The Château de Vaudreuil—which was used by subsequent governors, and as a boys' school, and was destroyed by fire in 1803—is known from a number of images, including drawings in the National Archives of Canada, and a drawing attributed to the painter and sometime architect William Berczy (1744-1813). Like the Aubert de la Chesnaye house, it was planned in the shape of an 'H', with the principal block flanked by a pair of pavilion wings projecting towards the roadway and the garden behind the house. (The flanking wings suggest the towers of Champlain's second *habitation* at Quebec [**1.22**]; although built a century apart, both buildings trace their roots to the châteaux of the French aristocracy.) Elegant curved

staircases led up to a shallow court, which provided access to the distinguished entrance, framed by classical pilasters and a high entablature. Two principal storeys were elevated atop a high basement, and dormer windows illuminated an attic contained within the hipped roofs. The façade was symmetrical, with a horizontal string course in the stone walls defining a line between the ground and upper floors.

These were all features of fine French buildings of the day—with the wings, curved staircases, and their walls controlling one's approach by first offering only a tantalizing oblique and incomplete view of the château: the visitor's full attention was finally focused on the dominant, classically framed central entrance. Once through the door [**2.34**], there was an equally contrived view through the principal reception room (*salle*) to the walled garden and the prospect of Mont Royal beyond. These are the same kinds of manipulations of space and vistas that occurred in European Baroque public buildings of the day, including those as grandly conceived as the Château de Versailles. But in Montreal they were used on a much smaller scale, and with less refined detail (due in part to the hardness of the local greystone). To the right of the *salle* was the four-room domestic unit, called an *appartement*, that had been characteristic of French palaces since the sixteenth-century Château de Chambord. It comprised a private reception room (*antichambre*), sleeping-room (*chambre*), dressing-room (*cabinet*), and closet (*garde-robe*). Here the continuity of the *appartement* was interrupted by privies and a staircase. A second, incomplete, *appartement* was situated in the left-hand wing.

The Château de Vaudreuil, and the house of Aubert de la Chesnaye, represent the architecture of the ruling class. They are 'academic', 'high', or 'polite' architecture—formal, contrived, based on study, and consciously produced to express power, wealth, and authority. They can be analysed in terms of architectural style (the Baroque, in the case of the Château de Vaudreuil). One person (the architect or engineer) designed the building, and a separate person or group (the contractor and artisans) built it. The architect or engineer often considered himself an artist; this is seen particularly vividly with Chaussegros de Léry, who signed and dated most of his drawings [**2.4**] in the same way as an artist signs a painting.[95] In contrast, the house of the ordinary colonist is 'folk' or 'vernacular' architecture, built according to craft tradition without a conscious reliance on design, rules, or architectural

2.33 Château de Vaudreuil, Montreal, Quebec, 1723-6. Drawing attributed to William Berczy, *c*. 1802. Archives du Séminaire de Québec.

2.34 (*below*) Main-floor plan, Château de Vaudreuil, Montreal, Quebec, 1723-6. Drawing by David Byrnes, after Chaussegros de Léry.

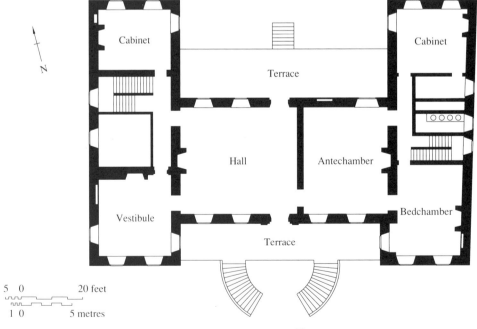

style. It was usually conceived and built by one person (or group of people). The former activity may be called 'architecture' and the latter 'building'; or the one 'art' and the other 'craft'. Whatever words are chosen, these represented two separate strains of building in the eighteenth century, just as classical and popular music represent two strains of that medium—and as today a new architect-designed house may be contrasted with a builder-constructed tract home.

Religious Architecture

The churches of New France, like the colony's houses, developed a strong vernacular tradition that combined sources in the buildings of the motherland with the skills, materials, and social and environmental conditions found in the colony. The 'high' academic architecture of the churches built by the ruling classes, represented by the bishop and the religious orders, contrasts with the folk architecture of the parish churches—although the former provided a number of key architectural models that were followed, with important changes, in the vernacular parish churches.

The initial religious activity in New France was focused on bringing Christianity to the natives. From the point of view of church administration, the entire colony was considered to be a mission, and the missionary orders had control over religious life. All churches—not only the front-line missions discussed in Chapter 1—were technically mission chapels.[96]

Centralized religious authority came to New France in 1659 in the person of François-Xavier de Montmorency-Laval de Montigny. Laval's primacy over the religious affairs of the colony was promoted by the Jesuits and affirmed by the Pope, and in 1674 he became the first Bishop of Quebec. His rise to power coincided with the colony's coming under royal administration in 1663 and the intensive development efforts under Intendant Jean Talon. The King granted Laval political powers that in some respects equalled those of the governor. One of his first acts was to establish the Séminaire de Québec (in 1663), laying the groundwork for a Canadian-educated clergy whose allegiance was directed towards the Bishop and Rome. He also ensured that the colonists would maintain their ecclesiastical loyalty by discouraging parochial autonomy and developing an architectural church-form that was identified with his office.[97]

Laval was succeeded in 1688 (although he served as acting bishop between 1700 and his death in 1708) by Bishop Jean-Baptiste de La Croix de Saint-Vallier, who, perhaps unwittingly, allowed the parishes a greater degree of independence. The decentralization of ecclesiastical power by Saint-Vallier and his successors fostered the development of an architecture that was more distinctively Canadian.

The church architecture of the colony has been divided by architectural historians Alan Gowans and Luc Noppen into three periods. The first, which Gowans calls the Heroic Age and Noppen describes as the Period of Establishment, extends from 1608 (the settlement of New France) to 1663 (the establishment of royal administration). The second, from 1663 to 1700, is the Age of Laval (Gowans) or the Period of French Influence (Noppen). The period from 1700 to the British Conquest in 1760 was described by Gowans as 'New France becomes *Canadien*' and by Noppen as 'The Elaboration of a Quebec Architectural Tradition'. The first of these three periods was introduced in Chapter 1. The discussion that follows treats the second period in two parts: the churches (and associated buildings) of the religious orders and the parish churches; and the third period in the context of a selection of eighteenth-century parish churches.

The churches of the religious orders

The Jesuits, Récollets, and Sulpicians were all active builders in the young colony, constructing a number of important churches, chapels, religious houses, and seminaries during the age of Laval. Exquisite monuments in their own right, they would also have a long-lasting influence on the architecture of New France.

The Jesuits, who came to New France in 1625 to work with the natives, established their headquarters in Quebec. In 1647 the Order began to build a college in the Upper Town, and in 1666 work was begun on an ambitious **Jesuit Church [2.35]** next to it. One hundred feet (30.5 m) long by 30 feet (9.2 m) wide, it was the largest church in the colony at its consecration in 1676. Its appearance in 1759, when it was nearly a century old and had undergone alterations, is known from engravings of views drawn by military artist Richard Short after the Conquest. It had a cruciform plan with a pair of towers standing nearly free from the façade and flanking the entrance (probably stairtowers providing access to the galleries) and a tall belltower (*clocher*) over the crossing. The right-hand tower,

2.35 The Jesuit Church and College, 1640s-70s, Quebec, Quebec. Drawing by Richard Short, 1759; engraving by Charles Grignion. NAC/C-354.

2.36 (*below*) Interior of the Jesuit Church, Quebec, Quebec, 1666-76. Drawing by Richard Short, 1759; engraving by Anthony Walker. NAC/C-351

which originally touched the corner of the college quadrangle, was incorporated into the college building (or removed) when that structure was enlarged in the late 1720s, and so it is does not appear in Short's view. The drawing shows pilasters and an entablature articulating the façade into two storeys with three bays; this too may have been an alteration of about 1730, attributed to Chaussegros de Léry, that was applied over a previously plain elevation. The exterior side walls were unornamented stone. The nave and transepts were capped by hipped roofs covered with slate.[98]

The interior [2.36] was clearly splendid; many visitors to Quebec commented on its beauty. The French Jesuit chronicler Pierre-François-Xavier de Charlevoix (who taught here in 1709-13, and later travelled by canoe to New Orleans) wrote:

It is very much ornamented on the inside; the gallery [une Tribune] is bold, light, and well-wrought, and surrounded by an iron balustrade of excellent workmanship, which is painted and gilded. The pulpit is all gilt, and the work both in iron and wood is excellent. There are three altars, handsomely designed, and some good pictures. There is no vaulting, but the flat ceiling is handsomely ornamented....[99]

The Baron de Lahontan, who was in Quebec in 1684 and 1690, described the interior as 'fair, stately, and well lighted', and the altar as being

adorn'd with four great Cylindrical Columns of one Stone; the Stone being a sort of Canada Porphyry, and black as Jet, without either Spots or Veins.[100]

Short drew the interior, in a shambles after the bombardment, looking from the crossing towards the altar retable, the classically treated wall ornamentation whose three sides fit within the curved apse that terminated the building. (The retable is called a 'reredos' in English churches.) This may not have been the altar described by Lahontan: Alan Gowans has suggested that the original one was a free-standing baldachin with a canopy in the manner of the Church of the Val-de-Grâce in Paris (and, before it, St Peter's in Rome), versions of which subsequently adorned churches throughout the colony.[101]

The size, the expensive and permanent materials (Charlevoix said that the slate roof was unique in Canada), and the rich ornament of the Jesuit Church indicate the Jesuits' determination that it should assert the Order's influential position in the religious and educational life of New France. So too does the design, which was surely prepared in France (although the architect's name is not known). Its essential characteristics reflect the principal Jesuit churches in France: the college church at La Flèche (where Laval spent ten years as a student) and the Church of the Jesuit Noviciate in Paris, both of which were inspired in turn by the Jesuits' mother church in Rome, Il Gesù. Gowans has shown that the Quebec church followed these French Baroque prototypes in features such as the Latin-cross plan, the round apse, the clocher above the crossing, and the hipped roof over the façade. All of these elements, however, were modified—and simplified—in response to the climate, materials, limited artisans' skills, and frontier environment of the colonial centre.

Included in the Short engraving is the Jesuit College of 1647-50, which was enlarged in the 1730s and 1740s to become a quadrangle more than 200 feet (60 m) square with a central courtyard. (The larger property contained a wooded garden and was enclosed in the eighteenth century by a pallisaded fence.) It was a three-storey stone building (two storeys where the grade rose), with an attic contained within the steeply pitched roof. Horizontal string courses separated the floors, and a pedimented frontispiece framed the main entrance. Peter Kalm was very impressed by the College and its palatial character. He called it 'the finest building in town' and described it at length:

The building the Jesuits live in is magnificently built, and looks exceedingly fine, both without and within, which makes it similar to a fine palace. It consists of stone, is three stories high, exclusive of the garret, is covered with slate and built in a square form like the new [royal] palace at Stockholm, including a large court. Its size is such that three hundred families would find room enough in it, though at present there were not above twenty Jesuits in it....There is a long corridor along all the sides of the square, in every story, on both sides of which are either cells, halls, or other apartments for the friars. There are also their library, apothecary shop, etc.[102]

Père Pierre-Antoine Roubaud, a Jesuit missionary, declared (in 1770) that the building was 'entirely constructed in France', meaning that the stone was prepared in France, numbered, and shipped to Quebec as ballast. This would refer only to the cut-stone trim, since the walls were built of rubble stone, but it is still a considerable amount of masonry. If Roubaud—described as 'one of the most precious rascals in Canadian history'—is to be believed, then the Jesuit College represents a remarkably early instance of prefabrication.[103]

The Jesuit Church and College both survived the bombardment. After the Conquest the Church served for a while as a British army depot and was demolished in 1808; the College became a military barracks and was torn down in 1878.

Construction of a new **Récollet Church [2.37]** in Quebec, replacing Notre-Dame-des-Anges and dedicated to Saint-Antoine, was begun in 1693 to designs by a French Récollet architect, Juconde Drué (1664-1739)—a pupil of the celebrated painter (and sometime architect) Frère Luc. The less-élitist attitude of the Récollets—unlike their rivals the Jesuits, they worked closely with the people and recruited *Canadiens* (including craftsmen) to their Order—ensured that they enjoyed good relations with the governors of the colony. Frontenac provided financial assistance for the construction of the church, and he and Governors Callière, Vaudreuil, and La Jonquière were all buried there. After the Conquest the church was used for a while for Anglican worship; but it, and the adjacent monastery of Saint-Antoine, were destroyed by fire in 1796. When, a few years later, the Anglican Cathedral [4.51] was built on its site, the British Conquest was proclaimed in a particularly symbolic way.[104]

The Récollet Church is also known primarily through engravings of Richard Short's drawings. His exterior view shows its location on Place d'Armes and a wing of the attached monastery. (The Cathedral of Notre-Dame, identified by its broad tower, stands behind a row of burned-out houses, and the spire of the Jesuit Church is in the centre distance.) It was simpler in plan and massing than the Jesuit Church (corresponding to the Récollets' simpler attitudes), having a longitudinal nave and sanctuary with no transepts, and it was covered by a simple gabled roof. It appears that the altar (east) end was originally flat, but was replaced by a semicircular choir within fifteen years of completion. A *clocher* with a tall spire (a *flèche*) rose above the east end. The towerless façade was treated with a pilastered doorway and three statued niches. Two windows beside the upper niche seem to illuminate a gallery, and a circular 'bull's-eye' window pierces the point of the gable. The side elevations appear to have been unornamented stone.

Short's view of the interior [2.38] after the British

bombardment shows that the walls had wood panelling to the height of the sills of the arched windows, and that the nave was covered by a barrel-vaulted wood ceiling. A handsome retable stood in front of the choir: four engaged columns on pedestals articulated a three-part composition, with the wider central portion containing a painting (*The Assumption of the Virgin*) and capped by a pediment; a small statue stands on top of each column. A pair of side-altars flank the central one, and a curved communion rail separates the sanctuary from the nave.

The Jesuit and Récollet Churches were familiar and greatly admired landmarks in Quebec during the French regime. Although their respective designs differed in many ways, they were to have an enormous impact on the design of eighteenth-century parish churches.

The third major religious order active in New France, the Sulpicians, made their base in Montreal. Their church of Notre-Dame de Montréal (1672-83, with many later additions; see also page 248) had a Latin-cross plan and showed the influence of Sulpician churches in France. The plan was prepared by Dollier de Casson, the Superior of the Sulpician Order in Canada (and, by dint of his position, the seigneur of Montreal). A new two-storey classical façade, intended to have twin towers—only one was actually built—was designed in 1722 by Chaussegros de Léry, surpassing the magnificence of both the Jesuit Church and the cathedral in Quebec, then newly enlarged. The client and the architect-engineer both belonged to what may be called the ruling class, and it was therefore appropriate that they should have turned to classical Baroque architectural forms for the façade.[105] '*La Paroisse*', as Notre-Dame was called, is best known for its replacement in the 1820s by a new Gothic Revival church, the present Church of Notre-Dame [6.9, 10, 11, 12], a building that had considerable influence on Quebec parish churches of the nineteenth century.

A short distance away from Notre-Dame de Montréal—and directly adjacent to the present church—the Order built its **Séminaire de Saint-Sulpice** (1683-4). It is the oldest building in Mon-

2.37 (*top right*) The Récollet Church, Quebec, Quebec, begun 1693. Drawing by Richard Short, 1759; engraving by P. Canot. NAC/C-361.

2.38 (*right*) Interior of the Récollet Church, Quebec, Quebec, begun 1693. Drawing by Richard Short, 1759; engraving by Charles Grignion. NAC/C-353

65

treal, although only a portion still stands. Dollier de Casson, or his successor Vachon de Belmont, may have been the designer. The Séminaire [**2.39**] has a symmetrical design, with two U-shaped wings (1704-12) arranged around open courtyards. The formal, classical plan—anticipating that of the Château de Vaudreuil—would have been expected of Montreal's religious and temporal authorities and contrasts with the simple craft tradition evident in the design and construction. Three storeys high in parts and four storeys elsewhere, the walls were constructed of the familiar random rubble stone opened up by rectangular casement windows, with little ornament other than the attractive door casing, added in 1740. A charming clock-tower over the entrance, with a small peal of bells on its top, was installed before 1701. A walled formal garden at the rear, a unique survivor of the early monastic gardens of Montreal, remains intact after three centuries.[106]

Other, smaller, orders were also active in the colony. One was the Company of St Ursula—better known as the Ursulines—who came to Quebec in 1639 with Mère Marie-de-l'Incarnation and dedicated themselves to the education of young girls. Their large convent in the Upper Town was built in stages after a fire in 1686 (which destroyed buildings that had replaced those consumed by a previous fire in 1650). Three seventeenth-century portions survive, forming two sides of a large quadrangle. The principal craftsmen were carpenters Pierre Ménage (who built the Jacquet house) and Jean Caillé, and masons Guillaume Jourdain and Sylvain Dupleix. The walls are built of rubble stone two feet (60 cm) thick; those of the St Augustine wing has cut-stone dressings and the others are covered with *crépi*. The window heads are segmental arches and the windows are 12-paned casements that open inwards. Evidently concerned about the risk of yet another fire, the builders covered the steep roofs with tin 'tiles' laid diagonally and used masonry fire-breaks here for the first time in Quebec (visible in the Franquelin view of Quebec, **2.3**).[107]

2.39 Séminaire de Saint-Sulpice, Montreal, Quebec, 1683-4. Photograph by Brian Merrett.

2.40 Retable, Ursuline Chapel, Quebec, Quebec, 1726-36. Photograph by Daniel Lessard. Ministère des Communications (Quebec), Service de la photographie.

The **Ursuline Chapel** was built within the convent in 1718-22 by François de Lajoüe; the building was demolished in 1901 and the magnificent interior fittings were preserved and reinstalled in a new structure, designed by David Ouellet (1844-1915) and completed in the following year. The architectural sculpture was executed in 1726-36 by cousins Noël Levasseur (1680-1740) and Pierre-Noël Levasseur (1690-1770), members of a dynasty of outstanding artists founded three-quarters of a century earlier by brothers Jean and Pierre Levasseur. The centrepiece is a superb four-column retable [2.40]. The other furnishings include a lavishly carved pulpit, climaxed by the trumpeting angel of the Last Judgement standing on top of the sounding board. In 1759 a British army chaplain delivered the funeral eulogy to General Wolfe from this pulpit, and the purported skull of Wolfe's opponent, General Montcalm (one of three 'Montcalm' skulls!), is preserved in the Ursulines' museum.[108]

Parish churches

Parishes were not formally delineated in New France until 1721, but the religious needs of the European residents were accommodated long before that time. In the early years of the colony Quebec, Trois-Rivières, and Montreal each had a community church built with the help of the orders, and several churches were built as well in the area around Quebec by the local residents.

The seventeenth century In 1633 the Jesuits built in Quebec's Upper Town the wood church of Notre-Dame-de-la-Recouvrance—where, two years later, Champlain was buried. The church was soon destroyed by fire and was replaced in 1647 by Notre-Dame-de-la-Paix—for twenty years the only stone church in the colony. When it was named the city's parish church by Bishop Laval in 1664, it became in effect the first parish church in New France. A decade later it was upgraded to be the cathedral of Laval's new diocese and became the first cathedral in North America north of Mexico. The church was cruciform in plan. The nave— 80 feet (24.4 m) long by 38 feet (11.6 m) wide— terminated in a semi-circular apse, with deep lateral chapels forming a transept. A *clocher* rose above the crossing.[109]

The Cathedral of Notre-Dame de Québec was constructed around the Church of Notre-Dame-de-la-Paix. Between 1684 and 1697 a tower was built beside the entrance and the nave was lengthened by architect and master mason Claude Baillif (c. 1635-98/9), likely a native of Normandy with connections to Paris, who had come to Quebec at Laval's invitation to teach at the École des Arts et Métiers that was connected to the Séminaire.[110] Baillif's ambitious plan for an imposing two-towered façade was not completed, nor was a design for the improvement of the façade proposed in 1744 by Chaussegros de Léry. The cathedral was badly damaged during the bombardment of 1759. It was repaired and improved inside and out in several stages by members of the Baillairgé family, a dynasty of talented architects who were active in Quebec for two hundred years. The first phases of work were done between 1768 and 1818 by Jean Baillairgé (1726-1805) and by François Baillairgé (1759-1830), Jean's son. François's son Thomas Baillairgé (1791-1859) proposed a new façade in 1843; though it was begun, like almost every other component of the cathedral it was never completed. A fire gutted the building in 1922, but the repairs that followed restored much of Thomas Baillairgé's classically inspired work. The cathedral of today [4.61], which has been recognized as a basilica, is imposing in its scale, but its details reveal the piecemeal manner in which it was built.[111]

Although Notre-Dame-de-la-Paix is now buried deep within the cathedral, it was known well and long enough in its original form to have become a model for parish churches erected under Laval's authority. The Bishop undertook a vigorous campaign that resulted in the building of fifteen new churches of stone, and others in less permanent materials, before 1700. Some were built by the seigneurs—Pierre Boucher, for one, built a 50-foot-long wood church at Boucherville in 1670 to help make his seigneury more attractive to settlers. Most were financed by money raised by Laval, either by acquiring grants from the King, by tithing the population, or by taking surplus funds from the Séminaire. Laval announced his intentions in 1663:

> As it is necessary to build several churches for... divine service..., I order, though without prejudice to the obligation that the faithful have in each parish to contribute to the building of churches, that when the annual expenses have been covered, all the rest [of the Séminaire's funds] shall be spent on the construction of churches, or in...other good works for the benefit of the Church, according to the orders of the bishop.[112]

Laval built a number of churches on his own seigneuries on the Beaupré shore and the Île d'Orléans. At least two were built of *colombage*, one of wood, and six of stone.

A pair of sketches [2.41, 42] drawn between 1681 and 1686 by the Jesuit Père Claude Chauchetière, illustrating a chapel built in 1678 at the Iroquois mission at Sault Saint-Louis (Caughnawaga, now known as Kahnawake), gives a good idea of the use of *colombage* in church construction. The first shows a carpenter at work on the roof structure; the walls are framed in closely spaced timber posts awaiting the masonry infill. The second sketch depicts the completed chapel (with lightning striking it): the façade has been covered with horizontal boards, with the timber frame of the gable left exposed (the side wall is not shown); the gabled roof has bellcast eaves and a small belfry set on the ridge over the entrance, and an arched door leads into the building.[113] A building that used *colombage*

2.41 (*below left*) A log chapel at Sault Saint-Louis, Quebec, 1678. Sketch by Père Claude Chauchetière, *c*. 1681-6. Archives Départementales de la Gironde, Bordeaux, France.

2.42 (*below*) Lightning strikes near the log chapel of Sault Saint-Louis, Quebec. Sketch by Père Claude Chauchetière, *c*. 1681-6. Archives Départementales de la Gironde, Bordeaux, France.

2.43 Église Sainte-Anne de Beaupré, Sainte-Anne de Beaupré, Quebec, 1689-95. Photograph by Livernois Ltd., 1870s, MU/no. 107170.

pierroté was the Church of la Petite-Rivière-Saint-François (1777), which was photographed before its demolition in 1903.[114]

Église Sainte-Anne de Beaupré [2.43] represents the more substantial parish churches of the age of Laval. On the Beaupré shore, a short distance below Quebec, Sainte-Anne has long been an important pilgrimage site. As early as 1665, five years after the construction of the first (wooden) church, Mère Marie-de-l'Incarnation wrote:

> Seven leagues from here there is a village called Petit-Cap, where there is a church dedicated to St Anne where Our Lord works great marvels for this blessed mother of the very blessed virgin. The paralysed are seen to walk, the blind to recover their sight, and those sick with various maladies to recover their health.[115]

The wood church was too small to accommodate the many pilgrims who flocked to the site and so, in 1676, a new and larger stone church was built, 80 feet (24.4 m) long and 28 feet (8.5 m) wide. This second church was 'repaired' (in fact, largely rebuilt) between 1689 and 1695 under the supervision of Claude Baillif, who added large side-chapels and thereby gave it a cruciform plan. He also designed a *clocher* (in 1696), and may have undertaken other work on the church as well. Further repairs were done in 1787, but without making any significant changes to the appearance, and the church was demolished in 1878—fortunately not before it had been photographed.[116]

As altered by Baillif, Sainte-Anne de Beaupré resembled Notre-Dame-de-la-Paix, with its Latin-cross plan, side-chapels, and semicircular apse (which appears from an interior photograph to have been as wide as the nave). The exterior treatment shows plain rubble-stone walls, with cut-stone at the corners and around the openings. The façade is pierced by an arched door and a bull's-eye window, the sides by small arched windows. In its massing and its steep roofs—a gable over the nave and *pavillons* over the chapels, with slightly bell-cast eaves—the church bears a decided resemblance to farmhouses of the time. The rectory is seen beyond the church.

The interior was ornate, with rich architectural and sculptural decoration that included a retable designed by Jacques Leblond de Latour (1671-1715), an artist-priest from Bordeaux who came to Quebec to teach painting and sculpture at the Séminaire. The curé of Sainte-Anne de Beaupré proudly wrote to a friend in France in 1734:

My church is one of the finest and best ornamented in Canada. You may think this is not very much, but make no mistake: let me tell you that the country parish churches of France are not comparable to those where I live.[117]

Many of the features seen at Sainte-Anne de Beaupré—and, before it, at Notre-Dame-de-la-Paix—were repeated in the other churches built by Bishop Laval. This homogeneity among the parish churches symbolized the Bishop's firm control over his communities of worshippers. The first church of Sainte-Famille (1669) on the Île d'Orléans had almost the same dimensions as Notre-Dame-de-la-Paix (80 by 36 feet, or 24.2 by 11 m), and those buildings that were smaller, such as the church at Beauport (1677), retained similar proportions (60 by 30 feet, or 18.3 by 9.2 m). By 1700 most churches were being built, or refitted, with side-chapels—in effect, transepts—including Saint-Joachim de Montmorency (1685-6) and Saint-Laurent on the Île d'Orléans (1695; lengthened in 1708 by architect Jean Maillou). This 'transept plan', as it was called by Gérard Morisset, remained popular even beyond Laval's time.[118] Earlier churches tended to place the *clocher* over the crossing, as in the Quebec prototype, although with time belltowers came to be built at the entrance end. The original parish church of Notre-Dame-de-la-Paix, by serving as a model for other parish churches, was being canonized, so to speak, and in the very same years (1684-97) that it was being transformed into a cathedral by Claude Baillif.

As with the domestic architecture of New France, general parallels are seen between the churches of New France and those of the French countryside, but no specific models for the churches of Laval can be found in Normandy or Brittany. Alan Gowans reasoned that it might be more appropriate to seek a source in the Île-de-France, the region around Paris, and then discovered a forebear in **Église Saint-Pierre-et-Saint-Paul [2.44]** at Armenonville-les-Gatineaux, a town about 10 miles (16 km) north of Chartres. Built in 1658 by the local seigneur, and essentially finished by 1676, the church at Armenonville shares many features in common with those of the Quebec region. The façade has similar proportions, with the steep gable, slightly turned-up eaves, arched door with keystones, circular window, and niches with statues of the saints (as at Notre-Dame-des-Victoires, Quebec, which is described below). The *clocher*, located over the entrance, is composed of a drum, lantern, and *flèche*, although it is larger in proportion to the building than those with which we are familiar. The dimensions of the French church are about 60 feet (18.3 m) by 20 feet (6.1 m), and the nave is augmented by a single sacristy to one side. The interior features plain plastered walls, a king-post wood truss, and a wood ceiling divided into small painted panels—possibly a clue to the original interiors of the seventeenth-century churches of Quebec.[119]

Rather than interpreting the Armenonville church as a direct source for those in New France, Gowans suggests instead parallel convergences of the rural craft (vernacular) tradition with academic ideas from the court in Paris. Such academic influences are best seen, in the colony, in the elegant churches built in Quebec for the religious orders.

The only one of Bishop Laval's churches to survive to our day in a condition that in any way resembles its original appearance is Notre-Dame-des-Victoires, a chapel-of-ease for his new cathedral. The church was begun in 1687 on Place-Royale in Lower Town [2.2] and is one of the most familiar historic buildings in Quebec. It was built on the site of the storehouse of Champlain's second *habitation* (the *magasin du Roi*; 1.22) and some stones from it were used in its construction. The church was originally dedicated to the Infant Jesus, but its name was changed twice in response to miracles that saved the people of New France from British invaders. In 1690, after five days of seige by Admiral William Phips and his naval force, the citizens of Quebec became desperate. The annals of the Hôtel-Dieu reported:

As the situation grew more alarming, public prayers redoubled in the city. The citizens had implored the Blessed Virgin to act as their patron saint and protect them. The ladies had pledged word to go on pilgrimage to the Lower Town church if the Blessed Virgin obtained their liberation.[120]

Their prayers were heeded when Phips gave up the seige. Bishop Laval expressed the gratitude of the community by renaming the church Notre-Dame-de-la-Victoire (Our Lady of Victory). The second miraculous event occured in 1711, when another

2.44 Église Saint-Pierre-et-Saint-Paul, Armenonville-les-Gatineaux, France, c. 1658-76. Photograph by Alan Gowans, for Gowans, *Church Architecture in New France* (1955).

English fleet, this one commanded by Admiral Hovenden Walker, sailed up the St Lawrence River, supported by land forces approaching from the south. Once more the citizens appealed to the Virgin Mary and once more their prayers were answered. A sudden storm destroyed ten warships, the naval attack was abandoned, the army retreated—and the name of the church was pluralized to Notre-Dame-des-Victoires.

The church was begun in 1687 to designs by Claude Baillif. Work was stopped a year later because of a dispute with an adjacent property-owner; the building was covered in and usable, but unfinished. Construction resumed in 1723, when Jean Maillou extended the nave to 72 feet and built a permanent façade. The gable front was articu-

lated by a doorway surrounded by pilasters and an entablature, three small niches containing statues, and a bull's-eye window and a smaller square opening at the peak. The façade was a simplified version of the Récollet Church. Luc Noppen has suggested that Baillif's original façade, if built, would have been more ornamented, somewhat like his work at the Cathedral of Notre-Dame de Québec; but by the early eighteenth century the European architectural models were being adapted to the colonial context by colonial-born designers such as Maillou, and consequently the academic features were reduced to their essentials.[121]

The façade and the interior of Notre-Dame-des-Victoires changed considerably in the course of the many rebuildings and restorations it endured over the subsequent two and a half centuries (most recently in 1967). Its external appearance in the eighteenth century is known from an engraving of a drawing by Short made after the British attack: it shows as well that the church, and all the adjacent buildings on Place Royale, were entirely burned out and left in ruins. The most evident exterior changes since that time have been the opening up of the niches into windows, the insertion of a second bird's-eye window in the point of the gable, and the erection of a *clocher* over the entrance, rather than in its original location over the middle of the church.

The eighteenth century   The churches of Laval became the basis for those built under his successor, Bishop Saint-Vallier, although he remained somewhat in the shadow of his predecessor until Laval's death in 1708, and he certainly lacked the first bishop's charisma. It was Saint-Vallier who officially delineated parishes in 1721. He created eighty-two, making them for the most part coterminous with the seigneuries, and he insisted that each should have a fixed *curé* (in 1720 there were only twenty incumbent parish priests in the colony). In order to counter this new parochial independence with some semblance of central ecclesiastical control, Saint-Vallier strove to maintain standardization in church design.

Evidence of this is found in 'the Maillou plan' [**2.45**], a crude drawing in the archives of the Séminaire de Québec that was likely produced in the first dozen years of the eighteenth century. It shows the plan and exterior view of a simple church, three bays long, the nave terminating in a semicircular apse and the façade elaborated by a door (framed in cut stone), a niche, and a circular window. A multi-tiered *clocher* rises above the entrance (which, we have seen, was becoming increasingly popular, superseding its earlier location near the east end). An inscription on the back of the drawing reads: 'Church designed by Mr Jean Maillou. It is not wide enough; only 30. and we need 36. . . .' This, the most basic of church plans, follows an important model from the previous generation, the chapel of the Palais épiscopal in Quebec (1693-1700), Saint-Vallier's personal place of worship, which had been designed by Claude Baillif.[122] (The large palace had been begun in 1692 on the site of Indendant Talon's former house. It was altered by Chaussegros de Léry in 1743 and rebuilt by Thomas Baillairgé in 1844.)[123]

The progeny of the Maillou plan can be seen in **Église Saint-François-de-Sales** [2.46] on the Île d'Orléans. A small wood chapel had been built here in the 1680s; another, twenty years later. In 1732 archdeacon Eustache Chartier de Lotbinière noted that the latter was in poor condition and 'ordered

2.45 Plans for a church by Jean Maillou, *c*. 1700-12. Archives du Séminaire de Québec.

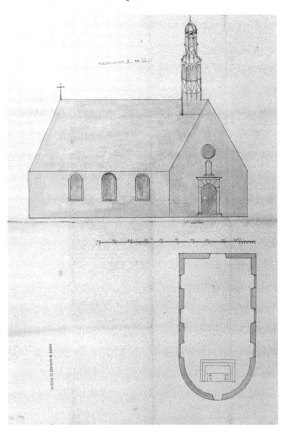

2.46 Église Saint-François-de-Sales, Île d'Orléans, Quebec, 1734-6. Photograph by Edgar Gariépy. ANQ, Collection initiale/P600-6/N-1174-27.

2.47 (*opposite*) Plans, sections, and elevations of Église Saint-François-de-Sales, Île d'Orléans, Quebec, 1734-6. Ramsay Traquair Archive, no. 45.01/005 100/1, MU.

the inhabitants and parishioners to collect and bring to the site the stone necessary to build a stone church.' Mason Thomas Alard of Quebec supplied additional stone. An unnamed person was paid 4.10 French pounds in 1734 'to have the plan of the church made', and the building was erected between 1734 and 1736. Whoever it was that prepared the design followed the essentials of the Maillou plan. (His paltry fee allowed for little creativity!)[124]

The handsome façade of Saint-François has the familiar pyramidal shape and features, but the proportions are broader than in earlier churches, such as Notre-Dame-des-Victoires, since the width of the nave has been increased to 36 feet—the same dimension that is recommended on the back of the Maillou plan. Three niches contain statues of Christ and Saints Francis and James. The three longitudinal bays of the nave, which has no transepts or side-chapels, follow the same source. An

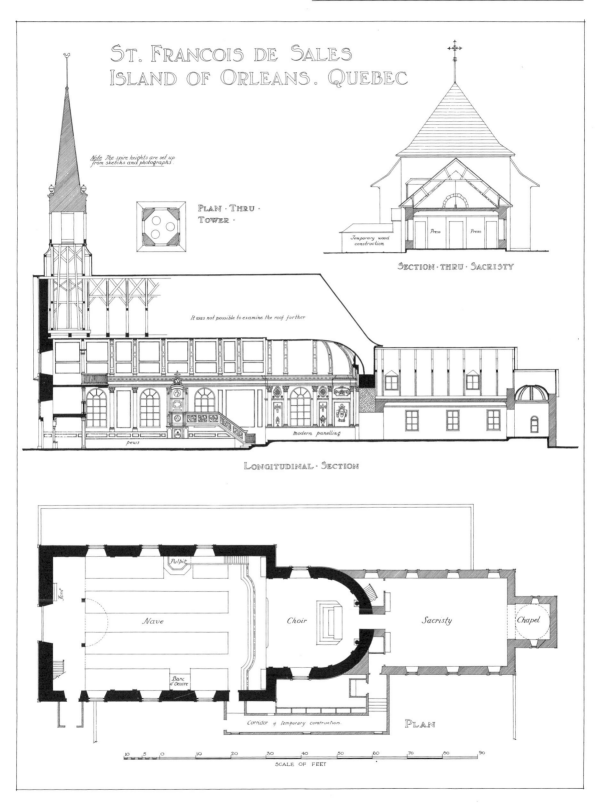

ST. FRANCOIS DE SALES
ISLAND OF ORLEANS. QUEBEC

Note. The spire heights are set up
from sketches and photographs.

PLAN · THRU ·
TOWER ·

Temporary wood
construction

Press   Press

SECTION · THRU · SACRISTY

It was not possible to examine the roof further

modern panelling

pews

LONGITUDINAL · SECTION

Tent

Pulpit

Nave   Choir   Sacristy   Chapel

Banc
d'Oeuvre

Corridor of temporary construction.   PLAN

SCALE OF FEET

73

2.48 Interior of Église Saint-François-de-Sales, Île d'Orléans, Quebec, 17th and 18th centuries. IBC/76.1044(45).

element of the plan [2.47] that differs from Maillou's drawing is that the choir is narrower than the nave, which allows a secondary altar to be placed on each side of the choir arch. This feature follows the plan of the Récollet Church and reveals the importance of that church as a model. (Gérard Morisset has described this kind of plan as '*à la récollette*'.)[125] The two superimposed galleries at the west (entrance) end were built in 1782 and about 1815 respectively. Other parish churches of the time followed the Maillou plan more closely, having a choir that was the full width of the nave; one example is the church of Saint-Étienne at Beaumont, begun in 1727.[126]

The magnificent painted and gilded woodwork of the interior of Saint-François [2.48], which provides a remarkable contrast with the simplicity of the exterior design, is the work of several leading artisans of nineteenth-century Quebec. Although installed well after the end of the French regime, its style continues generations-old Quebec traditions. The wall and ceiling decoration were produced between 1835 and 1844 by the sculptor André Paquet *dit* Lavallée (1799-1860), who was executing designs by Thomas Baillairgé, with whom he apprenticed.[127] The nave is simply treated, with a low wood dado and Corinthian pilasters at intervals; these carry a cornice and continue as decorated bands that follow the curve of the vaulted plaster ceiling. The choir is more elaborately finished. Corinthian pilasters divide its wall (actually extensions of the retable) into alternating broad and narrow bays, and an architrave moulding separates each of these bays into an upper and a lower panel. The beautifully carved wooden ornament includes flower-filled urns, crosses of oak leaves and acorns, wreaths of flowers, and other naturalistic forms contained within conventional classical motifs such as cartouches and rosettes, and is carried into the coved ceiling. The centrepiece of the retable, another reminder of the Récollet church, is a large painting of St Francis contained within a frame comprising two engaged columns supporting a semicircular pediment, above which is a dove in rays of glory.

The general composition of the retable follows the interior design principles of eighteenth-century France, particularly those seen in the work of the period of Louis XVI. Thomas Baillairgé was quite familiar with European sources. Much of his work continues the Baroque and post-Baroque classical tradition, which he learned while training with his father, François Baillairgé, who had studied in Paris at the Académie royale de peinture et de sculpture (and who painted the altarpiece); Thomas also had his own fine architectural library.

Other decorative items of distinction inside the church of Saint-François-de-Sales include the fine

2.49 Église Ste-Famille, Île d'Orléans, Quebec, begun 1743. IBC/77.1017(45).

pulpit (by Louis-Xavier Leprohon and Louis-Thomas Berlinguet, completed 1844) and the baptismal font (by Olivier Samson, 1854). The high altar was carved in 1771-3 by François-Noël Levasseur (1703-94) or his workshop. As was the custom in New France, the decorative work was executed in wood rather than plaster, which was the more common material in France.[128]

Saint-François is typical of many Quebec churches in that it was never 'completed', but rather evolved; improvements to the building have continued through the centuries. A large sacristy was erected behind the choir in 1877 to designs by David Ouellet, and the *clocher* is a work of the 1960s (replacing one erected in 1863), designed by Gérard Morisset and André Robitaille in the manner of a tiered French-regime steeple. Exterior wood siding (like houses, many churches were covered with clapboards)[129] was removed at that time, and the original stonework was revealed.

The Île d'Orléans boasts other distinguished churches as well, notably **Église Sainte-Famille** [2.49], one of the finest parish churches in the colony. Among the larger and more affluent parishes in New France, Sainte-Famille was the headquarters for all of the missions on the island and attracted particular attention from its seigneur, Bishop Laval himself. The community's first church, begun in 1669, had the same dimensions as Notre-Dame-de-la-Paix and was one of the earliest in the colony to be built of stone. Perhaps as a consequence of using a new technique, it was poorly constructed and the walls required frequent repair. It seems also to have been roofed only with thatch. Work on the present church was begun in 1743, and the imposing building was opened for worship three years later and consecrated in 1749 by Bishop Pontbriand.[130]

The Jesuit Church in Quebec served as a model for Sainte-Famille. Their plans are similar, with a pair of detached stairtowers (originally covered only by roofs without spires) flanking the entrance, side-chapels that produce a Latin-cross form, and a choir that is as broad as the nave. Sainte-Famille is 105 feet (32 m) long and 45 feet (13.7 m) wide, larger than the Jesuit Church. The European academic tradition represented by the Jesuit model has been tempered and simplified by the craft tradition of the Quebec artisans, as is appropriate for a parish church. Instead of pilasters on the façade, the decoration is restricted to five niches that contain statues of the members of the Holy Family (Christ and Saints Mary, Joseph, Anne, and Joa chim—the precious originals, carved by the Levasseurs, have been replaced) and the roof is gabled rather than hipped; both these features appeared on Maillou's façade of 1723 for Notre-Dame-des-Victoires.

The towers of Sainte-Famille were heightened in 1807 and their roofs replaced with the present *clochers*; the central *clocher* at the gable peak was designed in 1843 by Thomas Baillairgé. The cut-stone voussoirs and the cornice over the door, the lovely central arched window, and the bull's-eye windows beside the top niche are also later alterations. The original sacristy behind the choir was replaced by the present sacristy in 1852. The exterior walls were formerly covered with *crépi* to protect the masonry, but a recent 'restoration' has exposed the texture of the stone.

The beautiful interior represents the work of a number of leading artisans, including several who worked at nearby Saint-François. The original decoration was by local joiner Gabriel Gosselin; other contributors over the course of the next century included the Levasseur family, Thomas Baillairgé,

2.50 Chart, conceived by Luc Noppen, illustrating the evolution of religious architecture in New France, 1640-1760. Redrawn by David Byrnes.

Pierre-Florent Baillairgé (Thomas's uncle), and Louis-Bazile David (trained in the famous Montreal workshop of the woodcutter and sculptor Louis-Amable Quévillon and his family). The walls of the nave and the choir are divided into two-tiered panels by pilasters, as at Saint-François, and the magnificent high altar features a row of miniature columns and a cornice supporting a canopy composed of six free-standing scrolls surmounted by a cross whose summit is more than sixteen feet above the floor. The coved ceiling is patterned with lozenges filled with rosettes and articulated with bands in shallow relief.

The churches of Sainte-Famille and Saint-François are characteristic of the many eighteenth-century parish churches in New France because they were based on the Quebec prototypes of the previous century—which in turn owed much to academic buildings in the Baroque style of seventeenth-century France—but the exterior forms have been simplified and assimilated by the developing colonial craft tradition. The rich interiors, on the other hand, became showpieces of sculpture and decorative design.

Luc Noppen has compiled a chart [2.50] that illustrates the principal models for these parish churches—Notre-Dame-de-la-Paix, its metamor-

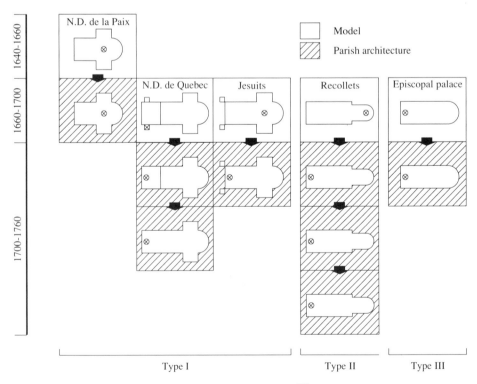

2.51 The three chapels at the summit of the Calvary, Oka, Quebec, 1740-2. Photograph by Edgar Gariépy, *c*. 1925. ANQ/P600-6/GH 273-22.

phosis into Notre-Dame de Québec, the Jesuit Church, the Récollet Church, and the chapel of the Palais épiscopal—and shows their progeny in three parish-church-types: the Jesuit plan, seen in the churches built by Laval (Type I; Morisset called this a 'transept plan'); the parish churches that follow the Récollet plan, with a choir that is narrower than the nave (Type II); and the simple Maillou plan (Type III). The chart illustrates the manner in which the European-designed prototypes were disseminated through the colony and became the basis for a Quebec architectural tradition.[131]

The essence of the parish church form was used as well for small mission chapels and processional chapels. At the Indian mission originally known as 'village du Lac des Deux-Montagnes' and now called Oka (Kanehsatake), southwest of Montreal, a Calvary consisting of seven small stone buildings (each representing a Station of the Cross) was built by the Sulpicians on one of the two mountains behind the village. Four oratories—trapezoidal structures with hipped roofs—are encountered one by one as a person ascends a trail through the forest, and **three chapels** [2.51] with gabled roofs

stand together at the summit. A large painting illustrating an episode of Christ's Passion was contained in each of the buildings. The intent of the Calvary was to evangelize the Indians by trying to interpret the scene of the Passion through the use of natural sites that they encountered while rising to the top of the mountain; it was felt that they would find them non-threatening.[132]

Each small building in the complex—erected in 1740-2 by the French-born Sulpician missionary Hamon Guen (1687-1761)—resembled a simplified parish church. As the paintings quickly suffered from exposure to the weather, they were replaced by wood bas-reliefs carved about 1775-6 by François Guernon *dit* Belleville. Used at first only by natives, the Calvary at Oka became a popular pilgrimage site for Montrealers in the nineteenth century. Since the chapels and the sculptures began to show the effects of vandalism, steps were taken in the 1970s to restore and secure the Calvary.

Acadia

The Acadians were the French settlers of today's Maritime Provinces. The name 'Acadie' is a corruption of 'Arcadia', celebrated by the Roman poet Virgil as a sylvan paradise of classical Greek culture. But the Acadians of New France settled in a land that was anything but a paradise, and they endured a troubled and insecure history. The first European settlers arrived in 1604 with de Monts and resided first at Île Sainte-Croix and then at Port Royal (pages 16-21), but they either returned to France or were dispersed in 1613 by the English-American raider Samuel Argall. Britain disputed the French claims to the area, settled some hundred or so Scots at Port Royal, and named the region Nova Scotia; but the Treaty of Saint-Germaine-en-Laye returned Acadia (and New France) to France in 1632. New colonists were sent out from France, despite subsequent British claims to the land, and the first official census, held in 1671, recorded an Acadian population of more than 400. Most came from the west central portion of France—as had Champlain and de Monts—and had sailed from the port of La Rochelle in Poitou, well south of Normandy and Brittany, the principal homeland of the Quebec colonists.[133]

The tidal marshlands of the Bay of Fundy (called the Baie Française) had rich alluvial soil. The settlers reclaimed the land for agriculture—and as a by-product harvested salt, useful for preserving cod—with a system of sod dikes and wood sluices (*aboiteaux*) with swinging doors (*clapets*) that prevented saltwater from entering at high tide.

The Acadians spread out along the east and north coasts of the Bay of Fundy, forming settlements especially in the Minas Basin (Bassin des Mines) and Chignecto Bay. France showed relatively little interest in the colony, and Acadia became a kind of no-man's-land between the British interests in New England and the French in New France. Consequently it was often a battleground. French policy was directed more at maintaining good relations with the Indians—the Micmacs in today's Nova Scotia and the Abenakis in today's New Brunswick and Maine, both of them Algonquian groups—than at assisting or protecting the European settlers. The Acadians generally got along well with the natives, largely because they never attempted to inhabit their hunting and fishing grounds.

In 1713 France ceded Acadia to Great Britain by the Treaty of Utrecht. The Acadian population was then only about 1,600. But by 1750 it had increased to between 10,000 and 12,000 (compared with 55,000 in New France and 1.2 million in the American colonies).[134] Despite their small numbers, and even though they had remained neutral throughout the wars between the European powers, at the beginning of the Seven Years' War the British authorities decided that the French minority posed a threat to security. Under the pretext of the Acadians' refusal to swear an oath of allegiance, the British expelled the entire Acadian population in 1755. It took some eight years, but virtually all the Acadians in the Maritimes were rounded up and deported by being loaded onto outbound ships. Their houses were burned and their land was confiscated and given to (or reserved for) new American settlers. Many relocated in Quebec, Louisiana (where they became known as Cajuns, a corruption of 'Acadians'), the West Indies, and France.[135]

Acadians were permitted to return to the Maritimes after 1763 on the condition that they take an oath of allegiance. Those who came back were resettled in small groups scattered on the north and east coasts of today's New Brunswick, at Baie-Sainte-Marie in western Nova Scotia, around Malpèque and Rustico on Prince Edward Island, and in parts of Cape Breton—communities that are sometimes described collectively as New Acadia. The land in most of these areas was infertile, and so these farming people were forced to learn to fish or cut wood.

Little evidence remains of pre-Expulsion Acadian buildings, particularly of private dwellings: not a single confirmed building stands—though manors and forts have fared marginally better. Nevertheless, recent documentary research and archaeological excavations, as well as a critical analysis of surviving post-Expulsion building, permit a glimpse at early Acadian architecture.

The manor and the fort

More than thirty seigneurial grants were made in Acadia in the seventeenth century, but the seigneurial system was largely unsuccessful there and had little effect on development. Few seigneurs took up their grants, and most of those who did were more interested in trading furs and fish than in settling their lands. Many were driven away by the frequent British raids. The resident seigneurs, wealthy merchants, and others in a position of power seem to have lived in fortified dwellings throughout the century. Governor Isaac de Razilly, who arrived in

2.52 Mount House, on Grimross Island, St John River, near Gagetown, New Brunswick, *c.* 1670s. Photographed in the 1930s. PANB/P4-2-1.

1632 with '300 hand-picked men' to re-establish the colony, set up his first base at La Hève—a short distance south of today's Lunenburg, on the south shore of Nova Scotia—in a 'little fort (*fortin*) of wood that served as both a storehouse and a manor house.'[136] Later in the century Jean Serreau de Saint-Aubin lived at Pesmocadie (Passamaquoddy) on the Sainte-Croix River in a palisaded dwelling, and Richard Denys de Fronsac lived in the Mirami-chi district in 'a little fort of four bastions formed of stakes.'[137] Richard's father Nicolas Denys—a trader from La Rochelle with fishing and lumber interests, and a colonial promoter with more failures than successes to his credit, who had come over with Razilly—described his residence at Nipisiguit or Nepeguis (today's Bathurst, New Brunswick):

> My habitation...is on the shore of the basin....It is where I was obliged to withdraw after the fire at my Fort Saint-Pierre on Cape Breton Island. My house there is flanked by four small bastions with a palisade whose pickets are 18 feet high; with six cannon in batteries....I have a large garden.[138]

These 'little forts' were more properly trading posts than manors.

Denys's house was reportedly built of stone,[139] as were other houses built by wealthy new arrivals from France. **Mount House [2.52]**, a picturesque stone ruin near Gagetown and Jemseg, about half-

way between today's Saint John and Fredericton on the St John River, is believed to have been built in the 1670s by Pierre de Joybert de Soulanges et Marson, who received large grants of land from Governor Frontenac. Joybert's daughter would have been born here; she later married the Marquis de Vaudreuil, the governor of Montreal and gover-nor general of New France (whose palatial Mon-treal residence was described above). The British attempted to burn Mount House when the Acadi-ans were expelled, but it survived and was inhab-ited for a while by James Peters, a Loyalist from Long Island. The house is now in an advanced state of ruin, although enough survives of its $2\frac{1}{2}$-foot-thick stone walls to reveal that it was a three-storey dwelling built carefully by skilled craftsmen.[140]

A number of forts—larger and more substantial structures than these fortified dwellings—were erected throughout Acadia by the French military forces. Commander Joseph Robineau de Villebon built several at the end of the century for defence against English attack, and they are known through early maps and drawings. **Fort Nashwaak (Fort Saint-Joseph)**, built in 1692 at the junction of the Nashwaak and St John Rivers, near present-

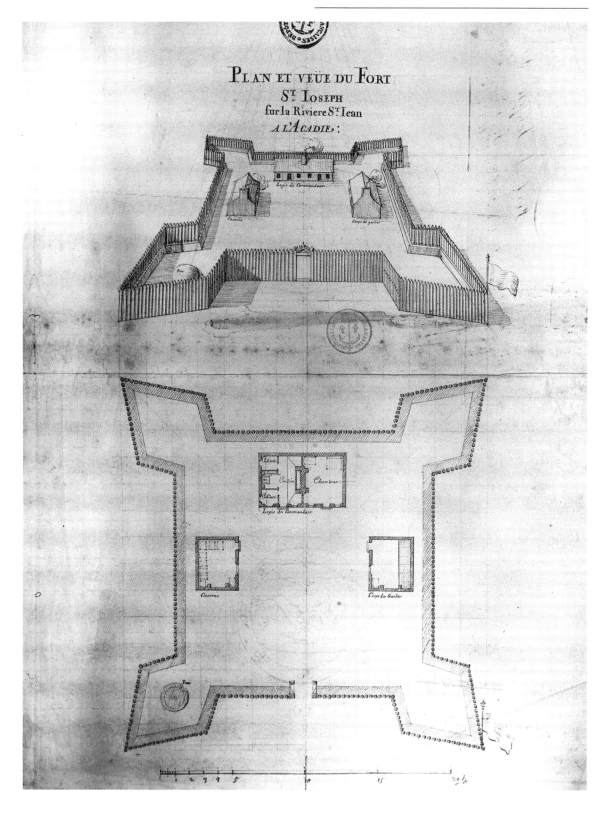

PLAN ET VEÜE DU FORT
St. IOSEPH
fur la Riviere St. Iean
A L'ACADIE :

day Fredericton, and Fort Saint-Jean, built in 1699-1700 at the mouth of the St John River, were both clusters of buildings protected by square palisades with bastions at the corners. (The palisade walls that connect the bastions are called 'curtains'.) Fort Nashwaak [2.53] contained only three buildings—the commander's house, flanked by barracks, and the officers' quarters—and was about 100 feet (30 m) square. The commander's house was a gable-roofed structure divided into two rooms with a chimney and stone wall between them; one room was used as a kitchen, chapel, and general living space, and the second was a bedroom. The other two buildings seem to have had a single room with chimneys at the ends.[141]

The same arrangement was adopted at Fort Pentagoët, begun in 1635 as a defence against British incursions at the southern edge of Acadian territory and destroyed in 1674 by a Dutch adventurer. An important French fortification whose site has been extensively excavated by archaeologists is located in the town of Castine on Penobscot Bay in the State of Maine. The compound was about 80 feet square (24.3 by 23.5 m) and the buildings and fortifications were constructed of rubble stone.[142]

The best known of the French forts in Acadia is Fort Beauséjour, located near today's Sackville, New Brunswick. Begun in 1751, its plan (or 'trace') was in the form of a pentagon, with a bastion at each of the five angles, following the more developed state of military engineering in the eighteenth century. The shorter curtains and lesser angles were supposed to be more easily defended, but it was nevertheless captured easily by the British in 1755 before its completion. The fortress was renamed Fort Cumberland and kept armed for another eighty years; the ruins have been stabilized by Parks Canada and now form the centrepiece of Fort Beauséjour National Historic Park.[143]

Forts much like these were built across Canada: in eastern and central Canada by the French and the British, and in the West by the fur-traders of the Hudson's Bay Company and North West Company, the American whiskey traders, and the North-West Mounted Police. A selection will appear in subsequent chapters. Some were tested in battle, but most never saw action.

2.53 *Plan et veue du Fort St-Joseph sur la rivière St-Jean à l'Acadie, 1692.* Archives nationales, France. Dépôt des Fortifications des Colonies, Amérique sept. c39; reproduced from a photograph in the NAC, c-15701.

The builders of the manors and the forts were all people from France who were living in Acadia only temporarily, strangers in a strange land. True Acadian architecture is not found here, but rather in the houses of the second- and third-generation immigrants, the people who were committed to making their permanent home in the new territory.

The Acadian house

Life in Acadia was chronically insecure, since its geographical (and strategic) position between the flagship colonies of France and Britain rendered its settlements vulnerable to frequent attack and destruction, despite the inhabitants' profession of neutrality. At the earliest raid, Samuel Argall's rout of Port Royal in 1613, the attackers took everything of use from the buildings, and this pattern was repeated for a century and a half until the Expulsion. Since destruction and rebuilding were recognized as being inevitable, the Acadians' architectural response—reinforced by economic necessity—appears to have been to build insubstantial houses of impermanent materials.

Pre-Expulsion houses No confirmed pre-Expulsion Acadian dwellings are known to have survived.[144] What little is known about them has come down from scattered early accounts, crude cartographical images, and inconclusive recent excavations. A discussion of the houses must therefore rely heavily on textual evidence. The records provide useful information about building materials and use, but they give us little idea of what an Acadian house actually *looked* like.

Early impressions of Acadian villages and houses by both residents and travellers make constant reference to poor construction and equally poor living conditions. Characteristic of these is a description of Port Royal, the community that developed near Champlain's *habitation* and the capital of the colony, written in 1688 by Governor Des Friches de Meneval (under whose command Port Royal fell to Admiral William Phips two years later):

> Port Royal is a place that hardly has any shape any longer, and what is there is composed of about twenty miserable houses of mud and wood (*de boue et de bois*).[145]

Soeur Chausson of the Congrégation des Filles de la Croix, who visited Port Royal from La Rochelle in 1701, noted in a letter:

Acadia is a very miserable district of Canada; the houses there are only made of *colombage* covered with straw; there is no stone at all....All of the inhabitants there are poor....Our church is in hideously poor condition. It is covered only with straw, the walls are only made of *colombage*, the windows are simply paper.[146]

The Sieur de Dièreville offered his impressions on a visit of 1699:

The Houses [at Port Royal] are built rather far apart, & are nothing more than Cottages, very badly constructed (*fort mal bousillées*), with chimneys of clay....

[The parish priest] went with me to see a house, which I leased; it is the largest in the place & served formerly as the Church; it is composed of three rooms, downstairs, with attics above & a cellar of masonry under the middle apartment.[147]

A few years later another visitor, Baron de Lahontan, echoed Dièreville's observations:

The Capital or the only City of *Acadia* [Port Royal], is in effect no more than a little paultry Town,...only a handful of Houses two Story high.[148]

Charles Morris, who surveyed Acadian settlements in 1748, described the buildings at Grand Pré as

low Houses fram'd of timber and their Chimney fram'd with the Building of wood & lined with Clay except the fireplace below....

He also noted a few stone houses in the centre of town.[149] The impermanent nature of the houses referred to by most of these observers is supported by the unkind story that piles of manure, for which the Acadians had no use, grew so large around their farms that the buildings sometimes had to be moved.[150]

Evidence indicates that the prevailing method of construction for pre-Expulsion Acadian houses was a timber frame with an infill of clay and hay—the local materials, 'tamped clay and saltmarsh hay'—or what was called *colombage bousillé* in New France. This is consistent with Meneval's description of houses being built of mud and wood, with Dièreville's comment that they were *mal bousillées*, with Soeur Chausson's use of the term *colombage*, as well as with other early accounts. It is also supported by recent research on Fort Anne, at Port Royal, which shows that most of the frame buildings built in that fort between 1701 and 1710 by French soldiers and Acadian day-labourers were constructed of upright timbers with infill of clay and straw.[151]

This building technique is called 'wattle-and-daub' construction in the English and American architectural literature. Horizontal rails (or struts) were typically inserted at intervals between the vertical posts of a timber frame, and the spaces between the posts and the rails were usually further subdivided with vertical staves and horizontal woven branches or reeds ('wattles'), before being 'daubed' with a mixture of clay, horsehair, and other materials. The method was common in the vernacular architecture of sixteenth-century England and France; and timber frame with wattle-and-daub infill (using clay and straw) was also utilized widely in New England during the colonial period.[152] The Acadian settlers may therefore have brought over the technique from France, or else learned it from New England.

Alphonse Deveau, who observed a number of ruined buildings in Nova Scotia believed to be pre-Expulsion houses—at Belleisle in Annapolis County and at Upper Clements, although none have been confirmed by scientific evidence—found a large quantity of clay that had been burned and become somewhat like unformed bricks. This is consistent with our knowledge that the British burned the Acadians' houses, and also with the use of *colombage bousillé*. The dimensions of the houses Deveau described were typically 18 by 24 feet (5.5 by 7.3 m), with a cellar beneath the centre of the house (Dièreville and several others cited cellars) and a chimney on the east wall (the prevailing wind is from the west). A number of writers, including Dièreville, referred to clay chimneys, or to wood chimneys covered with clay.[153]

Other construction methods were also recorded. Some houses were apparently built of horizontal logs. A Monsieur de Gargas, the *écrivain principal* of Acadia, reported in 1687-8 that at Port Royal:

All of the houses are low, made of pieces of wood, one on top of another [*faites des pièces de bois, une sur l'autre*], and covered with thatch; the one in which the governor lives being the only one covered with boards.[154]

This would seem at first to contradict the descriptions of Port Royal cited above, leaving us to wonder whether the *bousillage* or a covering of *crépi*—the top coat of a clay-like substance—may have concealed the underlying structural system and led Gargas merely to guess at the materials. Other evidence, however, also points to the Acadians' hav-

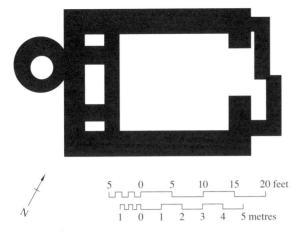

5   0   5   10   15   20 feet

1   0   1   2   3   4   5 metres

N

2.54 Plan of House 1 at Belleisle, late 17th century. Drawing by David Byrnes, after plan in Christianson, *Belleisle 1983* (1984).

ing built log houses. The Acadians who hid in New Brunswick immediately after the Expulsion, hoping to escape detection by the British, built with square logs, and they must have been familiar with the method previously. As Gamaliel Smethurst reported, while travelling from Bathurst Harbour to Fort Cumberland (Beauséjour) in the fall of 1761:

> The Acadians make themselves a winter house in two or three days. They cut down a number of pine trees, suitable to the occasion, square them, and place them upon one another, fastening them with trunnels ['treenails', or wood pegs], and fill the crevices with moss; they cover their houses with slabs and bark. They are very good broad axe men.[155]

A trunnel, however, is unnecessary in a horizontal log structure, and so this passage may refer to a timber frame with horizontal log infill (*poteaux en coulisse*).

A glimpse at an Acadian house is provided by archaeological evidence from the only convincingly dated pre-Expulsion house to have been excavated professionally. The site is at Belleisle, a village about 5 miles (8 km) up the Annapolis River from Port Royal that was settled in the 1670s. Two of about twenty houses were excavated by the Nova Scotia Museum in 1983, one thoroughly. **House 1** [**2.54**], as it is called, was likely built in the late seventeenth century, and was certainly occupied in the early eighteenth century. It showed evidence of having been destroyed by burning. The foundation, made of local basalt fieldstone laid three to four courses high, measures 38 by 25 ft (11.5 by 7.5

m), with a cellar below the central portion. The house consisted of a single living area, with what may have been a storage area along a short side. The principal feature was a large fireplace, along the opposite (west) wall, which was connected to a circular exterior oven. The fireplace was lined with locally made bricks and the hearth was tiled in slate, with a small compartment—possibly for storage or for warming feet—at either side. (A similar arrangement of fireplace and oven has been observed in the plan of a vernacular house in the Vendée region of France, near La Rochelle.) The walls seem to have been covered with a 2- to 2½-inch (5- to 7-cm) coating of local clay, mixed with a marsh-grass binder, and covered with a smooth clay finish on one side (probably the interior) and retaining the impression of wood grain on the other. This suggests that the wall structure was wood—either horizontal squared logs, or *poteaux en coulisse*—and not wattle and daub, which is presumed to have been the more common material. Evidence shows that the roof was likely thatched.[156]

The observations at House 1, and the previously cited documents, lead to the preliminary conclusion that, in addition to wattle and daub, the Acadians used one or another kind of log construction (horizontal bearing walls, or log infill in a timber frame). If they knew the horizontal-log technique in the seventeenth century, as builders in New France almost surely did (see page 51), then a strong case can be made for the French settlers' having been familiar with this important building system before the English colonists, and possibly even before the Swedes and Germans introduced the technique to the American colonies. The source for the technique may well have been Governor Razilly, who was in Scandinavia studying log structures before coming to Acadia to establish the colony.[157]

Masonry, which was often used for Acadian forts and manors, was only rarely utilized in houses. A document of 1704 records the sale in Port Royal of 'a house of brick and wood',[158] presumably *colombage briqueté*, but this was a rare and special large house—boasting a kitchen, a parlour, and five small rooms—that was being purchased by the Récollet missionaries. Elsewhere Captain John Knox saw 'a row of indifferent brick houses, between twenty and thirty in number', at Beaubassin in 1757.[159]

There were sawmills in the colony, and so sawn boards were available, as well as hewn logs. A sawmill was operating in Port Royal by 1692, and one was built at Nashwaak (New Brunswick) in 1695 by Mathieu Damours de Freneuse.[160] Colonial official Mathieu de Goutin wrote in 1707 that 'the drought was so severe this autumn, that the sawmills [*les moulins à planches*] were unable to cut.'[161] Many of the mills may have been light, portable structures. De Goutin noted in 1699 that the founders of Chipody 'even have a mill ready to be transported to their land'. Although some mills were surely powered by rivers and creeks—such as the ones that went dry in 1707—several were undoubtedly tidal mills.

Roofs were normally covered in thatch of straw or reeds, as was recorded in many descriptions (and discovered at Belleisle). De Gargas said that in Port Royal only the governor's house was covered with boards, but sawn wood was often seen as a roofing material. Dièreville noted in 1699 that the people 'cover [with fish] the houses whose roofs are planks, in order to dry them in the sun.'[162] Shingle roofs were also seen by early observers.

Houses were typically one storey high with an attic and a cellar—what is described as a $1\frac{1}{2}$-storey house—with 'only a handful' (Lahontan's words) two storeys high. This is corroborated in a **1686 bird's-eye plan of Port Royal [2.55]** by Franquelin, which indicates the town plan as well as the appearance of the buildings. Sixteen buildings in one cluster (some of them probably large outbuildings) were loosely arranged in a linear fashion parallel to the shore, along what might be described as a main street. Many had gardens enclosed within picket fences. Although the houses were only sketched, their forms are clearly shown. Three in the group are identified. The largest was the governor's house (7), which was the only one with a *pavillon* roof (retaining the meaning of the French palace/château roof-form), as well as the only one roofed in boards, as de Gargas reported. The other two buildings named were the residence of Sieur le Borgne (8) and one of two Englishmen's stores (*maison d'un anglois*, 6). The others all had gable roofs (Gargas said they were thatched), with the entrance in the long side or the gable end. Only one—the store—clearly had windows illuminating an attic; the others seem to be only one storey high. The second store (5) was a short distance away, and it too had a *pavillon* roof, as well as a flagpole on the ridge. The parish church (2) stood away from the village, along one side of a fenced garden, and was surrounded by a double row of trees; next to the church were a house (presumably the manse) and

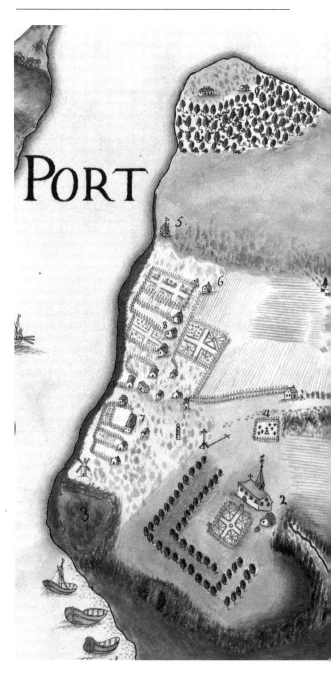

2.55 Detail from *Plan tres exact du terrain ou sont sçituees les maisons du Port Royal et ou lon peut faire une Ville considerable*, by Jean-Baptiste-Louis Franquelin, 1686. Original at the Bibliothèque nationale, Paris France; cartes et plans, Service hydrographique, PF 133-8-2. Reproduced from a 1933 transcript in NAC/NMC 34343.

an outbuilding. The church, with a *flèche* in the centre of its gable roof, is shown with its entrance not in the gable end, but on a long side, facing the garden. (If this depiction is accurate, it might suggest a source in the New England Protestant meeting-house, including the relationship to the town common.) The cemetery (4) was on the other side of the church. A windmill stood at one edge of the village (near a ruined fort, 3), and a water-powered mill was nearby.[163]

Robert Hale of Beverley, Massachusetts, left a detailed description of the arrangement and furnishing of an Acadian house that he visited in 1731:

They have but one Room in yr Houses besides a Cockloft, Cellar, & Sometimes a Closet. Their Bedrooms are made something after ye manner of a Sailor's Cabbin, but boarded all round about the bigness of ye Bed, except one little hole on the Foreside, just big eno' to crawl into, before which is a Curtain drawn & as a Step to get into it, there stands a Chest. They have not above 2 or 3 chairs in a house, & those wooden one, bottom and all. I saw but 2 Muggs among all ye French & ye lip of one of ym was broken dowen above 2 inches. When they treat you with strong drink they bring it in a large Bason & give you a Porringer to dip it with.[164]

A single room was typical, since only one room could be heated adequately by the fire in a single hearth located on an exterior wall.

Post-Expulsion houses   After the Treaty of Paris (1763) that ended the Seven Years' War, many Acadians returned to their homeland and established new communities along the coast, living peacefully beside the newly arrived English-speaking colonists. A fascinating description of the Acadian house built at this time was provided in 1795 by Captain John MacDonald in a report he wrote to J.F.W. DesBarres, the governor of Cape Breton Island and Prince Edward Island. MacDonald was visiting Minudie, near Amherst, which had been resettled in 1768; but he could equally have been describing House 1 at Belleisle, built several generations earlier:

The premises of every one seem to be a house from 18 to 25 feet long & as many in breadth without porch or partition but the outer door opening immediately into the sole room. There are generally two doors, the one being that which

is used. The chimney, of which the lower part is stone & clay, & the higher part is clay wrought upon cross bars of wood between a wooden frame, is in the remotest part from the door. The Beds are on both sides of the house from chimney to the doors. In the end of the house opposite to the chimney, the pots and water vessels lie on the floor, and the Milk & Milk vessels are disposed of on shelves, together with their bowls, muggs &c: As they all sleep, eat, cook, smoke, wash &c: in this house or room, I need not say it must look black & dirty enough particularly as the houses are now old.

Behind the Chimney on the out side is an oven of clay, the opening to which for bread & fire is on the In side back of the chimney. The oven rests on a square wall of Loggs or Stone around an appartment three or four feet in the square, where a few pigs enter on the out side, and lie warm from the heat of the chimney & oven.

In their Barns they are more Sumptuous. They are from fourty to fifty feet in length—from twenty to thirty in breadth & from ten to fifteen high, the lower story destined for the cattle—and the upper for the corn, Hay, and threshing floor: At a distance they sett off the whole place.

I had almost forgot to mention that their houses have a cellar under ground for the roots &c to which they descend by a trap door in the floor.[165]

A handful of extant houses have been identified by scholars as having been built in the years immediately following the Acadians' resettlement, when Captain MacDonald wrote his report. They may well have continued the types built before the Expulsion, but since the New Acadians were creating new communities under changed political and environmental conditions, there is no assurance that their houses were identical to pre-Expulsion ones.[166]

Rodolphe Bourque observed *colombage bousillé* in a few early post-Expulsion houses, one of which was the **Germain Dugas house** [2.56] in Upper Caraquet, New Brunswick, which was likely built some time after 1770. Bourque described it as being built of posts and beams mortised, tenoned, and pegged together, with vertical studs spaced a little less than three feet apart. Horizontal rails were inserted between the studs at intervals of about six to eight inches. Clay, mixed with marsh hay, was packed into the spaces and then covered with a plaster (what would have been called *bousillage*).

The house had a livingroom, kitchen, and two bedrooms on the ground floor (not necessarily the original layout); and a staircase in the corner of the kitchen led to the upper floor, which had two small bedrooms and a large attic beneath the eaves. The house sat on a foundation of stone and tamped clay, with a cellar in the centre reached by a trap door in the kitchen.[167]

A number of post-Expulsion log buildings have also been identified. Father Anselme Chiasson published in 1969 a photograph of a house in Falmouth, Nova Scotia, built of horizontal logs with dovetail joints, which he claimed was built shortly after the Acadians returned to the area.[168] Frame buildings with exterior boards and no clay infill were also built. The Joseph à Hilaire Boudreau house at Barachois, New Brunswick, on Northumberland Strait, was built shortly after 1789—probably about 1795—and survives, although moved and much altered, as a barn. It was larger than many houses, 24 by 34 feet (7.3 by 10.4 m), with the ground floor divided into two rooms, heated by a central chimney; an attic and a stone cellar occupied the full area of the house. The joints of the timber frame were mortised and tenoned, and it was covered with hand-sawn horizontal cladding.[169]

2.56 Germain Dugas house (partially dismantled) at Caraquet, New Brunswick, built after 1770. PANB.

The 'old' Acadian houses that are best known today were mostly built in the nineteenth century, by which time any distinctive features of the original Acadian houses might well have been lost through several generations of close contact with English neighbours. Several of these houses have been moved to the Acadian Historical Village near Caraquet, NB, and restored. Many were built using horizontal logs with dovetail joints. The oldest house at the Village, the **Martin house from Sainte-Anne** (*c*. 1783), is an important exception because it may be early enough to indicate the appearance of a pre-Expulsion Acadian house [**2.57**]. The walls are opened up by a door and a window on one side, and by two windows on the other. The gable roof has a medium pitch, much lower than the roofs on Quebec houses of the time and closer to the slope of a Nova Scotia or New England house.[170]

Some log houses at the museum village, such as the Doucet house (*c*. 1840)—also from Sainte-Anne originally—have an exterior cladding of shingles over the logs, also a characteristic Maritime and New England feature. Others are built of wood frame with exterior siding of shingles or boards.

Clarence Lebreton, the chief curator at the Acadian Historical Village, has studied the prevalent post-Expulsion house-forms. Horizontal logs prevailed—sometimes dovetailed and sometimes with

2.57 Martin house, St Anne, New Brunswick, *c*. 1783 (now at Acadian Historical Village, Caraquet, New Brunswick). Misho Studio Ltd/Ltée. Courtesy of Village Historique Acadien.

the logs fitted into the corner posts—laid on top of each other and secured with tongues and grooves. Stoves were substituted for open hearths, allowing the plan to be subdivided into two rooms. In the middle years of the nineteenth century—a time of nationalism, when the Acadians began to express themselves as a people—the austerity of the early period gave way to more spacious, comfortable, and elegant housing. The dominant construction method was the wood frame clad with vertical boards, and houses often had a second storey, with both floors divided into several rooms with plastered walls.[171]

The question remains: to what extent did early Acadians develop a distinctive architectural form? It is clear that they were a group distinct from the Québécois. They originated in a different region of France, encountered different geographical and political conditions, were not controlled so strongly by the Church, and never achieved material prosperity. Their houses were likewise dissimilar. The two most common building materials in New France, stone and *colombage pierroté*, were not

used by the Acadians. Driven by political insecurity and economic necessity, the Acadians built houses that were smaller and constructed of less-permanent materials, primarily *colombage bousillé* (wattle and daub) and *pièce sur pièce à queue d'aronde* (horizontal logs with dovetail joints). A single chimney, joined to an exterior clay oven, usually occupied an end wall, in contrast to the central and paired chimneys of Quebec, and a stone cellar lay below the house. The scanty evidence suggests that roof slopes may have been lower than those in Quebec.

Acadian houses looked more like the houses of the English settlers of Nova Scotia than those of the French settlers of Quebec. Whether the Acadians and the Nova Scotians learned from one another, or whether both responded to a common environment, it is probable that geography was a more compelling determinant than cultural origin.

CHAPTER 3

BRITISH AND AMERICAN SETTLEMENT ON THE ATLANTIC COAST

WHILE FRANCE was building a vigorous colony in the St Lawrence valley, the first English-speaking settlers were establishing communities along the Atlantic coast. Seventeenth-century settlement was much sparser in today's Canada than in the warmer and more fertile American colonies to the south. In Newfoundland, English (as well as French) fishing stations along the coast evolved into small permanent settlements, of which the town of St John's emerged as the strongest, but most seventeenth-century attempts at establishing agricultural colonies there and in Nova Scotia failed. Despite the precariousness of settlement in both regions, the early buildings in their scattered communities marked the beginning of a strong tradition of British architecture that was to dominate Canada outside Quebec in the centuries that followed.

English-speaking settlement began in earnest in the 1750s, when the British government encouraged large contingents of Protestants from Britain, the American colonies, and the European continent to immigrate to the shores of Nova Scotia in order to provide a bulwark against French and Catholic influence. Two decades after Britain's military triumph over France in 1763 ended the Seven Years' War, large numbers of refugees loyal to the British Crown fled the new United States of America and settled in maritime and central Canada, augmenting the anglophone population and bringing about the formation of New Brunswick and Upper Canada (Ontario). To the provinces of British North America, large numbers of people from Britain and the US followed in subsequent decades.

As part of their cultural baggage, the new arrivals brought their architectural traditions. The earliest structures were built more for survival than for show, adapting vernacular building techniques

from the mother countries. But as communities and institutions became established, a distinctive Anglo-Canadian architecture developed. The symmetrical arrangement of floor plans, façades, and town plans that evolved, which differed from the more organic manner of designing buildings and communities practised by French Canadians, often put appearance ahead of comfort.

The dominant architectural manner was the Georgian style. Derived from the eighteenth-century buildings of Britain, it was imported simultaneously from Britain and the US—whose buildings were themselves transplants from British sources. In Canada this Georgian legacy was modified in response to environmental, economic, and practical necessities, but it also developed distinctive regional differences. The buildings of Newfoundland and the Maritime Provinces are discussed here, and those of Upper Canada in the next chapter.

Newfoundland

Fishing stations

It is not known how long fishermen from England, France, Portugal, and the Basque country worked the coastal waters of Newfoundland and Labrador before the sixteenth century—when, it is thought, the English and French began to build seasonal fishing stations on the rocky, windswept coast of Newfoundland and the Basques built whaling stations in Labrador. The first to erect temporary stations in Newfoundland may have been the English, who established posts along the eastern shore of the Avalon peninsula (where the present-day city of St John's lies), and on nearby Conception and Trinity Bays. The French preferred Placentia Bay, to the south, and the northeast coast. The fishermen needed the land-based facilities to dry cod and other fish, since they lacked easy access to the salt required to preserve fish in a wet, or 'green', state. They cured their catch on stages, called flakes— sometimes simple platforms, and sometimes elaborate tiered structures covered with roofs and supplemented with storehouses and primitive houses.[1]

The earliest of these temporary dwellings were crude structures, now known as tilts, that provided only the most basic type of shelter. (A 'tilt', which came to mean any rough shelter, was synonymous with 'cabin' or 'shack'.) Tilts were constructed of vertical poles (usually slender spruce-logs—common along the exposed shore—with their bark 'unrinded', or left on) set in a trench and arranged to produce a single rectangular room. The spaces between the vertical logs were filled with moss. The caulking process was called 'chinsing' or 'chintzing', a term later corrupted to 'chinking'. A roof was provided by rafters consisting of poles resting on a longer ridge pole and covered with bark, boughs, boards, sods, or slabs of wood. The floor was packed earth or boards. A window might be made with a shutter set on cloth or leather hinges. An open fire on flat stones provided heat for cooking. Smoke was allowed to escape through a hole in the roof.[2]

Tilts were built as seasonal shelters by migratory fishermen not only along the coast of Newfoundland but also in Labrador. In Newfoundland they provided the initial year-round house when families began to settle there. The best period illustration of an early Newfoundland shelter of this kind is French rather than English. Published in 1722 in Bacqueville de la Potherie's *Histoire de l'Amérique septentrionale*, it shows a **sod-roofed house [3.1]** at Placentia.[3]

Tilts were used into the twentieth century as family homes and winter houses rather than as parts of fishing stations. Sir Richard Bonnycastle— an army officer, military engineer, and author— described a tilt in 1842:

It was, perhaps, about eighteen feet long by fourteen in breadth, for I did not measure it correctly, as it was surrounded by fences and snow, and consisted of one apartment only, in which the whole family...were squatting round a scanty fire....

This dwelling, which was as lofty as a barn, was built of poles or sticks of very small diameter, placed upright, irregularly together, and braced every here and there. The chimney, formed of

A. *Maison sur la quelle un Mouton paist.* B. *Cour de la Maison.* C. *palets ou pierre.*

3.1 Sod-roofed house at Placentia, Newfoundland. From Bacqueville de la Potherie's *Histoire de l'Amérique Septentrionale* (Paris, 1722), Volume I, after p. 16. Special Collections, University of British Columbia.

rough unmortared stone, adjoined the roof, which was also of poles at one gable end, and was finished above the ridge pole with boards, or short slabs of wood. The roof had been covered with bark and sods, and some attempts had originally been made to stop or caulk the crevices between the poles, both of the roof and walls, with moss or mud; but these substances had generally disappeared, and in every part of this wretched dwelling, was the light of heaven visible, and everywhere must the rain have fallen in it, excepting towards the gable, opposite the chimney, which had some pains taken with it, and where the unfortunate family slept in their rags.[4]

Tilts were also described by other early visitors—including the Reverend Edward Wix in 1835 and the Reverend William Wilson in 1866. Wix observed that winter tilts were located at a distance from summer-houses, situated along the shore, and wrote:

> The structure of the winter tilt, the chimney of which is of upright studs, stuffed or 'stogged' between with moss, is so rude that in most of them in which I officiated the chimney has caught fire once, if not oftener, during the service. . . .
> The chimneys of the summer-houses in Fortune Bay, are better fortified against the danger, being lined within all the way up with a coating of tin, which is found to last for several years.

Wix also noted a particularly crowded dwelling:

> One tilt was visited by me on this island, the dimensions of which were only twelve feet by ten, and I found living in it a man and his wife,—the master and mistress of the house,—two married daughters with their husbands and children, amounting, in all, to fifteen souls![5]

Wilson called the tilt 'perfectly original', but this was not so. The rectangular hut constructed of vertical poles (slender logs) was a common architectural response to the need for temporary shelter in a hostile environment. Some New England settlers used this construction technique in the first half of the seventeenth century, describing it as 'palisado'; the current term is 'palisade'. The walls of vertical stakes were often reinforced with 'wattles' (withes of willow or hazel) woven between them and daubed with clay; the dwelling that resulted is known as a wattle-and-daub cabin. Forked sticks ('crotchets') supported a short ridge pole, which carried a roof of poles covered with sod or thatch. The New Englanders soon abandoned vertical logs in favour of a frame house, but French builders in Quebec and the Mississippi basin retained the form (*pieux en terre*) into the eighteenth century. A number of European cultures, including British and Scandinavian, had developed similar shelters in earlier times, and homesteaders in the Prairies would resort to it in the years around 1900.[6]

The tilt form survived into the middle of the twentieth century as a summer shelter for fisher

3.2 Tilt, Lockston Path Pond, near Trinity, Newfoundland. Photograph by David Mills, 1972.

men and a winter shelter for loggers. The photograph of a **tilt** [3.2] on Lockston Path Pond, 10 miles (16 km) from Trinity on Trinity Bay, was taken by David Mills in 1972. Diagonal poles help to secure the structure, since vertical and/or horizontal members without diagonal braces are potentially unstable. In 1974 Shane O'Dea found a tilt on the King's Cove Road, built about 1950 by a Bonavista man for use in logging. Eighteen by 12 feet (5.5 by 3.7 m) in plan, and 6 feet (1.8 m) high at the ridge, it had walls made of unrinded spruce trees set into the earth, and the roof was built of 'slabs'—the half-round boards that remain after a log is squared. No chimney was apparent, but it once had a stove, as did other tilts along the same road. Openings were provided by a door fabricated from vertical boards and an unglazed window.[7]

In the last two centuries tilts were erected side-by-side with later building-forms. A photograph of about 1900 shows a **summer fishing settlement at Logy Bay** [3.3] set in a barren landscape near St John's. A vertical-log tilt—buttressed by diagonal shoring—is nestled among three houses that appear to be constructed of wood frame and clad in coarse horizontal siding.

Seventeenth-century settlements

Sir Humphrey Gilbert sailed to Newfoundland in 1583 and claimed the island for England. Permanent settlement was discouraged by the Crown, partly owing to the vigorous lobbying of the powerful fishery interests in the west of England—the West Country merchants. As late as 1806, British law stipulated that 'neither house, nor chimney, nor barn, was allowed to be erected, nor any business other than fishing business permitted without the sanction of the Governor.'[8] The statute, however, was poorly enforced, and year-round fishing communities gradually gained a toe-hold on the rocky coastline. Chief Justice Reeves reported to the authorities in Britain in the 1790s that 'it must be understood that Newfoundland is no longer a place resorted to only by mere fishermen', and that the colony 'has been populated behind your Back.' In 1799 Captain Ambrose Crofton observed that:

> Newfoundland...[has] more the appearance of a Colony than a fishery from the great number of People that have annually imperceptibly remained the Winter who have Houses, Land and Family's....[9]

In 1824 a judicial decision finally gave formal recognition to the private ownership of property.[10]

The first effort at a planned settlement occurred in July 1610, when 39 colonists, led by Alderman John Guy of Bristol, arrived at St John's. Finding a number of houses around the harbour, they proceeded to Cupers Cove (today's Cupids) in Conception Bay. They built a settlement there that was intended to secure English fishing interests on behalf of the London and Bristol Company for Newfoundland, and the settlers were also requested to send back to England masts, spars, and deals (sawn boards) for ship-building. Guy de-scribed the buildings, and the palisade within which they were enclosed:

> From the first of October [1610] until the sixteenth of May [1611] our company had bin imployed in making of a store-house for our habitation, which was finished about the first of December; with a square inclosure of one hundred and twenty feet long and ninetie foot broad, compassing these two houses, and work house to work dry in; to make boats or any other work out of the raine; and three pieces of ordinance are planted there to command the harboroughs upon a platform made of great posts, and rails, and great poles sixteene foot long set upright round about, with two plankers to scoure the quarters.[11]

The community at Cupers Cove survived, but did not prosper, in part because settlement was not necessary to tap the island's fishery resources.[12] Guy's habitation was begun only five years after Champlain's *habitation* (both used the same word) at Port Royal, which was located some 1,000 km to the southwest, and only three years after the first successful American settlement at Jamestown in the Colony of Virginia. The various seventeenth-century settlements in Newfoundland, Virginia, and the Caribbean were parallel attempts by the

3.3 Summer fishing settlement, Logy Bay, Newfoundland. Photograph *c*. 1900. PANL/C2-37/NA 3698.

England of James I to colonize and settle the New World.

In 1616 the London and Bristol Company sold the southern half of the Avalon peninsula, including the harbours of Ferryland and Renews, to Welsh promoter and author Sir William Vaughan. In 1620, when his colony at Renews failed, Vaughan sold some of his land—including Ferryland, about 50 miles (80 km) south of St John's—to Sir George Calvert (who became the first Baron Baltimore in 1625). In 1621 Captain Edward Wynne and twelve men arrived at Ferryland, where they founded the colony of Avalon.

In the first year the settlers built for Calvert the **Mansion House** (or Manor House) at Ferryland, almost certainly the largest structure in Newfoundland in the seventeenth century [3.4]. Although preliminary archaeological excavations of the Ferryland settlement have been undertaken, no verified physical evidence has yet been found of the Mansion House. It is described in a letter that Wynne sent to Calvert in July 1622:

It was All hallowtide before our first range of building was fitted for a habitable being. The which being 44 foot of length, & 15 foot of breadth, containing a hall 18 foot long, an entry of 6 foot, & a cellar of 20 foot in length, and of the height betweene the ground floore and that over

head about 8 foote, being devided above, that throughout into foure chambers, and four foot high to the roofe or a halfe storie. The roofe over the hall, I covered with Deale boords, and the rest such thatch as I found growing here about the Harbour, as sedge, flagges and rushes, a farre better covering than boards, both for warmth & litenesse. When I had finished the frame, with onely one Chimney of stone worke in the hall, I went forward with our kitchin, of length 18 foot, 12 foot of breadth, and 8 foot high to the eves, and walled up with stone-work, with a large Chimney in the frame. Over the kitchen I fitted another Chamber. All which with a staire case and convenient passages both into the kitchin and the rooms over it were finished by Christmas Eve....[After Christmas:] For addition of building, we have at this present a Parlour of foureteene foote besides the chimney, and twelve foot broad, of convenient height, and a lodging chamber over it; to each a chimney of stone worke with staires and a staire case, besides a tenement of two rooms, or a storie and a halfe, which serves for a store house till we are other wise provided.[13]

Wynne's description is not easy to interpret. Attempts to reconstruct the design have concluded that the plan was the 'longhouse' or 'single-pile'

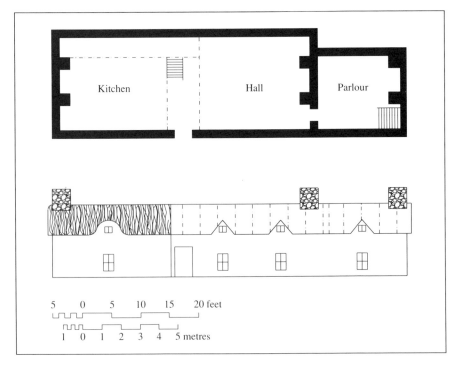

3.4 Robert Barakat's hypothetical plan and elevation of Lord Baltimore's Mansion House, Ferryland, Newfoundland, 1622. Drawing by David Byrnes.

type, with the rooms located side by side (or end-to-end) in a single range—a plan that became common in Newfoundland houses. These conclusions have been encouraged by the Fitzhugh Map of Ferryland of 1693, which seems to show the house as being linear with four gables—though it has been suggested that the draftsman never visited Ferryland and that this is only one of several inaccuracies in his map.[14]

A different interpretation of Wynne's letter leads to the alluring possibility that Lord Baltimore's house may have had a central entry with the hall and parlour along the front and the kitchen and storeroom at the rear, anticipating the 'double-pile' plan (two ranges of rooms, one behind the other) that would become common in the great houses of Britain after 1650, and in its overseas colonies early in the eighteenth century.[15]

Whatever the plan, the exterior walls were likely framed in wood (Wynne says 'I had finished the frame'), with stone or stone infill used in the kitchen and perhaps elsewhere. The kitchen was 'walled up with stone-work'. If this refers to infill, the technique would have been similar to the *colombage* used in New France at this same time (see page 48). The Mansion House was probably one-and-a-half storeys high, the second floor being contained within the slope of the roof (Wynne's 'halfe storie'). The house was roofed partly with sawn boards ('deal') and partly with thatch.

Near the Mansion House, about four acres were enclosed as a 'plantation' by a seven-foot-high palisade 'for the keeping off of both man & beast.' The posts and rails were sharpened at the top and fastened with 'spikes and nayles'. In an attempt at economic self-sufficiency, the colonists built—in addition to their dwellings—a forge, saltworks, a wharf, and probably a sawmill, and at the time of Wynne's writing they were turning their attention towards a brewhouse and more housing. They planted crops from seeds, which they had brought from England, and appeared quite committed to their new home.

By 1625 the growing settlement numbered about 100 people. Lord Baltimore visited for the first time in 1627, and a year later he and his family wintered there. They found it too cold and in 1629 he decided to 'quitt my residence, and to shift to some other warmer climate of this new world, where the wynters be shorter and lesse rigorous.'[16] He and his son, Cecil Calvert, later the second Baron Baltimore, subsequently founded the Colony of Maryland, whose capital city bears their name. The Fer-

ryland settlers remained, however, likely under a governor left by Baltimore. Sir David Kirke subsequently governed Avalon for a period, and the colony continued to attract settlement. Ferryland was sacked by the Dutch in 1673 and again by the French in 1696. The Mansion House at Ferryland may have survived the first onslaught, but not the second.

Attempts such as this to establish English colonies in Newfoundland by patent may be considered to have largely failed. Nevertheless, the island was home to some of the earliest English colonial plantations in the New World, and future archaeology will likely reveal the forms of the buildings and the subdivision of the land. The would-be 'planters' (as those who founded plantations or colonies were called) probably did not appreciate the difficulties of the land and the climate, nor the shortness of the growing season. Some West Country merchants continued to pressure the English government against settlement; and while the residents were never forcibly evicted, England offered them little protection against raids. A deportation order of 1675 was never enforced. Sir John Berry, who was sent out to remove the colonists, reported that settlement should be encouraged as protection against the French, but that the number of settlers should be kept small in order to provide a more efficient fishery.

St John's By the time of Sir Humphrey Gilbert's arrival in 1583, there were certainly temporary shelters located at St John's. The unauthorized villages that had been established by the fishermen survived and slowly grew. In 1676 the English eastern shore of Newfoundland was home to 1,490 persons scattered among 30 communities. The largest was St John's, with 185 inhabitants; the smallest was Torbay, with fourteen. The vast majority—some 1,286 of the 1,490 residents—were servants (likely indentured employees), and so the committed 'permanent' population was only a few hundred. Most had come from the south and west of England, the south of Ireland, and the Channel Islands.[17]

Vertical-log construction was dominant in the seventeenth century. A decade before the census of 1663, Plymouth surgeon James Yonge described the appearance of St John's:

> The houses are made of a frythe of boughs, sealed inside with rinds, which look like planed deal, and covered with the same, and turfs of earth upon, to keep the sun from raning them.

The 'frythe of boughs' refers to thin poles or sticks, and so the houses Yonge observed were constructed like tilts, only their builders had taken care to give the interior a finished appearance with bark ('rinds. . .like planed deal'), and bark and sod provided the roof. Historian Paul O'Neill, who quoted Yonge's description, goes on to say that by 1697 'these sod-roofed tilts were replaced by shingle or clapboard houses,'[18] but other contemporaneous sources show that tilt-like structures continued to be built alongside more substantial ones.

John Downing, son of the governor of that name and a resident of St John's, reported in his *Brief Narrative* (1676) that the inhabitants' 'stages and houses are covered with New England and the country's boards' (i.e. weatherboards that were sawn locally as well as in New England, with which there was active trade), but that the 'comers out of England'—the seasonal fishermen—stripped the bark off trees ('rinding', mentioned above) to protect their structures, and that this practice was 'done not only for 18 foot Cooke Rommes [cook rooms] but to cover whole stages and lodging houses.'[19] The superior stability of frame construction was appreciated, but the marginal economy often made it unavailable. The two structural systems—frame and vertical logs—co-existed, as is shown in a letter of 1680, in which the writer distinguishes between them: '. . .the best sort with sawd plancks from the foundations up. . .others with whol timber joyn'd together, standing stake wise.'[20]

The first military defences at St John's were built in 1693, when Captain Christian Lilly of the Royal Engineers designed a square fortification with corner bastions, surrounded by palisades and a ditch. Named Fort William, it was destroyed three years later, along with the whole town, by a force of French raiders led by Pierre le Moyne d'Iberville. A new Fort William, surrounded by a wooden palisade, was built in 1697, and more skirmishes followed.[21] The battles severely damaged the town, as Lilly noted in 1715:

> The habitations which (except about half a dozen) are but little value, no better than such huts as us'd to be built in the Army during winter campaigns.[22]

Evidently the tilts remained predominant.

A measure of peace finally arrived in 1713 with the signing of the Treaty of Utrecht, which gave Britain undisputed control of Newfoundland and allowed unimpeded growth for the first time.

Eighteenth-century maps provide a glimpse of the growth of St John's. By 1728 the town had a church, a dozen substantial merchant premises, and many smaller dwellings, stages, and flakes, although fewer than 300 people stayed during the winter. Early settlement occurred on the north shore of the harbour, where the land was relatively level. Even there, the uneven terrain, an indifference to planning, and the lack of a formal land-division system produced a somewhat haphazard arrangement of houses. Buildings appear to be perched randomly on the hilly landscape. Pathways between the houses and the flakes became narrow winding streets, principally the Upper Path (today's Duckworth Street) and Lower Path (Water Street). While a casual arrangement of this kind was adequate for a small village—and is evident today in many of Newfoundland's outports—as St John's grew it became increasingly impractical in terms of communications and because of the threat of fire.

The most common house-form seen in the early maps was a small 1- or $1\frac{1}{2}$-storey dwelling with a gable roof and central chimney. On the waterfront, the fishing stage was often an extension of the house. A map of 1751 shows numerous kitchen-gardens and at least one ornamental garden, suggesting the residents' increasing commitment to their community.[23]

As the eighteenth century drew to a close, St John's became increasingly established, and it expanded as a succession of governors granted land to notables and soldiers. Governor Sir Erasmus Gower noticed the change in 1804 when he returned to St John's after a long absence:

> Having served on the Newfoundland station eighteen years ago, I was, on my arrival this year, forcibly stuck with the change which had taken place at St John's, where the trade has increased to such a degree that the north side of the harbour is now taken up with Merchants' Stores Wharfs &c for the purposes of trade, and the Fishing Stages with many of the Flakes, and other erections for curing fish, removed to make room for them.[24]

Gower had had much to do with bringing about these changes, since he had laid out a relatively straight street 200 yards (183 m) back from the shoreline (the present Gower Street), with lots along it, and encouraged their lease.[25] By 1800 St John's had more than 500 private houses (there were 42 in 1735 and 226 in 1762) and growth was even more rapid after 1800, particularly after 1813, when Sir Richard Keats, the governor, removed

3.5 The town and harbour of St John's, Newfoundland. Engraved by Henry Pyall from a watercolour by William Eagar, 1831. NAC/C-3371.

restrictions on building and land occupation. Immigration from Ireland began in the late eighteenth century and continued for some time. Flimsy structures remained the rule; merchant and future premier Charles James Fox Bennett recalled that when he came to St John's as a boy in 1806,

> the whole area was nearly covered with flakes on which to dry fish; the houses, if they could be called such were, with very few exceptions, all of a temporary character.[26]

The city continued to grow, stimulated by the need to rebuild after several major fires between 1816 and 1819. An Act 'to regulate the rebuilding of the town of St John's' was passed in 1818, setting the width of Duckworth and Water Street at 40 feet (12.2 m) and requiring that new buildings respect this; establishing four cross streets 'to serve as Fire breaks'; and declaring that all new buildings on Water Street be 'built and made entirely of stone or bricks, and covered with slates or tiles.'[27]

The appearance of St John's after the rebuilding that followed those fires is seen in a superb **view by William Eagar [3.5]**, which was engraved and published in London in 1831. Drawn from just above the Queen's Battery at Signal Hill, Eagar's panorama shows the busy harbour with a continuous row of docks, warehouses, and other mercantile buildings along the breadth of the north (far) shore. Water Street is at their rear (barely visible); Duckworth Street is the next street, a short distance up the hill; and further up, to the right of centre beyond a knoll of undeveloped land, is Gower Street. To the left of the vacant land, with a hipped roof and a small cupola on its porch, is the Anglican church. Below the church is the classical courthouse. The large building in the distance at the right is Government House, set in its landscaped grounds, and just to its right is the Commisssariat (both are described below).

Despite the attempts to render the city safer from fire, a succession of major fires continued to ravage St John's. Few buildings survive from before the mid-nineteenth century because disastrous blazes in 1846—which destroyed most of the buildings in the Eagar view—and 1892 levelled most of the downtown area.

By 1870 St John's was firmly established as the service centre for the Newfoundland fishery, which it remains today. Because the fishery was the basis of the economy, all trade was focused there. A good idea of the waterfront commercial developments of the mid-1800s is provided by the **Murray Premises** [**3.6**], a cluster of early buildings at Beck's Cove and the largest group of survivors of their kind. They consist of between six and ten structures (because of the organic way in which they blend together, it is hard to determine their number) that were erected, in stages, in the middle of the nineteenth century—though portions of some may go back further. They were built on pilings sunk into the harbour floor. Most are three storeys high, with masonry walls and heavy timber frames supporting the floors. Some have exterior wood-frame walls with brick infill—a form of the centuries-old technique of brick-nogging (*colombage*). Several—including the Goodrich Building and the Levitz Building—have survived to the present, bearing the names of their builders or long-time occupants,

A.H. Murray and Company, a prosperous mercantile firm, operated out of these buildings for three-quarters of a century. When their preservation became threatened, the Newfoundland Historic Trust and other groups secured the property, obtained its commemoration as a national historic site, and rehabilitated the buildings in 1979 for modern retail, restaurant, and office use, and as a branch of the provincial museum. They form a lively and important component of the larger Water Street historic district.[28]

The Newfoundland house

The Mansion House of Lord Baltimore was an exceptional architectural event. The characteristic Newfoundland house is seen rather in the homes of ordinary fishermen and labourers. Searching for such 'folk' or 'vernacular' architecture—whether in Newfoundland, Quebec, or the rest of Canada—has been an activity of the cultural geographer and folklorist (architectural historians have followed their lead). Professionals in the first two disciplines have developed techniques for identifying vernac-

3.6 The Murray Premises, St John's, Newfoundland. HWS/SSS/NF SJ CM 1.08.

ular house-forms on the basis of structure, materials, plan, and profile, and discuss them primarily in the context of the diffusion of folk-culture in rural areas, where traditional types have persisted with minimal influence from urban culture.

Newfoundland has provided fertile ground for study of this kind. Since no buildings remain from the seventeenth century and very few, if any, remain from the eighteenth, our understanding of the early Newfoundland house is limited to examples from the nineteenth century and later. Nevertheless, careful study and interpolation by several scholars have given us an impression of the early development of the Newfoundland house-form.

3.7 Partially dismantled house, showing full-studded construction at Old Bonaventure, Trinity Bay, Newfoundland. Photograph by David Mills. PANL.

When year-round residents required permanent dwellings, they turned from the tilt to 'studded' (also called 'full-studded') structures that were built of logs ('studs') squared with a pit-saw or adze and set vertically on a wood sill [3.7]. Some or all of the studs were tenoned or dovetailed into the sill, while others might be connected only with dowels. Spruce and fir, predominant in Newfoundland, are soft woods that are ideal for use as studs. The sill was usually either set on a low stone foundation or supported by posts (called 'shores'). Being squared, the logs fit together more tightly than the unrinded round logs of the tilt—which technically is also a studded form. (In some cases the logs were split or sawn along their length, and the rounded sides were left exposed on the outside.) The gaps between the studs might be filled with moss, paper, rope, or rags to provide protection from wind and rain. The walls were usually sheathed on the exterior with horizontal clapboard or shingles, and with wide vertical or horizontal boarding on the interior. In some cases diagonal braces were let into the studs. Floor-joists were set on a plate nailed to the wall and carried through the studs for additional stability. Studded structures were used in Newfoundland by all the major immigrant groups—English, Irish, French, and Scottish—and were found in every bay, among all economic classes, and in both simple and ornamented designs.[29]

The full-studded wall is a primitive structural form that had long since been succeeded in Europe first by close-studded construction (in which narrow spaces were left between the studs, as in the *colombage* of New France) and then by the timber frame, with its widely spaced verticals. (In eighteenth-century Europe, full studs were used only for interior partitions.) Authorities on full-studded Newfoundland houses have debated—without resolution—whether they represent the reintroduction of an obsolete European form in a land where wood was abundant, or whether they are not a medieval survival at all, but rather the universal response of an unsophisticated settler to a new situation.[30]

The most common arrangement of rooms in the Newfoundland house was the two-room hall-and-parlour plan, with the house being only a single room deep. The hall—used for family living and for cooking—was often called a kitchen. The smallest houses of this kind, such as the **Lar Norris house** [3.8] in Witless Bay, are only 13 by 20 feet (4 x 6 m)

3.8 Plan of the Lar Norris house, Witless Bay, Newfoundland. Drawing by David Byrnes, after Gerald L. Pocius.

3.9 Plan of the Rose Williams house, Bay Bulls, Newfoundland. Drawing by David Byrnes, after Gerald L. Pocius.

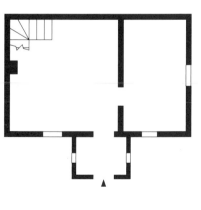

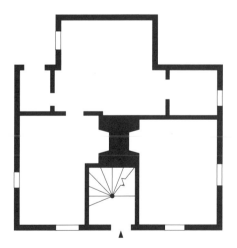

3.10 House, Port Rexton, Trinity Bay, Newfoundland. Photograph by David Mills. PANL.

in size. The Norris house has a chimney on the gable end and a staircase in the corner leading to a sleeping loft for children.[31]

Houses often had a second row of rooms, containing a porch and a pantry, across the rear of the house, as at the **Rose Williams house [3.9]**. The rear rooms were usually covered by a shed roof with a distinct slope, as in the Paddy Crane house, Ferryland; or, less often, by a flat roof. This lean-to, which might be original or added, is a common Newfoundland feature known as a 'linhay' (pronounced 'linney') or a 'back kitchen'. The everyday entrance to the house was—and remains—into the linhay rather than through the front door. The original purpose of the linhay may have been for livestock.[32]

In the 1970s David Mills undertook a detailed and methodical study of 258 houses in four communities in Trinity Bay, most of whose original residents had come from Devon or Dorset. He concluded that the 'first-generation house', which succeeded the temporary tilt and persisted as the basic house type between 1650 and 1850, was this one- or one-and-a-half-storey cottage, with an attic reached by a ladder or corner stairway and having a linhay that was covered by a shed roof with a distinct slope. An example of this type is the **house at Port Rexton [3.10]**, Trinity Bay (demolished in the 1980s): it has a clearly differentiated linhay and is expressed as a single storey on the façade (not visible in the photograph). After examining 65 examples, Mills found that the average floor area was 21'-8'' (6.6 m) wide by 20'-3'' (6.2 m) deep, and that 45 had studded walls. (The remainder were framed.) He notes that full two-storey houses—

with either a continuous roof-slope (called a 'saltbox' roof, a term borrowed from New England), or a flat roof over the linhay—are later second- and third-generation house-forms that did not appear in Trinity Bay until after 1860.[33]

In 1819 Lewis Anspach described a house of this kind that was earlier than the oldest documented survivor:

> The common dwellings consist only of ground floor, or at most of one-storey; the materials, except the shingles, are the produce of the Newfoundland woods; the best sorts are clapboard on the outside, others are built of logs left rough and uneven on the inside and outside; the interstices being filled up with moss, and generally lined with boards planed and tongued. This filling with moss the vacancies between the studs to keep out the weather, is there called chinsing....They have only one fireplace in a very large kitchen.[34]

Differences in house-form occur among all the regions of Newfoundland, but in no area other than Trinity Bay have the houses been subjected to the same degree of investigation.

A relationship between house-type and ethnic origin has been discerned, although the analysis is preliminary and is based on a relatively small sampling. In Newfoundland-English houses, a central hall (or 'entry') was often inserted between the living-hall and the parlour, with the staircase at the back; the roof was frequently gabled, and the chimney (or chimneys) would usually be located on the side, as in the Taylor-Fraize house (c. 1825) at Carbonear. In Newfoundland-Irish houses, a large chimney was often placed in the centre, eliminating the possibility of a central hall, as in the Neary house (c. 1850) in Portugal Cove. The roof was generally hipped, as in the vernacular architecture of southern Ireland, and its use in Newfoundland may have been the survival of a regional tradition.[35]

Houses were also built with three rooms (other than an entry) and no linhay, having a bedroom, kitchen, and parlour on the ground floor, as at the Stacia Power house, Bay Bulls. Roofs might be hipped or gabled, with the chimney off-centre—which has been described as a Newfoundland interpretation of the three-room plan that is found throughout the West of England and Ireland.[36]

Newfoundland houses are best appreciated in their setting. At some of the more isolated outports time has stood relatively still, and so recent photo-

3.11 View of Greenspond, Newfoundland. Photograph by Douglas Richardson.

3.12 House belonging to Malcolm Rogers being relocated from Fox Island to Flat Island, Dover, Newfoundland. Photograph by Bob Brooks, 1961. NAC/NFB/PA-154122.

graphs can give an excellent impression of appearances a century or more ago. A group of houses in **Greenspond** [3.11], a nearly treeless island community in Bonavista Bay that is reached only by boat, represents such outports well. 'Winding with the winding shore', Greenspond's broad and narrow paths follow the topography, obeying no regular pattern, and the houses are not oriented uniformly, but the picket fences and their natural clustering link the buildings well. Most of the houses in this photograph have gabled roofs (several of them red) and all are covered with clapboard that is painted white or yellow with brown or green trim; they vary in size from $1\frac{1}{2}$ to $2\frac{1}{2}$ storeys. Many are set off the ground with a broad porch, called a 'bridge', on their lower (south) side.[37]

After Newfoundland joined Confederation in 1949, federal assistance encouraged the formation of new industries and the adoption of new methods of fishing, with the result that many fishermen moved from the outports to do wage labour in the towns. In the 1950s and 1960s the provincial and federal governments offered people cash incentives to relocate from the remote coves and islands. Some of the 20,000 people who accepted the offer demolished their houses, many left them standing, while others floated their residences to a new site. The photograph [3.12] shows Malcolm

Rogers' house being towed from Fox Island in 1961.[38]

In the eighteenth and nineteenth centuries the merchants and the wealthy planters naturally built larger houses than the coastal fishermen. Their design was likely inspired by the houses of well-to-do merchants of Dorset and other southwestern English counties with strong ties to Newfoundland.[39] Some of the larger houses in the colony were two rooms deep, following the 'double-pile' plan of England (and perhaps of Lord Baltimore's house). **Blenheim House [3.13]** (1786, demolished *c*. 1930s), built at Placentia by the Sweetman family and subsequently used as the first Placentia cable office of the Anglo-American Telegraph Company, had a double-pile plan with a central hall, two chimneys, and a hipped roof.[40] Some houses with this plan have gable roofs, such as Retreat Cottage, Kenna's Hill, St John's, built for merchant John Murch Brine around 1834.[41] These are Georgian houses, a type that was to dominate English Canada in the early nineteenth century, though they remained relatively uncommon in Newfoundland.

Most larger houses, particularly those of the merchants, were frame dwellings. Full-studded construction would have required a prohibitive quantity of wood, particularly in a large building. Prefabricated house-frames were frequently shipped to St John's from Nova Scotia, New Brunswick, Prince Edward Island, and New England and sold at auction, although many were also sawn and assembled locally.[42] With the frames likely came a greater familiarity with the house-forms of the Maritimes and New England.

While stone construction is found in a number of communities—including Ferryland, Brigus, and Harbour Grace—stone was never common in Newfoundland, though Ferryland boasted several stone houses. The stone house of planter Sir Arthur Holdsworth (*c*. 1770; demolished *c*. 1920) was 24 by 60 feet (7.3 x 18.3 m), with three rooms on the ground floor, four rooms above, and a spacious attic, and it was covered with a low hipped roof. A parlour, counting house, and shop were on the ground floor, and a 'ware-room' for the storage of goods was in the attic—a series of rooms similar to those in some merchants' houses in England.[43] The Freebairn-Coffey house at Ferryland (demolished), which may have been begun in the eighteenth century as a private house or as the Anglican rectory, had at least one storey built in stone.[44] A much smaller stone barn in Brigus seems to have been built about 1820 as a stable with a residence

3.13 Sweetman's Blenheim House, Placentia, Newfoundland, 1786. Photograph by the Hon. W.J. Browne, *c*. 1930. Collection of Shane O'Dea.

above—possibly a coach house on the property of Charles Cozens.[45]

By the middle of the nineteenth century the Newfoundland house had assumed a variety of forms, yet maintained a consistent character. The original dwellings—which were partly a natural response to a difficult environment, and partly a transference of old-world vernacular forms—were primitive and temporary shelters. In time they developed into permanent types that were influenced both by the familiar dwellings of England and Ireland and by the newly learned house types of the Maritimes and New England.

Public buildings

As the communities of Newfoundland grew, so did their need for buildings for assembly, education, the administration of justice, and religion. The first public buildings were barely differentiated from houses, but in time they developed distinctive architectural types.

The Georgian form is seen in two St John's buildings with important official functions. The earlier one is **Commissariat House [3.14]**, a wood structure built in 1818-19 to designs by (and under the supervision of) the Royal Engineers to accommodate the Assistant Commissary General of the British garrison in Newfoundland, William Lane. Six, rather than the customary five, bays wide, with a tall hipped wing pierced by dormer windows, the design sacrifices symmetry for convenience.[46] The other is **Government House [3.15]**, built 1827-31 as the residence of the governors of the colony. The initial plans were drawn up by Sir Thomas Cochrane before he came out to Newfoundland to take up his appointment as governor. The commanding officer of the Royal Engineers, Lieutenant Colonel Lewis, complained:

> The plans furnished by his Excellency are very defective in detail and if they had been made by a professional man the errors in question would not have happened.

The governor's secretary retorted that the Colonel had no business judging the conveniences of a plan drawn up by His Excellency. The building of Government House was begun under the direction of Lewis. After he demanded (and received) a transfer

back to England, it was continued by his two successors, with the governor interfering and ordering changes. Constructed of red sandstone with Portland stone trim, the rigidly formal house has a five-bay, two-storey Georgian façade with a two-bay wing extending at either side; a corridor running form one side to the other creates a double-pile plan. The interior decor displays taste and quality.[47]

As will be discussed below with the buildings of the Maritimes and Upper Canada, the Georgian style, characterized by a formal symmetry and the use of classically inspired ornament, came to be considered mandatory for buildings of the ruling class—so much so that in 1829 the Chief Justice of Newfoundland noted that Commissariat House and Government House were the only two houses in St John's suitable as a residence for a person in his appointment. (He was given the use of neither!)[48]

Schools did not evolve a distinctive form until the middle years of the nineteenth century. The grammar schools at Harbour Grace and Carbonear,

3.14 (*left*) Commissariat House, St John's, Newfoundland, 1818-19. Centre for Newfoundland Studies Archives, Joseph R. Smallwood Collection/5.04.360.

3.15 Government House, St John's, Newfoundland, 1827-31. Photographed in 1901, during a Royal Visit. PANL, B7-167/VA5-19.

both built about 1844, were large hipped-roof buildings indistinguishable from houses.[49] And in the early years of the colony there were no meeting-halls at all. The first courts of Newfoundland, for instance, convened either in the open or in fishermen's tilts.[50]

A system of justice was introduced slowly to Newfoundland. Three courthouses were built in the eighteenth century: at St John's (1730), Placentia (1774), and Burin (before 1775). The first court of civil jurisdiction was established in 1791, but the wooden courthouses that were subsequently built at Harbour Grace (1807) and Trinity (1811) were financed by local subscription and not by the British government. Little is known about the appearance of any of these buildings.[51]

In 1825 Newfoundland was divided into three judicial districts and a Supreme Court was created, establishing the first permanent judicial system for the colony. Four years later the ban on settlement was lifted, encouraging a rapid growth in population. New courthouses were built in Harbour Grace and St John's. Built in 1830-1, the **Harbour Grace Courthouse [3.16]** replaced the previous structure, barely twenty years old, which was already in a 'decayed and dilapidated state—almost entirely unfit for any purpose whatsoever.' Governor Cochrane commissioned two designs—one in

3.16 Courthouse, Harbour Grace, Newfoundland, 1830-1. Photograph by Fern E. Graham, 1988.

stone, the other partly in stone and partly in wood—and the authorities in London approved the more substantial stone building. The courthouse was designed and built by Patrick Kough (or Keough, 1786-1863), a master builder from St John's who had come from Ireland in 1804, and who may have been Newfoundland's first professional designer of buildings. Constructed of random-coursed stone, it is a rectangular two-storey building covered by a hipped roof, with the courtroom located on the upper floor and reached from the street by wooden staircases. The quality of detail and the symmetry set the courthouse apart from houses of the time. The doors feature classical wooden casings, with pilasters, a broken pediment, and a fanlight with fine curved mullions (whose panes have the pointed-arch form of the Gothic Revival); the window surrounds and arched heads are carefully constructed of brick.[52]

Newfoundland was granted representative government in 1832, and the local Assembly assumed the responsibility of constructing and maintaining its public buildings. For the first time colonists had an opportunity to express their own aspirations in public architecture. Two impressive buildings erected in St John's in the late 1840s not only reveal this new initiative but also demonstrate the acceptance of the Georgian classicism and its development into Neoclassicism—styles that had been used for public buildings in Britain and Ireland for a century. The **Colonial Building [3.17]**, the seat of

the new government, was built in 1846-50 to designs by Irish stonemason and architect James Purcell. Built of limestone quarried near Purcell's home in Cork, the two-storey hipped-roof building features an Ionic portico with six columns 30 feet (9 m) high supporting a pediment containing the Royal arms. The usefulness of the portico as a setting for special occasions can be seen in the photograph as a crowd has gathered to hear Governor Sir Ralph C. Williams, on the steps, proclaim His Majesty George v king on 9 May 1910. The ceilings of the Council Chamber and Assembly Room—well-appointed rooms each 30 by 50 ft (9.1 by 15.2 m)—were painted in 1880-1 by Alexander Pindikowski. A fresco painter from Poland who had been convicted of forgery, he served his fifteen-month sentence by painting ceilings in the Colonial Building, in Government House, and the Athenaeum (a library and society for learning in St John's), and was released one month early for good service.[53]

The other building in this manner was the Courthouse and Market, erected in 1846-7 with Patrick

3.17 Colonial Building, St John's, Newfoundland, 1846-50. Provincial Archives of Newfoundland and Labrador/C1-126.

3.18 Anglican Church, Placentia, Newfoundland, 1787. Collection of Shane O'Dea.

Kough as supervising architect. The Georgian features included classically inspired door and window surrounds and projecting frontispieces on the façade (capped by a cupola with a clock) and the long side (topped by a pediment).[54]

Until the early nineteenth century, churches were simple structures with few embellishments, like the **Anglican Church at Placentia** (1787), which is representative of Newfoundland's eighteenth-century religious architecture [**3.18**]. A wooden building with clapboard siding and a hipped roof, it differs externally from domestic building of the day only by its larger windows and the oversized tower. The doorway has classical trim, but so too do the doorways of many houses of the time.[55] Only after 1820 did the merchants and other members of the community begin to express their social and religious aspirations by building churches with more claims to style and high design.

The Maritimes

Pre-Loyalist Nova Scotia

Anybody who has driven through the Maritime Provinces and New England has noticed the striking resemblance between the buildings and towns of those two regions. Cultural and social ties between the coastal provinces and the 'Boston states' have always been strong. This affinity is usually attributed to the many Loyalists from New England who settled in Nova Scotia after the American Revolution. Migration to the area, however, began a full generation earlier. By 1776, some 20,000 people had already settled in Nova Scotia (which then included today's New Brunswick), half of them from the American colonies (mostly New England) and the other half directly from Britain.[56]

The first extensive English-speaking settlement in Nova Scotia occurred in the middle of the eighteenth century as a result of several government-initiated schemes. Their principal motive was strategic, intended to reduce the French threat to the New England colonies, a situation that had been aggravated by the return of Fortress Louisbourg to France in 1748. The instigators were Governor William Shirley of Massachusetts, who wanted to see a buffer between his colony and the French stronghold, and the Board of Trade and Plantations, an advisory commission to the King that was concerned with colonies around the world, and whose president was Lord Halifax. The result was the extension of British (and New England) influence and control along the northern Atlantic seaboard.

Halifax In March 1749, probably at Shirley's suggestion, the Board of Trade and Plantations offered free land and passage to people who were willing to move from Britain to Nova Scotia. Three months later Colonel Edward Cornwallis and the warship *Sphinx* led a convoy of thirteen transports carrying 2,576 hopeful settlers—many of them cockneys—across the Atlantic to the New World. Cornwallis's first dispatch upon his arrival, at what was known as Chebucto harbour (the future Halifax), rang with optimism:

> The harbour itself is full of fish of all kinds. All the officers agree the harbour is the finest they have ever seen. The country is one continued wood; no clear spot is to be seen or heard of. I have been on shore in several places. The underwood is only young trees, so that with difficulty one is able to make his way anywhere.[57]

Early in July the immigrants, their leaders, and soldiers from Annapolis and Louisbourg gathered to hear Cornwallis take the oaths of office as Governor and Captain General of Nova Scotia. After a day of celebration, called Natal Day, the new arrivals set down to the business of building a colony. The governor's enthusiasm quickly waned as he noted that 'the number of industrious, active men proper to undertake and carry on a new settlement is very small.' The Church of England missionary, the Reverend William Tutty, agreed with Cornwallis's assessment, although from a different perspective. He considered the populace 'a set of profligate Wretches. . .so deeply sunk into all Kinds of Immorality, that they scarce retain the Shadow of Religion.'[58]

A 10-acre (4-hectare) townsite was laid out by military engineer John Brewse (or Bruce, d. 1785) and Boston-born Captain Charles Morris (1711-81), the first Surveyor General of Nova Scotia, and the settlement was named Halifax after the president of the Board. Halifax was an instant colonial town planned and built with military expediency, a statement of British rule in a French- and Indian-dominated land, and also the first permanent British community on today's Canadian mainland. The town's plan and its buildings reveal British imperial values that were to prevail for more than a century.

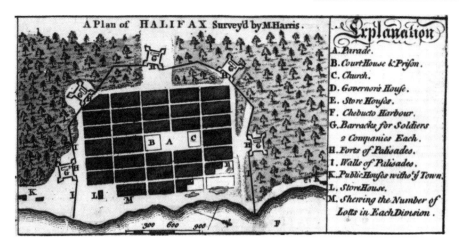

A Plan of HALIFAX Survey'd by M. Harris.

Explanation

A. Parade.
B. Court House & Prison.
C. Church.
D. Governor's House.
E. Store Houses.
F. Chebucto Harbour.
G. Barracks for Soldiers 2 Companies Each.
H. Forts of Palisades.
I. Walls of Palisades.
K. Public Houses witho'y Town.
L. Store House.
M. Shewing the Number of Lotts in Each Division.

3.19 'Plan of Halifax, Nova Scotia surveyed by M. Harris', 1749. Detail from *A Map of the South Bank of Nova Scotia and Its Fishing Banks*, engraved by T. Jefferys and published in 1750. NAC/NMC-1012.

The **plan of Halifax [3.19]** was a regular gridiron extending five blocks along the harbour and seven blocks up the hillside. The two blocks in the centre were reserved for the church (C on the plan), the courthouse (B), and a parade-ground (A)—the hub of temporal and religious authority—and the remaining blocks were divided into sixteen house lots each with a frontage of 40 feet (12.2 m) and a depth of 60 feet (18.3 m). No allowance was made for the topography except where the shoreline and the slope cut off two corners of the grid. In vivid contrast to the 'natural' plan of St John's, whose initial development occurred in response to topography and the needs of the fishery without government intervention, Halifax was laid out in a formal plan that was imposed on the constraints of the landscape by an imperial government. (Louisbourg, the nearby imperial outpost of France, had also been planned on a grid, but its regularity was less rigorous and was allowed to be interrupted in places by natural features and interfering buildings.) The grid at Halifax was enclosed by a fortified palisade with a citadel at the top of the hill [5.21-2] overlooking the harbour.

The settlers were immediately faced with the massive task of building houses. Cornwallis, who stayed on as governor, explained how he obtained a labour force:

> I have constantly employed all the carpenters I could get from Annapolis [where Britain maintained a garrison] and the ships here to build log houses for stores. I have likewise offered the French at Minas [Acadians] considerable wages to work, and they have promised to send fifty men to remain until October.[59]

Lots were drawn in August, and, as Cornwallis remarked, 'now everyone knows where to build his house, a great many houses are begun, and many huts, loghouses already up, for about half a mile on each side of the Town.'[60] Log construction—presumably using horizontal logs in the manner of the Acadian labourers—seems to have prevailed in the houses built outside the palisade because it provided a measure of defence. Cornwallis noted that the structures located outside the palisade were 'mostly Loghouses musket proof', and Shirley wrote in advance of the settlement that the settlers should 'commonly make ... their dwelling houses ... of Log Timber, defensible against Musquetry which is the only artillery the Indians can bring against them.'[61]

Within the town, frame construction prevailed. The barracks and officers' quarters were built from frames and lumber that had been purchased in Boston at considerable cost. (Dissatisfied with what he was being charged, Cornwallis sent a Lieutenant Martin to Boston in August to try to negotiate a better price.) It has been suggested that many of the private houses were prefabricated in Boston or New York and sent to Halifax by American merchants who were eager to exploit the new Nova Scotia market.[62] This solution, with its tone of military expediency, may have been the only way in which the 2,500 settlers could be housed before the onset of winter. Prefabrication was consistent with the method of house-frame construction current in New England. Timbers were customarily cut and hewn where it was most convenient for the carpenters to do this work. The frame would be prepared, the major units marked with numbers at their intersecting joints, and the frame then disassembled and transported to the building site for re-erection.[63] A letter written by a new arrival on 28

July 1749 confirms that sawn wood was being imported in large quantities (although it does not cite building-frames):

> ...one gentleman is preparing to erect a saw-mill [but meanwhile] we have received constant supplies of plank and timber for building our houses, and also fresh stock and rum in great quantities, 20 schooners coming in on one day.[64]

An indication of the appearance of the first dwellings may be found in the engravings of careful drawings of Halifax made in 1759 by Richard Short. A view of **Hollis Street** [3.20], Halifax, looking up George Street, shows the typical houses as being $1\frac{1}{2}$ storeys high, sheathed in clapboard, and having roofs that are variously gabled, gambrel, and hipped, some pierced with dormer windows and with the ridge generally parallel to the street. A number of buildings along Barrington Street are row-houses providing multiple dwellings. Short shows the Governor's house on Hollis Street as a two-storey building, six bays wide, with a hipped roof, dormers, and a pair of chimneys at the ridge. Its large scale clearly dominates its neighbours, emphasizing the importance of the Governor. The uniformed soldiers serve as a reminder of the community's military role. To the left of the Governor's house is the the Protestant Dissenters' Meeting House (1754, later called St Mather's and then St Matthew's Church); to its right a fence surrounds the first Governor's residence and administrative offices. Behind them, in the right distance, is St Paul's Church.[65]

3.20 View of Hollis and George Streets, Halifax, Nova Scotia, showing part of the Parade and Citadel Hill. Drawing by Richard Short, 1759; engraving by François Antoine Avenline. NAC/C-2482.

The **Anglican Church of St Paul** [3.21], the first house of worship built by the Church of England in today's Canada and the oldest building still standing in Halifax, was erected at the south end of the Parade Ground in 1750. The Reverend William Tutty identified the source for the design when he described St Paul's as having followed 'exactly the model of Marybone Chapel'. He was referring to the church now known as St Peter, Vere Street, in Marylebone, London [3.22], built in 1721-4 to designs by James Gibbs (1682-1754). St Peter's was illustrated as Plates 24 and 25 of Gibbs's celebrated *A Book of Architecture* (1728), which contained 150 plates of designs for buildings and decorative details—some of which were executed and others not. Frequently used as a source for designs by architects and builders in Britain and the US, Gibbs's work was the most popular architectural 'pattern book' of its century, and had a tremendous impact on the architecture of the American colonies.[66]

St Peter, Vere Street, was the very church attended by Lord Halifax, president of the Board of Trade and Plantations, and his Lordship's intervention in the design of St Paul's has been suggested, although not substantiated. According to historian Beckles Wilson, Lord Halifax 'sought out the architect of St Peter's, got the plans, and sent them out to Nova Scotia.'[67]

3.21 (*above*) The Church of St Paul, Halifax, Nova Scotia. Drawing by Richard Short, 1759; engraving by John Fougeron. PANS/N-150.

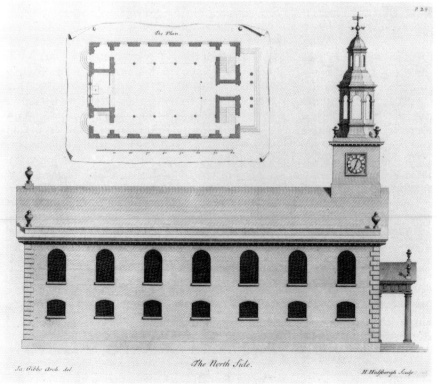

3.22 Marylebone Chapel (St Peter, Vere Street), London, England. Side elevation and plan by James Gibbs, 1721. From James Gibbs, *A Book of Architecture* (1728). By permission of the British Library.

The components of St Paul's were cut and fitted in Boston to follow the Gibbs plan and then disassembled and shipped to Halifax. Tutty wrote in March 1750: 'It begins to thaw apace and as soon as the frost is quite gone, the foundation will be hard and I hope finished for the church by the time it can arrive from Boston.' A report written in July continues: 'The Frame of the Church is now erecting & I am in hopes that we shall be able to assemble it in about 2 months time.' Cornwallis echoed these sentiments: 'I expect the Frame of the Church will be here next month from New England, the plan is the same with that of Marybone Chapel.'[68]

The anonymous designer clearly borrowed from St Peter to build St Paul's. The two churches share the same rectangular plan, number of bays (seven), and side-elevations with two tiers of arched windows—one placed above, and one below, the U-shaped interior gallery. Both also have pediments at the ends, a large 'Palladian window'—a window with three openings, the centre one arched and wider—at the liturgical east end (south by the compass), and an attractive three-stage tower over the entrance culminating in a cupola and weathervane. St Paul's translates the brick walls and stone quoins of the English source into wood. It even has the quoin-like window surrounds that Gibbs frequently used, even though these do not appear in the published view of St Peter's, making St Paul's more Gibbsian than the printed prototype—or indicating that the designer had a direct knowledge of the London church, which possessed this feature. The only significant deviation is in the interior, which uses plainer finishes and simplifies Gibbs's tall, round columns and heavy Classical ornamentation into easier-to-fabricate square wood posts in two tiers. Two-tiered square posts are found in several churches by Gibbs's illustrious predecessor, Sir Christopher Wren, and are seen as well at Christ Church (Old North Church) in Boston (1723), a prominent landmark in the city where St Paul's was fabricated.[69]

The structure of St Paul's follows the common New England technique, which in turn was adapted from the buildings of England: timber frame with brick 'nogging' or infill—similar to the colombage briqueté of New France. The bricks were made locally. As Cornwallis noted in July 1750, '30,000 bricks have been burnt here that prove very good.' The church opened for services on 2 September 1750, although it was not completed for another five years.

St Paul's has been altered by an extension to the north front—the detailed appearance of the original façade was never recorded—and by the addition of side aisles (1812), the replacement of the rectilinear glazing pattern with Italianate mullions, the removal of the window surrounds (1858), and the addition of a chancel at the south end (1872). Nevertheless, it stands today as the oldest Protestant church building in Canada, and the only building to remain from Cornwallis's Halifax.[70]

The integration of English and American sources achieved at St Paul's established a prototype for British public buildings in the new Canadian colony. The simplified treatment of the European model, and the reliance on wood, are characteristics transferred directly from New England. These modifications resulted from the technical and budgetary constraints of New World building, and from a taste for plainness that was influenced by Massachusetts Puritanism.

Although many of Cornwallis's original settlers did not survive the first winter, Halifax grew steadily in population and size with the arrival of additional boatloads of immigrants. Many came from Britain and New England—Governor Shirley encouraged migration northward to Nova Scotia—but their numbers were considered insufficient to secure the new colony. Consequently the British government recruited several thousand Protestant Europeans, many of them German-speaking and most of them farmers.

The first of these 'foreign Protestants' arrived in 1751. Some stayed in Halifax and formed a German enclave just north of the original townsite. Their legacy is seen today in the **Little Dutch Church** [3.23]—also called the Old Dutch Church—('Dutch' being a corruption of 'Deutsch'). Constructed of logs and covered with clapboards, it seems to have been built as a house and moved to the site in 1756. The steep roof and small window tucked under the eaves may be seen as Germanic features that contrast with the gentler roof slope and visible window heads of the buildings erected by the English. The small church—originally only 20 by 29 feet (6.1 x 8.8 m)—was extended 11 feet (3.4 m) in 1760 to make room for the belltower with its tall spire. It held the bell from the convent at Louisbourg, which had fallen to the British two years earlier. The bell is now in Montreal.[71]

Lunenburg In 1753 most 'foreign Protestants' were escorted by Lieutenant Colonel Charles Lawrence from Halifax southwest to Merliguesh harbour, a former French settlement that had already been cleared, and there they formed the town of Lunenburg. A gridiron plan was once again laid out on a hillside, most of the 48 blocks being divided into 14 building lots each, measuring 40 by 60 feet (12.2 x 24.4 m). The plan, which was signed by Charles Morris, was made compact for defensive purposes. Only the central, north-south King Street was wide. The four central lots were set aside for public use, and a palisade and two fortified blockhouses protected the settlement. In addition to allocating the lots in the townsite, the Board of Trade and Plantations sent over livestock and encouraged 100 German families to settle farm-lots in the surrounding countryside.[72]

The industrious settlers set to work building themselves houses, and two months after the first landing Lawrence wrote that 'Most of them are well under cover. All of them have gardens and many of them good Framed Houses.'[73] Lawrence distributed 500 feet (150 m) of sawn boards and 250 nails to each family—useful, but not nearly enough for a frame house. The sawn lumber was apparently in-

tended only for the roofs or other auxiliary components, because the evidence suggests that the early houses were framed not with sawn wood but with hewn timbers, likely adopting the post-and-groove (*poteaux en coulisse*) technique that had been used in New France. In the 1860s historian M.B. DesBrisay interviewed a number of elderly inhabitants of Lunenburg in an attempt to determine the nature of the first dwellings. He described a house, then still standing, that was built in 1757 in the grooved-post technique. Its original portion was 26 by 14 feet (7.9 x 4.3 m), with vertical posts set on sills that were 'made of the best pine, free from sap. The walls were filled in with hewed timber, between the shingling, and inside boarding.' The posts were 9 feet (2.7 m) high, but the lower floor had walls only 6 feet (1.8 m) high, and the rooms on the upper floor (apparently a half-storey accommodated within the slope of the roof) were

3.23 Little Dutch Church (Old Dutch Church), Halifax, Nova Scotia, *c*. 1750s. Photograph by Joseph Rogers, *c*. 1870. PANS, Joseph Rogers Collection/N-34.

3.24 Romkey house, Lunenberg, Nova Scotia, *c*. 1770s-90s. Photograph by Harold Kalman, 1978.

'still lower'. Although the roof of this house, which was built for a brewer named Kailer or Koehler, is not described, DesBrisay stated that a number of the early houses were thatched.[74]

Historian W.P. Bell notes that several houses built in this grooved-post manner have been found in Lunenburg County, and that Lawrence wrote to England asking for whipsaws, which were used for cutting the grooves in the posts. Bell maintains that 'variants of this same type of building may be seen today in parts of Switzerland or the Black Forest of Germany', from where many of the settlers had come; but the source was likely closer to their new homes, in the buildings of New France and Louisbourg.[75]

Other houses in Lunenburg were built of vertical logs. DesBrisay describes houses 'constructed of round poles' 6 feet (1.8 m) high set into the ground to form a structure about 18 or 20 feet (5.5 to 6.1 m) square. Another nineteenth-century historian, Beamish Murdoch, noted:

... the tradition is, that many dwellings were put up of pickets—that is, small trees cleared of branches, and set up vertically in rows close together, and then fastened with strips of board

nailed on, afterwards roofed and covered in, thus forming small wooden cottages. This has been confirmed in several instances, on the repair or pulling down houses where the pickets with the bark on have been found.[76]

This early house-type would have resembled the Newfoundland tilt. Whether or not the form was developed independently on the island and the mainland colony may be the subject of speculation; however, the migration of French-speaking settlers from Newfoundland to Louisbourg in 1713 would have brought the tilt-form closer to mainland Nova Scotia. These Lunenburg 'tilts' may well be the 'huts' that Colonel Lawrence referred to on several occasions.

By 1754 Lunenburg had 319 houses, ten huts, five sawmills, a church, and a stone jail. No buildings from this initial period survive. The oldest structure in town is considered to be the **Romkey house [3.24]**, which has been dated as early as 1760 but was more likely built between 1774 and 1798 by Jacob Üllshe (now Hilchey). It is constructed of solid plank walls with beaded clapboard sheathing and lath and plaster on the inside surfaces. Built on a steep slope just above the waterfront, it has $1\frac{1}{2}$ storeys on Pelham Street and $2\frac{1}{2}$ at the rear. The rooms are just over 6 feet high. The gambrel roof (this characteristic early Nova Scotia form is de-

110

scribed below) is sheathed in vertical boards up to 18 inches (45 cm) wide and fastened with hand-wrought nails. The front slope of the roof, which tradition says was originally thatched, used to have two small dormer windows; the present hipped and bayed dormer, a characteristic local feature called a 'Lunenburg bump', was surely added later. Two small dormers, likely original, are found on the rear slope.[77]

Other towns James I granted New Scotland (Nova Scotia) by charter to Sir William Alexander in 1621. The few seventeenth-century attempts at Scottish settlement were unsuccessful, and no buildings from this period have been identified. Scottish settlers came to Nova Scotia in large numbers towards the end of the eighteenth century. The first Highland Scots arrived on the *Hector* in September 1773 after a difficult eleven-week voyage. They landed at Pictou, on the north shore, poorly prepared to face the winter. Seventy of two hundred remained there for the first winter, living in bark-covered huts, and the small community gradually took root and was reinforced by additional immigrants. The oldest surviving building in Pictou is a small $1\frac{1}{2}$-storey wood house on Deacon's Hill built in 1788 for John Patterson, who had arrived on the *Hector*. Stone, particularly local Wallace sandstone, came into widespread use by the new Scottish arrivals early in the nineteenth century as the town's prosperity increased. The **Pictou Men's Club [3.25]** is a compact stone cottage built around 1827 as the residence of Henry

Blackadar. The two rooms in the attic are so low that the doorways are less than 6 feet (2 m) high. The Pictou region remains one of the few in Nova Scotia where stone buildings are common. Many houses, including the Pictou Men's Club, have five-sided bayed dormer windows like those in Lunenburg.[78]

Several towns besides Halifax and Lunenburg were built to formal plans. Particularly important was the plan for Charlottetown (1768), part of an initiative to accommodate new settlers who would replace the expelled Acadians of Prince Edward Island. The island was then called the Island of Saint John—an anglicization of its original French name—and was administered as part of Nova Scotia; but in 1769 it became a separate colony, and in 1799 it was given its present name in honour of Edward, Duke of Kent, then living in Halifax. The plan for Charlottetown was originally prepared in 1768 by Charles Morris (1731-1802), son of the Surveyor General of Nova Scotia and himself a future Surveyor General, who was working under the direction of Samuel Holland (1728-1801), a veteran surveyor and military engineer who had been appointed Surveyor General of both the Province of Quebec and the Northern District of North America in 1764. The plan was amended in 1771 by surveyor Thomas Wright (*c*. 1740-1812). The now-familiar gridiron has a central open square (Queen Square), with lots around it reserved for public purposes; these are surrounded in turn by town lots, in which are interspersed four smaller squares. Further from the core are pasture and farm lots.

3.25 Pictou Men's Club, Pictou, Nova Scotia, *c*. 1827. Photograph by Larry Turner, 1988.

3.26 View of Queen Square, Charlottetown, Prince Edward Island, *c*. 1860. Painted by Spencer Macky, *c*. 1924. Public Records and Archives Office of Prince Edward Island/Acc. no. 2320/5-1.

Queen Square [3.26] was developed as planned, with all of the major institutions clustered around it. A view of about 1860 (painted by Spencer Macky, *c*. 1924) shows the second generation of public buildings, most of them designed by architect Isaac Smith (*c*. 1795-1871): from the left we see St Paul's Anglican Church (Smith, 1833-6), the Colonial Building (Smith, 1843-8, now called Province House, **3.54**), and the Round Market House (Isaac Smith, 1823), which is surrounded by farmers' carts. At the right is the earlier Legislative Building and Courthouse, erected in 1811 to a design by John Plaw (1745-1820), an accomplished English architect and the author of three early pattern-books on rural architecture, who immigrated to the island colony in 1809. The public uses of Queen Square continued into the twentieth century, the newest major addition being the highly acclaimed Confederation Centre of the Arts (1964, **15.62**).[79]

This rational, symmetrical, and urbane town-plan, based on a gridiron street-pattern relieved by public open spaces at regular intervals, was adopted throughout Britain and her overseas colonies in the eighteenth century—as at Savannah, Geor-gia (1733), and Edinburgh New Town (1767)—even when it was somewhat impractical in relation to the local topography. It represents the classical ideal of Georgian England—the imposition of geometrically perfect forms on an imperfect world—and contrasts with the unstructured manner in which Quebec and Montreal grew in the years before the Conquest. The hierarchical nature of the Georgian town-plan mirrored the order and power structure of British society. Order was particularly important to the colonial administrators—notably the Board of Trade and Plantations, to which surveyor Samuel Holland was responsible—because it was a superb expression of imperial expansion and control.[80] A similar classic design was soon to appear in Anglo-Canadian buildings, in the architectural style known as Georgian.

Settlers from New England Governor Shirley of Massachusetts continued to encourage settlement in Nova Scotia. As an indication of his enthusiasm, one of his ideas, proposed in 1753, was to relocate the Acadians from the Saint John area and the Chignecto Isthmus to the Annapolis area of Nova Scotia, and to replace them with 1,000 families from New England and Northern Ireland.[81] In addition to its intended military advantages, this scheme would locate New England fishermen closer to their fishing grounds off Nova Scotia.

Two years later, in 1755, as relations between Britain and France deteriorated further, Charles Lawrence—now the Governor of Nova Scotia—expelled the Acadians from their homeland in Nova Scotia. Lawrence offered the cleared, fertile farmlands that had been vacated by the Acadians—'plouwlands, cultivated for more than a hundred years past'—free for the taking to any Protestants who wanted them. Even though the Church of England was nominally the established denomination, Lawrence proclaimed that

> Protestant dissenters from the Church of England, whether they be Calvinists, Lutherans, Quakers or under what denomination whatsoever, shall have free liberty of conscience and may erect and build meeting houses for public worship.

He appealed to New Englanders by promising to establish new townships and provide military security. Many responded by immigrating to Nova Scotia. Most who came were concerned for their freedoms: freedom of religion and freedom from military autocracy.[82]

The New Englanders who settled in Nova Scotia took with them—in some cases all too literally—much of their material culture. As we read about one migrant from Cape Cod:

> When Edmund Doane formed the strange project of emigrating to Nova Scotia, he had his two-storey house taken down, the posts cut shorter to make it one storey, and the roof made something like our present mansard roofs. He hired a vessel, got his house frame and material on board...and set sail.[83]

3.27 Calkin house, near Grand Pré, Nova Scotia, 1766-8. Photograph by Heather Davidson.

Doane's house was subsequently lost at sea, but others like him did arrive in Nova Scotia with house frames, building materials, and furniture as well as their social and political values. (As we have seen, some Newfoundlanders resorted to the same venture two centuries later.) A number of communities of farmers from Rhode Island and Connecticut settled in the old Acadian areas around the Bay of Fundy; many fishermen from Massachusetts relocated along the South Shore of Nova Scotia, particularly around Barrington, Yarmouth, Liverpool, and Chester; and others, mainly farmers, accepted land—between 250 and 2000 acres (100 to 800 hectares) each—in the Annapolis Valley.

The first group settled the four western townships on Minas Basin, on the south shore of the Bay of Fundy. They were called 'planters', as were their predecessors in seventeenth-century Newfoundland. The houses of several first-generation Nova Scotia planters survive. Most began as small 1½-storey buildings, with only one or two rooms on the ground floor. They grew larger and more formal over time, evolving to accommodate growing families and increasing prosperity.

The **Jeremiah Calkin house [3.27]** near Grand Pré is one such dwelling. (It has been moved.) Calkin, his wife Mary, and their three children arrived in Horton Township from Connecticut in 1765, and built their house between 1766 and 1768. The ground floor originally consisted of one open room with a chimney along the side wall and a staircase leading up to the sleeping loft. Like many other houses built shortly after the Expulsion, it may have been constructed on top of an Acadian cellar. A decade or two later—likely by the early 1780s, by which time Calkin had established himself as a planter, acquired additional land, and fathered nine children—the house was extended to one side and to the rear, with a sloping 'saltbox' roof placed over the rear addition. The original loft was divided into two bedrooms, and two more were located in the upper floor of the addition. A central hall off the front door now provided entry to a house that was much larger and more gracious than it had formerly been.[84]

A gambrel roof covers the house. This roof-type is characterized by having two slopes: a relatively flat slope at the top and a longer, steeper one rising from the eaves and usually pierced with dormer windows. The gambrel roof—commonly known by that name in the US, and more often called a mansard roof in Canada—had been used in seventeenth-century England and was popular in

eighteenth-century New England. It provided more space and headroom in the loft than a low-gable roof, and used shorter rafters than a steep-gable roof, but it required complex framing. Indeed, if the anecdote about Edmund Doane transporting his house frame by boat is accurate, the gable roof may have been modified to the gambrel form to make it easier to ship. This shape also provided a way to avoid paying taxes on the upper floor (houses used to be taxed according to the number of storeys). While the gambrel roof did not endure, it had its moment of popularity in pre-Loyalist Nova Scotia, and some Loyalist buildings in New Brunswick continued the form. It was not until its re-introduction as the mansard roof, with the Second Empire Style of the late nineteenth century, that the form left its mark on the Canadian landscape.

The best known of the dwellings of this period is the **Simeon Perkins house** [3.28] in Liverpool, on the South Shore of Nova Scotia. Perkins came to Nova Scotia from Norwich, Connecticut, in 1762 when he was 28. He was a businessman with good connections: his cousin and sometime business associate became a general on George Washington's staff, and his first wife, Abigail, whose untimely death may have led him to emigrate, was a cousin of the Governor of Connecticut. Perkins

3.28 Perkins house, Liverpool, Nova Scotia, begun 1766-7. Nova Scotia Supply and Services, Visual Communications/20426.

3.29 Original ground-floor plan (conjectural) of the Perkins house, Liverpool, Nova Scotia, 1766-7. Drawing by David Byrnes, after Allen Penney.

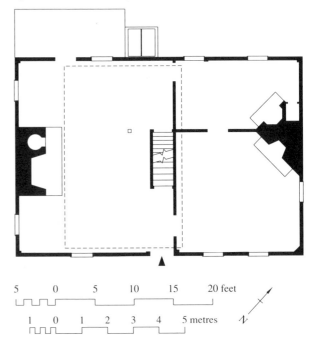

quickly established himself as a merchant and leading citizen of the new town—Liverpool had been planned only in 1759—and was later to serve as a magistrate, judge, town clerk, and county treasurer, as well as colonel in the Queens County militia during the American Revolution.[85]

Perkins built his house in 1766-7. It was originally a small one-storey building [3.29] with two rooms on the ground floor, an attic above, and a small cellar—possibly the cellar of a former Acadian house. The gable roof-form seen in the photograph was used commonly in Nova Scotia, as was the gambrel, although having a much lower slope than the gable roofs in New France. At each end of the roof was a chimney, one of them triangular at the base to provide a corner fireplace in each of the two rooms—another feature of early Nova Scotia houses. The construction is wood frame; vertical posts rest on sills that lie directly on the sandy soil, and the studs and rafters were supplemented by a single layer of vertical boards on the walls and a double layer of boards on the roof. The wall-boards were clapboarded and the roof shingled.

Although New England is better known for its two-storey houses, dwellings of the Perkins type were built there as well. As architectural historian Allen Penney has noted, the Moses Farnham house at Uxbridge, Massachusetts, 40 miles (65 km) north of Norwich, is very similar in plan to the Perkins house (the common features include the corner fireplaces) and was built at the same time, although in brick. Perhaps because of Perkins' limited means—he was a trader, but never a very successful one—and because of the frontier nature of the new Nova Scotia community, his house followed the smaller of the New England models.

Perkins remarried, and he and his second wife, Elizabeth, had eight children. The growing family forced Perkins to enlarge his house. In 1781 a new kitchen was added on the left, enclosing the former outside chimney, and the attic was opened up with dormer windows; a new wing was built at the rear in 1792 to make a T-shaped plan. The interior finishes were gradually upgraded as well, progressing from bare boards to paint, wallpaper, and finally plaster. The result is a somewhat rambling house that was continually being renovated to meet the needs of the day. The house was restored in 1949 and again in 1982. It is now operated by the Nova Scotia Museum and the Queens County Historical Society, which has erected a large museum building next to it that overwhelms the historic house it was intended to interpret.

The Calkin and Perkins houses are typical of those built in Nova Scotia in the 1760s by New Englanders of modest or moderate means. Their original plans, and those of other buildings of the time, had either a single room on the ground floor or a large room and one or two small rooms beside it, similar to the familiar hall-and-parlour plan that was seen in the houses of Newfoundland. The chimneys were usually located against the end walls, a feature of English housing, and not in the centre, as was prevalent in New England. It has been suggested that the central-chimney plan was characteristic in Nova Scotia at this time, but few buildings with this form have been documented.[86]

New Englanders also came to other parts of Nova Scotia. The Township of Barrington, on the southern tip, was founded in 1759 by forty families from Cape Cod, most of them involved in the fishery. The settlers began to arrive in 1761, and many others came in the decades that followed. At first the residents traded almost entirely with Boston. Their villages and houses understandably resembled those of Massachusetts.[87]

John Crowe of Yarmouth, Massachusetts, and several others built 'palisaded' houses with walls of vertical poles (and not a wood frame)—Crowe's dwelling survived for a century and a half, although it was much altered—but most erected frame buildings. The Sargent house at Barrington Head, built by John Porter in 1769, was a $1\frac{1}{2}$-storey dwelling constructed with an oak frame and covered with a gambrel roof.[88]

Most settlers from Massachusetts were Congregationalists—Puritans who dissented from the Church of England—and their houses of worship rejected the traditional longitudinal orientation and liturgical appurtenances of the English church. The **Meeting House at Barrington** [3.30], built in 1765, is a transplant of the Dissenters' most characteristic public building, the meeting house, and is the only survivor of five such buildings erected in Nova Scotia before 1770. Originally used for both Congregationalist worship and town meetings, the Barrington Meeting House consists of a single room 36 by 30 feet (11 by 9.2 m), wider than it is deep, with the pulpit on the long side opposite the entrance, a gallery on the other three sides, and without an altar or a chancel. The architecture reflects the Dissenters' emphasis on the spoken word in that it enables every worshipper to sit at about the same distance from the pulpit. The treatment is plain and unostentatious both inside and out. The exterior is treated as a two-storey gable-roofed building, looking much like a large house. The timber-frame structure is clad with shingles, a popular material in Massachusetts. (It was originally covered with clapboard; the shingles were probably introduced shortly before 1800.) The most prominent ornament is seen in the understated pilasters at the corners and a classically derived fascia board beneath the eaves, although all of the interior mouldings exhibit graceful classical profiles [**3.31**].[89]

Construction was directed by Joshua Nickerson, a local shipbuilder; he was assisted by carpenter Elijah Swaine, one of a number of Quakers from Nantucket who had come to Barrington and were free to worship at the Meeting House. The wood brackets that support the structure above the ceiling are in the form of 'ship's knees', familiar to shipbuilders. Although the building was used for meetings by 1767, completion took several decades because the congregation was poor and somewhat divided. In 1786 the Meeting House was described as still being without doors or windows. The present finishes may date from that decade, or from repairs carried out in 1817 under the direction of chief carpenter David Doane (a relation of the early migrant who lost his house at sea).

The outward appearance closely resembles the New England meeting houses of the period, such as the meeting house at Sandown, New Hampshire, built in 1773-4. The two are similar in scale and proportion, but the building at Sandown displays more refined classical detail, owing to its having been built by an older, more established, community. Nova Scotia buildings rarely achieved the elegance of their American counterparts: elegance never seemed to be an objective. The transfer of the New England model to the Nova Scotia frontier resulted in a greater directness and simplicity of form.

So ecumenical is the form of the Meeting House at Barrington that the original Congregationalists—who opened their doors to 'all preachers of the Gospel'—were succeeded by Baptists, Methodists, Presbyterians, and Anglicans. Each denomination left its mark: the Methodists built the high pulpit and the gallery, and the Presbyterians installed the pews and flat ceiling. The building is now administered by the Nova Scotia Museum and is open to the public.

The boundaries of early Nova Scotia took in the expanse of land to the north of the Bay of Fundy that is now New Brunswick. The first New Englanders came to this region in 1760, and within

3.30 The Meeting House, Barrington, Nova Scotia, 1765. Photograph by Larry Turner, 1988.

3.31 Interior of the Meeting House, Barrington, Nova Scotia, 1765. Photograph by John de Visser.

three years settlements were established at Portland Point at the mouth of the St John River—now the city of Saint John—and at Maugerville and Sackville. Many of the early settlers brought the frames and boards for their houses with them; thus Captain Francis Peabody, from Essex County in Massachusetts, was able to raise his house at Portland Point in just three days in 1762.[90]

One group of fifty families from Essex County, Massachusetts, established the farming community of Maugerville on the St John River, about 60 miles (100 km) inland from the Bay of Fundy. Here, deeper in the frontier, it was more practical to build log houses, as did settler Hugh Quinton and many of his neighbours.[91] Staunch Congregationalists, the people of the community began to build the **Maugerville Meeting House [3.32]** in 1775. It followed the traditional New England form, but unlike the Meeting House at Barrington, it had a tower at the west end, with an octagonal belfry and a tall spire over a square base that gave it a decidedly longitudinal axis. Towers occured on some New England precedents, the most renowned being Old South Meeting House in Boston (1729-30), which also had an octagonal stage with arched openings below the spire.

In 1776, when the American Declaration of Independence was proclaimed, most of Nova Scotia's Yankees quickly expressed their allegiance to the Crown. The residents of Yarmouth, for example, asserted their loyalty and their desire to remain undisturbed in December 1775:

> ...all of us profess to be true Friends and Loyal Subjects to George our King. We were almost all of us born in New England, we have Fathers, Brothers, and Sisters in that Country; divided betwixt natural affection to our nearest relations, and good Faith and Friendship to our King and Country, we want to know, if we may be permitted at this time to live in a peaceable State....[92]

The Congregationalists of Maugerville, on the other hand, sympathized with the Americans, and resolved 'to submit ourselves to the government of Massachusetts Bay.' They soon found themselves surrounded by newly arrived neighbours who were loyal to the British cause. Tensions increased as the years went by. The Congregationalists responded imaginatively and tactfully, in the winter of 1789, by transporting their meeting house, the most visible symbol of discord, 5 miles (8 km) down the St John River to a new site at Sheffield.[93]

3.32 Maugerville Meeting House, Sheffield, New Brunswick, 1775. Photograph by John de Visser.

The Loyalists in the Maritimes

The settlers who displayed hostility to the residents of Maugerville—New Englanders who had arrived during, and immediately after, the American Revolution of 1775-83—represented only a tiny portion of a huge migration. It is estimated that fully one-fifth of the residents of the American colonies remained loyal to the Crown. Regarded as traitors to the Revolution, between 80,000 and 100,000 Loyalists fled the United States, about half of them to Canada. Settling in Nova Scotia, parts of Quebec, the St Lawrence River valley, and the Niagara Peninsula, most of them came in 1783 and 1784. The Loyalists were welcomed—indeed, enticed—by the British government, which offered them generous grants of land as incentives. They were a highly mobile group of refugees, however: many disillusioned Loyalists subsequently moved back to the United States.[94]

The Loyalists were diverse in their make-up, and in their values:

> Loyalists were women as well as men; black and Indian as well as white; Dutch and German and

117

French as well as British; Baptists and Methodists as well as Anglicans; fishermen and frontiersmen, artisans and poor farmers as well as office-holders and merchants; Whigs as well as Tories; rebels against established authority as well as its upholders.[95]

What they had in common was a period of living in the American colonies, the experience of revolution, and a respect for Britain. These factors, combined with the ambiance of newly developing English Canada and its young building traditions, succeeded in fostering a consistent architecture from the Atlantic seaboard to the Great Lakes.

Some 30,000 Loyalists came to the Maritime Provinces alone—far more than the 20,000 settlers who were already there at the outbreak of war. Half of the Loyalists who came to the Maritimes settled on the north shore of the Bay of Fundy. They vastly outnumbered the existing residents, who were a combination of New Englanders who had arrived before the Revolution, Acadians who had returned after the Treaty of Paris in 1763, and natives. The Loyalists petitioned for separate colonial status from Nova Scotia, and in 1784 the new province of New Brunswick was proclaimed by its first Governor (later called Lieutenant Governor), Colonel Thomas Carleton, a career soldier who was the brother of Sir Guy Carleton, the former governor of Quebec who became in 1786 Commander-in-Chief of British North America as Lord Dorchester.

The same types of towns and buildings that developed in pre-Loyalist Nova Scotia continued into the beginning of the Loyalist period without apparent changes. Within a decade or two, however, the buildings erected by people of means became increasingly formal and sophisticated in design, reflecting the growing affluence of Nova Scotia society and the greater confidence of its young establishment.

Early towns One group of Loyalist refugees settled at the mouth of the Penobscot River, at Castine, south of today's Bangor, Maine, the site of the former French Fort Pentagoët. Some 700 civilians and soldiers were living there in 1783 when they learned that the international boundary would be located further north, at the St Croix River. Most of them immediately left the American territory and re-settled nearly 125 miles (200 km) further up the coast at St Andrews, at the mouth of the St Croix River on Passamaquoddy Bay, which the French had considered to be the centre of Acadia.[96]

The new arrivals sailed north with all their possessions crammed aboard a flotilla of large and small vessels. The first group from Castine arrived on 3 October 1783, and others soon followed. They took with them their furniture, the 'priceless mahogany', silver plate, damask, linen, family portraits, and brass-studded trunks. Many even disassembled the frame houses they had built so quickly, conveyed them by schooner, and re-erected them at St Andrews. Robert Pagan, a Scottish-born merchant (and future influential politician), brought both his house and his store; the coffee house that had been used for secret meetings of the would-be refugees was rebuilt on Water Street. Pagan also helped to settle a boundary dispute between Britain and the US by using a copy of Champlain's map and doing some archaeological investigation to identify Île Sainte-Croix, and thereby help determine which river was the St Croix and locate the new international boundary.[97]

St Andrews was laid out by Surveyor General Charles Morris on a regular plan much like that of Halifax and Lunenburg, but at St Andrews the plan was a checkerboard with square blocks—similar to many New England towns—and not a rectangular gridiron.[98] The plan had three divisions of 20 or 25 blocks (excluding the irregular water-lots), each with a public reserve of two blocks. The blocks are 320 feet (97.6 m) square and contain eight building lots each 80 by 160 feet (24.4 by 48.8 m). The street names left no doubt about political loyalties: King, Queen, Prince of Wales, Princess Royal, and the first names of the royal children.

The town was built quickly, assisted by the government's providing sawn lumber, nails, and glass. The trader William Pagan (Robert's elder brother) reported on the progress in May 1784, barely a half-year after the first settlers had arrived:

> We have now about ninety houses up and great preparations making in every quarter of the town for more. Numbers of inhabitants are daily arriving and a great many others are hourly looked for from different quarters....I can with pleasure assure you that the land is in general very good abounding with large quantities of hardwood, all kinds of fine timber of a large growth and very handy to the water where most vessels can safely anchor. There are a number of falls of water where saw mills can be erected but only two on the Scuddock yet up.[99]

With a fine year-round seaport, good land and mill sites, and prospects for the lumber and fishing industries, the future prosperity of St Andrews seemed assured. William Pagan was ready to 'supply the whole British West India Islands with Boards, Plank, Scantling, Ranging Timber, Shingles, Clap Boards and every other species of Lumber that can be shipped from any part of New England, oak staves excepted.'[100] Indeed, St Andrews was the centre of the West Indies trade for half a century. Its prosperity today derives from tourism, which has been stimulated by the many well-preserved historic buildings.

3.33 (*above*) Crookshank house, St Andrews, New Brunswick, *c*. 1760s-70s; re-erected *c*. 1784. CIHB/04105000800107.

Some houses may remain from the first wave of building. It is often speculated that the **Joseph Crookshank house** [3.33] on Queen Street was one of those moved from Castine. The residence of a ship's carpenter, it might have been built as early as the 1760s. The two-storey, three-bay frame house is shingled, with a side entry and an internal chimney. The eave of the gable roof is lower at the back (because it continues over a shed-like rear room) than at the front, following the so-called 'saltbox' form characteristic of houses in Connecticut, Massachusetts, and Long Island.[101]

Loyalists were also arriving in large numbers at Parr Town and Carleton, at the mouth of the Saint John River. In 1785 the two communities were incorporated as Saint John, a city that would become Canada's most important commercial port in the first half of the nineteenth century (see page 243).

As his capital, Governor Carleton chose Fredericton, at the site of the former Acadian village of Ste Anne, 60 miles (100 km) up the St John River. The plan, laid out by military surveyor Lieutenant Dugald Campbell, is the familiar British imperial gridiron with rectangular blocks. A few eighteenth-century buildings remain, including the **Jonathan Odell house** [3.34] on Brunswick Street. This 2$\frac{1}{2}$-storey wood structure, with a gable roof and four massive chimneys, was built between 1785 and

3.34 Odell house, Fredericton, New Brunswick, *c*. 1785-95. PANB/P5/288.

1795 as the residence of the Honourable Jonathan Odell, a physician, Church of England clergyman, poet, and spy from New Jersey who was rewarded for his loyalty to the Crown by being appointed New Brunswick's first Provincial Secretary. Architectural historian Stuart Smith identifies this as the first house in the province 'intended to reflect the taste, social importance, and wealth of its occupant', citing the abandonment of the central chimney and dominant kitchen—although he notes that the house is 'curiously modest, almost hesitant in its decoration and elaboration.' The Odell House presents a four-bay front to Brunswick Street, but has its entrance around the corner on the gable end, which is protected by a one-storey porch. The kitchen wing (barely visible through and above the left side of the porch) was removed in the 1960s. Today the building serves as the Deanery of Christ Church Cathedral [6.32].[102]

Two early Fredericton inns featured a gambrel roof over a two-storey frame. (This popular New England roof-form evidently afforded the most efficient way of providing a third floor, needed in a busy inn.) One was the British American Coffee House on Queen Street (demolished), built *c*. 1784, which was the temporary home of Governor Carleton while Government House was under construction; the other is **McLeod's Inn [3.35]** on Waterloo

Row, built in 1785. Both buildings were extended after their initial construction, and so their original width is uncertain.[103]

The largest influx of Loyalists to the Maritimes converged on Shelburne, Nova Scotia. The optimistic arrivals—who came from New England and the central colonies, as well as from Virginia and North Carolina—believed that they were laying the foundations for another Boston or New York and grandly named the town after British Prime Minister Lord Shelburne. Many of them had organized in New York as the Port Roseway Association in November 1782 (Port Roseway being the original name of the site) to negotiate the terms of settlement with Governor John Parr and other Nova Scotia officials. They expressed their fond hope that, with assistance, 'the Associates will form a Settlement, not only Happy for themselves, but... an ornament to the British Empire.' The Nova Scotia government agreed to provide a survey, military security, and free land, without prejudicing any claims for compensation for war losses, providing that no grantee would transfer his land until after he had made improvements to it.[104]

The first contingent of settlers arrived at Shelburne in May 1783: 1,686 property-owning men, women, and children; 415 servants; and 936 freed slaves listed as servants. Many more followed, some from as far away as Florida and Jamaica. It is estimated that by the end of that year the community had a population of 10,000 people—larger than

3.35 McLeod's Inn, Fredericton, New Brunswick, 1785. Photograph by Isobel Louise Hill.

3.36 View of Shelburne, Nova Scotia, showing houses used as barracks. Drawing by William Booth, 1789. NAC/C-10548.

Montreal or Quebec, and double that of Halifax.[105]

The town was constructed at breakneck speed. Eight months after the arrival of the first settlers, Governor Parr wrote to Lord Shelburne (in December 1783) that

> the most considerable, most flourishing and most expeditious [town] that ever was built in so short a time is Shelburne. 800 houses already finished, 600 more in great forwardness, and several hundred lately begun upon, with wharfs and other erections.[106]

In a report prepared in September 1784, Benjamin Marston said that 1,127 buildings had been constructed between May 1783 and February 1784, and that another 250 to 300 houses and stores had been built since then. Of the first group, Marston noted that 80 were temporary structures intended only for the first winter, 231 were frame houses, and the remainder were log houses 'built of pieces of timber framed together at the ends', which, with the addition of clapboards, could be made into permanent buildings. Describing the most recently built group, he reported that 'these later buildings are altogether framed houses and most generally large, commodious, and some of them elegant buildings.'[107]

Historian Marion Robertson has described the early houses of Shelburne in some detail. Among the log houses, she notes that some were constructed from round logs connected at the corners with their ends projecting (i.e. saddle notches); others were better built, using square logs framed together at the corners (probably dovetail joints); and huts were made of vertical poles covered with strips of bark (a reminiscence of the tilt). The framed houses were built from sawn or hewn wood. Settlers brought lumber with them, but some was purchased from Nova Scotia or New England mills. Shelburne also had saw-pits and sawmills of its own, using 'the very wood that grew where the town now stands.' Boards could be produced in sufficient quantity to cover the walls of six to ten houses a week. Some tools and hardware were provided by the government, but not enough to meet the demand.[108]

Drawings and watercolours of **Shelburne [3.36]** from the late eighteenth and early nineteenth centuries show a variety of houses and commercial buildings between one and two-and-a-half storeys high and covered with gable and gambrel roofs. Central chimneys appear to predominate. Shingles and clapboards provided exterior finishes. Small-paned double-hung windows and panelled doors, many with transoms, are evident. The overall impression is of a densely built-up town with simple but substantial housing.

The best preserved of the early Shelburne buildings, which includes the only store to survive from the first era of construction, is the **Ross-Thomson House [3.37]** on Charlotte Lane. Scottish-born brothers George and Robert Ross reached Shelburne by way of Florida and prospered as merchants trading with the US, the West Indies, and England. By 1785 they had built a pair of attached two-storey buildings on Charlotte Lane: the one on the north was a store, covered with a gambrel roof, and behind it, to the south, was their gable-roofed house. The Rosses were assisted by fellow Aberdonian Robert Thomson, and in 1815 sold the house and the business to the Thomson family. The two-part building, owned by the Nova Scotia Museum, is operated by the Shelburne Historical Society.[109]

Shelburne's moment in the sun was brief. The Port Roseway Association had sited the town by a superb harbour, but foolishly chose an area with little arable land. When the government stopped distributing food in 1787, residents began to leave, many of them returning to the US. Some may have taken their houses with them. By the 1820s Shelburne's population had dropped to around 300. Today, just over 2,000 people live there; the economy is based on fishing and tourism.

House-types of the Loyalist era

The houses of St Andrews, Saint John, Fredericton, Shelburne, and the many other Loyalist communities in the Maritimes owe much to the pre-Loyalist buildings of Nova Scotia and New England, as well as to the building traditions of Britain. In Atlantic Canada, two principal types of houses were dominant in the late-eighteenth and early-nineteenth centuries: the Cape Cod cottage and the Georgian house. The former is a relatively unpretentious vernacular homestead that was used by both unestablished settlers and the relatively well-to-do. The Georgian house, on the other hand, is larger and more ostentatious, with its origins in Euopean high architecture. As its clear links with Georgian England made it a symbol of British power and authority, it was preferred by owners with strong British or Loyalist ties who wanted to assert their commitment to the traditional order.

Not every house, of course, fits into one of these two classifications, nor is there even a consensus on the terminology. But these two house-types are

3.37 Ross-Thomson House, Shelburne, Nova Scotia, early 1780s. HWS/SSS/SH RW 1.02.

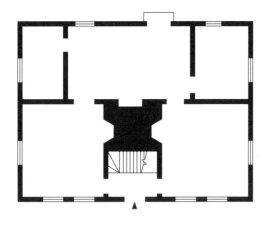

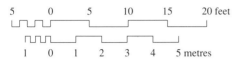

3.38 Plan of a Cape Cod cottage. Drawing by David Byrnes, after Peter Ennals.

3.39 House at St Margaret's Bay, Nova Scotia, 19th century. Photograph by Deryck Holdsworth, 1978.

particularly useful to study: the Cape Cod cottage as a basically vernacular form; and the Georgian house, which—though having its origins in high ('polite' or 'academic') architecture—quickly entered the vernacular.[110]

The Cape Cod cottage This name is used widely in Nova Scotia to describe a vernacular house-form whose origins are found in New England, and whose Canadian version was derived, if somewhat loosely, from the type of house that was prevalent on Cape Cod. The true 'Cape Cod house' (rather than 'cottage'), as it is found on that Massachusetts peninsula, is constructed with a timber frame. It faces south, is $1\frac{1}{2}$ storeys high (the half-storey refers to the attic within the slope of the roof), and has a gable roof, single chimney (often serving multiple hearths), shingled exterior walls (sometimes with clapboard on the south and north), windows that typically have nine panes on the upper sash and six on the lower (referred to as nine-over-six windows, sometimes rendered 9/6), and a small entry (what today would be called a hall) and a steep staircase squeezed between the front door and the chimney. A second room, or range of rooms, is located behind the chimney. In its simplest form, the Cape Cod house has a single room and a loft, with the chimney located against a side wall, much like the earliest houses in seventeenth-century Plymouth, Massachusetts; but it is also found with two rooms of about equal size, one at either side of the

chimney (in which case it is called a 'double-house'), or with a large room at one side and a small one at the other (called a 'house-and-a-half' or, in modern terminology, a 'three-quarter-house').[111]

The **Cape Cod cottage** [3.38] of Nova Scotia shares most of these features. Peter Ennals and Deryck Holdsworth have prepared a plan of its typical Nova Scotia form, which is redrawn here. They see little difference between the pre-Loyalist and Loyalist houses of this type, other than an apparent tendency over time towards symmetry, often achieved by adding to the original mass to create a double-house. In Nova Scotia the roof may be hipped, gabled, gambrel, or saltbox in form. The pre-Loyalist version of the Cape Cod cottage may be better illustrated by the original form of the Simeon Perkins house [3.29]. Both had a living-hall extending the full depth of the house, to the left of the entry, and two smaller rooms at the right. They deviated from the archetype in having a chimney on each side wall instead of one in the centre (probably to help cope with the colder Canadian winters).[112]

A **house at St Margaret's Bay** [3.39], Nova Scotia, identified by Ennals and likely built in the nineteenth century, is a good example of the Cape Cod house-and-a-half. The shallow eave is only a single shingle course over the windows on the front elevation, and the house is heated by a single central chimney.[113]

123

North Hills [3.40] at Granville Ferry, in the Annapolis Valley, is a house with an interesting, if still somewhat cloudy, architectural history. In its present form it is an exemplary Cape Cod cottage: $1\frac{1}{2}$ storeys high, twelve-over-twelve windows, and shingled walls. It differs from the model in that the gable roof is of the saltbox type, having a lower eave at the rear than in the front, and in having a chimney on each of the side-walls. The original house, however, was much smaller. It consisted only of the portion behind the door and the two windows to the left. The date '1702' carved on a beam, while not necessarily authentic, has led to speculation that the house could have been built shortly after the first New England traders came there in the late seventeenth century. The right-hand portion, which made it into a double-house, may have been constructed by Paul Amberman, a Loyalist from New York who purchased the house in 1784. Subsequent additions were made to the left side and in the rear (not visible in the photograph). In 1964 retired banker Robert B. Patterson bought the Amberman house, as it was then known, and redesigned the interior; exterior changes were also made that included replacing the four-panel windows with early-looking small-paned sash windows. Patterson placed his fine collection of furniture in the house, and bequeathed house and collection to the Nova Scotia Museum, which operates it as a museum jointly with the Historic Restoration Society of Annapolis County.[114]

The basic Nova Scotia house was larger than its Newfoundland counterpart, which was usually only one room deep (although it was often extended by a linhay). Owing to Nova Scotia's greater prosperity—and its residents' compulsion to display their means—many houses (such as the Perkins house and North Hills) underwent a continual program of improvements that, among other things, added symmetry as well as space.

The Georgian house The second house-type was a more formal structure that exhibited the owner's influence and affluence, and was clearly read as an expression of British imperial order. Where the Cape Cod cottage was a vernacular house-type, whose form followed its use as a homestead, the Georgian house was artificial and contrived; its archetype was the European palace. Symmetry and regularity were its guiding principles, and the expression of authority and upward mobility was its social function. In its most characteristic

3.40 North Hills, Granville Ferry, Nova Scotia, possibly begun *c.* 1700. Nova Scotia Museum.

Canadian form, the Georgian house is two storeys high and five bays wide, with the entrance placed in the centre of the long side. The façade is usually treated quite austerely and in a single plane; what little decoration there is will be concentrated around the front door and perhaps the ground-floor windows.[115]

A superb Georgian house that is a perfect study in proportion and elegance is **Acacia Grove [3.41]**, built between 1811 and 1817 at Starr's Point, King's County, in Nova Scotia's Annapolis Valley. Every door, every window, every bit of trim seems to be exactly right. The two principal storeys are five bays wide, with the middle bay (containing the door and an upstairs window) ever so slightly wider than the others to provide a subtle emphasis on the centre. The walls (for many years covered by a protective coating of whitewash) are constructed of light red brick made from clay found on the property. The basement walls, only a part of which appears above grade, are rubble stone, faced on the front with dressed Wallace stone (a grey-and-blue sandstone quarried at Wallace, Nova Scotia).[116]

The entrance is approached by a pair of straight stairs that lead to a small pedimented porch supported by columns. A finely detailed semicircular fanlight and sidelights surround the door. It opens onto a rectangular entrance hall, at the end of which a second door—a repetition of the entrance—gives access to the staircase hall [3.42]. The drawing-room and dining-room are on either side of the central hall on the ground floor, and the family bedrooms are on the second floor. Chim-

3.41 Acacia Grove, Starrs Point,
Nova Scotia, 1811-17. Nova Scotia
Supply and Services, Visual
Communications/27720.

3.42 (*right*) Ground-floor plan of
Acacia Grove, Starrs Point, Nova
Scotia, 1811-17. Drawing by David
Byrnes, after Arthur W. Wallace.

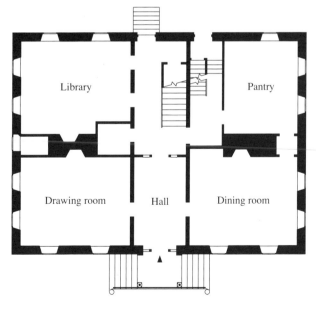

Library

Pantry

Drawing room

Hall

Dining room

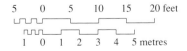

5   0   5   10   15   20 feet

1   0   1   2   3   4   5 metres

N

neys are located at either side in the centre of the partitions that divide the rooms. The attic beneath the broad hipped roof contains the servants' bedrooms, which are illuminated by gabled dormers. The kitchen is in the basement. The floor plan is a generous 52 by 40 feet (16 by 12 m). The interior finishes are of high quality, with fine woodwork appearing throughout, particularly in the panelled surrounds of the ground-floor windows and fireplaces.

Acacia Grove was built by a man of high social and political position: the Honourable Charles Ramage Prescott. Born in 1772 in Halifax to parents who had come from the American colonies before the Revolution, Prescott was a wealthy merchant who retired from business in 1811 and built his large Annapolis Valley house on a 100-acre (40-hectare) tract of land facing the Cornwallis River. He quickly became involved in the affairs of the Cornwallis community, served in the legislature and the legislative council (the cabinet), and devoted the remainder of his time to horticulture. Prescott brought many varieties of fruit trees and flowers from Europe and planted them on his estate. He did much to develop Nova Scotia's embryonic apple industry, producing plant varieties specifically for the Nova Scotia climate: he introduced the Gravenstein apple to the region, and helped to establish the Fruit Growers' Association.

Visitors raved about Prescott's garden. *The Times* praised the property as a showpiece of the era's 'taste for improvement', and an aspiring poetess named Emily published these verses in the *Novascotian*:

> Here are flowers of ev'ry hue—
> Fragrant, beautiful to view;
> From the lovely Pansy, bright
> Breathing love—emitting light,
> To the stately Dahlia, tall,
> Looking round with pride on all.
>
> Here survey, of every kind
> Fruits, the choicest you can find;
> Luscious Grape, and Peaches rare,
> Golden Plumb and mellow Pear;
> Rosy Apples, blushing through
> Foliage touched with Autumn's hue—
> They look as fair as Mother Eve's,
> Without the serpent 'neath the leaves.[117]

The house and grounds come as close to a Georgian 'gentleman's country seat' as the Maritimes had yet produced. They were well maintained for a half-

century following Prescott's death in 1859, but a succession of indifferent owners early in this century led to their deterioration. The grove of acacia trees that gave the estate its name was cut down. Mary Allison Prescott, the great-granddaughter of the first owner, bought the property in 1932 and restored it. Following her death in 1969 Acacia Grove was purchased by the provincial and federal governments. It is now open to the public under the administration of the Nova Scotia Museum.

The Georgian style of Acacia Grove prevailed in British colonies around the world in the eighteenth and early nineteenth centuries. The term 'Georgian' derives from the first four British monarchs named George, whose combined reigns spanned the years 1714 to 1830. It is used to describe a formal and refined architecture based on classical Greek and Roman sources as interpreted by Renaissance and post-Renaissance architects of Italy and Britain—particularly the group of designers known as the Palladians.

The most respected Renaissance proponent of the buildings of classical antiquity was Andrea Palladio (1508-80), who designed many villas and public buildings in the region around Venice, and gained wide recognition through his architectural treatise, *I Quattro Libri dell'Architettura* (The Four Books of Architecture, 1570). His restrained classical manner was introduced into England early in the seventeenth century by Inigo Jones (1573-1672), and was revived a century later by a coterie of architects and connoisseurs centred on Colen Campbell (1676-1729) and architect and patron Richard Boyle (1694-1753), third Earl of Burling-

3.43 Marble Hill, Twickenham, England, 1724-9. River elevation. Photograph by Harold Kalman, *c*. 1968.

ton, and the leading figure of Neo-Palladianism. Illustrated books formed an important component of the new movement. Campbell published *Vitruvius Britannicus* (3 vols, 1715-25), a compilation of plates of recent British work that displayed 'antique simplicity' in the manner of Palladio and Jones; Palladio's treatise was translated into English by Giacomo Leoni (published 1715-20), and again by Isaac Ware (published 1738); and Burlington's protégé William Kent published *Designs of Inigo Jones* (1727).

This group of enthusiasts and their followers, known after their idol as 'Palladians', altered the course of British building away from the bombastic manner of the English Baroque. During a relatively brief period (*c*. 1715-50), they introduced a sparsely decorated manner based on principles of harmony and proportion—called either the Palladian style or the Palladian phase of the Georgian style. A seminal building is **Marble Hill** (1724-9), Twickenham, an exquisite villa (the word 'villa' is itself classically derived) on the Thames, a short distance west of London [**3.43**]. Designed by Henry Herbert (*c*. 1689-1750), the ninth Earl of Pembroke, a friend of Lord Burlington, and by Roger Morris (1695-1749), it has two storeys above a ground-level 'basement' and is covered by a low hipped roof. It is five bays wide, and the three central windows are emphasized on the entrance façade by a projecting four-pilaster-wide pedimented temple front with a rusticated base. (The pilasters are omitted on the river elevation, which is seen in the photograph.) The wall planes are flat, the relief shallow, the corners crisp, the walls cream stucco.

3.44 Crowinshield-Bentley house, Salem, Massachussets, begun 1727. Photograph by Harold Kalman, 1972.

Architects outside the immediate circle of Lord Burlington pursued similar objectives. One of these was James Gibbs, the designer of St Peter, Vere Street, which we have seen was the source for St Paul's Church, Halifax. Buildings by Gibbs and his contemporaries are also classically inspired but are not so pristinely simplified as those of the Palladians. The same design principles also percolated into the work of minor architects and builders throughout England and Scotland, who often omitted pediments, pilasters, and most other overt references to antiquity. The British buildings in this manner and period are collectively described by the general term 'Georgian'.

Generic Georgian had an enormous impact on the British colonies. The five-bay, two-storey Georgian house appeared in New England and the Middle American colonies (and the Caribbean) beginning in the second quarter of the century. It is seen in the McPhedris house in Portsmouth, New Hampshire (begun 1718), where it is faced in brick and originally had a double-gable roof; and in the **Crowinshield-Bentley house** [**3.44**] in Salem, Massachusetts (begun 1727), with clapboard siding and a gambrel roof. More classical references appear in the John Vassall (Longfellow) house in Cambridge, Massachusetts (1759); it has the same classical forms and symmetry, but its use of giant ground-to-cornice pilasters and dormer windows, the somewhat vertical proportions, and the textured clapboard wall surfaces all deviate from Palladian models. The true Palladian style was followed in the American colonies only in the hands of a few architects, notably the Yorkshire-born Peter Harrison (1716-75) in Rhode Island.

Palladianism did not appear in Canada in its pure form. Canadian builders who followed classical models found sources in the less-rigorous Georgian vernacular that immigrants from Britain and the US brought as a part of their cultural experience—and it was further simplified by the frontier conditions. They supplemented this knowledge with details that were available in accessible British architectural books published by Gibbs, Abraham Swan, William Pain, and others. Some buildings that reveal a concerted effort to incorporate classical forms can be described as 'Palladian-Georgian'.

Georgian houses, mostly simpler in design than those in the US, began to be built by men with political power in Nova Scotia and New Brunswick, as well as in Upper Canada, towards the end of the eighteenth century—fully three-quarters of a century after the introduction of the style in the US.

Their symmetry, palatial connotations, and restrained classical ornament provided an effective expression of wealth and authority. An important prototype was the second Governor's House in Halifax [3.20], built about 1757, a prominent two-storey wood building—in effect, the young colony's palace—that was six (rather than the canonical five) bays wide. The transfer of the Georgian style to the Maritimes was principally by way of Britain, whereas in Upper Canada there was a closer architectural link with the US. The earliest known appearance of a Georgian façade in Newfoundland was at Blenheim House [3.13] in Placentia, in 1786. Since there was relatively little American influence on the island colony, this is further evidence of the style's coming directly from the British Isles.

Documented Georgian houses in the Maritimes were almost all erected after 1800 (several in Upper Canada were earlier). A rare eighteenth-century example was Westcock, the residence of Amos Botsford, Speaker of the New Brunswick legislature, built in the Chignecto area in 1790. Covered with a hipped roof and having a small pediment-like gable over the entrance, it burned down many years ago. Another was the Naval Commissioner's house at Halifax, built in 1785. A fine frame Georgian house on Water Street in St Andrews has been

dated 1784; if the date is correct, the house would be a Maritime prototype by a recently arrived Loyalist immigrant.[118]

One of the best known of the many wooden Georgian houses in the Maritimes is the aptly named **Loyalist House [3.45]** at Union and German Streets in Saint John. It was built between 1810 and 1817 by David Daniel Merritt, who came with his parents to Saint John from Rye, New York, in 1783, when he was nineteen. The younger Merritt prospered as a merchant. The property remained in the Merritt family for 150 years and is now a museum. The façade has the now-familiar two storeys and five bays, with an arched fanlight over the front door, which is reached by a double staircase. The plan has a central hall, with a curved staircase, two parlours on one side, and the dining-room and kitchen on the other. Each of the public rooms has its own fireplace, with a restained wood mantel, under one of the four large chimneys placed within the outside walls. The interiors are decorated with delicate plasterwork displaying reeding and other classically derived motifs. The house is covered by a low hipped roof.[119]

Wood was also the most common material in early Prince Edward Island, although local red sandstone became popular towards mid-century.

3.45 Loyalist House, Saint John, New Brunswick, *c.* 1810-17. Photograph by Margaret Coleman, 1991. PC.

3.46 Belmont, Bird Island Creek, near East Royalty, Prince Edward Island, 1810. Photograph *c*. 1915. Public Archives and Records Office of Prince Edward Island/Acc. no. 3466/HF 73.373.68.

Belmont (1810), the house of the Honourable George Wright, the Surveyor General—at Bird Island Creek near East Royalty, overlooking the Hillsborough River—is a fine wood Georgian residence with a Palladian window over the entrance and nine-over-six-pane windows elsewhere, and a pilaster at either side of the façade [**3.46**].[120]

Despite the availability and affordability of wood, and the large number of skilled carpenters, stone was considered by society to be a more dignified, and therefore a more desirable, building material. Some builders attempted to satisfy fashion by painting wood to look like stone (as had often been

done in the US in the eighteenth century), particularly in status-conscious Halifax. One observer of Georgian Halifax noted that visitors to the city

> universally acclaimed its appearance, at least when they first viewed it from shipboard, and frequently after they landed—although they were disappointed to discover that the slate- tile- and shingle-roofed houses were only wood painted to look like freestone.[121]

Many old houses in Halifax have stone on the façade and the more common wood on the other three sides. In contrast, Kingston, Ontario, where limestone is commonplace, has a number of residences with showy wood façades and stone on the other three elevations.

Masonry predominated in the region around Chignecto Bay, the inlet off the Bay of Fundy that separates Nova Scotia from New Brunswick, and elsewhere when brick or stone was available, skilled masons were handy, and the owner was able to afford the expense. Many of Chignecto's settlers came from England, especially Yorkshire, a region where stone construction was prevalent. A fine Georgian house by one such squire is the **Keillor house** [**3.47**] at Dorchester, New Brunswick (1813), at the head of Chignecto Bay. It was built of stone with a truncated hipped roof and wings on the sides. The builder was a Yorkshireman, John Keillor, who had come to New Brunswick in 1774 at the age of fifteen, with his stonemason father, and rose to become Justice of the Peace. The cut-stone façade was probably placed over the earlier coursed rubble stonework, perhaps by John Keillor's son Thomas, who inherited the house in 1840.[122]

The most impressive urban Georgian house in the Maritimes is the **Black-Binney House** [**3.48**] in Halifax, built by the Honourable John Black, a leading merchant, a member of the legislative council, and president of the North British Society. He was the senior partner of Black, Forsythe and Company, a firm that represented Scottish merchants in the city. Some time between 1815 and 1819 he built for himself and his family this grand residence on Hollis Street, adjacent to Government House. It has the familiar five-bay façade, augmented by a low third storey below the eaves of the hipped roof, and with an attic storey illuminated by dormer windows. Massive chimneys with multiple flues rise above the eaves at either side. The front elevation is faced with granite ashlar from Aberdeenshire, Scotland, and the sides are built of

3.47 Keillor house, Dorchester, New Brunswick, 1813. Photograph by Harold Kalman.

local ironstone and Cumberland County sandstone. The handsome entrance, which is ornamented with side panels and an elaborate transom with delicate tracery, leads to the now-customary central hall and staircase.[123]

John Black would have looked out his window and seen Government House, a building whose central portion also has the five-bay composition of the Georgian house. He may well have coveted the office of its occupant and expressed this desire in his own house, which emulates the design of the official residence, although on a smaller scale.

Black died in 1823 at the age of 59. His house went on to aquire an impressive lineage of occupants. It was owned for a time by Black's son-in-law, James Boyle Uniacke, who was premier of Nova Scotia from 1848 to 1854, and then by the Right Reverend Hibbert Binney, Bishop of Nova Scotia. It later became a residence for the YWCA and then apartments. In 1965 the house was rehabilitated to serve as the headquarters of the Nova Scotia Division of the Canadian Corps of Commissionaires.

The Georgian house rapidly achieved a close association with the upper ranks of the Nova Scotia establishment. Its formal and well-proportioned composition expressed political authority and cultivated good taste. Most Georgian houses seem to have been built by new arrivals from Britain and not from the American colonies; the latter may have shown a preference for the Cape Cod cottage. (No study has been made of the correlation.) The reason may be more socio-economic than aesthetic, reflecting the fact that a large proportion of the Nova Scotians who achieved power and wealth were of British origin. However, many men of American descent who managed to gain high office and riches, such as Charles Prescott and David Merritt, also built Georgian houses.

The fully developed Palladian-Georgian house-type seen in the US and Britain, with the central bay highlighted as a columned classical frontispiece, rarely appeared in the Atlantic provinces. An exception is **Uniacke House [3.49]**, which has a decidedly American flavour. It was built in 1813-15 by Richard John Uniacke, one of whose sons would marry the daughter of John Black and take over his Halifax mansion. The elder Uniacke left his native Ireland in 1774, at the age of 21, and went to Philadelphia to seek his fortune. He worked as a trader in the Maritimes until his arrest in 1776—reportedly by John Keillor of Dorchester—as an American sympathizer. As he was being led to Hali-

3.48 Black-Binney House, Halifax, Nova Scotia, 1815-19. Photograph by A.W. Wallace, *c*. 1930s. NSM/76.116.47.

3.49 Uniacke House, Mount Uniacke, Nova Scotia, 1813-15. Photograph by Bob Anderson. Industry Science and Technology Canada.

fax for trial, Uniacke admired a beautiful vista with a lake. 'Here', he said, 'is where I shall have my home.' And so he would. Charges were dropped and Uniacke returned to Ireland to study law. Five years later he was back in Halifax, where he amassed considerable wealth and attained to a number of important political offices, including that of Attorney General.

Uniacke received a grant of 1,000 acres (400 hectares) some 30 miles (50 km) west of Halifax—at the spot where he had commented on the view—a property that he eventually extended to 11,800 acres (4,720 hectares) and named Mount Uniacke. In 1813, when he was 60, he began to build his grand country residence on the estate. The salient feature of the large wooden house is its classical portico, whose four posts rest on a broad veranda and rise two storeys to support a pediment. This temple front looks both forward and backward—it is ahead of its time in foreshadowing the Neo-Classical style of later decades (see page 299), yet is somewhat retardataire, since the source would seem to lie in the freestanding porticoes of the Palladians. The spindly proportions of the square (rather than round) columns and the curious semi-circular window in the pediment (which illuminates a room in the attic) possess a somewhat clumsy naïveté. Behind the portico lies a variant of the Georgian façade, in which the central bay is widened to allow three openings. The two extra

windows on the main floor are treated as sidelights and are enclosed within the shallow arch that surrounds the door. The roof behind the pediment was originally flat, surrounded by a railing.[124]

The grounds were fully developed. Uniacke cultivated some of the property and imported cattle to graze on the rest. He built barns, a coachhouse, a conservatory, and cottages for the workers. The old post road from Windsor to Halifax ran close to Mount Uniacke, making the estate a conspicuous landmark. Uniacke House remained in the family until 1949, when it was acquired by the province. It is now one of the many historic buildings operated by the Nova Scotia Museum.

Public buildings

The Georgian style and its classical forms lend themselves particularly well to public buildings. One initiator of the Georgian style in the Maritimes was HRH Prince Edward, the fourth son of George III—and the future father of Queen Victoria—who arrived in Halifax in 1794 to take command of the garrison. Prince Edward deplored 'the miserable state of all the Works and Public Buildings', and set out at 'very great exertion' to make the town more defensible and more attractive in a manner based

3.50 Prince's Lodge Rotunda, near Halifax, Nova Scotia, c. 1794. MMCH.

on the prevailing British royal taste.[125] His achievements during his short stay—he was in Halifax from 1794 to 1798 and again in 1799-1800, when he returned as Duke of Kent and Commander-in-Chief for British North America—were considerable. Most of his architectural work was military (see page 227), but he contributed non-military buildings as well.

Prince Edward's earliest designs were at Prince's Lodge, his Halifax home on Bedford Basin, 6 miles (10 km) from Halifax, lent to him by Governor John Wentworth. The Prince spent considerable effort and money developing the estate, improving the house, and designing a landscape on the Picturesque principles of the English landscape designer Lancelot 'Capability' Brown (1716-83). For four years he lived there in happiness with his mistress, Thérèse-Bernardine Mongenet (who called herself Julie de St-Laurent). The only surviving building is the **Prince's Lodge Rotunda** (or Music Pavilion, *c*. 1794), a circular classical temple surrounded by a colonnade and surmounted by a broad dome and a spherical finial [**3.50**]. The pavilion—which looks somewhat like a truncated version of Bramante's Tempietto in Rome (a Renaissance landmark built in 1502)—was inspired more directly by the circular Temples of Aeolus and Victory designed by Sir William Chambers (1723-96) and built between

3.51 Town Clock, Halifax, Nova Scotia, 1802-3. Photograph by Harold Kalman.

1757 and 1763 in Kew Gardens, near London, the royal park that Prince Edward had known as a child. He provided a direct transplant of a Palladian ornamental pavilion in an attempt to transform his Nova Scotia environment into a familiar British garden.[126]

As Duke of Kent he gave the citizens of Halifax a more public monument in the classical manner: the **Town Clock** (or Garrison Clock) on Citadel Hill [**3.51**]. The legislature had voted £50 for a public clock in 1761, but to no avail. Prince Edward ordered a large timepiece from Vuillamy, the royal clockmakers, and discussed the design of the clock tower with Captain William Fenwick, a Royal Engineer whom he had seconded for military work. The clock was not built until 1802-3, after the Prince's departure, to Fenwick's designs and under the supervision of architect Isaac Hildreth (1741-1807), but it surely reflects Prince Edward's intentions. The wooden structure is a multi-level affair: atop a square base, which provided a residence for the clock-keeper, rise a circular Doric colonnade, an octagonal stage supporting the four faces of the clock, an arcaded belfry, and a domed roof surmounted by a ball. Three 125-pound (57-kg) weights and a 12-foot (3.7-m) pendulum (which still operate faithfully) hang in the centre of the structure. Bramante's Tempietto again provided a point of departure, but it and other sources have been synthesized into a gem of colonial Georgian design. Bishop Plessis of Quebec praised the clock when he arrived in Halifax harbour in 1815: 'The most striking building is the one containing the public clock.' As architectural historian Alan Gowans has observed: '... its logical and orderly organization of forms expresses the spirit of men who felt that they controlled their environment as firmly and consistently as they controlled time with their clocks.'[127]

Governor John Wentworth praised Prince Edward's 'zeal and industry in the minutiae of tactics, architecture, and domestic economy', and evidently also agreed with his taste in buildings, because he showed similar, if grander, taste in the building of the third (and present) **Government House** [**3.52**] in Halifax. A member of a patrician family from New England, Wentworth had served as Governor of New Hampshire (as had his uncle and grandfather), gone to England during the American Revolution, and subsequently immigrated to Nova Scotia as a distinguished Loyalist. He succeeded John Parr as governor in 1792 and inherited as his residence the second Government

3.52 Government House, Halifax, Nova Scotia, begun 1800. Nova Scotia Supply and Services, Visual Communications.

House. Wentworth argued that the building had been quickly erected from green lumber and was in poor condition, and eventually convinced the legislature to authorize a new residence.[128]

The architect of the new Government House was Isaac Hildrith, a native of Yorkshire who in 1770 moved to Virginia, where he designed military defences at the outbreak of the Revolution. He spent part of the war years in England and Jamaica, and landed at Shelburne as a Loyalist in 1783. He designed Christ Church in Shelburne, and was involved in survey work for the proposed Shubenacadie Canal (see page 209) between Minas Basin and Halifax.[129]

Hildrith was appointed both architect and master builder of Government House, making this the first architect-designed building we have encountered in the Maritimes. The initial estimates were reviewed in 1799 and the cornerstone laid on 11 September 1800. Sir John and Lady Frances Wentworth moved into their new residence in 1805, but work continued for several years—as did problems about the rising costs of the building.

Government House combines a three-storey, five-bay, cut-stone central block (the now-familiar Georgian façade), having a rusticated and arcaded ground floor and fine ashlar above it, with a narrower two-storey wing at either side, their bowed projecting ends facing Barrington Street. The dignified elevation on the Hollis Street side (seen in the photograph—originally the principal entrance but now the garden side) features tall pilasters between the windows and a Doric portico above the curved entrance stairs. The roofs are hipped. The result is an impressive ensemble with a level of grandeur and sophistication that had not been seen before in the Maritime colonies. The sources of the design are found in Georgian Britain. Architectural historian Elizabeth Pacey has noted its similarity to the architecture of Yorkshire, which was home both to Wentworth's English relatives and to Hildrith—particularly houses such as Denison Hall (1786) in Leeds and the buildings of John Carr (1723-1807), the leading Yorkshire architect of the later eighteenth century—and she speculates that Wentworth may have procured plans through his family.[130]

A second, even grander, Halifax landmark was erected only a few years later: **Province House** (1811-19), the home of Nova Scotia's legislature and now Canada's oldest seat of government [**3.53**]. Charles Dickens called it 'a gem of Georgian Architecture' when he visited Halifax in 1842.[131] Province House is as close as Canadian architecture came to a classic Palladian-Georgian design, particularly the version of Palladianism seen in England in the second half of the eighteenth century. The design and construction were directed by a take-charge committee of the legislature. The records indicate that painting contractor John Merrick (*c.* 1756-1829) produced the designs and that masonry contractor Richard Scott (who is named in the cornerstone as the architect) provided supervision; however, neither had prior experience on a building of this scale. Merrick may have delivered a design that had been procured in England; this is

3.53 Province House, Halifax, Nova Scotia, 1811-19. Drawn and engraved by Charles W. Torbett, [1829]. From T.C. Haliburton, *An Historical and Statistical Account of Nova Scotia*, Volume 2 (1829), NAC/C-108970.

supported by a report that in 1798-9 a legislative committee purchased in London 'Plans, Sections &c for the State House and Government House.'[132]

Province House presents a 140-foot-long (42.7-m) elevation of Wallace sandstone on each of its sides. The taller Hollis Street elevation resembles the time-honoured Palladian country-house façade, with a rusticated ground floor serving as a base for the two smoothly finished upper storeys and projecting at the centre to support a columned-and-pedimented Ionic portico. On the Granville Street side, where the grade is higher, the column bases are closer to the ground, producing a more urbane and public appearance. On both façades the emphasis placed on the end bays—by the projection, the pilasters, and the pediments—is more characteristic of British architecture after 1750 than of the earlier work of Lord Burlington's circle. Province House shares design principles with Wardour Castle, Wiltshire, designed by James Paine (1717-89) and built in 1770-6, although the two are quite different in their details. The public rooms inside are magnificently finished in orna-

3.54 Province House, Charlottetown, Prince Edward Island, 1843-8. Photograph by Ted Grant, 1972. Canadian Museum of Contemporary Photography/NFB Collection/72-1723.

mented plasterwork inspired by the exquisite decorative work of Scottish architects Robert and James Adam.

Government House and Province House forged the link between Georgian architecture and government authority. The official British classical style was perpetuated in military and public buildings in Halifax and the other Maritime capitals, including Admiralty House in Halifax (1814-19), the Barracks in Fredericton (c. 1824-7), and the Commissariat (1818-19) and Government House (1827-31) in St John's, all designed or executed by the Royal Engineers; the first Province House in Fredericton (built by R. Smith and F. McBeath, 1802; destroyed by fire in 1880); Government House in Charlottetown (Isaac Smith, 1832); and the somewhat later Colonial Building (1846-50) in St John's. It was used as well for countless courthouses. A prolific exponent of this style was architect John Elliott Woolford (1788-1866) of Fredericton, who gave that city its Government House (1826-8) and King's College (1826-9, now the Arts Building at the University of New Brunswick) and also designed York County Gaol in Fredericton (1830).[133]

The most elegant Georgian public building in the Maritimes is **Province House [3.54]** on Queen Square in Charlottetown (1843-8), designed by Yorkshire-born architect Isaac Smith, the leading Island architect of the time. Originally called the Colonial Building, it was the scene of the Charlottetown Conference of 1864 that led to Confederation. It replaced the earlier (1811) Legislative Building and Courthouse (at the right in **3.26**) by John Plaw, which had a gable end to the street and a low wing on either side. Although it sported some classical ornament, Plaw's building differed from its successor and from other Georgian buildings we have seen, having been built before the style became *de rigueur* for the public edifices of the Maritime colonies.[134]

Churches

Many churches were built in Nova Scotia during the Loyalist period, and a fine selection of early religious buildings survives. Both the Church of England and the nonconformists continued to attract their share of adherents. In the period before the American Revolution, as we have seen, each had a distinctive form for its houses of worship: the Anglican Church used the traditional British longitudinal plan and a tower, as at St Paul's, Halifax; whereas the Congregationalists and other dissenters preferred the plain American meeting-house form, as at Barrington. In the last decades of the eighteenth century, the church and the meeting house began to lose their distinct architectural identities, reflecting the integration of the two founding English-speaking communities.

3.55 St Mary's Anglican Church, Auburn, Nova Scotia, 1790. Photograph by Twila L. Robar-De Coste.

St Mary's Anglican Church [3.55] at Auburn, Nova Scotia, is an exquisite little frame church built in 1790 by a Loyalist congregation in the Annapolis Valley. The residents of the community included the Right Reverend Charles Inglis, the first Bishop of Nova Scotia, who praised St Mary's as 'the neatest, best finished church in the province.' The church has the traditional Anglican plan, with its entrance in the west end through the base of the belltower, a nave 37 feet (11.3 m) long (the side galleries were built in 1826), and a chancel opposite the door. The various elements are similar to, but far simpler than, those of St Paul's in Halifax. The panelled front door displays the high-quality craftsmanship that is characteristic of the whole building. It is framed by a classical pediment and pilasters with a profusion of delicate mouldings. The motif of the round arch and keystone is carried around the building in the tall windows and the Palladian window at the east end, which was retained when the chancel was enlarged in 1890.[135]

William Matthews, who was not from the Auburn area, built the church with the assistance of three local workmen. Lumber came from a nearby stand of pine trees; the frame was hewn and the clapboards and shingles whip-sawed on the site. The frames for the doors and windows, and the nails, were brought from Halifax, and lime for the plaster came from Saint John.

Around 1797 at Clementsport, about 45 miles (72 km) to the west, an Anglican Loyalist community of English and Dutch descent built **St Edward's Church** [3.56]. This unique fusion of the church and meeting-house has two doors: one in the west end, beneath the small belfry; the other in the middle of the broad south side, as in the Meeting House at Barrington. The chancel identifies the building as an Anglican church.[136]

The **Old Covenanters' Church** [3.57] at Grand Pré, Nova Scotia, was built by members of a Congregationalist sect from New England who accepted an Irish Presbyterian, the Reverend James Murdoch, as their minister. It replaced an earlier log church that had been constructed about 1767. As built in 1804-11, it had a pure meeting-house form, with the entrance located on the broad side. Traditional box pews fill the ground floor. Across

3.56 Old St Edward's Church, Clementsport, Nova Scotia, *c*. 1797. Photograph by John Lavers.

from the door stands the original three-tiered pulpit with its large acoustic sounding board [**3.57**]. The front elevation, five bays wide with two rows of elegant small-paned windows, looks like a Georgian house of the day. A belltower was added at one end in 1818—tradition says that it was done to compete with the new house of worship built by the local Methodists—radically changing the building's appearance and making it look from a distance much like a conventional church.[137]

As the nineteenth century progressed, the architectural forms of the various denominations grew even closer, and eventually merged. The North West Range Meeting House at North West, four miles from Lunenburg, was built for Baptist worship in 1818-20 on an oblong plan similar in proportion to that of the Old Covenanters' Church, and with two tiers of windows on the broad side. The entrance, however, was in a narrow side, and the pews faced the opposite end, where the pulpit and elders' chairs were located.[138]

3.57 Old Covenanters' Church, Grand Pré, Nova Scotia, 1804-11. Photograph by Gauvin and Gentzel, 1933. NSM/33.73.

3.58 Interior of Old Covenanters' Church, Grand Pré, Nova Scotia, 1804-11. Photograph 1933. PANS.

3.59 St George's Church, Halifax, 1800-1 (the Round Church). Copyright Heritage Recording Services, PC 1993.

Mention should also be made of **St George's Church** in Halifax, better known as the 'Round Church' [**3.59**]. Built in 1800-1 for the German congregation that had worshipped in the Little Dutch Church, St George's was erected under the personal sponsorship of the Duke of Kent, who wanted it to accommodate the troops from the garrison as well as its regular worshippers. He obtained funds and commissioned plans from naval builder William Hughes, who may have been assisted by John Merrick. Its circular nave, with a gallery running around 270 degrees of the circle and a cupola on the outside, is unique in Canada and represents one more effort by Prince Edward,

Duke of Kent, to introduce classical geometric forms to Halifax.[139]

From the classic formality of the Georgian style adopted by the power élite, to the unaffected responses to everyday needs expressed by the vernacular building-types of the working and middle classes, the Atlantic colonies developed a distinctive Anglo-Canadian architecture. Based on British architectural traditions, but learned in part through the intermediary of American forms and techniques, the designs of these buildings met the needs of the Canadian environment, both social and physical. A parallel situation was occurring in Upper Canada, where an architecture was being produced that had many general similarities but was distinguished by a number of regional differences.

138

CHAPTER 4

CLASSICISM IN UPPER AND LOWER CANADA

AN ESTIMATED 7,000 Loyalists left the United States for Canada by crossing the frontier from upstate New York and western Pennsylvania into portions of today's Ontario and Quebec. Some were refugees who lost their homes with the signing of the Treaty of Paris; others were members of Loyalist corps that had fought in New York State. Many had been farmers before the war. Disbanded army units were kept together, as were the various ethnic groups. Many Mohawks who had remained loyal to the Crown, and whose land had been bartered away to the Americans, followed their chief, Joseph Brant, to settle on a large tract of land granted to them on the Grand River (in southwestern Ontario). Other Loyalists moved to the Niagara peninsula and to the area around today's Windsor.

The new arrivals comprised a vocal English-speaking minority in what was then the large province of Quebec. A series of petitions for self-rule resulted in the Constitutional Act of 1791, which created the provinces of Lower Canada (Quebec) and Upper Canada (Ontario), separated by the Ottawa River. As Upper Canada was essentially empty, the settlers had to clear the land for agriculture, lay out new towns, and form new communities.

The new Upper Canadians who became leaders of the province first built in a manner similar to that of the Atlantic Provinces. Soon, however, their architecture developed a more consistent and rigorous version of Georgian Classicism, because they found this style to be an effective and appropriate way to articulate for the young province an image that conveyed self-confidence and control, and that declared loyalty to the British Crown and British values.

Georgian Classicism is 'classical' in its relationship to the architecture of classical antiquity (ancient Greece and Rome); it is 'Georgian' because its way of maintaining that relationship was through the architecture of post-Renaissance Italy, as it was interpreted in the Britain of the Georges. The essence of the style is its regularity and symmetry, achieved with the judicious use of classical ornament. Georgian buildings exhibit calm, order, and good taste—just as the authors of the British North America Act would later decree that Canada should be characterized by peace, order, and good government. The design of Georgian buildings (and also of towns) is inherently logical and self-contained, consistent with Alexander Pope's statement that art is 'nature improved'. Everything has its place, and that place is determined by reason; nothing should look as if it happened by accident. Building materials were simply a means of achieving those ends. The natural patterns of the textures of materials were often concealed, or disguised, to produce the finished effect that was sought.

The Georgian architect's method was to follow tradition, to borrow from the past whatever might be seen as good; originality for its own sake was not encouraged. Canada was a young country, barely into its adolescence, and it welcomed the architectural hand-me-downs of its big brother to the south and its parent across the sea. Although the government of Upper Canada discouraged American republican social and political practices, the version of Georgian in that province—ironically—was more indebted to high-style building (particularly pre-Revolutionary architecture) in the new United States than in Nova Scotia and New Brunswick, partly because proportionately more Upper Canadians came from the US, and partly because they lacked the Maritimers' Puritan streak, and could therefore interpret classical architecture in a more literal and showy manner.

Even the simpler vernacular buildings of the majority, who were not in a position of wealth or authority, reflected the classicism of the ruling class. Symmetry, order, and decorum became the universal architectural values of the day.

Those Loyalists who settled in the cities of Lower Canada, and in its Eastern Townships south of the St Lawrence, joined the French-speaking people of that established province. But many of them quickly achieved a disproportionately dominant political and economic presence, which they expressed in the conspicuous Englishness of their buildings. Their classicism was so appealing that its principles were eventually adopted by the leading francophone architects.

This chapter describes, first, the architecture of Upper Canada, from its beginnings in the 1780s through the first third of the nineteenth century; then the buildings of the small, but powerful, English-speaking population of Lower Canada; and concludes by looking at their influence on the architecture of the French-speaking majority.

Upper Canada

The land survey

Sir Frederick Haldimand, governor of Quebec at the end of the American Revolution, made sound arrangements to accommodate the new arrivals. In May 1783 he dispatched Surveyor General Samuel Holland to examine the territory along the north shores of the western St Lawrence River and Lake Ontario—good land that was virtually unpopulated and would provide a strategic buffer against American aggression. Natives had mostly abandoned the region after the Iroquois wars, and Europeans used it only as a springboard to the interior.[1]

Holland developed a system of rapid surveys to form townships in anticipation of the massive immigration. He created eight 'Royal Townships' along the St Lawrence and five 'Cataraqui Townships' along the water around today's Kingston and Bay of Quinte. In Haldimand's mind, these formed an extension of the seigneurial system, and he instructed Holland to form 'distinct Seigneuries or Fiefs', with lands allotted to settlers according to their status and rank.[2]

In 1789 Lord Dorchester (formerly Sir Guy Carleton)—the new governor of Quebec—responded to the continued immigration by issuing regulations for surveying additional townships. He provided models for two highly structured types: 'water townships' along navigable waterways and 'inland townships'. The latter were remarkable because they imposed an ideal plan on the landscape without reference to natural geographical features—much as Jean Talon had done with his unsuccessful town plots of a century earlier—and provided a powerful symbol of European imperialism in the New World. The inland townships were to be 10 miles (16 km) square, with a public square at the centre, surrounded successively by one-acre (0.4-hectare) building lots, a 'town reserve', a 'town park' with pasture land and gardens, and finally farm lots of 200 acres (80 hectares). Lord Dorchester's scheme was unworkable because, as urban-historian John van Nostrand has noted, 'the ideal township was, on the one hand, not ideal enough to complete its conquest of nature, and, on the other, too ideal to allow for its practical application.'[3]

A revised **land survey system [4.1]** was created in 1792 by the new acting deputy surveyor general, David William Smith, for the first Lieutenant Governor of Upper Canada, John Graves Simcoe. A rigid churchman and military officer, Simcoe promoted British institutions, disallowed the establishment of town meetings modelled on the New England experience, and strove to 'inculcate British Customs, Manners, & Principles in the most trivial, as well as serious matters.'[4] In his survey Smith devised what has come to be known as the 'chequered plan', in which townships were 9 miles (14.4 km) wide and 12 miles (19.2 km) deep, each with fourteen 'concessions' of twenty-four 200-acre (80-hectare) lots. Within the twenty-four lots were scattered seven that were reserved for the Crown and the clergy. This provided large blocks that could be sold to important landowners, yet ensured that government control was retained throughout the township. Used with only minor variations throughout Upper Canada, the system has been charged with encouraging the growth of a ruling oligarchy—which came to be called the Family Compact—and, in turn, stimulating a kind of class system in building.[5]

The first towns

The earliest buildings were erected for expediency and not for show, providing shelter with local materials that were used in a straightforward and unornamented manner. Within a generation, however, when the newcomers were securely settled in their new country, their confidence and aspirations rose. Upper Canadians who were in a position of

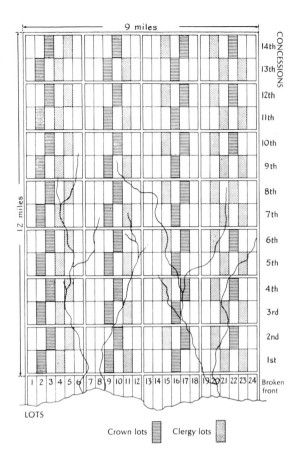

9 miles

12 miles

CONCESSIONS

14th
13th
12th
11th
10th
9th
8th
7th
6th
5th
4th
3rd
2nd
1st
Broken front

| 1 | 2 | 3 | 4 | 5 | 6 | 7 | 8 | 9 | 10 | 11 | 12 | 13 | 14 | 15 | 16 | 17 | 18 | 19 | 20 | 21 | 22 | 23 | 24 |

LOTS

Crown lots   Clergy lots

4.1 A diagram of D.W. Smith's 'chequered plan' for the land survey, showing the lots reserved for the Crown and the clergy, 1792. Drawing by Courtney C.J. Bond. From Gerald Craig, *Upper Canada* (1963).

power now began to exploit architecture as a vehicle for expressing their increasing wealth and sophistication. They came to see their first-generation structures as being too plain and utilitarian, and demanded a new, more refined style of building that would express their cultural and political values. Georgian Classicism proved to be the perfect medium for this.

By the end of the eighteenth century, three towns on Lake Ontario had become dominant: Kingston, at the eastern end of the lake; Newark (now Niagara-on-the-Lake), situated where the Niagara River flows into the lake; and York (present-day Toronto), across the lake from Newark. Kingston quickly became an important commercial and military base. Newark was made the first capital of Upper Canada in 1792 and consequently attracted

residents (and builders) of considerable stature and talent. Two years later, however, Governor Simcoe moved the capital to York, and that town soon surpassed the others in size and importance, ultimately becoming the dominant city in Upper Canada. Newark was burned by the retreating American army in 1813 and all of its original buildings were destroyed. The town was rebuilt, but its political role had been assumed by York and its commercial importance was soon diminished by the construction of the Welland Canal, which created a navigable bypass around Niagara Falls. With its many fine early-nineteenth-century buildings, Niagara-on-the-Lake flourishes today as a tourist mecca that is not only close to Niagara Falls but has been culturally enriched by the Shaw Festival.

A selection of early buildings in Kingston provides an introduction to the development of Upper Canada's architecture. Houses in Newark and York are included in the discussion of domestic architecture that follows.

Kingston   In his land survey of the St Lawrence front, Samuel Holland was particularly enthusiastic about the prospects of Cataraqui (later to be renamed King's Town), located next to the ruins of the French Fort Frontenac. He told Haldimand that its grounds 'will cover a Sufficient space for a Town, the harbour is in every respect Good, and most conveniently situated to command Lake Ontario.'[6] This area received a further boost when, in July 1783, Sir Guy Carleton urged Haldimand to settle at Cataraqui a group of Loyalist refugees who were about to leave New York City. A townsite was surveyed by Deputy Surveyor General John Collins in October. The familiar gridiron plan was gored to accommodate the curved waterfront, with a wedge-shaped space between the two grids reserved for the public common and marketplace.

The first buildings were those erected for military personnel and some private houses that were brought to Kingston by raft from Carleton Island, 10 miles (16 km) to the southeast, much as St Andrews' first buildings were floated there from Castine. At least three, and likely five, of these timber-framed transported houses, all of them built by 1783, survived into the twentieth century. One remains, although much obscured by later alterations: the William Coffin house at Gore and King Streets, a $1\frac{1}{2}$-storey cottage with a gable roof, dormers, and a chimney at each side. Its appearance in 1834 is known from a watercolour made by Harriet Dobbs Cartwright. The **Nathaniel Lines house**

4.2 Lines house, Kingston, Ontario, *c*. 1783. Photograph by Fern E. Graham, 1983.

[**4.2**] at Earl and Ontario Streets was better preserved, but it was destroyed by arson in 1988, shortly after having been moved to 'safety'. A photograph taken five years earlier shows it as two joined $1\frac{1}{2}$-storey cottages, each with an off-centre entrance and end chimneys. The left-hand (western) portion, with its shed dormer windows, was believed to have been original; the other half may have been built at the same time or slightly later. The house had been re-faced with modern siding. Although its structure was not investigated, another house in this group, the Simcoe house (demolished early in this century), was reported to have been built 'with internal beams and struts like a barn. Between the struts it was insulated with rubble and lime, a typical form of early construction'—that is, half-timber or *colombage* construction. Both are similar in their general form to the Cape Cod cottage [**3.38**], although they display significant regional differences in that the eaves of the Ontario houses were several feet (nearly a metre) higher than the tops of the windows, and they have end rather than central chimneys.[7]

0   20 feet

0   5 metres

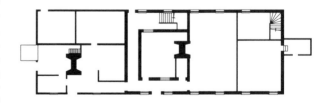

4.3 Plans of the Cartwright house, Kingston, Ontario, *c*. 1784. Drawing by David Byrnes, after a drawing by Captain M.C. Dixon, R.E. (1815) in the NAC/NMC5128.

142

A surviving plan for the **Cartwright house [4.3]** in Kingston, which may have been built as early as 1784, shows the utilitarian nature of the first buildings and their indifference to formality or symmetry. This was almost certainly the home of the Honourable Richard Cartwright, an Albany-born merchant who subsequently served on the Legislative Council and as a military officer. The plan consists of a single range of rooms with circulation spaces arranged in a seemingly haphazard way. The entrance to the principal two-storey block opens onto a narrow corridor that leads to two living-rooms on the right, a smaller room (possibly Cartwright's office) ahead, and to a staircase around to the left. Six bedrooms of varying sizes are situated upstairs. The one-storey block to the left appears to be a small attached cottage. Cartwright later recalled (through romantic eyes) the primitive conditions that existed in 1784, when he built his first Kingston house, at a time when 'this province was...a howling wilderness'. He maintained that there had been nothing 'except the movable hut of the wandering savage', and 'the solitary establishment of the trader in furs.'[8]

At the end of the eighteenth century, the duc de La Rochefoucauld-Liancourt noted somewhat scornfully that none of Kingston's buildings was more distinguished than the next, and that

> considered as a town, [it] is much inferior to Newark .... Kingston may contain a few more buildings, but they are neither so large nor so good as at Newark. Many of them are log-houses, and those which consist of joiner's work, are badly constructed and painted ....
>
> The houses...are built of wood, for reasons which it is extremely difficult to discern. The town is seated on rocky ground; and not the smallest house can be built without the foundation being excavated in a rock, a sort of stone which affords the twofold advantage of being easily cut, and of growing hard, when exposed to the air, without cracking in the frost. The inhabitants allow that, if bricklayers were procured even from Montreal (for there are none in this place), building with stone would be less expensive than with wood. They grant that, in addition to the greater solidity of such buildings, they would afford more warmth in winter, and more coolness in summer.[9]

Masons who could work with the excellent blue-grey limestone on which Kingston sits had indeed arrived. In 1792, shortly before La Rochefoucauld's visit, Elizabeth Simcoe, the wife of the new Lieutenant Governor, noted that Kingston 'is a small town of about fifty wooden houses and merchants' storehouses. Only one house is built of stone. It belongs to a merchant.'[10] This first of the stone buildings that have made Kingston so distinctive was a $2\frac{1}{2}$-storey **house and store for John Cumming and Peter Smith [4.4]**, built in 1792. A pho-

4.4 Cumming and Smith house and store, Kingston, Ontario, 1792. MTRL/John Ross Robertson Collection/T15308.

tograph taken early in the twentieth century, by which time the building had been somewhat altered, shows an undecorated structure with a steep gabled roof and an asymmetrical five-bay façade facing Ontario Street and the harbour. The high pitch of the roof and the dormer windows reflect current French practice, and suggest the presence of a French-Canadian work-force—a situation that was recommended by La Rochefoucauld and is supported by the knowledge that tradesmen from Montreal (as well as some from Niagara) were sent to Cataraqui in 1783.[11]

By the first decades of the nineteenth century, stone construction became the rule rather than the exception in Kingston, and the Georgian style provided the characteristic design vocabulary. The plain buildings of a generation earlier were no longer acceptable to increasingly sophisticated tastes. The new classical flavour of the growing city is seen in a **view along King Street** [4.5], drawn in 1829 by James Pattison Cockburn. In the left fore-

4.5 King Street, Kingston, Ontario. Drawing by James Pattison Cockburn, 1829. Collection of the Agnes Etherington Art Centre, Queen's University. Gift of Chancellor Agnes Benidickson, 1987.

ground is St George's Anglican Church, a stone structure that was built in 1825-7 to designs by Thomas Rogers (1778/82-1853), an English-born and -trained architect who settled in Kingston and maintained an active practice both there and in York. Rogers' church replaced a wooden church of the same name that had been erected nearby in 1791-2 by carpenter Archibald Thomson (seen here in a somewhat romanticized watercolour sketch). Characteristic of buildings by and for newly arrived Loyalists, the earlier **St George's** [4.6] was a straightforward, yet well-proportioned, gable-roofed structure, 40 by 32 feet (12.2 by 9.8 m), with a belfry and spire rising over the east end. In its proportion and handling it resembles St Edward's [3.56] at Clementsport, NS, although St George's had two tiers of windows, not one. As the young Kingston society matured, however, its church was soon perceived as being inadequate. The ever-critical La Rochefoucauld sneered that it 'resembles a barn more than a church', and Bishop Jacob Mountain described it in 1813 as a 'long low, blue wooden building, with square windows, and a little cupola or steeple, for the bell, like the thing on a brewery placed at the wrong end of the building.'

4.6 Reconstructed view of St George's Church, Kingston, Ontario, 1791-2. Watercolour, 19th century. From a negative at Queen's University Archives/PG-K, 65-1. Original at the Anglican Diocese of Ontario.

The parishioners, for their part, wanted a new church of 'more convenient dimensions and more durable materials'.[12]

The outcome was the church seen in Cockburn's watercolour. Five bays long and built of Kingston limestone, it is distinguished by a tall entrance tower that rises in several diminishing stages to an arched belfry. The pilasters at the corners of the upper tiers, the rusticated treatment of the wall around the doorway, the graceful arched windows of the nave, and the cut-stone window surrounds combine to produce a new level of classical elegance (although less so than the Ionic portico that Rogers initially proposed and that was rejected by the building committee).[13] Even this church soon became inadequate for the congregation, and it was enlarged at intervals through the nineteenth century, culminating in the work of architect Joseph Power (1848-1925) that produced the large, domed St George's Cathedral of today.

Beyond St George's in Cockburn's watercolour, further north on King Street, is seen the **Courthouse** (1823-6), which was built to designs by John Leigh Okill. Traveller James Buckingham described it in 1843:

Among the public buildings, the Court House is the most prominent. It stands near the centre of town, opposite to the principal hotel, and within a few yards of the English church. The Court House has a front of about 100 feet, a depth of 200 feet, and is about 60 feet in height. The front has a pediment, above and behind which rises an octagonal tower, with lantern and cupola, to a height of from 60 to 70 feet above the road, making the whose elevation, with the terminating spire, about 150 feet. The interior is spacious and well arranged; and on the upper floor is one of the best fitted Court-rooms in the province. The Town Jail is in the rear of this Court House.[14]

Chief Justice William Campbell considered it to be the finest building of its kind in Upper Canada. (His own house in York [**4.20**] shared many of its features.) The layout is known through floor plans prepared by Rogers in 1839. The Courthouse was demolished in 1855; the site was used for the present Customs House.[15]

The hotel that Buckingham mentioned is the tall gable-roofed building seen on the other (east) side of King Street in Cockburn's watercolour. Built in 1807 as Edward and Robert Walker's Hotel, and later known as Daley's and then the British-American, it accommodated many distinguished visitors to Kingston, including Charles Dickens in 1842.[16] The three small houses on the right are remnants of early Kingston that seem entirely out of scale with the newer, grander structures. Those beyond the Courthouse and hotel, closer to the city core, are newer and larger residential and commercial buildings, two and three storeys high. Some have end gables with chimneys in them, others hipped roofs with internal chimneys; all were certainly built of limestone.

Kingston's prosperity was based on its economic role as a trans-shipment point, and on being a military garrison. When Lord Sydenham (Charles Poulett Thomson) undertook to carry out the recommendations of the Durham Report in 1841, he chose Kingston as the first capital of the united Upper and Lower Canada. Kingston's brief moment on the national stage, when it served as the capital for only three years, led to a new wave of development. Some of the impressive public buildings of that era will be discussed below.

Domestic architecture

In towns and in the countryside throughout the new province, both Loyalists and Britons made Georgian Classicism the dominant manner for the houses of the landed gentry. People without wealth and power built and lived more simply, some in log houses and others in dwellings of frame, brick, or stone; the most characteristic features of Georgian design, however, filtered down into the vernacular and affected modest housing as well. This section looks at the different kinds of houses that were common in Upper Canada in the first half of the nineteenth century.

Georgian houses The Georgian style arrived in Upper Canada—as it did in Nova Scotia and New Brunswick—simultaneously from the US and Britain at a time when it was already old-fashioned in both of those places. An important prototype was the wood-frame **D.W. Smith house** (*c*. 1794) at Newark (Niagara-on-the-Lake); as David William Smith was a draftsman (he became Surveyor General of Upper Canada in 1798), he likely designed it himself. When compared with the Cartwright house, it shows the greater maturity occasioned by the intervening decade and the more sophisticated milieu of the capital. Smith, a British-born army officer, was posted to North America in 1790 and soon resigned from the military to enter the civil service and then the political arena as a trusted subordinate of Simcoe. He gained a seat on the Executive Council and he

and his family then accumulated more than 20,000 acres (8,000 hectares) of choice land in 21 townships—a striking example of how the survey system (of which he had been in charge) benefited people who controlled policy and patronage—and who would later be known, by such opponents as William Lyon Mackenzie, as members of the Family Compact.[17]

The Smith house was burned in 1813, but drawings [4.7] prepared by Captain Robert Pilkington of the Royal Engineers in 1798 (when Smith left Newark to go to York and put the house up for sale) show a fully developed Georgian plan and elevation, similar to many seen in the American colonies before the Revolution and in the Maritimes after it. Forty by eighty feet (12.2 by 24.4 m), the plan features a central staircase hall that leads to a pair of rooms on either side on the ground floor, and to one large and two smaller bedrooms upstairs. Each room was heated by a fireplace, and the chimneys rise within the exterior walls of the main block. Balanced wings at either side share the ground-floor chimneys. The rigidly symmetrical elevation has the familiar five bays and two storeys. Classical detail is applied liberally: a pedimented Ionic porch stands before the entrance, the windows have Roman surrounds, and giant pilasters at either side support a dentilled cornice. The gabled roof is truncated to provide a deck with railings. La Rochefoucauld wrote:

> In point of size and elegance the house of Colonel Smith...is much distinguished from the rest. It consists of joiner's work, but is constructed, embellished, and painted in the best style; the yard, garden, and court are surrounded with railings made and painted as elegantly as they could be in England. His large garden kept in good order.

The 'large garden' made up only a small part of the 4-acre (1.6-hectare) lot, which was formally planted with trees and parterres. Without any doubt, Smith had achieved the image of English prosperity that was expected of the leaders of the young province.[18]

A similar design is rendered in stone at **Homewood** [4.8] in Maitland, a small community in the Royal Townships on the St Lawrence River, about halfway between Kingston and Cornwall. It was

4.7 (*opposite*) Plans and elevation of the D.W. Smith House, Newark (Niagara-on-the-Lake, Ontario), *c*. 1794. MTRL/D.W. Smith Papers/B15-39.

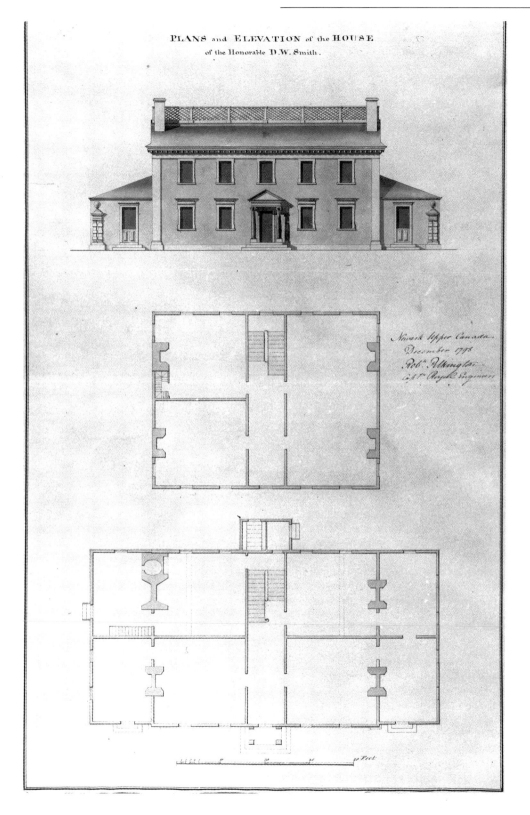

PLANS and ELEVATION of the HOUSE
of the Honorable D.W. Smith.

4.8 Homewood, Maitland, Ontario, 1800-01. Ontario Heritage Foundation.

built in 1800-1 for Dr Solomon Jones, who was born in Connecticut, studied medicine in Albany, and fought in the Loyalist forces under Sir John Johnson during the American Revolution. The reward for his service was a 500-acre (200-hectare) grant. He built a log dwelling in which he and his growing family lived until he was ready to build this handsome stone house some fifteen years later.[19]

It was built by Louis Brillière, a master mason from Montreal. French-Canadian influence is seen in the steep gabled roof and the use of random fieldstone. Otherwise it is thoroughly Anglo-American in its proportions and detail. The central bay is emphasized by its greater width and by the treatment of the door and upper window. Both openings are broadened with vertical sidelights (possibly the earliest surviving doorway whose sidelights are original), and a small rectangular transom lies over the door. A small porch originally stood before the entrance (the columned portico is new). The windows are finely crafted double-hung sashes with twelve small panes in each sash. The central hall—used by the Joneses as a dining-hall, because one of the two principal rooms served as the doc-

tor's surgery—extends just over half the depth of the house, and the staircase is enclosed within partitions. The wing at the left is an addition of the 1920s or 1940s. The house was purchased by the Ontario Heritage Foundation in 1974. An earlier house, and one of few eighteenth-century survivors, supports the notion that the steeply gabled roof was common, if not prevalent, in the early permanent buildings of the Loyalists. This is the **White House [4.9]** near Amherstview, just west of Kingston, built in 1793 by Loyalist William Fairfield. Here the steep roof flares out at the eave to cover a two-tiered veranda across the five-bay façade. Both the roof and the gallery are characteristic of Quebec, but in this case there is no documentation to support the presence of a French-Canadian (or any other) builder, and it would be imprudent to jump to such a conclusion. The White House has a wood frame, with the space between the studs filled with rubble brick and stone—a survival of either the nogging of New England or the *colombage* of New France—and the walls are covered with horizontal clapboard siding, which Fairfield knew well from his native Vermont.[20]

In the early nineteenth century, after the initial Loyalist influx was over, and in a period when immigration was mainly from Britain, roofs be-

4.9 The White House, near Amherstview, Ontario, 1793. Photograph by Ralph Greenhill.

4.10 Fraserfield, the Alexander Fraser house at Fraserfield, Ontario, *c*. 1812. HWS/SSS/92 WN RS 1.02.

came lower in pitch, and usually hipped in form. This is the case at **Fraserfield** [**4.10**], an imposing house that was probably begun about 1812 by Colonel Alexander Fraser, a Scottish-born officer who served in the Canadian Fencibles during the war and received a grant of land near Williamstown in Glengarry County. He was elected to the Legislative Assembly and was later appointed to the Legislative Council. The house has a main block flanked by a pair of wings, with a hipped roof and a cupola—the last an uncommon feature in English Canada, although it is often found in Britain and the US. The walls were built of rubble stone, plastered and grooved to imitate cut stone. A wide veranda once stood in front of the main block (it has been replaced by a small portico), and cut-stone quoins emphasize the corners.[21]

William Thomson, who had arrived almost penniless with his family from Roxboroughshire, near Edinburgh, in 1817 and settled down to farm a 360-acre (144-hectare) grant of land, built the austerely beautiful **Maplelawn** (*c*. 1831-4) on the Richmond

149

Road in Ottawa (then a part of Nepean Township). The house [**4.11**] has similar proportions to Fraserfield, although without the cupola or wings. Maplelawn offers a perfect statement of Canadian Georgian taste—a full century after the Palladian style appeared in Britain, and a half-century after it fell out of popularity both there and in the US. Trying, perhaps unconsciously, to recreate the order and ambience of their Scottish homeland, new Canadians like Thomson clung to a familiar architectural style. The coursed limestone walls of his house feature quoins and a simple belt-course below the ground floor. The recessed doorway has sidelights and a graceful elliptical fanlight, features that by now were common in Upper Canada, particularly in the Ottawa valley. The windows are twelve-pane casements, a type more popular in Quebec than Ontario, with interior shutters that are stored within the finely crafted casings. The well-preserved interior has finely crafted woodwork throughout. The house, and its walled perennial garden, have a secure future in the custody of the National Capital Commission.[22]

Although the last two houses were built by Scots

4.11 Maplelawn, Ottawa, Ontario, *c*. 1831-4. Photograph (1980) courtesy Public Works Canada, Heritage Recording and Technical Data Services. Original with CIHB/06107011900529.

4.12 Fort Johnson, near Amsterdam, New York, 1763. Historic American Buildings Survey/NY-29-FORJO 30-1-10. From the Collection of the Library of Congress.

rather than Americans, it would be simplistic to suggest that the hipped roofs merely indicated the Scottish origins of the owners or builders. Houses of all immigrant groups were lower in profile now than earlier, reflecting increasingly classical tastes and the larger number of Scottish and English masons in the work-force. Loyalists as well as Scots were familiar with low hipped roofs, which had been used widely in American buildings since pre-Revolutionary times. Sir John Johnson—the commander of a Loyalist regiment and subsequently a British government official who helped to settle Loyalists in the St Lawrence valley—had two such Georgian houses in his family before the Revolution: **Fort Johnson** (1749), a stone building [**4.12**] near Amsterdam, New York, where he was raised; and Johnson Hall (1763) in Johnstown, New York, a wood house finished to imitate stone, to which he moved in 1774 after the death of his father, Sir William Johnson. (A third family home, Mount Johnson, no longer stands.) Fort Johnson is very much like Maplelawn and countless other houses built in Upper Canada during the first third of the nineteenth century. Johnson himself built two

similar residences in Lower Canada, one at St-André d'Argenteuil (in the seigneury that he was granted) and one at St-Mathias de Rouville.[23]

York quickly surpassed Kingston and Newark as the focus of power and sophistication in Upper Canada. Its growth was steady once Simcoe identified it as the capital in 1796. Surveyor Alexander Aitken had laid out a simple gridiron plan in 1793 and, in true British imperial manner, the original ten blocks expanded on the grid, generally ignoring the rivers and ravines that make up the topography. Lots on Front Street (facing the lake) and the 100-acre (40-hectare) properties north of Lot (Queen) Street were reserved for Simcoe's senior officials. York was not a Loyalist town. In 1797 Loyalists made up only one-quarter of the population, and their proportion subsequently decreased. Most of the original houses in York were utilitarian frontier structures. In 1809 there were 14 round-log houses, 11 one-storey and 27 two-storey squared-timber houses, and 55 one-storey frame houses.[24]

4.13 Elevation of Maryville Lodge, York (Toronto, Ontario), 1797. MTRL/D.W. Smith Papers/B15-90.

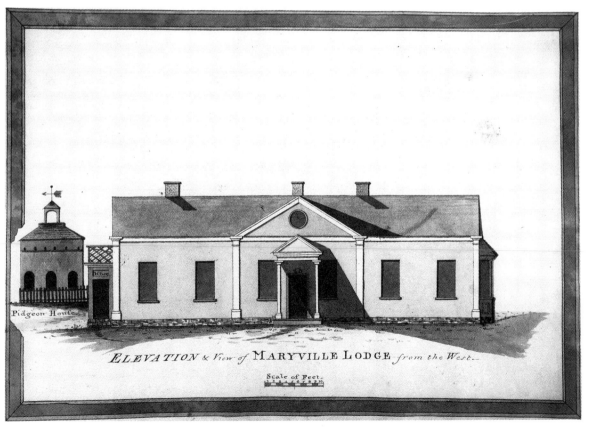

ELEVATION & View of MARYVILLE LODGE *from the West.*

Scale of Feet

In contrast to the artisans and tradesmen, the government officials who came from Newark immediately adopted the Georgian style. In 1797—only a few years after he had erected his fine Newark house—D.W. Smith built **Maryville Lodge** [**4.13**] in York, where he owned a little over 100 acres. Again, he was probably its designer. Built of wood (painted yellow) and constructed around a small pre-existing house, it was only one storey high, yet it had a central pediment, pilasters, and a classical portico, all features of developed two-storey houses. The plan was a double-pile, two ranges of rooms deep, without a full central hall; the kitchen formed a separate wing in the rear,

connected to the house by a passage (and consequently less of a fire hazard). Smith described Maryville Lodge as a 'Cottage', a term that denoted its single storey. While the house—at the northeast corner of King and Ontario Streets—may have been lacking in size, it was situated on a large property, with orchards, vegetable gardens, servants' quarters, and stables.[25]

The years shortly after 1810 saw the introduction of an important variant of the Georgian house, one that soon became associated with the ruling class in Upper Canada. The earliest instance, in Newark, was the **house of William Dickson** [**4.14**], a prosperous Scottish-born merchant, lawyer, land specu-

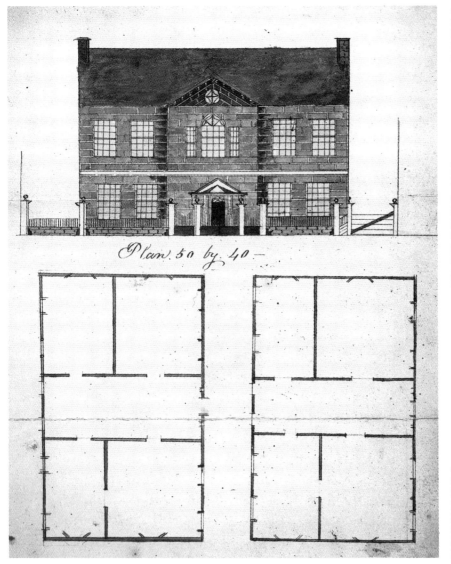

4.14 Plan and elevation of the William Dickson house, Newark (Niagara-on-the-Lake, Ontario), *c.* 1811. NAC/NMC-126555.

4.15 (*right*) Winslow Hall, Buckinghamshire. England, 1699-1702. Royal Commission on the Historical Monuments of England/BB89,1029. Reproduced from a photograph in the copyright of the *Victoria County History* by permission of the General Editor.

4.16 (*right*) Cliveden, Germantown (Philadelphia), Pennsylvania, 1763-4. Photograph by Jack Boucher. Historic American Buildings Survey/PA-51-GERM, 64-3. From the Collections of the Library of Congress.

lator, and politician. He immigrated in 1785 to join his cousin, who was in partnership with Richard Cartwright. Around 1790, at the age of 21, Dickson moved to Newark and built a residence that he claimed was 'the first brick house in the province.' By 1812 he had replaced this with a larger brick house—built around 1811 (he claimed to have built it in the year before the war), and not in 1787-90 as has generally been maintained—seen in the illustration.[26] The house was the repository of a magnificent library of more than 1,000 books that Dickson brought over from England.

As described in Dickson's claim for compensation after its destruction by the Americans, the house was two storeys high with the familiar five-bay width and gable roof. Unlike the previous houses, however, the central bay now projected forward, containing a pedimented entry and a Palladian window on the second floor, and was topped by a pediment (or gable) with a circular window. A belt-course marked the division between the two floors. The central hall led to two rooms on each side, each of which had a fireplace along the gable end. The walls misleadingly look as if they were built of stone; the material is identified by Dickson's claim, which describes 'a Brick house, two Storeys high, with Lofty Garrets above and cellar below.'[27]

Many precedents for a five- (and seven-) bay house, with a projecting and pedimented frontispiece, are found in the US and Britain, where prototypes appeared towards the end of the seventeenth century. An early example is **Winslow Hill [4.15]**, Buckinghamshire (1699-1702), probably designed by Sir Christopher Wren (1632-1723) for William Lowndes, Secretary of the Treasury. By the early eighteenth century this composition was becoming common in England and Scotland, usually with a hipped roof—a type that became popular in the 1750s and 1760s in the American colonies, as in Britain, and subsequently in Canada. It was often built by members of the political establishment. One example, with a gabled roof, is **Cliveden** (1763-4) at Germantown, Pennsylvania, the residence [4.16] of Benjamin Chew, Attorney General of Pennsylvania.[28]

This embellished variant of the Georgian style, characterized by the central projection and pediment, came to be favoured in Upper Canada by members of the Family Compact and other government officials in York. Their builders would have recognized that the design was common in England among modestly scaled eighteenth-century suburban and country houses. Foremost among such residences in York—owned by people in the inner circle of power—were The Grange, the home of D'Arcy Boulton, Jr; The Palace, owned by the Reverend John Strachan; and the Sir William Campbell house, home of the Chief Justice. All were built of brick, a favourite material in the young capital; bricks made from local clay and lime from Kingston had been available in York since 1796.[29] Neither for these houses, nor for the Dickson house, have the architects' names been identified.

The Grange [4.17], the earliest of the three, was built in 1817-18 by D'Arcy Boulton, Jr, the oldest of

4.17 The Grange, Toronto, Ontario, *c*. 1817-18. Art Gallery of Ontario, Toronto.

4.18 Drawing-room, The Grange, Toronto, Ontario, *c*. 1817-18. Copyright Toronto Star/v138-12. Toronto Star Syndicate photograph/u138-12.

several sons of the sometime Solicitor General and Attorney General of Upper Canada, D'Arcy Boulton, Sr. The elder Boulton was born in England and had settled in Augusta Township, Upper Canada, by 1802, after living for a short time in the US. When William Lyon Mackenzie formed his list of the 'Family Compact' in 1833, the names of Boulton and his four sons stood at the top. All rose to prominence. The younger D'Arcy was trained as a lawyer, but chose to hold only minor government positions and dabble in business while he turned his attention to leading the life of a gentleman on his suburban estate. The Grange—which originally commanded a 100-acre (40-hectare) property west of the town centre—was originally planned by Boulton in 1808, when he was 23, but construction was delayed for a decade because of the war.[30]

The house has the familiar Georgian five-bay, two-storey façade, with the three central bays projecting slightly beneath a central pediment, in the centre of which a circular window illuminates the attic. It had a wooden portico, which was later replaced (see below). The design concept is similar to that of the Dickson residence (which had burned down four or five years before The Grange was begun), although only the central bay of the Newark house projected forward from the rest of the block. The proportions of The Grange are more horizontal, a characteristic emphasized by the low hipped roof (framed by end chimneys), the elegant cornice and broad pediment, and the shutters of the finely crafted windows, all of which give it a firm relationship to the land and a definite air of stability and permanence. A broad central hall leads to all of the principal rooms on the ground floor which feature fine plaster cornices and fireplaces with classical motifs [4.18]. The bedrooms are on the second floor, and the kitchens and services are in the basement.

This particular elevation occurs with variations in the work of Palladio (e.g. the Villa Emo at Fanzolo, 1560-5), and recurred in many contexts in British architecture of the seventeenth and eighteenth centuries. Many smaller houses of the late Stuart and early Georgian periods (such as Eagle House, Mitcham, Surrey, 1705), as well as a design for a house in James Gibbs's *A Book of Architecture* (1728), have the same arrangement of parts as The Grange. The Palladians were particularly fond of the composition. It can be seen—with pilasters on the entrance façade, and without them on the river fronts—at Marble Hill (*c.* 1728, **3.43**), and as the basis of many 'villas', modestly scaled suburban residences of the well-to-do, designed by second-generation Palladians, such as Sir Robert

Taylor (1714-88), whose Danson Hill (*c.* 1760-5), Bexleyheath, Kent, has no pilasters (like The Grange). In the minds of Boulton and his British-born contemporaries, this arrangement was the tried-and-true architectural solution to the suburban villa, which The Grange aspired to be.[31]

The Grange was enlarged and altered, first by Boulton, and then in the 1880s by Goldwin Smith—the distinguished Oxford professor of history (and later advocate of commercial union with the US) who had married Harriette, the widow of Boulton's son, William Henry. Smith built the stone portico we know today, with its handsome Doric columns and entablature facing south. Harriette Smith bequeathed the house to the Art Gallery of Toronto, and it now forms a part of the Art Gallery of Ontario. The house was restored in 1971 by architect Peter Stokes (b. 1926) and interior consultant Jeanne Minhinnick. Although the property has been subdivided, the grounds in front of the house have been preserved as Grange Park, and partially restored (by Commonwealth Historic Resource Management Limited, 1983).

The **John Strachan house** (1818) was similar in design, but larger and broader [4.19]. Strachan

4.19 Strachan house (The Palace), Toronto, Ontario, 1818. Photograph *c.* 1885. MTRL/T11528.

came from Scotland to Kingston in 1799 as a tutor to the children of Richard Cartwright and other prominent members of the community. He was ordained in the Church of England in 1803 and not only rose in the ranks of the Church but came to influence government. He acquired wealth through his marriage in 1807 to a Montreal widow, Ann Wood McGill, who had inherited the fur-trade fortune of her first husband, Andrew McGill. As a teacher Strachan educated many sons of the governing class (including D'Arcy Boulton, Jr, and several of his brothers) at his school in Cornwall, thus ensuring that he would long remain close to people in power. He also passed on his fervent belief that Upper Canada had to be kept British and free from 'democratic' American ways. Appointed rector of York in 1812, he became archdeacon in 1827 and Bishop of Toronto in 1839—when the popular name of his house, The Palace, became appropriate.[32]

Not surprisingly, Strachan chose an embellished Georgian form for his house on Front Street West. The three projecting central bays were dressed up with pilasters beneath the pediment, and a columned wood portico stood in front of the door. The ensemble was impressive in a manner unprecedented for houses in the province. A pair of tall chimneys rose from each side of the low hipped roof, and the large twelve-over-twelve windows were shuttered. Dr William Warren Baldwin, another member of the privileged class and an amateur architect, praised Strachan's house as 'magnificent'. Others described it as the 'finest house in the town', built by a man who 'gave entertainments that outshone those of the Lieutenant Governor, and rode about in a grand coach with a hemispherical top.' Strachan's brother James is said to have remarked: 'I hope it's a' come by honestly, John.' Strachan lived here until his death in 1867, by which time the railways were transforming this once-fashionable residential area along the shore of Lake Ontario into a commercial district. The gracious residence faded into the Palace Boarding House and was demolished in 1896.

The seven-bay Georgian façade finds respectable antecedents in both Britain and the US. A late Stuart forerunner is Apsley House (1695), Bedfordshire; an American one—which Strachan would likely not have known, but that shows the elevated status of people who lived in residences of this kind—was Governor Tryon's Palace (1767) in New Bern, North Carolina, designed by the English architect John Hawks.[33]

4.20 The Campbell House, Toronto, Ontario, 1822. Photograph by William Toye.

The **William Campbell House** (1822), which reflects the same Georgian image of gentility, has the more typical five bays and lacks the pilasters of The Palace. But it still impresses the passer-by with its handsome and harmonious appearance, complemented by the columned porch that was added in the restoration of 1972 [**4.20**]. The two red-brick storeys rise from a stone foundation. The details are more refined than in The Grange—as can be seen in the thinner glazing bars, the tracery of the fanlight and the elliptical window in the pediment, and in the more vertical proportions, which illustrate technical and stylistic developments over the few years since The Grange was built. Campbell, another Scot, had come to Canada as a soldier in a Highland regiment and first settled in Nova Scotia. He served as Chief Justice of Upper Canada from 1825 to 1829, when he was knighted. In 1972 his house was moved from its original location on Duke Street (later Adelaide Street East) to Queen Street West at University, and it is now the proud home of the Advocates Society.[34]

The Georgian manner became established throughout Upper Canada, and versions of the Campbell House soon appeared across the province. Several fine examples are found in Perth, an attractive community that had been settled in 1816 by discharged soldiers on half-pay, and by Scots civilians who were promised 100 acres (40 hectares) of land, free tools, and food for six months. In the early 1980s the historical architecture of Perth received national attention when the city was selected as the first demonstration project for

Heritage Canada's Main Street program (see Chapter 15). Two outstanding Georgian houses in Perth, built nearly two decades apart, are The Summit (1823), the residence of James Boulton; and the Matheson house (1840), an austerely handsome sandstone dwelling built by Scots-born soldier and politician Roderick Matheson, which now serves as the Perth Museum. Perth, and other communities in the Rideau valley, benefited from the presence of skilled Scottish and Irish stonemasons, particularly after the completion of the Rideau Canal. They exploited the abundant limestone and sandstone resources in the area, and gave the region a distinctive architecture of stone.[35]

The house now called **The Summit** (1823) was built of brick and not stone by James Boulton, the seventh child of D'Arcy Boulton, Sr. He became a lawyer in 1822 and the following year, at the age of 22, set out to make his career. He moved to Perth, hung up his shingle as the town's first lawyer, purchased the choicest property in town (a quarter-block at the top of the hill at Drummond and Harvey Streets, across from the Anglican church, next to the Catholic church, and near the Courthouse), and built his elegant residence [4.21]. James Boulton sought to become a dominant figure in Perth, as had his father and brothers in York, and he expressed his ambition by modelling his house

on The Grange, which his older brother, D'Arcy, Jr., had built six years earlier. Both are brick houses with a Georgian five-bay front, a central-hall plan, a hipped roof, paired chimneys at the sides, and a frontispiece consisting of a gable over the central bay and a classical entrance portico. The design clearly announced James Boulton's pedigree, and his sophistication. The details of the façade of his house differ from those of The Grange, however, in some significant respects. The three central bays do not project forward, and the roofline is broken, not by a classical pediment but by a simple gable that is aligned imperfectly with the windows beneath it. These features suggest that the Perth house may have been the work of a local builder who followed Boulton's instructions faultily. The changes give it some characteristics of a regional house-type that was being developed in the Rideau valley area during these very years: the central-gable house, in which the eave over the entrance is interrupted by a gable.[36]

A later owner of the Boulton house, railway contractor and merchant Hugh Ryan, named it Tara Hall and built a two-storey brick wing at the west (left) side in the late 1870s. He also altered the

4.21 The Summit, Perth, Ontario, 1823. Photograph by Harold Kalman.

interior. In 1897 the house was named The Summit by a subsequent owner, Mary Jane Hicks.

The central gable is seen in a more modest (but no less elegant) one-storey house in Perth, **Inge-Va** [**4.22**]—which means 'come here' in Tamil. This attractive stone house, set well back from Craig Street on an attractively landscaped lot, was built in 1823 or 1824 by the Reverend Michael Harris, the Anglican rector. It was originally $1\frac{1}{2}$ storeys high, with a straight eave across the front and gables at the ends. Illuminating the ground floor are superbly crafted 24-pane double-hung sash windows, and around the front door sidelights and an elliptical transom. The second floor would have been fairly dark, as light was admitted only through the small windows in the side gables. The second owner, lawyer Thomas Radenhurst, had acquired the house by 1832. He married a daughter of the prominent Toronto politician Thomas Ridout and, like his father-in-law, was a Reformer who opposed

4.22 Inge-Va, Perth, Ontario, *c*. 1823-4. Photograph by Ralph Greenhill.

4.23 McMartin house, Perth, Ontario, *c*. 1830-2. Photograph by Harold Kalman.

the privileges of Tories such as the Boultons. Radenhurst appropriately chose to live in a more proletarian house-form, one anchored in the Perth region and the Rideau valley. Nevertheless he felt obliged to add a touch of refinement, in keeping with his stature, and inserted the prominent front gable, with its large arched window, to provide light to the upper hall and create an air of greater distinction.[37]

A third prominent lawyer of Perth—Daniel McMartin, the Ontario-born son of a distinguished Loyalist family from New York—built yet another kind of house. The imposing brick **McMartin house** (1830-2) on Harvey Street, a block below The Summit, boasts a five-bay façade of which the three central bays are contained within an elegant engaged arcade [**4.23**]. Cut stone is used for quoins, as a belt course between the two storeys, and for the window heads. Three cupolas crown the truncated hipped roof. The McMartin house shares many features with late-eighteenth-century Adamesque classicism in Britain, and with the parallel Federal style in the US—revealing McMartin's American roots. Both styles—which had run their course in their respective countries when the McMartin house was built—followed Georgian classicism.[38]

The three social-climbing lawyers were bitter rivals. Both McMartin and Boulton had attended Strachan's Cornwall Grammar School and law classes together, and their enmity may have had a long history. In April 1827 McMartin challenged Boulton to a duel, but Boulton declined the challenge; he said that he had no chance of hitting his opponent, since McMartin was no thicker than a broomstick. They quarrelled again in 1831; McMartin posted printed handbills charging Boulton with perjury, and Boulton responded by horsewhipping McMartin in public. Boulton and Radenhurst were no kinder towards each other. In 1830 Radenhurst dragged Boulton to the ground, and the two agreed to a duel in New York State, but it never took place.

The relationship among the three went from bad to worse, culminating in Canada's last fatal duel, in which Boulton and Radenhurst were both implicated. Two young law students, John Wilson (who was boarding at Boulton's house and tutoring one of his children) and Robert Lyon (a student of Radenhurst and a relation by marriage), had a dispute over a young woman, Elizabeth Hughes. Their argument led to a duel with pistols on 13 June 1833. Lyon was mortally wounded and carried to Inge-Va, where he died. In the trial that followed,

Wilson was acquitted for having adopted 'the only alternative which men of honour thought open'. Boulton, who testified, was criticized for not having done enough to prevent the duel. This humiliation ended Boulton's career in Perth, and he soon left town. The night before his departure a group of townspeople marched past his house carrying torches and a hanging effigy. Boulton, however, re-established himself in a new law practice in Niagara (formerly Newark), and in 1835 invited John Wilson to join him there. Wilson, who married Elizabeth Hughes, accepted the invitation and went on to a successful career as a soldier, politician, and judge.[39]

The commanding residences of the three volatile lawyers of Perth (by which they are remembered today) reflected, in their differences, the men's backgrounds and personalities. But in their symmetrical five-bay façades and gracious classical detail, all three celebrate the triumph of Georgian architecture in Upper Canada. Inge-Va and the McMartin house are both owned, and have been restored, by the Ontario Heritage Foundation.

The Georgian house was so pervasive a symbol of polite Upper Canadian society that it formed the central feature in needlework produced by teenaged girls as part of their domestic studies. A sampler [**4.24**] embroidered in 1854 by fifteen-year-old Elizabeth James Hicks of Perth depicts a masonry house with the central-gabled façade of The Sum-

4.24 A sampler featuring a house embroidered by Elizabeth James Hicks of Perth, Ontario, 1854. Collection of Larry Turner.

mit and the fan-lighted doorway of Inge-Va and the McMartin house. The house is set formally behind a tidy lawn enclosed by a picket fence. The same composition is found in at least three other Perth-area samplers of the day, revealing the popularity of the image.[40]

Log houses Most Upper Canadians could not afford the expense of a two-storey frame or masonry house, and many who could did not aspire to such grandeur. Georgian Classicism will be set aside while we look at alternative kinds of housing.

From the last years of the eighteenth century until well into the second half of the nineteenth, the first house to be built by a new settler in the region we now know as Ontario was almost always made of logs. This was a matter of expediency more than choice: a log house was quick and cheap to build—the logs were obtained while clearing the land, and volunteer labour was usually available to help with construction. Most people recognized that the log house was a stop-gap measure and would soon be replaced by a more substantial building; indeed, a frame, stone, or brick dwelling often followed before many years had passed.

Log building was once thought of as the quintessential invention of the American pioneer, but this 'log-cabin myth' was debunked more than a half-century ago. The technique in which logs are laid horizontally on top of each other and are connected at the corners is now generally accepted as having been introduced to North America by the Swedes, who settled near the mouth of the Delaware River in the seventeenth century; and it was also used by early German settlers in Pennsylvania. As we have seen, French colonists in Quebec and Acadia used this manner of building in the eighteenth century and possibly also in the seventeenth, in which case one might be able to establish a case for their primacy. In any event, the technique was adopted by English-speaking Americans only in the eighteenth century, long after they had become accustomed to frame construction. This log building-form spread through the central Canadian frontier.[41]

It was quickest to use round logs, but if the time was taken to square the logs with an adze, their flattened tops and bottoms would butt against each other and offer much better protection against the weather. 'Chinking' (called 'chintzing' in Newfoundland) the spaces ('chinks') between the logs with moss, clay, slats, or wood wedges provided fairly good insulation.

The weight of a log wall is borne at the corners, and so the kind of joint (also called a 'notch' or a 'key') is vital to the wall's stability. The simplest form is the 'saddle notch', known to most of us from children's toy logs, in which round logs overlap at the corners and are held together with saddle-shaped cuts near their projecting ends. Squared logs might be joined with a 'simple lap', in which the ends are cut narrower and overlap with the ends of the adjacent logs. As the saddle notch and the simple lap allow movement in the walls, a 'tie log' sometimes connected the centres of opposite walls (near the top) to hold them together, or else wood pins might be inserted through the joints to strengthen them.

More complicated to make, but providing greater strength and stability, is the 'dovetail' joint, in which the laps are angled and fit together somewhat like the pieces of an interlocking wood puzzle. In a 'half-dovetail' joint one face of the lap is angled and the other flat; and in a 'full-dovetail' joint both faces are angled to resemble the flaring tail of a dove. A well-keyed dovetail joint requires considerable carpentry skill and provides a tight fit with a correspondingly high degree of strength and stability. Dovetail notching is found in the middle Atlantic colonies of the US, where it was likely brought over by both Swedish and German settlers, and in the early buildings of New France. It re-emerges in the early nineteenth century in central Canada as well as in Wisconsin, Minnesota, and the Upper Midwest. French- and English-speaking builders both used it extensively, and the joint-type became common among Métis builders on the Prairies (see also pages 352-5).[42]

Although sizes varied considerably, the basic log house in Upper Canada was often about 16 by 20 feet (4.9 by 6.1 m), which in 1798 were stipulated in a general regulation as the minimum dimensions for houses.[43] Twenty feet was also a length of log that was easily obtainable from clearing the property and could be handled by two men. A single log was typically about 8 to 11 inches (20 to 28 cm) in diameter, and a house might be eight or nine logs high to the eave. Cutting and reinforcing openings for doors and windows took time and skill, and so their number is usually related to the degree of permanence intended. Temporary dwellings might have only a door and a hole in the roof to allow smoke to escape, whereas a house intended to be lived in for a considerable length of time would boast milled and glazed windows.

The standard log house was one storey high with

a sleeping loft that was reached by a steep corner staircase or a ladder. The main floor might be treated as a single room in smaller structures, or divided by partitions into two or three rooms, the largest being the kitchen—actually a multi-purpose living-hall—with a large fireplace. The roof was usually gabled and shingled, although sometimes it was covered with bark or with 'scoops' (see page 230). The gabled peak would be framed and covered with boards rather than built of logs. Interior finishes might be bare logs, plaster, paper, or wood panelling.

The terms 'shanty', 'cabin', and 'house' are all used to describe log dwellings, and while there is no clear-cut line dividing one from another, they represent an ascending level of construction, finish, and permanence. 'Shanty' usually refers to a rough one-room structure with a simple shed roof, whereas 'cabin' and 'house' describe gable-roofed buildings. A watercolour painted in 1830 by James Pattison Cockburn and depicting **Maitland's Rapids** on the Rideau River shows both a shanty and a house [4.25]. The shanty, near the centre of the picture, was built of round saddle-notched logs pierced only by a door and has a gently sloped scoop roof (not evident in the painting) made of logs cut in half along their length and scooped out to conduct water off the roof; the house has rough-

4.25 Log house and shanty at Maitland's Rapids on the Rideau River, Kilmanock, Ontario. Watercolour by James Pattison Cockburn, 1830. Royal Ontario Museum/942.48.10.

hewn squared logs with a door and a small window, and is covered by a steeply sloped roof finished in wide boards, perhaps purchased at the sawmill in nearby Merrickville.

Shanties and houses of this kind continued to be built one and two generations later. A shanty that was very similar to the one at Maitland's Rapids, for example, was built by Thomas McDowell in Palmerston as late as 1862 and photographed at that time; its scooped roof clearly slopes to shed water.[44] Houses similar to the one illustrated by Cockburn were constructed throughout the nineteenth century. Both types of buildings were products of the prevalent environmental and economic conditions, and of their relationship to the frontier, rather than of any particular time.

Many early log houses are still standing, and many more are known from photographs. It is difficult, however, to assign a precise date to any of them because property records relate to the land and not the building, and a particular house may well not have been the first one on the site. A number of log houses in Upper Canada, known

4.26 Log house near Yarker, Camden Township, Ontario, *c*. 1820-40, Photograph, *c*. 1900. Lennox and Addington County Museum and Archives, Napanee, Ontario, Camden Township History Collection/N3827.

from early photographs and believed to have been erected in the first three decades of the nineteenth century, have the door at the centre of a long side with a small window next to it (as in the house at Maitland's Rapids), and no other windows except for a small one in the gable to illuminate the loft. A **log house near Yarker** [**4.26**], Camden Township, likely built between 1820 and 1840, represents this dominant early type. The photograph of about 1900 shows Jonathan and Tillie Elliott and their daughter standing in front of their house. Later houses often placed a window at either side of the door, and perhaps another in an end wall. Some larger log houses have been documented as well, such as one 23 by 33 feet (7 by 10 m) that used to stand on Dawes Road in East York, Toronto, believed to have been built *c*. 1810-15, with round logs and saddle-notched joints.[45]

A log house of a different kind was built north of York by Governor John Graves Simcoe for himself and his family. Simcoe, who lived first in a tent and then in the garrison, in 1793 obtained a 200-acre

(80-hectare) property on the west bank of the Don River, just north of the present intersection of Bloor and Parliament Streets. In 1795-6 he built a summer residence there that he named **Castle Frank** [**4.27**] after his son, Francis. Elizabeth Simcoe, the Governor's wife, described its construction:

> It is...built on the plan of a Grecian Temple, totally of wood the Logs squared & so grooved together that in case of decay any log may be taken out. The large Pine trees make Pillars for the Porticos which are at each end 16 feet high.[46]

The house measured about 50 by 30 feet (15.2 by 9.2 m), and its walls were apparently built in the grooved-post technique of New France. The construction technique was confirmed by historian Henry Scadding, who noted that 'its walls were composed of a number of carefully hewn logs, of short lengths.'[47]

Castle Frank was a rustic temple in a picturesque landscape setting, the garden ornament of a person of refinement that was conceived in the same spirit (and at the same time) as the Prince's Lodge Rotunda [**3.50**] at Halifax. With its solid sides and open ends, its classical source was more Roman than Greek, but Mrs Simcoe may be forgiven her imperfect knowledge of architectural history. European precedents for this kind of rustic building abound, but they tended to be ornamental buildings on large country estates rather than actual residences. Mrs Simcoe revealed her appreciation of the picturesque qualities of Castle Frank in the sketches she made of it. The Simcoes lived in the house for only three weeks in the summer of 1796 before they were recalled to England. The building was left to deteriorate, and it burned in the 1820s.[48]

The Roman temple was a particularly American (not Canadian) architectural obsession at this time. For the Virginia State Capitol at Richmond (1785-98), statesman and talented amateur architect Thomas Jefferson (1743-1826) and French architect Charles-Louis Clérisseau (1721-1820) used as their model the Maison Carrée, a Roman temple at Nîmes. Jefferson intended that the building should provide an appropriate architectural symbol for the new American republic. Two generations later,

American architect Alexander Jackson Davis (1803-92) would publish a plan for a domestic version of a Roman temple in his *Rural Residences* (1837), calling it an 'American cottage'. Canadians are left to wonder how the staunchly imperialist Simcoe would have felt had he known the manner in which his American neighbours used the model that he chose for his own house.[49]

Cottages and other houses When the inhabitant of a log house accumulated enough capital to afford the materials and the labour for a new dwelling, he usually built a frame or masonry house and relegated the original one to the role of an outbuilding. The same was done when a barn was replaced. A simplified description of the evolution of a typical Ontario homestead, from a humble

4.27 Castle Frank, near York (Toronto, Ontario), 1795-6. Sketched by Elizabeth Simcoe in 1796. Archives of Ontario, Simcoe Collection/132.

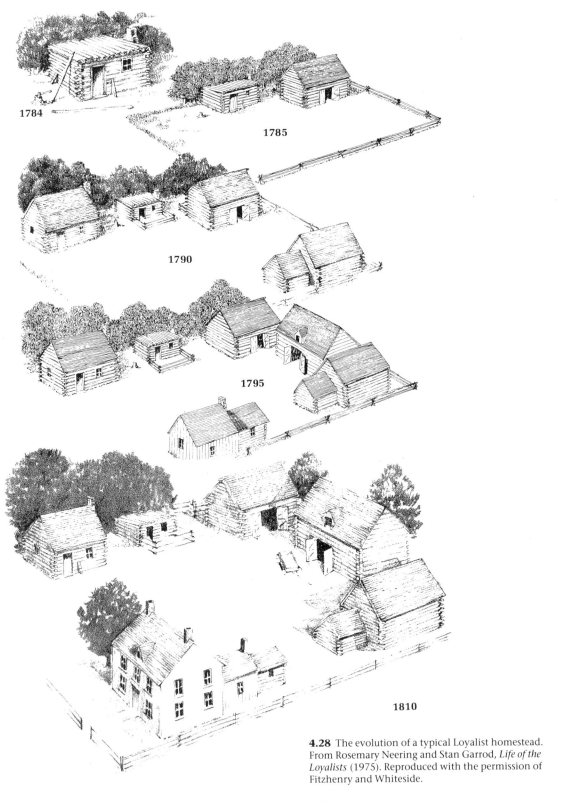

1784

1785

1790

1795

1810

4.28 The evolution of a typical Loyalist homestead. From Rosemary Neering and Stan Garrod, *Life of the Loyalists* (1975). Reproduced with the permission of Fitzhenry and Whiteside.

4.29 Street house, Streetsville (Mississauga), Ontario, 1825. Photograph by John J.-G. Blumenson.

shanty to a substantial complex made up of a two-storey Georgian house and a complex of log buildings, is shown in the accompanying sketches [**4.28**].[50] In parts of eastern Ontario, particularly in the Ottawa valley, the rural landscape is still

4.30 Bradley house, Clarkson (Mississauga), Ontario, *c*. 1830. Photograph by John J.-G. Blumenson.

dominated by picturesque farm complexes of this kind, with clusters of log buildings and fences that define barnyards and fields.

One-and-a-half-storey frame and masonry houses (their 'half-storey' consisting of a bedroom floor contained within the slope of the roof) were particularly common throughout Upper Canada. Two houses in today's city of Mississauga, just west of Toronto, illustrate the range of types. The **Timothy Street house** (1825) in Streetsville is five bays wide (similar to a double Cape Cod cottage, although with end chimneys rather than a central one, and is believed to have been the first brick house in Peel County [**4.29**]. The **Lewis Bradley house** (*c*. 1830) in Clarkson, built by a Loyalist family on the shore of Lake Ontario (but moved inland in 1963 and now the Bradley House Museum), is only three bays wide, again with a central entrance [**4.30**]. This frame house is sheathed in clapboard and covered with a saltbox roof—which extends further, and is lower, at the rear than the front. Its 24-pane (12-over-12) windows, classical door surround, and fireplace mantels reveal a high standard of craftsmanship despite the modest size of the house.[51]

From the 1830s onwards, the most common house-type built in Upper Canada, often called an

Ontario Cottage, was 1½-storeys high with the principal gables on the sides and a secondary gable over the entrance. This central gable, known as a 'peak', was both utilitarian and ornamental: it permitted a large window to illuminate the upper floor and gave the house an air of distinction, similar in effect to a full-blown classical pediment in a two-storey house, but at lower cost.

The central gable was sometimes added to a house with a straight eave, as at Inge-Va in Perth. The Rideau valley has many stone houses similar to Inge-Va. Thunderwood Farm (c. 1840) in North Gower township is typical: three bays wide, with a fine elliptical fanlight and sidelights surrounding the door, it has an elegant 24-pane window at either side. The central gable has a smaller 8-over-12 window.[52] This house-type became popular in the middle years of the century, when it acquired some Gothic Revival detail; it is therefore commonly described as a Gothic Cottage [11.14].

A second variant of the 1½-storey house is the Regency Cottage. The adjective refers to the regency (1811-20), when George III was insane, of his son who became George IV; 'cottage' denotes its single-storey appearance. The Regency Cottage has a low profile, usually provided by a low-sloped

hipped roof; it often has wings at either side (sometimes a later addition), a broad veranda extending along one or more sides, and oversized windows, giving the house an intimate relationship to the landscape—often picturesque, and near water. Classical detail is used, though sparingly. This type of house tended to be favoured by people who had made their money in commerce.

Inverarden [4.31], near Cornwall, is an early Regency Cottage with an interesting history. It was built in 1816 on a 750-acre (300-hectare) site on the St Lawrence River by John McDonald (McDonald of Garth), a retired wintering partner of the North West Company who had built the trading posts at Fort Augustus (later Fort Edmonton) and Rocky Mountain House (Alberta). A Highland Scot, as were most of the fur-trade company's other directors, McDonald retired and with his first wife, Nancy—the Métis daughter of fur trader Patrick Small—purchased a farm at Gray's Creek, near Cornwall (near the retirement homes of former partners Simon Fraser, Hugh McGillis, John McGillivray, David Thompson, and Duncan Cameron). He named the house Garth, after his family's estate in Perthshire; Inverarden is a later name. As initially built it was 44 by 34 feet (13.4 by 10.4 m), with a large kitchen and servants' rooms in the basement and an unfinished attic. The walls were constructed of fieldstone 2½ feet (75 cm) thick and finished in stucco. The windows are casements, a

4.31 Inverarden, near Cornwall, Ontario, 1816. Photograph by Harold Kalman.

4.32 Riverest, L'Orignal, Ontario, *c*. 1833. Photograph by Ralph Greenhill.

French form common in this region close to Lower Canada, and four chimneys rise from the low hipped roof. The simple plan has a drawing-room and a dining-room on either side of the central hall, with two smaller bedrooms behind them. The wood panelling and the plasterwork reflect classical decorative themes. McDonald furnished the house with modish Regency furniture imported from England.[53]

The bay-windowed wings were added shortly after McDonald's future son-in-law, retired trader John Duncan Campbell, moved into the house in 1821. A dormer was inserted above the entrance in the 1880s, but it was removed when the house was restored by Parks Canada in 1976-8. McDonald's Garth has now become the Inverarden Regency Cottage Museum. Interpreting the lives, wealth, and taste of the fur traders of the North West Company, it is administered by the Stormont, Dundas and Glengarry Historical Society for the City of Cornwall.

A second, more developed, Regency Cottage in Eastern Ontario is **Riverest** [4.32] at L'Orignal. It was built about 1833 by locally born merchant John Wurtele Marston on land along the Ottawa River that had formed a part of the seigneury of Longueuil—the only seigneury to have been included within the boundaries of Upper Canada. Marston's residence may have been the work of master-builder William Moody, who had come from Montreal and was responsible for several private and public buildings in the L'Orignal area that share features with Riverest.[54]

Riverest is built of sandstone with a principal central-hall portion, 40 by 29 feet (12.2 by 8.8 m), and a one-room wing at either side about 17 by 20 feet (5.2 by 6.1 m). The original entrance—on the north side, facing the river and a scenic view of the Laurentian Mountains—established a close link between the house and the landscape. The casement windows on both sides were enlarged with semi-circular fanlights and sidelights to produce a Palladian motif. Both the front and back façades of the main block originally featured a lovely full-width veranda with arched trellises between the posts. Only the south veranda (away from the view) survives; the entrance is now located on this side.

Although all the elements are fully integrated into a unified design, the wings and the veranda appear to have been additions erected a few years later than the main block, possibly as early as 1837. The building stones of the wings are larger than those on the main block, and the walls are not keyed to each other; differences are also found in the beams, floorboards, window frames, and cornices. Nevertheless, Riverest remains an exceptionally attractive Regency Cottage whose parts blend together in full harmony.

Low, hipped-roof houses with verandas (and often with wings at either side), appeared in British colonial architecture around the world during the late eighteenth and early nineteenth centuries, particularly in climates that were warmer than Canada's. There are parallels between the Regency Cottage, the 'great house' of the British Caribbean, and the colonial bungalow of India—the last a form that would have an enormous influence on residential architecture in Canada nearly a century later.

Other early Ontario dwellings were a full two storeys high but had fewer than the five bays characteristic of the Georgian house. A particularly well-crafted example of this form is the **Ebenezer Doan house** (1819) at Sharon, a former religious community in East Gwillimbury Township, now about 30 miles (50 km) north of Toronto. Doan—who was descended from the Doanes of Cape Cod, whom we met in the discussion of Nova Scotia architecture—was a carpenter and farmer who came to Upper Canada from Bucks County, Pennsylvania, with a number of relatives and fellow members of the Society of Friends, looking for land and religious freedom. The house [4.33] has been moved onto the grounds of the Sharon Temple Museum [4.45].

Three bays wide, it has a central door leading directly into a large hall-kitchen (extending to the wall on the right), which was traditionally the focus of family life and here emphasized the value placed on the family by the Doans and their Quaker community. Two smaller rooms (probably parlour and bedroom) are on the left, and an enclosed staircase is at the rear. Other small, enclosed spaces are storage adjuncts to the hall-kitchen. John McIntyre has traced the 'diffusion' of vernacular house-forms that produced the Doan house, showing that this three-room plan was common in the houses built by Pennsylvania Germans ('Pennsylvania Dutch'), and also in houses in the north and west of England and in Wales, where most Pennsylvania Quakers had come from. The three-bay façade could be seen among both English and German houses in Bucks County, although in that American region stone was the most common building material. The Doan house, therefore, combines traditional British, German, and American precedents—which would have been familiar to its carpenter-builder and were rendered in the wood-frame construction that was favoured in the area around Toronto. McIntyre suggests that 'Doan's house can be seen as a symbol of conservatism and accommodation in a new land'.[55]

If the low cottage and the three-bay house may be seen as being simpler in form than the Georgian standard, some other houses were more elaborate. The **Barnum house** (*c*. 1819-20) at Grafton is one of the most classically inspired Upper Canadian houses of the period [4.34]. Eliakim Barnum—a 'Late Loyalist' born in Rutland, Vermont, in 1783, the year the American Revolution ended—came to

4.33 Doan house, Sharon, Ontario, 1819. Photograph by Harold Kalman, 1976.

4.34 Barnum house, Grafton, Ontario, *c*. 1819. Photograph by Ralph Greenhill.

Canada by 1810, at the start of yet another North American war. He quickly established himself as an active, and affluent, member of the Grafton community, operating a tavern, milling grain, and eventually amassing 5,000 acres (2,000 hectares) of land. Conservative in his politics, he was a sometime commander of the Third Northumberland Regiment, and was an opponent of the reforms advocated by William Lyon Mackenzie.[56]

Barnum called his house The Poplars. Although the identity of his builder or architect is not known, it has been suggested that he came from New York State. This distinguished white frame house, built of white pine (now painted white), features a central two-storey block treated like a Roman temple-front, with its gable oriented towards the road and four Doric pilaster strips supporting low segmental arches, an entablature, and a pediment. A one-storey wing at either side continues the pilaster-and-arch motif. The façade is sheathed in flush boards whose joints are hardly perceptible and imitate cut stone, whereas bevelled clapboard siding with articulated edges covers the side walls; the frame is heavy timber. Classical triglyphs and mutules, features of the Doric order, decorate the frieze, and the level of craftsmanship, inside and out, is high.

Temple-like houses were rare in Ontario at this time (although Joseph Keeler, another native of Rutland, built a very similar house in Colborne about 1820),[57] and look forward to the classical revivals of mid-century (see page 299). They are more common south of the border in upper New York State and New England, where they often have free-standing columns rather than applied pilasters. One of the most American of Loyalist buildings, the Barnum house ironically played an important role in the rediscovery of historic Ontario architecture. Eric Arthur (1898-1982), Professor of Architecture at the University of Toronto and a devoted champion of early Ontario building (as well as a strong proponent of modernist architecture), discovered the Barnum house in the 1930s while on a sketching trip with his students. He purchased it and passed its title on to the Architectural Conservancy of Ontario, in whose founding he had been instrumental. The Conservancy operated the house for a short while as a museum, then leased it out. It is now the Northumberland County Barnum House Museum, and is owned by the Ontario Heritage Foundation.

The variety of house-types in early Upper Canada was noted by keen building-watchers of the day. Royal Engineer John Mactaggart offered his own observations in *Three Years in Canada* (1829):

...everyone builds his house or cottage according to his fancy; and it is not a difficult thing, in passing through the country, to tell what nation the natives of the house hail from, if we are aware of the whims and conceits that characterize them. Thus a plain rectangular house of brick or stone, with five windows and a door in front, and a window perhaps in either gable; the barns, sheds, stables and offices at a respectable distance behind...is the dwelling of an honest English farmer. The wealthy Lowland Scotsman follows the same plan nearly: there is not such an air of neatness and uniformity but there is more livestock about the doors....

A house larger than either of these, chiefly built of wood, and painted white with nine windows and a door in front, seven windows in either gable, and a semi-circular one above all, almost at the top angle of the roof, the blinds painted green, the chimney stocks highly ornamented, and also the fan-light at the door; the barns, stables, etc. off at a great distance;...it is almost needless for me to say that this is the mansion of Jonathan [a name for Americans] or the U.E. Loyalist from the United States.

A house nearly as large as the American's but built of stone and high roofed, having two tall chimney stocks growing out of either gable; an attempt to be showy and substantial, without rhyme or reason...was intended for the abode of a person who had made a few thousand pounds in the fur trade—a wild, pushing, Highland-man who had often seen the remotest regions of the North-west.[58]

The choice of building material was related partly to cultural origin, as Mactaggart suggested, but it also depended on economic and geographical factors. The 1851-2 manuscript census for Canada West records the type of house (shanty, round-log, squared-log, frame, brick, or stone), occupation, and place of birth of every resident of the province. Brian Coffey has analysed samples of this data and found that among non-log houses, Scots used stone (17 per cent) and brick (13 per cent) most often, and frame (70 per cent) the least, whereas about 85 per cent of the Irish, American, German, English, and Ontario-born residents lived in frame houses. Nearly one-quarter (24 per cent) of

all Irish settlers and nearly one-half (46 per cent) of all rural labourers still lived in shanties—far higher than the numbers for other cultural and occupational groups. As might be expected, merchants and innkeepers, who stood high on the social ladder, owned the most substantial houses: 61 per cent of those in towns and villages lived in brick or stone houses, far more than any other group. The statistics reflect as well the geological facts that stone was more available in Eastern Ontario than elsewhere, and that the most suitable clays for brick were found around Toronto. Frame dwellings, of course, required a nearby sawmill.[59]

Another factor that may have influenced the choice of building type and material, although to a far lesser extent, was taxes. As is the case today, owners of larger houses had to pay more in annual taxes. An act passed by the Legislature of Upper Canada in 1807 taxed houses according to their construction and the number of storeys, superseding the previous act, which had taxed according to the number of fireplaces. Six categories were created, each with an incrementally higher tax rate:

> Round logs
> Square timber, one storey
> Square timber, two storeys
> Framed under two storeys
> Brick or stone of one storey with not
>   more than two fireplaces
> Brick or stone of two storeys with not
>   more than two fireplaces

The first category, round logs, was no longer taxed after 1811, and the definition of 'square timber' was amended to include timber hewn on two sides. At the same time a surtax was added for storeys over two; a one-storey house was defined as referring to 'houses one story and not two stories', and included what we call a $1\frac{1}{2}$-storey house; two-storey frame houses were included with those of brick or stone.[60]

Some historians have suggested that the tax structure posed a disincentive to replace log houses with those of frame, brick, or stone; but this has been overstated. As William Cattermole—a spokesman, albeit a land promoter, of the time—wrote: 'The tax on a [frame] house is so minute, that it can never become a motive to deter [the settler] from building.'[61] In 1831 the owner of a two-storey brick house in most districts paid annual taxes of five shillings, less than a day's wage for skilled labour.

Residents of early Ontario could choose from among a variety of house-types. The log shanty and

4.35 'English Barn' near Dacre, Ontario. Photograph by Dudley Whitney.

simple log house were forced upon all but the very few wealthy settlers by economic and environmental realities; but once a resident achieved a degree of stability, many alternative kinds of housing—based on a combination of aesthetic, cultural, economic, and geographical factors—became available.[62]

4.36 Schmidt-Dalziel barn, Vaughan Township, Ontario, *c*. 1809. Black Creek Pioneer Village, Toronto.

Barns The house was only one of several buildings that the settler was required to erect. Agriculture required a variety of outbuildings for crops and stock. The principal cash crop in the early and middle years of the century was wheat, and this required a barn, in which the farmer would store and thresh the grain. A stable provided stalls for horses and storage for hay. As dairy farming grew in importance, particularly in the decades following 1860, when Manitoba's wheat production began to predominate and Ontario compensated by developing a cheese industry, a cow barn (or cow shed) would be needed to shelter cattle and store hay. Smaller sheds were also required for other purposes. Barns and other farm structures were often built of logs, although frame and stone were also used.

The basic 'English barn'—so called because it was the prevalent form in both England and New England, and subsequently in Upper Canada throughout the nineteenth century—had two 'mows' (areas for storing grain) and a central threshing floor, with a large door in the middle of each long side. Each mow was, in effect, an independent log structure, and the two were united under a single roof. A loft was often included to hold fodder. Some smaller barns had only one mow, with the threshing floor and doors conse-

quently located off-centre.[63] A **barn near Dacre** [**4.35**], built along the Opeongo Road in the second half of the nineteenth century, shows the larger two-mow form; the later additions to the left of, and behind, the barn are typical of the way in which farm buildings grew as the needs increased.

This same form was repeated, in ever-varying sizes and proportions, in both log and frame construction. The gable roof prevailed in Ontario, although hipped gables and a gambrel roof also appear.

Another type of barn is the 'bank barn', in which a stone-walled stable is placed on the ground floor and the mows (often enclosed by log walls) form a second storey above it. An earth ramp (a 'bank') gives carts access to the threshing floor. The source of this two-tiered type is the Pennsylvania barn, and the best early survivor in Ontario is the impressive **Schmidt-Dalziel barn** [**4.36**], built by 'Pennsylvania-Dutch' settler Johannes Schmidt (John Smith) in Vaughan Township, north of York, about 1809. The lower level is a stable, used to house the stock that Schmidt had sent to him from Pennsylvania, while the upper level contains the mows and the threshing floor. Both storeys were built of massive logs, with the floor plan an impressive 50 by 28 feet (15 by 8.4 m). Heavy floor beams allow the upper floor to project 8 feet (2.4 m), creating an overhang (called a *laube*, or 'overshoot') that provides additional floor space and shelters the animals from bad weather. The Schmidt-Dalziel barn is now located at Black Creek Pioneer Village, an outdoor museum just northwest of Toronto. In a recent restoration, inappropriate windows were inserted in the mow to allow the barn to function as a museum, but otherwise it retains its original form.[64]

Public buildings

In Upper Canada the first task was to settle the rapidly growing population and ensure its survival, then to establish a social and political identity, and finally to try to make its impact felt elsewhere in British North America. Governor Simcoe, his successors, and other officials at the various levels of government recognized that impressive public buildings were an essential component of a program of self-aggrandizement. In York and other towns, as at Kingston, the initial structures, which had been erected hastily and cheaply during the period of settlement and adjustment, soon became physically and symbolically inadequate. Within a generation they began to be replaced by new and gracious Georgian buildings.

The evolving threshold of adequacy can be seen in the legislative buildings (called 'Parliament Buildings' in Upper Canada) that were required to carry on the business of government. In February 1796 Simcoe reported that he intended to build temporary legislative buildings at the eastern end of his town plan that would comprise the wings of a future government house:

> I am preparing to erect such Buildings as may be necessary for the future meeting of the Legislature; the plan I have adopted is, to consider a future Government House, as a Center, & to construct the *Wings* as temporary Offices for the legislature, purposing that so soon as the Province has sufficient Funds to erect its own Public Buildings, that They may be removed elsewhere.[65]

Master carpenter William Graham drew up plans for the buildings and superintended their construction, which was undertaken in 1797-8 by Ephraim Payson, the government bricklayer, and David Thomson (d. 1834), a stonemason. Since the city had good clay deposits but no good source of building stone, these craftsmen set a precedent for using brick as the predominant material for York's public buildings. The two separate wings of the first Parliament Buildings were each 40 by 24 feet (12.2 by 7.3 m) and joined by what the Honourable Peter Russell, who became Administrator upon Simcoe's return to England, described as 'something like a Colonade'. Russell wrote Simcoe in England in December 1797:

> The Two wings to the Government House are raised with Brick & completely covered in. The South One, being in the greatest forwardness I have directed to be fitted up for a temporary Court House for the Kings Bench in the ensuing Term, and I hope they may both be in a condition to receive the Two Houses of Parliament in June next. I have not yet given directions for proceeding with the remainder of your Excellency's plan for the Government House, being alarmed at the magnitude of the expence which Captain Graham estimates at (£10,000) I shall however order a large Kiln of Bricks to be prepared in the Spring.[66]

No adequate view of these first Parliament Buildings exists. In a letter to US President Thomas

4.37 Third Parliament Buildings, Toronto, Ontario, 1832. Lithograph by W.K. Hewitt from a drawing (1835) by Thomas Young. MTRL/John Ross Robertson Collection/T-10249.

Jefferson, John Strachan exaggeratedly called them 'two elegant mansions', and noted that they were situated 100 feet (30 m) apart.[67] The buildings were burned by the Americans in 1813, in retaliation for which the British burned the President's house in Washington—which had to be painted to cover the charring and has since been known as the White House.

The first Parliament Buildings were replaced in 1820 by a new structure that looked more like a fine private dwelling than the seat of government. Its front elevation was similar to that of John Strachan's house of one year earlier (two storeys high and seven bays wide, with the centre portion projecting), although it lacked the central pediment and pilasters.[68] The same Georgian manner evidently served both the residences and administrative offices of the power élite. It was also used for their places of business, as in the Bank of Upper Canada, whose directors included Strachan, D'Arcy Boulton, Jr, and other members of the Family Compact. Similarly composed to the second Parliament Buildings, the bank was built in 1825-7 to designs by Dr William Warren Baldwin (1775-1844), another director of the bank. The building still stands on Adelaide Street East at George Street, although its appearance has been changed by many subsequent alterations.[69]

Fire destroyed the second Parliament Buildings in 1824: this time it was caused by an overheated flue, and not enemy action. If this 1820 structure is seen as transitional design, hovering midway between the temporary and the eternal, the **third Parliament Buildings** that opened in 1832 on Front Street West, between Simcoe and John Streets, certainly aspired to the latter—a reflection of the rapid growth and increasing prosperity of both the town and the province. The government of Upper Canada expressed its coming of age with a mature Georgian building designed by the most respected architect in the province. The commissioners for the new building obtained plans in 1828 from Thomas Rogers of Kingston (after a competition they had held two years earlier that produced a winner, the little-known Joseph Nixon, but no design that could be carried out). Construction proceeded slowly, partly because of the bankruptcy of contractor Matthew Priestman and two of his subcontractors, and partly because it was decided that additional offices were needed: plans for two wings were executed by James G. Chewett (1793-1862). Parliament finally moved into its new quarters in 1832.[70]

A lithographed view of the new buildings [4.37]—drawn in 1835 by Toronto architect and artist Thomas Young (1805-60)—shows the intended design: the four-column classical portico was regrettably never built. Executed in brick with stone trim, the building had a central entrance that led to a corridor opening onto the chambers of the Legislative Council (on the left, beyond the tall windows with pedimented heads) and the Legislative Assembly (to the right, with similar windows), each the full height of the building. The wings that extended to either side, in two storeys, were treated more plainly. All three blocks were covered with low hipped roofs. The composition follows the general lines of many Palladian-Georgian country houses built in Britain a century earlier, with its porticoed main block, flanking wings, coherent geometry, and gentle classical ornament (the influence of this style was still potent in the young colony). After the union of the Canadas in 1841, the capital of the Province of Canada was ambulatory: Toronto succeeded Montreal as the capital in 1849-51 and replaced Quebec City in 1855-9. In between, and until Confederation, the buildings were put to other uses. They were replaced by the present Ontario Legislative Buildings in 1893 and demolished in 1903.

The musket-bearing soldiers and the grazing horse in Young's view are a reminder that York was still a young garrison town. In 1828 it had only 2,000 people; six years later, when it was incorporated as the city of Toronto, immigration (mostly from Britain) had increased its population to 9,000. The growing community had become the financial and service centre for the region—but the edge of the frontier was still not far away.

Scottish-born builder John Ewart (1788-1856), one of the unsuccessful competitors for the third Parliament Buildings (although he acted as superintendent there for a year or more), designed and built several important buildings for the privileged class at the end of the 'plain phase' of York architecture. One was Upper Canada College on King Street West, conceived on the model of English public schools and built in 1829-31 near the Parliament Buildings and Elmsley House, which was built (where Roy Thomson Hall now stands) by John Elmsley, Chief Justice of Upper Canada, in 1798, and purchased in 1815 as a residence for the lieutenant governor. Upper Canada College consisted of five separate but linked 2-storey brick buildings, the central building containing classrooms and offices, and the others providing residential space for teachers and boarding pupils.[71] Two other buildings attributed to Ewart are the Home District Courthouse and Jail (1823-4) on King Street East.[72]

Ewart was also responsible for the first portion of **Osgoode Hall** (1829-32), the headquarters of the Law Society of Upper Canada, which was named after William Osgoode, the first Chief Justice of the province. Ewart's three-storey house-like building

4.38 Osgoode Hall, Toronto, Ontario, begun 1829. Photograph by Harold Kalman.

in red brick [4.38], the present East Wing (seen at the right, behind H.B. Lane's later portico), was apparently designed in association with Dr William Warren Baldwin. Members of the Law Society demanded that it be 'in the plainest manner', and Ewart complied. Historian John Ross Robertson described it as 'a plain matter-of-fact brick building' containing two storeys and an attic. Its unassuming aspect, and domestic central-hall plan, were appropriate to its functions as a courtroom, law library, lounge and dining space for judges and lawyers, while also providing boarding rooms for

portico to Ewart's wing, duplicated it with a second wing at the west, and replaced the Baldwin bedroom wing, creating a central block with an egg-shaped dome to light the new library. The end pavilions feature projecting porticoes composed of an arcaded ground floor faced with rusticated stonework, four Ionic columns that support a finely detailed pediment in front of the two upper storeys, and classically detailed window surrounds that are embellished with pediments on the middle floor. The central block—nine bays wide (an awkward ten on the arcaded ground floor), with tall

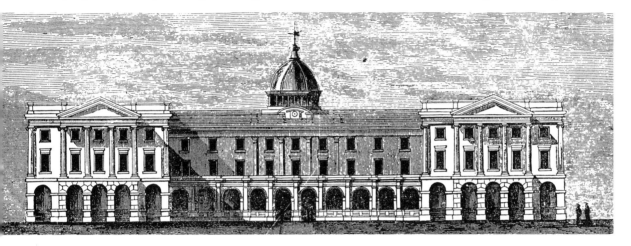

4.39 Addition to Osgoode Hall, Toronto, Ontario, 1844-5. Elevation by Henry Bowyer Lane. From W.H. Smith, *Smith's Canadian Gazetteer* (1846). NAC/C-3261.

articling students. In 1833 Dr Baldwin added a three-storey wing of student bedrooms.[73]

While suiting the tastes of York, a decade and a half later Osgoode Hall did not please more discriminating Torontonians. During and after the Rebellion of 1837-8, the Baldwin wing was used as a military barracks; and when the soldiers left in 1843 the building was in poor condition. The Law Society had also grown to the point where it needed more space, including accommodation for the Courts of Chancery and Queen's Bench. For renovations and additions, the Benchers turned to the English-trained architect Henry Bowyer Lane (1817-78), who maintained an active practice in Toronto during his short sojourn there from 1842 to 1847. (He was related to the Boultons, and had come to town under the patronage of William Henry Boulton—who was a member of the Law Society's building committee.) In 1844-5 Lane transformed Osgoode Hall into a Palladian-Georgian public building [4.39]. He added a new stone

pilasters on the central bays of the two upper floors—was rebuilt in 1857-60 (see page 178).

Although Lane's use of classical references may have been more rigorous and consistent than Upper Canadians were accustomed to, its source remains in the Georgian buildings of eighteenth-century Britain. The components, and the proportions of the end bays, look back to Palladian prototypes—such as Colen Campbell's house for Lord Herbert in Whitehall (*c.* 1723-4), which was illustrated in *Vitruvius Britannicus*; or to a second-generation Palladian building such as Isaac Ware's Wrotham Park, Middlesex (1754). But in provincial British centres the form was still used in the early nineteenth century, as at the Isle of Wight Institution (1811) and the Guildhall (1814)—both in Newport, Isle of Wight, and both designed by the celebrated John Nash (1752-1835). The effect of the ensemble of Osgoode Hall, with a domed and broad central block linking end units with pedimented columns, is a reduction and simplification of a composition such as Sir William Chambers' Somerset House (begun 1776), the most celebrated of the public buildings of Georgian London.[74]

4.40 Courthouse of the Johnstown District (now the United Counties of Leeds and Granville), Brockville, Ontario, 1841-5. Photograph by Harold Kalman, 1979.

An Upper Canadian prototype for Lane's treatment of the end pavilions of Osgoode Hall may be seen in the proposal by James G. Chewett for the Newcastle District Courthouse at Cobourg (then called Amherst), prepared in 1828. (The courthouse was built somewhat differently in 1829 to a design by Archibald Fraser.) Chewett's seven-bay façade, with a projecting Ionic portico, also looks back to English country houses of the 1720s.[75] An executed courthouse in this style is the handsome **Johnstown District Courthouse [4.40]** in Brockville (now the courthouse of the United Counties of Leeds and Grenville), built in 1841-5 to designs by Toronto architect John G. Howard (1803-90), who re-used a competition design he had prepared in 1838 for a Toronto courthouse. This Brockville landmark is one of the most elegant designs in the Palladian-Georgian manner and, like Lane's work at Osgoode Hall, marks the final flowering of the style in the 1840s. The building's fine interiors include a large double-height courtroom. Its exterior is distinguished by a larger-than-lifesize wood sculpture of *Justice* on the peak of the pediment; the original figure has been retired to the indoor security of the Rideau District Museum and replaced by a reproduction.[76]

Howard left a legacy of fine buildings, including many accomplished churches. Known as John Corby in his native England, and trained there, he immigrated to York in 1832 and changed his name. He is best known for the Provincial Lunatic Asylum at 999 Queen Street West, Toronto (1846-50), an immense four-storey limestone-and-brick building 584 feet (178 m) wide, whose breadth was held together by a masterly composition that culminated in a higher-domed central pavilion. (It was tragically demolished in 1976.) Howard's own house, Colborne Lodge (1837), is a Regency cottage that still stands in High Park, the large estate that he donated to the City of Toronto.[77]

Most of the buildings that have been considered to this point continue the Georgian style, which, as we have seen, emerged in both Maritime and central Canada at the end of the eighteenth century. The later and more embellished variants—those with projecting central pavilions, pediments, and porticoes—look back specifically to the Palladian phase of the Georgian style, which flourished in Britain in the second quarter of that century. The latter differ from the former in their greater complexity and more refined details. The Johnstown District Courthouse (1841-5) and the William Campbell House (1822) in Toronto, for example, show greater richness, as well as a more liberal use of classical features, than do Homewood (1800-1) or Fraserfield (*c*. 1812), and the same can be said of comparable houses in the Maritimes. These changes represent the development of a single style, from a plain phase to a more mature and embellished phase, and not the introduction of a new style. The earlier phase may be called Georgian and the later one Palladian-Georgian (or simply Palladian); both are stages in Georgian Classicism.

Architectural historians have been inconsistent in their terminology. Numerous other names have been used to describe these styles, including Loyalist, Regency, Neo-Classic, Neoclassical, and Classical Revival. The last three, however, are alternative terms for a later style that made a conscious attempt to leap over the architecture of the recent past and revive the lost classical architecture of antiquity—in contrast to Georgian Classicism, which is characterized by its continuity with the buildings of the sixteenth century through the eighteenth.[78]

Some buildings that have been discussed, such as the Colonial Buildings at Charlottetown and St John's, combine a Palladian approach to design with a somewhat more literal interpretation of classical detail than their predecessors'. They are best considered as a late and developed phase of the Georgian style, rather than as Neoclassical, because they represent the Georgian approach to the past: their architects continued to interpret classical antiquity as it had percolated through the successive renditions of Palladio, Inigo Jones, the circle of Lord Burlington, and such 'late Palladians' as Sir William Chambers.

The term 'Neoclassical', on the other hand, is best reserved for an alternative approach to architectural design, one that attempted to revive the forms of ancient Greece and Rome more directly, reflecting their rediscovery by European antiquarians and architects in the late eighteenth and early nineteenth centuries. This approach is characteristic of a new romantic and historicist perspective on architecture (and on culture in general)—one in which forms from the past were chosen consciously and deliberately because of their symbolism and associations. Neoclassicism of this kind was seen in a private and somewhat capricious manner at Castle Frank in the 1790s, made its first public appearance in Canada in the 1820s, and was a significant style until about 1860. It is considered with other revival styles in Chapter 6.

Some buildings defy rigid classification into one style or the other. An example is the monumental **Kingston City Hall** (1843-4), which offers a sophisticated fusion of the Georgian and Neoclassical styles, while looking ahead to the heavier yet more dynamic Victorian design [**4.41**]. The construction of the City Hall came about as a result of the short-lived economic boom occasioned by Kingston's designation in 1841 as the capital of the United Provinces of Upper and Lower Canada. The municipality announced a competition for a combined town hall and market in June 1842, and two

4.41 City Hall, Kingston, Ontario, 1843-4. Copyright 1994 Sparks Studio, Kingston, Ontario.

months later George Browne (1811-85) was named the winner; Alfred Brunel (1818-87) came second and John Howard third. (Howard's unsuccessful entry formed a basis for the design of his Provincial Lunatic Asylum in Toronto.) The Belfast-born Browne, who had worked in Quebec and Montreal before coming to Kingston in 1841, was eager to undertake a building of this scale; the result was an architectural triumph, although its progress was marred by quarrels and cost overruns.[79]

The British army officer and engineer, Sir Richard Bonnycastle, praised the completed building:

The Town Hall is probably the finest edifice of the kind on the continent of America, and cost £30,000, containing two splendid rooms of vast size, Post-office, Custom-House, Commercial Newsroom, shops, and a complete Market Place, with Mayor's Court and Police-office, and a lofty cupola, commanding a view of immense extent.[80]

The large limestone building was originally T-shaped, with a broad elevation 250 feet (75 m) wide facing Ontario Street and the Lake Ontario waterfront, and a deep wing at the rear containing the market. (The 'market shambles' was destroyed by fire in 1865 and was never rebuilt, but the open space, known as Market Square, has retained the original commercial function.) The composition of the façade follows Georgian precedent in its treatment as two storeys, with a rusticated ground floor supporting a smooth upper storey whose windows are contained within segmental and round arches respectively, and in the emphasis on the central portico and the dome above it. (The dome was originally hemispherical; the taller profile, clocks, and crowning cupola are later alterations that followed a fire in 1909.) Browne's personal choice of the 'primitive' Tuscan order, with its bare shafts and simple capitals and bases, is more of a Neoclassical gesture than a Georgian one. The portico was removed in 1956 and restored ten years later; the interior was restored by architects Harry P. Smith (1905-83) and Neil MacLennan in 1971-3.

The massive scale and assertive projection of the portico and the end pavilions, as well as the dynamic counterpoint of the design elements, deviate from the lighter, more static Georgian style. They look back to the English Baroque of Sir John Vanbrugh and Nicholas Hawksmoor—the style that preceded Palladianism and provided an important source of inspiration for the buildings of the Victorian age. Palladian-inspired designs were at last being perceived as old-fashioned.

Changing tastes are particularly evident in a design rationale for Osgoode Hall prepared in 1855 by Montreal architects Hopkins, Lawford, and Nelson as a part of their proposal for further additions to the Toronto building:

The style of architecture of the present building is inappropriate to the purposes of Courts of Law, from its too great lightness, and we consider that for such a city as Toronto, and for such a building as the Law Courts perhaps the most important in the place, a more massive and more imposing style should be adopted.[81]

The architects' submission was not accepted, and the new work was carried out instead, in 1857-60, by Toronto architects Frederic W. Cumberland (1820-81) and William G. Storm (1826-92). Cumberland and Storm did indeed adopt 'a more massive and more imposing style', yet one that sensitively respected the existing building. The front portions of the two wings were left unchanged (although they were made deeper), and Lane's central block was replaced by new construction. The portico motif was retained, but the proportions and details were all new, including placing an emphasis on the ends of the portico by doubling the columns and widening the base, using both round- and flat-headed windows, placing a full attic storey above the entablature of the portico, creating a picturesque silhouette by breaking up the parapet with finials, and varying the wall textures. (See **4.38**.) These are all features of the heavier and more eclectic architecture of the High Victorian age, a style that was just then coming into its own, and will be introduced below.[82]

Churches

Religious architecture in this country did not achieve a consistent Georgian style in the way secular buildings did. The earliest churches in Upper Canada exhibited a variety of forms, their characteristics dependent on the denomination and the means of the congregation, as well as on the nationality of the builders. Churches built for Anglican worship were generally straightforward rectangular buildings with a spire or tower at one end—simplified cousins of the Nova Scotia churches of the late eighteenth century. The altar was at the east end and the pulpit was usually located closer to the congregation, either against or near a side wall. The first St George's Church at Kingston (1791-2) was built in this way [**4.6**].

Mohawk Church Grand River, U.C. The oldest Episcopal Church in Canada. Here Peter Jones was baptized, and 2 here Capt.ⁿ Brant was buried

The oldest house of worship in Ontario, erected a half-dozen years before St George's, is St Paul's Church on the Six Nations Reserve near Brantford. Construction was authorized in 1784, and the church was built a year later, by order of Governor Haldimand, for the Mohawk Loyalists who had fought with the British forces during the American Revolution. The building is now known as **Her Majesty's Chapel of the Mohawks**, having received a royal dedication in 1906. The builders were John Smith and John Wilson, Loyalists from the Mohawk Valley of New York State and longtime friends of Joseph Brant, the Mohawks' celebrated leader. The church is clad in clapboards and is presumed to have a timber frame with log infill, materials that were common in upstate New York (as well as in Quebec). Three years after its completion, the Reverend John Stuart of Kingston wrote that 'the church is about sixty feet in length and forty-five in breadth, built with squared logs and

4.42 Mohawk Chapel, near Brantford, Ontario, begun 1785. From P.W. Jones, *History of the Ojebway Indians* (1861). Special Collections, University of British Columbia.

boarded on the outside and painted—with a handsome steeple bell, a pulpit, a reading desk and Communion table, with convenient pews.'[83] It contained at least three box pews, intended for Brant and his family and for white members of the congregation.

The church has been altered many times—first in 1799, when the tower was rebuilt and the church repaired (by Captain Robert Pilkington) after being struck by lightning. Subsequent changes included the relocation of the entrance from one side to the tower. Its appearance around 1850 is seen in a view [4.42] published by the Reverend Peter Jones in *History of the Ojebway Indians* (1861): it had a square chancel and round-arched window heads. The church remains in use, much admired for its age and the circumstances of its construction.

179

A church that combines French and English building practice is **St Andrew's Presbyterian Church** (1812-18) at Williamstown in Glengarry County, north of Cornwall [4.43]. A group of Highland Scots Loyalists settled there in 1787 and formed the first Presbyterian congregation in Upper Canada, under the direction of the Reverend John Bethune, a Loyalist from North Carolina who had been born on the Isle of Skye. Their first church was built of logs. The initial attempt at a permanent stone church ended in failure, as it collapsed during construction; the second try was successful. François-Xavier Rocheleau (d. 1812), a mason who was reportedly from Quebec City and had worked in Kingston, built the walls in the manner known to him, with uncoursed rubble stone. Rocheleau died before construction was finished and was succeeded by his foreman, John Kirby. The longitudinal plan, 68 by 36 feet (20.7 by 11 m), places the pulpit at the centre of a long side in the manner of the Church of Scotland. The characteristically French-Canadian walls are balanced by a number of British elements, notably the tracery in the round-arched windows, whose thick horizontal glazing bars near the springing of the arch create the impression of a Palladian arch. The steeple, made by Pierre Poitras of Montreal, resembles a Quebec *clocher*. It holds a bell that was produced in 1806 by Mears of London and donated to the church by fur-trader Sir Alexander Mackenzie, one of several directors of the North West Company who lived in the neighbourhood. Because of the shortage of skilled craftsmen in the early years of settlement in eastern Ontario, Quebec artisans were employed along with English-speaking ones—we have seen this both in Kingston and at Homewood—and St Andrew's represents the consequent fusion of two ways of building.[84]

Logs, usually left exposed, were commonly used for the first churches, as they were for the initial houses. An early extant log structure is St Elmo Congregational Church (1837) near Maxville in Glengarry County; another is Providence Church from Kitley Township, also in eastern Ontario, built about 1845 for the use of any denomination and now preserved at Upper Canada Village.[85] The Roman Catholic congregation of St Andrews West, near Williamstown, whose members emigrated directly from Scotland, also built a log church in the 1780s. Its stone foundations were excavated in 1938, revealing that the log building measured 18 by 24 feet (5.5 by 7.3 m). It was replaced in 1801 with a rubble-stone church having a steep gabled roof and rounded eastern end—built by Quebec artisans and looking like a Quebec church; it now serves, with its roof lowered, as the Parish Hall. Its gilded tabernacle was made by sculptor Philippe Liébert of Montreal. The historic cemetery of St Andrews West contains the graves of fur-trader Simon Fraser and Sir John Sandfield Macdonald, the first premier of Ontario.[86]

Methodism was a vital force on the Upper Canada frontier, particularly in the Niagara and Bay of Quinte regions. Many Methodists were among the Loyalists and 'late Loyalists', and included itinerant preachers on horseback whose ways were well adapted to frontier society. Their early meeting-houses were unadorned buildings, nearly square in

4.43 St Andrew's Presbyterian Church, Williamstown, Ontario, 1812-18. Photograph by Ralph Greenhill.

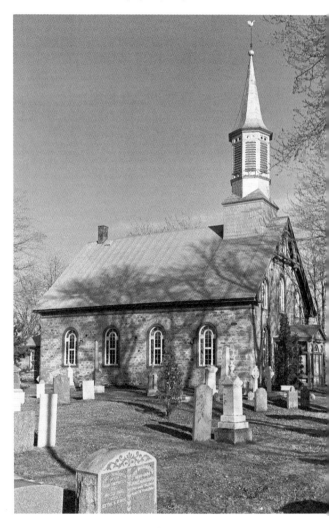

4.44 White Chapel, near Picton, Ontario, 1809-11. HWS/SSS/ONT 80 P1 CH 1.05A.

plan, similar to those of both the Methodists and the Congregationalists in the Maritimes, New England, and—the immediate source—the central United States. (Even though the origins of the two denominations were different, they adopted similar building-forms.) The earliest survivor, the Methodist Meeting House at Hay Bay (near Adolphustown), was built in this manner in 1792, and was described two decades later by the Reverend Anson Green: 'The house is 30 by 36 [feet] with a gallery; it is painted blue on the inside and is rather a blue

looking affair altogether.' As the building was subsequently enlarged and drastically 'restored', the present structure does not well represent its early appearance.[87]

The **White Chapel** (or **Conger Chapel**) near Picton, built between 1809 and 1811 on land donated by New Jersey Loyalist Stephen Conger, provides better evidence of the early appearance of Methodist meeting-houses. The community possessed a sawmill, and so the construction is frame with clapboard siding [**4.44**]. Also roughly square in plan, it has two levels of delicate 12-over-8 windows, the upper ones illuminating the gallery that runs around three sides of the building and is reached by a corner stair. The interior is a picture of attractive simplicity. The raised panelled pulpit is covered by a sounding board to project the preacher's voice to the congregation, all of whom sit on straight-backed benches within close range, on the ground floor and in the gallery. A few pictures hang on the walls, lamps are attached to the hewn posts that support the gallery, and a bookcase and a small organ stand beside the pulpit. There are no fancy fixtures, liturgical trappings, or decorative items to divert the worshippers' attention from the spoken word. The building has endured few changes, although a draft vestibule now helps to keep out the cold winter wind.[88]

4.45 Sharon Temple (and David Willson's study), Sharon, Ontario, *c*. 1825-30. Archives of Ontario/Acc. 2768-5.

A remarkable and unique house of worship is **Sharon Temple** (*c*. 1825-30) at Sharon, north of Toronto [**4.45**]. It was built by the Children of Peace (sometimes called Davidites), the followers of David Willson, a native of upper New York State who had crossed Lake Ontario and joined the Society of Friends. A mystical experience inspired Willson to speak out loudly at a monthly meeting of the Friends; when he continued his disruptive ways he was expelled. He and five other families withdrew from the Quakers and settled in Sharon. They and their followers deviated from the established group in such indulgences as their love of music, their intricate service, and their particular observance of feast days (notably Thanksgiving).

In 1825 Willson was instructed by a message to erect a temple. He appealed to his associates for assistance:

> *Oh! friends and workmen, come to me,*
> *If you accept the plan,*
> *We'll build a throne of liberty,*
> *An equal rest for man.*

Willson had no experience in architecture, but with the help of master builder Ebenezer Doan he directed his followers to erect a handsome structure that is rich in symbolism. The temple, as it was called, is sited on a level plain, enclosed by a fence (now gone) and sheltered from Yonge Street by a row of maple trees. David Willson's elegantly arcaded study is seen at the left. The temple is 60 feet (18.3 m) square—representing 'square dealing with all the world'—and built in three tiers, which stand for the Trinity. The four doors face the four compass points, because people from all directions were expected to come to worship. Forty windows— each divided on the three levels into 72, 60, and 54 panes of glass respectively—flood the interior with light. One row of interior columns bears the names of the apostles; other posts are designated 'Faith', 'Hope', 'Love', and 'Charity'. In the centre, surrounded by the columns, is the Ark, a model of the lowest tier of the temple. The ground floor was used for worship, the second storey as a musicians' gallery. At the top, more than 70 feet (21 m) above the ground, are clusters of pinnacles reaching upwards and a gilded ball inscribed 'Peace'.[89]

The Children of Peace survived its founder by only a few years. Sharon Temple has fortunately been preserved by the York Pioneer and Historical Society, and has been used in recent years for a highly successful summer music festival, a tribute to its builders' love of music.

As Upper Canada grew, the new churches of the various denominations began to lose their distinctive characteristics. The dissenters began to place towers at the entrances of their churches, as at White's Methodist Church (1841) in Hastings, although its squat proportions and lack of a belfry distinguish it from the Anglican norm.[90]

The Church of England—and also the Church of Scotland—came closest to adopting a consistent Georgian style, as might be expected by the manner in which the Toronto establishment embraced Georgian for its houses and public buildings. St George's Anglican Church in Kingston (page 000), built in 1825, was an early attempt at a gracious stone building with liberal classical ornament. It has a similar composition and massing to that of an English Georgian church—such as the one at Hardenhuish, Wiltshire (1779), designed by John Wood the Younger (1728-81) of Bath.

The style was developed further at **St Andrew's Church of Scotland [4.46]** on Church Street, York, designed and built in 1830-4 by John Ewart for a congregation that was an important one in Toronto life; a founding member was William Lyon Mackenzie. St Andrew's was built of brick, stuccoed and scored to imitate stone. The tower was placed at the entrance, as at St George's, but the entablature and the pilasters supporting it were continued around it so that the lower portion appeared to be a central projection of the façade (as on a Georgian house). Tall and elegant round-arched windows— separated by pilasters—illuminated the nave, and a square-headed door and window, with carefully detailed classical surrounds, were inserted into the entrance bay. These details around the entry may be considered to be Neoclassical features, but the overall intent was not one of reviving a lost classical past, but rather of continuing—as in St George's—an eighteenth-century building tradition. The upper part of the tower and the spire were added by John Howard in 1841; the church was demolished in 1878.[91]

Another building in this mode was **Christ Church, Hamilton [4.47]**, built in 1837-42 to designs by Robert Charles Wetherell (d. 1845), the architect of Dundurn Castle, the Regency villa of Sir Allan MacNab overlooking Hamilton harbour. (The powerful MacNab family participated in the building committee for the church.) Pilasters, paired at the corners, separated the tall round-headed windows, and the cornice continued around the tower. The latter was embellished with a projecting portico, which created a dynamic Baroque focus on the entrance when viewed in combination with the tall spire and the intermediate stage (whose columns supported a broken entablature and urns, in the manner of John Soane's Holy Trinity Church, Marylebone, London, built 1826-7). Christ Church is seen here in a drawing made in 1842 by visitor Thomas Glegg. It remained this way for only a decade. The Georgian style was soon eclipsed by the Gothic Revival, and additions in that manner were made in 1852; but twenty years later Wetherell's church was demolished to allow the completion of the present Gothic Revival building.[92]

4.46 (*above*) St Andrew's Church of Scotland, Toronto, Ontario, 1830-4. Watercolour by John G. Howard, 1840. MTRL/John Ross Robertson Collection/T-10706.

4.47 Christ Church, Hamilton, Ontario, 1837-42. Sketch by Thomas Glegg, 1842. Archives of Ontario/Acc. 4579 S12407.

Lower Canada

When New France became a part of British North America with the Treaty of Paris (1763) there were few immediate changes in the day-to-day lives or the physical environment of the residents. The new governors, of course, were British and not French, but most social and cultural institutions remained as they had been. The British authorities wanted to establish a good relationship with their new subjects and permitted the French to retain both their language and French civil law. The Quebec Act of 1774 left the seigneuries and parishes intact, and fixed boundaries that were similar to those of New France. The parish priests were allowed to retain their considerable influence, although the power of the religious orders was suppressed. The Constitutional Act of 1791 divided the colony of Quebec into the provinces of Lower and Upper Canada, each with an elected Legislative Assembly in the British tradition.

Changes certainly occurred—but over time, and

4.48 Courthouse (Palais de Justice), Quebec, Quebec, 1799-1803. Photograph *c.* 1870. ANQ/P547/431-2.

largely as a result of the small but vocal English-speaking minority that settled in Lower Canada, primarily in the cities of Quebec and Montreal. English, Scots, and Americans came as suppliers and contractors to the British army, and then moved into general commerce, many of them becoming involved in the fur trade. The St Lawrence merchants acquired considerable wealth and economic power; they also achieved a significant impact not only on the politics, but also on the built environment of the province. The anglophone community began to build their houses, churches, and commercial buildings in the Georgian manner—partly because this was the style to which they were accustomed, and partly because it made a potent statement of their increasingly important economic, political, and social position within the predominantly French province. Their buildings had a secondary effect as well, since they left a deep impression on a generation of Quebec-born architects, and inspired them to introduce elements of classicism into their own buildings. The remainder of this chapter traces the impact of Georgian architecture on the buildings of both the English- and French-speaking communities in Lower Canada.

4.49 Courthouse, Montreal, Quebec, 1799-1803. Drawing by James Duncan. From Newton Bosworth, ed., *Hochelaga Depicta* (1839). NAC/C-13342 (top).

The architecture of the English-speaking minority

Secular buildings The British institutions that were introduced into Lower Canada were initially accommodated in the existing French-regime buildings that had been appropriated by the government, but in time new public buildings were required. Georgian Classicism was invariably used, not only because it was the only style that was familiar to the authorities, but also because it provided an unmistakable expression of British sovereignty.

The first significant architectural statements made by the new government were courthouses—symbols of British secular power—erected in Quebec City and Montreal in 1799, four decades after the Conquest. They responded to the requirements for new courts of law and judicial districts that were stipulated by legislation in 1793. The **Courthouse (Palais de Justice**, 1799-1803) in Quebec was built on a portion of the land on Place d'Armes that had been occupied by the Récollet order, whose monastery and church were destroyed by fire in 1796. Half the site was allocated to the courthouse and half to a new Anglican cathedral [**4.51**]. Construc-

tion of the courthouse [**4.48**] was overseen by a military engineer, Captain William Hall, who served with the Royal Artillery and was stationed at the Quebec garrison. The design was almost certainly by the talented sculptor, painter, and architect François Baillairgé (1759-1830), who submitted a plan in 1799; and an active role was taken as well by Jonathan Sewell, one of the three commissioners responsible for the work, who was a lawyer and a powerful member of the Legislative Assembly. Sewell revealed in a letter to Hall that he had done his homework by consulting architectural treatises. Baillairgé corroborated Sewell's involvement in a note in his personal journal, dated June 1799:

> The 23rd, made and delivered a plan of the ground floor and the first floor yesterday evening with the elevations of a building for the audience rooms and courtrooms proposed to be executed in Quebec, with the various offices, vaults, etc., directed by Mr Suel [*sic*], the King's advocate, one of the three commissioners for this building.[93]

Baillairgé's design—if indeed it was his, and not Hall's, that was built—follows classical models, with which he was familiar from his studies in Paris. The courthouse was a stone building, two storeys high with a basement, and covered by a low hipped roof. The broad principal façade, 120 feet (37 m) wide, was divided into nine bays, the three central ones projecting slightly and capped by a pediment. Rusticated stonework was used on the first floor in the central portion around the triple-arched entrance portico—a detail that confuses somewhat the usual distinction between a rusticated basement and smooth main floor, and may show Baillairgé's familiarity with French, rather than British, classicism. Quoins were inserted at the corners; otherwise the walls were smooth ashlar and the windows flat-headed casements. The cornice was rendered in 'the tuscan order . . . on account of its propriety, its durability, its safety from fire and its superior degree of ornament.' The spacious courtroom and ancillary chambers were located on the upper floor, and judicial services on the lower one. In 1873 the building was destroyed by fire and replaced by the present courts.

The **Montreal Courthouse [4.49]** was similar in design, although it shows a more developed Palladian-Georgian composition. Built in 1799-1803, it was more liberally ornamented, and the end bays—illuminated by Palladian windows—projected as pavilions, as did the three central bays. The designer has not been identified. François-Xavier Daveluy was the builder, and construction was overseen by William Gilmore. This building, too, was destroyed by fire, in 1844.[94]

4.50 Sewell house, Quebec, Quebec, 1803-5. Photograph by Harold Kalman, 1976.

When we realize that the Quebec and Montreal courthouses preceded most of the institutional structures in the other provinces, their considerable significance begins to emerge. In 1800 Quebec, Montreal, and Halifax all had populations of about 8,000, whereas York had a mere 300—so the cities of Lower Canada and the Maritimes might be expected to take the lead. But an added factor was the government's urgent need to assert its power by using a British style that contrasted forcefully with the indigenous institutional vernacular.

In 1817 nine of the city's leading merchants formed the Bank of Montreal, the oldest chartered bank in Canada. Eight were originally from England, Scotland, or the US; Austin Cuvillier was the sole French Canadian. The directors purchased a strategic site at the corner of rue Saint-Jacques and rue Saint-François-Xavier—adjacent to Place d'Armes, the Church of Notre-Dame, and the Séminaire de Saint-Sulpice—and in 1818-19 they erected the Bank of Montreal, the first purpose-built bank building in the country. The architect has recently been identified as Andrew White (c. 1783-1832). The classically inspired edifice was three storeys high and six bays wide (not the customary five or seven), with a low Doric portico in front of the two central doors. The walls, built of local limestone ashlar, were relieved by belt-courses between the floors and by quoins, and the building was covered by a low hipped roof whose eaves formed a cornice. Four relief panels of Coade stone

set over the ground-floor windows—depicting Commerce, Agriculture, Navigation, and Arts and Manufactures—were the first example of narrative relief decoration on bank buildings. The banking chamber and directors' offices occupied the ground floor, which was 16 feet (4.9 m) high; the vaults were in the basement and the 'cashier' (manager) lived on the second floor. (The use of the third floor is uncertain.) The characteristically Canadian restraint of its design may be contrasted with the overt Neoclassicism of American banks of the time; the Bank of Montreal looks far more like a gentleman's townhouse than a temple of commerce. Despite the reticence, traveller Edward Allen Talbot praised it as 'by far the finest edifice, either public or private, in the Canadas'. The much more imposing second bank was erected next door in 1845-8 (see **5.52**, where both are illustrated).[95]

Georgian principles also found their way into domestic architecture. One of the most uncompromisingly British of Quebec houses, as might be expected, was the **residence of Jonathan Sewell [4.50]**, the man who directed the construction of the Quebec Courthouse and donated the funds for building Holy Trinity Chapel (1824, on rue Saint-Stanislas; architect George Blakelock). The son of the attorney general of Massachusetts, the young Sewell and his family went to England during the Revolution and later went to New Brunswick. Jonathan Sewell moved to Quebec in 1789 to practise law. He was a devoted imperialist who held several high political offices, including a thirty-year stint as Chief Justice of Lower Canada (during which time he was also Speaker of the Legislative Council). Advocating the anglicization of all Canadian children through the schools, he eliminated the French legal code, replaced the seigneurial system with freehold land-tenure, and reduced the position of the Roman Catholic church. In short, he had little tolerance for the customs or practices of the French-Canadian majority. The architectural expression of his personality, and politics, was a house that declared its Britishness, and was conspicuously different from those of his French-speaking neighbours. Built on the rue Saint-Louis in Quebec in 1803-5, it has the familiar five-bay Georgian elevation and central-hall plan. The gable roof is lower in pitch, and the stone walls are smoother in texture, than Quebec custom ordained. The house originally had a fanlight over the door, a cornice below the eaves, and a wing to either side, but these features have been removed— perhaps because they were seen, consciously or

not, by subsequent owners as being out of character with the other buildings of the city.[96]

The streets of both Quebec and Montreal were gradually infilled with Georgian buildings. James Pattison Cockburn's 1830 view of Quebec's Hope Street (rue Ste-Famille, **2.5**) shows the contrast between the British-style townhouse in the left foreground—with its imposing height, classical door surround, and bow window—and the lower French-regime house beyond it. The tower of the Anglican Cathedral on the axis of the street competes aggressively with that of the Catholic Cathedral on the left.

The Georgian house-type—often with the pedimented central portion that was so important a part of the Upper Canada landscape—appeared frequently in Lower Canada, particularly in the Eastern Townships, east of Montreal, which received heavy Loyalist settlement, in part because the colonization roads made them more accessible (see page 211). A splendid example is the Joshua Copp house, Georgeville (c. 1816); many others survive as well.[97]

Churches The same process of anglicization also occurred in religious architecture. Just as Upper Canada had Bishop Strachan, so did Lower Canada have a clergyman who ardently defended British institutions and traditions: Bishop Jacob Mountain. Born in Norfolk and educated at Cambridge University, Mountain was appointed in 1793 as bishop of the new Anglican diocese of Quebec, which originally included all of Lower and Upper Canada. (In 1839 his episcopal see was subdivided to create Strachan's bishopric, the Diocese of Toronto.) Mountain glumly noted that the English Protestant community in Quebec, Montreal, and Trois-Rivières worshipped in borrowed spaces, and he determined to replace these with purpose-built Anglican churches. During his tenure Mountain oversaw the construction of some sixty church buildings.

His earliest architectural achievement was the construction of a cathedral in Quebec. The Protestants in that city first worshipped in the Récollet Church (the adjacent monastery was used as a military prison); when the Récollet complex was destroyed by fire in 1796, the Anglican community co-opted the house of worship of the other once-powerful order and moved to the Jesuit Church. Mountain complained that it was 'in all respects insufficient for our purpose, small, dark, dirty, and ill-suited to receive a decent assembly of people'—a

far cry from the praise that had been heaped on the chapel a century earlier. He petitioned to England for funds to build a new church, arguing that 'nothing, I believe, would tend more effectually to give weight and consequence to the Establishment than a proper Church at Quebec, exclusively appropriated to our Worship.' Mountain received permission, money, and land. Construction of a new **Holy Trinity Cathedral** [**4.51**] began in 1800 on one half of the Récollet site, which was ample to allow a treed open space around the building. In 1804 the new cathedral was consecrated as the first purpose-built Anglican cathedral outside the British Isles.[98] (St Paul's in Halifax became a cathedral in 1787,

4.51 (*opposite*) Holy Trinity Cathedral, Quebec, Quebec, 1800-4. HWS/SSS/QUE 82 QC CH 2.09.

4.52 St Martin in-the-Fields, London, England, 1726. From James Gibbs, *A Book of Architecture* (1728). By permission of the British Library.

when Charles Inglis was consecrated as Bishop of Nova Scotia, but it was built as a parish church.)

The design and construction of Holy Trinity Cathedral were entrusted to two members of the Royal Artillery garrisoned at Quebec: Captain William Hall (who was participating in the construction of the courthouse) and Major William Robe (1765-1820). The latter left a valuable description of the building that identified the authorship of the plans: 'The general plan of the Church was given by Captain Hall of the Royal Artillery, the detailed plans of the several parts were drawn by myself. . . .' He identified the principal workmen (most, led by master mason Edward Cannon and his three sons, were English), and explained the sources for the design:

> The general dimensions of this Church were in great measure taken from those of St Martin's-in-the-Fields, but the state of materials and workmanship in Canada made a plain design necessary. . . . The east and west ends are ornamented with pilasters of the Ionic according to Palladio and supporting a modillion cornice and pediment but without a frieze: this idea was taken from the Pantheon at Rome so executed, and was done to give more boldness to the pilasters for the intended height of the building. The pilasters project less than Palladio's rule directs, owing to the Point[e]-aux-Tremble[s] stone, which, in the then state of the quarries, could not be got in masses large enough without an enormous expense.[99]

James Gibbs's St Martin-in-the-Fields (1726), on London's Trafalgar Square (perhaps the most widely admired of eighteenth-century English churches) was a more elaborate version of St Peter, Vere Street [**3.22**], with a free-standing portico and pilasters along the side elevations. Like St Peter, it was illustrated in Gibbs's *A Book of Architecture*. St Martin provided a model for many American churches, including Christ Church (1727-54), Philadelphia, and St Michael's (1752-61), Charleston, South Carolina, both of them Anglican (later Episcopal).[100] When Robe and Hall turned to Gibbs for a source for the Quebec church, they were acting within good Georgian practice by using classical sources as they had been interpreted by Palladio and the architects of eighteenth-century England—and they supplemented this with a glance at one Roman source, the Pantheon, in what could be described as a tangential Neoclassical gesture.

St Martin-in-the-Fields [**4.52**] consists of a rectangular block, with a large free-standing portico at the entrance and a tall tower and spire that rise from the body of the church just behind the portico. The exterior walls exhibit rich classical detail, including tall pilasters between the windows (as was seen at the later St Andrew's, York) that are paired at the corners (as would occur at Christ Church, Hamilton). Many of the individual features of Gibbs's design are based on the London churches of Sir Christopher Wren, but the ensemble is far more monumental than Wren's churches, as well as being more ornate than the work of the strict Palladians.

The nature of the 'plain design' becomes clear when Holy Trinity Cathedral is compared with St Martin-in-the-Fields. The overall proportions and massing may be similar, but the free-standing six-column Corinthian portico of St Martin has been reduced to four thin Ionic pilasters (the Ionic capital is easier to carve than the Corinthian one) superimposed on a blind arcade, and the pilasters have disappeared entirely along the side elevations. The tower follows the general lines of the English source, with a square base surmounted by a stage with four clock faces, an arched octagonal tier, and a spire; but at Quebec each of the stages has been simplified and one omitted entirely. A similar process of abridgement occurred in the interior [**4.53**], which has been marvellously preserved. As in the London church, 'giant' columns—also changed to Ionic from Corinthian—rise past the galleries to support the arches of the coved ceiling, and a Palladian window illuminates the chancel. A number of other features (including Gibbs's ornate plaster ceiling) have been simplified or omitted. English oak was used for the fittings, including the pulpit and reading desk, which are located at the east end of the nave, outside the chancel, as was the practice in Anglican churches. A special Royal pew was reserved for the King or his representative.

The similarities to the English model were far more important to the people of the day than were the deviations from it. Holy Trinity Cathedral was clearly perceived as a forceful symbol of British authority. Bishop Mountain declared the power of the British ruling class by building the cathedral in the British manner using British workmen, without making compromises to its surroundings (other than modifications that were necessitated by the available materials, skills, and funds). His model was by now long out of fashion—St Martin-in-the-Fields had been built three-quarters of a century

earlier—but, if anything, its venerability made the new cathedral all the more familiar and reassuring. Bishop Mountain's message was enhanced by the cathedral's prominent location in the Upper Town, near the escarpment and the venerable Château Saint-Louis (which had been appropriated for British military purposes and would be given a Georgian frontispiece in 1808-11).[101] Its aloofness was heightened when walls were built around the cathedral close about 1818, under the supervision of Lieutenant Colonel Elias Walker Durnford (1774-1850), a Royal Engineer.

These associations did not go unnoticed. Joseph Bouchette, a keen observer of buildings in the Canadas, called the cathedral

4.53 Interior of Holy Trinity Cathedral, Quebec, Quebec, 1800-4. HWS/SSS/QUE 78 QC CH 2-24.

...perhaps, the handsomest modern edifice of the city; and though not highly decorated, the style of architecture is chaste and correct. In the interior, a neat and unostentatious elegance prevails, wherein ornament is judiciously but sparingly introduced.[102]

Bishop Mountain would have been pleased that his building was appreciated as being 'modern' and displaying 'elegance' and 'taste', for these were the very qualities that he meant to be recognized as British.

The Quebec cathedral was built earlier than the Georgian churches in Upper Canada described above, and it served as an important source for them. A number of other Anglican churches were subsequently built in Lower Canada on the same theme. The most celebrated was **Christ Church**, **Montreal** [**4.54**], which also follows the Wren-Gibbs lineage, although without adopting a specific source. The Montreal merchants were ready to express their bid for power and recognition in stone, and they chose a site on rue Notre-Dame, a short distance from the French-Catholic parish church of that name. After considering proposals by a number of architects, the building committee chose the plans of William Berczy. An itinerant German-born painter who occasionally dabbled in architecture, Berczy may have studied architecture in Vienna in the 1750s. He had travelled in England and the US before coming to Upper Canada and then to Montreal, so he had first-hand experience of Georgian Classicism. Bishop Mountain laid the first stone of Christ Church in 1805. Construction progressed slowly because of changes to the design that were needed to increase the church's capacity as the English-speaking community grew. The first services were not held in the church until 1814, and it was not completed until 1821. Like its Quebec predecessor, Christ Church had a rectangular body with a tall spire—which became a Montreal landmark—and a suggestion of a portico created by applied pilasters supporting a pediment, here rendered in the Doric order. The Georgian character of the façade was reinforced by the classical window surrounds, the recessed panels and carved swag over the door, the parapet over the cornice, the quoins at the corners of the building, and the tower.[103]

Christ Church was very much admired. American traveller Benjamin Silliman called it the most beautiful building in Montreal; Edward Talbot said that the steeple 'is acknowledged to be superior to

4.54 Christ Church, Montreal, Quebec, 1805-21. Drawing by James Duncan. From Newton Bosworth, ed., *Hochelaga Depicta* (1839). NAC/C-13332.

anything of the kind in British North America'; and Joseph Bouchette wrote, before its completion, that 'it promises to become one of the handsomest specimens of modern architecture in the Province.'[104] The old parish church of Notre-Dame—and, by extension, the French-speaking Catholic community of Montreal—had been eclipsed by this architectural upstart. No matter that it was *retardataire*; like Holy Trinity Cathedral in Quebec, Christ Church made a powerful declaration of British values. Two such assertive architectural statements instantly made the French vernacular building traditions seem tired and old-fashioned. The Roman Catholic church would soon respond aggressively to this Protestant architectural challenge by building a new and more 'modern' Church of Notre-Dame in the Gothic Revival style. And after the Georgian Christ Church was destroyed by fire in 1856, the English community retaliated with a new and more correctly Gothic church. This clash between the two cultures on the architectural battlefield of Montreal will be described in Chapter 6.

4.55 St Stephen's Anglican Church, Chambly, Quebec, 1820-2. Photograph by Harold Kalman.

Classical churches were built to serve the English-speaking residents of Lower Canada by all the denominations that served them. Three other examples are St Andrew's Presbyterian Church (1809-10) in Quebec, which shares many features with the Anglican cathedral (its builder, John Bryson, had worked on the cathedral); the British Wesleyan Methodist Chapel (1820-2, demolished) in Montreal, whose five-bay façade adopted the composition commonly used for Georgian public buildings, as had John Wesley's City Road Chapel (1770) in London; and Holy Trinity Chapel (1824-5) in Quebec, a chapel-of-ease to the cathedral designed by George Blaiklock (1792-1828), which imitates the Methodist Chapel and adds a broad pediment and cubic belfry. The recessed (rather than projecting) central bays, blind arcades, and baseless Greek Doric columns of both the Methodist Chapel and Holy Trinity Chapel are Neoclassical features that look ahead to the full-blown classical revival.[105]

Some churches were more respectful of local custom. In the lovely Anglican church of **St Stephen's, Chambly**, [4.55], built in 1820-2 to serve the garri-

son in that fortified community, 15 miles (25 km) east of Montreal, English and French building traditions reached a happy compromise (as they had at St Andrew's in Williamstown). The semicircular apsidal end and the rubble-stone walls (described in the building contract as 'thick stone') are characteristic of Quebec churches, whereas the Palladian window illuminating the chancel, the Tuscan porch and pediment of the façade (not visible in the photograph), and the layout of the interior galleries represent the Gibbs-derived British manner.

This fusion of two traditions reveals the contributions of the two people most responsible for the project: the Reverend Edward Parkin (1791-1844), a missionary sent by the Society for the Propagation of the Gospel (known as the SPG) and the incumbent priest at Chambly, who played an active role in construction and took credit for the design; and François Valade, the builder, who styled himself as a 'carpenter and joiner'. Valade retained two local masons, François Morier and Louis Duchatel, to build the exterior walls.[106]

French classicism

The English of Lower Canada may have had difficulty seeing the world through the eyes of the French, but the local population had little trouble in recognizing what the English were doing. However they felt about the messages inherent in the new Georgian buildings, Quebec-born architects and their clients evidently admired their classical design. Beginning around 1800, a number of French-speaking architects began to introduce classical elements into their own buildings, many for institutions that represented the old order.

The French classicism of the early nineteenth century began not so much as a direct effect of British classicism as a parallel initiative to look at the architecture of antiquity, in this case as it was interpreted by French architects and theorists of

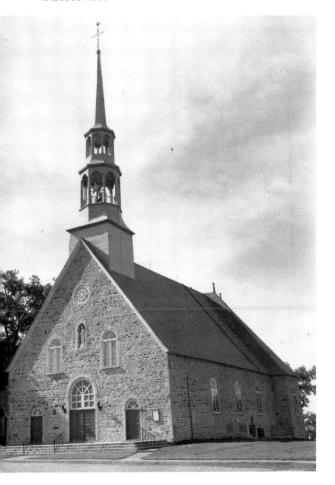

4.56 Église Sainte-Marguerite, L'Acadie, Quebec, 1800-1. IBC/15667 H-9.

the seventeenth and eighteenth centuries. Towards mid-century, however, the interaction between the two cultures in Lower Canada brought the two architectural movements closer together.

For the first thirty years after the Conquest, Quebec architecture maintained a strong continuity with the past. Buildings that had been destroyed during the war were repaired or replaced by artisans who continued to use the familiar forms and techniques they had learned during the French regime. There was an upsurge in church-building after 1790 as the economic situation improved. The Catholic Church used this opportunity to assert its position by deliberately reviving traditional architectural church-forms as a gesture of nationalism and an expression of authority.

An important landmark in this parish-church revival was **Église Sainte-Marguerite [4.56]** at L'Acadie, built in 1800-1 under the direction of Abbé Pierre Conefroy (1752-1816), the vicar-general of the diocese of Quebec for the Montreal region. Everything about the church follows the traditions of the old regime. Its plan has roots that go back to the churches of Bishop Laval (e.g. **2.43**) and provides a compromise between the Jesuit plan (with transept) and the Récollet plan (transeptless, with a choir that is narrower than the nave): the nave is intersected by transepts, each containing a lateral chapel, and the choir, which is narrower than the nave, terminates in a deep semicircular apse. The gabled façade has a tall arched central door flanked by two lower doors, with two arched windows (illuminating the gallery), and a niche on the second level and a circular oculus (lighting the organ tribune) in the gable. The walls are built in the customary rubble stone, the steep roofs have slightly flaring eaves, and a *clocher* with an open belfry rises from the peak. In essence it is a larger version of a church such as Sainte-Anne de Beaupré [**2.43**], built more than a century earlier; it is 120 feet (36.6 m) long and 50 feet (15.2 m) wide.

The church at L'Acadie represents a determined revival—or a remarkable survival—of the church traditions of New France. (The question of survival versus revival took on more importance a few decades later, and is discussed in the context of the Victorian stylistic revivals in Chapter 6.) The design can be attributed to Abbé Conefroy, who prepared model specifications and drawings for churches in the Montreal region and then oversaw the construction of many of them. His own parish church of Sainte-Famille at Boucherville (1801) is very similar to the church at L'Acadie, and also acknowledges the new classical taste by framing the entrance with a pediment and a pair of pilasters in ashlar. It survives in good condition, but it suffered a fire in 1843 and was somewhat altered during the subsequent repairs. More than twenty new churches followed what has come to be called the 'Conefroy plan'. All share the basic characteristics of the church at L'Acadie, although each has some individual features.[107]

These churches provide an introduction to French classicism, not because of the presence of classical features (although some are evident, particularly in the fine interiors), but because they represent the first awareness of the Quebec parish church as a definable building tradition that was worthy of being revived and improved, and even of being used for nationalistic purposes. Abbé Conefroy's adaptation of the architecture of the recent past (i.e. a century or so earlier) follows the same principle that was being used by English-speaking architects in their own buildings of the day.

Outside the Montreal region, and therefore beyond Abbé Conefroy's sphere of influence, a number of modest, older parish churches were 'modernized'—and a few new ones built—with monumental new façades that were entirely unlike the Québécois tradition. Several, including **Église Saint-Louis [4.57]** at Lotbinière (1818, on a nave of 1750-1) and the church at Louiseville (1804, demolished 1917), acquired façades with two towers, a *clocher* over each, and a triangular pediment applied to the gable that rises between them. The pediment responded to the new English taste; the towers recalled Sainte-Famille on the Île d'Orléans [2.49] and the few others like it that were based on the Jesuit church in Quebec; they may also acknowledge Chaussegros de Léry's partially executed proposal for Notre-Dame in Montreal (1722). Another member of this group was Église Sainte-Geneviève-de-Berthierville, which was renovated with a twin-towered façade in 1818-19. Evidently inspired by the work at Louiseville, the neighbouring parish, the wardens decided 'to raise the gable squarely to the height of the towers, with a cornice and balustrades'. They further showed their admiration for the English taste by getting in touch with Edward Cannon, the master mason for the Anglican Cathedral; he provided them with a scheme for improvements that formed the basis for the work.[108]

These two parallel efforts at introducing a new style were undertaken by parish priests and their

artisans. The next step involved a teacher and a professional architect who turned to the classical tradition as it had been interpreted by the architects and theorists of Renaissance and post-Renaissance France. The former, and the leader in this regard, was Abbé Jérôme Demers (1774-1853), who was a generation younger than Abbé Conefroy. A teacher and superior at the Séminaire de Québec, Demers was an architectural theorist who likely never designed a building on his own but had a significant impact on the architects and architecture of the province. He taught a course on architectural principles at the Séminaire and wrote a text for his students that he called *Précis d'Architecture* (1828); although it was never published, it received wide circulation. This was the first architectural treatise written in Canada, and Demers was the country's first professional teacher and theorist of architecture.

He was born in a village on the south shore of the St Lawrence near Quebec. Although he never went to France, Demers showed a keen awareness of French architecture and theory that was probably acquired from books and from his friendship with

4.57 Église Saint-Louis, Lotbinière, Quebec, 1818. IBC/73.17(45).

194

François Baillairgé, who had studied in Paris at the Académie royale de peinture et de sculpture. Demers's chief inspiration was the *Cours d'Architecture* (1771-7) of Jacques-François Blondel, professor at the Académie royale d'architecture. Blondel promoted a rational architecture that would combat the excesses of the Rococo style; his taste was for the forms of antiquity as codified by Italian and French architects and theorists of the post-Renaissance period, among them Giacomo da Vignola (1507-73) and Claude Perrault (1613-88)—a parallel, but different, genealogy from that of English Georgian classicism. Demers followed Blondel in this regard. His primary doctrine was the need for a 'pure classical architecture'. For Demers, 'classical' meant 'pure', 'universal', and 'based on absolute principles of beauty', and implicitly followed the style of Louis XVI, the French counterpart to late Palladian classicism. He believed that 'foreign' styles would destroy Quebec culture, and he labelled as foreign all the new revivals, including Gothic, Egyptian, and Chinese.[109]

The architect who actualized the theories of Demers was Thomas Baillairgé (1791-1859), the son of François and a student and protégé of Demers. The two collaborated closely for a number of years. Baillairgé provided the plates and models to accompany the *Précis d'architecture*, and Demers helped the young architect gain commissions, and coached him in design during the early period of his practice.[110]

An important example of the dynamic Demers-Baillairgé collaboration is **Église Saint-Charles-Borromée [4.58]** at Charlesbourg. The parishioners wanted to replace their aging church, which had been begun in 1695, so they consulted Abbé Demers in his capacity as vicar-general of the diocese. Demers determined the location and dimensions of the new church; then he helped Baillairgé prepare plans for the building, which was constructed in 1828-30. They searched for rules that they might use to organize the various components, following the rational academic method Demers espoused. The façade follows the lead of the twin-towered chuches of the previous two decades, such as Saint-Louis de Lotbinière, but everything is here precisely plotted within a tightly geometric design. The bases of the towers form an integral part of the façade rather than being seen as separate from it; they are articulated by shallow projections and decorative quoins, and their verticality is emphasized by the doors, the bull's-eye windows, and niches (containing statues of Saints Augustine and

4.58 Église Saint-Charles-Borromée, Charlesbourg, Quebec, 1828-30. HWS/SSS/QUE 81 CB CH 1.01.

Peter). The broad pediment unifies the three divisions of the façade (as did the pediment at the Anglican Cathedral), and appears to rest securely on the tower bases. A Palladian window occupies the centre. A perfect square can be described around the façade (up to the point of the pediment and the base of the *clochers*), and if this square is divided into quarters, the boundary lines of the segments neatly locate all the principal elements, including the tower bases, the bottom of the pediment, and the bases of the niches and the Palladian window. Baillairgé's drawing for the façade shows pilasters and an entablature around the main entrance, but these were omitted. Cut stone is used only at the corners and in the surrounds of the openings, and the walls are built of rubble stone covered with *crépi* and whitewashed. The result, however, is less of a visual than a theoretical triumph, as the façade looks clumsy and immature, even if (or perhaps because) reason accounts for every element; this may be due to both Baillairgé's immaturity and Demers's participation.[111]

The floor plan, like that at L'Acadie, offers a synthesis of the Jesuit (transept) and Récollet plans, which had competed for a century and a half: the nave opens onto a pair of transepts (each of which contains a side chapel), and the choir is narrower than the nave and terminates in a flat east end. The fine interior decoration was designed by Thomas Baillairgé and executed by his close associate, André Paquet (1799-1860), beginning in 1833. The general lines of the choir walls and retable follow those of the eighteenth century, as seen in a church such as Saint-François-de-Sales, although at Charlesbourg everything is more architectonic and structured.

Thomas Baillairgé succeeded to the position of diocesan architect of Quebec after his father's death in 1830, and he subsequently designed a number of other large churches. Many offer variations on the Charlesbourg theme; these include Église Sainte-Croix de Lotbinière (1835) and **Église Saint-François-Xavier** (1839-49) at Saint-François-du-Lac [**4.59**], in both of which a curved gable is substituted for the pediment; and Sainte-Geneviève at Pierrefonds (1837-44), where the pediment is supported by four pilasters, under which are three large arched openings, possibly inspired by the church of Notre-Dame in Montreal [**6.9**]. Baillairgé's increasing maturity is revealed in the harmony and balance that are evident in the designs. He was also responsible for several smaller churches; these, such as Saint-Joseph at Lauzon (1830-2), follow the precedent of the churches of Abbé Conefroy although, as might be expected, they reveal more discipline in their proportions.[112]

The most important church design by Thomas Baillairgé, but one that was never fully carried out, was a monumental classical proposal for the façade of the **Cathedral of Notre-Dame de Québec** [**4.60**], one of three alternative elevations he prepared in 1843. The frontispiece is dominated by giant pilasters of channeled ashlar that support a Doric pediment and contain the entrance and a large arched window; the end of the roof gable rises in several tiers above and behind the pediment, and curved volutes beside the pilasters make a graceful transition to the lower wings of the façade. These wings contain secondary doors and windows, and also mask the bases of the two towers, which rise in four square stages to their climax in domes, spires, and crosses. Besides possessing a powerful coherence of their own, the elements of the façade respond as well to the interior design of the cathedral, which was built largely to designs by

4.59 Église Saint-François-Xavier, Saint-François-du-Lac, Quebec, 1839-49. Photograph by Bernard Vallée. Ministère des Communications, fonds des moyens de communications (Québec).

4.60 (*right*) Elevation of Notre-Dame Cathedral, Quebec, Quebec. Thomas Baillargé, 1843. Archives de Notre-Dame-de-Québec.

François Baillairgé (1818). A journalist noted that the towers were intended to 'correspond to the façade in taste conforming to the times.'[113] Unfortunately the towers were never finished; the frontispiece, and half of the north (left) tower, were built to Baillairgé's design, but it was never completed above the third stage; and the south tower is very different in appearance from the architect's intentions [**4.61**].[114]

As time passed, the distinctions between the classicism of the English- and French-speaking communities became rather meaningless. A landmark that sums up the general acceptance of classical architecture in Lower Canada is the **Hôtel du parlement (Assemblée nationale)** in Quebec [**4.62**], built by a succession of architects between

4.61 Notre-Dame Cathedral, Quebec, Quebec. MMCH/2340.

1831 and 1852; and destroyed by fire in 1854, shortly after its completion. Since its formation in 1792, the National Assembly had been using space in the Palais épiscopal. Plans for a purpose-built Parliament Building were solicited from British architects in 1811 (see page 257), but to no avail. Finally in 1831 the government acquired a second episcopal palace, located further west in the Upper Town near the Plains of Abraham, and Thomas Baillairgé was commissioned to alter and add to the existing building, adapting it to become a parliament building. The project took twenty years to execute, and a number of other architects participated in the process and made changes to the Baillairgé plan, namely Louis-Thomas Berlinguet (1790-1863), Pierre Gauvreau (1813-84), and George Browne. The outcome was nevertheless surprisingly coherent. The central block and two projecting wings of the U-shaped complex enclosed a forecourt (seen in the lithograph with the ever-present drilling soldiers), somewhat in the manner of Osgoode Hall. The four-column Ionic portico of the central portion rested on a rusticated and arcaded basement and supported a pediment; a tall dome rose beyond it. The projecting wings terminated in a pedimented three-storey façade that screened the hipped roof behind. The frontispiece looked to eighteenth-century Britain, the dome more to seventeenth-century France; the ends of the wings resembled the church at Charlesbourg and Baillairgé's early attempts to define a Quebec classicism; and the relative plainness of the walls in combination with these classical features recalled the traditional institutional architecture of the French regime, and a building such as the Hôpital-général [**2.1**].[115]

Such were the fusions and compromises that came about in the course of developing a public architecture for Lower Canada. The Hôtel du parlement seems to make as many concessions to diverse influences as did the politicians who debated behind its walls. The building represents a late flowering of the Georgian Classical tradition, in that the path from antiquity led through the theory and buildings of seventeenth- and eighteenth-century intermediaries; the architects' approach was one of continuity, of maintaining and developing a single established tradition that was seen as being the one and only proper way to design buildings.

The next generation of architects would approach the past very differently, through a kind of historical discontinuity. Their aim was to learn more about all the different styles and traditions that made up European (and ultimately non-European) architectural history, and to select from the past the forms that were most closely associated with the needs of the present. This revivalist phase in Canadian architecture will be examined in Chapter 6. First, however, we shall look at a number of other kinds of buildings and structures that were current in the first half of the nineteenth century.

4.62 Hôtel du parlement (Assemblée nationale), Quebec, Quebec, 1831-52. Lithograph by Sarony and Major. ANQ/P600-5/GH-772-13.

CHAPTER 5

BUILDING FOR COMMUNICATIONS, DEFENCE, AND COMMERCE

BY THE early years of the nineteenth century most of the arable land close to the ocean and the principal inland waterways was being farmed, so it was continually necessary to develop new tracts further inland. Settlers put pressure on the government to improve the fledgling transportation system and provide them with military security. Only with assured communications could the colonists reach their land, receive regular supplies, and develop industry and trade. For its part, the military needed better transportation to improve defences—a priority that became particularly evident during the War of 1812-14.

The transportation and building needs of settlement, defence, and trade sometimes coincided, sometimes conflicted; nevertheless, public and private interests combined to develop an extensive communications system that served them all reasonably well. The waterways, roads, and railways that were constructed in the decades before Confederation were important in their own right, but they also succeeded in stimulating new settlement and trade. As a result of the country's immense scale, Canada quickly established itself as a world leader in transportation and communications technology, a position it maintains. Combining imported (primarily British) and domestic engineering expertise and capital, Canada achieved a primacy in these endeavours by demonstrating that necessity is indeed the mother of invention. This may be contrasted with early Canadian architecture, in which (as we have seen) the country's builders were often followers rather than leaders, since tried-and-true architectural imagery and practical building solutions met the needs of the young country perfectly well.

This chapter begins by looking at the communications and defence systems—the lighthouses, canals, roads and railways (and their bridges), and fortifications—that were built in British North America, and considers the systems themselves as engineering achievements, as well as the buildings that were directly associated with them.[1] The text then discusses land development in the interior and building for industry, two activities that were stimulated by new construction in the transportation and military sectors. It concludes with a brief overview of Canada's two leading mercantile cities in the mid-nineteenth century, Saint John and Montreal, whose growth was the outcome of the development of transportation and commerce.

Developing a Transportation System

Lighthouses

Until the end of the eighteenth century, coastal and inland waterways provided the only viable means of travel. Shipping encountered numerous natural hazards—we often forget how common shipwrecks were—and so lighthouses were erected to make both coastal and inland shipping safer. Often located on isolated islands or promontories, lighthouses were a challenge to build and maintain. Their design was a structural and utilitarian issue, although aesthetic concerns were usually addressed as well. The rudimentary solution was to construct a tall, sturdy tower and place a light at its peak. Most early lighthouses were built of masonry, and a slightly tapered shape provided structural stability (as well as a stable appearance).

5.1 (*opposite*) Lighthouse, Louisbourg, Nova Scotia, 1731-3. Archives nationales (France), Dépôt des fortifications des colonies, Amérique sept./C.171; reproduced from a photograph in the NAC/C-15674.

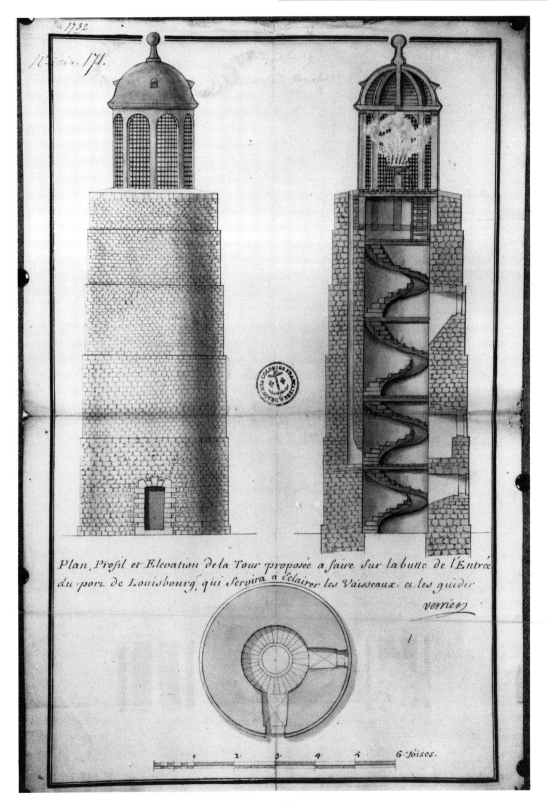

Plan, Profil et Elevation de la Tour proposée a faire sur la butte de l'Entrée du port de Louisbourg, qui servira a éclairer les Vaisseaux et les guider

Lighthouses made an important statement of government authority, built as they were in remote locations on the fringe of the empire (or, later, the dominion). Meticulously maintained, often with attractive lawns and gardens, they effectively symbolized dominion from sea to sea. Most were built by governmental departments of works—be they French, British, Canadian, or provincial. The names of individual designers have rarely come down, although drawings for many are retained by the Department of Transport and the National Archives of Canada.[2] Official records, however, cannot indicate the extreme engineering and personal difficulties that must have been encountered in erecting these buildings in their remote, exposed locations.

The **Louisbourg lighthouse [5.1]** was likely the first in Canada, although an earlier one may have been constructed at Placentia, Newfoundland, in 1727. Built in 1731-3 and sited on a rocky promontory at the entrance to the harbour of Louisbourg— the first landfall for many ships coming to New France—the Louisbourg lighthouse was a circular stone tower 70 feet (21.4 m) high, tapered slightly in five recessed stages and reinforced with iron supports. It supported a cupola-shaped lantern that

was reached by an internal spiral staircase. Even without reflectors, the light was visible for 18 miles (29 km) in clear weather. Illumination so strong generated a lot of heat, and because of faulty design the sperm-oil lamps caused a severe fire in the wood lantern-housing in 1736. The lantern was rebuilt in stone with brick vaulting and restored to service two years later. The lighthouse lasted twenty years before it was destroyed by the British attack in 1758. Engineer A.M. Verrier, who designed many of the buildings at Louisbourg, was responsible for the design; his signature appears on the drawings in the National Archives of Canada. Its substantial ruins were dismantled in 1923 by the federal government.[3]

The oldest lighthouse still in use in North America is the **Sambro Island lighthouse [5.2]**, built in 1758-60 on a small island outside the entrance to Halifax harbour. Its stone tower is octagonal rather than circular, an angular shape that was occasionally used for other North American lighthouses of the period, including the one at at Sandy Hook, New Jersey (1764), the oldest standing lighthouse

5.2 Lighthouse, Sambro Island, Nova Scotia, 1758-60. Nova Scotia Supply and Services, Visual Communications/12847.

5.3 Lighthouse, Cape Spear, Newfoundland, 1834-6. Photograph by Wayne Sturge. Industry Trade and Technology, Newfoundland and Labrador.

in the US. Construction of the Sambro Island light was authorized by the Legislative Council of Nova Scotia in the same year that the Louisbourg lighthouse was destroyed, an act symbolic of British domination over the French and an indication of Halifax's succession as Canada's principal Atlantic port. Funds for its construction were provided partly by a tax on liquor and partly by a lottery, with one thousand tickets sold at £3 each and prizes as high as £500; this novel scheme actually provided a surplus that went towards completing the interior of St Paul's Church [**3.21**]. In 1907 the tower was raised from 62 feet (18.9 m) to 82 feet (25 m); the original cast-iron lantern was replaced only in 1969.[4]

Towers came in a variety of shapes and materials. The Gibraltar Point lighthouse (1808) on Toronto Island in Lake Ontario, the second-oldest lighthouse in Canada, is a hexagonal limestone tower; the Cap-des-Rosiers lighthouse (1854-8) near Gaspé is a tapered circular limestone tower faced with brick and reaching 112 feet (34.1 m). In 1905 a 41-foot (12.4-m) cylindrical iron tower, later reinforced with concrete buttresses, was built at the north end of Belle Isle, between Newfoundland and Labrador. In most tower designs the lightkeeper's dwelling was a separate building, although at Cap-des-Rosiers the residence was attached to the base of the tower.

While the tower is the most effective form for achieving height, and consequently illumination range, an alternate design placed the lantern on the roof of the keeper's house. This was practicable when the lighthouse was located on a high natural promontory and did not require much additional height. **Cape Spear lighthouse** (1834-6) at the approach to St John's harbour—the oldest surviving light in Newfoundland, at the most easterly point in North America—is a good example of this type [**5.3**]. It was built and maintained by the British government. The base is a two-storey square wood building covered by a hipped roof and made symmetrical by the use of false windows. In good Newfoundland domestic tradition, linhays were added to the keeper's house over the years. The lantern is in the centre and supported by a stone core. Its lighting apparatus was taken from the light at Inchkeith, near Edinburgh, which had been installed in 1816. Replaced by a concrete tower in 1963, the Cape Spear lighthouse has been restored and opened to the public by Parks Canada.[5]

203

Another type of lighthouse has a tapered wood tower set on a stone foundation built into the end of the keeper's house. This design was common in the 1870s and is seen both on the Great Lakes—as in the **Gore Bay lighthouse** [5.4], officially the 'Janet Head light station' (1879) on Manitoulin Island, Georgian Bay—and in coastal waters, as in the West Point lighthouse, Prince Edward Island, on Northumberland Strait (1876; the dwelling has been demolished).

Lighthouses made their début on Canada's west coast in 1860 with the construction of the Race Rocks lighthouse, protecting shipping on the wet and windswept Strait of Juan de Fuca, and the nearby **Fisgard Island lighthouse** [5.5] across the harbour from the Esquimalt naval base. Both were near Victoria, and both were circular towers—the former brick, the latter sandstone, with attached brick dwellings. Fisgard Island keepers William and Amelia Bevis complained in 1861 that 'Every room...is so Damp that when the Frost sets in, all the plastering and whitewash will come off', and noted that the driving rain had 'a complete run through doors and windows.' The keepers and the building suffered equally. After only a dozen years in service the Fisgard Island light had to be coated

5.4 Gore Bay lighthouse (Janet Head light station), Manitoulin Island, Ontario, 1879. Photograph by R. Walker, 1990. Canadian Coast Guard.

5.5 Fisgard Island lighthouse, near Victoria, British Columbia, 1860. Photograph by Harold Kalman, 1992.

with a generous layer of Portland cement and three coats of 'best white paint', and new windows were installed. These repairs succeeded and, still in use, the lighthouse stands today as an interpreted national historic site (see also page 391). Race Rocks, at the southern tip of Vancouver Island, also remains in service.[6]

At the outer entrance to Burrard Inlet and Vancouver harbour the Point Atkinson lighthouse, whose two-tone fog horn is very familiar to Vancouverites, is a 41-foot (12.6-m) hexagonal reinforced-concrete shaft, with six exterior buttresses, that was erected in 1912 to replace a structure built in 1875. The tallest and oldest of the buttressed lights in British Columbia is at Estevan Point on the west coast of Vancouver Island. Its 100-foot-high (30.5-m) octagonal shaft of reinforced concrete, poured with a flying buttress at each of its angles, was built in 1909-10 to the bold design of military engineer Colonel William Patrick Anderson.[7]

Illumination technology was constantly being improved. Early lamps used sperm oil (produced from sperm whales), but it often smoked and caused carbon deposits that reduced the light. The Argand burner, introduced in 1782, eliminated smoking by improving combustion. Subsequent enhancements included the invention of kerosene (coal oil) in 1846 by Abraham Gesner of Nova Scotia, and the use of vapour lamps, including acetylene (another Canadian development), and finally electricity. The light was intensified first by the parabolic reflector, then by the dioptric lens, and finally by revolving and flashing electric lights.

In recent years many lighthouses have been automated (a central station monitors their activities automatically), and others have been replaced by electronic navigational aids. These latest technological advances threaten to end a remarkable era of government presence and public service by putting the last of Canada's solitary and committed lighthouse-keepers out of work.

Canals

In the early years of exploration and settlement, ocean-going ships were able to ascend the St Lawrence River as far as Montreal. Further inland, canoes and boats could navigate the extensive river systems, but frequent portages were necessary around rapids. These were fine for the canoes of the *coureurs de bois* and other fur-traders, but they were inadequate for military or large-scale mercantile needs.

Inland shipping was made possible by canals that were constructed to enhance abundant natural water routes. Canals required far more than the excavation of channels. The locks, dams, and weirs that regulated the flow of water and enabled navigation were significant engineering achievements, and they were supplemented by the buildings that were erected at lock stations for maintenance and military security. Most of Canada's canals were built by the British and Canadian governments to bypass rapids and waterfalls, or as shortcuts between navigable waterways, in contrast to the many canals in the United States and Europe that were created by private enterprise to blaze new routes.[8]

The St Lawrence River and its tributary, the Ottawa, provided access to the Canadian interior for the early explorers, but both were interrupted at points by rapids that required portages. The country's first canals were intended to bypass these obstacles, particularly on the St Lawrence, where ocean-going ships could ascend the river only as far as Montreal and the Lachine Rapids. In 1680 François Dollier de Casson, the superior of the Sulpicians and the seigneur of Montreal, initiated a mile-long (1.6-km) canal that was intended to go around the rapids—thinking the work could be done in two months—but it was never completed.[9]

Construction on the first operational canal system was undertaken in 1779-83, with four small military canals that skirted the Cascades, Cedars, and Côteau Rapids, above Montreal between Lac St-Louis and Lac St-François. The largest of the four, at Côteau-du-Lac (subsequently an important railway junction), was 7 feet (2.1 m) wide and had three locks; the others were 6 feet (1.8 m) wide with a single lock. The depth was a scanty $2\frac{1}{2}$ feet (76 cm), yet this was enough to accommodate canoes and the small *bateaux* that were capable of carrying up to 40 barrels of flour.

The project was undertaken at the request of Governor Sir Frederick Haldimand under the direction of Captain William Twiss (1745-1827) of the Royal Engineers.[10] This élite military regiment—made up of highly skilled engineers who built many other British government initiatives described in this chapter—was assigned specific construction projects of strategic importance, including canals, bridges, and forts, as well as the task of laying out entire towns. Two other regiments were also involved in Canadian engineering projects: the Royal Sappers and Miners (a 'sapper' was a person who wielded a shovel), who sometimes worked under the direction of the Royal Engineers and were amalgamated with them in 1856; and the Royal Staff Corps. These military units often retained civilian contractors to help them with construction.[11]

The problems of supplying the Great Lakes during the War of 1812, and the advent of steamboats on the St Lawrence—the first was John Molson's *Accommodation*, launched in 1809—quickly made the first-generation canals obsolete. A proper Lachine Canal was built in 1821-5 by the government of Lower Canada, under the direction of British engineer Thomas Burnett. It was $8\frac{1}{2}$ miles (13.6 km) long, between 36 and 48 feet (11 and 14.6 m) wide at the surface and 28 feet (8.5 m) at the bottom, and had seven stone locks, each 20 feet (6.1 m) wide and 100 feet (30.5 m) long, with 5 feet (1.5 m) of water over the sills. The Governor, Lord Dalhousie, maintained that the locks were built of 'the finest masonry I ever saw'—a tribute to the work of Scottish-born mason John Redpath.[12] (No longer in use, the Lachine Canal is being developed as an urban park.)

Proposed at the end of the War of 1812-14, when there was fear of a new American attack on Upper Canada, the 123-mile (200-km) Rideau Canal (1826-32) was built along the Rideau and Cataraqui river systems, between the Ottawa River at Bytown (Ottawa) and Lake Ontario at Kingston. The circuitous course of the canal was intended as an alternative route for carrying military traffic from Montreal to Lake Ontario, beyond the range of American artillery (although it was never used for this purpose). Lieutenant-Colonel John By (1779-1836), of the Royal Engineers, directed the enormous undertaking.[13]

The engineering achievements of the **Rideau Canal** were considered among the technological wonders of the world. Forty-seven locks and fourteen dams were constructed from limestone, and many more temporary dams were erected during construction to hold back the relentless water. About 18 miles (29 km) of the route are through artificial canals, and the remainder follows the natural courses of rivers and lakes. The waterway was cut by hand through virgin forest, and many of the labourers employed by the Royal Engineers and private contractors—probably several hundred of them at least—succumbed to malaria. Colonel By—wisely arguing to his superiors in England that the canal should be built to serve commercial steamboats as well as military traffic—succeeded in gaining approval to make the locks 33 feet (10 m) wide rather than the planned 25 feet (7.6 m). (By

had argued for 50 feet, or 15.2 m.) The locks are 134 feet (40.9 m) long and have a draft of $5\frac{1}{2}$ feet (1.7 m) over the sills. Defensive blockhouses (described below) were built at many of the lock stations. The **dam at Jones Falls** [5.6], 60 feet (18.3 m) high and 350 feet (107 m) along the top, was more than twice as high as any dam in North America. It was built by contractor John Redpath (1796-1869), who had previously worked on the Lachine Canal (and subsequently became Canada's premier sugar refiner).

A splendid series of eight locks built into a ravine at the **Ottawa River entrance** [5.7] to the canal (now in mid-town Ottawa) lifts boats the first 80 feet (24.4 m). The illustration, a lithograph made from a drawing of 1839 by W.H. Bartlett, bestows a romantic and sublime grandeur on the stately ascent of locks, with their mighty stone walls securing the wooden gates. The locks are built of solid limestone—quarried from the embankments at either side—and are set on inverted stone arches. The first stone was laid on 16 August 1827 by Captain John Franklin, who was on his way back to England after having explored the Mackenzie River. To the right of the locks in the illustration is the Commissariat, constructed of stone in 1827 (the oldest surviving building in Ottawa, it is now a museum). Opposite is the Royal Engineers' building—creating a strong sense of classical symmetry, an essential ingredient of imperial planning. The latter no longer stands—nor does the Sappers' Bridge (1827, replaced in 1912), which encloses the landscape at the top and defines the entrance; the steamship terminal (seen with a steam-powered sidewheeler at the dock); or Colonel By's stone residence (*c*. 1829, destroyed by fire in 1849) on the hill to the left, which is now known as Major's Hill Park (after Major Daniel Bolton, who succeeded Colonel By in 1832). The embankment on the right—the side of Barrack Hill, which accommodated the Sappers' barracks and their hospital—Colonel By wisely reserved for government buildings, and in 1857 the land beyond it was selected as the site for the Parliament Buildings.[14]

At the head of the locks, Colonel By laid out a townsite that he named Bytown after himself; the community was renamed Ottawa in 1855. Masonry contractor Thomas MacKay (1792-1855), who built the Bytown locks, went on to yet bigger things, erecting and operating a large mill complex at the falls of the Rideau River—the natural obstruction that had forced the construction of the Bytown locks. MacKay's house, begun in 1838 as a fine Regency villa on a 100-acre (40-hectare) estate, was later leased by the government to become the residence of the Governor General. Enlarged several times, the house—now known as Rideau Hall—was acquired by the government in 1868.[15]

The building of the canal stimulated the development of this part of eastern Ontario, bringing it

prosperity first through commerce and then as a government centre. Another impact of the canal was the settlement of many skilled stonemasons—most of them Scottish—in the Rideau Valley, and the consequent development of a fine regional building tradition in stone.[16] Many official buildings flanked the waterway, including lockmasters'

5.6 Dam on the Rideau Canal at Jones Falls, Ontario, *c*. 1827-30. Watercolour by Thomas Burrows. Archives of Ontario, Thomas Burrows Collection/Book I, no. 53.

5.7 (*below*) Entrance locks to the Rideau Canal at Ottawa, Ontario, 1827-31. Drawn by W.H. Bartlett, engraved by J.C. Armytage. NAC/C-2367.

houses (some wood and others stone) and military blockhouses (see page 227). In addition, hotels and commercial buildings were erected at a number of 'intersections', where roads subsequently crossed the canal system. In 1972 the Rideau Canal was transferred from the Department of Transport to the ministry responsible for parks and is now a national historic site, maintained for recreational boating by Parks Canada.

Just as Canadian control of the Great Lakes trade was enhanced by the canals on the St Lawrence and Ottawa Rivers, it became threatened by American construction of the Erie Canal (1817-25), which extended from Lake Erie to the Hudson River and provided a water route from the upper Great Lakes to the Atlantic Ocean. Canadians countered by building the Welland Canal through the Niagara Peninsula to connect Lakes Ontario and Erie, bypassing Niagara Falls and eliminating a long portage.

The first Welland Canal (1824-9)—there have been four, as a result of continual expansion and relocation—was constructed as a commercial venture by private enterprise. (The canal has been government-owned since 1841.) The principal promoter was St Catharines businessman William Hamilton Merritt, in honour of whom the canal

was sometimes known as 'Merritt's folly'. A sometime soldier and politician who was born in Westchester County, New York, Merritt was a dedicated entrepreneur—he styled himself 'a projector'—who was intent upon transforming Upper Canada into a beehive of commercial activity.[17] Another backer, and the president of the Welland Canal Company, was George Keefer, whose sons Samuel Keefer and Thomas Coltrin Keefer watched the first two schooners navigate the canal on 20 November 1829. (Perhaps inspired by this experience, both sons later became brilliant engineers.)

The canal had some 40 wooden locks, 100 feet by 22 feet and 7 feet deep (30.5 by 6.7 by 2.1 m), and was provided with a towpath for horses, mules, and oxen. Its upper terminus, at the mouth of the Welland River (formerly Chippawa Creek), emptied traffic into the swift-flowing Niagara River just above the Falls. In 1833 it was extended to reach Port Colborne on Lake Erie. This was the first of many continuing improvements to the canal, which was largely rebuilt in 1845, 1887, and 1931, each time with bigger (and fewer) locks. The 1,380-foot-long (421-m) Humberstone lock at Port Col-

5.8 Hydraulic lift lock, Peterborough, Ontario, 1896-1904. Photograph by Harold Kalman.

borne is the largest lock in the world.[18] The Welland Ship Canal, as it is now called, serves as a vital link in the St Lawrence Seaway (1954-9), the newest of the many enhanced natural waterways in the St Lawrence River/Great Lakes basin.

Another remarkable canal structure is the **Hydraulic lift lock [5.8]** at Peterborough, Ontario, built in 1896-1904 as a part of the Trent-Severn Waterway. Two large lock chambers stand side by side—one at the lower level, the other at the higher. When boats enter the locks, water is pumped into the upper chamber to make it slightly heavier; it drops as the lower chamber rises, creating a counter-balanced situation that offsets the enormous weight of the water. This was the first lift lock in North America and, at 65 feet (19.8 m), the highest lift in the world. Taking advantage of concrete, then in its infancy, engineers Richard B. Rogers and Walter J. Francis also created the world's largest 'massed' (unreinforced) concrete structure.[19]

One of several canals built in the Maritimes was the Shubenacadie Canal (1826-61), joining Halifax harbour to the Bay of Fundy. The merchants of Halifax and neighbouring Dartmouth promoted its construction to try to draw the Fundy trade away from Saint John. Delayed by insufficient funds and a ruptured dam, the $53\frac{1}{2}$-mile-long (86-km) waterway opened in 1861, with seven locks and two marine railways, but it was a commercial failure. One cause of its early demise was the construction of a fixed railway bridge over the canal, signalling the triumph of rail over canal traffic. Portions remain, but are not in use.[20]

Canals had a considerable impact on the growth of British North America. They provided direct opportunities for commercial and industrial development, at their ends and along their routes. The subsequent growth of Montreal at the Lachine Canal, of Ottawa at the entrance to the Rideau Canal, and of the eastern Niagara peninsula at the Welland Canal are examples of their impact. Perhaps more important, canals improved access to the interior for people and goods, and made the hinterland available for settlement.

Roads

In the early years of settlement, overland transportation was possible only on foot or on horseback along unimproved trails. In 1734 a road linked Montreal and Quebec, and one between Halifax and Lunenburg, begun in 1767, may have been the first in the Atlantic colonies. Two 'great roads' were completed between Halifax and the Bay of Fundy early in the nineteenth century, but they were very rough. The stage that began operation in 1816 took nine hours to travel the 45 miles (70 km) between Halifax and Windsor.[21]

Upper Canada provides a well-documented example of the development of a comprehensive road system. The earliest land routes were the well-developed networks of Indian trails. Many followed waterways; some served as portage routes. The first Europeans used and improved the Indian trails—one was the Iroquois Trail that went from Queenston to Hamilton, which defined a route that is paralleled by today's Queen Elizabeth Way—and they also opened new roads to assist settlement and defence.

The most celebrated of the new roads were two that were begun in 1793 by Governor Simcoe: Yonge Street, which ran from York (later Toronto) north to a point near the lake that bears his name; and Dundas Street, which extended eastward from York to the Bay of Quinte and westward through Hamilton towards London. Simcoe envisioned London's becoming the 'grand Mart and Imporium of the Western World', situated as it was at the focus of the Great Lakes and trans-Appalachian trade routes. In the southwest, the Talbot Road—from Fort Erie on the Niagara River to Sandwich (Windsor) on the Detroit River—was built between 1804 and 1811 by Thomas Talbot, a promoter of settlement in the region and the person after whom the town of St Thomas was named. These roads certainly stimulated settlement, although new arrivals had to go 15 miles (25 km) or more beyond the roads in their search for land.[22]

The widths of developed roads were established by statute. In 1777 the King's Highroad was fixed at 30 feet (9.2 m) wide, and byroads at 20 feet (6.1 m); this was changed in 1824, so that public highways were to be between 40 feet (12.2 m) and 66 feet (20.1 m) wide—far wider than was necessary.

East-west road allowances—one chain (66 feet, or 20.1 m) wide—were provided as a part of the original land survey, dividing tiers of lots into 'concessions'; and north-south sideroad allowances of the same width broke the concessions into smaller blocks. The number and spacing of the roads varied as changes occurred to the survey system being used at the time (see page 140), but more important was the provision that was being made for a dense network of communication. Those concession roads that followed a line where a route was needed became part of the highway system; others remained minor access roads. Before settlement, road allowances might be no more than rights-of-way indicated by surveyors' stakes or notched trees in the forest; only when the land was settled were they usually opened into actual roads.

When the time came to build the roads, trees were felled to a width sufficient for a wagon, and the stumps were cut low enough to be cleared by the wagon wheels. If the land was high and dry few, if any, improvements to the surface might be made. However, the swamp and muskeg that made up much of the country required the construction of a firm surface. The least-expensive method involved taking logs that had been obtained by clearing the road and placing them across muddy depressions (perpendicular to the direction of travel) to create a 'corduroy' road: the illustration, drawn by Titus Ware in 1844, shows a **corduroy road** [5.9] in Orillia Township. Minor streams could be bridged with logs laid parallel to the travel route. Such a roadway was solid (until the wood rotted), but unbearably bumpy in a wagon. Anna Jameson described a bone-jarring trip over a road of this kind:

> The road was scarcely passable; there were no longer cheerful farms and clearings, but the dark pine forest and the rank swamp, crossed by those terrific corduroy paths (my bones ache at the mere recollection), and deep holes and pools of rotted vegetable matter with water, black, bottomless, sloughs of despond![23]

Plank roads, consisting of wooden planks nailed to stringers or beams, were far smoother than corduroy roads. The first plank road was built in 1835-6 east of Toronto, and portions of Yonge Street were planked shortly afterwards. Covered with sand, this provided a cheap and fairly durable surface, although the maintenance needs were so high that the method was soon abandoned. Paving began in Ontario in 1837 as a result of the methods developed in Britain by John Macadam, which involved covering a layer of stones with layers of increasingly fine gravel. Though more durable, it was considerably more expensive. True 'macadamization' was rare in Canada, although paving became widespread several decades later.[24]

The first wave of post-Loyalist colonization, in the 1820s, occurred inland from Lake Ontario northward to the fringe of the Canadian Shield. When Catharine Parr Traill and her family settled in eastern Ontario in 1832, she found the first part of the road north from Cobourg adequate for a

5.9 Corduroy road, Orillia Township, Ontario. Drawn by Titus Ware, 1844. MTRL/T14377.

wagon. At Rice Lake her party boarded a steamboat, then transferred to a scow in shallow water. Beyond Peterborough they hired a wagon and two horses, and found the going rather rough:

> There was no palpable road, only a blaze on the other side [of the lake]...encumbered by fallen trees, and interrupted by cedar swamps, into which one might sink up to one's knees....What is termed in bush language a *blaze*, is nothing more than notches or slices cut off the bark of the trees to mark out the line of the road....[Further on] our progress was slow on account of the roughness of the road, which is beset with innumerable obstacles in the shape of loose blocks of limestone, with which the lands on the banks of the river and lakes abound; to say nothing of fallen trees, big roots, mud-holes, and corduroy bridges over which you go jolt, jolt, jolt, till every bone in your body feels as if it were being dislocated.[25]

This was in September, a relatively dry time. In spring, the roads were a sea of mud and quite impassable; in winter, transportation by sleigh was relatively easy.

Roads were built to help the movement of settlers in other parts of the country as well. In the Eastern Townships of Lower Canada—between the seigneurial settlements south of the St Lawrence River and the US border—the land was surveyed and first settled in the 1790s with the arrival of the Loyalists. In order to provide communication with Quebec City—and to help divert the townships' economy in that direction, rather than towards the United States—two roads were built south from Lévis, across the river from Quebec. The Craig Road, which led southwesterly to the town of Richmond, was begun in 1809 by Sir James Craig, Governor of Lower Canada; the Gosford Road, which was proposed in 1805, was completed to the US border by 1838. Cheaply built and poorly maintained, they attracted only a smattering of British settlement in their respective areas, which in the second half of the nineteenth century were largely bypassed by the railways. As a result the population grew slowly, and the economy stagnated.[26]

A characteristic building found along the roads was the inn, tavern, or stopping-place, where a traveller might have a meal and spend the night.

5.10 Campbell's Inn, near Port Talbot, Ontario. Sketch by Anna Jameson, 10 July 1837. MTRL, by permission of J.D. Bain.

Campbell's Inn [5.10] on the Talbot Road, which was visited and sketched by Anna Jameson in 1837, was indistinguishable from a private log house. Jameson described it as a 'log-hut and a cattle-shed. A long pole, stuck into the decayed stump of a tree in front of the hut, served for a sign.'[27] Inns in more established regions were often better constructed. Cook's Tavern (*c.* 1822) is a handsome stone Georgian building that was originally on the riverfront in Williamsburg Township, serving traffic along both the St Lawrence River and the King's Highway between Montreal and Kingston. It is now located at Upper Canada Village near Morrisburg, Ontario (with its barn, and the 'historical representations' of its drive-shed and bakehouse).

English visitors regularly found the conditions at inns to be unacceptable. As Edward Allen Talbot wrote:

> The beds are indifferent, and from four to ten are crowded in one room, destitute of curtains, etc. and swarming with fleas and bugs. In such houses there is no such thing as comfort or privacy.[28]

In the more remote regions of the Upper Canadian hinterland, inns catered for lumbermen as well. The roads that were built in mid-century often had stopping-places every 10 miles (16 km) along the way. Most—such as Jeffery's Lumbermen's Hotel at Rockingham, on the Peterson Road, were also built as oversized log houses.[29]

Railways

Wagons could not be depended on to transport heavy loads, because of the difficulties encountered in providing a firm, level roadway; and many of the new inland communities were inaccessible from waterways. The answer was found in the railway. This section looks at Canada's early railways and some of the station buildings. (A number of railway and road bridges are introduced in the following section. Post-Confederation railways and their buildings are discussed in Chapter 9.)

As early as the sixteenth century European miners moved ore in small carts or wagons ('trams'), with flanged wheels that ran along wooden rails. A small horse-powered railway (or 'tramway') appears to have been used to haul quarried stone to Louisbourg in the 1720s, and an inclined railway, pulled by a steam-powered winch and cables, was installed to bring stone to the Quebec Citadel (see below) in the 1820s.[30]

It was a short—but crucial—step to place the steam engine on wheels and to pull cars behind. This invention of the self-propelled locomotive (literally 'motion to a place') occurred in England in the first decade of the nineteenth century. In 1830 the Liverpool and Manchester Railway, designed and built by George Stephenson (1781-1848), became the world's first successful commercial railway.

5.11 St Lawrence and Atlantic Railroad Station, Longueuil, Quebec, c. 1848. Collection of the late Omer Lavallée.

Canada's earliest railways followed soon afterwards. They served much the same purposes as canals, in that they provided portage routes between two adjacent navigable waterways. The first was the Champlain and St Lawrence Rail Road, which in July 1836 inaugurated service along $14\frac{1}{2}$ miles (25 km) of pine rails between St-Jean-sur-Richelieu, a town that was accessible from Lake Champlain, and Laprairie, across the St Lawrence River from Montreal. The locomotive was the 6.5-ton *Dorchester*, tiny by later standards, which was built in England by Robert Stephenson (1803-59), the son of George Stephenson. In combination with steamboats on Lake Champlain and the Hudson River, and a ferry across the St Lawrence, the little railway created a viable shipping route from Montreal to New York, increasing the prosperity of both cities, and of the smaller trans-shipment points along the route. Wood-framed 'station houses ... 100 feet by forty feet (30 by 12 m) ... substantially built and ... finished without unnecessary expense' were erected at both ends of the line in 1835-6. Although they were never illustrated or photographed, it has been suggested that an extant wood structure at 129 rue Jacques-Cartier in St-Jean may be the original station building.[31]

Other early 'portage railways' provided routes around the Lachine Rapids (1847) and smaller rapids on the Ottawa River (1854). The Northern Railway was built in 1851-5 to connect Lake Ontario, at Toronto, with Georgian Bay, at Collingwood—a centuries-old portage route to the western interior. The portage system provided an early example of what is today called 'intermodal transportation', in which goods are moved by more than one transport mode (e.g., the modern freight container, which may be carried by ship, train, or truck).

Evidence of the appearance of the earliest stations is seen in a drawing (dated 1855) of the **St Lawrence and Atlantic Railroad Station** [5.11] in Longueuil, Quebec (also across the river from Montreal), which inaugurated service in 1848. Likely built in that year, the station was a plain rectangular structure, with a large arched opening at the end (flanked by what appear to be pilasters) through which the train emerged, and penetrated by windows and doors on the long side. Its form was not unlike that of a barn: this is why architectural historian Carroll Meeks has called this early station-type (which appeared in the US in the late 1830s) a 'train-barn'. The terminus of the Montreal and Lachine Railroad, whose initial run was in 1847, was similar (if a twentieth-century painting by Adam Sherriff Scott is to be trusted), although the gable-roofed brick structure was illuminated by

5.12 Grand Trunk Station, Port Hope, Ontario, 1856. Photograph by John J.-G. Blumenson. Ontario Heritage Foundation.

small clerestory windows and ventilated by a cupola. Pioneer railway-builder Alexander Millar provided locomotives for both lines: it may therefore be possible that the two also shared station designs.[32]

'Trunk lines', or 'main lines' (as opposed to 'short lines'), were long-distance railways that carried traffic between major cities and regions. Their potential economic impact was immense, as were their political advantages. The Durham Report of 1839 suggested that a trunk railway would be essential to the union of the Canadas. This notion was repeated in the British North America Act of 1867, and the promise of a railway to the west coast succeeded in luring British Columbia into Confederation in 1871. Indeed, Canada may be the only country in the world in which a railway played a significant role in the attainment of nationhood. Other benefits of railways were also evident. In 1832 British engineer Henry Fairbairn recognized that a trunk line in British North America would attract settlers away from the United States.[33] The military were slow to recognize the advantages of railways in transporting soldiers, although their value in this respect was proved during the North West Rebellion of 1885 with the movement of troops to Manitoba on the new Canadian Pacific Railway.

The Grand Trunk Railway was the first, and also the most important, of Canada's early trunk lines. An ambitious campaign of construction and amalgamation during the 1850s created an 800-mile line (1300 km) from the all-weather seaport at Portland, Maine, to Sarnia at the southern tip of Lake Huron, by way of Montreal and Toronto. In Canada West alone, some 14,000 men and 2,000 horses were employed at one time. The principal builders were the English firm of Peto, Brassey, Jackson, and Betts, which had constructed railways around the world and built the Montreal-Toronto section; and the Russian-born Canadian civil engineer Casimir Gzowski (1813-98), who built the portion from Toronto to Sarnia and part of the line from Montreal to the US border. Both firms combined engineering design and contracting, a practice typical of the era. (The two tasks are usually separated today.)

Financed largely by English capital (and having its head office in London), the Grand Trunk Railway was built to British railway standards, using permanent materials to make structures that were designed to last. Its stations along the route were solidly constructed of stone. They were standardized, simple, utilitarian buildings that provided a compromise between the pragmatic approach of the engineer and the more design-conscious approach of the architect. Several are still standing, including the **Grand Trunk Station** (1856) at Port Hope, Ontario [5.12]. Most were compact, symmetrical, thick-walled, one-storey buildings with deep and regular courses of stone and round-arched openings. The low-pitched gabled roofs with deep overhanging eaves provided the platforms with some shelter from the weather. Inside, a central hall led on one side to a general waiting-room and a ladies' waiting-room, and on the other side to the ticket and telegraph offices, baggage-room, and storeroom. The operator's desk was contained within a projecting bay, whose windows at either side permitted him to see up and down the track. The designer may have been Alexander M. Ross (d. 1862), the Chief Engineer of the Grand Trunk, or Thomas Seaton Scott (1826-95), the future federal chief architect (see Chapter 9), who served for a time as architect to the railway.[34]

5.13 European and North American Railway Station, Saint John, New Brunswick, 1860. Canadian National Railways/X32160.

The other important early trunk line was the Intercolonial Railway, which linked the Maritime colonies with Quebec. Such a line was made one of the conditions of Confederation. Conceived in the 1840s, the Intercolonial was finally completed in 1876 after the Dominion government took over lines built by Nova Scotia and New Brunswick. Sandford Fleming (1827-1915), considered to be the leading engineer in Canada, surveyed the route and became chief engineer of the railway. His pragmatic approach to railway construction advocated quality without ostentation:

> With the exception of the few localities where towns called for extended accommodation, it was held that there was no necessity for much expenditure on station buildings: and it was held to be wholly unnecessary to spend money through the wilderness portions of the line on costly buildings. . . . A railway of a high standard is in fact a simple problem. It does not exact magnificence of design, or works which astonish by their display or cost. Architectural monuments have no place on public works like the one in question, and many well known structures can be regarded as mementos of useless expenditure.[35]

5.14 European and North American Railway Station, Moncton, New Brunswick, *c*. 1857-60. Canadian National Railways/53027.

Five stations on the Truro-Picton Landing line, built by the Nova Scotia government under Fleming's direction and completed in 1867, were shingled timber buildings, 60 feet (18.3 m) by 30 feet (9.2 m), that combined passenger and freight facilities; the station at New Glasgow was larger and built of stone.

One component of the Intercolonial Railway was begun as the European and North American Railway (ENAR), which linked Maine, New Brunswick, and Nova Scotia. The New Brunswick section was begun in 1853 by Peto, Brassey, Jackson and Betts. The first ENAR **Station at Saint John** (1860; demolished), New Brunswick, was a three-storey gabled board-and-batten structure [5.13] designed much like an oversized house, with a projecting bay and a long wooden train shed attached (on the right). The hood mouldings above the windows, the buttress on the side, and the finial-like projections at the parapet all place the building within the Gothic Revival. Its deviation from our popular image of a station serves as a reminder that this was a building-type that developed over time: early designers searched widely for an appropriate form. Gothic Revival features, well known to the builders of the ENAR, were common in English stations; the prototype was Temple Meads station at Bristol, built by the gifted engineer I.K. Brunel in 1839-40.

The first stations in the smaller New Brunswick communities were more cheaply built. The ENAR **Station at Moncton** (*c*. 1857-60; demolished), New Brunswick, then a small shipbuilding commu-

nity of 800, was a $1\frac{1}{2}$-storey frame building [5.14] with a steep gabled roof and a flared eave providing shelter at trackside—a tiny precursor of the typical station of the future. Many of the early stations, including Moncton's, were rebuilt by the Intercolonial in 1872 to a standard two-storey frame design with a mansard roof. (The same design could also be seen in the Quebec portion of the line, as at St-Simon, Quebec.) Located at the junction of the lines to Quebec, Maine, and Nova Scotia, Moncton was selected by the Intercolonial as the site for its head offices and shops, and the town subsequently prospered as an important railway centre. The Intercolonial became part of the Canadian National Railways in 1919. The closure of the CNR's Moncton shops in 1988 dealt a harsh economic blow to the city.[36]

Many of the stations built in the early decades of the railways were simple structures in the vernacular of the area and were scarcely differentiated from houses. The Sherbrooke terminal of the Sherbrooke and Eastern Townships Railway (1874) was a plain, wood, gable-roofed building finished in vertical boards; while the station at High Falls, Ontario (*c*. 1885), on the Kingston and Pembroke Railway (known affectionately as the K & P or the 'kick-and-push'), was built of squared logs with dovetail joints and a 'scoop' roof of hollowed logs, such as the lumbermen used for their camboose shanties (see below).[37]

By the end of the 1860s Nova Scotia, New Brunswick, and the Canadas were well served by railways. Prince Edward Island and Newfoundland obtained lines in the 1870s and 1880s respectively (both were abandoned in the 1980s). The transcontinental railway—a trunk line conceived and built on a much larger scale than the Grand Trunk—began to take shape in the 1870s and was completed in 1885 (see Chapter 9).

Bridges

In the same way that land and rapids posed obstructions to marine traffic and required canals or railways to bypass them, rivers obstructed road and rail traffic and required the construction of bridges. Canada's expansive and difficult terrain has continually inspired engineers to seek ever-more daring solutions to bridging rivers, and as a result Canada has remained at the forefront of international bridge design.

The first span across a major river in Canada was

5.15 Union Bridge and Chaudière Falls, linking Ottawa, Ontario (left) and Hull, Quebec (right), 1826-8. Engraving after a drawing by W.H. Bartlett. From N.P. Willis, *Canadian Scenery*, 2 (1842) NAC/C-2369.

the **Union Bridge** [5.15] over the Ottawa River, built in 1826-8 by the Royal Engineers to allow them to move construction supplies to the Rideau Canal. The first land link between Upper and Lower Canada, this bridge connected Bytown with Wright's Town—today's Ottawa and Hull—over the turbulent Chaudière Falls. The extemporaneous design was directed by the Royal Engineers' John Mactaggart (1791-1830) and Thomas Burrowes (1796-1846?). The bridge hopped, skipped, and jumped across the falls from one rocky island to another in seven independent stages. The two northernmost spans were stone arches of cut limestone, one dry masonry and the other mortared, and were built by Hull's founder, Philemon Wright, after an arch by canal mason Thomas MacKay had failed. The other gaps were crossed by wooden truss bridges, three flat and two arched, all built by contractor Robert Drummond. The longest span, 212 feet (64.7 m) across the 'Great Kettle', was first achieved with a temporary rope suspension bridge that was reported safe to cross, 'although the at-

tempt...was not made without some consciousness of danger.'[38] It was replaced by a daring arched truss, reinforced with iron chains, that collapsed during construction, was rebuilt, and held for seven years before its final tumble into the white water below. Engineer Mactaggart remarked on the political importance of the bridge when he quoted a letter that he had read in the press:

> This bridge on the Chaudiere is the only point where the two Provinces can be connected on their water boundary. This, therefore, is a *solid* step to the union of the Provinces, a question long in agitation among our politicians.[39]

Wood was the most popular material for bridges because it was reasonably cheap and strong. The roadway was generally supported by a truss—a built-up section composed of small members arranged in a configuration based on the triangle, whose geometry prevents it from deforming. The various patented trusses were named after their designers: the Town (invented by American architect Ithiel Town), Burr, and Howe trusses (the last strengthened with iron tension rods) were the most popular in the nineteenth century.

The problem with wooden bridges, of course,

5.16 Covered bridge, Hartland, New Brunswick, 1896. Industry Science and Technology Canada.

siding was usually applied vertically; in Quebec, horizontally; in Nova Scotia, shingles were popular. At the beginning of the twentieth century Quebec had at least 1,000 covered bridges and New Brunswick 400. Even though most have disappeared, those provinces retain the largest concentration of survivors in the world. The **covered bridge** (1896) **at Hartland**, New Brunswick, which crosses the St John River in seven spans with a total length of 1,282 feet (391 m), is the longest covered bridge in the world [**5.16**]. Like many others in the province, it was built as a toll bridge and subsequently (in 1900) taken over by the government. Covered bridges everywhere were called 'kissing bridges' because of the opportunities they offered amorous couples.[40]

The best way to prevent bridge failures was to use materials that were more permanent than wood. Iron superseded wood in truss design because of its greater strength as well as its superior durability, particularly for railway bridges, and stone was usually used for piers and abutments. Sandford Fleming argued successfully that the Intercolonial Railway should build its bridges of iron, not timber, and all but three erected under his direction were constructed of iron trusses set on stone piers.[41]

was that they deteriorated quickly and required ongoing maintenance. In order to protect them from the weather and prolong their life, they were often covered with a roof. The trusses were usually sheathed with wood siding that stopped just short of the roof, admitting light while keeping out moisture; sometimes windows were inserted in the sides. The exterior treatment varied from region to region, just like buildings: in New Brunswick the

5.17 Victoria Bridge, Montreal, Quebec, 1854-9. Composite photograph by Notman and Sandham, 1878. MMCH/47427-II.

217

A tubular design—using solid metal walls and a roof rather than open trusses—was adopted for the remarkable **Victoria Bridge** [5.17], which spanned the St Lawrence River between Montreal and Longueuil to close the last link in the Grand Trunk's international system. The site for the crossing, and the principles on which to build, were both chosen by civil engineer Thomas C. Keefer (1821-1915). The river was broad and rough, and the bridge had to be rigid enough to take high-speed trains. The design was undertaken by English engineer Robert Stephenson, and by his architectural specialist Francis Thompson (active 1839-54). They were assisted by GTR engineer A.M. Ross and by James Hodges (1814-79), engineer to Peto, Brassey, Jackson, and Betts. Planned in 1853 and built in 1854-9, the Victoria Bridge was officially opened in 1860. The ceremony was the main reason for the celebrated Canadian visit of the nineteen-year-old Prince of Wales (later Edward VII).

The Victoria Bridge (seen in the distance in the panorama of Montreal, **5.53**) was notable for its novel form of construction, as well as for being the longest bridge in the world. Twenty-five spans—each one a large tube composed of riveted wrought-iron plates that formed an enclosed box girder—extended some 6,592 feet (2 km), and the approaches brought the total length to nearly two miles (3.2 km). The ironwork was prefabricated in England, and some 118,000 separate pieces, 'punched, marked, and ready for putting together', were transported to Montreal for assembly on the massive stone piers. The wedge-shaped piers were built of solid limestone resting on the river bottom, with their points facing upriver so as to provide a cutting edge that would withstand the massive, crushing ice-floes that clog the river every spring.[42]

The opening ceremony was a momentous event—appropriate for what was praised as the eight wonder of the world:

> ... an engine, snorting and chugging, pulled the Prince's car of state towards the bridge as loyal crowds pressed close. It passed between trophies of locomotive wheels, and just before the entrance to the tube it stopped. The Prince alighted and climbed to a platform covered with scarlet cloth where he was received by James Hodges. He was handed a silver trowel. A derrick lifted the cornerstone, the Prince spread some mortar, the stone came down; three raps of a mallet from the Prince and the crowd began to cheer. Then the royal train entered the tube to its

centre. There the Prince placed a last silver-headeded rivet (which was later hammered in by some mechanics) as the wood-smoke from the engine, hanging thickly in the tunnel before disappearing through the outlets in the roof, nearly asphyxiated him.[43]

The Prince of Wales praised the bridge as being 'unsurpassed by the grandeur of Egypt or Rome'.

The tube was a structural success but a traveller's nightmare. Ventilation and lighting were negligible. Extending the Prince's metaphor, one observer described the 'Egyptian darkness' of the smoke-filled tube. Despite the discomfort, no changes were made until 1897-8, when the need for a double track caused the tube to be dismantled, the piers widened, and a new open steel truss constructed.[44]

Spans that carry railways across depressions in the land where there is little water are called viaducts or (if made of wood or steel open-work) trestles rather than bridges. The structural challenge is one of height and length rather than clear span, since foundations can be placed almost anywhere along the base of the depression. The Grand Trunk Railway built several impressive viaducts in which an iron superstructure was placed on tall stone piers. The GTR Viaduct (1854-5) at Georgetown, Ontario, crossed the Credit River Valley with a graceful structure that was 931 feet (284 m) long and 115 feet (35 m) high. The tracks were laid on the top of (rather than through) eight tubular girders sitting on sandstone piers. As with its stations, the GTR followed the British system of

5.18 Quebec Bridge, Quebec, Quebec, 1900-17. HWS/SSS/QUE 81 QC BR 1.08.

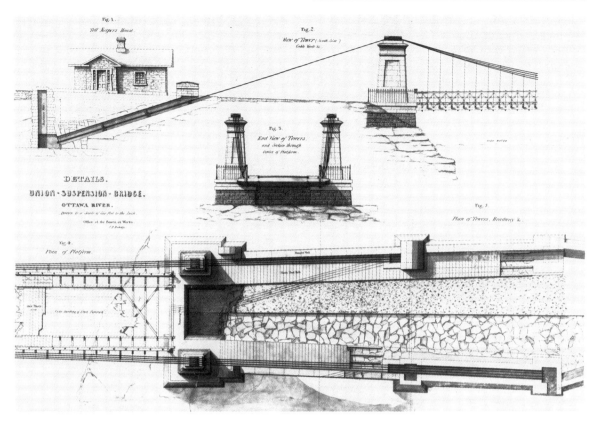

5.19 Elevations and plan of part of the Union Suspension Bridge, Ottawa, Ontario, and Hull, Quebec, 1843. Drawing by F.P. Rubidge. NAC/NMC-16940.

using permanent materials with a high initial cost but low maintenance expenses. This impressed the talented architect and railway engineer F.W. Cumberland (see page 289), who admired the Grand Trunk's adoption of 'more substantial character than had previously obtained either in the United States or Canada, [being] founded indeed on the British system.'[45]

The expansion of the railways later in the nineteenth century—particularly the building of the transcontinental Canadian Pacific Railway, completed in 1885—led to new techniques and the development of increasingly longer bridges. The replacement in the 1870s of iron with steel—which was stronger, particularly in tension—stimulated the development of the cantilever truss, in which the bridge was constructed by building out (cantilevering) the superstructure from fixed abutments or piers to a meeting-point at mid-span. The *ne plus ultra* of cantilever design was reached in 1900, when the National Transcontinental Railway began work on the **Quebec Bridge** [5.18], crossing the St Lawrence just upriver from Quebec City. Engineers P.J. Szlapka and Theodore Cooper proposed structural members of stupendous dimen-

sions, including an 1800-foot (550-m) central span of conventional truss design that was to be supported at each end by the outsretched arms of the cantilever trusses. In the summer of 1907, two years after work had begun on the superstructure, the south arm of the incomplete bridge collapsed, killing eighty-two people. An enquiry found the engineers at fault in their calculations, but not in their principles. A new Quebec Bridge was built on the same system, with five engineers collaborating in the design, but this time a faulty jack caused the loss of the central section and eleven more lives. The Quebec Bridge was finally completed in 1917 and remains in use as the longest trussed span in the world.[46] The illustration also shows the Pierre Laporte Bridge, a suspension bridge of the 1970s that carries highway traffic across the river in a single, seemingly effortless, sweep.

The suspension technology was first used a century and a quarter earlier to replace the span of the Union Bridge that had fallen into the Ottawa River. The **Union Suspension Bridge** [5.19], built in

1843, was an iron suspension bridge designed by the half-brother of Thomas C. Keefer, the talented Samuel Keefer (1811-90), in his capacity as chief engineer to the Department of Public Works, a position he held from 1841 to 1853. Two pairs of stone towers were erected and wire cables, three inches in diameter, were strung over each, their ends anchored in the ground. The roadway, which spanned 243 feet, was suspended from the cables and stiffened by a light metal truss. The drawing shows the components clearly. The design resembled that of the first successful metal suspension bridge in North America, the Fairmount Park Bridge in Philadelphia, built the previous year. The northern approach crossed the two limestone spans built in 1826-8 [**5.15**].

The Union Bridge's tapered towers, with their flaring cornices, were thought of as being in the Egyptian style and adding an 'architectural' quality to this work of engineering. The Egyptian allusion

was repeated in an unexecuted design by Samuel Keefer for a suspension bridge at Bout de l'Île, at the west end of Montreal Island (1844),[47] and in the much-admired Niagara Suspension Bridge (1851-5) over the Niagara Gorge, designed by American engineer John A. Roebling (1806-69), who adopted what he called 'imposing gateways erected in the massive Egyptian style.'[48] The Egyptian Revival, and other styles from antiquity, were popular for bridges because decorating a span with the features of an architecture that had withstood the test of time could instil public confidence in the suspension bridge—a stucture built on a principle not yet perfected. Public suspicion was justified when it became clear that some suspension bridges were singularly short-lived. The one at Grand Falls, New Brunswick (by Edward Serrell, 1852), lasted only five years, and that at Montmorency Falls, Quebec (by Samuel Keefer, 1853-6), was poorly built and collapsed a week after its opening, taking with it a woman, a boy, a horse, and a cart. Although they lacked rigidity, suspension bridges—including

5.20 Alexandra Suspension Bridge, Spuzzum, British Columbia, 1863. BCARS/10294.

Roebling's at Niagara—were accepted for railway use.[49]

The first suspension bridge in the West was the **Alexandra Bridge [5.20]** at Spuzzum, British Columbia, built over the Fraser Canyon in 1863 as part of the Cariboo Wagon Road. Engineer Andrew S. Hallidie (1836-1900)—a manufacturer of wire rope who developed the first cable-car system in San Francisco—designed the bridge for contractor, and future Lieutenant Governor, Joseph William Trutch. Pyramidal towers, made of immense 20-by-20-inch (51-cm) wooden timbers, supported twin $4\frac{1}{2}$-inch (114-mm) wire cables that carried a roadway with a clear span of 268 feet (81.7 m). Though they had no pretense to architectural style, these towers expressed a direct approach to construction.[50]

Suspension bridges are ideally suited for long spans above turbulent waters or deep gorges where intermediate piers cannot be built. The technique has continued into the present century, as at the Lions Gate Bridge, which links Vancouver with the north shore of Burrard Inlet (1937-8: Monsarrat and Pratley, engineers; Robinson and Steinway, consulting engineers; Palmer and Bow, architects), and the graceful Alex Fraser Bridge over the Fraser River at Surrey, BC (CBA-Buckland and Taylor, 1987-8), a 'cable-stayed' suspension bridge whose main deck span is the longest of its type in the world—just one more 'first' among Canadian achievements in transportation structures.[51]

Military Defences

The improvement of the transportation network was motivated to a large extent by military considerations. The most evident part of the defence strategy was, of course, the maintenance of a system of fortifications. Britain inherited the remains of the French military defences when she gained control of Quebec, but many of these structures were antiquated and had been ravaged by war. Louisbourg was in ruins and Quebec City had suffered considerable damage. One might have expected an immediate initiative to rebuilt the country's forts, but this did not happen. British policy towards the defence of Canada was directed by the interests of the imperial government and not necessarily by those of the colony. Economy was a high priority. Westminster was more likely to react to a specific military threat than to take a proactive role

in building the country's defences. It never adopted a comprehensive defence scheme, despite several thoughtful attempts to create one. What resulted was a series of stop-gap measures of limited effectiveness. Fortunately for Britain—and for Canada—the inadequate fortifications were never tested.

A great deal of capital was invested in the Rideau Canal as a reaction to fear of an impending American invasion. Even then, Colonel John By's persuasive arguments for permission to make the locks wide enough for commercial as well as military traffic ultimately earned him a reprimand for having spent too much money.

The Rideau Canal and the rebuilding of the Halifax Citadel were two of many recommendations for improving Canadian defences that were made in 1825 by a Royal Commission headed by Sir James Carmichael Smyth of the Royal Engineers. Most of the Smyth Commission's suggestions went unheeded—a result that was characteristic of Westminster's *ad hoc* approach to crisis management.

Forts

The British interest in defending Canada began with the settlement and fortification of Halifax as a counter-move to the French fortress at Louisbourg [2.6, 7]. The series of works carried out over the next century at the Halifax Citadel revealed Britain's lackadaisical attitude towards defending the colony, particularly in time of peace, and also the tendency to use cheap construction techniques that led to high maintenance costs and the need for frequent rebuilding.

The first defences at Halifax (1749) were designed by Governor Cornwallis's chief engineer, John Brewse, and were built by the soldiers with civilian assistance. The installation consisted of five square stockaded wood forts with corner bastions connected by a palisade (a continuous row of vertical wooden posts inserted into the ground and often sharpened to a point at the top) and strung around three sides of the town. The harbour formed the fourth side. The central fort, located on the rise behind the town, was called the Citadel. Each of the five forts could accommodate about 100 men.[52]

This was replaced within a dozen years by the second Citadel, an octagonal wooden blockhouse with a cupola built on the highest ground and surrounded by earthworks. Construction began in

1761, was suspended in 1763 at the end of the Seven Years' War, and was resumed a decade later. Neglected in peacetime, the earthworks fell victim to the weather and were in ruins by 1784.

The presumed threat of military action with France in the 1790s led to the construction of the third Citadel (1795-9)—called Fort George—under the command of HRH Prince Edward, the Duke of Kent, who was stationed at Halifax. Captain James Straton of the Royal Engineers designed a rectangu-

lar fortress with four bastions connected by 'curtains' (walls). The barracks within were large enough to accommodate 650 soldiers, and guns stood on its reinforced flat roof. This fort, too, was built cheaply of logs and earth, and it also deteriorated quickly. It was repaired and augmented during the War of 1812; but by the time the Smyth Commission visited it in 1825, the earthworks were in poor condition. The Commission criticized the practice of building temporary fortifications and

5.21 Plan of the fourth Halifax Citadel, Halifax, Nova Scotia, begun 1828. From: 'Nova Scotia. Plan of Barracks', 1862. NAC/RG8M, 84503/27, Item 10/C-108107.

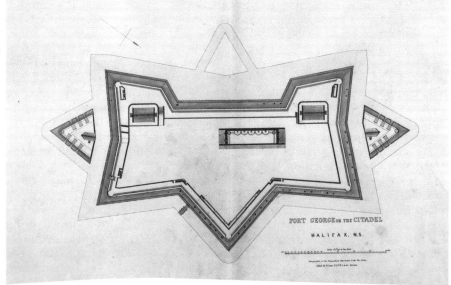

5.22 (*below*) West ravelin, Halifax Citadel, Halifax, Nova Scotia, begun 1828. Photograph by Royal Engineers, *c*. 1879. PANS, Royal Engineers Collection/N7367.

urged that the Citadel be rebuilt in permanent materials—one of its few recommendations that the British government followed.

The fourth **Halifax Citadel** [5.21], also called Fort George, which stands today as a popular tourist attraction, was planned in 1825 by Colonel Gustavus Nicolls of the Royal Engineers. It was begun three years later, and was built to ever-changing designs over the course of the next quarter-century by a work-force made up of the Royal Sappers and Miners, the Royal Staff Corps, and civilians under contract. It was designed and built in the form of a narrow eight-pointed star less than 150 feet across. Nicolls explained 'that the trace [the outline plan] has been formed more to answer the extent and nature of the ground than according to any regular system of fortification.'[53] Four of the points were demi-bastions; the other four were 'ravelins' (freestanding triangular outworks) located outside the ditch and intended to protect the curtains between the bastions [5.22]. Behind the ditch's outer wall, called the counterscarp, is a passage with short-range firing positions for defending the walls from attackers within the ditch.

Whether through incompetence or because of orders to cut costs, Nicolls' design was a failure. The ironstone walls of the 'escarp' (the side of the ditch below the wall) were built too thin, and in 1830 two portions collapsed. Other compromises included the use of two-sided demi-bastions rather than full diamond-shaped bastions (which offer far superior defensive positions), the lack of any provision for drainage, and the retention of the old powder magazine, whose site was so high that its roof was visible from outside the fort!

Nicolls was sent to Quebec in 1831 and was replaced over the next seventeen years by four different commanding Royal Engineers. Each tried to correct the problems left by his predecessor. The major revisions were a redesigning of the east face, replacing two demi-bastions and a ravelin with a continuous wall having three salient points; and an increase in the number of 'casemates', vaulted chambers built into the ramparts (walls). The principal structures within the fort are the stone Cavalier Barracks (1830-2), with its two storeys of casemates and gun emplacements on the roof (revealed by vertical slits, or loopholes, along the top of the long walls), and two new powder magazines (1840s).

The Halifax Citadel was built according to archaic principles associated with Vauban (page 32), who based his own seventeenth-century work on earlier French and Italian theory. It was obsolete even before the first stone was laid in place, when European military technology was relying on the detached fort. The Crimean War (1854-6) would reveal the inadequacy of British defensive systems against rifled artillery; but even after this, only

5.23 Halifax Dockyard (the King's Yard), Halifax, Nova Scotia. Photograph *c*. 1867. NAC/C-4480.

5.24 Quebec Citadel, Quebec, Quebec, 1820-31. Photograph by Jean Audet. PC.

minor improvements were made to the Citadel. Fortunately it never had to withstand an attack. As Colonel Nicolls had recognized, its true role was as the symbolic guardian of British North America's Atlantic seaboard.[54]

The Citadel was complemented by other military installations at Halifax. The largest was the **King's Yard** [5.23], or the Halifax Dockyard, which was the headquarters of the British North American fleet between its establishment in 1759 and its removal to Bermuda in 1819. The Yard contained dozens of buildings. Some, such as the large Mast House (1759) and the Sail Loft (1769), were utilitarian; many were residential; others, including the Naval Hospital (1784), provided specialized services. Most were simple but substantial wood frame buildings with gabled or hipped roofs and dormers, but some were more pretentious; for example, the Commissioner's Residence (1784) was given fine Georgian dress. Many of the buildings have been lost to fire and demolition, but the survivors convey a sense of the original scale of the complex. The Yard was defended by three small forts around Halifax Harbour, and it was a hive of activity during the War of 1812. A number of buildings remain, although many were destroyed by the Halifax Explosion of 1917.[55] The defensive installations at Halifax also included three Martello Towers (discussed below) and additional works on George's Island. (For the important Pacific naval base at Esquimalt, see **8.28, 29**.)

At Halifax the British had to build a defensive system from scratch, whereas at Quebec they inherited what was left of the French defences after the end of the Seven Years' War. As elsewhere, there was constant pressure to keep costs down and to undertake work only in reaction to a specific threat.

Very little work was done on improving the defences at Quebec until after the unsuccessful American siege of Quebec in 1775-6. Construction of a temporary citadel on Cape Diamond was begun in 1779 under the direction of Captain William Twiss (whose canals on the St Lawrence were discussed above), but activity ceased with the Treaty of Paris in 1783. A more elaborate defence plan comprising work proposed for several locations was completed in 1799 by Chief Engineer (and subsequently Inspector General of Fortifications) Gother Mann (1747-1830). Although a number of repairs were made and some new structures erected, progress continued to be slow.

Finally, sixty years after the British Conquest, work was begun on a permanent **Quebec Citadel** (1820-31). The motive behind approval of the construction at this particular time was likely economic: helping to protect the lucrative commercial trade on the St Lawrence. Most of the labour was supplied by soldiers. As at Halifax, the design—by the new Chief Engineer, Colonel Elias Walker Durnford (1774-1850)—followed the centuries-old system of bastioned fortification. A series of pointed stone bastions, intended to cover all possible angles of attack, are connected by broad curtains that are protected by ravelins built across the moat from their mid-point, with gun positions trained on the curtains. One face sits atop the cliff, Cape Diamond. The attractive star-shaped geometry, created by the stone walls and the earthworks, is best appreciated in aerial photographs [**5.24**].[56]

The Quebec Citadel and the other fortifications received minor improvements in the next three decades, and then were turned over to the Dominion government in 1871 with the departure of the British army. The Governor General, Lord Dufferin—who recognized the historical, symbolic, and scenic value of the old fortifications—intervened to save the Citadel, and many of the surviving stone fortification walls built in the French regime, from demolition, in an important early initiative at heritage conservation. He proposed that the old *enceinte* be opened up to allow urban traffic to penetrate it, and that a series of new gates be built. Dufferin summoned fellow Irishman W.H. Lynn (1829-1915), 'a very clever architect I happen to know at home, who has a *specialité* for picturesque mediaeval military construction.' Lynn visited Quebec in 1875, and the **St Louis Gate** (1878) [**5.25**] and Kent Gate (1879) were built to his designs. Dufferin also built himself a residence at the Citadel, and extended the walkway along the escarpment that is now known as Dufferin Terrace (seen in front of the Château Frontenac, **9.18**). The two gates are romantically inspired works from a later age than the walls and are based on a conception of what fortifications *should* look like. Nevertheless these battlemented and turreted Victorian enhancements form part of the *tout ensemble* that make up the fortifications of Quebec, and have helped to make the city one of the great tourist meccas of the world.[57]

The British fortified a number of sites in Upper Canada as defensive measures against the French, the natives, and finally the Americans. The first was Fort Erie (1764), a wooden fort at the south entrance to the Niagara River that was intended to protect the supply route through the Great Lakes; the most important ones were at the two entrances to Lake Ontario: Kingston at the northeast, and Niagara-on-the-Lake at the southwest.[58]

Like so many other sites, Kingston had vital military, naval, and commercial strategic value, located as it was at the entrances to both Lake Ontario and the Rideau Canal. The British inherited decaying Fort Frontenac from the French and made some repairs to it, but in 1788 the fort was declared 'altogether defenceless' and the repairs 'could not be expected to last long.' It nevertheless took the War of 1812-14 to stimulate new military construction. The outcome was a large system of harbour installations defending the city and its busy naval dockyard, which reached the peak of activity during the War and was closed in 1852. These defences included two forts.

Fort Frederick began as a blockhouse to defend the Kingston dockyard, but during the Oregon Crisis of the 1840s it was upgraded with earthworks and bastions to provide a proper battery. It was later abandoned and became the site of the Royal Military College. **Fort Henry** [**5.26**], located a short distance away, was built as a small fort in 1813-16 and reconstructed on a larger scale in 1832-6 under the direction of Lieutenant Colonel John Ross Wright and Major (later Sir) Richard Bonnycastle (1791-1847) of the Royal Engineers. It is a six-sided limestone structure with vaulted casemates and protected by a ditch, 30 feet deep and 40 feet across, and a stone counterscarp. Fort Henry was never

5.25 St Louis Gate, Quebec, Quebec, 1878. Photograph *c*. 1880. ANQ, collection initiale/P600-6/N673-1.

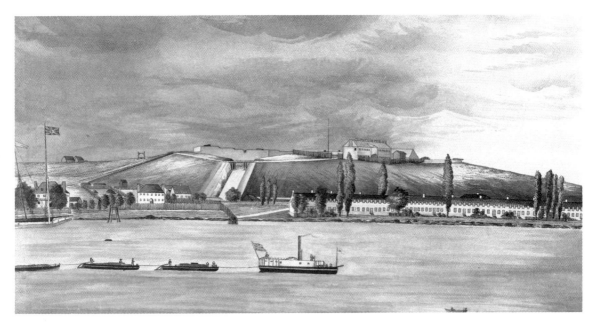

5.26 View from Fort Frontenac of Point Frederick and Fort Henry, near Kingston, Ontario. Drawn by Lt.-Col. Henry Francis Ainslie, 1839. From 'Views in the Canadas'. NAC/C-510.

attacked and its most important military use has been as a prison; nevertheless, it has been preserved and interpreted in modern times as the mighty citadel of Upper Canada.[59]

At Niagara-on-the-Lake (then called Newark), at the other end of Lake Ontario, the British built Fort George. The first fort (1796-9) was a collection of buildings—blockhouses, storehouses, and others—surrounded by a wooden palisade, bastions made of earth embankments with timber facing, and a ditch. The fortifications were improved in 1812-13, but on 26 May 1813 the Americans attacked Fort George, burned the wooden buildings to the ground, and occupied it for half a year, making renovations to the defences. The British recaptured the fort in December and the withdrawing Americans burned the town of Newark. Fort George was again repaired, but was soon superseded by nearby Fort Mississauga (1812-15), which was located on a more strategic and defensible site. Fort George is now operated as a historic site by Parks Canada.[60]

The British built a number of other forts on the Great Lakes. The best known is Fort York (1813-15) at Toronto. The remaining eight of the original eighteen buildings were restored by the city and are operated by the Toronto Historical Board.

Blockhouses and Martello towers

Forts were the principal, but by no means the only, components in military defence systems. The British used other building types as well, sometimes in isolation and sometimes in association with forts.

The basic defensive building was the blockhouse, built to withstand attack from musket-fire and arrows. The building-type originated in New England during the seventeenth-century French and Indian Wars. Although many variations existed, a blockhouse was typically a two-storey structure built of horizontal squared logs, often covered with clapboards or shingles to protect the logs from weathering. The upper storey overhung the first so as to provide 'machicolations'—openings in the floor through which the defenders could fire downward on attackers who had reached the walls. Narrow loopholes and wider portholes in the walls provided positions for musket and ordnance fire.

Most blockhouses were self-sufficient defensible posts that combined the functions of barracks, magazine, and storeroom. Many were isolated stations built along military waterways. Others formed part of a larger defensive system, as at Halifax and Kingston. They usually stood within a wooden palisade that formed the first line of defence.[61]

The oldest in Canada is the **Fort Edward Blockhouse** (1750) in Windsor, Nova Scotia, named after Governor Edward Cornwallis. The fort [**5.27**] was built by Major Charles Lawrence to defend the main route between Halifax and the Annapolis Valley from the French and the Indians. It consisted of the blockhouse, two barracks, and a storehouse set within a 250-foot-square (76-m) palisade wall with bastions. The blockhouse measures 18 feet, 6 inches (5.6 m) on each side, with an overhang of 17 inches (43 cm) all round, and is built of squared pine logs, 6 by 9 inches (15 by 23 cm) and nailed at the corners (although most blockhouses were dovetailed). The walls were probably clapboarded or shingled soon after construction, and are now covered by a steep hipped roof. The building was prefabricated in Halifax and carried to Fort Edward by the soldiers of the 45th Regiment.

Built a half-century later, the blockhouses along the Rideau Canal were similar in design. Colonel By proposed twenty-two, one at each strategic point, with the innovation of having the ground floor built of stone (salvaging left-over masonry from the excavations for the locks). Because of the projected cost, this recommendation was rejected in favour of defensible lockmaster houses. Undaunted, Colonel By built five blockhouses on his own initiative. The Kingston Mills Blockhouse (1831-2) is typical of the group, 28 feet (8.5 m) square with the ground-floor walls of stone. Clapboard covers the walls of the upper floor. The entrance is on the second storey, allowing the ladder to be removed in the event of attack.

Other Canadian blockhouses were variants on this theme. The largest and strongest was the Fort

5.27 Fort Edward Blockhouse, Windsor, Nova Scotia, 1750. Photograph by Larry Turner, 1980.

Wellington Blockhouse (1838-9) at Prescott, Ontario, which was 50 feet (15.3 m) square and had stone walls on both storeys. The most sophisticated was the Madawaska Blockhouse (1841) near Edmunston, New Brunswick, whose top floor was set at an angle of 45 degrees to the lower storey.

The other important self-sufficient defensive installation was the Martello tower, a circular masonry structure, usually about 30 to 35 feet (9.2 to 10.7 m) high, with a flat roof (called a 'terreplein') on which was mounted ordnance. There were usually two storeys inside, the lower one for storing powder and supplies and the upper one used as barracks. The thick walls—often thickest on the most exposed side—and the bomb-proof arched design provided security from attack, although the towers would not withstand sustained breaching artillery fire. The circular shape allowed the cannon to be fired at any angle. The tower was entered at the second floor by a wooden ladder that could easily be removed in the event of an attack. The name 'Martello' derives either from the Bay of Mortella in Corsica, where a tower built by the Genoese withstood British naval bombardment in 1793-4, or from the Italian *martello*, meaning 'hammer'. British military engineers built such towers on Minorca in 1798-1801, and the name came into use shortly afterwards. More than seventy were built along the south coast of England in 1805-8. All were constructed of brick and used strictly for coastal defence.[62]

Sixteen Martello towers were built in Canada between 1796 and 1846—five at Halifax, one at Saint John, four at Quebec, and six at Kingston—and many more were proposed but never constructed. They differed from the British prototypes in that they were intended to defend against attack by land as well as sea, and because they were built of stone rather than brick. These towers were popular because they were permanent, gave an impression of strength, required little manpower, were relatively cheap, and had low maintenance costs. They were much better able to withstand artillery attack than wooden blockhouses. None of the Canadian towers were ever subjected to attack, however, so there is no way of knowing how effective they would have been in action.

The first three Martello towers in Canada—and arguably the first in the world—were erected at Halifax in 1796-9 under the command of the Duke of Kent, who named them after other members of the royal family. Captain James Straton, the engineer for the third Citadel, was the designer. The

Prince of Wales Tower (1796-9), at Point Pleasant, defending the North West Arm, is the earliest of these prototypes [**5.28**]. Constructed of ironstone rubble, it is 72 feet (22 m) in diameter and 26 feet (7.9 m) high, with the walls 8 feet (2.4 m) thick at the base and 6 feet (1.8 m) at the top. A hollow circular masonry pier, rising through the centre and creating a room 16 feet (4.9 m) in diameter within it, helped to support the 3-foot-thick (92-cm) timber terreplein that could carry ten pieces of ordnance. Loopholes in the wall permitted musket fire, and larger embrasures in the parapet provided firing positions for the cannon. The Prince of Wales Tower was altered somewhat over the years, but has been restored by Parks Canada as a national historic site. The other two, the Duke of Clarence's Tower and the Duke of York's Tower, lost their upper storeys in the nineteenth century, and only the basement of the latter is still standing.

Later Martello towers were thinner in their proportions. Six towers were erected at Kingston in 1845-8 to strengthen the city's defences. Three were built on land and heavily fortified, and were 'among the most technologically advanced of any Martello towers in the world.'[63] In 1846-7 the **Fort**

5.28 Prince of Wales Tower, Halifax, Nova Scotia, 1796-9. Photograph *c*. 1870. PANS/Notman Studio Collection, No. 1692/N-5308.

5.29 (*right*) Fort Frederick Tower, Kingston, Ontario, 1846-7. Plans and section, 1846. NAC/NMC-24730.

Frederick Tower [**5.29**] was built within the fort of that name as its battery keep and barracks. Sixty feet (18.3 m) in diameter and 45 feet (13.7 m) high, it has a limestone ashlar wall that is 15 feet (4.6 m) thick towards Lake Ontario and 9 feet (2.7 m) thick facing land. A central circular pillar of solid masonry helps support a stone arch and the ashlar terreplein, providing a flat bomb-proof roof 6 feet (1.8 m) thick. Three pieces of long-range ordnance were mounted on the terreplein. Four 'caponiers' (looking somewhat like feet), with loopholes, project at the base to provide short-range firing positions that command the ditch. The basement was used as a magazine and contained a cistern, and two levels of barracks were located above. The present conical roof is a later addition installed to provide protection from the weather.

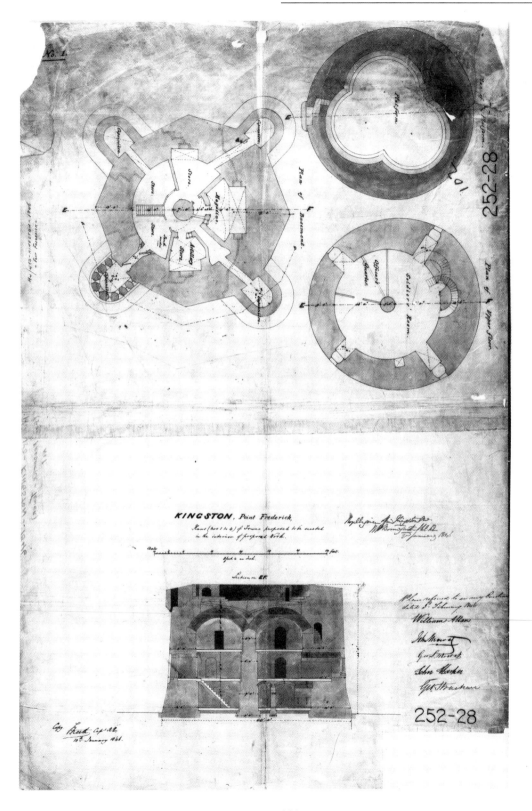

Building for Commerce and Industry

By the early years of the nineteenth century much of the arable and accessible land in eastern Canada was settled and being farmed. The continued influx of new immigrants, many of them displaced Scottish and Irish tenant-farmers as well as American land-seekers, created the need to open up additional land for settlement—a new 'interior', away from the principal waterways. The improving road and rail transportation systems helped to make this possible, as did the military protection. Vast tracts became available, in part by the initiatives of private speculators and in part by government-directed activities [12.1, 3, 4]. By mid-century many 'pioneers' had reached the edge of the Canadian Shield.

Industry went hand in hand with the opening of the interior. Lumbermen cleared the first-growth timber in advance of the farmers; mills provided the new settlers with sawn wood and processed their agricultural products. Business considerations also lay behind the scheme to build the colonization roads, as lumber barons demanded better access to the rich timber lands in the Huron and Ottawa Tract as repayment for their industry. Roads were seen as being necessary to

> facilitate and cheapen the supplies to the Lumbermen, and stimulate the farmer to raise larger crops, for which he would find a ready home and cash market, and employment for himself and teams, in transportation, during the winter.[64]

The poor soil prevented most farmers from harvesting the large crops envisioned by the government road-builders, but the lumber industry certainly benefited from the roadways, as did the farmers and their teams in winter. The growth of the square-timber trade in the first half of the nineteenth century required that logging operations had to be extended deeper and deeper into the wilderness frontier. Trees were felled in winter, and the logs were skidded on ice and snow to streams and rivers, where they were driven and rafted downstream after the spring thaw.

Camboose shanties

A logging gang spent the winter season in a large temporary bunkhouse known as a **camboose shanty** [5.30]. A distinctive building-type that was developed for the needs of the logging industry in the northern woods, it was found, with regional variants, in Upper Canada, Lower Canada, and New Brunswick. The camboose shanty was constructed by the lumbermen (sometimes called 'shantymen') of large horizontal pine logs more than a foot in diameter, and saddle-notched at the corners; it had walls that often stood 6 to 8 feet (1.8 to 2.4 m) high, with a floor that sometimes sank below grade to expose less of the exterior walls to the winter weather. The spaces between the logs were chinked with moss and pieces of wood. A low-sloped gabled roof was made of 'scoops': half-logs of pine that were hollowed out like troughs and laid side by side with the hollow side up, with a second set placed on top of them hollow side down. The result was a roof (constructed much like pantiles, the clay roofing material we know as Spanish tile) that shed moisture very effectively.[65]

The central interior feature was the large camboose fireplace, an open hearth often ten feet (3m) square that was used for cooking, heat, and light [5.31]. A large square log chimney above the fireplace carried away the smoke and provided light and ventilation. Bunks were placed in single or double tiers along the walls. There was usually only one door, and no windows, in order to conserve heat. Fifty to sixty men might be accommodated in a camboose shanty 40 feet (12.2 m) square; many shanties were around 30 by 40 feet (9.1 by 12.2 m) in size; and some were as small as 12 by 16 feet (3.7 by 4.9 m), sleeping only five or six men. The arrangement of bunks and fires recalls that of the Iroquoian longhouse [1.5]. Both may have been independent discoveries of a plan that could accommodate a large group of people in a heat-efficient manner.

Camboose shanties were used from the 1820s to around 1900. Their demise was brought about in part by the introduction of the stove, which replaced the need for the camboose fireplace, as well as by the building of the colonization roads and railways. Easier access into the forested interior meant that the lumber companies could build semi-permanent camps from which the loggers were dispersed for short periods into more isolated areas.

Mills

The success of a new community—as land transportation would remain difficult for some time—depended to a large measure on its being able to

5.30 Camboose shanty, Lake Travers, Black River, Ontario, *c*. 1900. Archives of Ontario/Macnamara Collection/Acc. 2271/s5154.

5.31 (*below*) Interior of a camboose shanty. Photograph 1900. NAC/C-25718.

Cook's Department

take the raw materials it produced and process them into usable products. Within a few years of their founding, the villages of Guelph in Canada West [12.1], and Stanley, NB [12.4], had sawmills that made boards from logs and gristmills that made flour from grain, as well as blacksmiths who forged horseshoes, tools, and hardware. Guelph's brewery and two distilleries provided alternative ways of processing locally grown grain. Settlers in sheep-raising areas would have carding, weaving, and perhaps fulling mills; and other communities might boast any number of other industrial enterprises. Families that did not have access to a mill would have to use hand processes, which included a small grinding mill, a mortar and pestle, a hand-sieve for making flour, and hand-cards and spinning wheels for making cloth.

A 'mill' originally referred to a building used for grinding grain, and also to the machinery that did the grinding. (A household coffee mill retains this use of the word.) The term came to refer to any building or mechanical device that yielded a manufactured product through a repetitive process. (The term 'factory' was originally used to describe a large fur-trading post—one was York Factory [13.9]—but came to describe a large manufacturing facility that used more complex processes than a mill.) Mills require a source of power, and until the latter part of the nineteenth century that power was usually derived from water. Mills were therefore often sited where a river or stream intersected the road network. They provided nodes of settlement, many of which grew into villages.

Most early mills were 'custom mills' that did custom work for individual farmers. In economic terms the farmer was both the source of raw materials and the market for the processed product. Cash was scarce, so payment was often made through barter, or by offering the miller a percentage of the crop. This practice was gradually replaced, through the nineteenth century, with 'merchant mills'—commercial operations in which the miller purchased and processed raw materials (made available by the development of non-subsistence agriculture) and then sought markets for his products. This was a more capital-intensive activity that required easy access to both the materials and the markets. It was made possible by improvements in transportation—especially the introduction of railways—and the concentration of markets in cities and large towns. Merchant mills often differed from custom mills in the greater efficiency of their technology and their increased scale, although a

custom miller could progress to a merchant operation without making any physical changes to his mill.

Nineteenth-century mills were typically constructed with a conventional heavy timber frame in which wood posts (or columns) supported wood beams. The weight of the machinery, and the vibrations caused by its movement, required large-dimensioned members that were securely braced, with the posts usually one foot (30 cm) square or larger. Early in the century the beams were mortised into the posts, but in time iron beam- and joist-hangers were used. Since fire was always a significant risk, true 'mill construction' was developed in which a continuous row of joists were spiked together to form a solid, fire-resistant floor, replacing the customary plank floor resting on spaced joists. The exterior walls might be made of wood, stone, or brick, and in many small-scaled mills there were no walls at all: simply an exposed frame supporting the machinery and a roof.

Although water was the usual means of powering early industry, windmills and animal power were used as well. Towards the end of the nineteenth century steam power was introduced, followed by electricity, which remains the primary source of industrial energy.

Water-powered mills Water power operates by the action of a moving stream turning a wheel that powers machinery through a system of gearing. A stream that provides a reliable flow and an

5.32 Mill, Varennes, Quebec, 1719. IBC, Fonds Gérard Morisset/16355-D-5.

5.33 Mill, Napanee, Ontario, begun 1786. Sketch by Elizabeth Simcoe, 1795. Archives of Ontario/f47-11.

adequate fall of water is essential. A dam or weir is generally built across the stream and a headrace constructed to carry water to the point where there is a good vertical fall; the mill and wheel are built at this location.

Waterwheels—which were usually mounted on the outside of the mill—came in several types: an overshot wheel, in which the water falls on top of the wheel on the side further from the source; an undershot wheel, in which the water runs beneath the wheel; a breast wheel, in which the water falls on the side of the wheel closer to the source; and a tub wheel, located at the foot of the fall. Each had its advantages in certain situations. The turbine—an internal wheel in a cast-iron housing that was far more efficient and functioned well in winter—was invented in France in 1827 and began to replace water wheels in Canada in the second half of the century.[66]

Mills were built by the earliest settlers in New France. The first water-powered gristmill in North America was built on Île Sainte-Croix in 1604 (page 18), and every subsequent community of any size had a mill to grind grain and perform other functions. The stone **mill at Varennes** [5.32], Quebec (moulin Lussier), built in 1719, resembles a house in its massing and materials, but it is entered on the gable end, and a shed extension along one long side contains the mill machinery.[67]

A number of tide mills were built at the mouths of creeks or rivers or on tidal estuaries in the Maritimes, taking particular advantage of the massive tides on the Bay of Fundy. Tidewater was trapped behind the mill and flowed through the waterwheel as the tide receded. At least twelve tide mills operated in Nova Scotia from 1780 to 1880. Many utilized a tide machine invented in 1821 by Robert Foulis, a Scotsman who moved first to Halifax and then to Saint John, where he became a successful miller.[68]

Advanced milling techniques were brought to Canada by American entrepreneurs and through publications. The early settlements of the Loyalists and other American immigrants generally included mills—which, in some cases, were provided by the government. The first grist- and sawmill in Upper Canada was built by the government at Newark in 1783 at the instigation of Peter and James Secord, farmers from New Jersey; Captain William Twiss provided the iron machinery and assisted generally. Robert Clark (b. 1744), a Loyalist from Dutchess County, New York, was hired by the government in the same year to build and operate a gristmill at Kingston Mills, 6 miles (10 km) above Kingston. In 1785 Clark was again retained to build a **sawmill** (opened 1786) and a **gristmill** (opened 1787) **at Napanee** [5.33]. In 1792 the Napanee mill became the property of the Honourable Robert Cartwright, who hired Clark to erect a new mill (built of lumber, like its predecessors) and repair an existing one. This mill complex was sketched in 1795 by Elizabeth Simcoe, who gave us one of the earliest images of an industrial building in Upper Canada.[69]

5.34 View of Wrightstown (Hull), Quebec. Painting by Henry Du Vernet, 1823. NAC/C-608.

Another American, Philemon Wright, was the first industrialist to harness the power of the Chaudière Falls on the Ottawa River, the waterfall that was subsequently crossed by the Royal Engineers' Union Bridge. In 1800 Wright—with his family, five other families, and 25 men Wright had recruited—completed a month-long 500-mile (800-km) trek from their farms in Woburn, Massachusetts, to make a new home on the site of today's Hull, Quebec. Wright received a grant of 12,000 acres (4,800 hectares) and built an agricultural and industrial community that became known as **Wrightstown [5.34]**. He built a two-storey frame sawmill and gristmill by 1802. His principal venture was cutting down the magnificent stands of white and red pine, an activity that was initially challenged by nearby Algonquin and Iroquois chiefs. In 1806 Wright made entrepreneurial history—and initiated a major Canadian export industry—when he lashed together hundreds of logs, and thousands of sawn boards and staves, to make a timber-raft that he navigated down the turbulent Ottawa River, around Montreal, and down the St Lawrence River to Quebec City. Here the raft was disassembled and the lumber sold for distribution in lumber-starved Europe, which was sorely missing the shipments of Baltic timber halted by the Napoleonic blockade.

The timber resources of the Ottawa Valley, and the renewable energy of the Chaudière, combined to make this the most heavily developed hydraulic site in the country. Development and redevelopment were continuous. Industrialist E.B. Eddy, who came from Vermont in 1854 and manufactured matches, generated hydro-electric power here for the first time in 1881 (to illuminate his mill), and began making pulp and paper eight years later. By the end of the century some 350 million board-feet of lumber were cut at the Chaudière Falls every year (enough to be stacked into a cube higher than the Peace Tower).[70]

A single water-wheel might power several different kinds of mills simultaneously. For example, in Ontario's Lanark County in the 1830s there were mills in Clayton, Smiths Falls, Perth, and Almonte that all used one water-wheel to card wool, grind grain, and saw wood.

Every significant community soon had one or more sawmills—which were needed to provide lumber for building a settlement—just as every town has its lumberyard today. Thomas Need, who settled for ten years (1832-42) on Sturgeon Lake, Canada West, wrote in 1838:

> The completion of the sawmill was an event of vast interest to all the inhabitants of the settle-

ment, who looked to exchange their rude shanties in a little time for a neat frame house.'[71]

By the middle of the nineteenth century, Nova Scotia and Ontario each had more than 1,000 sawmills powered by water.[72] The McDonald Brothers' Sawmill in Sherbrooke Village, NS, is a working reconstruction (built in the early 1970s) of a sawmill that had been erected between 1826 and 1829 and was abandoned by 1900. The two-storey frame building contains the running gear on the lower floor and a reciprocating (up-and-down) saw on the upper level. Power is provided by a breast wheel 12 feet (3.7 m) in diameter that is capable of 35 revolutions per minute.[73] The reciprocating saw was eventually superseded by the circular saw and the band saw, which were far more productive.

In Ontario sawmills were also typically two storeys high, built of frame construction, often sheathed with vertical boards, and covered by a broad gabled roof. Smaller mills were contained within a rectangular building, whereas others had wings and sheds added as needed. The gable ends

often contained characteristic diamond-shaped windows, and dormers frequently provided additional illumination. The Boyd Sawmill at Bobcaygeon, Peterborough County, was acquired in 1851 by Mossom Boyd, a leading lumberman in the Trent watershed, and was rebuilt in the early 1870s. The lumber was sawn on the upper level, which was accessed by a raised platform covered with tramway tracks.[74] The **Perley and Pattie sawmill** (1856), Ottawa, had no fewer than fourteen tilted windows, varying in size between nine and sixty-four panes, in one end elevation [5.35]. The builder's instincts for decoration are seen as well in the belfry on the roof, which probably served no useful function. Different regions favoured different architectural details. Bagnall's Sawmill at Hunter River, PEI—built in the 1840s and still operating in modern times—has walls clad in shingles and is illuminated by conventional rectangular windows in the gables.[75]

5.35 The Perley and Pattie sawmill, Ottawa, Ontario, 1856. Photograph 1872. MMCH/78889-I.

Equally important to the survival of early communities was the gristmill. The grain-milling process had made important technological advances in the United States in the late eighteenth century, and these were transferred into Canada a short time later. American inventor Oliver Evans discovered how to use the power that drove the millstones to carry out the other processes, such as cooling and separating, and he used belt drives, elevators, conveyors, and chutes to automate the operation. He published his methods in *The Young Millwright and Miller's Guide*, which went through fifteen editions between 1795 and 1860.[76]

Because of the constant threat of fire from spontaneous combustion, gristmills were often built of stone—or, especially later in the century, of brick (rather than wood)—and consequently many have survived into modern times. The mills were typically rectangular buildings covered by gable roofs and illuminated by numerous windows, usually symmetrically arranged. When the milling procedure became more complex, as recommended by Evans, additional storeys were necessary to allow the grain to be lifted up by bucket elevators and dropped through chutes as they passed from one process to another. **Watson's Mill [5.36]** at Manotick, Ontario, built in 1859-60 of a heavy timber frame with coursed rubble walls of limestone and operated by Moss Kent Dickinson and Joseph Currier, has been restored to simplified working conditions and opened to the public. Incoming grain was cleaned by a separator and raised by an elevator to be stored in one of many bins. When it was time for grinding, the grain was dropped into the millstones—originally there were four 'run' (pairs) of stones—and ground. The grist was raised to the attic, cooled in an auger (screw-type) conveyor, and then dropped into a bolter where the flour and bran were separated and bagged. The mill was originally powered by six turbines, cast in Ottawa in 1859; today three are in operation. In 1862, two years after the mill opened, Currier's young wife Anne stood too close to a spinning shaft, and it caught her skirt and hurled her to her death. Currier immediately sold his interest in the mill to Dickinson, but millers and visitors have continued to encounter the ghost of Anne Currier. The last operator was Harry Watson, who purchased the mill in 1946.[77]

Mills of this kind were built across the country. A number of others have been restored as well, including the **gristmill at Keremeos [5.37]**, British Columbia, built in 1877 by English-born rancher

5.36 Watson's Mill, Manotick, Ontario, 1859-60. Courtesy of the Rideau Valley Conservation Authority.

Barrington Price. He imported machinery from the US and Britain to produce flour from grain grown in the Similkameen Valley. Before then, flour had to be packed in from Colville, Washington, some 170 miles (270 km) away. Water is carried along a wooden flume to an overshot wheel, which powers the machinery. A rational, functional structure, the Keremeos mill, like the mill at Manotick, was built with little pretence to high architectural style.

5.37 Gristmill, Keremeos, British Columbia, 1877. Photograph by Harold Kalman, 1977.

The two are very different in appearance, however. The British Columbia mill was constructed of squared logs, dovetailed and pegged at the corners, with a variety of window and door openings; whereas the Ontario building was built of stone and has regular and symmetrical windows. Each followed the prevalent manner of building seen in the houses of its time and place.[78]

New technologies introduced in the later nineteenth century revolutionized Canadian gristmilling. A machine called the middlings purifier allowed the wheat to be ground in several stages ('breaks') to produce a 'stronger', more glutinous flour; this was followed around 1880 by the roller process, which was much more efficient than grinding with stones. Finally, the widespread use of steam power—tentatively introduced much earlier, perhaps first in a sawmill and a mine in Nova Scotia in 1827[79]—eliminated the need to locate mills along rivers and allowed them to be situated in large cities near rail and water transportation routes, where they could receive shipments of prairie wheat and then distribute the flour to a large market. These developments encouraged millers to increase their scale of operation and shift to a merchant, rather than a custom, operation.

The need for constant upgrading to keep a mill competitive is well illustrated in the history of **Wood's Mill [5.38]** at Smiths Falls, Ontario. In 1823 Irish-born Loyalist Thomas Smyth built a crude sawmill—a timber frame structure without any exterior wall sheathing—at this cataract along the Rideau River, and two years later it was purchased by American-born Abel Russell Ward. When the mill site was flooded by the building of the Rideau Canal, Ward built a $1\frac{1}{2}$-storey wood-frame gristmill, about 60 feet (18 m) square, nearby in 1831. A few years later he added a carding mill and a sawmill. In 1852, in order to increase his capacity, Ward erected a $3\frac{1}{2}$-storey limestone mill equipped with interconnected machinery on all the floors. His mills were purchased in 1880 by Alexander Wood, who had been born in Upper Canada to a Loyalist family and was a partner in the successful Frost and Wood Foundry of Smiths Falls, one of Ontario's largest manufacturers of farm machinery. Wood immediately installed middlings purifiers in the stone mill and began to take shipments of prairie wheat by rail; and in 1887 he installed a five-break roller system, retaining five run of stones as well, and raised the roof from a gable to a more capacious mansard. Finally, in 1890-2 Wood built a new turbine-powered four-storey limestone mill on the site of the old wooden mill and constructed a large grain elevator between it and the 1852 mill for storing the incoming wheat.

5.38 Wood's Mill (at right), Smiths Falls, Ontario, 1852-92. Photograph by William J. Topley. NAC/PA-8803.

Alexander Wood died in 1895, and his successors were not able to make the mill pay, in part because of vigorous competition from the large steam-powered flour mills in Montreal and Toronto. The mill was operated in the early 1920s by the United Farmers' Co-operative Company, an early co-op, but with little success. The elevator was dismantled and, in the 1950s, the newer mill building was converted into apartments. In 1990 the entire mill complex was adapted (by Barry Padolsky) to become the Rideau Canal Museum, interpreting the history of the canal and its industries, and to house the offices of Parks Canada's Rideau Canal administration.[80]

The elevator at Wood's Mill stored grain that was about to be milled. Larger grain elevators were built along the railway as part of the national grain-transportation system: in prairie towns, where the grain awaited shipment from the growing region to market (see page 000); in major cities, such as Toronto and Calgary, where it was stored before being milled or malted; and at the major transshipment terminals—particularly Fort William (Thunder Bay), Montreal, Vancouver, and Prince Rupert—where the grain was held before being loaded onto ships. The massive concrete elevators built in the early 1900s along Montreal's harbour (most of which have been demolished) were particularly impressive for their scale, and their direct response to function. The European modernist Le Corbusier illustrated and praised their 'primary forms' in his architectural polemic of 1923, *Vers une Architecture* (published in English as *Towards a New Architecture*, London, 1927).

The textile industry used entirely different technical processes, although its mills adopted similar architectural forms. The principal steps in wool cloth production are carding, in which the fibers are blended, cleaned, and combed; spinning; weaving; and fulling, in which the woven cloth is cleaned, shrunk, and felted. In the early nineteenth century some processes were carried out at home (particularly spinning and weaving), and some might be done in mills that specialized in the respective processes. The Wile Carding Mill at Bridgewater, NS—built in 1860 and now administered by the Nova Scotia Museum—and the Asselstine Woollen Mill (*c.* 1840), a weaving mill now located at Upper Canada Village, are two of countless specialized mills that were built in eastern and central Canada and are now interpreted to the public.[81]

The British woollen industry had already seen the development from a small-scale custom mill to a semi-automated merchant mill—which was, in effect, a textile factory. In 1790 Samuel Slater moved from Derbyshire to Pawtucket, Rhode Island, where he introduced English textile machines and milling methods to North America. His cotton mill, known as the Old Slater Mill (1793), did carding, spinning, and other processes in one sequence of operations. The technology was subsequently transferred from the US to Canada.[82]

One of the largest textile mills in Canada was the **Marysville cotton mill** [5.39] at Marysville, New Brunswick, located just east of Fredericton on the Nashwaak River. In 1862 a giant of a man named Alexander 'Boss' Gibson bought an existing unprofitable sawmill and 200,000 acres (80,000 hectares) of timber (most of it from the New Brunswick and Nova Scotia Land Company). Determined to make the mill work, he refitted the water-powered sawmill and before long was producing lumber for the British, American, South American, and Australian markets. In the 1880s he added a lath mill and a steam-powered shingle mill.[83]

Encouraged by the incentives offered by the federal government's National Policy, 'Boss' Gibson decided to diversify into textiles, and in 1883-5 he built a large mill to process cotton imported from the southern US. The principal building, designed by architects Lockwood and Greene of Boston, is typical of the brick cotton mills of the US. It is a remarkable 418 feet (127.5 m) wide by 100 feet (30.5 m) deep, four storeys high, with exterior walls of locally produced brick—three feet (90 cm) thick at the foundation and two feet (60 cm) at the roof—and an internal frame of local spruce and southern pine. The symmetrical main elevation, facing the river, has a central entrance tower flanked by broad wings that are illuminated by arched, mullioned windows; the mammoth structure contains some 518 windows in all. The mill was large enough to accommodate 1,100 looms and 60,000 spindles, although it never worked at full capacity, and it was enlarged later in the 1880s with a dye house and several warehouses.

The Marysville cotton mill had machines for all the processes—including picking, carding, spinning, dying, and weaving—required to take cotton in its raw state and produce finished cloth. They were powered by two 650-horsepower steam engines with ten boilers (there was a smokestack 155 feet [47.3 m] high) and these also provided heat. The mill was illuminated by more than 800 carbon-arc electric lights, which drew their power from a dynamo in the basement. Many of the foremen

were recruited from Lowell, Massachusetts, the largest textile community in New England (and now a National and State Historic Park interpreting the textile industry). In 1887 Gibson manufactured 1.86 million pounds (837,000 kg) of cloth, valued at more than half a million dollars; and at the same time he produced wood products, valued at another quarter-million dollars, and a million bricks.

To accommodate the 500 cotton-mill workers, Gibson built an entire town [5.40], including some fifty brick duplexes (which he rented out at $40 to $50 per year), two hotels, two stores, a school, a large Gothic Revival Methodist Church (which was later stripped of its monopoly by the arrival of an

5.39 View of the Cotton mill, Marysville, New Brunswick, 1883-5. PANB/P87-12.

5.40 Workers' houses at Cotton Mill, Marysville, New Brunswick. Photograph by G.T. Taylor, *c*. 1890s. PANB/P5-318A.

Anglican church), and his own ornate brick mansion. Houses had been built for the sawmill workers before Gibson's takeover.[84]

Cotton manufacturers in Ontario and Quebec eventually waged—and won—a price war with Gibson, and in 1907 he lost control of the Marysville mill to the Canadian Coloured Cotton Mills Co., which closed in 1954. Subsequent attempts at operating the mill also failed. The gradual decline industry, as well as a number of devastating fires, have reduced the size of Marysville, but the mill and many of the residences remain standing on the picturesque site along the river. The New Brunswick government rehabilitated the mill in 1986, and it now accommodates the offices of the Department of Tourism, Recreation and Heritage and is known as Marysville Place.

Many single-industry resource communities developed across Canada in the last two centuries. A number of these are discussed in Chapter 13.

Windmills People think of the windmill as a quaint and picturesque feature of the landscape of Holland and other European countries without realizing that it was employed widely in Canada, well into the present century, in locations where an insufficient head or flow of water was available to power a waterwheel. Windmills generate power from moving air in the same way that waterwheels and turbines use moving water. Since the sails must face into the wind to generate power efficiently, the mill itself rotates with the wind, much like a weather vane. In a 'post mill' the entire structure turns on a fixed post to catch the wind, whereas in a 'tower mill' only the cap rotates above a fixed tower. (The latter was also called a 'smock mill'.) Sails were made of wood slats (or vanes), or of a wood frame covered with canvas.[85]

Windmills were common in New France. The earliest one recorded was built at Ville Marie (Montreal) in 1647, and in the following century there were at least eight windmills along the St Lawrence River between Île-aux-Coudres and Montreal, as well as several others in each of those locations. A **windmill at Île-aux-Coudres [5.41]**, built in 1772, still survives and may well be typical of the group. It is a tower mill with a circular stone base and a conical cap out of which the sails project. The power generated by the sails and their horizontal shaft is transferred by gears inside the building to a vertical shaft that rotates the millstones.

British settlers built windmills in both the Maritimes and Upper Canada. Halifax had one before 1761, and William Lowden built two wind-powered sawmills near Pictou, Nova Scotia, in 1788-92. An old **post mill at Chezzetcook [5.42]**, east of Halifax, was photographed in the 1930s. The square gable-roofed mill building, and the supports for the sails, sat on a wooden turntable that rotated to catch the wind.[86]

A large stone tower mill at Prescott, Upper Canada, was built in 1822 for grinding grain. It was captured during the Rebellion of 1838 because its height and strength made it seem to be a defensible position on the St Lawrence. Two hundred rebels held out here for five days and surrendered only when confronted with three armed British warships. Despite a valiant courtroom defence by a young Kingston lawyer named John A. Macdonald, eleven were hanged and sixty exiled to Australia. The sails of the Prescott windmill were removed after a half-century of service, and since 1873 the landmark tower has served duty as a lighthouse.[87]

Windmills were a natural solution on the Prairies, since few rivers had sufficient drops in elevation to provide adequate water power. The Red River Settlement in Manitoba had a functioning windmill by 1826, and at least twenty windmills and five watermills were in operation in the 1830s and 1840s.[88] The Mennonites in southern Manitoba commonly used windmills as well, in part drawing on their experience with the technology learned in Holland, Germany, and elsewhere in Europe. They bought three Red River windmills in 1876 and installed them in East Reserve communities; a steam-powered mill was built at Reinfeld in the same year. A new **windmill at Steinbach [5.43]**, Manitoba, was built in 1877, using the char-

5.41 Windmill, Île-aux-Coudres, Quebec, 1772. Photograph by T. Ratté, 1949. ANQ/E6-7/72299.

acteristic tower (smock) design. The cap of the windmill rotated on a metal track at the top of the octagonal tower. A change in wind direction would cause the small 'fan' at the rear to turn, which would rotate the whole cap until the sails faced directly into the wind (somewhat as a helicopter works). In 1879 the mill was dismantled and moved to Rosenort, where the photograph was taken. J.F. Galbraith, a neighbour of the Mennonites, described their mills in 1900:

> A quaint institution of the Mennonites when they first came to Manitoba, was their flour mills. These are of very ancient pattern, the buildings being of octagonal construction and pyramidal in design, and a good deal more capacious than they appear to be at first sight. They had a height of about 30 feet. The grinding power was derived from the wind, and the great arms and huge sails of the motor looked decidedly pretentious from underneath. Several of these mills are still standing and are a novel sight in this country.[89]

None of the early windmills survive today, but an operating reconstruction of the Steinbach-Rosenort windmill was built in 1972 at the Mennonite Heritage Village in Steinbach, incorporating some machinery from an early-nineteenth-century mill in Schleswig-Holstein.[90]

Other industrial buildings

Canada's first venture into heavy industry was **Les Forges du Saint-Maurice**, an iron foundry located on the St-Maurice River a few miles above Trois-Rivières. The plant was first proposed in 1729 by Montreal businessman François Poulin de Francheville, but it went into only limited production in 1734, a year after his premature death. The foundry began to be rebuilt in 1736 under the direction of French ironworks master Pierre-François Olivier de Vézin, using the more advanced process of indirect reduction with a blast furnace rather than the original direct-reduction method. The new plant was first fired up in 1738 and began to extract iron from the bog-iron along the river's shore, burning charcoal made from hardwood logs. Several of the structures were designed by the royal engineer Chaussegros de Léry (see page 32).[91]

The French Crown acquired the foundry a few years later, and the site was actively developed and improved until work was interrupted by war in 1760. The young Scotsman Matthew Bell took over

5.42 (*below left*) Windmill, Chezzetcook, Nova Scotia. Photograph *c.* 1930. From a negative held by NSM/N-3459; original at PANS.

5.43 Windmill, Steinbach, Manitoba, 1877. Moved to Rosenort, Manitoba, 1879. PAM/N13826.

operation of the plant in 1793—by now it was owned by the British government—and he made many additional improvements. Among his manufactured products were stoves, ploughs, bedframes, and the engines for John Molson's steamboat, *Accommodation*. Bell lost control of the ironworks in 1846, but by then it was already losing ground to newer and more technologically advanced plants. Les Forges du Saint-Maurice failed to keep up with the times and stopped production in 1883 after 150 years of operation.

The foundry consisted of a large complex erected over the years, including the blast furnace, two forges (where the reduced ore was made into iron), a moulding mill, a bellows building (the bellows was powered by a waterwheel), several storage facilities, many dwellings, and the *grande maison*, which served as the administrative headquarters. Some buildings were of stone, others of wood; all were constructed in the utilitarian vernacular manner of their day. Most fell quickly into ruins, but several fragments survived. Parks Canada restored portions of the complex, beginning in 1984, using a novel and effective interpretive approach in which the surviving remains—the original **blast furnace** (built *c.* 1737 by Chaussegros de Léry) and the two forges—were protected by contemporary symbolic structures erected around them [**5.44**]. Designed by architects Gauthier, Guité, Roy of Quebec City, they are aluminum 'space frames' (frameworks assembled from small members) finished in bronze, with the original chimney, bellows, and waterwheel replicated in steel painted bright red. These structures, explains their architect, 'suggest the outline of vanished historical elements in the landscape.'[92]

Early foundries—like Les Forges and the Marmora Ironworks at Marmora, Ontario, founded in 1823—were located close to the source of the iron. As railways became available to transport the ore, it was more efficient to locate the plants closer to the sources of power and the markets.

By the third quarter of the nineteenth century the economies of eastern and central Canada had gone far beyond the primary processing of resources in mills and foundries, and developed numerous secondary industries. Every community of size boasted its factories, which manufactured everything from wagons to furniture, from soap to shoes; and its food-processing plants, such as refineries, breweries, and distilleries. On the whole, the design of these buildings exhibited a straightforward, no-frills, vernacular approach that was in-

5.44 Blast-furnace complex, Les Forges du St Maurice, near Trois-Rivières, Quebec, 1984. Photograph by Jean Audet, *c.* 1985. PC.

tended primarily to serve their utilitarian functions—in contrast to the more style-conscious architecture of other building-types. Nevertheless, they usually achieved a pleasing sense of balance and proportion.

The commercial cities

In the early decades of the nineteenth century several towns were developing as focuses of trade and commerce. Montreal and Quebec, whose populations in 1820 were about 20,000 each, were already well established; other, smaller, urban centres were Saint John, Halifax, Trois-Rivières, and Kingston. York (Toronto) was smaller, with a population of only 1,500, but it would eventually overtake the lot.

All grew quickly into cities as the century progressed. Each developed as a reasonably self-sufficient economic unit, with its own industrial and financial infrastructure, and attempted to achieve commercial dominance within its own trading region. Just as each city strove for economic independence, so too did it develop a distinctive architectural character, deriving from the values and experiences of its residents as well as from the materials and technical skills available to them. This was the heyday of regionalism, an era that preceded the arrival of standardization in commercial ventures and in building types. The chapter concludes with a brief look at Saint John and Montreal, the two most important commercial cities in the middle years of the nineteenth century. Several buildings are treated in more detail in other chapters.

Saint John Throughout much of the nineteenth century Saint John, New Brunswick, was the third largest city in British North America (after Montreal and Toronto) and the largest on the eastern seaboard. Settlers from Newburyport (near Boston), led by James Simonds and James White, came here in the 1760s to Portland Point, as the site of the future city was then called, and immediately exploited its industrial potential. They erected a sawmill and were soon exporting lumber, lime, and fish to New England and Newfoundland. A large contingent of Loyalists settled in the area, and Saint John was incorporated in 1785, making it Canada's oldest incorporated city.[93]

The Napoleonic blockade in the 1790s threatened Britain's source of timber from the Baltic region, and so Britain turned to Canada and her other colonies for wood. Although all of British North America benefited from these events—the timber rafts Philemon Wright floated to Quebec were a response to this opportunity—Saint John was in an especially strong position to do so, since it had a superb natural harbour as well easy access by river to an immense hinterland with good timber. Exports began as unprocessed timber, but by the 1830s this was changing to an emphasis on sawn lumber. A strong sawmill industry developed—in 1851 Saint John and the adjacent towns had 26 sawmills, most of them large, with an average employment of 28 men. The timber trade fostered a shipbuilding industry, and by mid-century Saint John boasted the largest fleet in British North America.[94]

A number of financial institutions emerged to provide the industrial and commercial activity with a strong monetary infrastructure. The Bank of New Brunswick became Canada's first chartered bank in 1820 and was soon followed by other banks, insurance companies, and trading companies. The commercial interests—timber, shipbuilding, shipping, and banking—were all directed at the British timber trade. Colonial preference was removed in the 1840s, but Saint John was strong enough to stand the new international competition.

The merchant class was descended from the Loyalist élite, and, as might be expected, the city's finer houses and public buildings showed a decided American influence. David Daniel Merritt's Loyalist House [**3.45**] is representative of many. The opulence to which many merchants aspired can be seen in the fine painted decoration in a group of houses on Prince William Street, built in 1859-60.[95]

The early public and commercial buildings of Saint John were dominated by the Greek and Roman Revivals (page 300), which were paramount in the United States but gained only an insecure toehold elsewhere in Canada. Many presented a dignified temple front to the street. The **Germaine Street (Queen Square) Methodist Chapel** [**5.45**] of 1839—with its prim pedimented gable, stately Doric pilasters, classical window and door heads,

5.45 Germaine Street Methodist Chapel, Saint John, New Brunswick, 1839. Photograph *c*. 1865. New Brunswick Museum/ x11309.

and balustraded fence, all rendered in wood—projects an image of dignified classicism. But the design seems somewhat incongruous next to the adjacent vernacular houses, whose side gables, shutters, and location right up against the street give them a familiar New England/Maritime appearance. (In the background of the early photograph is the spire of Trinity Church, an Anglican church built in 1854 to the designs of Fenety and Raymond; it also had a columned entrance portico.) The adjacent building also has a classical front, which is treated as two storeys with Adamesque recessed arches on the ground floor and pilasters above; and the building next to that features large store windows capped by a broad entablature. The Roman Revival is also seen in the Bank of New Brunswick (*c*. 1826) on Prince William Street [**6.49**]. The stone Courthouse (by John Cunningham, 1826-9) on Sydney Street was a fine Georgian-Palladian composition in the spirit of other public buildings in the Atlantic colonies and Upper Canada.[96]

The Gothic Revival also reached Saint John in good time. It is seen in St John's Church (1824; **6.7**); the Cathedral of the Immaculate Conception

5.46 Mechanics' Institute, Saint John, New Brunswick, 1840. Photograph *c*. 1890. New Brunswick Museum.

5.47 Interior, Academy of Music, Saint John, New Brunswick, 1872. Engraved from a drawing by Edward John Russell, *c*. 1872. Gift of the New Brunswick Historical Society (w6725). New Brunswick Museum.

(*c*. 1853), which served the city's rapidly growing Irish population; and the ENAR Station [5.13].

The affluence of Saint John led to the development of a number of vital social institutions. The New Brunswick Philosophical Society was formed in 1836, and led to the founding of the **Mechanics' Institute** [5.46], an educational and cultural centre for working people that in 1840 was built in wood in the Neoclassical style—a little Ionic temple designed by Edwin Fairweather (1793-1868).[97] Three large theatres were built in the fifteen years after 1857, culminating in the **Academy of Music** (1872), a sumptuous concert hall that accommodated more than 1,100 people in the orchestra, dress circle, and gallery [5.47]. The classically ornamented interior was finished in carmine and lavender, accented with gold leaf, bronze, blue, and yellow. Six private boxes, with white lace curtains and crimson fringes, were inserted in the 38-foot-high (12-m) proscenium arch, which was painted light blue. The large stage had 72 wings and 20 flats, and the curtain, scene-paintings, and mechanical effects were all provided by Boston artisans. Architect Moses Washburn was also from Boston, reflecting

how much New England continued to dominate the culture of New Brunswick.[98] Skating, another social pastime, was accommodated by the enormous, domed Victoria Rink.

Saint John reached its peak in the 1850s and 1860s. Sailing vessels and steamships connected the city to ports in Britain, the West Indies, Australia, and the United States, and railways provided convenient access to New England and Quebec. A horse-drawn street-railway system was inaugurated in 1866, only five years after those in Montreal and Toronto. The population rose above 40,000.

Characteristic of this 'commercial era' in Canadian urban development, as it is called by urban historian Gilbert Stelter, the central core of Saint John became filled with a concentration of commercial and industrial functions and buildings that overshadowed the old imperial institutions, and as time progressed these were improved and enlarged. In the 1860s a new generation of brick and stone commercial buildings, typically four or five storeys high, began to replace earlier wooden structures. A photograph of **King Street** [5.48], looking towards the harbour and taken around 1867, shows a few of

5.48 King Street, Saint John, New Brunswick. Photograph *c*. 1867. NAC/C-1649.

5.49 Courtney Bay, near East Saint John, New Brunswick, with ships under construction. Photograph by G.T. Taylor, *c*. 1860. PANB/P5-361.

these new masonry structures overshadowing the earlier wood ones.

As new subdivisions were opened up in the middle of the century, the original gridiron plan was largely continued, but a decline in central planning authority led to fragmented and irregular street patterns. Wood remained the predominant material in residential areas. As Stelter has pointed out, 'Throughout the commercial era [Saint John] was larger and more prosperous than its regional rival, Halifax.'[99]

Outlying working-class districts were less ordered and retained a distinctly maritime flavour. **Courtney Bay [5.49]**, a shipbuilding community near East Saint John, is seen in a photograph of *c*. 1860 to have a profusion of two- and three-storey frame hotels, houses, and stores, almost all of them with gabled roofs whose ridges run parallel to the front. Several have sheds at the rear. The density indicates the success of the community, and the ships under construction in the background reveal the source of its prosperity.

Confederation in 1867 had an adverse affect on the economy of Saint John—and on the Maritime Provinces generally—as central Canada began to compete successfully with local manufacturers and soon overshadowed New England as the dominant neighbouring power. Although Saint John was highly industrialized, most of its factories were small and could not compete with the large manufacturers in other cities. The growing economic woes were compounded by the tightening British market for lumber and ships after 1873.

Worse still, disaster struck Saint John on 20 June 1877. A fire that started innocently enough in Henry Fairweather's storehouse on York Point Slip spread out of control in the hot wind and quickly destroyed more than 1,600 buildings. Before the day was done 200 acres (80 hectares)—some two-fifths of the city—lay in ashes and more than

5.50 King Street, Saint John, New Brunswick, in 1899. From *Art Work on the City of Saint John* (1899). New Brunswick Museum.

246

13,000 people were homeless. The city's wooden buildings did not stand a chance against the wind-whipped flames, and many new brick and stone structures were destroyed in the inferno as well. Aid came quickly, including more than $25,000 from people in Chicago, who had suffered a similar fire six years earlier, and a relatively meagre $20,000 from the federal government in Ottawa.[100]

The fire proved to be a blow from which Saint John never fully recovered. The city was rebuilt, mostly in brick, as can be seen in a photograph of **King Street** [5.50] taken in 1899 from a vantage point close to that in the earlier picture. Many important new public buildings were erected, including an immense Custom House (1877-81; see **10.8**), indicating the volume of the city's trade. Nevertheless, Saint John's day in the sun had passed. Even Macdonald's National Policy, and its incentives to strengthen manufacturing in the Atlantic provinces, had no lasting effect. The commercial focus remained at Market Square, but in the twentieth century that district fell into disrepair as the city slumped. After a century of use and decline, the post-fire buildings of Market Square were

rehabilitated in the 1980s [**15.94**] as part of a downtown revitalization initiative that attempted to restore the once-great city's lost pride.[101]

Montreal Its uniquely strategic location at the head of navigation on the St Lawrence River, at its confluence with the Ottawa River, made Montreal Canada's largest and most prosperous city for a century and a half. It was the trans-shipment point where, in the seventeenth century, goods were transferred from boats to canoes, and in the nineteenth century from ocean vessels to lake boats and trains.

The first permanent settlement, called Ville-Marie, began in 1642 with few commercial motives, when forty colonists led by the Sieur Chomedy de Maisonneuve arrived with the intention of converting the native peoples to Christianity. A recently discovered plan, drawn in the early days of the settlement, shows that it was arranged much like Champlain's Sainte-Croix [**1.17**].[102] Ville-Marie soon became the centre of the fur trade. With prosperity came an increase in population—from 625 in 1665 to 2,025 in 1706.

The Sulpician priest Dollier de Casson, in his capacity as seigneur of Montreal, laid out the first streets in 1672, together with his surveyor and notary, Bénigne Basset. Rue Notre-Dame, the principal street, was aligned in a northeast-southwest direction (east-west by local custom), along a natu-

5.51 Plan of Montreal, Quebec, attributed to Levasseur de Néré, 1704. Original at the Centre des Archives d'Outre-mer, Archives nationales (France); Dépôt des fortifications des Colonies, Amérique sept., A468. Reproduced from a print held by the NAC/C-21752.

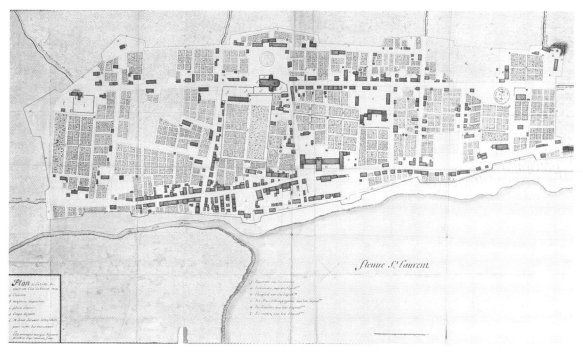

ral ridge and parallel to the river. The parish church of Notre-Dame was erected in the centre of the roadway, directly on its axis, in the tradition of continental European planning, and the Séminaire de Saint-Sulpice [2.39], of which Dollier was the superior, was built near it. Two other streets were laid out roughly parallel to Notre-Dame, and seven perpendicular to it, making up what is today called Old Montreal.

A plan [5.51] drawn in 1704—perhaps by Levasseur de Néré, and intended as a proposal for new fortifications—indicates these and other improvements. The very broad rue Notre-Dame is seen running from left to right near the top, with the church in the centre, an open square (the future Place d'Armes) above it, and the Séminaire just below and to the left of the church. The street closer to the river is rue Saint-Paul, originally a path from the fort at Pointe-à-Callières (beyond the left edge of the plan) to the Hôtel-Dieu (the hospital, which is the largest building in town, seen near the centre of the plan) and the Chapel of Notre-Dame-de-Bonsecours (one of the buildings further to the right); the path was widened to 24 feet by Dollier. The roadway north of Notre-Dame (at the top) is rue Saint-Jacques, which two centuries later would be the financial centre of Canada. The other large institutional buildings are the convent of the Soeurs de la Congrégation, the structure east of the church and set back a distance south of rue Notre-Dame; and the churches of those traditional rivals, the Récollets and the Jesuits, located at the extreme west and east ends of rue Notre-Dame respectively. The large walled garden in the centre belongs to the Séminaire. Most of the buildings have large gardens behind them: about twice as much land is covered by gardens as by buildings.[103]

The town was now surrounded by a wooden palisade with projecting bastions at intervals. It was described by Soeur Morin of the Hôtel-Dieu:

> ...there is at present a kind of town surrounded with stakes of cedar, five or six feet high, bound together with heavy nails and wooden pegs, and this for the past ten years. This is how towns in Canada are surrounded; there are several large gates which are used as entrances and exits and are closed every evening by army officers maintained there by the King of France for our defence, should our enemy wish to worry us; they open both gates in the morning at regular hours, etc.[104]

The palisade began to be replaced in 1716 with a stone fortification wall under the direction of Chaussegros de Léry. Completed in 1744—and therefore built at about the same time as the fortress of Louisbourg—the walls provided a powerful symbol of French sovereignty, and indicated the King's commitment to the colony and the fur trade.

Montreal had an irregular gridiron plan that followed the natural topography and placed the symbol of religious, rather than temporal, authority in the centre of town. It lacked the rigidly parallel streets and equal distances between blocks that would so obsess British surveyors a half-century later at Halifax [3.19] and other new towns. These essential features—a long and dominant main street ('rue principale'), which usually followed a pre-existing transportation route, and a centrally located parish church—remain characteristic of communities throughout Quebec.

Montreal greystone (a hard limestone) became the predominant building material, in part because an ordinance of 1721, which followed a disastrous fire, prohibited the use of wood for house-building. The by-law recommended stone for walls and non-combustible materials such as slate, tile, or tin to cover roofs. Tin roofs became very popular later in the century, and have remained so throughout French Canada.[105]

Montreal's phenomenal economic and physical expansion began shortly after the British conquest of New France. A group of powerful merchants—mostly Scottish, but also English and American—formed the North West Company in the 1780s and used Montreal as a base for their head-to-head competition with the Hudson's Bay Company. The city also became the port and trans-shipment point for goods destined for, and coming from, the growing population of Upper Canada. In time Montreal developed a strong and diversified economy with a large manufacturing sector that required an ever-increasing work force. After the War of 1812-14 immigration from Britain and Ireland increased Montreal's population beyond that of Quebec City in the 1820s, and by the 1830s residents of British origin had become the majority. French Canadians, in turn, began to pour into the city from rural areas, and by Confederation *they* formed the majority.

The new anglophone merchant class brought its own institutions, architecture, and urban design, giving the western portion of the city a decidedly British flavour. Early in the nineteenth century several powerful merchants—including Simon McTavish, his nephew William McGillivray, and Joseph Frobisher—built grand suburban mansions on the slopes of Mount Royal, creating a posh residential area separate from the commercial district. (None of these early manors survive.) The merchant élite formed the Bank of Montreal (1817) and the Committee of Trade (1822), the Church of England built Christ Church (a cathedral after 1850), and merchant James McGill donated his estate for the formation of the university that bears his name. French Canadians were represented on some boards of directors and organized their own commercial and public institutions, but they were overshadowed by the English-speaking merchants.

The early-nineteenth-century buildings erected for these institutions displayed British Classicism—not the American-inspired Greek and Roman Revivals seen at Saint John, but rather the Georgian Palladian-Gibbsian tradition of England and Scotland. Christ Church [4.54], built on rue Notre-Dame in 1805-21, was indebted to James Gibbs's St Martin-in-the-Fields, like its Quebec City namesake. The first **Bank of Montreal** [5.52] (1818-19; seen at the left of the photograph) had the air of the townhouse of a well-to-do resident of Edinburgh or London. In 1845-8 the Bank built an imposing Neoclassical building next door (in the centre), designed by John Wells (1789-1864) and featuring a large freestanding classical portico.[106]

The conscious use of British models is seen particularly well at McGill College (1839-62), now the Arts Building of McGill University. An architectural competition for the new institution was held in 1838-9, just as the Durham Report was advocating the establishment of an English Protestant college in Lower Canada:

> There exists at present no means of college education for Protestants in the Province: and the desire of obtaining a general and still more, professional instruction, yearly draws a great many young men into the United States. I entertain no doubts as to the national character which must be given to Lower Canada: it must be that of the British Empire.[107]

The commission was awarded to the young London-born John Ostell (1813-92), who was just becoming one of the city's leading architects and won over competitors as strong as John Wells and George Browne. As completed in two building campaigns, McGill College was a perfect Palladian composition. A central three-storey block featured a cupola—which Ostell felt would make the college a landmark visible from 'distant points of view'[108]— and a classical portico. Ostell intended a double (two-tiered) portico, like Palladio's Palazzo Antonini at Udine; as executed, the low baseless Doric

5.52 Bank of Montreal, Montreal, Quebec, 1818-19 (left), 1845-8 (centre). Photograph c. 1865. MMCH/MP090/74.

5.53 View of Montreal, Quebec, from Mount Royal. Photograph 1865. NAC/C-453.

columns acknowledge the Greek Revival. In 1862 the central block was connected by low links to a wing at either side, in the manner of countless English Palladian country houses.

In a **panoramic photograph of Montreal [5.53]** taken from the mountain in 1865, McGill College is seen from the rear—just below the oval municipal reservoir. The McGill estate—undeveloped in the photograph, but now filled with university buildings—extends beyond the college southward to Sherbrooke Street, and from University Street at the left (east) to McTavish Street on the right. The twin towers of the Church of Notre Dame, in the old city of Montreal, are seen silhouetted against the St Lawrence River at the left, and the Victoria Bridge extends across the river to the south shore. Other buildings and districts will be identified later in this section.

In 1801 the Parliament of Lower Canada authorized the demolition of the (by then) old stone walls of Montreal, which stood in the way of urban development, and also—although this was left unstated—comprised the most visible artifact from the former French regime. The walls came down during the next dozen years; three commissioners (including James McGill) were appointed to oversee the work. Parliament instructed that there be 'a regular plan' with 'commodious Streets...and convenient places reserved for Squares in time to

come.'[109] In other words, a British town plan—a regular gridiron with wide streets punctuated by public squares—was superimposed on the plan inherited from the French. A number of significant improvements were carried out, including a riverfront terrace that would serve also as a dike and a fire-break, several canals to improve drainage and sanitation, the enlargement of the Champ-de-Mars to form a military parade, and the creation of a number of squares (among them Place Jacques-Cartier and Victoria Square). Place d'Armes, the focus of Old Montreal, was extended to become a proper square with the demolition of the old parish church (which, it will be recalled, had been built in the centre of the street) and its replacement by a magnificent new Notre-Dame Church at the edge of the square [6.9], directly opposite the Bank of Montreal. New defences were built after 1818 on Île Sainte-Hélène, overlooking the entrance to the Port of Montreal.

As the population of Montreal mushroomed—from 25,000 in 1825, to 45,000 in 1844, 140,000 in 1881, and 468,000 (not including the rapidly growing suburbs) in 1911—the city expanded, with many of the new arterial roads following the seventeenth-century land division. Housing became an increasingly important commodity. Multiple housing has always been dominant in the city, where renters have long outnumbered home-owners. The south and east sectors, whose inhabitants were primarily French and Irish working-class, developed densely because of the need to locate a large population within walking distance of work or (after its introduction) of public transportation. (Horse-drawn streetcars were introduced to Montreal in November 1861, two months after Toronto inaugurated the first such system in Canada.[110])

Two- and three-storey brick-faced tenements with flat roofs, built right up to the sidewalk, sprang up everywhere. The mid-century **houses on rue Wolfe [5.54]**, in the Terrasse Ontario (a neighbourhood a distance east—beyond the left side—of the 1865 panoramic view), are typical, in that they contain dwelling units stacked one above the other. The suites were small—usually two to a floor, two rooms deep—but they were well lighted and ventilated, since every room had outside windows and the units had cross ventilation. A steep and narrow staircase reached from a door at the front led to the upper suites. The entire structure usually consisted of a solid wall of two-inch planks nailed to heavy timber uprights, with the planks covered by a veneer of brick. This system of 'plankwall'

construction, a direct descendant of grooved-post construction, remained prevalent in Montreal until the 1970s.[111]

A separate building was often located at the back of the property and reached through a passage or carriageway cut through the main building. The upper units of the rear structure were generally accessed by exterior staircases that rose from the courtyard.

The first outside stairs were built in the 1820s and 1830s, before the advent of the courtyard buildings, and were located in the side or rear wall. Towards mid-century they began to be used to provide access to the separate rear building. Around 1900 houses were generally set back from the street and built three or more storeys high, as in the **houses on rue Jeanne-Mance [5.55]**, near where Sherbrooke Street meets the left edge of the 1865 photograph. Built of brick over a plankwall structure, they represent a type [5.56] that was popular throughout the inter-war period. Exterior staircases at the front—providing access to the second and third floors, with wood porches at all levels—were often curved in order to take up less

5.54 Houses, rue Wolfe, Montreal, Quebec, mid-19th century. Photograph by Jean-Claude Marsan.

space, and had distinctive cast-iron railings. They subsequently became the characteristic feature of Montreal working-class housing, though they were dangerous in winter. Until they were prohibited in the middle of the twentieth century, builders continued to use them because of the economies they provided.

The west side of the city was mainly anglophone and middle class and developed with both single-family dwellings and row houses whose units were located side by side, typically faced in stone with decorative wood and stone trim. The most elegant of the rows was **Prince of Wales Terrace [5.57]** on Sherbrooke Street West, built in 1859-60 on a portion of the McTavish estate in the heart of the English-speaking enclave that was to become known as the 'Golden Square Mile'. Its rear elevation can be seen extending beyond the right edge of the 1865 view of Montreal. The building was designed as an eight-unit upper-income speculative row by the respected architects William Footner (1799-1872) and George Browne for Hud-

5.55 Houses, rue Jeanne-Mance, Montreal, Quebec, early 20th century. Photograph by Harold Kalman.

5.56 (*below*) Plan of a typical house on Plateau Mont-Royal, Montreal, Quebec, early 20th century. Drawing by David Byrnes after Jean-Claude Marsan.

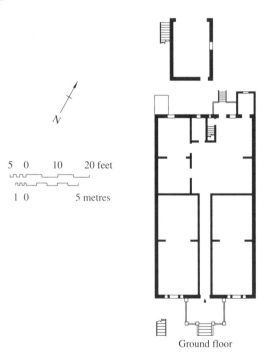

Ground floor   Second floor   Third floor

son's Bay Company Governor Sir George Simpson. The ashlar façade (with brick party walls), parapet balustrade, central pediment, giant pilasters, and entrance porticoes produced an elegantly classical British appearance that was clearly reminiscent of the terraced residential rows of London, Bath, and Edinburgh. The terrace remained in use until the 1960s and 1970s, when it was demolished in two stages: a portion for a hotel, and the remainder to make way for a building of McGill University. Other, similar, rows are seen in the panorama, including one on McTavish Street directly above the Prince of Wales Terrace—Prince Rupert Place, built in 1863 by contractor Ferdinand David.[112] Above the Square Mile, Mount Royal Park was developed as one of the continent's finest urban parks [12.5].

A new commercial and institutional district, catering for English-speaking Montrealers, developed along Ste Catherine Street, south of Sherbrooke. The tall spire seen in the panorama of the city, above and slightly to the right of the cupola of McGill College, is that of Christ Church Cathedral, on Ste Catherine. The considerable distance between the Square Mile and Old Montreal—centred

on the Church of Notre-Dame—can be appreciated in the photograph.

As the century progressed, the west and central areas of the city became filled with Victorian row houses of a different kind, typically with rough-faced walls of greystone, mansard roofs, and attractive picturesque detailing in the form of balconies, porches, and finials.

The reason for Montreal's steady increase in population was its burgeoning commerce and industry. In the 1830s the Port of Montreal received an average of 100 ships a year with an overall tonnage of 23,137; by 1860 this had increased to 261,000 tons for ocean-going vessels and 530,000 tons for inland boats, and by 1877 the tonnage exceeded $1\frac{1}{2}$ million.[113] In addition, the city became a major railway centre with the arrival of the Grand Trunk and Intercolonial Railways, followed in the 1880s by the Canadian Pacific Railway and many short feeder lines. The port and the railways provided a considerable amount of direct employment—large

5.57 Prince of Wales Terrace, Montreal, Quebec, 1859-60. Photograph 1860. MMCH/MP082/74.

terminal grain elevators were built along the harbour, and both the Grand Trunk and the Canadian Pacific had their shops in Montreal—and offered an opportunity for the development of a strong manufacturing sector.

The earliest commercial buildings were warehouses erected near the waterfront, reflecting the city's initial commercial activity as a trans-shipment centre. The so-called **d'Youville Stables** [5.58] are a group of $2\frac{1}{2}$-storey stone former warehouses erected around a central courtyard. The U-shaped portion at Place d'Youville, built in 1827-8 by canal masons Thomas MacKay and John Redpath for brothers Jean and Tancrède Bouthillier, were used for the storage of potash. (Produced from wood ash and used for soap-making, potash was the first export product from the subsistence farms of the St Lawrence and Ottawa valleys.) The **Blaiklock Warehouses** (1846-57), located directly behind on rue de la Commune (formerly Water Street, and seen at the right of the photograph), provided general warehousing and served for a while as a customs house. They too were built of greystone ashlar with a gently-pitched gable roof, adapting the Quebec domestic vernacular for commercial purposes. The two related groups of buildings were

rehabilitated in 1967-8 for restaurant and retail uses as a part of the revitalization of Old Montreal.[114]

The first area to be industrialized was located further west, along both banks of the eastern portion of the Lachine Canal. The canal was enlarged in 1840s and water power was released for private industrial use, bringing about considerable development in the 1840s and 1850s. The areas known as Griffintown (after its Irish inhabitants), Pointe-Saint-Charles, and Sainte-Anne became filled with flour mills, textile mills, factories, tanneries, and warehouses, all of them competing for space with densely packed tenements. Stonemason John Redpath turned industrialist and erected the **Redpath Sugar Refinery** [5.59] along the edge of the canal that he had built. In 1854 a seven-storey stone-and-brick refinery—the first in Canada—two brick sugar warehouses, and other brick buildings containing stables, iron- and tin-works, and gasworks were all built to designs by engineers Milne and Milne. It was a typical self-contained industrial complex, with easy transportation provided by the canal. The twin towers of Notre-Dame

5.58 d'Youville Stables, Montreal, Quebec, 1827-57. Communauté urbaine de Montréal.

5.59 Redpath Sugar Refinery, Montreal, Quebec, 1854-6. Lithograph 1854. Courtesy the Redpath Sugar Museum, Toronto, Ontario.

5.60 (*below*) Merchants Manufacturing Co., Montreal, Quebec, 1880-1916. *La Presse*, 17 July 1909. Bibliothèque nationale, Montreal/Fonds Maiscotte/v.5 #35.

dominate the view of the city in the background of the lithograph. The plant has been enlarged and modernized many times over the years, including the replacement of the original refinery by a new brick structure in 1907-8.[115]

Factory complexes proliferated along the canal. One of several large cotton mills erected in Montreal (and elsewhere in Canada) in response to the tariff protection provided by the National Policy was the **Merchants Manufacturing Company** [**5.60**] on rue Saint-Ambroise, the principal employer in Saint-Henri. The plant's work-force was primarily female, and this was the site of the first strike in Montreal's textile industry, in 1891. The initial portion of the immense factory was erected in 1880-2 to designs by a firm from Providence, Rhode Island. The building was enlarged four times between 1892 and 1916, when it was part of the Dominion Textile Company's manufacturing empire and achieved a floor area of more than 360,000 square feet (34,000 m^2)—making it the second-largest plant in the country. The design was characterized by relentless red-brick façades that are opened up at every structural bay and on each floor by windows, and are punctuated at intervals by staircase towers and large smokestacks. The composition was repeated in large industrial buildings throughout Canada and the US, and perfectly expressed the scale, wealth, and monotony that characterized big industry.[116]

At the beginning of the present century Montreal was a teeming metropolis, a large urban centre with some of the magnificence—and all the problems—of major cities everywhere. (Its churches, mansions, and office buildings are discussed in Chapter 6, 10, and 11.) The city had a diversified and cosmopolitan population, secure economic and social institutions, a strong industrial base, and well-developed transportation systems—all the culmination of a long period of progress in communications and commerce. It also experienced overcrowding, housing shortages, poor sanitation, and inadequate educational opportunities. The many social and economic sectors that participated in creating Montreal are clearly visible in its buildings and its urban form.

CHAPTER 6

THE RETURN TO THE PAST: THE VICTORIAN REVIVALS

EARLY IN the nineteenth century a new attitude towards architecture reached Canadian architects and builders, by way of Europe and the United States. No longer were buildings designed from within a single contemporary and living stylistic tradition, as had been the situation until that time—whether it was the folk heritage of New France or the Georgian lineage of British North America. Now architects were able to make a conscious selection of style from among various alternatives. This new approach is revealed in a pair of unexecuted designs produced in 1811-12 for a proposed new **Parliament Building** at Quebec by English architect Jeffry Wyatt (1766-1840), who in later life became known as Sir Jeffry Wyatville. Wyatt was one of at least five people who responded to a competition; the others were François Baillairgé, joiner William Morrison (1766-1842), a Mr Cushing, and English architect Joseph Gandy (1771-1843). Of these, only Wyatt's and Gandy's drawings have survived.[1] Even though none of the entries were constructed, the competition marks an important turning-point in Canadian architecture. (A Parliament Building was eventually created out of an existing episcopal palace, with work beginning in 1831 to designs by a succession of architects; see **4.62**).

Wyatt submitted two alternative schemes for the exterior design of the building, each one based on a different historical style of architecture: one revived the forms of Greek antiquity, the other those of the Gothic era of medieval Europe. As Wyatt wrote in the text that accompanied his submission, '[three drawings] Are Gothic Designs made to the same Plan & openings of Windows &c as the Grecian Design.'[2] The central feature of the entrance elevation of the 'Grecian' scheme [**6.1**] is a six-column Ionic portico capped not by the familiar Georgian pediment, but rather by a horizontal en-

tablature and parapet, on the top of which Wyatt suggested that 'Statues might be well placed....'. The projecting frontispiece proposed for the Gothic design [**6.2**] features tall pointed arches, on the sides of which are pairs of buttresses topped by pyramidal pinnacles. The parapet displays the saw-toothed profile whose projections are called battlements (or crenellations). The outer bays of the façade provide further contrasts: the windows of the Greek version have bracketed surrounds, whereas those of the Gothic one have hood mouldings and the end buttresses are capped by little turrets. The same kinds of features appear on the other elevations as well. The high arched windows that illuminate the high-ceilinged chambers of the legislative council and legislative assembly on the sides, for example, have semicircular heads in the first design and pointed, double-curved 'ogee' profiles in the other one. Since both sets of elevations for the Quebec building responded to the same floor plan—a rigidly symmetrical arrangement of rectilinear rooms—the differences between the two lie solely in their decorative vocabularies.

Joseph Gandy's design [**6.3**] also adopted what his generation called the Grecian style, and what we now describe as the Greek Revival style. Its entrance façade is dominated by a row of six Doric columns, the absence of bases identifying them as taken from the severe Greek rendition of the Doric order. (The bottoms of the columns are smooth, and not fluted like the rest of the shaft, but these are not bases.) The portico is composed 'in-antis', or between projecting walls—another feature associated with the buildings of ancient Greece.

The turn to Greek and Gothic Revivals, and the idea of proposing alternative designs for a single building, may have been radical in Canadian architectural experience but represented the 'state of the art' in England, where the penchant for dressing up

A Design for the Entrance Front of the Government House for Quebec

A Gothic Design for the Entrance Front of the Government House for Quebec

buildings in revivals of historical styles had emerged more than a half-century earlier. The Greek Revival designs of Wyatt and Gandy may not look very different to our eyes from the Georgian Classicism of a later Canadian building such as the Third Parliament Buildings in Toronto (1832; **4.37**), but to contemporaries they were quite distinct. As we have seen, the Toronto building represented a stage in the continuum of architectural development, from Renaissance Italy, through eighteenth-century Britain, to the nineteenth century. The Greek features in the designs for Quebec, on the other hand, were inspired by the recent rediscovery of classical Greek architecture by European antiquarians, and the Gothic elements reflected a corresponding new appreciation of early English building. In both cases, architects leap-frogged over current models in their desire to revive a dead architectural style—just as the builders of the Italian Renaissance had resurrected the manner of ancient Rome. The revival of long disused classical Greek (and also Roman) architecture can be described as a renewed classicism, or Neoclassicism, distinct in spirit from the unbroken classicism of the Georgian tradition.

The return to the past is characteristic of the

romantic movement that was beginning to dominate European arts and letters in the late eighteenth and early nineteenth centuries. Romanticism displayed an affinity for historicism and the remote. It cultivated personal feelings, showed an aesthetic interest in picturesque irregularity, and was obsessed with the associations that could be attached to things from the past. Romanticism is often contrasted with classicism, an intellectual strain that sought reason, order, and decorum, and is characteristic of the age of rationalism. (This 'classicism'—embodied in the poetry of Pope and the music of Haydn, as well as in Lord Burlington's interest in the Neo-Palladian movement [pages 126-7]—was influenced by, but was not directly equivalent to, the 'classicism' of the arts and architecture of antiquity. Romantic artists also drew on antique sources for their purposes, as in the Neoclassicism of Wyatt, Gandy, and the Canadian architects who will appear later in this chapter.)

The option of producing designs in different modes was characteristic of the new eclectic attitude of the romantic age. ('Eclecticism' is derived from the Greek word for 'choose'.) A style could now be selected from among alternatives because it was considered appropriate to a particular project; or features from more than one style could be combined in a single building—procedures that

6.1 (*above left*) Parliament Building, Quebec, Quebec. Unexecuted design by Jeffry Wyatt, 1811-12. NAC/NMC-2358.

6.2 (*left*) Parliament Building, Quebec, Quebec. Unexecuted design by Jeffry Wyatt, 1811-12. NAC/NMC-2361.

6.3 Parliament Building, Quebec, Quebec. Unexecuted design by Joseph Gandy, 1811-12. NAC/NMC-4924.

would have been unthinkable in previous eras. Jeffry Wyatt's uncle, James Wyatt (1746-1813), belonged to the first generation of British architects who thought in this way. He (and his contemporaries) worked in a variety of modes, including the Palladian, Neoclassical, and numerous medieval revival styles, including Early English Gothic, castellated, and Tudor.

The question *why* Jeffry Wyatt proposed the Neoclassical (Greek Revival) and Gothic Revival alternatives may be inferred. The Neoclassical mode was surely selected because it was considered to be *au courant* for important public buildings; this was influenced to a considerable extent by examples set by prize-winning student designs at both the Royal Academy in London and the Académie Royale d'Architecture in Paris, and by the *grand prix* awarded by both schools, which sent students to Rome to study classical buildings. The reason for using Gothic is less certain. In the absence of documents recording the intentions of either Wyatt or Sir George Prevost, the Canadian governor-in-chief, it may be suggested that Wyatt associated British institutions with early English architecture, and hence saw it as being appropriate for a public building. A generation later this link became explicit—it was demonstrated in 1835, when the Gothic or Elizabethan styles were specified for the new Parliament Buildings at Westminster—but in 1812 Gothic was being used in Britain only for churches, villas, and country houses. Indeed, Wyatt's design for Quebec is probably the earliest Gothic Revival design for a government building in Europe *or* America.[3]

Once the architect's vocabulary was widened to

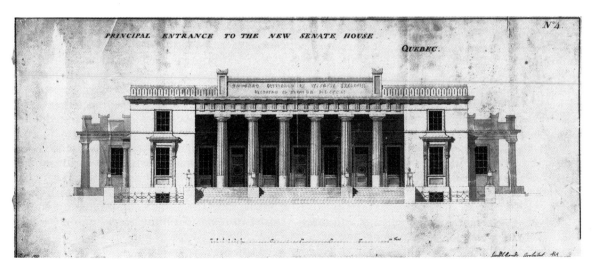

6.4 New Haven Green, New Haven, Connecticut. Trinity Church, 1814-17; Connecticut State Capitol, 1827-31; Centre Church, 1812-15. Engraving by L.S. Punderson, *c*. 1850, after his drawing of *c*. 1831. Yale University Art Gallery, Gift of Anson Phelps Stokes.

admit a choice of styles, specific meanings could be attached to the various alternatives. For example, the selection by Thomas Jefferson of a Roman temple as the source for the Virginia State Capitol in 1785 explicitly associated the ancient Roman republic with the new American nation (page 163), and this precedent had a long and fertile progeny in the US.[4] Canadians did not take architectural politics quite so seriously as Americans, but the history of building in Canada during this period is nevertheless rich in the use of romantic associations—beginning with the competition drawings by Wyatt and Gandy. Even if they received little exposure in Canada (they were exhibited at the Royal Academy in London in 1812-13),[5] they were perfectly timed to inaugurate the new romantic era.

A vivid early venture into eclecticism, and one that would have an indirect impact on Canadian building, could be seen across the border in New England, at New Haven Green in New Haven, Connecticut. An engraving [**6.4**] shows four adjacent buildings, three of which were designed by architect Ithiel Town (1784-1844). The second building from the right is Center Church, built in 1812-15 for Congregationalists; adopting an established architectural style for the religious denomination of the New England establishment, it is in the Federal style, the American counterpart of Georgian Classicism. On the left is Trinity Church, built in 1814-17 for an Episcopal congregation and designed in the Gothic Revival style. Between them is the Connecticut State Capitol (1827-31), a Neoclassical venture that follows the example for government building set by Jefferson in Virginia. Town used three modes for three different purposes. The respective associations would have been clear to the people who saw and used the buildings.[6]

Nineteenth-century Canadian architects, like their American counterparts, revived a large number of historical styles, from Egyptian to Baroque. This chapter examines the romantic revivals in Canada, from their origins until the third quarter of the nineteenth century, focusing on the two most popular and tenacious ones: the Gothic Revival and Neoclassicism.

The Early Gothic Revival

Church architecture

The Gothic Revival was introduced into Canada as a mode for religious buildings, because of the associations with medieval churches and cathedrals—and, by extension, with an earlier and supposedly purer Christianity. The first, tentative, use of the style consisted simply of the introduction of a few pointed-arched windows—the most elemental components that are clearly identified with Gothic—on a building that would otherwise be described as Georgian. This is seen in **Christ Church at Karsdale [6.5]**, Nova Scotia, a small Anglican church a short distance down the road from the reconstruction of Champlain's *Habitation* at Port Royal. Built for a Loyalist community in 1791-3—Bishop Charles Inglis certified that it had been completed 'according to contract' in July 1793—and originally known as St Paul's, this plain clapboarded building is remarkable only for the three pointed Gothic windows along each of its sides. (The tower and the small chancel were likely added a few years later.)[7]

Unassuming as they may be, these windows represent the earliest known use of Gothic features in Canadian architecture. Whether or not they alone are sufficient to make Christ Church, Karsdale, a Gothic Revival building poses more of a philosophical than an architectural question. This is like asking whether a child whose face is made up as a clown on Hallowe'en is, in fact, a clown. Most people would respond that the child is a clown only to those who choose to see him or her as being one. Christ Church can be viewed similarly.

In the following decades a few other rural Protestant churches in Nova Scotia adopted Gothic components. The **Goat Island Baptist Church [6.6]**, on the main road between Annapolis Royal and Digby, has windows with mouldings that are very similar to those in the nearby church at Karsdale, and extends the Gothic features to the tower and to corner pilaster strips (looking like emaciated buttresses) with pointed heads. Gothic elements are used more consistently than at the Karsdale church (to continue the Hallowe'en analogy, the child has donned a clown's costume as well as its face). The Goat Island church is believed to have been built in 1810-11, although this date is undocumented; if it is accurate, the church could qualify as the earliest-known consistently Gothic Revival building in Canada, contemporaneous with Wyatt's submissions for the Quebec Parliament Building.[8]

Far more consistent in its application of Gothic Revival features is **St John's Church [6.7]**, Saint

6.6 Goat Island Baptist Church, near Deep Brook, Nova Scotia, *c.* 1810-11. Photograph by Barry Moody.

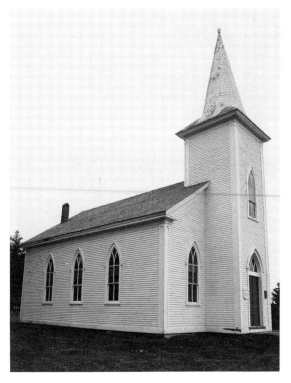

6.5 Christ Church, Karsdale, Nova Scotia, 1791-3. CIHB/0200400000071.

John, New Brunswick, built in 1824 and known locally as 'The Stone Church'. It is seen in a photograph of 1863; the pediment to the left belongs to the Mechanics' Institute [5.46]. Every building except the church has been demolished. St John's was built as a chapel-of-ease for Trinity Church, and acquired its own parish (and its present name) in the 1840s. The church council reportedly stipulated that the new church should be in the Gothic Revival style. The designer was probably the Irish-born Lloyd Johnston (1767-1842), although the inconclusive evidence points also to a certain Mr Crookshank and to John C. Cunningham (1792-1872). St John's was built of roughly dressed stone, quarried in England, which was said to have been brought over as ballast in sailing ships.[9]

The plan and composition are familiar: a rectangular box with a gable roof, a three-bay façade, and a central entrance tower that projects slightly forward. This composition had been used frequently in the eighteenth century, as at St Mary's, Auburn, NS [3.55], although it was not as common as the tower that rose from within the perimeter of the building, as at Trinity Church, Saint John (seen in the background of 5.45), and the Canadian prototype of them all, St Paul's in Halifax [3.21]. Both

treatments of the tower were derived from English Georgian models promoted by James Gibbs and his contemporaries. The gable-end on the façade is articulated with a horizontal band that is a vestige of the base moulding of the pediment that crowns many Georgian façades. What is new at St John's is the Gothic-inspired ornament. The windows on the front elevation and along the sides have pointed arches and are subdivided by Gothic tracery and mouldings. The entrance doorway is capped by a double-curve ogee moulding. The roofline in front features battlements and spiky finials; taller finials with cherubs' heads at their bases and a myriad of knob-like 'crockets' rise from the corners of the tower.

This superficial application of Gothic features in St John's on what is otherwise a Georgian shell—accomplished far more rigorously here than in the rural Nova Scotia churches seen previously—is characteristic of the earliest phase of the Gothic Revival. Because of the inherent mixture of stylistic elements and the changing aesthetic, the style is sometimes described as Georgian Gothic Revival, Picturesque Gothic Revival, or Regency Gothic. I prefer the term Early Gothic Revival, since by the 1820s the Georgian period was nearing its end (buildings of similar design had appeared in Britain a half-century earlier, during the Georgian period), and because picturesque principles had not yet

6.7 St John's Church, Saint John, New Brunswick, 1824. Photograph, 1863. Major J.M. Grant Collection, Partridge Island Research Project.

262

permeated Canadian sensibilities. St John's stands with one foot in the classical-Georgian tradition and one in the new romantic-Gothic manner associated with the era of Queen Victoria. Such buildings mark the transition from one era to the next.

St John's is similar in composition and appearance to Ithiel Town's slightly earlier Trinity Church in New Haven, suggesting a continuing transfer of architectural ideas from New England to New Brunswick, as had occurred throughout the previous half-century. Although their details differ, both have a tripartite façade, pediment-like gable, sloping battlements, and an articulated tower with tall corner finials and lower central ones. Architectural historian William Pierson has suggested that the model for Trinity Church may be found in no less a source than James Gibbs's popular *Book of Architecture*, in which the plate of Gibbs's eighteenth-century church, All Saints, Derby, and its early-sixteenth-century tower (the only Gothic structure illustrated), share many features with St John's.[10]

Town's hints about why he used the Gothic mode for the Episcopal (Anglican) Trinity Church may be applied to St John's. Writing at the time of its completion, Town stated of Trinity Church that

...the Gothic style of architecture has been chosen and adhered to in the erection of this Church,

6.8 St Mary's Cathedral, Halifax, Nova Scotia, 1820-30. Lithograph by Sarony and Major after a painting by J. Clow, published between 1845 and 1857. PANS/N1420.

as being in some respects more appropriate, and better suited to the solemn purposes of religious worship.[11]

He went on to reveal that he used roughly dressed masonry (a feature also of St John's) because he appreciated its picturesque qualities, which he associated with the Gothic. The walls, he wrote, were built of

... a hard granite... laid with their natural faces out, and so selected and fitted, as to form small but irregular joints, which are pointed. These natural faces present various shades of brown and iron-rust; and when damp, especially, the different shades appear very deep and rich; at the same time conveying to the mind, an idea of durability and antiquity which may be very suitably associated with this style of architecture.

If only the architect of St John's had been as articulate, the motivation for its radical design (for Canada) would not have to be inferred from a second-hand source.

An early Gothic Revival church in Canada's Atlantic colonies, built by a different religious denomination, is St John's Presbyterian Church at Belfast, PEI, erected in 1824-6 for a community of Highland Scots who had settled on the Island under the sponsorship of the Earl of Selkirk. It was built by carpenter and joiner Robert Jones (c. 1779-?), a native of Paisley, to replace a log church of 1804. Constructed of wood, rather than stone, the exterior is clad in shingles. The tower is unusual in that it rises in a series of four diminishing stages, culminating in finials and a tall spire.[12]

Parallel with these initial Protestant ventures into the new style, the Roman Catholic community also began to adopt the Gothic Revival for church-building. The first Catholic church of this kind—and, if the Goat Island church is dated prematurely, the earliest significant Gothic Revival building in Canada—was **St Mary's Cathedral**, Halifax (originally called St Peter's), built in 1820-30. The cathedral as it appears today is principally a product of the 1860s and 1870s, although much of the original building material survives beneath the later alterations. Its original appearance is known from several paintings and prints of the 1840s.[13]

The diocese was formed in 1817 as the Vicariate Apostolic of Nova Scotia. In June 1820, Bishop Edmund Burke wrote to the Archbishop of Dublin:

We have just begun to build a cathedral here which will cost us at least ten thousand pounds sterling. The extreme length of the church is 106 feet and the breadth 66 feet, the walls lime and stone, cut stone in the whole front.[14]

The cathedral was ready for worship by late 1829. The diocesan records and Bishop Burke's papers, examined by architectural historian J.P. McAleer, do not identify the architect. Burke was known to have taken an interest in engineering, and he might well have been partly responsible for the design.

The original exterior form, known best from a lithograph published after 1845 from a painting by J.S. Clow [6.8], consists of the Georgian arrangement of a rectangular block, gabled roof, and articulated tower that was seen also at St John's in Saint John. The windows on the façade and along the sides again have pointed-arched heads and are subdivided into smaller elements by decorative tracery. Battlements and pinnacles appear at the top of the tower. The paper-thin appearance of the walls, which seem to lack depth or substance (accentuated in the painting, perhaps, but seen as well in the other churches of this era), is also characteristic of the Early Gothic Revival.

The same blend of Georgian and Gothic occurs in the parish house to the right of the church. Its rectangular $2\frac{1}{2}$-storey mass, covered by a medium-pitch gable roof, is representative of many Georgian houses in Nova Scotia and New Brunswick, but once again the decoration deviates from this tradition. A projecting entrance vestibule has the now-familiar pointed arch over the door; the windows on the side elevation have straight heads, but with Gothic-inspired projecting mouldings (called 'hood' mouldings) along the top and the upper portion of the sides.

The interior of St Mary's also follows the Georgian model of the 'galleried box', but adopts Gothic forms more extensively and consistently than outside. Clustered piers terminate in moulded capitals and support quadripartite groin vaults (presumably fashioned from plaster). According to an early drawing, the sanctuary wall appears to have continued the motif of pointed arches over freestanding clustered piers—possibly painted illusionistically and not actually constructed in three dimensions—with a semi-circular apse (probably used as a sacristy) that is covered by a half-dome extending out behind it. If McAleer's careful reading of the early visual evidence is correct, St Mary's would have had 'the earliest full-scale Gothic Revival interior in Canada.'[15] He suggests that a model may have been St Patrick's Cathedral in New York, an early Gothic Revival church built in 1809-15 to designs by French-born architect Joseph F. Mangin. Joseph-Octave Plessis, the Roman Catholic Bishop of Quebec from 1808 to 1825 (and the cleric who consecrated Edmund Burke as Bishop), showed considerable enthusiasm for Gothic architecture, and specifically for St Patrick's (and its *trompe-l'oeil* sanctuary) when he visited New York in 1815, and he may well have participated in the selection of the style for St Mary's. Curiously, Plessis used classical models and not the Gothic Revival for his own Cathedral of St-Jacques in Montreal [6:65, 66], which was begun in 1823.

It was not St Mary's, however, but a Roman Catholic church in Montreal that became the most important landmark in the Early Gothic Revival: the immense Church of **Notre-Dame in Montreal** [6.9], built on Place d'Armes between 1823 and 1829 to replace the aging church that had been erected in 1672-83 (and whose façade had been designed in 1722; page 64). Notre-Dame was under the control of the Sulpicians, the powerful society of secular priests who held the title of seigneurs of Montreal. The Sulpicians' temporal and

6.9 Church of Notre-Dame, Montreal, Quebec, 1823-9.
Photograph by Armour Landry, courtesy Franklin Toker.

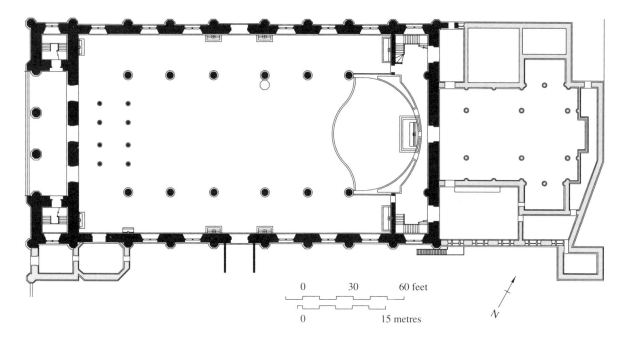

6.10 Plan of the Church of Notre-Dame, Montreal, Quebec, 1823-9. Drawn by David Byrnes.

6.11 (*below*) Interior of the Church of Notre-Dame, Montreal, Quebec, 1823-9. Engraving of a drawing by W.H. Bartlett *c*. 1842 from N.D. Willis, *Canadian Scenery*, 2 (1842), NAC/C-2358.

spiritual aspirations led them to go to whatever lengths might be necessary in order to procure an appropriately impressive contemporary design—in no small part motivated by the threat to their jurisdiction posed by the announced construction of Plessis's Cathedral of St-Jacques, and also by competition from the Anglicans' newly completed Christ Church nearby [4.54].[16]

The wardens of Notre-Dame determined that their new church should be very large, seating between 8,000 and 9,000 people, and so they instructed the building committee 'to bring over an architect from the United States or from Europe, if it seems suitable.' The committee was strongly represented by members of the new merchant class, men who were open to bringing about change within their institutions. They selected James O'Donnell (1774-1830), an Irish Protestant who was practising in New York. Although O'Donnell had never built a Catholic church, he had designed at least four major buildings in New York and had just completed Christ Church in the Gothic Revival style for the Episcopalians of that city.[17]

The new parish church of Notre-Dame, which served all of Montreal, was the largest church in either Canada or the US and remained so for half a century. Some 255 feet (78 m) long and 122 feet (37 m) wide [6.10], the interior is spanned by a complex wooden truss that originally supported a tin roof (replaced by copper in 1872) and a painted wood-and-plaster ceiling. The exterior walls are built of cut and coursed Montreal limestone, $2\frac{1}{2}$ feet (75 cm) thick, with 2 to $2\frac{1}{2}$ feet of coursed rubble inside.

Notre-Dame's imposing Gothic Revival façade features a recessed triple portico above which are niches with statues of saints and a battlemented parapet. A pair of tall towers, 210 feet (64 m) high (completed in 1843, after O'Donnell's death, under the supervision of John Ostell), enclose the composition. All of the openings have pointed arches, and the decorative tracery, crenellations at the parapet, and octagonal colonettes at the corners and along the sides continue the Gothic theme. As at St Mary's Cathedral, Gothic ornamental features are placed on what is essentially a Georgian form, although the twin towers deviate from the Gibbsian model. Although the interior [6.11] was far larger than any Canadian precedents, having a nave and side aisles with two tiers of galleries, its plan and decoration followed St Mary's and English sources. The clustered piers, pointed arches, and painted ceiling tracery continued the Gothic theme.

O'Donnell's interior was renovated in 1872-80 to designs by Victor Bourgeau (1809-88) in a more convincing version of the Gothic Revival, creating a highly decorative effect that continues to dazzle worshippers. The nave was painted in silver, gold, blue, azure, red, and purple, and illuminated by three octagonal skylights (in response to complaints that it was too dark); and the ceiling was enhanced by a network of decorative ribs that was similar to a design by O'Donnell. Bourgeau's reworking of the sanctuary was nothing short of spectacular [6.12]. He blocked off the east window and inserted a reredos almost 80 feet (24 m) high to contain a series of large statues in white pine that had been carved in Paris by sculptor Henri Bouriché in 1872-5. A central *Crucifixion* is surrounded by four Old Testament prefigurations and surmounted by the *Coronation of the Virgin*. To either side six polychromed plaster statues of saints, produced in Quebec, stand on pedestals

6.12 Sanctuary of the Church of Notre-Dame, Montreal, Quebec, 1872-80. Communauté urbaine de Montréal.

within niches, above the mahogany choir stalls. Between and around these statues appears a filigree of interlaced arches, columns, and pinnacles—the many colours dominated by blue and gold, and all illuminated with a mystical light provided by a fourth, concealed, skylight.

In 1888-91 the chapelle du Sacré-Coeur was added beyond the choir by Henri-Maurice Perrault (1828-1903) and Albert Mesnard (1847-1909); this ornate sacristy was burned by an arsonist in 1978 and restored in the following two years.

The Gothic Revival was familiar as a mode for churches in England and Ireland in the 1820s, and had been used hesitantly for this purpose in the US for nearly two decades—in churches by O'Donnell, among others. The exterior design of Notre-Dame bears a particularly close resemblance to that of St Paul's Church (1817-18) in Alexandria, Virginia, designed by Benjamin Henry Latrobe (1764-1820), which has the same triple-arched recessed portico and similar proportions. The membrane-like thinness of Notre-Dame's Gothic elements, and the Georgian-like regularity and symmetry of its design, show a family resemblance to the widely known 'Commissioners' churches'—many of which were in the Gothic Revival—that were erected in England after 1818 by the Church Building Commissioners. Indeed, the *Albion* of New York may well have been referring to the Commissioners' Churches when in 1824 it wrote that the style of Notre-Dame, then just under construction, was 'strictly and purely gothic, from the best models now existing in Europe.'[18]

Notre-Dame had an interesting relationship with the chapel of St Mary's Seminary (1806-8) in Baltimore, recognized as the first important American church in the Gothic Revival style. St Mary's was a sister Sulpician institution whose directors had close relations with those of Notre-Dame. The architect of St Mary's, Maximilian Godefroy (1765-1840?), was, like many of the Montreal and Baltimore Sulpicians, a political refugee from France.[19] The use of Gothic forms in both St Mary's Chapel and Notre-Dame, as well as in St Mary's Cathedral, Halifax, suggests that the Roman Catholic Gothic Revival in North America began as a concerted Sulpician initiative.

The new style of Notre-Dame was accepted favourably by many Montrealers. There were a few objections, however, notably one by Abbé Jérôme Demers (page 000), who in 1824 criticized the Gothic manner and said that the classical style was more suitable for a Catholic church; he submitted to the building committee an alternative design for Notre-Dame by his protégé, Thomas Baillairgé.[20]

Alan Gowans suggested in 1952 that the twin towers of Notre-Dame neatly recalled both those of its namesake cathedral in Paris and the twin-towered tradition of French-Canadian churches. Although pundits of the day did not remark on this parallel, a critic for Montreal's *La Minerve*, writing in 1866, described the Montreal church and noted that 'Notre-Dame de Paris…has nearly the same dimensions.' He continued: 'One sees by the size of the façade, if by nothing else, that this church belongs to the family of those great basilicas of the Old Continent.'[21]

Too firm a connection between the churches of Montreal and Paris (which O'Donnell had never visited) should not be assumed, nor should one assume that twin towers automatically roused images solely of French and Catholic church architecture. O'Donnell and his clients were also motivated by competition with the aggressive new English architecture of Montreal. The towers of Notre-Dame bear no less a likeness to the ones that flank the main (west) entrance of that bastion of Anglicanism, Westminster Abbey in London, whose towers were planned by Sir Christopher Wren and built after his death, in 1735-45, to designs by Nicholas Hawksmoor.

O'Donnell himself is irritatingly enigmatic about the reasons for his choice of style and does not refer at all to the towers. In a note that sounds somewhat like Ithiel Town's apology for Trinity Church, New Haven, O'Donnell wrote in 1824 to François-Antoine LaRocque, the secretary of the building committee (in response to the objection from Demers), that 'I…formed a few rough sketches in the Gothic style, as I considered it more suitable to your materials, workmen, climate, wants and means etc.' He noted that his sources were to be found in early, rather than late, Gothic:

> And as to the florid style of Gothic work, it neither suits your materials, workmen, Climate or even had you the means, the plane and simple style divested of its ornaments, comports more with the purpose of your Edifice…[22]

Notre-Dame provided a distinct contrast not only with the traditional churches of French Canada and the Georgian churches of the Anglicans, but also with the Georgian design of the recently completed Bank of Montreal (1818-19, **5.52**) across the square. Just as the three buildings on New Haven Green used different modes for differ-

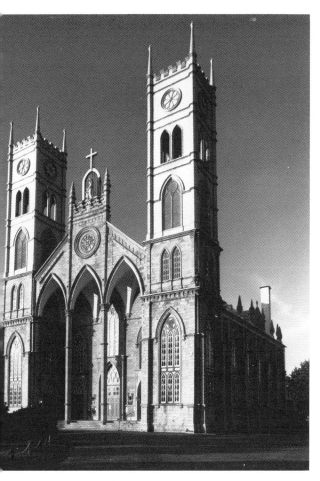

6.13 Parish church at Sainte-Anne-de-la-Pérade, Quebec, 1855-69. HWS/SSS/QUE 81 SP CH 1.01.

churches, such as the large **parish church at Ste-Anne-de-la-Pérade** [**6.13**], Quebec (designed by Casimir Coursol and built in 1855-69), directly imitated Notre-Dame. Its twin towers stand like bookends on either side of a portico made up of three tall, free-standing pointed arches.[24]

The Early Gothic Revival began to gain wide acceptance in Upper Canada in the 1820s, initially with Anglicans, among whom the style became virtually universal for churches by the 1840s. Three early ones in that province are St Thomas, a wood church in the town of that name (1822-4); St James, Maitland (1826-7), designed by Irish-born architect and builder Arthur McClean (1779-1864), built of stone; and the brick church of St Mary Magdalene at Picton (1825-7), which was later altered with a new tower and an extended east end.[25] The growing Gothic imperative is seen in the remodelling of St John's, Bath (a small community near Kingston), in the 1820s; although the stuccoed wood church was only thirty years old (it had been built in 1793-5), the congregation evidently felt compelled to add Gothic ornament and a battlemented tower.[26]

An attractive yet unpretentious church that is characteristic of this group is **Christ Church Burritts Rapids** [**6.14**], along the Rideau waterway

6.14 Christ Church, Burritts Rapids, Ontario, 1831. Photograph by Ralph Greenhill.

ent modes for different abodes, so too did those on Montreal's Place d'Armes. The church and the bank may not have had the same architect, but they did have, in part, the same client. Two men sat on both the vestry of Notre-Dame and the board of directors of the Bank of Montreal: the powerful LaRocque (a retired fur-trader, who succeeded in placing three relatives and two business partners, in addition to himself, on the church's building committee) and Joseph Masson, reportedly the wealthiest French-Canadian merchant.[23]

Notre-Dame and its style had a considerable influence on church-building in Quebec. Within eight years of its completion, four Catholic churches in Quebec were built with Gothic Revival features, and for three-quarters of a century the Gothic Revival remained one of several styles used for church architecture in the province. Some

of Ottawa. In July 1829 the community determined to build a stone church; at a subsequent meeting the question of the material was put to the residents and wood defeated stone by 12 votes to 5. As the building committee did not discuss style, Gothic must have been assumed. Completed in 1831, the elegant clapboarded church has an entrance tower with battlements and finials at the top—as well as classically inspired quoins at its corners—and slender pointed-arched windows along the nave. The builder was likely Arthur McClean, who is also credited with having constructed the church at Maitland and several others in the region.[27]

The other Protestant denominations in the Canadas also began to use the Gothic Revival for their churches in the 1830s, sometimes adopting different models. Montreal's Scottish community built **St Paul's Presbyterian Church** (1834; replaced 1867), which was somewhat more explicit in its Gothic references and deviated from the familiar entrance-tower scheme [6.15]. A row of four buttresses terminating in pinnacles dominated the façade, which also featured battlemented parapets and pointed arches around the door and windows. The design was attributed to a Mr Thompson of London—possibly Francis Thompson (1808-?), who practised both there and in Montreal—and credit for the supervision was given to John Wells (page 301). Gothic was used as fancy-dress that was interchangeable with other stylistic fashions—a characteristic of the Early Gothic Revival. Writing

6.15 St Paul's Presbyterian Church, Montreal, Quebec, 1834. Illustration by James Duncan from Newton Bosworth ed., *Hochelaga Depicta* (1839).

in the late 1830s, Montreal chronicler Newton Bosworth noted that the front 'is entirely Gothic' and that 'the interior of the building is Grecian.'[28]

All of these early churches apply Gothic ornament to a classic Georgian rectangular plan and a simple box-like building. They reveal the enduring popularity of the Wren-Gibbs plan, which persisted throughout the British sphere of influence for more

6.16 Joshua Chase house, Sheffield Mills, Nova Scotia, *c*. 1799. CIHB/02002800000149.

than a century. The next phase of the Gothic Revival would finally abandon the Georgian form in the search for an expression that was more closely related to medieval building. This Victorian Gothic Revival will be introduced after a glimpse at secular building.

Secular architecture

Although the Gothic alternative for the Parliament Building in Quebec was not built, the Early Gothic Revival was nevertheless used for domestic, institutional, and public architecture as well as for churches—although not so widely. Secular buildings, like religious ones, began with the arbitrary (and sometimes whimsical) application of Gothic detail on an otherwise Georgian body. An example is the **Joshua Chase house** [6.16] at Sheffield Mills,

Nova Scotia, in the Annapolis Valley, built around 1799 (and also known as the Burgess house and the Swetnam house). The 1½-storey centre-plan house is Georgian in all respects but the pointed-arched window in the gable over the entrance. If this window is indeed original, as was asserted by investigators from the Heritage Trust of Nova Scotia, it would represent the introduction of Gothic windows into domestic building in the same decade (and in the same part of the colony) as at Christ Church, Karsdale.[29] This house-type became a prototype for the popular Ontario Cottage, which first appeared in Upper Canada in the 1820s and gained in popularity over the course of the next half-century [11.14-17].

Gothic features soon appeared on institutional buildings as well, as in the **National School** (1822-4) in Quebec City, a Protestant benevolent organi-

6.17 National School, Quebec, Quebec, begun 1822-4. Photograph 1868. MMCH.

271

zation that educated orphan children. Initially a long and relatively low building, its original appearance is known from a watercolour painted in 1829 by James Cockburn; but it is seen here in an 1868 photograph [6.17], taken after the addition in 1842 of a compatible top storey by H.M. Blaiklock (1790-1843). (Since Blaiklock immigrated to Quebec from London only in 1823, he could not have designed the original school.) A gable roof runs parallel to rue d'Auteuil, and a cupola (that appeared atop the original building as well) rises from the centre of the ridge. The entrance is contained within a projecting gabled vestibule in the centre of the long side, which is illuminated by a large pointed-arched window with an ogee hood. Gothic ornament was applied liberally. The casement windows (the most common window-type in Quebec) are grouped in pairs and threes beneath flat-headed hood mouldings, and the glazing pattern has painted arches. The building has been the property of the Jesuits since 1904, and is now known as Maison Loyola. Just beyond the National School in the photograph looms the side of the slightly earlier Church of the Congregation (1818, now the Jesuit Church), whose round-arched windows were still untouched by the Gothic Revival.[30]

The Gothic Revival style may have been selected for the National School because of the institution's Protestant religious affiliation. The religious link is also suggested in the Protestant Orphan Asylum in Montreal, which had a similar function and was built in the same year (1822). A building about which little is known other than in an early image that shows a datestone, it also had a determined display of Gothic windows. Whichever of the two was built first was likely the first secular building in Canada with a consistent application of Gothic features. Both were built shortly before Notre-Dame in Montreal, and may also represent the first use of Gothic detail in Lower Canada.

The other reason for the choice of Gothic may have been the association of the style with collegiate architecture in Britain—a motivation that would later become very important in both Canada and the US.

The first Canadian college to acknowledge this association and adopt the Gothic Revival was **Bishop's College** [6.18] in Lennoxville, Quebec. (The first American educational building in the style was Kenyon College in Gambier, Ohio, 1827-9.)[31] The original Bishop's College building of 1846, the three-storey brick structure seen at the right of the illustration, has a raised and crenellated frontis-

piece, with a row of buttresses terminating in finials. A pointed-arched entry is contrasted with the flat hood mouldings over the windows. The additions to the left included an auditorium, a primary school, the chapel, and a faculty residence; all were completed by 1865 in a later version of the Gothic Revival. Bishop's College had been founded in 1843 under the sponsorship of George Jehoshaphat Mountain, the third Anglican bishop of Quebec (after whom it was named), and its architectural style was certainly intended to express an association with Britain. In the previous era Georgian Classicism would have been used without a second thought; now it was proper to choose an appropriate historical mode for the building.[32]

Another Anglican bishop, John Strachan of Toronto, founded **Trinity College** [6.19] in that city in 1851 with the intention of establishing its allegiance to the Church of England, which both Oxford and Cambridge Universities maintained. Strachan raised support in Britain from several sources, including the Society for the Propagation of the Gospel in Foreign Parts, and he brought back the plans for St Aidan's Theological College in Cheshire (by Thomas Henry Wyatt and David Brandon, 1850) as a model. A proposal by the Irish-trained Toronto architect Kivas Tully (1820-1905) was chosen over one by the firm of Cumberland and Ridout, who were then building Strachan's St James' Cathedral. Tully intended to produce a large range of buildings around a landscaped quadrangle, but tight finances led to the building of only the front block in 1851-2, centred on the entrance on Queen Street West (opposite what is now called Strachan Avenue). His design, two storeys high with a continuous gable roof, respected the model of St Aidan's and also included explicit references to Tom Tower at Christ Church, Oxford, and to New Court, St John's College, Cambridge, the latter an early work of the Gothic Revival (by Rickman and Hutchinson, 1825-31). This eclectic use of different specific sources is characteristic of the Victorian phase of the Gothic Revival, which will be introduced below. Between 1877 and 1894 the Toronto architect Frank Darling (1850-1923) made several additions, including a chapel and a pair of wings. Trinity College was demolished in 1956.[33]

As mentioned above, the Early Gothic Revival had several versions. One variant that was particularly appropriate for secular architecture was the castellated mode—the name given to the attempt to make buildings resemble medieval castles. This was introduced to the public buildings of Upper

6.18 Bishop's College, Lennoxville, Quebec, begun 1846. NAC/C-84075.

6.19 (*below*) Trinity College, Toronto, Ontario, 1851-2. MTRL/T-34761.

6.20 London District (now Middlesex County) Courthouse, London, Ontario, 1828-31. Archives of Ontario/Acc. 3619 S12569.

6.21 (*below*) Plan of the second floor, Middlesex County Courthouse, London, Ontario. Drawn by David Byrnes after a drawing of 1839.

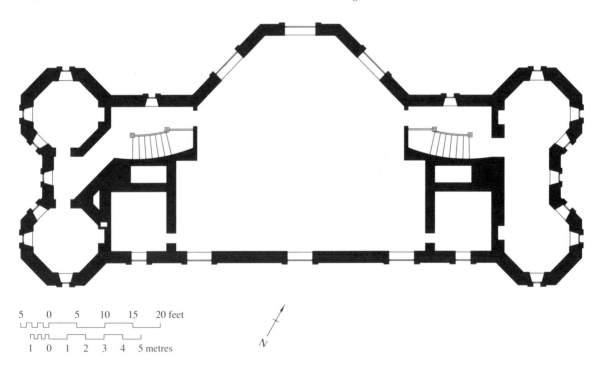

Canada in the **London District Courthouse** (1828-31), subsequently called the Middlesex County Courthouse [**6.20**]. Governor Simcoe originally chose the site of London as the capital of Upper Canada. Located on the River Thames, in the Township of Westminster, in the County of Middlesex, the future town and its environs were appropriately named for this intended role. It was York (Toronto), however, that was ultimately named the provincial capital; so London had to settle in 1826 for becoming the seat of the London District. Formal settlement began in that year.

The legislature of Upper Canada reserved 4 acres (1.6 hectares) for a courthouse and jail, appointed five commissioners to be responsible for building the combined structure, and authorized the commissioners to borrow £4,000 for this purpose. Evidently the legislature intended that a suitable monument asserting the power of the colonial government should be erected quickly. The president of the Commission was the powerful Colonel Thomas Talbot, a former private secretary to Governor Simcoe who was the leading promoter of settlement in the London District. The Commission advertised for an architect even before the townsite had been selected and surveyed. The following spring it accepted the plans prepared by John Ewart.

This remarkable courthouse, as built between 1828 and 1831, was a large building, some 100 feet (30.5 m) by 50 feet (15.2 m) in plan and 50 feet high, dominated by massive octagonal towers at the four corners. The now-familiar Gothic ornament includes battlements along the parapet, a trio of tall pointed-arched windows and doors on the elevation, and buttresses at the base of the towers. The walls are built of brick faced with stucco, with stone foundations. Behind the massive façade lay a symmetrical arrangement of rooms, with the county offices and jail cells located on the lower storey and the courtroom and judges' chambers on the second floor [**6.21**]. (A low attic contained additional cells.) A large angled bow extended at the back towards the bluff over the river, much like the bow on the garden front of Georgian British and Irish country houses. (Major additions and alterations in 1877-8, by Thomas H. Tracy [1846-1925], and in 1911, by Arthur P. Nutter [1874-1967], transformed the exterior appearance and interior layout, but retained the castellated manner.) The sharp-tongued Anna Jameson, who visited London in 1837, wrote: 'The jail and court house, comprised of one large, stately edifice, seemed the glory

6.22 Malahide Castle, County Dublin, Ireland. Photograph courtesy Irish Tourist Board.

of the townspeople. As for the style of architecture, I may not attempt to name or describe it; but a gentleman informed me, in rather equivocal phrase, that it was "*somewhat gothic*".'[34]

Ewart had used an elegant pilastered-and-pedimented Georgian design for the Home District Courthouse and Jail in York (1824),[35] and so it is evident that Gothic was chosen for a specific reason. The London Commission did not formally stipulate a style, but Colonel Talbot, a landed aristocrat, likely indicated a preference for the castellated manner. He would have seen the mode as an appropriate architectural image of authority, declaring the court to be the stronghold of law and order. Local legend also holds that the courthouse was intended to resemble Talbot's Irish ancestral home, **Malahide Castle** [**6.22**] in County Dublin, and indeed there is a strong resemblance between the two in the arrangement of the corner towers (circular at Malahide) and battlements. It was no secret that Talbot had long wanted to build himself a castle at Port Talbot, his Lake Erie home: in 1794 he is said to have welcomed Simcoe to the 'Castle of Malahide'—referring to the tent he had erected on the site—and he called the log house that he eventually built there by the same pretentious name. Ewart's willingness to follow Talbot's wishes would seem to be borne out by the Commissioner's recommendation that Ewart be given a lot of his choice, 'as he appears liberal in his views of building the Gaol & Court House.'[36]

A watercolour view [6.23] of the London courthouse, painted around 1835 by George Russell Dartnell, gives us some insight into the romantic view of the Gothic Revival held by people of the age. Through the manipulation of perspective and lighting, the artist makes the courthouse seem very much more vertical and keep-like—far more like the popular idea of a castle than it appears in reality.

The castellated mode of the London courthouse would seem to have been Talbot's personal choice for an appropriate model from history. While it may have been in tune with the architectural currents of the time, however, the style gained only a precarious foothold in courthouse-building in Upper Canada, and none elsewhere in Canada. The Wellington County Courthouse in Guelph (1842-4), designed by Thomas Young, repeated the corner towers—although here they are square—and battlemented parapets, featuring flat-headed windows with drip mouldings rather than pointed arches. The jail was constructed as a separate octagonal building just behind the courthouse. The Halton County Courthouse in Milton (by Hutchinson Clark and David Murray, 1854-5) was a third county building in the Gothic Revival manner.[37]

The Gothic Revival found wide acceptance in residential design, in which the romantic aspects of the new style are most evident. It began as a picturesque plaything for the houses of the wealthy, but eventually entered the vernacular, with the help of published images in the popular literature as well as real-life examples from church-building.

Holland House [6.24], Toronto, represents an early milestone. The residence of Attorney-General Henry John Boulton—brother of D'Arcy, owner of The Grange—it looked out onto a driveway and garden on Front Street. Holland House was begun in 1831 in a Georgian design (perhaps not unlike that of The Grange), but the next year Boulton commissioned John Howard, who had just arrived in Toronto from England, to redesign it. Howard cloaked the house entirely in Gothic garb; even its chimneys (along the side walls) were partly hidden by turret-like enclosures. The new garden façade on the south featured a semi-circular loggia that rose to become a medieval tower; the battlemented parapet of the tower was repeated as a balustrade over the loggia. Pointed Gothic arches in the loggia, and surrounding the French doors of the tower, were complemented by flat-headed windows on either side—all with Gothic hood mouldings. (In the remodelling, a new entrance was created on the north front, facing Wellington Street.) Constructed of brick, over which a layer of stucco was scored to resemble stone—another bit of theatre in the design—the house was a delightful fantasy. It was demolished in 1904.[38]

Boulton, like Talbot, clearly intended to create an associative link with old England. Holland House was the name of his sometime home in England, a Jacobean manor just west of London that was built early in the seventeenth century. That the two houses bore no resemblance to each other made no difference whatsoever; what counted was that Boulton's Toronto residence was identified in people's minds with an idea of the London one, which was remote in time and place, and therefore attractive to romantic sensibilities. Association was more important than a physical resemblance. The design of the new Holland House resembled the 'castle-houses' that sprang up in the English countryside and were illustrated in English architectural books of the period, and formed a part of the Early Gothic Revival. One source may have been the remodelling of Windsor Castle by Jeffry Wyatt in the 1820s. Holland House is closer in scale and treatment, however, to Luscombe in Devonshire, whose gardens and house were created in 1799-1804 by the talented and prolific team of landscape architect Humphry Repton (1752-1818) and architect John Nash (1752-1835). In a description of Luscombe that is equally applicable to the new Holland House, Repton explained how the character of the site determined the appropriateness of

> ... giving to the house the character of a Castle which, by blending a chaste correctness of proportion with bold irregularity of outline, its deep recesses and projections producing broad masses of light and shadow, while its roof is enriched by turrets, battlements, corbels, and lofty chimneys, has infinitely more picturesque effect.[39]

Repton's comments reveal how the Early Gothic Revival was closely interwoven with a growing taste for the picturesque, a new aesthetic principle that developed out of eighteenth-century English landscape design and was subsequently applied to architecture. The picturesque was defined by its theorists as showing the qualities of irregularity, roughness, and variety of form, colour, and texture—attributes implied, or cited, by Repton and that emerge in Early Gothic Revival buildings. They are seen, for example, in the finials of Wyatt's Gothic design for the Quebec Parliament House and of most of the churches seen above, in the towers of the London District Courthouse and Holland House, and in the coarse masonry of St John's Church. They became far more ingrained in the next phase of the style, introduced in the following section, and in the domestic architecture and pattern books of the day, which are discussed in Chapter 11.[40]

Other houses in the Toronto area experimented with the castellated mode. One that incorporated this into its name as well as its form was Castlefield, built in 1832 by James Hervey Price, an English-

6.24 Holland House, Toronto, Ontario, 1831. Photograph *c*. 1880. MTRL/T-11149.

6.25 Elizabeth Cottage, Kingston, Ontario, 1841-3. Photograph *c*. 1880. Queen's University Archives/PG-K 80-15.

born attorney and politician, on his property north of York. (It was demolished in 1918.) Like Holland House, the garden front had a raised central portion—flat, rather than curved, and with corner turrets—that was topped by crenellations.[41]

A different version of the Gothic Revival, one that lacked castle-like features and had a more urbane setting, is seen at **Elizabeth Cottage** (1841-31) in Kingston, designed for his family's own use by architect Edward Horsey (1809-69). As originally built, and as seen in the photograph [**6.25**], the house was a $1\frac{1}{2}$-storey Ontario cottage with aggressive Gothic detailing, including bay windows, bargeboard, and a high central peak that masks a conventional gable roof. The main body of the house was a self-contained block, with a separate stable wing connected by a wall. A second, lower, stone wall with a decorative iron railing was constructed along the street. The Gothic features that grace this limestone house are profuse, especially on the entrance wing that projects towards Brock Street. These include scalloped bargeboard in the central gable and beneath the eaves, several doors and windows with pointed-arched heads, and projecting bay windows with decorative tracery beneath the central gable and to either side of the entrance. The decorative vocabulary provides a do-

mestic parallel to the churches of the day. The house stands, although with alterations. The name 'Elizabeth Cottage' (commemorating Horsey's daughter) was given in 1955 when, in accordance with the will of Horsey's granddaughter, the house became a retirement home.[42]

The connection between Gothic Revival houses and churches is underscored in the **Bishop's Palace** (1845) on Church Street, Toronto, the residence of the Roman Catholic prelate, built adjacent to St Michael's (Roman Catholic) Cathedral (1845-8).

6.26 Bishop's Palace, Toronto, Ontario, 1845. Photograph by William Toye.

Both the Cathedral and the Palace (now the rectory) were designed by William Thomas (*c*. 1799-1860), arguably Toronto's pre-eminent architect at the time and the founder of an architectural dynasty that became active in several provinces (see page 000). Before coming to Toronto in 1843, Thomas had an active career in England as a builder and designer. He was president of the Toronto Society of Arts in 1847-8 and in 1859 became the president of the country's first professional architectural association: The Association of Architects, Civil Engineers and Public Land Surveyors.[43]

The Bishop's Palace is a three-storey building (the third storey was a later addition) with a projecting frontispiece and wings [6.26]. Projecting bays, pointed gables, corner turrets, and decorative surfaces use a gothic vocabulary to create a picturesque aspect. Sculpture is used to good effect, and includes a panel over the entrance with the episcopal arms, and dripmoulds beside the doorway carved with the heads of Bishop Michael Power and architect Thomas. The Palace is built of the same grey brick and stone trim as the Cathedral, which is an effectively designed Gothic Revival church perched at the edge of the ecclesiological movement—a new phase in the style that will now be introduced.[44]

Ecclesiology and the Victorian Gothic Revival

Background in England

Around 1840, shortly after Queen Victoria's accession to the throne, a new intensity began to infuse the Gothic Revival in Britain. A serious and archaeological interest in the Gothic architecture of the Middle Ages was combined with a rejection of current liturgical practices in the Church of England—the former the result of the work of antiquaries and architects, the latter of theologians and academics. The two converged in the university community of Cambridge and produced strong pressures on church-builders to model their designs closely on Early Gothic parish churches. This 'parish church revival', as it is called in Britain, had a profound influence on the design of churches—and, ultimately, on buildings of all kinds—in Canada.

The first decades of the nineteenth century saw an increasingly studious interest in England's Gothic past. Gothic was no longer regarded as a quaint style that was useful for decorative ornament. Architect John Rickman (1776-1841), who made careful studies of Gothic buildings, and provided nomenclature that is still used today, discerned several distinct sub-styles: Early English, Decorated, and Perpendicular. He also generated an appreciation of the unique characteristics of individual historical monuments. Rickman's work was paralleled by that of historians and illustrators such as John Britton (1771-1857), whose prodigious output included the fourteen-volume *Cathedral Antiquities of England* (1814-35), and Augustus Charles Pugin (1768-1832), who prepared and published careful measured drawings and views of Gothic buildings and details in *Specimens of Gothic Architecture* (1821-3) and later books.[45]

Independently of the work of the architects, a number of voices within the Church of England demanded the rejection of the Protestant domination over the Church and a restoration of Anglo-Catholic high-church theology. The Oxford (or 'Tractarian') Movement, led by John Henry Newman and others, gained a strong following that peaked around 1840. Newman converted to Roman Catholicism in 1845, but others continued the 'Counter-reformation' from within the Church of England. The Church responded by introducing revisions to its liturgy. The changes rejected some of the simplified practices that had been in effect since the Reformation and returned to the ceremony of the Middle Ages. One such change that had considerable impact on architecture was the placement of the service within a chancel that was physically separated from the nave and often hidden from view by a choir screen.[46]

The new and earnest interest in Gothic, and the shift to the liturgical right, first came together in the writings and designs of Augustus Welby Northmore Pugin (1812-52), the son of A.C. Pugin and another convert to Roman Catholicism (in 1835). His polemical books posed a seemingly irrefutable link between the Gothic Revival parish church and good, moral, Christian, English life.[47]

The most important influence on Gothic Revival church design was the ecclesiological movement. This was initiated by the Cambridge Camden Society (after 1846 called the Ecclesiological Society), which began in 1836 as an association of undergraduates at Trinity College, Cambridge. The leaders were John Mason Neale (1818-66), Benjamin Webb (1819-85), and A.J. Beresford-Hope (1820-87). In 1841 the Society began publication of a periodical called *The Ecclesiologist*. The editors stated their interests in the first issue, proposing to consider topics such as

> Church Building at home and in the Colonies: Church Restoration in England and abroad: the theory and practice of Ecclesiastical Architecture: the investigation of Church Antiquities: the connection of Architecture and Ritual: the science of Symbolism: the principles of Church Arrangements: Church Musick and all the Decorative Arts which can be made subservient to Religion: the exposing and denouncing of glaring cases of Church Desecration: Criticisms upon Designs for and upon New Churches.[48]

The interest in 'the Colonies' would inevitably affect Canadian architecture.

The Society's architectural principles were simple: the Decorated phase (1290-1350) was the best period of the Gothic style, and its parish churches provided ideal models for new building. Architects, wrote Neale and Webb, should

> choose the glorious architecture of the fourteenth century; and, just as no man has no more than one handwriting, so in this one language alone will he express his architectural ideas.[49]

Such pronouncements led to the Victorian Gothic Revival (or what Kenneth Clark called the Ethical Gothic Revival), which is divided into two phases: Early Victorian and High Victorian. The Early phase of the Victorian Gothic Revival (or the Early Victorian Gothic Revival—not to be confused with the Early Gothic Revival) is characterized by buildings that were based on a single model or type and actually look as if they might have been built in the Middle Ages. High Victorian Gothic, on the other hand, produced buildings whose eclecticism combined a number of disparate sources, and that could only have been erected in the nineteenth century.

Canadian cathedrals

Ecclesiastics in Canada were naturally affected by these events in England. The Right Reverend John Inglis, Bishop of Nova Scotia, became a patron of the Cambridge Camden Society in 1839, the first North American cleric to be so honoured; and in 1845 the Right Reverend Edward Feild, Bishop of Newfoundland, was named the third. These men certainly looked to England for models for their new church designs. For example, *The Ecclesiologist* reported in 1845 that architect J. Cranstoun, who

had drawn a number of medieval parish churches for publication by the Oxford Architectural Society, had prepared a design 'for a church in the diocese of Newfoundland.'[50]

The Canadian cleric who best translated the theories of the Cambridge Camden Society into stone was the Right Reverend John Medley (1804-92), first Bishop of New Brunswick. A product of the Tractarian Movement, Medley had served for some time as rector of St Thomas, Exeter. He was interested in architecture, having studied it at Oxford, and founded the Exeter Diocesan Architectural Society, a provincial organization that corresponded with the Cambridge Camden Society. In 1841 Medley published *Elementary Remarks on Church Architecture*, which *The Ecclesiologist* was able to 'safely recommend' to its readers.[51] He had a fine library of architectural books, many of which remain in the Diocesan Archives in Fredericton.

Medley was called to Canada in 1845 and installed in Fredericton. He arrived on 10 June (five weeks after his consecration as bishop) and almost immediately turned his attention towards church building. Three years later he described his impressions of colonial church architecture (and, by implication, the Georgian church of 1794 that he inherited) to the Ecclesiological Society:

> Throughout the whole of North America no correct type of a church was formerly to be seen. The ordinary type seems to have been borrowed from the buildings erected by the Puritans, and from the different religious bodies who sprang up from time to time, the Church having no form of its own, nor having apparently any reference to the ancient churches in the mother country.[52]

Bishop Medley sought to remedy this situation by creating a 'correct type of a church' in Christ Church Cathedral and the smaller St Anne's Chapel at Fredericton. His architect for both was Frank Wills (1822-57), a talented but short-lived designer who had accompanied him from Exeter. The two buildings are significant for being Canada's first churches in the new Victorian phase of the Gothic Revival.

Wills described **St Anne's Chapel [6.27]** as 'the first ecclesiastical building erected in the British provinces on which ancient architecture has been attempted to be honestly carried out', and a modern authority has called it 'the finest small North American parish church of its date in the English Gothic Revival style.'[53] Begun in the spring of 1846 (its cornerstone was laid in May of that year), and

6.27 St Anne's Chapel, Fredericton, New Brunswick, 1846-7. PANB/P5-54.

6.28 (*left*) Interior of St Anne's Chapel, Fredericton, New Brunswick, 1846-7. Photograph by Phoebe B. Stanton.

consecrated in the following March, St Anne's was a chapel-of-ease that subsequently became a parish church.

The intimately scaled sandstone building offers an elegant interpretation of Early English Gothic. It consists of a single-cell nave, only 54 feet (16.5 m) long by 21 feet (6.4 m) wide, with a narrower and lower chancel some 20 feet (6.1 m) deep and an enclosed entrance porch on the side facing the street. An open belfry, with three bells, is perched atop the west end. The exterior treatment is plain and straightforward, dominated less by its ornament than by the richly textured sandstone (reminiscent of the picturesque stonework described two decades earlier by Ithiel Town). The interior [**6.28**] is more elaborate and colourful, with a tile floor, carved butternut pews and choir screen, a scriptural quotation over the chancel arch, and decorative tiles and rich stained glass at the chancel end.

The most important aspect of St Anne's that marks the transition to the new phase of the Gothic Revival is that it actually *looks* like a Gothic church. There is a strong resemblance to **St Michael's, Long**

Stanton, Cambridgeshire [6.29], a thirteenth-century church that had been championed by the Cambridge Camden Society in the mid-1840s. The Society recommended it as a model for colonial builders because of the simplicity of its forms. Wills—who evidently concurred with this sentiment—explained that he used the 'First Pointed' (i.e. Early English) style as inspiration for St Anne's because the masons were unable to execute the elaborate stone tracery characteristic of the Decorated phase.[54] Both the medieval and the modern church feature an austere gable end with a belfry at the peak and a low porch at the side. But the Fredericton chapel has a much steeper profile, omits most of the buttresses in favour of larger window openings, and favours an interior without side aisles, in contrast to the nave colonnade at St Michael's.

Some of Wills' details were copied from specific medieval prototypes—the cross on the porch gable, for example, was based on one in Norfolk—but the design of St Anne's Chapel was essentially a fresh and respectful interpretation of the Gothic parish church. This becomes clear when it is contrasted with St James the Less (1846-49), Philadelphia. Modelled far more closely on St Michael's than is St Anne's, and begun a few months after St Anne's, St James the Less was built directly under the supervision of the Ecclesiological Society, whose favourite architect, William Butterfield (1814-1900), furnished some of its designs.[55]

St Anne's Chapel also resembles the Church of St Lawrence, Tubney, at Oxford, built to designs by A.W.N. Pugin in 1844-6 and not consecrated until February 1847, a month before St Anne's. The Oxford church was never well known, nor (because of Pugin's Catholicism) was the identity of its architect revealed. Rather than a source for St Anne's, the two should be considered to be parallel designs—demonstrating just how up-to-date St Anne's Chapel was.[56]

The principal outcome of the Medley-Wills association—and an important landmark in North American architecture—was **Christ Church Cathedral** (1845-53) in Fredericton. The Ecclesiological Society and Butterfield had their hands in its design as well as that of St Anne's Chapel, although the story begins before their intervention, with Medley's determination to build an exemplary new cathedral that would be modelled on a particular English Gothic church. This followed the desires of the Exeter Diocesan Architectural Society, which had given him £1,500 with which to build a church 'after an ancient model of singular beauty and cathedral appropriateness.' Medley raised an additional £3,100 from members of his new diocese within two weeks of his arrival in Fredericton.

But *The Ecclesiologist* disapproved, because St Mary's was a mere parish church and therefore unsuitable as a source for a cathedral. The journal was especially critical because its chancel and transepts were lower than the nave, rather than the same height. William Butterfield offered to remedy this failing with a large central tower and a high chancel; his scheme was published in *The Ecclesiologist*, opposite Medley's comments on colonial church architecture and an appeal for funds. Another revised design, presumed to be by Wills, shows a pair of towers flanking the transept. Butterfield's scheme was ultimately followed—although with changes to the details of the tower, and with a spire that was closer to that of St Mary's, Snettisham.[58]

The foundation for the tower was laid in May 1849, and the stonework was mostly completed in that year. The chancel brought the length to 172

6.30 'The Proposed Cathedral Church, Frederickton, New Brunswick, adapted from St Mary's Snettisham, Norfolk'. Drawing by Frank Wills, 1845. PANB/MC223CA.

Wasting no time, he began work on the cathedral in August 1845 and the cornerstone was laid by the Lieutenant Governor, Sir William Colebrooke, in October. The nave and aisles were built by contractor Otis Small and completed by November 1847. This nearly drained the building fund, causing a slowdown in work. Frank Wills left for New York to pursue his career, and Bishop Medley went to England in search of financial support. He returned in September 1848 with £2,000 in donations, a further £1,000 from the Society for the Propagation of Christian Knowledge, and a fistful of suggestions from the Ecclesiological Society for altering Wills' design.[57]

Medley and Wills had chosen as their model the church of St Mary's, Snettisham, Norfolk [6.30, 31].

6.31 St Mary's, Snettisham, Norfolk, England. Photograph by Roger J. Smith.

feet (52.5 m) and the wood spire was constructed in 1851 to the height of 178 feet (54.3 m). Christ Church Cathedral was finally consecrated in August 1853. In a 'charge to the clergy' of his diocese, Medley found the opportunity to reflect on the principles that had guided the design of the building. He affirmed that

> ... my intention has been, that the Cathedral... should present to the minds of reverent and earnest churchmen, a type (humble indeed in its pretensions) of the glory and beauty of our common spiritual mother, in our Cathedrals at home [in England].

Medley noted that everything in the ornament and design had a precedent in English churches, based on the 'Middle Pointed' (Decorated) style, before Gothic architecture degenerated 'to mere frippery'. The correct precedents were related directly to the intended liturgy: 'I am as anxious not to go beyond our ritual, as not to fall short of it, where practicable.' Medley recalled that he had sent Wills, then only a draughtsman, to measure the church at Snettisham. (When Wills visited the church, the chancel and transepts were in ruins. Their present appearance is the result of a subsequent restoration.) The six-light west window at Fredericton was an exact copy of the one at St Mary's. The east window was modelled on that at Selby Abbey, since Snettisham's had been destroyed; and the side windows of the west end were taken from the east window of Exwick Chapel at Exeter, which Medley himself had built in 1841 to designs by architect John Hayward (1808-91), Frank Wills' mentor. *The Ecclesiologist* called this 'the best specimen of a modern church we have yet seen.' In his address, Medley went on to identify the sources of the choir roof, font, and other interior features. He acknowledged certain concessions to the Canadian climate, such as reducing the length of the transepts and the sizes of some windows in order to mitigate the problem of winter heating.[59]

The genaealogy was important to churchmen of the 1840s because it was believed that appropriate models would inspire correct religious feelings. The sources became metaphors for spiritualism. However, to lay observers of the time, as well as to those of today, what is impressive about Christ Church Cathedral is not its sources so much as their suc-

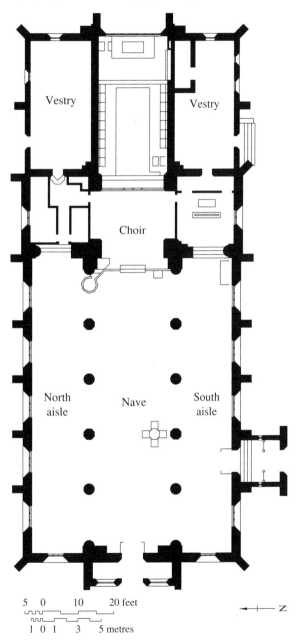

cessful synthesis in an effective and handsome composition [**6.32**]. Set on a lovely green, whose elms are said to have been planted by Medley to protect the cathedral from ice-floes on the St John River, the building rises in a carefully orchestrated *crescendo* from the base, past the low roofs of the aisles and the vestries, through the nave and

6.33 Plan of Christ Church Cathedral, Fredericton, New Brunswick, 1845-53. Drawing by David Byrnes.

6.32 (*left*) Christ Church Cathedral, Fredericton, New Brunswick, 1845-53. National Film Board/Photothèque/ 82-2490/IX 36554.

chancel, to the upward-pointing tower and the final climax in the cross at the peak of the tall spire. The walls were built of local sandstone, the trim of harder Grindstone Island stone from the Bay of Fundy; the dressings of the windows and doors are Caen stone from Normandy.

All the features seen in buildings of the Early Gothic Revival—buttresses, pointed-arched windows with elaborate tracery, gables, and finials—are present in the Fredericton cathedral, but they no longer appear to be incongruous, pasted-on ornament: they are perfectly integrated into the form and massing of the building, and have clearly become inseparable components of the larger whole. The result has nothing to do with a box-and-tower Georgian church in Gothic decorative garb; it is rather an integrated revival of Gothic form and Gothic feeling. Like St Anne's Chapel, it resembles an English church of the Middle Ages.

The same can be said of the impressive interior [6.33, 34], which is illuminated by the richly coloured light that passes through the stained-glass windows, most of which were installed in 1850-2 after additional fund-raising efforts by Medley. Large octagonal piers support the pointed nave arcade, above which the exposed wood trusses of the steeply pitched roof rest on large, curved wood brackets. The high altar at the east end, separated from the congregation in the nave by the communion rail, the crossing beneath the tower, and the deep chancel all follow the newly elaborated liturgy of the Church of England. The east wall is partially faced in tiles that were a gift of the Minton tileworks. William Butterfield designed the furniture in the east end as well as the communion silver.

Lightning struck the cathedral in July 1911 and started a fire that caused much damage, including the complete loss of the spire. This was rebuilt in 1911-12 by New York architect DeLancey Robinson (1872-1939) to resemble more closely that of St Mary's, Snettisham; the pointed stone gables at the top of the tower were added at that time. Additional masonry restoration work was carried out in the 1980s.

In bringing the Victorian Gothic Revival to Canada at Christ Church Cathedral and St Anne's Chapel, Bishop Medley introduced a new and earnest historicism that altered the design and meaning of ecclesiastical architecture. No longer was it sufficient for a church to evoke general associations with the Gothic past; it was now necessary that these associations be attached to specific buildings

6.34 Interior of Christ Church Cathedral, Fredericton, New Brunswick, 1845-53. Photograph by Roger J. Smith.

that were representative of a 'correct' age (the thirteenth and fourteenth centuries) and mode of worship.

The differences between Christ Church Cathedral and St Mary's Cathedral in Halifax or Notre-Dame in Montreal (both designed two decades earlier) are immense. The latter two are Georgian boxes embellished with the superficial application of Gothic ornament and detail, whereas Christ Church Cathedral is a reinterpretation of the English Gothic church in plan and massing, with detail that is integral with the overall design. The comparison clearly shows the change from the Early Gothic Revival to the Victorian Gothic Revival.

Medley and Wills proceeded with separate church-building careers that reinforced this new direction in architecture. Having created a spectacular new cathedral and a handsome chapel-of-ease in Fredericton, Medley went on to build a number of parish churches elsewhere in his diocese (pages 291-2). Wills left Fredericton for a short, but important, sojourn in New York, during which he had a decided influence on the design of Protestant Episcopal churches. He moved to that city in 1847, and a year later became the architectural expert of the newly formed New York Ecclesiological Society and an editor of *The New York Ecclesiologist*; he also published a number of articles and a book, *Ancient Ecclesiastical Architecture* (1850). In 1851 Wills went into partnership with Henry C. Dudley, who had also worked with John Hayward in Exeter, and the

two designed several churches in the American South.[60]

Wills returned to Montreal by 1857, when he received the important commission for that city's Anglican **Christ Church Cathedral** [6.35], which was to replace the large Georgian building [4.54] that had been destroyed by fire. The new church was built uptown on rue Sainte-Catherine, signalling the movement of the city's English-speaking community up the hill and to the west, into an area that would soon be the commercial core. Wills

6.35 Christ Church Cathedral, Montreal, Quebec, 1857-60. Photograph by Alexander Hamilton, *c*. 1870. NAC/PA-21698.

completed the plan and all the elevations except those of the east end, and supervised the laying of the foundations, when he died suddenly at the young age of thirty-five. He was succeeded by Thomas Seaton Scott (1836-95), who was to have a long and important architectural career in both private and government practice.

Wills and Scott produced a cruciform building in the Decorated style that was not unlike that of the Fredericton cathedral, but more profuse ornament was used to break up the surfaces into smaller parts and yield a more taut and energetic design. The proliferation of buttresses, spires, and windows, the projecting triple-arched western porch with its crocketed gables (based once again on Snettisham, although with French prototypes as well), and the roughly textured Montreal greystone combine to give a more picturesque effect that was to become characteristic of architecture after mid-century. The rose window over the porch is more French than English in inspiration. Inside, the nave arcade is supported by alternating octagonal and circular piers with the wooden roof structure exposed.[61]

Montreal's Christ Church Cathedral opened for worship in 1860 and was consecrated seven years later, when the debt had been reduced. The massive stone spire, which rose 230 feet (70 m), was built on a bed of unstable blue clay. Significant settlement was already detected before the church opened, and before long the spire began to lean noticeably. It was dismantled in 1927 and rebuilt by architects Ross and Macdonald in 1939-40 with a steel frame and a lightweight aluminum skin that had been cast from moulds taken from the original stonework and specially treated to resemble stone. In 1989-90 the cathedral was underpinned and a commercial mall was inserted beneath it.

The Ecclesiologist approved generally of the design for the Montreal cathedral, although it criticized the internal arrangements. The journal noted that Christ Church Cathedral would 'mark an epoch in transatlantic ecclesiology', being 'the largest completed cathedral in America of our communion.' The article stated that Toronto's cathedral, then still under construction, would be larger but 'on (we believe) a much inferior and less correct plan', and that 'the nave only has been erected' of the cathedral at St John's. The article concluded by expressing the hope that the Canadian cathedrals would have a 'reflex influence' on the church in the United States, where there was 'yet a sort of republican feeling.'[62]

These last two Anglican cathedrals mentioned by

6.36 Cathedral of St John the Baptist, St John's, Newfoundland, begun 1846. Perspective view from the *Illustrated London News*, 23 June 1849.

The Ecclesiologist, those in St John's and Toronto, were also important milestones in the development of the Canadian Gothic Revival. The **Cathedral of St John the Baptist** [6.36] in St John's, Newfoundland, rose out of the ashes of the great fire of 1846, which destroyed much of the city. Construction had already begun on a new stone cathedral, but the fire's heat left the stone unusable. Bishop Edward Feild, a churchman with decidedly Tractarian leanings, and recently made a patron of the Cambridge Camden Society, must have been inwardly relieved, because he had been unhappy with the cathedral planned by his predecessor, Bishop Aubrey George Spencer. 'I cannot tell you how I was disturbed by the prospectus for my Cathedral Church,' Feild wrote in 1844. He expressed his taste for the new verticality of the Gothic Revival in a letter to the Camden Society, criticizing the low-pitched roofs and clapboards of the frame churches in his diocese, and complaining that the 'succession of horizontal lines...[is] at first very strange and painful to English eyes.'[63] Horizontality, which was characteristic of the classical styles, would indeed have been distressing to picturesquely trained eyes.

Feild went to England to raise money for a new cathedral and relief for his diocese. While overseas he selected as the architect of his cathedral George Gilbert Scott (1811-78), who was in the early stages of a brilliant career (he was knighted in 1872) during which he was to build and restore hundreds of churches as well as design a number of important public buildings. His progeny included his family as well as his buildings, as he began an architectural dynasty that prospered—and remained the architects for the cathedral at St John's—for a century.

The Newfoundland cathedral was begun in 1846, and work on the nave was completed in 1850. Sandstone quarried from Glasgow and limestone from Ireland were used, together with local bluestone. Scott's design, published in the *Illustrated London News*, shows his respect for Pugin and ecclesiology in its reliance on early English sources and in the general simplicity of outline and detail: the St John's cathedral is much closer in treatment to the cathedral at Fredericton than the one in Montreal. The plain effect is emphasized in period illus-

6.37 St James' Cathedral, Toronto, Ontario, begun 1850. City of Toronto Archives/SC497#75

trations of the unfinished state. Work on the transepts and chancel was not undertaken until 1880-5, to designs modified by G.G. Scott, Jr, but another major fire in 1892 burned out the interior entirely. (Little remains of the first Scott's work.) The church was rebuilt soon afterwards—the work was supervised by John Oldrid Scott—and restoration continues to this day. It is still intended that a tower shall be built; the current design is by Sir Giles Gilbert Scott, whose firm continued as cathedral architect until the 1950s. The finishes and fittings are high in quality.[64]

Fire was responsible as well for the building of the new **St James' Cathedral** [6.37], Toronto, the seat of Bishop Strachan. In 1849 the ten-year-old Georgian cathedral was destroyed by a fire that devastated Toronto's business district. Gothic was selected for its replacement, so totally had architectural tastes changed in the intervening decade. Frederic W. Cumberland (1820-81)—a talented engineer and architect who had come to Canada from England in 1847—won the commission to rebuild it over competitors who included Kivas Tully and William Thomas, and he supervised its construction in partnership first with Thomas Ridout (1828-1905) and then with William G. Storm (1826-92), an English-born architect who studied with Thomas.

St James' is very much an urban church, tall and amply scaled. Like the other Canadian cathedrals, it has a nave and side aisles with a single tall tower at the crossing. It also contains a polygonal chancel and small transepts—a plan of which, as we have learned, *The Ecclesiologist* disapproved. The aisles were originally treated as raised galleries to provide more space for rentable pews; the raised floor was subsequently lowered to the level of the nave. The walls are constructed of buff-yellow local brick (known in Toronto as 'white brick') trimmed in Ohio stone, with stone used also for the piers of the nave arcade. The brick is exploited to its fullest, providing sophisticated and vigorous detail. Above the Decorated windows at the line of the eaves and parapets, Cumberland used arched corbels, a detail commonly found on the brick walls of Romanesque buildings.[65]

St James' Cathedral was mostly built in 1850-3, but a shortage of funds left it bereft of a spire and pinnacles. These and the side porches were completed in 1873 by architect Henry Langley (1836-1907). The tall spire and its picturesque silhouette made the cathedral an important local landmark for many years.

The Anglican cathedrals at Fredericton, St John's, and Toronto were built, or were substantially underway, by 1850. All were developed under the direction of English- or Scottish-born bishops who held conservative religious and political beliefs, and all were designed by architects who had recently arrived from—or, in the case of Scott, were still resident in—England. The Church of England created these monuments in the image of the great Gothic ecclesiastical architecture of the past, using them as an opportunity to reaffirm Canada's colonial status and to promote the High Church position. They stand in marked contrast to the Cathedral of the Holy Trinity in Quebec, built nearly a half-century earlier, which had adopted the then-modern Gibbsian box-and-spire design as its way of declaring the same loyalty to the motherland and its established religion.

Whereas in England it was the parish churches that initiated the Victorian phase of the Gothic Revival, in Canada the leadership role was taken by the cathedrals. The reason for this is obvious: England possessed a wealth of Gothic cathedrals that had been standing for centuries, while Canada was a young land with new dioceses. In St John's, Toronto, and Montreal, the Georgian churches that were being used as cathedrals fell victim to fire just as the Gothic Revival became pre-eminent for religious architecture. The bishops' urgent missions to rebuild them correctly went beyond mere utility to the creation of architectural symbols of the Anglican church's dominant position.

Parish churches

Anglican The cathedrals set an example that the smaller parish churches followed. Varied architectural responses occurred. In the more affluent urban parishes, churches were often smaller versions of the cathedrals—sophisticated masonry buildings with forms and details closely modelled on English sources, usually from the Decorated phase of Gothic. But in the rural and less wealthy parishes a serious attempt was made to develop an inexpensive church form that would respond more directly to Canadian conditions while still retaining sufficient links with the Gothic to serve as a symbol of Anglicanism.

In the well-to-do parishes that could afford the cost of masonry construction and the luxury of simulating an English building, the simplest church-form used was the one derived from St Michael's, Long Stanton, and St Anne's Chapel, Fredericton. The rectangular plan, with a nave but no aisles, was usually broken up by a porch or a chancel, and sometimes also by transepts or a tower. The end elevation appears triangular, with the profile of the gable continued down to the ground in the buttresses and often rising to a modest belfry (or 'bell cote'). Toronto's **St Stephen's-in-the-Fields [6.38]**—at the corner of College Street and Bellevue Avenue (beyond the western limits of the city when it was built in 1858)—is a fine example of the type. The architects were the newly formed partnership of Thomas Fuller (1823-98), who had recently arrived from England and Antigua, and Canadian-born Chilion Jones (1835-1912); a year later the partners would earn the right to design the Centre Block of the Parliament Buildings in Ottawa. St Stephen's is built of brick with stone trim (as was St James' Cathedral), and its foundation stone was laid by Bishop Strachan 'with an offering of corn, wine and oil'. It suffered a fire in 1865, but was restored within a year by the firm of Gundry and Langley.[66]

Several variants on this scheme were built, mostly of stone. One is St Alban the Martyr, Ottawa (1866-77), built for a parish made up of a number of Fathers of Confederation and cabinet ministers, begun by Fuller and completed by architect King Arnoldi (1843-1904), who worked with Fuller on the Parliament Buildings. St Alban's occupies a steeply sloping site and has a single transept, providing it with the picturesque asymmetry that was a valued aspect of the Gothic Revival.[67] A smaller version of the type is seen in the Anglican Church of the Messiah, Sabrevois, Quebec, built around 1855 in this Richelieu River community for the congregation of one of the most prosperous Anglican missions in Quebec.[68]

The most picturesque of the group, thanks both to its composition and its setting, is the **Chapel of St James-the-Less [6.39]** in St James Cemetery, Toronto. The chapel was designed by Cumberland and Storm, and built in 1857-61 in the a park-like cemetery laid out in 1842 by John Howard. A stocky belltower and tall, thin broach spire at one corner are balanced by the deep entrance porch. Built of grey sandstone with a slate roof and wooden porch, the church is as appropriate for its rural-like setting—atop a landscaped knoll—as the same architects' upright, urbane design for St James' Cathedral was for its downtown location.[69]

The Anglican Church recognized that a different type of building was indicated for parishes in newly

6.38 St Stephen's-in-the-Fields, Toronto, Ontario, 1858 (restored 1865). Photograph 1880s. MTRL/T-10812.

6.39 (*below*) Chapel of St James-the-Less, St James Cemetery, Toronto, Ontario, 1857-61. Panda Photography Limited.

6.40 (*below right*) St Mary the Virgin, New Maryland, New Brunswick, 1863-4. Photograph by Roger Smith.

developing areas where money or masons were less readily available. In an effort to improve the standards of design, Bishop Medley asked the Ecclesiological Society to provide 'small, plain models for wooden churches in the country'.[70] He offered his own solution in some attractive wooden churches that were erected in his New Brunswick diocese. Several were designed by his son Edward S. Medley (1838-1910)—a talented architectural amateur as well as a priest—and built in the early 1860s.

A short distance south of Fredericton, **St Mary the Virgin [6.40]** (1863-4), New Maryland, New Brunswick—the most striking and individual of the group—is a small aisleless church by Edward Medley with an entrance porch projecting asymmetrically from one side at the west end, and a polygonal chancel with a gable at the east end. The board-and-batten wall construction (consisting of vertical boards whose joints are covered with slender 'batten' strips) is articulated with horizontal mouldings and some diagonal 'stickwork' to provide a lively and varied surface; this treatment is sometimes referred to as the 'stick style'. Inside, the building is plastered in a manner that leaves the structural frame exposed. Bargeboards decorate the west and south gables of the steep roof, and a small spire rises from its ridge, emphasizing the vertical proportions. The design makes a final break with

the church-type that prevailed when the elder Medley came to Canada: the Georgian box with Gothic ornament, characteristic of the Early Gothic Revival and seen at the Goat Island Church in Nova Scotia.[71]

Edward Medley had followed the advice of *The Ecclesiologist*'s correspondent, the Reverend William Scott of Hoxton, who stipulated that a 'wooden church…must show its real construction' and 'discard rigorously and unceremoniously all that is essential to stone.' He wrote of 'that subdued humility, that retiring and unpretending dignity which ought to characterise a wooden church', and stressed that hood mouldings, buttresses, pinnacles, and other 'sham' elements were 'errors to be avoided'.[72]

Other architects also promoted model designs for cheaply built wooden churches that did not lose sight of ecclesiological principles. Frank Wills was one. Although most of his churches, built for parishes as far afield as Maryland and Louisiana, were constructed of stone, he used wood for Grace Church (1849-50, demolished 1951), Albany, New York, and published the design in his widely read book on ecclesiastical architecture. Better known still was Richard Upjohn (1802-78)—the architect of the much admired Trinity Church (1841-6), New York—who, like Wills, was an official architect of the New York Ecclesiological Society. In 1852 Upjohn published a 'Design for a Wooden Church' as a model for young congregations in rural areas—it featured a corner tower and a chancel and was finished in board-and-batten siding—and a number of his designs in this manner were executed in widespread American locations.[73] Vertical proportions, and the use of boards and battens, were also achieving widespread use in secular architecture, to a large measure by means of their promotion for houses in the popular publications of Andrew Jackson Downing (1815-52; see Chapter 11).

Wood was adopted across Canada for Anglican parish churches in the Gothic Revival. Encouraged by Medley's churches, the Atlantic provinces enjoyed a particularly splendid flowering of 'Carpenter's Gothic', in which builders exploited the decorative potential of that material. Skilled carpenters emerged in the West as well. One group of attractive wooden churches that successfully suggested the Gothic style without resorting to any 'sham' elements were those built in British Columbia for Bishop George Hills, including the delightful Christ Church at Hope [**8.40**] of 1860-1.

Roman Catholic While the ecclesiological movement was truly revolutionary, Anglicans did not have a monopoly on the Gothic Revival. Nor was the association of Gothic with a more meaningful kind of Christianity exclusive to the Church of England. A.W.N. Pugin and Cardinal Newman, after all, had converted to Roman Catholicism. As all the Protestant denominations came to adopt the Gothic Revival for their houses of worship, so did the Roman Catholics.

The Catholic Church had been fast off the mark with the Gothic Revival, and it continued to use the style to some extent. Several parish churches in Montreal turned to the style, producing a rather different version from that of the Anglicans. The preferred model was not a low-slung English parish church seen through picturesque eyes; instead, architects often followed the lead of Notre-Dame and other Early Gothic Revival churches by building a tall nave, a curved or polygonal apse, and a central entrance tower—the compositions often stressing verticality through the use of thin, spiky design elements. The buildings that resulted are not nearly so devoted to medieval models as were Anglican churches; if they resemble anything European, the image of a French cathedral is more appropriate than that of an English parish church.

St Patrick's Church [6.41], Montreal, built in 1843-7 to serve the city's rapidly growing Irish-Catholic population, developed naturally out of Notre-Dame. Architect Pierre-Louis Morin (1811-86) was assisted by Jesuit Father Félix Martin (1804-86)—both had come to Canada from France—and the final design decisions were made by their client, Sulpician Father Superior Joseph Vincent Quiblier, who had donated the land. Martin was surely familiar with French Gothic architecture; besides being from France, his brother Arthur had gained fame by publishing a significant book on the windows of Bourges Cathedral.[74]

St Patrick's is rectangular, with a curved apse (a more properly Catholic feature than the rectangular English chancel) and no transepts. Narrow buttress strips are inserted between tall, thin pointed windows. The central entrance tower, which barely projects from the plane of the façade, is sandwiched between a pair of slender octagonal turrets. The exterior severity—necessitated in part by the hard-to-work Montreal greystone and emphasized by the broad, barn-like roof—is relieved somewhat by the central rose window (not visible in the photograph), the crockets along the top of the gable, and the slender buttresses. The crockets

6.41 St Patrick's Church, Montreal, Quebec, 1843-7. Photograph by Brian Merrett.

recall the battlements of churches built a generation earlier, and in many respects the exterior of St Patrick's still looks back to the forms of the Early Gothic Revival.

Since the Sulpician Order had been responsible for building Notre-Dame as well as St Patrick's, it is interesting to notice the similarities between the two churches. St Patrick's seems less self-conscious and has a less-superficial application of ornament, showing the greater acceptance of the Gothic Revival after the passing of two decades. The grand interior, whose execution was supervised in 1848-51 by Victor Bourgeau (the architect, as well, of the present interior of Notre-Dame), features a nave and side aisles, separated by a high arcade with clustered Gothic piers and a ribbed vault, but no galleries. Bourgeau, a leading Quebec architect of the period, was the son of a farmer from Lavaltrie and had trained as a sculptor in the *atelier* Quévillon. He designed some twenty churches and remodelled another twenty-three, and was also the architect of several important institutional buildings. **Église Saint-Pierre-Apôtre** (1851-3) on rue de la Visitation in Montreal, in what was then the city's eastern edge, is his grandest church in the

6.42 Église Saint-Pierre-Apôtre, Montreal, Quebec, 1851-3. HWS/SSS/QUE 92 MO CH 8.01A.

6.43 Interior of Église Saint-Pierre-Apôtre, Montreal, Quebec, 1851-3. HWS/SSS/QUE 92 MO CH8.11.

Gothic Revival [**6.42**]. Gothic features run rampant, from the very French crocketed gable at the entrance to the flying buttresses, which span the gap between the nave walls and the heavy vertical buttresses; there is a gabled window illuminating the aisles between every two buttresses. Medieval precedent is followed in the structure as well as the form, since the ribbed vaults are built of stone and the flying buttresses function as supports, resisting the tendency of the arched vault to spread outwards at its springing. Behind the tall entrance tower the high nave, with full aisles, terminates in a full-height polygonal apse. The florid interior [**6.43**] also features articulated piers, a narrow projecting clerestory gallery, and fine stained-glass windows, anticipating the decorative qualities of Bourgeau's later interior of Notre-Dame [**6.12**]. Despite the many Gothic features, Bourgeau did not achieve in Saint-Pierre-Apôtre the feel of a European building, as did his Anglican colleagues, nor is it likely that he wanted to. Beneath its surface lie

hints of the Quebec parish church tradition: in the clearly articulated tower and nave, the *clocher*-like spire, the prominent shadow line of the eaves, and the concentration of decoration on the interior.[75]

Bourgeau's subsequent churches were increasingly removed from the Gothic. Saint-Joseph de Montréal (1861-2) is closer to the indigenous legacy of Quebec.[76] At **Église St-Barthélémy** (1866-7), Berthier, his monumental elevation [**6.44**] has the two-storey composition and twin towers of churches by Thomas Baillairgé (as at Saint-François-du-Lac, **4.59**); the pilasters, volutes, and pedimented top look also at the Italian Baroque; and the triple-arched entrance, as well as the towers and the niches between them, clearly recall Notre-Dame in Montreal.[77]

Québécois architects rarely came any closer to European Gothic sources than at Saint-Pierre-Apôtre, and they never accepted the Gothic Revival with the gusto of the English. A spirit of rivalry between the two founding nations kept the Gothic

6.44 (*above*) Église St-Barthélémy, Berthier, Quebec, 1866-7. IBC, Fonds Gérard Morisset/ 00616.619.A9.

Revival at somewhat of a distance. Bourgeau and other architects soon turned to the Italian Baroque for inspiration. (That interesting phase in Quebec architectural history will be described below.)

English-speaking Roman Catholics in Ontario and the Atlantic provinces embraced the Gothic Revival with considerably more enthusiasm. Being members of a minority, they probably felt a greater need for assimilation than for self-assertiveness. **St Basil's Church [6.45]** (1855-6), Toronto, which is attached to St Michael's College in the University of Toronto, is a highly competent exercise in the ecclesiological Gothic Revival. Scottish-born architect William Hay (1818-88) had come to North America by way of St John's, where he supervised the construction of George Gilbert Scott's Anglican Cathedral. The original plan for St Basil's provided for a cloister, a form with strong medieval and academic associations. The actual college building is less elaborate, and the junction between it and the church is quite abrupt.[78]

Hay revealed just how thoroughly he had observed Pugin's ethical interpretation of Gothic in an article that he wrote in 1853 to commemorate the death of the English architect:

> Christian architecture is the name given to that particular style of building, commonly called Gothic, which predominated in western Europe

6.45 St Basil's Church, Toronto, Ontario, 1855-6. Panda Photography Limited.

in the Middle Ages. It derived its origin from the efforts of Christians...to embody the principles and characteristics of their faith in the structures which they reared for the services of their religion. The name is used to distinguish it from Pagan [i.e. Classical] Architecture [which continues to be] the favourite style for civil and monumental Architecture...[79]

The non-Anglican Protestant denominations also showed an interest in the serious side of the Gothic Revival, particularly in Ontario. In the third quarter of the century in Toronto, Metropolitan Methodist Church (1870-2) on Queen Street East, Jarvis Street Baptist Church (1874), and the new Old St Andrew's Presbyterian (now United) Church (1877) on Jarvis Street, were all built to similar designs by the firm headed by Henry Langley. (It was known after 1873 as Langley, Langley and Burke: Henry Langley, his brother Edward Langley [d. 1897], and his nephew Edmund Burke [1850-1919]). Historian William Westfall sees an architectural similarity that blurs the sectarian distinctions between the denominations. After citing these churches—he might have added St Michael's Roman Catholic Cathedral (William Thomas, 1845-8, with the spire by Thomas Gundry [1830-69] and Henry Langley, 1865)—he suggests that church-builders were 'refashioning the Gothic into an Ontario style'.[80] While to some extent this was true, and Ontarians certainly revived the Gothic style with an earnestness that was lacking in other provinces, the observation does not take into account the differences in internal arrangements among the denominations, nor the evidently universal popularity of the architectural practices of Henry Langley.

The Gothic Revival found favour among the Protestant denominations in other provinces as well. Churches ran the gamut from large masonry landmarks in cities, such as St Matthew's Presbyterian (now United) Church in Halifax—designed by Cyrus Pole Thomas (of William Thomas and Sons) and built in 1858-9—to delicate exercises in Carpenter's Gothic, such as the United Baptist Church (c. 1862) in St Andrew's, NB, in which the board-and-batten siding and turrets on the picturesque façade contrast with common horizontal clapboard on the other elevations.[81] The Gothic Revival became the preferred mode in the developing West as well; a number of fine Gothic Revival churches there will be examined in the following chapters.

Secular architecture

The principles and forms of the Victorian Gothic Revival were based on Christian beliefs and historic churches, and so it remained primarily a style for religious architecture. Secular building lacked both the doctrine and the large number of extant models to nurture a dogmatic medieval revival. Instead, architects of the mid-nineteenth-century used the Gothic past as a springboard to achieve a freer, more eclectic, style that alluded to historical sources while emphasizing picturesque values. They were free to design buildings according to functional and aesthetic criteria without worrying about the ever-critical Ecclesiological Society's peering over their shoulders.

This attitude is seen at **Angela College [6.46]** in Victoria, a collegiate school for girls that operated under the auspices of the Anglican church, and therefore combined secular and religious programs. Established under the patronage of Baroness Angela Burdett-Coutts and designed by the Victoria architectural firm of John Wright (1830-1915) and George H. Sanders (also spelled Saunders), it was built in 1866 (see also page 393). The architects' proposed elevation shows a broad $2\frac{1}{2}$-storey front on Burdett Avenue, in which picturesque asymmetry is firmly entrenched. The entrance, located well to the right of centre, is announced by a gabled frontispiece and a tower. The gable, without the tower, is repeated at the left end (a secondary entrance projects from that side), and an off-centre spire rises from the roof. The gable peaks, tower, spire, dormer windows, and chimney stacks all break up the silhouette. Pointed arches are used for the entrance porches and second-floor windows, and casement windows divided by vertical mullions illuminate the ground floor. The design is characteristic of the Victorian Gothic Revival in that it does not feature the arbitrary application of Gothic ornament to a Georgian body, as did an Early Gothic Revival house (Elizabeth Cottage) or school (the original Bishop's College), but instead integrates the composition with the ornament. Only the three bays at the right (including the gable and the tower) were actually built. The brick building is now known as Mount St Angela, operated by the Catholic Sisters of St Ann.[82]

Similar intentions, rendered in a different 'dialect', occurred at the **Manoir Campbell [6.47]**, the manor house of the seigneury of Rouville at Mont-Saint-Hilaire, east of Montreal. Major Thomas Edmund Campbell, a London-born career soldier

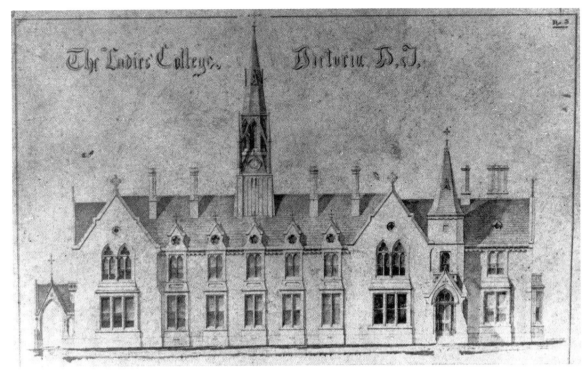

who married into an old French-Canadian family, purchased the property in 1844 from the descendants of the original seigneur. Having acquired a modest manor house that had been built in a classical mode some time between 1811 and 1841, Campbell before long determined to transform it into a country house in the Gothic mode. He re-

6.47 Manoir Campbell, Saint-Hilaire de Rouville, Quebec, 1853-60. Photograph 1980. Public Works Canada, Heritage Recording and Technical Data Services/05573001300125.

6.46 Angela College, Victoria, British Columbia. Proposed elevation by Wright and Sanders, 1866. BCARS/80045.

tained the Montreal architectural firm of John William Hopkins (1825-1905), Frederick Lawford (1821-66), and James Nelson (1830-1919), who undertook major alterations between 1853 and 1860. As at Angela College, the entrance is off-centre and is emphasized by a gabled frontispiece; here it features a bay window over the low-arched doorway and a pair of turrets serving as 'bookends'. A similarly scaled gable marks the bay on the right, balanced—but not duplicated—on the left by a two-storey bay window capped by a gabled dormer. Flat hood mouldings (also called 'labels') project over the casement windows. The decorative vocabulary is based on the Tudor phase of English architecture, which occurred at the end of the Gothic period. This variant of the Gothic Revival would become popular at the beginning of the twentieth century.[83]

As balanced asymmetry inspired by the picturesque gained currency over the formal symmetry of the Georgian era, irregular plans in the shape of an 'L' or a 'T' obtained broad acceptance. A Gothic Revival house of this kind, with a particularly interesting history, is **Earnscliffe [6.48]**, near Sussex Drive in Ottawa, built in 1856 or 1857 for John

297

6.48 Earnscliffe, Ottawa, Ontario, *c*. 1857.
CIHB/061070044000012.

MacKinnon, a son-in-law and business partner of mason, miller, and landowner Thomas MacKay (page 206). After MacKinnon's death in 1866 the house was purchased by engineer Thomas Coltrin Keefer (page 208), another MacKay son-in-law. A succession of residents followed. The most notable was Prime Minister Sir John A. Macdonald, who rented the house in 1870-1 and bought it a dozen years later, naming it Earnscliffe ('earn' means 'eagle' in Old English) and living here until his death in 1891. Macdonald extended the house in 1888 to designs by William Hodgson (1827-1904). Since 1930 it has been the residence of the British High Commissioner.[84]

Located on a picturesque site overlooking the Ottawa River, Earnscliffe has two principal wings that intersect at right-angles. The cut-limestone walls are accented with white wood trim that includes ornate bargeboard beneath the eaves and hood mouldings over the windows. The main entrance and the top window in one of the two façade gables have arched openings. The house is Gothic Revival more by association than in the spare use of

historical ornament, a characteristic of many domestic buildings after 1850. Lady Agnes Macdonald was very fond of 'the pretty, irregular large grey stone house which is now my home'—'irregular' being a reference to its picturesque qualities—and took great pleasure in the large garden and 2-acre (.8-hectare) grounds.[85]

Smaller houses also adopted features of the Gothic Revival. Some, such as The Cone at Port Hope, Ontario (begun 1858; **11.12**), have the pointed windows, board-and-batten siding, and vertical proportions of churches of the time; while others are related to the style more by suggestion. A profusion of English and American architectural books provided models for house-builders: the publications and the houses are discussed in Chapter 11.

In secular building, the Victorian Gothic Revival quickly evolved into High Victorian Gothic, a phase that offered a freer and more eclectic blend of historical sources, and whose name reflects the greater latitude in design by omitting the word 'revival'. The most important creation in the style was the Parliamentary complex in Ottawa (begun 1859); the buildings and the style will be described in Chapter 10.

Neoclassicism

The architecture of classical antiquity, which had long provided an ongoing source for building design, also experienced a determined revival. Once again romanticism provided the impetus for the rediscovery and renewed appreciation of the civilizations (and buildings) of Rome and, especially, Greece. Eighteenth-century European *cognoscenti* appreciated that the ancient era was distinct from the Renaissance, and that the classical cultures had disintegrated during the Middle Ages and been revived in the fifteenth century. The romantic spirit of the eighteenth century found a particularly satisfying outlet in archaeology—which is, after all, an all-consuming search for the past. Antiquarians and architects from a number of countries measured, drew, and published the buildings of the ancient world. Among the pioneers were the French scholar Julien David Leroy (1724-1803), whose *Les Ruines des plus beaux monuments de la Grèce* appeared in 1758, and the Englishmen James Stuart (1713-88) and Nicholas Revett (1720-1804), who published the first volume of their influential masterpiece, *The Antiquities of Athens*, in 1762. By the end of the century, folios of this kind had proliferated to the point where images of the ruins of Paestum, Palmyra, Baalbec, Split, and countless other sites were readily available in libraries.

European architectural theory of the time developed a rational, fundamentalist streak that was complementary to the nascent Greek Revival. Its spokesmen encouraged the reduction of architectural form to only those components that were required for structural and functional purposes. The French theorist Abbé Marc-Antoine Laugier (1713-69), whose *Essai sur l'architecture* (1753; first English edition 1755) was widely read in both France and England, went back beyond the Greek temple to depict an imagined little rustic hut, which he declared was the model from which all architecture was derived. Praising the directness of design represented by a structure composed only of columns, entablature, and gable, Laugier concluded that 'one should never put anything in a building for which one cannot give a solid reason.'[86]

The increased knowledge of ancient architecture led to its motifs' being incorporated into buildings in the style that we call Neoclassicism (a word that means 'new'—or 'renewed'—classicism). Some buildings in the manner made a distinct break with the Georgian-Palladian classicism. Such is the case

with Governor Simcoe's Castle Frank in Toronto (1795-6; **4.27**), whose simple composition was based on a Roman temple (although Elizabeth Simcoe called it a 'Grecian Temple'), with the columns and walls made of rustic logs. The spirit of romanticism is present in the picturesque landscape setting and the fact that the source of the building lay in the distant, golden past. The close relationship between Neoclassicism and rationalism is evident.

This kind of conceit may have been feasible in a private residence or a garden ornament, but it was far less practicable in an urban public building. For this reason, Neoclassical architecture generally presents a series of compromises with the ideals of the style, especially in Canada. Europe boasted antiquaries and connoisseurs who had visited and sketched the ancient ruins, and the United States adopted Neoclassicism as a symbol of its young republic; but in Canada the style had no experiential, theoretical, or ideological basis. Consequently, its more literal use never became firmly rooted. The major contribution of Neoclassicism in Canada was to reinforce the Georgian classical tradition at a time when it was being seriously threatened by the Gothic Revival.

Two strains of Neoclassicism appear in Canadian architecture in the second quarter of the nineteenth century. One, foreshadowed at Castle Frank, reveals the lessons of archaeology and rationalism directly. Buildings in this mode offer explicit renditions of classical models and reduce their components to columns, entablatures, and gables. The immediate source for Canadian architecture of this kind was found more in the buildings of the United States than in European publications and theory.

The other, less dogmatic, strain introduces Neoclassical elements into the Georgian-Palladian tradition, using colonnades, porticoes, and other features that are based more closely than previously on classical sources, but do not try to simulate antiquity. The Colonial Building at St John's, Newfoundland (James Purcell, 1847-50; **3.7**), provides a good illustration. At first glance it seems to be designed in the Georgian classical manner. However, when it is contrasted with the Province Houses in Halifax (1811-19; **3.53**) and Charlottetown (1843-8; **3.54**), it becomes evident that the six-column Ionic portico at St John's is far more dominant by dint of its rising a full two storeys (rather than being supported on a ground-floor rusticated arcade) and of its larger scale in proportion to the overall façade. This second strain does not represent a break with architectural currents so much as a modification of them, and it merged far more readily into the mainstream of Canadian architecture.

Leslie Maitland, the author of *Neoclassical Architecture in Canada* (1984), describes the first strain as the more 'advanced, rational side' of Neoclassicism, while she calls the latter its 'more conservative branch'. We maintain this distinction. Maitland also identifies American and British versions of Neoclassicism as corresponding to these two strains; but, as we shall see, the sources are not quite so clearly distinguished.[87]

Advanced Neoclassicism

A number of temple-like Neoclassical buildings were erected in eastern and central Canada, most of them in the Maritime Provinces, where American influence was strongest. Two wooden public buildings of this kind in Saint John, New Brunswick, were introduced in the last chapter: the Germaine Street Methodist Chapel (1839; **5.45**); and the Mechanics' Institute (1840; **5.46**). Both present austere gable ends to the street, with a row of columns or pilasters supporting an entablature and a triangular pediment—the elements that Abbé Laugier said belong on a building. The Germaine Street Chapel has pilasters, rendered in a Doric or Tuscan order that has been so simplified as to obscure the classical source. (Laugier disapproved of pilasters, preferring the unambiguous expression of support provided by the column, but it is unlikely that the designer of the Chapel had read the French theorist.) The Mechanics' Institute had four Greek Ionic columns 'in antis', meaning that the columns are inserted between the pilaster-faced ends of the side walls, rather than projecting as a distinct portico (in which case they are called 'prostyle'). The columns are also described as being 'engaged', since they touch the wall behind them. (The Greek Ionic order differs from Roman Ionic in that the 'echinus'—the bottom moulding of the 'cushion' that unites the two spiral volutes—has a curved rather than a straight profile.)

Freestanding columns appeared on the **Bank of New Brunswick** (*c*. 1826) in Saint John, the first chartered bank in Canada [**6.49**]. (It received its charter in 1820, two years before the Bank of Montreal, although the latter had been organized earlier.) Built of stone rather than wood, the bank presented an austere temple-front to Prince Wil-

6.49 Bank of New Brunswick, Saint John, New Brunswick, *c*. 1826. Photograph *c*. 1865, New Brunswick Museum/x11178.

liam Street. The Neoclassical theme was reinforced by a balustrade at the base of the columns and by the classically derived window and door surrounds (seen also on the Germaine Street Chapel and Mechanics' Institute in Saint John).[88] The bank, and most other Neoclassical buildings in Saint John, were destroyed by the fire of 1877.

The temple-form had first appeared in North American bank design only a few years earlier, at the Second Bank of the United States (later the Custom House) in Philadelphia, designed by William Strickland (1788-1854) and built in 1818-24. The directors of the Philadelphia bank had specified that the building should exhibit 'a chaste imitation of Grecian Architecture, in its simplest and least expensive form'; Strickland responded with a design based on the Parthenon in Athens, as illustrated in Stuart and Revett's *Antiquities of Athens*.[89] The principal motivation for the directors' choice of the Greek Revival was a romantic and aesthetic one, reflecting the infatuation with the Greek past shown by the Philadelphia establishment, particularly Nicholas Biddle, a Grecophile who was also a director and sometime president of the bank. A second, more implicit, reason for the style was the intended association of the institution of banking—then in its youth, and still seeking universal trust—with the strength and longevity of Greek architecture, which had, after all, stood for more than two millennia. This forceful association ensured that banks would retain allusions to classical temples for many generations to come. (The relationship would be notably pronounced at the beginning of the twentieth century with the renewal of classicism inspired by the teachings of the École des Beaux-Arts in Paris.)

Neoclassicism did not, however, gain acceptance for banks elsewhere in Canada during this period. The first Bank of Montreal (1818-19) on Place d'Armes in Montreal was built in a conservative Georgian manner [5.52]. When a new Bank of Montreal was built next door in 1845-8, Neoclassicism had become more widely accepted for banks. Architect John Wells's design featured a portico of six Corinthian columns rising a full two storeys, with a low third floor concealed within a high parapet, along the top of which was a row of Greek 'acroteria'—floral ornaments that create a broken silhouette not unlike Gothic battlements. This façade survives, although everything behind it was rebuilt at the height of Beaux-Arts influence by McKim, Mead and White [10.49]. The pedimented building seen beyond the Wells bank in 5.52 is the City Bank (1845), by the architects (Henry H. or James S.) McFarlane and Goodlatte Richardson Browne (c. 1813-55), which adapts the Greek orders in a two-tiered portico, with Doric on the ground floor and Ionic above.[90]

The temple-form appeared in other types of public buildings as well, mostly in the Maritimes—but only on a limited basis. The **Queen's County Courthouse** (1854) in Liverpool, Nova Scotia, is a handsome, and unique, instance of the temple's being used for this purpose [**6.50**]. Designed by local carpenter William G. Hammond and built in 1854 by George W. Boehner, it translates the Greek Doric order—characterized by its baseless columns (the square blocks beneath the columns are plinths, as distinguished from the circular bases seen on Roman Doric columns)—into superbly crafted wood. The Greek models, however, have been adapted, since the columns are spread wider apart, allowing *two* triglyphs (the three-bar vertical motif on the entablature) between each pair of columns, rather than the classically correct *one*. This triglyph frieze continues around the sides of the building. Behind the columns, the wood walls have been scored to resemble blocks of stone; the sides are covered with shingles. The interior contains a large courtroom with three chambers behind it: one each for the judge (in the centre, behind his bench), the jury, and the lawyers. The jail, which had formed a part of earlier courthouses, was accommodated in a separate building, a trend that began in the 1830s.[91]

6.50 Queen's County Courthouse, Liverpool, Nova Scotia, 1854. HWS/SSS/NS 81 LI CO 1.04.

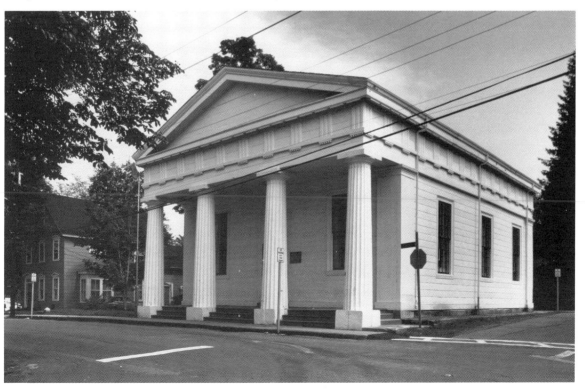

At the **Garrison Chapel** (1844-6) in Halifax, two Greek Doric columns *in antis* are flanked by portions of wall containing pairs of windows—the lower ones with pedimented heads—and framed by pilasters [**6.51**]. As the church was designed by a Colonel Calder of the Royal Engineers, it seems that the advanced mode of Neoclassicism had British as well as American sources of inspiration. The Halifax *Herald* reminisced in 1896 that the chapel had been the object of 'considerable criticism...for its lack of special ecclesiastical distinction' (surely meaning that it was not in the Gothic Revival!), but concluded that 'the building has thoroughly served its purpose'. It burned down in 1928.[92]

Other examples of *in-antis* and prostyle temple-like public buildings were erected in the Maritimes, but they were relatively uncommon—and were more so in central Canada. Toronto's **Seventh Post Office** (Cumberland and Ridout, 1851; altered by Henry Langley, 1874)—now the offices of the Argus Corporation—on Toronto Street has four Greek Ionic columns *in antis*, but features a flat parapet surmounted by a coat of arms, rather than

6.51 Garrison Chapel, Halifax, Nova Scotia, 1844-6. Photograph *c*. 1865. PANS/Joseph Rogers Collection/N-7368.

6.52 Seventh Post Office, Toronto, Ontario, 1851. Panda Photography Limited.

6.53 Temple Grove, Montreal, Quebec, 1836. Photograph *c*. 1870. MMCH.

the more common pedimented gable [6.52]. It was almost as if Toronto could not force itself to accept the gabled temple because of its Maritime connections.[93]

True Greek temples were surrounded on four sides by columns, but this arrangement hardly suited the requirements of Canadian urban architecture or the rigours of the climate, and so the Roman temple-form, with a portico only on one or both ends, provided the customary model. One of the few Canadian buildings to feature a portico on three sides (nearly as many as the Greek temple) was **Temple Grove** [6.53], the aptly named residence of John S. McCord on Côte des Neiges on the slope of Montreal's Mount Royal. A temple-like block with unfluted baseless Greek Doric columns—considered to be the most primitive (and particularly virile) among the classical orders—projected from a more conventionally designed pavilion. Set in a verdant and picturesque landscape, the house possessed a superb view of the city and the St Lawrence River. It was erected in 1836 by builder Paul Adams; the name of the architect is not known. It would be interesting to learn whether McCord was an enthusiastic Grecophile in the mould of Nicholas Biddle, who, also in 1836, added a portico based on the Theseion in Athens to Andalusia, his Philadelphia estate.[94]

If John McCord may be presumed to have been something of a romantic, his son, David Ross McCord, certainly was one. When David inherited Temple Grove in 1865, he made small but significant alterations that converted it into a shrine to the Battle of the Plains of Abraham, in which his grandfather (John's father) had fought. In front of the house he erected a terrace, which he dedicated to General James Wolfe (it is barely visible above the shrubbery in the photograph of *c*. 1870), and the terrace was accessed by sixteen steps, commemorating the sixteen regiments that took part in the battle. The house and main gate were forty paces apart, the same distance as between the English and the French armies. The younger McCord assembled an important collection of 80,000 Canadian historical artifacts, which he willed to McGill University; this led to the creation of the McCord Museum. Temple Grove was demolished in 1930s, after McCord's death. The great collection of photographs of Montreal's renowned Notman Studio, including the portrait of Temple Grove, forms part of today's McCord Museum of Canadian History.

The alterations to Temple Grove allude to another outlet for Neoclassicism—monuments to military heroes. The **Nelson Column** in Montreal was erected in 1809, only four years after Lord Nelson's decisive (and fatal) naval victory over France and Spain at the Battle of Trafalgar. British architect Robert Mitchell produced a tall stone column in the Tuscan order, which theorists considered to be the strongest and therefore the most appropriate of the classical orders for this purpose. The column—in Place Jacques Cartier, adjacent to the City Hall, seen here in an early photograph [10.30]—is set on a pedestal with circular relief panels commemorating three of Nelson's victorious battles, and wreaths and other decoration, all cast in London in artificial Coade stone; and a likeness of Nelson stands on the top. (The statue deteriorated and was replaced with a replica in 1981.)[95]

Its source is the free-standing monumental column of ancient Rome, the best known of which is Trajan's Column. Mitchell's immediate model, however, would have been the Monument (1671-7) in London that marks the spot where the Great Fire of 1666 began—a tall Doric column designed by Sir Christopher Wren, or his close associate Robert Hooke. Montreal's Nelson Column is but one in a series of monumental columns of this type erected at the beginning of the nineteenth century. Among them are the Nelson Columns in Edinburgh (1805) and Dublin (1808); the Colonne Vendôme in Paris (1806-10), which bears the figure of Nelson's prey, Napoleon; and the Washington Monument in Baltimore, Maryland (1815-29).[96] (The most famous Nelson Column—in Trafalgar Square, London—was built later, in 1839-42.) One may argue whether they are Neoclassical gestures, reviving a building-form from antiquity; or whether those in Britain and Canada are more properly described as Georgian, since they approach antiquity through the intercession of a 'modern' British architect. The differentiation, however, is moot, since the ancient Roman source would have been apparent to all knowledgeable observers.

The same conceit lay behind the first Brock Monument (1824-6) on the site of the Battle of Queenston Heights, Ontario, designed by Scottish-trained civil engineer Francis Hall, who submitted a Gothic design as well as the approved Tuscan one. The column was damaged by explosives in 1840, in an early instance of political terrorism. Its replacement was at first intended to be an obelisk 'in the Egyptian style' (although Rome had its obelisks as well, including the one in front of St Peter's)—a

6.54 Second Brock Monument, Queenston, Ontario, 1853-6. Photograph 1959. Archives of Ontario/RG 9-129-2, neg. 11-E-1659-2.

model earlier followed at the Bunker Hill Monument in the US (1825-42). This plan was given up in favour of a fluted column 'of the Roman Composite Order', raised on a high pedestal and supporting a colossal statue of Sir Isaac Brock with his right arm outstretched in the manner of a familiar Roman statue of Apollo. The architect of the second **Brock Monument** [6.54] was William Thomas, recently arrived from England; it was erected in 1853-6 and dedicated in 1859, after the 40-acre (16-hectare) grounds had been landscaped. The structure is an impressive 187 feet (57 m) high, taller than any in Europe other than Wren's Monument—which was a source for them all.[97]

The advanced and rational—one might also say radical—branch of Neoclassicism represented by temples and columns gained only limited acceptance in Canada. The McCords might try to make a temple symbolize Canadian history, but this was a facile gesture that would have held the interest of only a few connoisseurs. Lacking the political associations that it achieved in the American republic, 'hard-line' Neoclassicism had little future in Canada.

Conservative Neoclassicism

Canadians were far more receptive to the more conservative strain of Neoclassicism, in which elements derived from the new study of Greek and Roman antiquity became prominent features in buildings that otherwise continued the tradition of Georgian and Palladian classicism. This manner reached Canada directly from Britain, although still with some American influence, and reflected the impact of European Neoclassicism on the persistent British tradition of public building. The most common arrangement was to use a conspicuous Greek (or Roman) Revival portico as a central focus; another, more indirect, technique was to introduce ornament gleaned from modern publications of ancient architectural forms, or to make subtle changes to the composition that drew it somewhat apart from the Georgian heritage. While the association with buildings of the remote past was still intended, it was tempered by the greater continuity with more recent architecture.

The difference between the two kinds of Neoclassicism is seen by contrasting the conservative **Charlotte County Courthouse** (1839-40) in St Andrews, New Brunswick, which is typical of several built in the Maritimes at this time, with the more advanced Queen's County Courthouse in Liverpool, Nova Scotia [**6.50**], which had no imitators. The St Andrews building [**6.55**] features a four-column Tuscan portico (with the royal coat of arms in the pediment) on the long side of a one-storey gabled block—a composition that is similar to that of a generation of Georgian buildings, and quite unlike the temple-like end portico of the Liverpool courthouse. Like the Colonial Building at St John's [**3.17**], to which it is a smaller and simpler cousin, the Charlotte County Courthouse follows the tried-and-true British imperial tradition, modifying it only by the greater prominence given to the portico and by other classical detail. Builder Thomas Berry evidently recognized this, because he went beyond the contract plans and placed pilasters at the corners and beside the entrance door—incurring additional expenses that forced him to petition the legislature for more money (which he was granted). A row of large and handsome shuttered windows illuminates the interior, which consists of an entrance hall, the courtroom beyond, and offices for the judge and secretary. The building was constructed of local pine set on a stone foundation.[98]

6.55 Charlotte County Courthouse, St Andrews, New Brunswick, 1839-40. HWS/SSS/NB81 SA CO 1.01.

6.56 Bonsecours Market, Montreal, Quebec, 1844-7.
Photograph by Alexander Hamilton, *c*. 1870. NAC/C-24392.

A number of other public buildings of the time also represented a Georgian-Neoclassical fusion. The Kingston City Hall (1843-4; **4.41**) has a large Tuscan portico and a central domed cupola. It further deviates from some Palladian models in the accent on the end pavilions, which project forward and are raised with parapets: an emphasis on the extremities was characteristic of conservative Neoclassicism. The local newspaper recognized the innovative qualities of the new City Hall, describing it as being in the 'Roman Style of Architecture'.[99]

Similar in design is the large **Bonsecours Market** (1844-7) in Montreal, designed by William Footner (1799-1872). A mammoth 500 feet (152.5 m) wide, two storeys high throughout, and built of Montreal greystone [**6.56**], it too has a tall central dome and portico, this time with baseless Greek Doric columns, and with windows that are covered with flat heads (associated with Greece) rather than the circular Roman arches seen at Kingston. The columns were fabricated of cast iron and imported from England. Eager to identify a classical source, an early writer noted that 'the proportions of the [front and rear] porticoes are taken from those of the Propylaea of Athens'. The end pavilions are again emphasized, this time with the addition of attic storeys with gables on both the front and the rear (facing the harbour).[100]

6.57 Martock, near Windsor, Nova Scotia, 1790s, major alterations *c*. 1845. Photograph *c*. 1865, PANS/N-4281.

There was a public market here until 1964. The building also served as the Parliament of the United Canadas for a short while after the Parliament Building in Montreal was burned in 1849; and beginning in 1852 it hosted a number of municipal functions, for which there was a concert hall, a reception hall, and a magistrates' court. (These rooms were created by George Browne, the architect of the Kingston City Hall.) It is now given over to municipal offices. The façade on busy rue Saint-Paul is seen in the photograph, taken around 1870, with Chapelle Notre-Dame-de-Bonsecours (1771-3) beyond. Across the street, in the foreground, is Rasco's Hotel (1834-6), which was celebrated as the finest hotel in Canada.

Large Neoclassical porticoes found their way on to houses too. At **Martock** [**6.57**], near Windsor, Nova Scotia, Colonel Edward K. S. Butler transformed his family's two-storey frame house, built in the 1790s, into a grand classical manor. Around 1845 he built a four-column Ionic porch the height of the house: each column was made from a single tree and encased in wood carved to produce the flutes (vertical grooves). He added at either side a pair of lower wings with smaller Ionic columns. (Another wing appears at the rear.) The composition may have been inspired either by a Palladian house with low wings or by a Greek source such as the Erectheion at Athens, which has a pair of flanking porches. The relative historical accuracy is evident when it is contrasted with the Georgian Mount Uniacke [3.49] nearby. Martock has undergone many changes, such as the removal of the wings and the lowering of the roof, but it remains a gracious and imposing residence.[101]

6.58 St Andrew's Presbyterian Church, Niagara-on-the-Lake, Ontario, 1831. Photograph by Ralph Greenhill.

The Georgian-Neoclassical fusion may be seen as well in churches—perhaps best in one of the great monuments of the time, the lovely **St Andrew's Presbyterian Church** (1831) in Niagara-on-the-Lake, which was part of the rebuilding of that town after its destruction by the Americans in 1813. The red-brick church [6.58] has a tower with its tall spire over the entrance, and the delicate interior has a gallery on slender columns, in the manner of the Gibbs-inspired Georgian churches of the previous century, such as Holy Trinity Cathedral [4.51] in Quebec. But the façade differs from Canadian precedent in its six-column baseless Doric portico, whose pediment continues the roof-line to pro-

6.59 Commercial Bank of the Midland District, Toronto, Ontario, 1843-5. Panda Photography Limited.

duce a temple-church with a tall spire. (The spire was originally higher; it burned in 1854 and was replaced by Kivas Tully.) The exterior and interior designs of St Andrew's resemble—and were probably adapted from—plates in an American pattern-book: the sixth edition of *The American Builder's Companion* (1827) by the prolific and popular American architect, Asher Benjamin (1773-1845). The book, however, illustrated a Roman Doric portico, and St Andrew's adopted what was identified on a drawing as 'Cooper's Plan, the Grecian Doric'. This was surely a reference to James Cooper, a member of the congregation; he is presumed to have been the designer, and John Edward Clyde and Saxton Burr are known to have been the builders. Cooper changed other of Benjamin's details, such as omitting blind arcades along the sides and substituting flat for round heads over the doorways, all of which make the design less Roman. The plan was also altered so that the pulpit was at the entrance end, in keeping with the practice of the Church of Scotland, as determined by the minister, the Reverend Robert McGill. The exquisite woodwork is seen best in the portico, and in the tracery of the large windows.[102]

The work of Asher Benjamin—the Niagara church, which he influenced, can stand as an example—illustrates the cross-over from Georgian to Neoclassical. His earlier books (the first was published in 1797) were firmly rooted in Georgian design derived from British pattern-books, drawing on authors such as Sir William Chambers, William Pain, and Peter Nicholson; but he became increasingly aware, first, of the American Federal style, and then of the Greek Revival. The latter is particularly evident in Benjamin's *The Practical House Carpenter* (1830), which illustrates many Greek Revival designs, and states that 'the Roman school of Architecture has been entirely changed for Grecian.'[103]

Perhaps the most American of the spired temple-churches in Canada is Plymouth Trinity Church (1848) in Sherbrooke, Quebec, which has two Greek Doric columns *in antis*. It was built for a congregation composed of many people from Massachusetts, who named the church after the first settlement in New England.[104]

A final version of Neoclassicism appears in buildings whose principal development from the Georgian manner lies in the greater intensity and historical accuracy of the ornament, *vis-à-vis* architecture of the previous generation. The **Commercial Bank of the Midland District** (1843-5) on Wellington Street West in Toronto, designed by William Thomas, features what at first resembles a Palladian elevation in the manner of Government House in

Halifax (1800-7; **3.52**), with a rusticated ground floor, and two storeys of smooth ashlar masonry above, united by a single order of pilasters [**6.59**]. The composition and details of the two, however, are quite different. Whereas Government House placed an emphasis on the centre, with receding wings, in the Commercial Bank it is the outermost of the principal five bays that project and contain a concentration of decorative features, as well as two entrances (with steps)—although they are balanced somewhat by the raised parapet in the centre, topped by a golden globe. (The sixth bay on the left is recessed and not intended to be read as part of the composition; indeed, it was not visible when the building was seen from the east.)

The bank resembled a Roman or Italian Renaissance *palazzo*—appropriately, because of the association with classical stability and the great banking families of the Renaissance. There is profuse detail: carved leaf ornament (acroteria) on the ends of the parapet; 'anthemia' (ornament based on the honeysuckle) in the wrought-iron balconies of the principal storey; the stylized acanthus ornament of the pilaster capitals; and the 'eared' surrounds—so-called because the lateral projections near the top of the entrance, and of the window (a former entrance) that mirrors it on the left, resemble ears. The façade (and the pilastered mantel in the principal private office) surely found their sources in published pattern-books based on Greek and Roman buildings. In this century the building was turned into offices (and the entrance on the left into a window). But in the recent development for Bell Canada Enterprises that transformed the block from Wellington to Front (between Yonge and Bay), the façade of the Commercial Bank—including the sixth bay—was dismantled, restored (with the original two entrances), and moved some twenty yards to the south. It now fronts a modern office building within the galleria of BCE Place.[105]

Better documented in its debts to specific pattern-books is Quebec's **Music Hall** (Academy of Music, 1851-3), built on rue Saint-Louis in the capital city to designs by Charles Baillairgé (1826-1906), another member of that great artistic dynasty (the son of a cousin of Thomas Baillairgé). Used for concerts, plays, banquets, and balls, the Music Hall [**6.60**] was built by a private association led by Archibald Campbell, a notary and arts enthusiast. Like Toronto's Commercial Bank, it is a stone building based on the five-bay Georgian elevation. The Music Hall is light and delicate, with an emphasis on the central bays, whereas the compo-

6.60 Music Hall (Academy of Music), Quebec City, Quebec, 1851-3. Photograph by A. Charlebois. NAC/PA-24091.

sition of the bank is heavy and intense (their respective designs, in other words, fit their use). Architectural historian Christina Cameron has shown that Baillairgé drew heavily from ideas he found in the books of American architect and writer Minard Lafever (1798-1854), although she notes that Baillairgé never copied the source exactly. She traces the exterior ground-floor Greek order and the first-storey windows with their rosettes, as well as several interior decorative motifs, to plates in *The Beauties of Modern Architecture* (1835) and other books by Lafever. The richly finished interior was gutted by fire in 1900, but is seen well in an 1871 illustration [**6.61**] of a ball honouring the 60th Regiment: it had a coved ceiling, with banded plasterwork, church-like galleries supported by Doric columns, and the stage at the end was framed by an arched proscenium. The room was painted in white and gold (like Quebec churches), accented by the crimson curtain and touches of blue.[106]

The conservative strain of the Neoclassical style gradually blended into the mainstream of Canadian architecture. It was safe and comfortable, adaptable to buildings large and small, and therefore well suited to the cautious attitude of Canadian architects. The buildings illustrated have demonstrable links with the revival of Greek and Roman architecture, and therefore fit easily under the rubric of Neoclassicism. But many classically derived buildings of the time do not lend themselves so readily to this kind of analysis. As Neoclassicism and the other revival styles became a part of the vernacular, they drifted away from the consistent form and ideology that were displayed in the hands of trained architects.

Other Revival Styles

In the middle years of the nineteenth century the Gothic Revival and Neoclassical styles dominated Canadian architecture, but they were not the only revivals being practised at the time. Architects also experimented with a number of other historical models. Among the styles of antiquity, Egyptian architecture occasionally provided a source for new design, although with only limited success. We have seen that the Egyptian obelisk was considered a model for the second Brock Monument—although in the end the Roman column was adopted. One Egyptian Revival structure that was built in Canada was the Union Suspension Bridge (1843; **5.19**), linking Ottawa with Hull, which used the 'massive' antique manner to inspire confidence in the same way that banks relied on Greek and Roman forms. An early building in the style was a synagogue on rue Chenneville in Montreal (*c.* 1835?; demolished), described by Newton Bosworth in 1839 as being 'a fine specimen of the Egyptian style of architecture'. A somewhat crude line engraving by P. Christie shows it as having a temple form with two columns *in antis*; the windows, however, have 'battered' profiles—that is,

6.61 Interior of the Music Hall, Quebec City, Quebec, 1851-3. From *Canadian Illustrated News*, 25 November 1871, NAC/C-56604.

their sides taper in towards the top—a shape characteristic of the walls of Egyptian temples; this feature evidently was sufficient to create the link with that Mediterranean land.[107]

Other synagogues followed the same sources, apparently feeling that Egypt was sufficiently close to the Holy Land—and sufficiently distinct from Greek Revival churches—to be associated with Judaism. The **Shearith Israel Synagogue** [6.62] in Montreal, built in 1887-90 (and demolished *c*. 1960) for the oldest Jewish congregation in Canada (founded in 1768), was more determined in its Egyptian Revivalism. It not only incorporated the battered (sloping) form for the windows and doors, but also featured a portico of four lotus columns that had the inverted bell shape ('campaniform') capital with palm-frond patterns found in Egyptian colonnades.[108]

A medieval style that enjoyed a limited revival in the middle of the nineteenth century was the Romanesque, the form that preceded the Gothic. It too was used occasionally for synagogues, as at Temple Emanuel in Victoria (1863; **8.31**), in another attempt to distance Jewish houses of worship from Christian churches.

The first Romanesque Revival—so called to differentiate it from the Richardsonian Romanesque of the 1880s and 1890s (see Chapter 10)—achieved a significant triumph at **University College** (1856-9) in Toronto, the first teaching college in the University of Toronto [6.63]. Founded in 1853, it did not have a home until the Governor General, Sir Edmund Walker Head, authorized a huge government grant (£75,000) for a building in 1856. The commission was given to Cumberland and Storm, but Head, a scholar with a great interest in public architecture, involved himself in the design. He envisaged a truly 'modern' building, meaning that historical sources would be drawn upon to express the function of the university in the context of a picturesque interpretation of the past. John Langton, vice-chancellor of the University, reported that the choice of style was not easy:

... Cumberland drew a first sketch of a Gothic building, but the Gov. would not hear of Gothic and recommended Italian, shewing us an example of the style, a palazzo at Sienna which, if he were not Gov. Gen. and had written a book on art, I should have called one of the ugliest buildings I ever saw. However after a week's absence the Gov. came back with a new idea, it was to be Byzantine; and between them they concocted a most hide-

ous elevation...the Gov. was absent on a tour for several weeks during which we polished away almost all traces of Byzantium and got a hybrid with some features of Norman, of early English etc. with faint traces of Byzantium and the Italian palazzo, but altogether a not unsightly building and on his return His Excellency approved.

This kind of architectural schizophrenia was something new. University College marks the transition from the initial phase of Victorian revivals, in which one style was used consistently and unquestioningly, to the more freely eclectic High Victorian style, which will be discussed at length in Chapter 10. The building that emerged was primarily in the mode that Langton called Norman, and that we now call Romanesque. Langton found a good word to say about the ensuing stylistic compromise, noting that we 'may call it the Canadian style'.[109]

The architects' immediate source of inspiration was the University Museum at Oxford, then under construction, and the writings of its sponsor, John Ruskin (for both, see **10.4**); but they were also drawn to other buildings, including the Smithsonian Institution in Washington (by James Renwick, 1846-51). The Romanesque Revival not only lent itself to intricate ornamentation and patterning in stone- and brick-work, but also produced a suitably picturesque silhouette of towers, long roofs, gables, and chimneys in University Park, an area of dense foliage north of College Street that was surrounded (except to the north) by the built-up city.

The south front of University College, built around three sides of a quadrangle, is dominated by a massive central tower 100 feet (30.5 m) high over the main entrance, with the conical top of a round stair-turret rising above a corner. Other towers mark lesser entrances. Beige-grey stone moulded in seven different shapes (and somewhat darkened with time) is complemented by brick in a matching colour. The brick-work—mostly on the west front and the back—creates many variegated patterns, subtly increasing the textural richness of the detailing, which was an important aesthetic objective of Ruskin and High Victorian designers.

The glory of the building is the profusion and variety of its superbly crafted ornament, much of it sculptural, which seems to have been designed mostly by Storm, although some drawings of sculptural detail were signed by the clerk of the works, John Morris (d. 1904). A number of skilled craftsmen have been identified, including Charles Emil Zollikofer (b. 1829/30), a Swiss-German who may have been the master sculptor; Ivan Reznikoff, a Russian who was murdered in the tower, and whose ghost is said to linger there; and Reznikoff's assailant, appropriately named Paul Diabolos. All were presumably employed by the contractors—a partnership of brothers: John Worthington (1818-73) and James Worthington (1822-98), who had a payroll of about 350 men and owned stone quarries in Ohio. The Worthington Brothers' contract stated:

> The carvings of the beasts shall be executed in artistic style, bold in relief, sharp, true and graceful in outline, that near the eye delicate in finish, but that in lofty position having boldness and depth of cut in simple forms.[110]

The ornament is most intricately and impressively displayed in the much-photographed main entrance, where the thick walls allowed six concentric and receding impost arches and colonnettes to be carved beneath the central gable, all decorated (the gable with a lozenge pattern) and permanently transfigured by the play of light and shadow. The entrance is a characteristic Romanesque feature, as are the round-headed windows, the heavy buttresses, the arched corbels that project beneath the eaves and along the sloped parapets that flank the tower, and the general feeling of Romanesque bulk

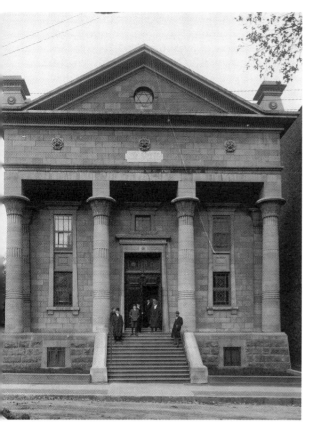

6.62 (*above*) Shearith Israel Synagogue, Montreal, Quebec, 1887-90. Photograph *c*. 1900. MMCH/10762.

6.63 University College, University of Toronto, Toronto, Ontario, 1856-9. Photograph *c*. 1859. NAC/C-21670.

and massiveness (which forms a contrast with the lightness of the Gothic Revival).

From the entrance one moves into a vestibule, with stone stairs on either side, and through an impressive carved-stone arcade into a two-storey atrium, lighted by stained-glass windows, with corridors leading from it on both sides. The mellow severity of the atrium is complemented by the floor of encaustic tiles—in earthy reds, yellow, and brown, accented in black and grey-blue—and by carved red-pine woodwork and ceilings. In 1890 a fire gutted the interior of University College, and many of the other interior features originated in the restoration that was completed two years later. In 1963 the three-storey Laidlaw Library (by Mathers and Haldenby) enclosed the north side of the quadrangle, a modern addition whose ground-floor arcade is in harmony with the old main building, the interior of which was again restored in 1970.

We have seen Toronto buildings designed by architect Frederic Cumberland and his various partners rendered in a number of historical styles, including the Gothic Revival (St James' Cathedral) and Neoclassicism (the Seventh Post Office), both of which were under construction in the early 1850s; and the Romanesque Revival University College, begun only five years later. This trio of executed buildings shows how the choice of historical style was dependent on the associations that were believed to be appropriate to the particular function, just as with Ithiel Town's three buildings on New Haven Green. To be sure, other factors might play a role—such as issues of cost, the client's or architect's tastes, or regional preferences—but these were all secondary. The Gothic Revival was selected for St James' because it was the only acceptable choice for an Anglican cathedral, and Neoclassicism for the Post Office because of the tradition that government buildings should be classical in design (although this would soon change with the competition for the Parliament Buildings in Ottawa). The previous use of the Romanesque Revival for a college building (Oxford) and research institution (Smithsonian) validated it for University College, although Langton's anecdote about the Head-Cumberland controversy shows that personal taste was also very much a factor.

Some architectural historians used to brand this stylistic mobility as 'insincere', but moralistic criticism of this kind misses the mark entirely. In the middle of the nineteenth century the choice of one style over another was based on convictions of appropriate expression. An architect might switch from Neoclassicism to the Gothic Revival (or one of the other modes) based on the program for the building, just as we choose between one suit of clothing and another depending on the nature of the social occasion to which it will be worn. If anything would have been judged immoral, it would have been making the incorrect choice of style. Jeffry Wyatt's submission of alternative designs for the Quebec Parliament Building, with which this chapter began, was his way of indicating that no firm precedents existed to guide him to the correct manner for the project, and so he left the choice to the client.

The Baroque revival

One final stylistic revival remains to be introduced, even though it takes us well past mid-century: the Baroque Revival, which became very important in Quebec church design. We have seen that French Canadians first used the Gothic Revival in the 1820s at the Church of Notre-Dame in Montreal, at the same time that the Anglicans were experimenting with the style. Although Notre-Dame had its following, and a number of architects, including Victor Bourgeau, used the style for both exterior and interior design, French Canada never adopted it with any enthusiasm. There were several reasons. One was a lingering commitment to the older Quebec tradition of church design, seen in the revival led by Abbé Demers and Thomas Baillairgé (page 000); another was that the Ecclesiological Movement had so identified the Gothic Revival with Anglicans and other English-speaking Protestants that Catholic Québécois did not feel entirely comfortable with the style. A third factor, and one particularly characteristic of the romantic period, was a search for an alternative historical style that might be associated more closely with Catholicism. That style was found in the architecture of the Italian Baroque.

Alan Gowans has related the story of the Baroque Revival in Quebec, and his compelling narrative may be summarized here.[111] It begins with the installation of Mgr Ignace Bourget as the second Bishop of Montreal in 1840. Bourget was determined to provide his diocese with new churches that were suitable to its size and wealth, and took on as his adviser the Jesuit Father Félix Martin, whom we met as a participant in the design of the

Gothic Revival St Patrick's in Montreal (1843-7; **6.41**). Martin was a historian and antiquary at heart. His eclecticism is seen in the parish church at Caughnawaga (now Kahnawake), which he designed at the very same time (completed in 1845) in the traditional manner of Quebec churches.

Faced with viable design options, Bishop Bourget chose a third alternative: the Baroque (also called the proto-Baroque or Mannerism) of sixteenth-century Italy, the period of the Counter-Reformation, seeing it as a potent symbol of the triumph of the Catholic Church. Bourget found an architect who could carry out his intentions in John Ostell (page 249), who had completed the towers of Notre-Dame. In 1849 the London-born Ostell, whom we saw as the first architect of McGill Uni-

6.64 Notre-Dame-de-Grâce, Montreal, Quebec, 1851-3. HWS/SSS/QUE 92 MO CH 51.02.

versity, began work on a new wing of the Grand Seminary of Saint-Sulpice and an Episcopal Palace for Bourget. He then designed Église Notre-Dame-de-Grâce (originally called Notre-Dame-de-Toutes-Grâces, 1851-3), in the Montreal district of that name. All had features of the Baroque style—partly as a result, Alan Gowans suggests, of Father Martin's advice. The façade of **Église Notre-Dame-de-Grâce [6.64]** has a three-bay ground storey and tapers, through the use of curved and stepped volutes, to a single pedimented bay at the top, with the organization provided by classical pilasters (Doric below and Ionic above) and entablatures. This composition was popularized (one might say canonized) at the church of Il Gesù in Rome—the mother church of the Jesuit order—built c. 1575-84 to designs by Giacomo da Vignola and Giacomo della Porta, and it became the standard seventeenth-century church-type in Italy, France, and throughout the Catholic world. The façade proportions of the Montreal church are narrower than those of Il Gesù; they are closer to those of French churches such as the Church of the Sorbonne (c. 1635) and the Val-de-Grâce (c. 1645) in Paris, although Notre-Dame-de-Grâce imitates neither. (Much of its interior decoration was undertaken in the twentieth century, and the belltower near the apse was built in 1927-8 to designs by J.-Omer Marchand.)[112]

Bishop Bourget regarded the many parish churches erected during his tenure as preliminaries to his principal project, a new cathedral for Montreal to replace the one built by Bishop Plessis, which was destroyed by fire in July 1854. We are told by church historian Olivier Maurault that a month after the fire Bourget went to Europe and

> visited several churches, but St Peter's in Rome inspired him so profoundly and vividly that...he conceived the audacious project of reproducing Michelangelo's masterpiece of genius....He communicated his enthusiasm to others.[113]

Three years later Bourget sent architect Victor Bourgeau to Europe. As a newspaper of the day reported,

> Mr Victor Bourgeau left last Monday on the *City of Baltimore* for Le Havre. The object of his voyage is to visit and study the principal monuments of Rome, especially the Basilica of St Peter's, on the model of which the new cathedral of Montreal will be built.[114]

Bourgeau's reaction was unexpected. He returned home after only eight days in Rome, indignant that

315

6.65 Cathedral Basilica of Saint-Jacques-le-Majeur (Marie-Reine-du-Monde), Montreal, Quebec, 1870-94, Communauté urbaine de Montréal.

the bishop should want to reproduce the great basilica (of which Michelangelo was only one of many architects) on so small a scale, and he advised strongly against it. Thereafter the use of Baroque forms in his own churches was limited, as at Saint-Barthélémy.

Bourget put his cathedral scheme aside for a decade, but revived it shortly after 1868, when the papal state was besieged by Italian troops and Quebec sent a contingent of 'Zouaves' to Rome to serve with the papal forces. Bourget seized the opportunity to argue that a replica of St Peter's would be a suitable symbol of Quebec's loyalty to the Vatican. This time his idea was approved. He chose as his designer Father Joseph Michaud (1823-1902), a priest with some amateur architectural experience. Michaud was appointed chaplain to the Zouaves and directed to make plans for reproducing St Peter's when he was in Rome. Construction began in 1870, but Michaud's limited skills in construction soon required that he be assisted by a professional—and Victor Bourgeau accepted the call. A third architect, Étienne-Alcibiade Leprohon, also participated in the work. The great dome was fin-

ished in 1886 and work on the building was finally completed in 1894.[115]

The **Cathedral Basilica of Saint-Jacques-le-Majeur** (now known as Marie-Reine-du-Monde) is indeed a reduced version of St Peter's and represents the peak of Victorian associationism [6.65]. The body of the cathedral follows the general form of St Peter's in its massing, with the nave and aisles leading to a centralized space in the form of a Greek-cross with ancillary chapels, covered by a large dome that faithfully reproduces much from the celebrated one by Michelangelo. The imposing broad façade, finished in ashlar, has columns, pilasters, a central pediment across its lower level, and an attic storey surmounted by statues of saints. Other than the façade and the dome, the exterior of the Montreal cathedral is finished in coarse grey-

6.66 (*opposite*) Interior of the Cathedral Basilica of Saint-Jacques-le-Majeur (Marie-Reine-du-Monde), Montreal, Quebec, 1870-94. Communauté urbaine de Montréal.

stone, devoid of decorative detail. The magnificent interior [6.66] captures much of the spirit of the Roman precedent, the high barrel-vaulted nave leading to a brilliantly illuminated crossing, in the centre of which is a *baldacchino* (by sculptor Victor Vincent, 1900) that reproduces the twisted columns and scrolled apex of Bernini's masterpiece in St Peter's. The effect of the ensemble is truly impressive, and certainly fulfilled Bourget's dream, although the Bishop died in 1885 and never saw his achievement in its entirety. The site, as well as the source, was symbolic, since Bourget located it next to Dominion Square on Dorchester Boulevard (now boulevard René-Lévesque), challenging the Anglo-Protestant domination of the new business district. A large statue of Bourget (by Louis-Philippe Hébert, 1903) stands near the entrance and expresses the church's dominion over the area.

The Baroque Revival did not die with Bishop Bourget. A number of parish churches in Quebec were built in the Baroque manner in the last years of the nineteenth century. Roman Catholics in other jurisdictions as well appreciated the association of their churches with those of Italy. The archdiocese of Toronto adopted this mode for several churches built between the 1880s and 1910s (e.g. **10.56-7**). Baroque principles also formed a component of the Beaux-Arts style of architecture, which dominated the design of public buildings in the early years of the twentieth century and was adopted with enthusiasm by many Catholic institutions.

CHAPTER 7

EARLY BUILDING ON THE PRAIRIES

SEVENTEENTH- AND eighteenth-century Euro-Canadian settlement inevitably occurred in the eastern portion of the continent. Explorers and *coureurs de bois* who ventured beyond the St Lawrence Valley and the lower Great Lakes brought back word of a vast western interior, dominated by what must have seemed to be an endless flat grassland prairie. They also noted the parkland fringe along the northern edge of the prairie, with its hills and fertile soils, and an inhospitable and infertile forest further north. Some reported a barrier of snow-capped mountains far to the west. These adventurous travellers also found aboriginal peoples thinly distributed across the land—living in close touch with the land and using its resources efficiently to construct shelters that also met the needs of their social organization and economy.

This was a new frontier, a quantum leap west of the earlier edges of settlement, a land where the terrain, climate, and indigenous peoples were all unfamiliar to the new arrivals. Their initial architectural responses to this new environment were directed at survival, as builders combined the materials furnished by the land with vernacular building traditions to fashion shelters. As on the earlier frontiers of eastern and central Canada, after an initial period of acclimatization had passed, the settlers began to express their social aspirations by emulating the forms and styles of polite, urbane architecture.

This chapter looks at the architecture in the western interior—of natives, Europeans, and people of mixed blood, from prehistoric times until the eve of the transcontinental railway in the 1870s and 1880s. It discusses the ways in which the different building traditions developed and were blended as the frontier moved westward from the basin of the Red River to that of the Saskatchewan.

Native Building

Until the nineteenth century, only native peoples were permanent inhabitants of the vast area between the Great Lakes and the Rocky Mountains, their ancestors having migrated there in the last two millennia—although nomadic hunters had occupied the plains as long as 10,000 years ago.

The prairie was inhabited by Plains Indians, who represented three distinct linguistic groups. Among those who spoke the Algonquian languages were the dominant Blackfoot Nation (known in the US as the Blackfeet), who lived in southern Alberta and adjacent Montana and comprised three tribes: the Blood, the Peigan, and the Blackfoot. The Plains Cree and Plains Ojibwa were a western extension of their Eastern Woodlands namesakes; although Algonquian-speakers like the Blackfoot, they were traditional enemies. The Assiniboine and Stoney Indians spoke Siouan languages. And the Sarcee of western Alberta, who were closely allied to the Blackfoot (and formed a part of the Blackfoot Confederacy), spoke Athapaskan. Hand gestures were often the only way in which the three groups could communicate with each other, yet all shared a nomadic culture that was based on the hunt for buffalo, or bison.

Plains Indians

The Tipi   The Plains Indians lived in portable conical shelters called tipis. A view of a **Plains Cree camp** [7.1] south of Vermilion, Alberta, photographed in 1871, shows a dozen tipis, with their entrances all oriented eastward, and a number of smaller frames used for drying and storing goods. The tipi consisted of a cover of buffalo skins sewn together and stretched tightly over a framework of peeled pine or cedar poles. The main structural frame consisted of either four poles or three, in either case supplemented with additional poles. The plan was ovoid, with the flatter and steeper side—which was more strongly braced—facing the prevailing westerly winds. The other, more gently sloping, side faced east. Above the entrance were two flaps (or 'ears') that formed the sides of the smoke hole and could be adjusted with moveable poles to regulate the draft. Women were responsible for making and setting up the tipi. Details of design and fasteners differed among the various tribes.[1]

The fire was lighted in the centre of the tipi and the inhabitants sat and slept in locations that were established by social custom, usually with the oldest man—the owner of the tipi—at the west, across from the door. His medicine bundle was stored there, and an altar for rituals was set up between his place and the fire.

A few of the tipis—perhaps one in ten among the Blackfoot—bore painted decoration, which transformed them into sacred lodges. (However, many decorated tipis would be set up together for special occasions, such as the sun-dance ritual.)

7.1 Plains Cree camp, south of Vermilion, Alberta. Photograph by Charles Horetzky, 1871. NAC/C-5181.

Each tribe had its distinctive iconography, which had both literal and cosmological interpretations. The **painted Blackfoot tipi [7.2]** illustrated here is typical of that nation's distinctive manner. The geometric designs at the top and around the base provide conventional borders. The dark portion at the top, usually painted black or red, represents the sky; the disks seen on the smoke flap symbolize certain constellations and stars. The cross-shaped emblem near the bottom of the sky, behind the external rear pole, has been identified as either the morning star or a moth (or butterfly) that brings dreams. The stripes below the sky may be clouds, a rainbow, or the trails of animal spirits. The dark band at the bottom, usually painted red, represents the earth; the disks are stars and the rounded projections above them are mountains or sacred places. The poles connect the earth to the sky and provide trails along which the people's prayers may reach the spirits.

Between these two regions lies a zone that represents another world that the principal occupant (or his direct ancestor) entered during a vision. A row of animals—here probably otter, but other mammals were depicted as well—occupy this zone and face the entrance. These supernatural creatures gave sacred powers, including the tipi, to the first Indian owner in the vision. The painted false door behind the pole signifies the entrance to

the home of the animal spirits, and reinforces the rear of the interior as the place of honour within the tipi.

After the skins wore out, usually every year or two, they were replaced. The paintings on the old tipi cover would be transferred to the new one, and so the designs passed on from generation to generation.

The Indians spent the summer and fall on the plain hunting buffalo, and the winter and spring in protected areas in river valleys—a mobility requiring that the dwellings be easily moved and re-erected. Dogs were originally used to transport the tipis while the people walked. This changed in the sixteenth century with the Spaniards' introduction of the horse to North America. Horses reached the Canadian Plains Indians by about 1750, allowing them to change their techniques of hunting and warfare and to transport larger and heavier tipis. The size of the covers increased from about six skins to between fourteen and twenty, and the number of poles often reached about twenty.

Evidence of prehistoric dwellings on the plains is found in tipi rings—circles of stones that are believed to have held down the bottoms of tipi covers. (Some of these tipi covers may have been tents in which important people were laid to rest after their death.) It is probable that tipi-like structures have been used for many thousands of years—

although scholars have not agreed on the meaning of the archaeological evidence.[2]

Other structures The Plains Indians developed sacred and ritualistic architecture as well. The sweatlodges of the Plains Cree were circular, dome-shaped structures about 4 feet (1.2 m) high and 6 to 8 feet (1.8 to 2.4 m) in diameter, made from willow withes and covered with robes, blankets, or tipi covers. Their function was similar to that of the steam bath and the sauna, although the sweatlodge offered a deeply spiritual experience—but it could be used only once, after which the frame was left standing.[3]

The Algonquian shaking tent spread to the Prairies [1.12], where it was used by the Blackfoot, the Cree, and the Ojibwa, and it was adopted as well by members of other language groups. Most consisted of light frames that were moved by the shaman, like those of the Eastern Woodlands Indians. Some tribes used miniature lodges that were not manipulated, and others simply erected screens to conceal the shaman.[4]

Two kinds of larger structural forms are known as well. One is the medicine wheel, a circle of stones or cairns that is larger than a tipi ring and of consid-

7.2 Blackfoot tipi. Canadian Museum of Civilization/58569.

7.3 Medicine wheel, Jelly Ranch, Saskatchewan. Saskatchewan Museum of Natural History.

erable antiquity. At least fifty wheels have been identified on the Canadian plains, usually located on top of the highest hill in the area. Those in Alberta, which have been carefully studied, are rarely more than 30 feet (9 m) in diameter, although some more than twice that size have been found on the US plains. Many have a central stone, or cluster of stones, and some—including the **medicine wheel** [7.3] at Jelly Ranch, Saskatchewan— extend outward as radiating spokes. In some medicine wheels, the spokes or the alignment of pairs of stones seem to point to astronomical features, such as solstitial sunrises or bright stars, while others appear to point to cairns or burial sites in the area. Their use (like that of similar stone circles in Europe) remains a puzzle.[5]

The other large structure is the buffalo jump, which consisted of long piles of rocks arranged in two converging rows and leading to the top of a cliff. Hunters would stampede buffalo herds into the funnel and over the precipice, where others waiting below would kill and butcher the animals. Every bit of the meat, bones, and hides was valued and utilized. This was carried out at a place called Head-Smashed-In Buffalo Jump (near Fort Macleod, Alberta) for nearly 6,000 years. Stone cairns were erected as far as 5 miles (8 km) from the kill site. The cliff is 60 feet (18 m) high and faces east so that the prevailing winds would carry the scent of the hunters away from the animals. The spot has been sensitively conserved and interpreted by the Alberta government, and selected as a UNESCO World Heritage Site.

The natives managed the buffalo stock well and sustained its numbers. The white hunters, however, did not—slaughtering the creatures by the thousands, primarily for their fur. The loss of the buffalo herds, in the second half of the nineteenth century, had a momentous impact on the Plains Indians. For a while they managed to cope, altering their diet and substituting canvas for buffalo hides for tipi covers. But they eventually lost their self-sufficiency, moved to defined reserves, and became dependent on government assistance.

The Forks and the Red River Settlement

The most strategic site in the early history of Western Canada was 'the Forks', the confluence of the Red and Assiniboine Rivers—two watercourses and their tributaries that provided the gateway to the western interior. They formed an extension to the St Lawrence River route and, as we shall see, also provided a western extension of the systems of land division and building that had been developed in the St Lawrence valley. Natives and Europeans alike competed vigorously for possession of the area. The junction eventually became the site of Winnipeg, the first city in the West. Beginning as the outpost of the trading empires that were centred in Montreal and London, the Forks quickly developed into an important nucleus in its own right, and exerted a decided influence on the hinterland.

The fur trade

The North West Company and Fort Gibraltar The fur-traders of the North West Company, the aggressive association of Montreal-based traders, were quick to appreciate the advantages of controlling the Forks. The site offered arable land, trees for building, and a base that led to rich sources of furs. (The fur-bearing animals in the immediate area were virtually exhausted by the beginning of the nineteenth century.) As Nor'Wester Daniel Williams Harmon wrote in his journal in 1805:

> The Forks or where the Upper [Assiniboine] and Lower Red River form a junction—and hereabouts the country appears to have a richer soil than at any other place, I have observed in this part of the world—and is covered with oak, Basswood, Elm, Poplar and Birch, etc., also here are Red Plums, and Grapes.[6]

Five years later John Wills began to build a post for the North West Company at the Forks. The first Fort Gibraltar (1810), as it was called, was dismantled and burned in June 1816 by territorial governor Robert Semple in a period of considerable tension that culminated later that month in the death of himself and twenty others colonists at the hands of a group of Métis and Indians under the mixed-blood leader Cuthbert Grant—supported by the

7.4 Second Fort Gibraltar (the first Fort Garry), Winnipeg, Manitoba, begun 1817. Sketched by Peter Rindisbacher, *c*. 1821. Glenbow Museum/Photo No. 1476 (58.42.4).

North West Company—in the Incident at Seven Oaks.

The descriptions of the Hudson's Bay Company's Colin Robertson (1816), and resident Jean-Baptiste Roi (1820), reveal that Fort Gibraltar consisted of a group of buildings within a well-fortified enclosure:

> Gibraltar...has two good bastions at the two angles of the Square, and the square is formed with oak palisades; eighteen feet in height, and proof against musketry, this is not only a strong place but very comfortable lodgings...
>
> It was a fort of wooden picketing, made of oak trees split in two, which formed its enclosure. Within the said enclosure were built the house of the partner (64' in length), two houses for the men (36' and 28' respectively), a store (32'), two hangards or stores, a blacksmith's shop, and a stable; there was also an ice-house with a watch tower [*guertie*] over it.[7]

Fort Gibraltar was rebuilt, beginning in 1817. A palisade constructed of 'excellent sawn oak piquets 14 feet above ground set very close together like a continued wall about 100 feet square' was erected around a cluster of new buildings.[8] The only known depiction of the **second Fort Gibraltar** [7.4], probably drawn in 1821 by fifteen-year-old Peter Rindisbacher, shows structures with both gable roofs and higher hipped roofs, whose dormers peek over the top of the palisade.

Fort Gibraltar—like the North West Company that built it—had a short but important life. Its primary significance is that it opened the way for the earliest and most important European settlement in Western Canada.

The Hudson's Bay Company and Lower Fort Garry The North West Company competed vigorously with the Hudson's Bay Company, the London-based organization, chartered in 1670, that had been granted trading rights to virtually all of today's northern and western Canada. The vast commercial empire was named Rupert's Land, after Prince Rupert, a cousin of Charles II. The heated and sometimes violent competition between the two organizations came to an end with their merger in 1821. The new conglomerate, which retained the name and the privileges of the Hudson's Bay Company, benefited greatly from the superior trading skills of the Nor'Westers.

The second Fort Gibraltar was renamed Fort Garry and became the busy headquarters of the Red

River District. However, a flood in 1826—one of many occasions in which the Red River overflowed its banks—caused considerable damage to the low-lying wooden trading post. The Governor of the Hudson's Bay Company, George Simpson, decided to avoid future floods by building a 'good solid comfortable Establishment...of stone' 20 miles (32 km) downriver, on high ground that was close to sources of construction materials (stone, lime, and wood) and had the potential for agricultural development. Construction on the site, named **Lower Fort Garry** [7.5], began in 1830.[9]

The principal building at Lower Fort Garry is the **Big House** (1831-2; **7:6**)—seen from the rear at the centre in the aerial photograph [7.5]—which was intended as the residence of the Governor and officers. It is a large $1\frac{1}{2}$-storey building with walls of rubble stone, quoins at the corners, and a steep hipped roof whose eaves flare to cover a broad veranda that extends around three sides. Two massive chimneys originally rose from the ridge (one has been removed). The roof, eaves, and veranda are all features of Quebec domestic architecture,

such as the Villeneuve [2.16] and Beauchemin [2.25] houses. Quebec influences could be seen as well in the annex, at the rear of the Big House, that was built in 1840 of *colombage pierroté* (timber frame with rubble-stone infill and covered with *crépi*—seen in a photograph [7.7] taken when the *crépi* was removed pending restoration), which had been the prevalent building technique in seventeenth-century New France.

The Company's use of French-Canadian builders accounts for this Quebec character. Although Lower Fort Garry was planned by the Governor, George Simpson, the buildings were erected under the supervision of Pierre Leblanc, who had filled a similar role at York Factory and Fort William. Of the team of stonemasons who worked under Leblanc, the only name that has come down is that of another Quebecker, André Gaudrie. (It may be presumed, however, that some of the masons at the Fort were Scottish.) Quebec provided the principal pool of artisans for the buildings of the fur-trade companies, and their presence in the Red River Settlement assured the perpetuation of their distinctive ways of building.

7.5 Aerial view of Lower Fort Garry, Manitoba, begun 1830. PC/Lower Fort Garry National Historic Site/3913.

7.6 The Big House, Lower Fort Garry, Manitoba, 1831-2. Photograph by Harold Kalman.

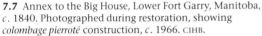

7.7 Annex to the Big House, Lower Fort Garry, Manitoba, *c.* 1840. Photographed during restoration, showing *colombage pierroté* construction, *c.* 1966. CIHB.

The Big House was surrounded by a picket fence, within which was a precinct reserved for commissioned officers and their guests—evidence of the rigid class structure maintained by the Company. The lawn was kept green and neatly trimmed, and plantings of annuals gave the appearance of an English garden.

Around the Big House are arranged a number of other buildings in which the operations of the trading post were carried out. They include the fur loft (which also served as a retail store), a granary, and a pair of warehouses. The fur loft and warehouse that flank the Big House are substantial $2\frac{1}{2}$-storey stone buildings, six bays wide, with hipped roofs, dormers, and two chimneys. Their narrow eaves, smaller windows, and absence of a veranda make them straightforward stone buildings without distinctive Quebec features; their rather dour quality may well indicate the hands of Scottish masons. They provided an important precedent for later stone structures along the Red River.

The buildings of Lower Fort Garry were surrounded by a stone wall with circular defensive bastions at the corners. Their general arrangement within a walled compound followed the models of Fort Gibraltar, York Factory, and other earlier British and Anglo-Canadian fur-trade posts. It mirrors the geometrical regularity that we have seen as typical of the British tradition of town-planning.

The new station was planned as a country estate as much as a trading post. Simpson intended to take up residence there and make it the administrative centre for all of Rupert's Land—but he failed on both counts. Simpson, and his young wife Frances, could not tolerate the frontier society, and they sailed for London in 1833 (though he and Frances returned to Lachine in 1834 and 1838 respectively). The main business of the Company never relocated entirely to Lower Fort Garry, because the operations required the population base and communications routes available at the Forks. The old Fort Garry, renamed Upper Fort Garry, continued to be maintained and expanded, forming the core of today's Winnipeg (see page 357).

Outside the walls of Lower Fort Garry grew a bustling village that was far more casual in its plan. It was inhabited by the administrators, miller, artisans, labourers, and others involved in the Company's non-trading operations. The structures included farm buildings, a gristmill (used also as a sawmill), and a brewery, as well as residences and service buildings. Lower Fort Garry developed as an agricultural centre that supplied provisions to posts in the western interior. Troops were stationed there during the Oregon crisis in the 1840s, and it played a minor role during the Northwest Rebellion.

The two Fort Garrys became the focus of the elaborate transportation system required to maintain the operations of the Company. This depended on York boats (durable boats that were propelled by oars and square sails, and that were named after York Factory, the principal post on Hudson Bay) on the rivers and lakes, replacing canoes; and on Red River carts along the growing network of trails. In the 1870s the York boat and the Red River cart were superseded by the steamboat and the railway respectively, and the revolution in transportation left Lower Fort Garry superfluous. The agricultural and industrial buildings were mostly sold for their materials, and the fort itself—used as the first provincial penitentiary and as a mental asylum—deteriorated badly.

In 1913 the fort was leased to the Motor Club of Winnipeg, and the Big House enjoyed the social activity it never achieved under Simpson. In 1951 the Hudson's Bay Company gave Lower Fort Garry to the federal government. The buildings within the walls were restored and reconstructed by Parks Canada, and they are now interpreted as a national historic site.

Settlement

The Hudson's Bay Company initially discouraged permanent settlement in the West, but found this policy increasingly difficult to maintain, partly because the very nature of its operations required the availability of a labour pool and a retail market. As a consequence, a large and diverse population became established at the Forks. In the first decades of the nineteenth century the Red River Settlement (as it became known) consisted of a number of separate European and mixed-race communities that were established within a few miles of the Forks. It was here, in the first non-native settlement west of the Great Lakes Basin, that fur traders, missionaries, Scots, Métis, and French Canadians combined to produce a distinctive way of building—featuring a structural system, transferred from New France, that would dominate the architecture of the West for generations.

Kildonan: The Selkirk Settlement Agricultural settlement reached the western interior as the result of the Hudson's Bay Company's sale in 1811 of 74 million acres (30 million hectares) of land straddling the Red River, for a nominal 10 shillings, to a forty-year-old Scots nobleman, Thomas Douglas, fifth Earl of Selkirk. The tract formed parts of present-day Manitoba, Saskatchewan, Minnesota, and North Dakota.

Lord Selkirk purchased the land (known as Assiniboia) as a way of fulfilling his personal ambition to settle destitute farmers and crofters from the Scottish Highlands in British North America. He had sent Scots to Upper Canada and Prince Edward Island in 1803 and 1804, and now turned his attention to the West. The Hudson's Bay Company was attracted by Selkirk's ambitious plan because it would provide food for trading posts, reduce the cost of importing provisions from England, and interfere with the provisioning routes of the archrival North West Company—and it could hardly refuse any proposal made by Selkirk, since he and his wife's family had recently acquired substantial financial control over the Company.[10]

The first contingent sailed from Scotland to York Factory in 1811, wintered there in makeshift huts, and reached the Red River only late the next summer. Captain Miles Macdonnell, whom Selkirk chose as the Governor of Assiniboia, selected a site on the west bank of the Red River, about two meandering miles (3 km) north of Fort Gibraltar, and called it Fort Douglas—now known as Point

7.8 View of the Selkirk Settlement, Manitoba.
Probably originally drawn by Lord Selkirk, 1817; copied by
A.R. Winning, 1930. NAC/C-8714.

Douglas—after his patron. Winter was approaching too quickly for construction to proceed, and so the weary group spent their second Canadian winter at the Hudson's Bay Company's post near Emerson at the present Manitoba/North Dakota border.

The Selkirk settlers finally began to move onto their properties near Fort Douglas in the spring of 1813. They named their settlement Kildonan, after the parish in Scotland from which many had come. The land on the Red River (as well as on the Assiniboine) was surveyed as long, narrow river lots, each with a frontage on the river, in the manner of New France.

A **view of the Selkirk settlement** [7.8], believed to have been drawn by Lord Selkirk when he visited the colony in 1817 (and known only in this copy by A.R. Winning), shows the appearance of the developing community. A number of one- and $1\frac{1}{2}$-storey houses and outbuildings, with medium-pitched gable roofs and the entrance in a long side, are scattered in the landscape. The attics are accessed by exterior ladders, suggesting the absence of staircases, and chimneys are not in evidence (perhaps the artist's omission), so that there are no clues about how the houses were heated. Stumps in the foreground suggest that the land had recently been cleared; the deciduous forest can be seen in the distance. A wood fence defines a field beside the road—probably the River Road (originally called the Selkirk Trail)—at the right.

This and other early views, as well as the few surviving buildings from the period, reveal that the predominant building technique was the grooved post—the *poteaux en coulisse* [7.9]—of New France. All the buildings in Selkirk's sketch have vertical posts at intervals of between about 3 to 10 feet (1 to 3 m). In this building system, wood sills—usually placed on a shallow stone foundation—served as the bases for the vertical posts, which were squared and prepared with tenons (tongues) at the bottom that fit into mortises (slots) in the sills. (In the

7.9 Detail of Red River frame construction (*poteaux en coulisse*). Drawing by Arthur Price. From Marius Barbeau, 'The House that Mac Built', *The Beaver*, December 1945, p. 11.

Arthur Price

327

eighteenth century, the posts were often set directly into the ground.) Horizontal infill logs filled the spaces between the posts, with tenons in their ends inserted into vertical grooves in the posts [2.24]. This construction technique was ideal for the environmental conditions. In an area where wood was available, yet limited in size and supply, a house could be built mostly with short logs. The posts had to be only about 8 feet (2.5 m) in length, and the only long members were the sills and the top wall plates. Few nails were needed, since wooden pegs were used as fasteners. The structure could endure extreme changes of temperature and humidity because the horizontal logs were free to expand and shrink without threatening its stability. Windows and doors were easy to insert, and the building was easily enlarged with the addition of more structural bays.

The grooved-post technique came west with the French-Canadian builders who worked for the North West Company (they used it, for example, at Fort William at the very beginning of the nineteenth century) and the Hudson's Bay Company. The system is found everywhere in Canada and the northern US where builders of French descent were active, and it remained the preferred manner among fur-trade builders of all nationalities. Because of its extensive use at the Red River Settlement, from where it spread further west, the technique is often referred to as the Red River frame, and sometimes as the Hudson's Bay style. Government builder Hugh Sutherland called it the 'Red River style' as early as 1877 (page 357), suggesting that the name was already in wide use. This text uses the terms Red River frame, grooved post, and *poteaux en coulisse* interchangeably. (The terms *pièce-sur-pièce*, *poteaux sur sole*, and 'post on sill'—which also describe this method of construction—are not used here because all three are non-specific terms that may refer to more than only the grooved post. The first denotes any kind of horizontal log construction, and the last two any kind of heavy-timber frame, as was discussed on pages 48-50.)[11]

Much of the initial construction at the Selkirk settlement was carried out by two carpenters named Bartenois and McLeod (the latter may have been either Scots or Métis), who also built a Hudson's Bay Company post on the east bank of the Red. Work continued in 1814 under the supervision of Peter Fidler (1769-1822), a veteran surveyor with the Company who had come to York Factory from England in 1788.[12] Fidler was busy at the Selkirk settlement in 1814:

7.10 St John's Anglican Church, St John's Parish, Manitoba, 1822-3. From John West, *Substance of a Journal* (1824). PAM/N13788.

> Mr. Fidler...built a convenient farm house, with barn stable cow house, sheep house, and hog stye and inclosed the whole within a strong fence of stockades $3\frac{1}{2}$ chains square. He built also the walls of a Government House two stories 64 x 22 feet a detached kitchen 23 feet x 17 feet a neat dwelling house, 23 x 16 (christened the 'Château').[13]

Fidler wrote on 6 August 1814 that '4 men are constantly employed at the large House—this day they got up all the posts and three logs high along the Front'. This was an evident reference to the grooved-post system of building.[14]

The first Selkirk settlers, and those who followed in subsequent years, suffered setback after setback. Besides being unprepared for the hard climate, they faced the growing hostility of the Nor'Westers and the Métis. But they persisted. A second Fort Douglas was built—incorporating some components from the recently destroyed first Fort Gibraltar—and an agricultural community developed alongside it. Despite a series of failed crops, the Red River Settlement grew and became increasingly self-sufficient through the 1820s.

The Anglican missionary John West, who had been sent for by the Hudson's Bay Company, built the **Church of St John's** in 1822 or 1823 to accommodate his mission—calling it 'a landmark of Christianity in this wild waste of heathenism.' A period drawing [7.10] shows that it was a log building in the Red River manner, with a post clearly visible in the centre of the gable end (as in several of the houses sketched by Lord Selkirk). A tower and a spire at the opposite end clearly express its religious function. The small building on the left was the community's school; the one on the right was a farmhouse. The log church was replaced in 1831 by one built in stone, and the site is now occupied by the large St John's Cathedral (by Prain and Parfitt, 1926) near Main Street, a short distance north of downtown Winnipeg.[15]

Presbyterians, who formed the core of the Selkirk settlement, did not obtain their own minister until 1851. Their first house of worship, Kildonan Presbyterian Church, is a limestone structure that was built in 1852-4 under the supervision of mason Duncan McRae, who will be introduced below. It stands today as a landmark to the Scottish pioneers.[16]

St Boniface The first church building in the Red River Settlement formed a part of Father Joseph Norbert Provencher's Roman Catholic Mission at St Boniface, erected in 1818 across the Red River from Fort Douglas. As he had done with the Anglicans, Miles Macdonell invited Bishop Plessis of Quebec to send a missionary, in the hope that the Roman Catholic church would replace the pesky Nor'Westers as the primary influence on the Métis, who were disrupting the Hudson's Bay Company's operations. (As so often occurred, the needs of commerce determined the course of social events.) Provencher and two companion clerics built a strong organization that served the Métis, converted Indians, a handful of German and Swiss mercenaries retained by Lord Selkirk to protect the colony after the Incident at Seven Oaks, and the growing number of French Canadians. Among the

latter were Jean-Baptiste Lagimonière and his wife, Marie-Anne Gaboury, who became the first non-native couple to live in the West when they wintered at the Forks in 1806-7, and to whom Lord Selkirk subsequently granted land at the mouth of the Seine River, near the St Boniface mission. They would become the grandparents of Louis Riel.[17]

The original mission church was about 50 feet (15 m) square—less than half was finished inside—and built of horizontal logs connected at the corners with dovetail joints. It, and its related mission buildings, were erected within a palisade wall. A second, and larger, **Church of St Boniface** was begun a year later. Early illustrations, including the one here [**7.11**]—drawn in 1823 by W.K. Kempt and copied by A.R. Winning—show vertical posts at intervals along the side and end walls, with log infill between them, indicating that the Red River frame had gained a firm foothold on the east as well as the west bank of the river. The large hipped-roof residence to the right was built in the same manner. The *clocher* atop the church was reportedly donated to the mission by Lord Selkirk. A third building, a cathedral, was erected in 1839. Its twin towers—fitted rather awkwardly on a square façade—and the pointed-arched windows clearly show the inspiration of the Gothic Revival and the twin-towered church tradition of Quebec. This attempt to transcend the regional vernacular and express a specifically French-Canadian character occurred a little more than a generation after the first settlement, by which time the residents were able to look

7.11 View of the Roman Catholic Mission, St Boniface, Manitoba. Drawing by W.C. Kempt, 1823; copied by A.R. Winning, 1929. NAC/C-1726.

7.12 Former Convent of the Grey Nuns, St Boniface, Manitoba, 1846-51. Manitoba Culture, Heritage and Citizenship; Historic Resources.

beyond merely coping with the environment and could try to come to terms with their own identity: an initial period of architectural sameness was followed by one that sanctioned differences. This same phenomenon will be seen among the other cultural groups in the frontier community.[18]

The importance of St Boniface received a boost in 1823 when the Hudson's Bay Company closed its post at Pembina, just south of the international border, and relocated its buildings and residents at the Forks. Many of the inhabitants were French-speaking Catholics who chose to settle in St Boniface. The community was further strengthened in 1844 when a new northwestern diocese was formed and centred there.

An impressive survivor from this era is the former **Convent of the Grey Nuns** (the Sisters of Charity of Montreal); it was built in 1846-51 and restored in 1964-7 (by E.J. Gaboury) to become a museum. Red River frame construction was used for the two-storey building [**7.12**], 100 by 40 feet (30 by 12 m), which showed a higher level of craftsmanship than many of its contemporaries. The exterior was subsequently covered with vertical siding, but the original structure is exposed inside.

The religious orders began a number of vital public institutions, including St Boniface College (which grew out of Provencher's mission school)

and the first hospital in the West (founded by the Grey Nuns). St Boniface was incorporated as a town in 1883 and as a city 25 years later, and it became a part of Winnipeg in 1971. The community retains its francophone character, and the historic centre remains dominated by the cathedral [**10.58**] and service institutions.

The Métis Derived from an archaic French word meaning 'mixed', 'Métis' is used generally to describe Canadians of mixed Indian-European descent, and more specifically to denote a social-cultural group descended from French, English, or Scottish fur-trader fathers and native mothers. Métis society was composed of permanent employees of the trading companies who lived in houses within or near the posts; subsistence farmers who cultivated gardens, and perhaps a few field crops, and engaged in seasonal hunting and freighting; and nomadic hunters and trappers whose ways of life resembled those of the natives. The last group followed the buffalo herds, and lived mostly in tipis or small log dwellings.[19]

Many Métis began to migrate westward to the Red River, around the time of the Selkirk settlement, as their traditional hunting grounds in the western Great Lakes (particularly on the American side of today's border) became occupied by Europeans. By the middle of the nineteenth century several established Métis communities formed a part of the Red River Settlement—principally at St Boniface, on the Red River south of the Assiniboine, and on the Assiniboine River itself, near White Horse Plains and St François-Xavier.

One important community was centred at St Norbert, located where the La Salle River flows into the Red and generally considered to be the southernmost point of the Red River Settlement. It was settled primarily by French-speaking Métis who had been released from fur-trading service as a result of the merger of the Hudson's Bay Company and the North West Company in 1821. These discharged employees, called freemen, chose to form a community there for several reasons. St Norbert lay on a trail to the buffalo-hunting grounds on the Grand Côteau du Missouri. It was also situated on the Pembina Trail, which linked Fort Garry with the head of the navigable Mississippi River at St Paul, Minnesota; and as commerce developed, residents of St Norbert were able to work as freighters.

St Norbert was surveyed into river lots, with narrow and deep properties having frontages on the

7.13 Pierre Delorme house, now at St Norbert Provincial Park, Manitoba, c. 1857-71. Manitoba Culture, Heritage and Citizenship; Historic Resources.

Red River in the system of land division that had been common along the St Lawrence. One of the earliest houses in the settlement was the dwelling of Jean-Baptiste Charette, a former carpenter with the North West Company. It may have been built as early as 1811. Although it was demolished in 1952, records indicate that it was a $1\frac{1}{2}$-storey building constructed of horizontal logs joined at the corners and covered with a simple gable roof. This building type was known in New France, and among the

Slavic and Scandinavian settlers in Wisconsin and northern Michigan, from where many Manitoba Métis had come. It became the typical house form of the prairie Métis throughout the nineteenth century, as will be seen below.[20]

More substantial (and still standing, although moved to St Norbert Provincial Park) is the **house of Pierre Delorme [7.13]**, a prosperous farmer of Pointe Coupée (now St Adolphe, near St Norbert) who used his residence as a roadhouse for the stagecoach along the Pembina Trail. It is seen in the photograph after it was moved and stabilized, but before receiving a new foundation. Built on the river some time between 1857 and 1871, the Delorme house was constructed of Red River frame, with the sill logs placed on a mortared foundation. The logs were chinked with a mixture of straw and mud. Interior partition walls were constructed with vertical posts set into the foundation logs, and were plastered (also with straw and mud) and whitewashed with a mixture of lime and water. A lean-to wing was built at one end. The Red River frame was well known to Métis carpenters, but it was a time-consuming method of construction that they rarely used for their own houses. J.C. Hamilton, a visitor in 1876, noted of the Delorme house that it was 'a model of the better class of Métis.'[21]

A surviving building that is of more historical than architectural interest is the Riel house at St Vital, the home of Louis Riel's mother and the place where the leader of the Northwest Rebellion stayed for several months in 1883. Built around 1882-3 of wood that was mostly reused from an earlier building, the main block was constructed of Red River frame. The original form of the previous building remains a matter for conjecture.[22]

Few, if any, typical dwellings of the Red River Métis survive from mid-century, and so we must rely mostly on descriptions and illustrations of them. Louis Goulet, who was born on the banks of the Red in 1859, describes his family home as having been constructed of squared logs, with mortise-and-tenon and dovetail joints, $1\frac{1}{2}$ storeys high, and twice as long as it was wide. The roof was covered with sod and hay. The chimney was constructed by fixing straight wooden poles, 10 to 12 feet (3 to 3.7 m) in length, side by side, and then applying a thick layer of clay both inside and out. Window openings were covered with rawhide. All woodwork—casements, frames, and doors—was handcrafted with the help of a hooked knife. The floors, too, were of wood; other houses of this period had only dirt floors.[23]

The Métis who migrated further westward in the 1870s brought these house-types with them. Their buildings in present-day Saskatchewan will be discussed below.

The Red River Settlement at mid-century By 1850 the Red River Settlement was a collection of 5,000 people. Despite their social and cultural differences, they had developed a reasonable homogeneity in architectural form. The two prevalent building systems were the Red River frame and rubble limestone—both the progeny of the fur trade; a third manner was horizontal log construction, which probably came by way of New France and the American Midwest.

The settlement had spread some distance from the Forks. To the north, the River Road followed the west bank of the Red as it passed through English- (and Gaelic-) speaking communities on its meandering route from the Forks to Lake Winnipeg. Most of the properties were river lots, although the curving river course did not allow all to be parallel. Beyond Point Douglas were the parishes of St John, Kildonan, and St Paul, where the descendants of the Selkirk settlers lived, with others from England. Further north lay the prosperous parish of St Andrew and its community of Grand Rapids (called Lockport, after the construction of a lock), whose large lots were inhabited by the gentry of the fur trade—many of them retired English employees of the Hudson's Bay Company and their Indian wives. An agreement made in 1817, between Lord Selkirk and Chief Peguis of the Salteaux Indians, gave the settlers in all these parishes the rights to use land only 2 miles (3 km) back from the river, and so they cut wood from the thinly settled east bank of the river. Further downriver was Lower Fort Garry and the native community in the Parish of St Peter. The rich heritage of the River Road is still visible, and co-ordinated conservation activity has enhanced and interpreted some of the remains.[24]

French Canadians were clustered near the mission at St Boniface, on the east bank of the Red. As was noted above, a large community of Métis settled along the Red River south of the Forks, and to the west along the Assiniboine. Many traders, and others who were dependent on commerce, lived at the Forks and at Upper Fort Garry, on the site of today's downtown Winnipeg.

Logs formed the principal building material—sometimes laid horizontally with corner joints, and sometimes forming a Red River frame. An example of the former is **Seven Oaks House [7.14]** at Kildonan (1851-3), a large two-storey dwelling with a high hipped roof and a sweeping veranda

7.14 Seven Oaks House, Kildonan, Manitoba, 1851-3. HWS/SSS/MA 80 WI RW 2.01.

7.15 St James Anglican Church, Winnipeg, Manitoba, 1853-5. Drawing *c.* 1860. PAM/N13794.

7.16 Interior of St James Anglican Church, Winnipeg, Manitoba, 1853-5. Photograph by John de Visser.

that now serves as a museum. It was built by John Inkster, a Scots-born settler who came over with the Hudson's Bay Company in 1821, and in 1832-6 acquired land near the site of the Incident at Seven Oaks. His first log house was a small dwelling that used the Red River frame; a portion of it stands to the right of the larger house that replaced it, which Inkster began to build in 1851. The 'new' house (on the left in the photograph) was constructed of oak logs from Baie St Paul that were floated down the Assiniboine River and sawn and hewn 7 inches (18 cm) square. They were laid on top of a stone foundation, butt-jointed at the corners, and fastened with wooden pegs. Although this is not usually as secure a means of construction as interlocking dovetail joints, the walls have stood for a century and a half. They were protected by horizontal siding on the outside, and by a layer of plaster nearly 2 inches (5 cm) thick on the inside; in addition, the walls were insulated with a lining of buffalo hair and fur. An 1858 photograph (not reproduced) shows the house with its attendant outbuildings, including the original cabin just to the left; it is seen with the porch and the siding, and so both may well be original.[25]

The Red River frame was widely used in all communities for both private dwellings and public buildings, although very few examples still stand. One survivor is **St James Anglican Church** (1853-5) on Portage Avenue in Winnipeg, the oldest wood church in Manitoba [**7.15**]. Built to accommodate the new settlers along the Assiniboine, west of the Forks, it was begun a year later than intended because the oak logs that had been floated from Baie St Paul (the same source as for Seven Oaks House) were lost in the flood of 1852. New logs were acquired, squared, and laid horizontally, their ends shaped with projecting tenons and inserted into grooves cut down the sides of posts, which had first been set upright at intervals on a timber sill. In 1967 the interior walls [**7.16**] were stripped of their plaster to reveal the structure.[26]

The gable-roofed nave of Old St James, as it is called, was originally preceded by a tall entrance tower with corner buttresses, crenellations, and finials—much like St John's in Saint John, NB (1824; **6.7**)—although the tower was removed in 1871 and replaced with a small belfry. The Reverend William Henry Taylor (1820-73), a missionary sent out by the Society for the Propagation of the Gospel, served as both pastor and architect. He described the church in a letter to the SPG, indicating how he was forging a compromise between

ecclesiological ideals and the pragmatic reality of the local materials, climate, and workmen:

> The building is 70 feet by 26. The tower 12 by 12, height to the eaves 17 feet. The roof has a sharp pitch—the windows narrow Lancet—the Communion is a high triple Lancet—all tolerably high and will throw a steady sombre light into the church. The roof is open to the ridge, the rafters, principals, purlins and struts being perfectly plain. The whole will, it is hoped, have a decent and becoming effect. It is quite a new thing in this country and many doubt of its answering. We are quite willing to try it and have not much fear as to its being sufficiently warm in winter as well as airy in summer. We make no pretense to ecclesiastical correctness—and no doubt have and shall fail in many points—but we have done our best in this case.[27]

In another letter he complained that 'workmen are scarce...and the difficulty in getting anything done correctly and properly with men who have never seen anything like they are required to do is great.'[28]

7.17 Church of St Andrew's-on-the-Red, Lockport, Manitoba, 1845-9. Photograph by Harold Kalman.

In her study of Red River architecture, Jill Wade explains that timber for building was cut from the stands of maple, elm, oak, aspen, and pine that grew in bluffs on the plains and along the Red River and Lake Winnipeg. Oak was generally used for the frame and pine for the floors. Other materials included hay for thatched roofs and mud for chinks, plaster, and fireplaces. Log and heavy timber frame remained the predominant methods of construction in the Red River area until well past mid-century—although as supplies of trees became depleted, it became necessary either to import timber, or to turn to other materials. Milled lumber first became available locally in 1856 when sawmill machinery, powered by a 25-horsepower engine, was brought to Winnipeg from Chicago.[29]

Stone, which had been used extensively at Lower Fort Garry, provided an alternative building material. Numerous substantial stone buildings once lined the River Road. Although many have been demolished, enough remain to remind the visitor of this rich heritage. The most familiar early stone building is the **Church of St Andrew's-on-the-Red** [**7.17**] at Lockport, which was erected in 1845-9 under the direction of the Reverend William Cockran (1796/1797-1865) of the Church Missionary Society. It replaced an earlier wood church (built in 1832), and stands as the oldest church building in Canada west of the Great Lakes. The simple gabled body is elaborated with a stalwart entrance tower capped by a wood belfry and spire. The church was built of limestone quarried a few miles downriver on the banks of the Red. Eighty by forty feet (24 by 12 m), the nave and chancel have windows with pointed arches, as do the tower and its wood belfry. These features, appearing here a few years earlier than at St James, mark the introduction to the West of the full-blown Early Gothic Revival, with its familiar box-and-tower composition—about twenty years after the style appeared in the East, and six years after pointed windows were used tentatively at St Boniface Cathedral.[30]

Credit for the design has been given to Cockran and his chief mason, Duncan McRae (1813-98). According to local legend, Cockran and McRae argued about the length of the church, the latter maintaining that it was too long for the congregation to hear the minister's voice. In order to settle their dispute, Cockran is said to have spoken from the front, while McRae stood at the back near the entrance. 'Duncan McRae,' Cockran intoned, 'they tell me that you drink more rum than is good for you. In future, curb your bestial desires and try to live a sober, righteous and godly life.' The mason heard the minister all too clearly and admitted defeat: 'I've changed my mind,' he said, 'the church is nae long enough.'[31]

Although the finishes at St Andrew's were simple, the workmanship was high in quality. The floors were hand-sawn from trees felled nearby, while the paint, glass, putty, and nails were brought from England. The interior retains many engaging historical touches, such as the original light fixtures (which have been electrified) and the kneelers covered with buffalo hide. Cockran was a popular clergyman whose simplified form of the Church of England service attracted Presbyterian Scots as well as Anglicans.

Whether or not he was affected by rum, Duncan McRae fell off a scaffold while building the tower of St Andrew's and was unable to do heavy construction for the rest of his life. Nevertheless, he had a long career erecting, and presumably designing, buildings in the Red River Settlement. Born in the Hebrides, he entered the service of the Hudson's Bay Company in 1837 as a stonemason at Upper Fort Garry. When his term of service expired five

7.18 Twin Oaks, St Andrew's Parish, Manitoba, *c*. 1858. Manitoba Culture, Heritage and Citizenship; Historic Resources.

years later, he worked for both the Company (largely at Lower Fort Garry) and other clients along the Red River. McRae's stone buildings were among the most prominent in the settlement. His ecclesiastical work includes St Andrew's Rectory, built across from St Andrew's in 1854; St Peter's Church (1853-4) and Rectory ('Dynevor', 1865) at Chief Peguis's Indian settlement below St Andrew's; Kildonan Presbyterian Church (1852-4); and Little Britain Presbyterian Church (1874) in St Andrew's Parish. As no architects have been identified for any of these buildings, it is generally assumed that McRae was the designer as well as the builder.[32]

Among McRae's secular buildings was **Twin Oaks** (*c*. 1858), an attractive, if austere, landmark just south of St Andrew's [**7.18**]. It was erected as a boarding school to be run by Matilda Davis (whose father was chief factor at York Factory, and whose brother was chief factor at Lower Fort Garry), so that she might provide a proper education for the privileged young women of the wealthy parish. Their families, having asked Davis to start the school, together contributed $12,000 to pay for her salary, the girls' expenses, and construction.[33]

A five-bay, two-storey limestone building with a hipped roof, Twin Oaks displays the formal Georgian composition that prevailed in the Maritimes and Upper Canada in the first third of the century, in buildings such as Acacia Grove and Government House in Nova Scotia, and The Grange in Toronto. The nearby St Andrew's Rectory exhibits the same composition and scale, although a veranda covers the first storey. (Neither has pilasters, pediments, or other of the more gracious accoutrements of the Georgian style.) The two buildings hosted activities that maintained British imperial values—private education and the established religion—in the young Red River Settlement, and both adopted an architectural mode that had been associated with the British power structure for more than a century. Although the style had long run its course in Britain and the US, and had recently fallen out of fashion in eastern Canada as well, it presented a fresh and meaningful social image on the western frontier.

This appearance in the Red River Settlement, in the 1840s and 1850s, of the Early Gothic Revival and Georgian Classicism (as well as the twin-towered French-Canadian church) tells us as much about the nature of the frontier as it does about the architectural imagery. It supports the 'frontier hypothesis', first posed in the 1890s by American historian Frederick Jackson Turner. Defining the frontier as the presence of free land on the western edge of advancing settlement, Turner suggested that society experienced a continuous process of rebirth at every stage along the moving frontier, as people and their institutions came into contact with primitive conditions. Turner's environmentally driven hypothesis—which addressed social and political institutions, and not buildings—is still being debated by Americans a century later. Canadian historians have disagreed in their acceptance of its relevance to this country.[34]

Few architectural historians, from either country, have cared to test the applicability of the frontier hypothesis to building—although the effect of environmental factors on architecture has always been acknowledged. Nevertheless, Turner's thesis would seem to be quite relevant. It is evident that masonry buildings, in a stripped-down version of eastern styles, emerged on the Red River frontier about a generation and a half after the first settlement, which had produced comparatively primitive log structures. This was the same sequence, and interval, as in the Maritimes and Upper Canada (where the initial buildings had been constructed of both log and frame). If Duncan McRae, and the Reverends Taylor and Cockran—transplanted Britons who never lived in eastern Canada—were indeed responsible for the design of some of the more developed buildings, then the source of their building-forms would be found in the 'rebirth' of pervasive Anglo-Scottish Georgian and Gothic traditions, rather than in a simple transfer from one Canadian colony to another. In other words, the Maritime, Upper Canadian, and Red River frontier societies all underwent a process of architectural rebirth that saw a transition from a first phase—in which the available materials and technologies were used to provide basic shelter—to a second phase, in which that technology was stretched to its limits in order to reproduce a more sophisticated architectural imagery. In the first phase the cultural differences among the inhabitants were suppressed; in the second, they were expressed.

This same phenomenon will be seen all along the advancing Canadian frontier: in coastal British Columbia in the 1860s and in the interior of that province and the Yukon in the 1890s, and in the western interior throughout this period. The Canadian experience differed markedly from the American one, in that the settlement of the West occurred over a few decades rather than over a century or more.

The Western Interior

The Red River Settlement developed for a number of economically driven reasons, not the least of which was to protect the interests of the Hudson's Bay Company and the fur trade. These interests remained a deterrent to the colonization of the western interior—the vast land that lay between the Red River and the Rockies. Nevertheless, from the 1850s on the activities of missionaries, law-enforcement officers, Métis, and a few bold home-steaders—as well as the activities of the Hudson's Bay Company itself—pushed the frontier further west, and established a network of settlements across the Prairies. These communities provided an infrastructure that prepared the western interior for the influx of immigrants that would arrive with the completion of the Canadian Pacific Railway.

Between 1857 and 1860 two official expeditions explored the western interior. The first was a British party led by Captain John Palliser, the other a Canadian group headed by geologist Henry Youle Hind. Both concluded that the interior was divided into two natural sub-districts: a fertile belt lying in a vast arc, from the Red River Settlement northwest to the Saskatchewan River valley and the Rockies; and the arid plains to the south of this, which came to be known as Palliser's Triangle, forming a northern extension of the 'Great American Desert'. Although the bleak outlook for Palliser's Triangle was subsequently discredited in order to encourage settlement along the railway line (whether the area is indeed arid is still uncertain), early reports encouraged interest in the agricultural possibilities of the northern parkland and prairie.[35]

Official British government policy towards the western interior long remained non-interventionist, in the hope that the Hudson's Bay Company—and later the government of Canada—would take the lead in bringing about change. Popular opinion in Britain nevertheless grew in favour of settlement. Beginning in the late 1840s, a number of writers and editorialists called for the colonization of the Prairies to link the Canadas with British Columbia and form a political union that would be a barrier to American expansionism. The London *Daily Telegraph*, for example, predicted in 1864 that 'the time must come when the two tides of civilisation flowing inwards from either shore will meet and coalesce.' Other writers were pessimistic about the possibilities of the Northwest. The *Edinburgh Review* insisted that 'there is very little prospect of rapid settlement in the region between Canada and British Columbia.'[36]

When Lord Carnarvon introduced the Confederation Bill in the House of Lords in 1867, he boldly predicted:

> The time also is not far distant when the broad and fertile districts to the west of Canada, now under the rule of a trading Company, will form part of the Confederation—perhaps it is not very far distant when even British Columbia and Vancouver's Island may be incorporated, and one single system of English law and commerce and policy extend from the Atlantic to the Pacific.[37]

Despite this acceptance of the one-Canada idea, the British government made no initiatives at colonization. The first actions came from the Hudson's Bay Company itself and from religious, rather than temporal, authorities.

The Prairies become Canadian

The Hudson's Bay Company After it amalgamated with the North West Company in 1821, the Hudson's Bay Company enjoyed several decades of unchallenged monopoly of the furs of the western interior. No longer bound by its charter to trade exclusively from Hudson Bay, the HBC built a network of trading posts—which it called 'houses' and 'forts'—that were served by water and land from Upper and Lower Fort Garry. Although the Company remained opposed to settlement, since it was felt that this would interfere with the trade in furs, many of its posts nevertheless became the basis for established communities as non-Company residents—natives, families, artisans, and merchants—settled around them. The Company also unwittingly encouraged development by nurturing a small army of carpenters and other tradesmen who were available to serve other clients.

The principal route to the interior was the Carlton Trail (also known as the Saskatchewan Trail), which led from Fort Garry to Fort Pelly, near the head of the Assiniboine River, and on to Carlton House on the North Saskatchewan River, within the area that Palliser had identified as the fertile belt. From there the trail continued to Fort Pitt and Fort Edmonton (on the site of the city of that name). Although a portion of this route could be travelled by York boats and canoes, by the 1860s it became a well-travelled overland trail negotiated by brigades of Red River carts.

7.19 Reconstruction of Carlton House, Carlton, Saskatchewan, begun 1810. Government of Saskatchewan/82-1174-177.

Carlton House [7.19] was established in 1810, some 45 miles (72 km) north of the present Saskatoon. It was occupied until 1885, when it was destroyed by fire during the Northwest Rebellion. As with most Hudson's Bay Company trading posts, a group of free-standing buildings (here ten) was arranged formally within a nearly square compound surrounded by a fortification wall that was defended by corner bastions, and everything was erected expediently out of wood. (It therefore differed from Lower Fort Garry, which was carefully built of stone.) The buildings deteriorated quickly and required rebuilding three times during the three-quarters of a century the post remained in business. The palisade wall consisted of vertical poles, or pickets, inserted directly into the ground. Early photographs indicate that the one-storey buildings were constructed with Red River frame and had steep gabled roofs. The illustration shows the recent reconstruction of the palisade and some buildings. White lines on the ground mark the location of other, unreconstructed structures.[38]

The HBC's trading monopoly was broken in 1849 by the Sayer trial, a legal decision favouring four Métis who had been charged with illegal trafficking in furs.[39] The Company reacted aggressively to this new challenge with a large capital-development program, expanding its already impressive network of trading posts to provide the natives with additional, and more conveniently located, establishments throughout present-day Saskatchewan, Alberta, and British Columbia. Most posts were similar to Carlton House (and Lower Fort Garry) in their somewhat formal arrangement of free-standing structures around an interior courtyard, within a boundary wall—a microcosm of the British imperial town plan introduced into Canada at Halifax. In all, between the 1780s and the end of the nineteenth century some 130 fur-trade posts were built between Hudson Bay and the Rocky Mountains. The largest district posts, which combined trade with administrative and service activities, contained more than twenty buildings (e.g. Fort Vermilion and Fort Chipewyan), while the smallest wintering posts had fewer than a half-dozen. Facilities provided storage for imported goods, furs, and provisions, shops for blacksmiths and carpenters, and residences for employees. The dwellings of the officers were larger and more comfortable than those of the labourers, reflecting their respective ranks; the differences between them were especially evident in the larger establishments.

The buildings within the many fur-trade posts across western Canada (and in the northern states) were predominantly constructed of Red River frame—the technique that is also called *poteaux en coulisse* (grooved-post), and the Hudson's Bay style—which developed in New France and came west with the French-Canadian carpenters retained by the North West Company and the Hudson's Bay Company. Anthropologist Marius Barbeau made this point convincingly in 1945, when many people still wrongly believed that the most common building-method used horizontal logs with corner joints. Barbeau found descriptions of the grooved-post technique in early journals from David Thompson's Saleesh House in today's Montana (1809) to Fort Reliance on the east end of Great Slave Lake (described by George Back in 1833).[40]

Although the Hudson's Bay Company in 1869 transferred Rupert's Land to the new Canadian government, its trading and retail activities continue—into its fourth century of operation.

The Missions   Religious organizations in Britain, Europe, and Canada were resolved to pursue their mission to convert the natives to Christianity. The Roman Catholic mission at St Boniface became the headquarters of an Apostolic Vicariate (similar to a diocese) in 1844, and the Church of England created the Diocese of Rupert's Land in 1849. Although both were based in the Red River Settlement, they formed a staging ground for further activity that was supplemented by the religious orders and missionary societies.

The order of Oblates of Mary Immaculate, which had been founded in France in 1816, and came to Canada in 1841 at the invitation of Bishop Bourget, joined the Roman Catholic missionary efforts initiated by the Quebec clergy. Their combined success is seen in the large number of French names among Alberta communities, including Lacombe, Leduc, Vegreville, Grouard, and Lac La Biche. In June 1842 Father Jean-Baptiste Thibault (not an Oblate) passed through St Boniface and arrived at Fort Edmonton, and a year or two later he established a mission in the former Hudson's Bay Company fishery station at Lac Ste-Anne, 50 miles (80 km) to the northwest. He encouraged the Métis to settle down to an agricultural life and invited the Cree to wor-

ship in peace away from their enemies, the Blackfoot—thus pacifying the region and enabling the fur trade to flourish. When Dr James Hector, of the Palliser expedition, visited Lac Ste-Anne in March 1858 he observed two villages of 30 or 40 houses each, but noted that the Métis had little heart for farming.[41]

A decade later the younger (and Quebec-born) Oblate Father Albert Lacombe succeeded Father Thibault. Lacombe arrived at Fort Edmonton from St Boniface in 1852, at the age of twenty-five; he spent the next sixty-five years in the West working with the Métis and the Indians, who knew him fondly as 'Man of the Good Heart'. The most important of Father Lacombe's establishments was the **Oblate Mission of St Albert** [7.20], 10 miles (16 km) north of Edmonton, which he founded in 1861 as a home for Métis. He and his companions built a log house and chapel for the priest, and dwellings for the twenty families who came from Lac Ste-Anne. Two years later the Grey Nuns arrived and soon established a convent, an orphanage, and a public school. The original log chapel was a cathedral for a short while in 1867, when St Albert was named a diocese (an honour later removed to Edmonton). It was replaced by a larger building in 1870, moved a short distance away, and later (in 1929) it was enclosed in a brick building and re-used as the Lacombe Museum. In the 1980s the historic log structure was moved to a more prominent location on the site, restored by the Alberta government—its Red River frame structure again revealed—and renamed the Father Lacombe Chapel.

7.20 Father Lacombe Chapel, Oblate Mission of St Albert, St Albert, Alberta, 1861. Photograph by Harold Kalman.

Behind its gable and *clocher* (beyond the trees at the right in the photograph) stands the Foyer Grandin, a 2½-storey frame building with a cross-gable roof and projecting frontispiece that was built in 1882-7. Intended as a hospital and orphanage, it was used instead as a residence for priests and young seminarians. As in Manitoba, the span of two decades marked the change from simple log building to a more sophisticated manner that expressed the ambitions of its builders—like the Foyer Grandin (named after Bishop Vital-Justin Grandin), which used a wood version of traditional Quebec institutional buildings, rather than the British Georgian style of the Red River Settlement. The chapel, and the residence, share a large property with a church and several monastic buildings.[42]

The Church of England also became involved in the western interior. In 1849 the Church Missionary Society sent the Reverend Robert Hunt and his wife Georgianna to Lac La Ronge—some 150 miles (240 km) north of Prince Albert in today's northern Saskatchewan—to establish a mission. The area was home to the Cree, and had been the site of a fur-trade post since 1781. The Hunts chose a site for their mission further north, along a major trade route on arable land on the English (now Churchill) River. They named it Stanley Mission,

7.21 Holy Trinity Anglican Church, Stanley Mission, Saskatchewan, 1854-60. Photograph *c.* 1925. PAM/N13793/Zachary M. Hamilton Collection 40.

after Mrs Hunt's family estate, and erected a parsonage, a school for Indian children, and several supporting buildings.

Between 1854 and 1860 Hunt built a large church. **Holy Trinity Church at Stanley Mission [7.21]** would have been noteworthy anywhere in Canada; in the northern wilderness it was a truly remarkable achievement. The tall wooden building is sited picturesquely at the water's edge. It has a tall nave and lower side aisles, a deep chancel, and an entrance tower and steeple rising some 75 feet (23 m). Local stone was used for the foundation and the structure consists of a heavy timber frame with mud-and-stone infill walls—another instance of *colombage pierroté*. This is attributable to the original carpenter's having been a Métis named Fox who had come from the Red River Settlement; he left in 1855 and was replaced by a Mr Sanderson. They were helped by many among the sizeable community of Cree who lived at the mission. The walls were covered with horizontal siding inside and out: more than 2,000 boards were cut and split by hand from 400 logs. (They have since been replaced with milled siding.) The pointed-arched stained-glass windows, made in England, give the building the Gothic Revival character that by now was so essential to an Anglican church.[43]

Hunt intended from the start that his church should be an impressive Gothic Revival monument, and he 'studied views and descriptions of more than 50 churches and chapels' in his search

for models.[44] He came from England with window frames, glass, hinges, and locks; additional building materials, including nails and roofing felt, were shipped from England during construction. Hunt fashioned the weathervane from an iron bedstead that he had used for a decade. The original spire became unstable and was removed in the 1920s, to be replaced two decades later with a lower, less elaborate one. The church is seen here, in a photograph taken in 1908, with its original spire and well-weathered siding. It continues to be maintained, a striking monument that symbolizes the vitality of the early agricultural missions. Holy Trinity Church has the distinction of being the oldest-known building in Saskatchewan.

The Methodists were also active as missionaries in the western interior. Fervent nationalists as well as purveyors of the Christian faith, they believed that their way was particularly well suited to the rigours of the West. The Reverend James Evans established a mission in 1840 near the Hudson's Bay Company's Norway House, at the northern end of Lake Winnipeg, and he used this as a base for work further west. The most important of the early Methodist missions was Victoria, located in Cree territory along the Carlton House-to-Edmonton wagon trail, 70 miles (110 km) down the North

7.22 Storehouse (1865) and Clerk's Quarters (*c*. 1866-7), Victoria Mission, Alberta. Photograph *c*. 1895. Provincial Archives of Alberta/G.2953.

Saskatchewan River from Edmonton. The community that developed is of particular interest because mission, fur-trade post, and agriculture combined in what was the first diversified settlement in the Canadian interior west of the Red River.

The Victoria mission was founded in 1862 by the Reverend George and John McDougall, a devoted father-and-son team from Ontario. George, who was superintendent of all Methodist missionary work in the West, left instructions for building the mission with twenty-year-old John (who was not ordained until 1872) and the Reverend Thomas Woolsey—and then returned to Norway House. He forgot, however, to specify a building system. The subsequent debate between the young John McDougall and Woolsey reveals that the two current manners of building with logs—the Red River frame and horizontal logs with corner notches— were regarded as viable alternatives. Woolsey advocated the former, with upright timbers set ten feet apart and grooved to accommodate horizontal tenoned logs; McDougall recommended using long logs laid horizontally. In the end Woolsey prevailed, and logs were cut and stockpiled through the fall and winter of 1862.[45]

In fact, only a temporary one-room log cabin and three outbuildings were constructed in 1863. Some of the logs were cut under the supervision of George McDougall himself, who had returned to the Victoria mission with his family. A carpenter named Larsen built the roof, floor, and windows.

The mission house was completed in August 1864. The eight-room structure, with four rooms in each of its two storeys, was built 'of logs, white-washed without and boarded within, amply forti-fied against the severest winds.' Lumber was 'whip-sawed', and the missionary party, aided by carpen-ter Larsen, had to 'straighten and plane and groove and tongue and bead, all by hand.' The windows were glass, surely a luxury in that remote location. A palisade of tamarack logs was built around the mission house in order, as John McDougall wrote, to 'command respect from the lawless around home, and be a great help from enemies who might come from a distance.' Other buildings in the mis-sion included a school (the first Protestant school west of Portage la Prairie and a building that for several years served also as the church) and a hospi-tal. Many settlers were attracted to the mission, most of them English-speaking people of mixed ancestry.[46]

The mission also attracted the Hudson's Bay Company, which established a new post at Victoria in the fall of 1864 and called it Fort Victoria. Lo-cated adjacent to the mission and just east of the school, it served as a small but productive compo-nent of the Company's network for three decades, providing Edmonton with a supply of high-quality furs. The first buildings to be erected were the **Storehouse** and **Clerk's Quarters** [7.22], seen side by side in an early photograph. The Clerk's Quar-ters, on the right, was likely completed in 1865, and the Storehouse by 1866 or 1867. One-and-a-half storeys high with a gable over the entrance, the Clerk's Quarters has the form of an Ontario cottage, yet grooved-post Red River frame was used in its construction—an interesting fusion of the Upper Canada form with the Hudson's Bay Company's preferred building method. The store, a larger building with a simple gable roof, was also con-structed with a Red River frame. It was said to have been built by Samuel Whitford and Joe Turner, Métis who had come to Victoria from the Red River Settlement.[47]

A map of Fort Victoria drawn by Chief Factor Richard Hardisty in 1874 shows seven independent buildings set within a palisade. Although all were oriented north-south or east-west, they were not grouped symmetrically, as were the larger posts. The Company also operated a grist mill nearby. The trading post was run sporadically until 1898, when it closed its doors for the last time.

George McDougall left the Victoria mission in 1871, by which time it was an established village with a permanent population of 150, augmented by the many natives who periodically set up camp around it. However, his goal of making farmers of the Métis was only marginally successful. The com-munity was one of few in today's Alberta that had been surveyed on the river-lot system (another was St Albert)—similar to that of the Red River Settle-ment and to the earlier form of land division in New France, but in distinct contrast to the grid system of the Dominion Land Survey.

Sandford Fleming described Victoria the follow-ing year:

> The church, (which is also used as a school-room) the Mission House, and Fort are all at the west end of the settlement. The log-houses of the half-breeds, (English and Scotch) intermingled with the tents of the Crees, extend in a line from this west end along the bank of the river, each man having a frontage on the river, and his grain planted in a little hollow that runs behind the houses, beneath the main rise of the ridge. Most of their hay they cut in the valley, on the other side of the ridge...The farming is on a very lim-ited scale, as the men prefer hunting buffalo, fishing, or freighting for the Company to steady agricultural labour...[48]

As the buffalo disappeared from the area, many Métis left. They were succeeded mostly by Euro-Canadians—first by migrants from the East, and then by European immigrants—and Victoria be-came known as the village of Pakan (named after a Cree chief who was a close friend of George McDougall). Victoria Settlement is now a provin-cial historic site. Of the original mission buildings, there are only two survivors: the Clerk's Quarters, now restored, and the Pakan Methodist Church, built in 1906.

The McDougalls continued their work among the natives and the whites. They are remembered in the McDougall Methodist Church on 101 Street in Edmonton (H.A. Magoon [1863-1941], 1909-10), which stands on the site of the log church that George McDougall built in 1873, and has been moved to Fort Edmonton Park. They were also closely connected with the mission to the Stoney Indians at Morleyville (now Morley), in the foothills west of Calgary. John McDougall began the mission buildings in 1873, and started con-struction of a frame church two years later. Origi-nally known as the **Morleyville Mission Church** and today called the McDougall Memorial United Church [7.23], the simple structure was built with

7.23 McDougall Memorial United Church, Morley, Alberta, *c.* 1875. Photograph 1953. Glenbow Archives/NA-1675-1.

materials brought from Fort Benton in Montana. A drawing of the late 1870s shows only a plain gable-roofed block, although a small hipped-roof tower has stood at the entrance end for many years. In its original form the church would hardly have differed from a plain Methodist meeting house of nearly a century earlier. Only the triangular heads atop the windows—a recollection of the Gothic arch—offered a concession to traditional church forms.[49]

The whiskey posts and the North-West Mounted Police During the early 1870s the Canadian prairie came as close as it ever did to the North American myth of the 'Wild West', as a result of the brief but significant whiskey trade in southern Alberta. American traders spilled over the border and established dozens of posts where they traded spirits with members of the Blackfoot Confederacy in return for buffalo robes and other furs. Most of the whiskey and other supplies came from merchants I.G. Baker and Company or T.C. Power and Brother Company, both located in Fort Benton, at the head of navigation on the Missouri River in today's Montana. The British government exercised no control over the Northwest, and the Hudson's Bay Company was not active in the area, so the trade went unchecked for several years. This episode was significant because it contributed to the decline of the natives by annihilating the buffalo herds and encouraging alcohol use. It also led to the establishment of Canadian sovereignty in the West. None of the posts still stand, but the remains of several have been identified.[50]

The first, largest, and most important of the whiskey posts was **Fort Whoop-Up** (originally called Fort Hamilton after one of its two partners) on the Oldman River (a source of the South Sas-

7.24 Yard of Fort Whoop-Up, near Lethbridge, Alberta, 1870. Photograph *c.* 1878. RCMP Archives, Ottawa/neg. 1240 (Old Forts).

katchewan River), near today's Lethbridge. Opened in 1869, it was burned by the Blackfoot and rebuilt in 1870 as a substantial complex protected by a palisade and two bastions. The new Fort Whoop-up [7.24] was built by William Gladstone, a former employee of the Hudson's Bay Company and a carpenter at Fort Benton. The post would have done the Company proud; indeed, a correspondent to the Toronto *Globe* said that 'in many respects it appears to be in advance of even the best Hudson Bay Company's forts I have seen in the Territory.'[51]

Although the documentary records and archaeological evidence are contradictory, Fort Whoop-Up was probably a rectangular compound about 150 by 120 feet (46 by 37 m), with buildings constructed along—and forming an integral part of—its western and northern walls. A smaller structure stood near the southeast corner. The buildings contained living quarters, artisans' shops, stables, and stores, and cellars provided additional storage space. Gladstone oversaw the cutting and squaring of some 6,000 cottonwood trees for the fort's construction. He built the palisade with logs set vertically; the bastions, located at opposite corners, were made of horizontal logs with corner lap joints (square-cut notches that were more common in the US than Canada); and the buildings used the familiar Red River frame, their openings kept small for defensive purposes. The photograph shows the ends of the two ranges of buildings, with the wall between them enclosing the well in the northwest corner. It was taken around 1878, when the fort was occupied by the North-West Mounted Police. (The story of how they came to be there will be told shortly.) The fort was for some time inhabited by settlers and squatters, but fires and the removal of wood for other structures ultimately led to its disappearance. Its reconstruction on a nearby site was based on faulty historical evidence.

The route from Fort Benton to the whiskey posts became known as the Whoop-Up Trail. In 1870-3 more than forty trading posts were built in the area. Some were surrounded by palisades, although with fewer and smaller buildings than at Fort Whoop-Up, while most consisted only of a rough log structure with a sod roof that was quickly and cheaply built but could not be well defended against Indian attack. (Some traders worked from their wagons, at far higher risk.) Many posts were named after traders (Conrad's Outpost, French's Blackfoot Crossing, Fort Weatherwax) and after events (Fort Standoff). Archaeological remains are all that are left of them.

The Canadian government responded decisively to the threat posed by the whiskey posts. Prime Minister Sir John A. Macdonald insisted that the law be respected in the West and in 1873 organized the North-West Mounted Police (NWMP) to enforce it. He insisted upon the strict discipline and high standards of a military regiment, and dressed the police in the scarlet tunics that the natives associated with the honour and fairness of the British redcoats. The first 150 recruits (their number soon doubled) assembled at Lower Fort Garry in October 1873 to begin training. The next July they began their legendary 'march west' to the land of the whiskey traders. The five-mile-long supply train—made up of some 275 policemen, 235 oxen and cattle, 310 horses, 187 carts and wagons, and 2 nine-pound field guns—travelled nearly 800 miles (1280 km) over the summer.

In early October 1874 the NWMP, under the command of Assistant Commissioner James Macleod, captured the vacated Fort Whoop-Up without incident and occupied it. For the force's headquarters Macleod chose a site 30 miles (50 km) further west along the Oldman River, and the recruits set out to build a post that they called Fort Macleod. This, the first architectural expression of government authority in the region, was built much in the manner of Fort Whoop-Up. The living quarters, stables, hospital, stores, kitchen, wash-house, and latrine were built in a row against a perimeter palisade, which was constructed of cottonwood logs cut into 12-foot (3.7-m) lengths and set upright in a square about 200 feet (60 m) across. The log walls were plastered with mud, and the roofs were covered with sod and sand.

The distinction between the buildings of the NWMP and those of the whiskey traders—the hunter and its prey—was blurred, since Fort Macleod followed the design of Fort Whoop-Up; both, moreover, were constructed loosely on the model of a Hudson's Bay Company post. To confuse matters more, doors, sashes, and furnishings at Fort Macleod were supplied by I.G. Baker and Company in Fort Benton. This large concern traded in groceries and general commercial goods as well as furs—and, as we have seen, whiskey. It maintained its own transportation system of bull teams and steamboats.

At all three kinds of establishments—the posts of the fur-traders, the police, and the whiskey-traders—the palisaded fort met the need for a building-type that could accommodate a remote outpost in relative security on the alien prairie. At a

7.25 Yard of the second Fort Macleod, Alberta, 1883. Photograph 1890. RCMP Archives, Ottawa/neg. 7360 (Old Forts).

more emotional level, it provided an architectural response to the loneliness and fear felt by many inhabitants in this open, unsettled land that lay beyond the settled frontier—a particularly Canadian response to the environment that literary critic Northrop Frye described as the 'garrison mentality'. The ordered arrangement of structures—and the tendency, at a number of fur-trade posts (such as Lower Fort Garry), to plant flowers and attain a domestic feeling—represented ways of coping with the sense of isolation.[52]

The structure of the posts, as well as their plans and landscaping, responded to the western environment, whose predominantly small trees led to the use of relatively short and thin logs. The Red River frame (used at Fort Whoop-Up and the Hudson's Bay Company posts) was a relatively permanent structural system that required a measure of carpentry skills; on the other hand, vertical logs (used at Fort Macleod) provided a more expedient—but less-sound—technique that could be employed by policemen who were less experienced as builders. The consequences of second-class construction at the NWMP post were predictable. 'This is the worst Fort I have been to yet, for comfort,' wrote Constable William Parker to his father. 'The buildings are miserable, mud floors and mud roofs, so that when it rains there is a devil of a mess.'[53] To facilitate improvements, Fort Macleod acquired a portable sawmill in the following year, although it was not put into working order until 1876.

In 1883 the original fort was abandoned for higher and drier land some $2\frac{1}{2}$ miles (4 km) to the west. The **second Fort Macleod [7.25]**—no longer the force's headquarters (which had been relocated to Regina) but now the home of 'D' Division—was built of sawn lumber, set on stone foundations and firmly spiked and braced. The complex was 484 feet (148 m) long and 254 feet (77 m) wide, with a number of free-standing buildings set near the palisade facing a central parade ground. The exterior walls were covered with tar paper and wood siding, and the roofs were properly shingled. Since brick was unavailable, the chimneys and stovepipes were made of zinc.

A substantial village grew up adjacent to Fort Macleod, periodically augmented by the tipis of large encampments of Indians who found security in the post. The original purpose of the settlement was to supply and service the force; but by the time the post was abandoned in 1922, the town of Fort Macleod had a vital economic life of its own as a service centre for a prosperous agricultural region. Largely dismantled, the fort was later reconstructed as a tourist attraction, although not accurately.

This pattern recurred as the NWMP erected a large network of posts across today's Alberta and Saskatchewan, most of which formed the nuclei of

345

western communities. In the spring of 1875 'F' Division established Fort Calgary at the confluence of the Bow and Elbow Rivers, north of Fort Macleod, near a whiskey post that had been set up by the I.G. Baker Company three years earlier. Materials were supplied by I.G. Baker for this police post as well. The fort was entirely rebuilt in 1882. The Baker store, some 100 yards (90 m) south of the barracks, quickly became a social and commercial centre for the surrounding area—serving the Mounted Police, Indians, traders, and travellers. Stimulated by the transcontinental railway, the post and commercial settlement soon grew to become the city of Calgary [**9.62, 63, 64**].[54]

The NWMP used similar building techniques at most of their posts, imposing the government's vision of peace and order on the virgin landscape. At Fort Walsh, established in 1875 in the Cypress Hills near today's Maple Creek, Saskatchewan, a palisade of vertical logs about 300 by 200 feet (90 by 60 m) enclosed a series of buildings that were mostly constructed with logs laid horizontally; roofs were made of poles covered with clay. The windows came from Fort Benton. When the fort was enlarged in 1880, bastions were added at two corners of the palisade. It was here that Superintendent James Walsh persuaded Chief Sitting Bull and his band of Sioux to return to the United States, averting a potentially major confrontation. Fort Walsh replaced Fort Macleod as the force's headquarters in 1878, and a village of 40-odd buildings sprang up overnight just outside the palisade. However, when the railway bypassed the post, the headquarters was moved in 1883 to the young town of Pile-of-Bones—soon to become Regina—and Fort Walsh was dismantled and deserted.[55]

The NWMP headquarters at Regina, begun in 1883, reveals the impact of the railway on building in the West. (The CPR reached Regina in August 1882.) The complex was built partly of 'section buildings' (also described as 'portable buildings'; today we would call them prefabricated buildings), which had been ordered from James Reilly & Co. of Sherbrooke, Quebec, and Logan and O'Doherty of Ottawa, and shipped by rail. They were intended for economy and expediency, although they may have also been seen as giving the force's architecture a touch of sophistication. Forty such buildings were erected at Regina; they varied in size between 12 by 16 feet (3.7 by 4.9 m; a kitchen) and 30 by 50 feet (9.2 by 15.3 m; stables). Commissioner A.G. Irvine reported, only months after their assembly, that he was dissatisfied with the prefabs:

The portable buildings had suffered very much, through the severity of the climate, and having been erected in mid-winter they received much rougher treatment than they otherwise would have done. The sections of which the buildings are composed separated, roofs leaked...and floors warped and twisted.[56]

Massive repairs were required. This early experiment in using mass-produced, mass-marketed building systems side-by-side with hand-built structures may not have succeeded, but it was the leading edge of a trend that would dominate the architecture of the West.

In the same years that the federal government erected simple log, frame, and prefabricated police outposts without any pretension to architectural style on the prairie frontier, it was building substantial masonry structures in a range of high styles in the cities and towns of eastern and central Canada. But so powerful were the levelling forces at the edge of settlement that to have built anything more elaborate would have been unthinkable.

Permanent settlement

The purchase of Rupert's Land from the Hudson's Bay Company in 1869 (the sale was consummated a year later) made the prairie a part of Canada and brought Prime Minister Macdonald's dream of a continent-wide nation a giant step closer to reality. Manitoba (the southern portion of the present province) entered Confederation in 1870—only three years after the maritime and central provinces had joined together—partly as a reaction to the Red River Rebellion of 1869-70, the first of two rebellions led by Louis Riel. British Columbia joined Confederation a year later. In these same years Macdonald began to prepare the way for a transcontinental railway that would tie the country together, although that momentous development would not be completed for more than a decade.

The shape of prairie settlement was determined by the Dominion Lands Act of 1872, which provided a uniform system for surveying and settling the land, based on American homestead legislation. Just as river lots had done in the St Lawrence valley, and the chequered plan in Upper Canada, the Dominion Land Survey provided for the orderly settlement of the prairie that met the economic and social needs of the time. Arable land was divided into townships, each made up of 36 sections of 640 acres (259 hectares). The basic homestead was a 'quarter-section' of 160 acres (65 hectares). Two sections in each township were reserved for schools. The survey drew lines on the land and gave the landscape the dominant pattern of squares, oriented to the points of the compass, that is so clearly visible as one flies over the Prairies. It conflicted with the river-lot system, which nevertheless remained intact in settled areas along the Red, Assiniboine, and Saskatchewan Rivers. The legislation provided for land to be given to new 'homesteaders' in return for a nominal fee and the fulfilment of certain conditions, including building a house and cultivating a part of the land within three years.[57]

The governments in Ottawa and Winnipeg addressed the matter of settling the young province by encouraging people in eastern Canada and overseas to immigrate. Ontario had run out of good arable land, and the attempt to settle marginal farmland in the Canadian Shield was largely unsuccessful, so many farmers from that province came to Manitoba to acquire larger and better properties. Francophones from Quebec and the New England states came as well. All adapted their traditions of building and organizing the land to the new conditions on the prairie.

Two groups of European immigrants who arrived before the railway were the Icelanders and the Mennonites. The Icelandic settlers left their island because their livelihood was threatened by Danish trade restrictions, an epidemic among sheep, and volcanic eruptions. Finding the soil, forest, and abundant fish around the southwestern shore of Lake Winnipeg to their liking, upwards of 1,500 people settled in the area between Gimli and Hecla Island in 1875-6, and more followed. (Some had first tried Kinmount, Ontario, but found the land there unsuitable.) They formed the colony of New Iceland, which featured a democratic system of local government. In 1881 it became a part of Manitoba as the boundaries of the province were expanded. Once sawn lumber was available, these new Canadians developed a wood-frame architecture that fitted comfortably into the late-nineteenth-century prairie vernacular. Many Icelanders remain in the Gimli area, as do vestiges of their early buildings.[58]

Mennonite communities The cultural and architectural patterns of the Mennonites who came to Manitoba in the 1870s were more distinctive.

A religious-cultural sect that traces its origins to the Anabaptist movement in sixteenth-century Holland, Germany, and Switzerland, the Mennonites were frequently forced to migrate in search of religious freedom. One group of Mennonites came to Upper Canada, by way of the US, after 1786, settling in today's Kitchener-Waterloo district in southern Ontario. A second found temporary refuge in Poland, Prussia, and then southern Russia; but the policy of 'Russification' in the 1870s brought nearly 7,000 Russian Mennonites to southern Manitoba with promises of military exemption and separate schools. A delegation examined the land in 1873, and a year later the first contingent arrived in Winnipeg by steamboat.

Eight empty townships east of the Red River and seventeen west of it (south of Winnipeg) were set aside for Mennonite settlement; these became known as the East and West Reserves. The Mennonites continued their traditional way of life, which included living in 'street villages' and not on their farms. The Dominion Lands Act required all settlers to build a house on their land, but this regulation was first waived and later enshrined in amendments that also gave the Minister of the Interior the discretionary right to allow groups of twenty or more families 'to settle together in a hamlet or village.' This 'hamlet clause' opened the door for many other cultural groups accustomed to village living.[59]

The Mennonites divided into groups, usually made up of friends who belonged to the same congregation and agreed to establish a village. A surviving agreement for Blumenort declares that the group desired to establish a village community such as it had been accustomed to in Russia, so that everyone would benefit equally from the wooded land, the arable land, and the meadows.[60] The Dominion Lands Act and the survey determined the size of the village land (the *flur*) and its boundaries, but within these boundaries the surveyors' 'metes and bounds' were ignored.

The values attached to agriculture and democracy are evident in the town plan. The distinctive arrangement of the 'street villages' along a main street, with the fields surrounding it, is still apparent in a number of communities, such as **New Bergthal** [7.26] in the West Reserve. Most village streets were laid out on high land or in a natural clearing and parallel to a creek, giving everybody access to water. Building lots for farming families had a frontage of about 200 feet (60 m), usually on both sides of the street, and the houses were set

back about 100 feet (30 m) to provide space for trees (at New Bergthal the street trees are cottonwoods), gardens, and fences. Lots were reserved in the centre of the village for the church and school. At one end of the village, sometimes along a side street, were smaller lots for the people who did not farm—tradesmen, retired farmers, and young married couples—and in time commercial buildings developed here. The village windmill (similar to **5.43**) was usually located at the other end of the street. The surrounding land within the *flur* was divided into a few large fields; the arable parts were further split into long, narrow strips for individual use—each villager being allocated the same number of strips—and those parts not suitable for cultivation were reserved as a common pasture. This provided a much more efficient division of land than the survey, which disregarded such key factors as soils and drainage. About 45 such villages were formed in the East Reserve and 70 in the West Reserve.

The Mennonite settlers first built a temporary dwelling that would provide basic shelter until there was time to build a more permanent house. Two kinds of temporary houses were common. One was the *sarai* [**7.27**], a tall structure about 25

7.26 (*opposite*) Aerial view of New Bergthal, Manitoba. Photograph 1959. National Air Photo Library, with the permission of Energy Mines and Resources Canada/A-16615-23: 17-7-59.

7.27 A *sarai* (Mennonite thatched house/barn), Manitoba. Photograph *c*. 1875. PAM/N10902.

feet (8 m) square, with steeply sloping walls in the form of a hipped roof, about 18 feet (5.5 m) high at the ridge, supported by poles and covered with thatch made from prairie grass. Separate parts were used by the family and the farm animals—combining the house with the stable was traditional among Mennonites. The family portion was sometimes lined with logs or shiplap (horizontal wood siding), which would then be re-used in the permanent house.

Many people in the East Reserve built a *sarai* only to discover that it did not effectively keep out the winter cold. Consequently later settlers, including most of those on the West Reserve, built a *semlin*, or sod house, which was considerably warmer. A *semlin* was constructed by excavating about a yard (1 m) into the ground and building a wall of sods about the same height above the hole. Poles extended across the walls were covered with sod to make the roof. The typical *semlin* was about 15 by 35 feet (4.5 by 10 m), with slightly more than half occupied by the family and the remainder by livestock. Klaas Wall of Neuhorst described his *semlin* in a letter sent to friends in Russia in 1876:

I want to report briefly how we constructed our dwelling. For our living quarters we dug an excavation to a depth of $2\frac{1}{2}$ feet. It is $29\frac{1}{2}$ long and its inside width is $12\frac{1}{2}$ feet. The inside walls and the floor were finished with boards. The roof, however, was first covered with split oakwood which was nailed into place, then plastered with clay

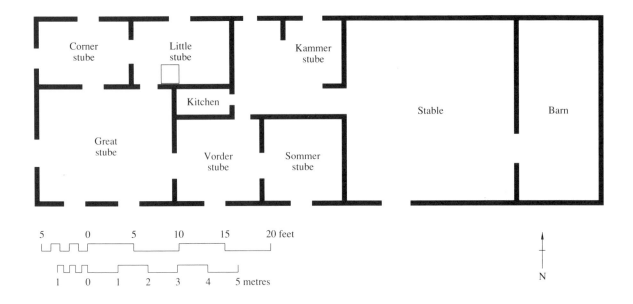

Corner stube	Little stube	Kammer stube		
Kitchen		Stable	Barn
Great stube	Vorder stube	Sommer stube		

| 5 | 0 | 5 | 10 | 15 | 20 feet |

| 1 | 0 | 1 | 2 | 3 | 4 | 5 metres |

N

7.28 Typical plan of a Mennonite house/barn, Manitoba. Drawn by David Byrnes after A. Klaus, *Unsere Kolonen* (1954).

7.29 Teichroeb house, Mennonite Heritage Village, Steinbach, Manitoba, 1892. Photograph by Harold Kalman, 1986.

and overlaid with earth. And so we believe we have a beautiful warm room prepared for winter.[61]

Both kinds of buildings were susceptible to spring flooding and neither was very comfortable. As one resident complained, 'There was sufficient good timber to build good farm houses, but no!—they had to build like in Russia.'[62] Although none of these temporary shelters survive, a *semlin* (without the stable) has been reconstructed at the Mennonite Heritage Village at Steinbach, in the East Reserve.

The permanent houses that were built after these shelters followed the traditional form of the **Mennonite house/barn** [7.28]. The two were connected to form a long, articulated building, with the end of the house facing the street. The typical complement of rooms comprised the *grosse stube* (great room), which was parlour and guest room; the *eckstube* (corner room), or master bedroom; the *klein stube* (small room), the bedroom for the girls and maidservants; and the *hinterhaus* (back of the house), used as the kitchen and dining-room. Sometimes partitions divided one or another of the rooms. The boys slept in the *sommerstube* (summer

room), an unheated bedroom next to the *gans* or corridor between the house and the stable. (The spelling of the German names varies with the dialect.) The entrance was near the centre of a long side, not facing the street. The centre of the house contained a large brick oven, built from floor to ceiling with hand-made bricks and used for cooking and heating. It was fired from the kitchen and fuelled with wood or bricks of manure. The barn, which was usually a bit wider than the house, contained stalls for the horses and cows (the stable) and often also a mow for hay and an area for implement storage (the barn).[63]

The house/barn is a folk building-form that can be traced back to medieval Frisia (the former North

7.30 Reinlander Mennonite Church, Reinland, Manitoba, 1876. Photograph by Edward Ledohowski, 1983. Manitoba Culture, Heritage and Citizenship; Historic Resources.

Sea nation that was subsequently divided between Holland and Germany). The Mennonites brought it from there to eastern Europe and then to Manitoba, making it one of the oldest vernacular house-types in Canada. The walls of the house/barn were almost always built of logs, and the roofs were thatched, since sawn lumber was unavailable at first, and then was too expensive to purchase. The Mennonites had built with brick in Russia and were unfamiliar with logs, so they learned construction techniques from their Canadian neighbours: dovetail and saddle-notched joints from the Ontarians, and Red River frame from the French and Métis.

The former Jake Thiessen house at Osterwick in the West Reserve, built *c*. 1878, is a rare survivor of the last type, which simplified the traditional method of building a Red River frame. Squared timbers were used for the uprights and mortised into a sill and a top plate; the infill logs were left in the round and simply wedged between the uprights (rather than fitted into a groove). Diagonal braces at the upper corners stabilized the wall. A thick coating of mud plaster (*crépi*) was applied to both sides and helped to keep the filler logs in place. External wood siding now conceals the logs.[64]

Other techniques were used as sawn lumber became available. The **Jacob Teichroeb house [7.29]**, built at Chortitz in the West Reserve in 1892, has walls built of 2-by-6 boards stacked on top of each other—a milled variant of the log house (called stack-wall or cribbed construction, the manner in which grain elevators were built). Horizontal wood siding protects them from the weather. (In time, sawn boards were applied to both the outside and inside of most log buildings.) Other than the walls, everything else follows the traditional Mennonite house-form. The barn was slightly wider and higher than the house. In 1967 the house was moved to the Mennonite Heritage Museum, where it has been restored and can be visited.[65]

As time passed, the Mennonites abandoned many of their building and planning traditions in favour of those of their neighbours. The strip fields were not suited to mechanization, and so many farmers left the villages and began to build houses on their quarter-section, often erecting separate structures like those of their non-Mennonite neighbours. Many who stayed in the villages built new houses that were oriented so that the long side faced the street, with an enclosed passage leading to the old barn behind it, giving the house-and-

351

barn complex a T-shape. Nevertheless, many street villages and house-barns remain, a testament to the strong cultural values of the Mennonites, the first non-English and non-French group to immigrate to the Canadian Prairies.

Churches and schools were simple, straightforward buildings that expressed the directness of Mennonite faith and education. The church was a rectangular building with a gabled roof. The entrance (often protected by a projecting draft vestibule) was originally located in the middle of one long side and the pulpit placed directly across from it, so that the minister could be heard clearly and to provide a sense of community. The men sat on one side and the women on the other. The plainness and the seating arrangement had much in common with Congregationalist and Methodist meeting-houses in the East, although the Mennonite church was only one storey high, longer in its proportions, and completely unadorned.

The **Reinlander Mennonite Church** (1876) in Reinland, the oldest Mennonite church in western Canada, was built this way, although the many alterations include moving the main entrance to an end [7.30]. (Placing the entrance at one end and the pulpit at the other became the established manner, similar to the arrangement of other Protestant churches.) Like that of other Mennonite churches, its construction was a community affair. Isaak Muller, who co-ordinated the project, told each farmer to bring a log 30 feet long, 8 inches wide, and 6 inches thick, planed on all sides; if the farmer could not find a tree this big, he was permitted to bring it in two sections. Carpenter Jacob Fehr finished the logs to the correct dimensions, and carpenter Abraham Dyck was in charge of construction. Every villager contributed labour, teams, and material. Building supplies that could not be made were purchased in Emerson.

Schools were similar in size and design. One side was used as the schoolroom and the other as the teacher's residence. The Mennonites had been promised the right to private education when they came to Canada, but the Manitoba government's Public School Attendance Act of 1916 forced them to be educated in English in public schools. The issue of education had led to the Mennonites' leaving Russia for Canada, and after 1920 many members of the community left Manitoba, some for northern Alberta and British Columbia and others for an entirely new life in Mexico.[66]

The architecture of the Métis   In preparation for the purchase of Rupert's Land from the Hudson's Bay Company, the Canadian government in 1869 sent surveyors to the Red River Settlement. This intrusion alarmed the Métis, by now a majority in the area, who recognized the imminent threat to the land rights they had enjoyed for decades without benefit of title. Despite the provision for the distribution of land to the Métis under the Manitoba Act of 1870, many chose to emigrate west (along the Carlton Trail) and south from the Red River to their hunting and wintering grounds, where the presence of the remaining buffalo herds promised the continuation of their traditional ways of life. Many congregated around the Oblate missions or in small clusters on the plains. Prince Albert, Lac La Biche, Qu'Appelle, St Laurent, Duck Lake, Batoche, and numerous other settlements were created or augmented by émigré Red River Métis between 1870 and 1875.[67]

In Manitoba, Métis houses had been built of both Red River frame and notched horizontal logs. The latter became the rule for Métis farm buildings in the western interior. Only occasional vestiges of mortise-and-tenon construction or grooved posts with tenons are found. The **Fayant homestead** (*c.* 1915) in the Qu'Appelle Valley, Saskatchewan, represents the predominant rural type [7.31]. It is a simple rectangular structure, $1\frac{1}{2}$ storeys high, with a gable roof (re-clad with asphalt shingles) and the

7.31 Fayant homestead, Qu'Appelle Valley, Saskatchewan, *c.* 1915. Photograph by Peter Charles, 1984.

7.32 Interior view of a Métis house. *Canadian Illustrated News*, 10:3 (3 October 1874). Collection of Harold Kalman.

entrance on the long side. A stovepipe protrudes through the ridge. The walls are constructed of squared horizonal logs connected at the corners with dovetail joints. It originally had a coating of mud-and-straw plaster on the exterior, applied to lath made from diagonally nailed twigs; a patch of plaster survives over the door, beneath the eave. (The Métis, like the house-builders of New France, used the verb *bousiller* to describe the rendering process.) Milled lumber was also used for ceiling joists—the joist ends can be seen along the façade—and some other components. Windows were generally 2-over-2 double-hung sash, usually milled, with plain frames.[68]

Such houses were usually unpartitioned within, allowing eating, sleeping, and general social activity to occur in a single space. An 1874 view of a Métis interior, although somewhat romanticized, shows a typical situation [7.32]. Planks cover the floors, and long pieces of milled lumber form tie-beams from the top of one log wall to the other; these were sometimes (although not here) planked to provide an attic storey. The room is sparsely furnished, with two tables and a pair of storage trunks in evidence. The usual clay fireplace at the end has been superseded by a cast-iron stove, used for both cooking and heating.

The houses in the new Métis settlements resembled those that had been built along the Red and Assiniboine Rivers, illustrating how a vernacular

building-type migrated from one frontier to another. The residence of Sampson Breland in Dumont, Alberta (also known as the Laboucane Settlement), built in 1880 and of the type described above, is very similar to the Breland house in St François, Manitoba, the family's place of origin, which was built by a relative who did not move west.[69]

The Métis also formed a number of small villages. One that was to figure prominently in the political development of Canada was Batoche, about 40 miles (65 km) south of Prince Albert on the South Saskatchewan River. Around 1872 François-Xavier Letendre (*dit* Batoche) established a ferry at the point where the Carlton Trail crossed the river, and there he erected a trading shop and storehouses. His business flourished, and throughout the next decade newcomers settled on river lots on both sides of the river. The village took Letendre's popular name, and was a bustling commercial centre until it became a focus of hostilities during the Northwest Rebellion. It was here, in May 1885, that about 900 Canadian militia under the command of Major-General Frederick Middleton defeated a force of fewer than 300 Métis and Indian fighters led by Gabriel Dumont. Louis Riel was captured and brought to trial, which resulted in his controversial execution.

In the east village of Batoche, a row of commercial and residential buildings developed in a linear strip (following the French tradition) along the Carlton Trail. Xavier Letendre was *'le seigneur de la mission'* and the leading citizen of the community. His substantial house, built in 1878, reflected his social and economic status. In size and finish it was worlds apart from the common Métis houses. Both the **Letendre (Batoche) house [7.33]** and Letendre's second store (1885) were built by Quebec carpenter Ludger Gareau. The house, 2½-storeys high, was faced in horizontal wood siding, with a cross gable in the centre of the façade (reminiscent of an Ontario cottage) and a veranda with a bell-shaped roof and pediment over the entrance. Bargeboard and pendants decorated the eaves, the window-heads had pediments on the first and second storeys, and arches surrounded the attic windows. A large wing extending to the rear is not visible in the photograph. Stone foundations defined a large cellar. This, and the other houses in the east village, no longer stand, and not even careful archaeological investigation has been able to reveal their structural system. The walls were

7.33 Letendre (Batoche) house, Batoche, Saskatchewan, 1885. Photograph *c.* 1890-94. Saskatchewan Archives Board/R-A5634-2.

likely erected of logs beneath the milled siding, but whether this was horizontal log or Red River frame is uncertain.[70]

The Roman Catholic **mission of Saint-Antoine-de-Padoue [7.34]** was founded near the village in

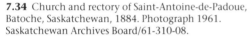

7.34 Church and rectory of Saint-Antoine-de-Padoue, Batoche, Saskatchewan, 1884. Photograph 1961. Saskatchewan Archives Board/61-310-08.

1881 and quickly became the spiritual centre of the district as well as Riel's military headquarters. The church and its rectory, both of which survive with scars from the Battle of Batoche, were built in 1884 by Ludger Gareau using the Red River frame covered with horizontal siding. The church has a plain, rectangular nave with an entrance tower and spire; its simple geometry, and the limitation of Gothic forms to its pointed-arched windows and *clocher*, make it representative of the Early Gothic Revival. The persistence of the style at so late a date is explained by the church's having been built on the ever-shifting frontier; the process of rebirth led to its being used here forty years after St Andrew's-on-the-Red and sixty years later than in eastern and central Canada. The two-storey rectory is plainer, more domestic, in treatment, with flat-headed double-hung sash windows. The church, the rectory (which is now a museum), and the cemetery in the foreground—which contains the graves of Gabriel Dumont and a number of Métis who died in the battle—form a part of Batoche National Historic Site, as do the partially excavated remains of the east village.

Towns

Small service communities often developed next to the posts of the Hudson's Bay Company and the North-West Mounted Police and adjacent to the religious missions. Some, such as Fort Macleod and St Albert, became important towns; a few, such as Calgary, Edmonton, and Regina, became major cities. Other communities developed independently from these historic posts because of their strategic geographical locations, their natural resources, or in anticipation of the railway.

Prince Albert and the building industry One of the important early communities was Prince Albert. Located in Palliser's fertile plain on the North Saskatchewan River, a short distance below Batoche and above its confluence with the South Saskatchewan, it was founded in 1866 as a Presbyterian mission under the leadership of the Reverend James Nisbet from Kildonan. He named the mission for Queen Victoria's popular consort. It experienced rapid growth in the 1870s because it was believed that the transcontinental railway would follow the valley of the North Saskatchewan.[71]

Prince Albert was the first community in what was then the Northwest Territories (it is now in Saskatchewan) to develop a mechanized building

industry. It and Winnipeg played important roles in the history of prairie building, taking the lead in the transformation from hand-building to the use of mass-produced commercial construction products. The first sawmill went into operation in 1876. According to some sources, the entrepreneur was a Captain Moore, who bought machinery in 'the east' and arrived with it in the summer of 1876, 'having been two months on the trail between Winnipeg and Prince Albert.' Others name Thomas Manley as the first sawmill operator, also in 1876.[72]

Lumbering and milling became important industries, fed by heavy demand for the products and the large stands of accessible timber. By 1880 mills were operated by Moore, Chester Thompson, and Thomas McKay, and a sash-and-door factory was opened in 1880 by Goodfellow Brothers and expanded a year later. By the end of the decade James H. Sanderson, who controlled extensive timber limits, was operating a sawmill, a lath mill, a shingle mill, and a sash-and-door factory. Moore and Macdonald, successors to Captain Moore, advertised in 1885 that they 'wish to inform the Public that they have on hand and for sale a half million feet of Dry Lumber, consisting of Matched, Dressed and Undressed.' Their stock included flooring, siding, sheeting, common lumber, dimension lumber, lath, and shingles. On another occasion it was noted that they sawed 'spruce from the North, lumber and shingles as well as pine and poplar.'[73]

Prince Albert also had the first brickyard in the region, which was started around 1879 by Thomas E. Baker. A store on River Street East, said to have been built by Baker in that year, is claimed as the first brick building in the Territories west of Winnipeg. Baker was described as using 'hand moulded' bricks, indicating that he did not have the benefit of a brickmaking machine.[74]

As it happened, the Canadian Pacific Railway chose a more southerly route and did not come near Prince Albert. The town's mills continued to supply lumber and other products throughout the region, servicing other towns through which the CPR did not pass, but in time the focus of economic activity shifted south. Its current prosperity derives from its being a service centre for mining, forestry, and agricultural activity in central and northern Saskatchewan.

Battleford and the territorial government In 1875 the government of Prime Minister Alexander Mackenzie passed the North-West Territories Act,

7.35 Commanding Officer's residence, Fort Battleford, Saskatchewan, 1876-7. RCMP Archives, Ottawa/neg. 742 (Old Forts).

which established a lieutenant governor and a territorial council resident in the Territories. The first capital (designated in 1876)—and, for a short while, the most important town in the western interior—was Battleford, which had previously been used only as a surveyors' work camp and a minor fur-trade post.

The NWMP immediately established a major base, called Fort Battleford, where an uncharacteristicly substantial community developed within the palisaded outpost. The **Commanding Officer's residence** (1876-7) is a substantial $1\frac{1}{2}$-storey building that was evidently intended as an impressive symbol of the new order being brought to the West [**7.35**]. It was designed in Ottawa by the Department of Public Works and built by Hugh Sutherland, the Department's local supervisor, and John Oliver, the foreman. The gabled roof, bargeboard trim, bay window, and milled window casings—all of which emulate Ontario houses of the period—assert government authority by contrasting with the simpler houses characteristic of the region.[75] Ironically, its closest rival in the Territories was Letendre's house at Batoche—foreshadowing the conflict between Ottawa and the Métis that would culminate in the Rebellion of 1885.

Oliver worked hard to obtain proper building materials.

> His [Oliver's] quest for large timber took him far afield, riding horseback, crossing lakes in a canoe and tramping through wooded areas. Some of his logs were cut 60 miles beyond Edmonton and rafted down the Saskatchewan. They were then hauled to the site of his work where he had set up his portable sawmill. Smaller timber was obtained from the neighbouring Eagle Hills. Soon lumber, shingles and laths were seasoning in the sun. Windows were being brought over the prairie from Winnipeg. Brick and lime kilns were set up for by good fortune suitable sand and limestone were plentiful.[76]

This reveals the huge amount of effort that went into building an extraordinary house and, inversely, shows how strong were the environmental constraints that led most people to build in the simpler vernacular.

Sutherland described the use of the Red River

frame, showing that the term was already in use in the 1870s:

> The walls of the buildings are constructed of hewn logs put up 'Red River style' joints of which are plastered with lime and sand on both sides—The inside of all walls are strapped, lathed with sawn lath, and plastered with good lime and sand in a first class manner. The outside of the buildings are again strapped and clap-boarded and all wood work both inside and out usually painted is receiving three coats of lead and oil paint.[77]

Unfortunately the lumber was not properly seasoned. The spruce clapboards shrank and the cottonwood (or poplar) rotted. NWMP Superintendent Walker reported in 1878 that

> what work is done does very little credit to those in charge of the works.... The base boards and casements were put on the inside before it was lathed and plastered consequently there is not plaster under them and as the lumber was not properly seasoned they have shrunk away from the plaster which makes the House very cold.[78]

It is tempting to draw morals about haste making waste and the folly of show without substance. Suffice it to say that the house impressed the territorial residents even if it left the Commanding Officer in the cold. It has been restored by Parks Canada, eliminating the defects that were so important a part of its history.

The adjacent Officers' Quarters (1884-8) at Fort Battleford (not yet built when the photograph of the Commanding Officer's Residence was taken) was distinguished by its mansard roof, a form that became popular for official government architecture in the more settled parts of the country during the 1870s. Milled lumber was still hard to get (Battleford was not on the railway), and so it too was built of logs, although it used horizontal logs with dovetailed notches instead of the Red River frame.

David Laird, the first Lieutenant Governor of the territory, set up his offices in Government House (1876-8). Also designed by the Department of Public Works, it was originally a large two-storey rectangular structure with a high gable roof and eaves-trim similar to that of the Commanding Officer's residence. It too strove to express an image of authority. Having been altered and enlarged many times—it subsequently housed, among other institutions, the Indian Industrial School (1883-1914) and the Oblate Fathers' St Thomas College (1931-72)—it currently stands vacant.

Outside the police and government precincts grew a significant town. Battleford's time in the sun, however, was short. The CPR announced in 1881 that it would route its line further south than originally intended, leaving Battleford, Prince Albert, and Edmonton without train service. The Territorial capital was moved to Regina in 1883, shortly after the tracks passed through that young city. This, and the political problems caused by the Northwest Rebellion, hurt Battleford's position. The Canadian Northern Railway finally reached the area in 1905, but it was located along the far side of the Battle River, stimulating the development of a new townsite called North Battleford.

Winnipeg: The first western city

The Hudson's Bay Company retained control over the Red River Settlement until 1849, when the results of the Sayer trial broke its legal monopoly. In 1849 also the American Territory of Minnesota was formed, and the city of St Paul quickly grew to be the major commercial centre in the Red and Upper Mississippi valleys. Canadian and American traders and politicians cast expansionist eyes on the Forks. Lower Fort Garry could no longer provide all of the goods and services that the growing colony required, leaving a vacuum that private entrepreneurs did not fail to notice.

By 1865 more than a dozen businesses had been set up near Upper Fort Garry. The most noteworthy was the Royal Hotel (with a general store on the ground floor), at the junction of the trails along the Assiniboine and Red Rivers. It was opened in 1862 by Ontario-born Henry McKenney, who had operated a store in Minnesota before coming to Winnipeg. Although McKenney was ridiculed for locating his premises on low land and about a half-mile (1 km) from the Fort and further still from Point Douglas, the businessman chose well. His was the first commercial establishment at the celebrated intersection of Portage Avenue and Main Street (originally called Garry Street)—soon to become the centre of downtown Winnipeg.[79]

The name Winnipeg—an Indian word meaning muddy water, and used to describe the large lake to the north—was first used in 1866 on the masthead of the Nor'Wester, replacing the newspaper's previous address: Red River Settlement, Assiniboia. The area around the Forks was still called Fort Garry, and the post office did not adopt the name Winnipeg until 1876.

A cluster of buildings grew up around McKenney's Royal Hotel, but the appearance of the young town was anything but impressive—as Methodist minister George Young tells us, in this description of his arrival in 1868:

> What a sorry sight was presented by that long-thought-of town of Winnipeg on the day we entered it! What a mass of soft, black, slippery and sticky Red River mud was everywhere spread out before us! Streets with neither sidewalks nor crossings, with now and again a good sized pit of mire for the traveller to avoid or flounder through as best he could; a few small stores with poor goods and high prices; one little tavern where 'Dutch George' was 'monarch of all his survey'; a few passable dwellings with no 'rooms to let', nor space for boarders; neither church nor school in sight or in prospect; population about one hundred instead of one thousand as we expected—such was Winnipeg on July 4th, 1868.[80]

Winnipeg's period of dynamic growth began with the Red River Rebellion and Manitoba's entry into Confederation in 1870. The population of 100 noted by Young grew to 8,000 by 1881 and more than 25,000 in 1891. The local economy was fuelled by an insatiable demand from the new settlers in Manitoba and the Northwest Territories for building materials, agricultural implements, and general merchandise. The factories and warehouses that responded to this need required capital and workers, which led in turn to the growth of the service sectors of finance and real estate. Its prosperity apparently assured, the City of Winnipeg was incorporated in 1873, subsuming Upper Fort Garry at the Forks and a portion of the Red River Settlement.

The open spaces soon filled in with streets and buildings, businesses and housing. A view of **Main Street** [7.36] taken around 1880, looking south from Portage towards Upper Fort Garry, shows how far the city had progressed since the Reverend Young's moment of disappointment a dozen years earlier. Broad plank sidewalks have been built. The street is in the process of being paved with cobbles (the poles indicate that electrical service was available) and is lined with wood and brick buildings, most of them two storeys high. The buildings on the left are distinguished by strong bracketed cor-

7.36 Main Street, south of Portage, Winnipeg, Manitoba. Photograph *c*. 1880. PAM/Elswood Bolt Collection/N13781.

7.37 City Hall, Winnipeg, Manitoba, 1884-6. Photograph *c*. 1913. PAM/N4728.

nices and Victorian Italianate ornament—rejecting the foursquare vernacular in favour of detail that is derived from historical styles. Some, like the brick building across the street that is second from the right, are true two-storey structures, with flat roofs; others, seen further down the street, are 1½-storey gable-roof buildings with false fronts (called boomtown fronts) that give the appearance of a full second floor. The signs (including the protruding boot on the left), merchandise, and carts indicate that the ground-floor frontages are in commercial use, while the upper floors appear to be occupied by residences and hotels.

The first railway in the region, the Pembina Branch line that led to the American border and St Paul, terminated at St Boniface and not Winnipeg. But in 1881 the Canadian Pacific Railway chose Winnipeg over Selkirk as a terminus—partly because of intensive lobbying by merchants and the city's offer of $200,000 and a railway bridge, and partly because CPR director, Donald Smith (later Lord Strathcona), was also a major shareholder in the Hudson's Bay Company, which owned a considerable amount of developable land near Upper Fort Garry. No longer was Winnipeg constrained by a frontier environment. It quickly became a full-fledged metropolis that emulated the Victorian architectural trappings of eastern cities.

The ebullient spirit of the young community could not have had a better symbol than the **Winnipeg City Hall** (1884-6), a landmark that was much loved and hated but was impossible to ignore [**7.37**]. Designed by architects (and brothers) Charles A. Barber (1848-1915) and Earle W. Barber (1855-1915), who headed one of several professional firms that quickly surfaced, it was lauded on completion as 'one of the handsomest and cheapest City Halls in the Dominion'. The grandiose composition terminated in an octagonal central clock tower and a stubby conical spire. Built of red brick with cream stone and terracotta trim, the assertive pile drew on a wide range of historical sources, all freely adapted to epitomize a kind of grandeur and the spirit of eclecticism. The overlapping pediments of the frontispiece, for example, recall the churches of Palladio (e.g. San Giorgio Maggiore in Venice, 1565), and the arch, gable, and stylized corbels of the portico seem to have a foot in the Romanesque period. The arcade below the clock is slightly Islamic, and the corner cupolas recall the profile of Eastern European domes. This is Victorian free composition at its best, and worst— an unrestrained *tour de force* that effectively (and, to present-day eyes, endearingly) expressed the unbridled dynamism of the city. Tastes change, and later generations could not endure the undisciplined

7.38 Empire Hotel (Cauchon Block), Winnipeg, Manitoba, 1882. Photograph by Henry Kalen, 1970.

style. The City Hall was condemned in 1956 by eminent British architectural historian Alec Clifton-Taylor as 'unbelievably ugly': he said that 'it was built at a time when artistic taste all over the world reached an absolute low'. Six years later it was demolished. The Leland Hotel, also demolished, is seen at the left of the photograph.[81]

The finest Winnipeg building in the Victorian Italianate style—the preferred style across the country for commercial buildings (see page 388)—was the **Empire Hotel** [7.38] on Main Street, designed by Louis-Arsène Desy (1856-1924) and built in 1882 near the buildings in **7.36**. It is supported by a conventional brick-and-wood structure, but the elaborately detailed façade consists of pressed-metal components that were supplied locally, by the Vulcan Iron Works (established at Point Douglas in 1874) and the firm of Linklater and Deslauriers. The elevation is treated in three stages. The ground-floor bays are separated by round columns that support an entablature. The two middle floors have round-headed arches on the second storey

and stilted-segmental arches above, each with fluted pilasters supporting the window heads and taller pilasters spanning both floors, and with balustrades below the third-floor windows. Above another cornice are the narrower arched windows of the top floor, grouped in pairs and triplets, with a third cornice and a balustrade above them. The superb detail features elaborate Corinthian capitals, leafed brackets, and a wealth of other ornament.

Delightful as its design may be, the building suffered continual bad luck. It was originally constructed during the boom of 1882 as a speculative office building (with shops on the ground floor) by Joseph Cauchon, the third Lieutenant Governor of Manitoba; but he never succeeded in renting the offices, and the Cauchon Block (as it was called) was foreclosed within a year. It was then adapted into residential suites—becoming one of the first apartment buildings in Canada—and endured three fires, including one in 1895 that killed three people and destroyed the interior. In 1904 it was converted, at considerable cost, into the Empire Hotel, but succumbed to competition and never attracted good clientele—even though Union Station was later built next to it. It was demolished in 1982; the metal components of the elevation were dismantled and now sit in storage, awaiting an opportunity to be reconstructed.[82]

A particularly lively group of commercial buildings, whose history is closely tied to Winnipeg's early prosperity, was erected nearby in the early 1880s on **Princess Street in Winnipeg [7.39]**, situated only a few blocks north of Portage and Main in Winnipeg's large, and architecturally impressive, warehouse district (now known as the Exchange District). Seen here in a photograph taken in 1900, they show some of the many design variations that could be achieved with classical and Italianate forms—in this case, with brick as the dominant exterior material. At the left, with the paired arched windows and the contrasting brick colour on the voussoirs, is the Henderson Block (1881), designed by Hugh McCowan (1841-1908), the only one of these buildings to have been demolished (in the 1960s). Its rooftop sign ('Undertaking'), made of sheet-metal letters attached to a wire fence, was common on commercial and industrial buildings of the time. To the right are two identical buildings: the Benson Block (then the Globe Hotel) and the Bawlf Block, both built in 1882 to designs by Barber

and Barber. Their fanciful elevations feature pediments at three levels—over the entrance, above the central third-floor window, and atop the ornate cornice—and exhibit a variety of brick patterns. Beyond them is a building erected in 1882 for the Harris Implement Company (later a part of Massey-Harris) and designed by James Chisholm (1841-1920). Its composition is similar to that of its neighbours, but the windows have different shapes, and the elaborate cornice is crowned by an arch rather than a triangle. The tallest structure, the four-storey Exchange Building—built in 1898 to the design of Samuel Hooper (1851-1911)—was the second home of Winnipeg's vital Grain Exchange, which controlled the rapidly growing grain trade throughout the Prairies. The vertical piers and horizontal spandrels of the façade, offering a direct expression of the timber posts and beams, are characteristic of this later period. The Grain Exchange (and the powerful Board of Trade) originally occupied the building at the extreme right of the block, built in 1892 (and now known as the Utility Building, with a fourth floor that was added around

7.39 Princess Street, Winnipeg, Manitoba. Photograph 1900. PAM/N4826.

1901-3). The architect was Charles Barber, who in 1900 was the principal of the Winnipeg branch of the Barber brothers' practice, which had moved to Duluth, Minnesota. Nicholas Bawlf, the builder of the Bawlf Block and originally a feed merchant, was a founder of the Exchange and financed both its buildings. After the ever-growing Grain Exchange moved to a yet-larger building in 1908, Hooper's Exchange Building had several occupants (including the Manitoba Theatre Workshop, 1974).[83]

Winnipeg dominated the prairie economy. The largest merchant empire—and warehouse—in the city was built by hardware dealer James H. Ashdown, a native of England who came to Winnipeg in 1868 (with the Reverend George Young) by way of Ontario and the mid-western US. He began humbly enough as a tinsmith; but his business quickly grew into a hardware operation with retail, wholesale, and manufacturing arms. By 1881 he had opened branches in Portage la Prairie and Emerson, and before long he was distributing hardware and building supplies throughout western Canada. In 1900 he sent an entire trainload of forty cars filled with hardware to customers in the West—the 'Ashdown special' was highly publicized all along its route. Ashdown became involved in politics as well as business, and served a term as mayor of Winnipeg.

His first building, which stood through the 1870s, was a modest 1½-storey wood structure with a boom-town front that was replaced by a larger building in the early 1880s. The third **Ashdown Warehouse [7.40]**, begun in 1895 on Bannatyne Avenue near Main Street, was much larger again, and it was expanded over the next two decades to achieve a floor area of more than 150,000 square feet (nearly 15,000 m²) on six storeys. The original portion, designed by S. Frank Peters (1847-1926), was four storeys high, eight bays wide, generous in scale, and featured three-storey-high arches with recessed spandrels between the floors. (This was a motif that had been popularized for warehouses by the Marshall Field Wholesale Store in Chicago [1885-7], one of the last buildings designed by the much-emulated American architect H.H. Richardson.) The Ashdown building originally terminated above the first row of small paired windows (an attic level of rectangular windows also capped the Marshall Field store). Between 1899 and 1911 the top two floors, and the horizontal additions, were carried out in five stages by architect J.H.G. Russell (1863-1946). The building has brick bearing walls and a heavy-timber structure, composed of wood

7.40 J.H. Ashdown Warehouse, Winnipeg, Manitoba, 1895-1911. Courtesy of the Planning Department, City of Winnipeg.

columns and beams, and floors made from two-by-sixes standing on edge and spiked together to form a solid, 6-inch-deep wood floor that would be very slow to burn in the event of fire. Today the Ashdown Block, and many buildings like it, are being converted to alternate uses, as inner-city warehouse districts in Winnipeg and elsewhere are supplanted by industrial areas with better highway access.[84]

The financial district developed along Main Street, northward from the corner of Portage Avenue, as a high-rent arterial that sliced through the Exchange District. Some monumental early-twentieth-century banks along the street are discussed in Chapter 10.

Although Winnipeg's first residents were primarily from Ontario and Britain, the city soon acquired a diverse multi-cultural population when large numbers of Europeans—particularly Poles, Germans, Ukrainians and Russians (including many Jews), and Scandinavians—settled there. The rich and the poor, and old and new Canadians, found their way into segregated residential neighbourhoods. The well-to-do, many of them pre-railway Manitobans, occupied large lots on tree-lined streets in the former Hudson's Bay Reserve west of the fort, between Portage Avenue and the Assiniboine River. People of moderate means lived west of the business and warehouse districts, north of

Portage. The 'north end'—the area along Main Street north of the CPR tracks, including Point Douglas and Kildonan—already contained old, and therefore inexpensive, housing, and became home to working-class immigrants. The area around Selkirk Avenue, named after the settlement of which it once formed a part, became the commercial and institutional focus of the north end, which was variously known as the foreign quarter, CPR Town, Shanty Town, and New Jerusalem.

A photograph taken around 1904, near the corner of **Dufferin and King Streets [7.41]**, gives a good idea of the poverty and planning chaos that characterized the north end. The many different kinds of dress indicate a variety of ethnic groups. Clotheslines, piled logs, and general clutter dominate the right-hand side. The chimneys rising from the low wood building in the centre suggest that it may have accommodated several families in separate rooms or suites. Behind is a tidy two-storey frame building, and the taller Dufferin Hotel stands in the background at the far left.

The various ethnic groups did not live in distinctive housing types, since most were tenants and not builders, and their residences were products of industrialized building processes that proved to be

7.41 Dufferin and King Streets, Winnipeg, Manitoba. Photograph *c*. 1904. PAM/N7961.

the great levelling influence in Canadian building. The individual groups expressed themselves not by their house-types, but rather in the ways in which they treated their properties: by paint colours, window decorations, gardens, and fences. The pattern of building had come full circle. The original settlers, who had succumbed to the power of the frontier environment, created an architectural sameness that transcended cultural distinctions. But by the middle years of the nineteenth century, differences began to be expressed in building. A generation or two later, however, the mass-production and distribution of building supplies and house-types blurred these differences.

By 1912 Winnipeg was a city of 166,000 people, with a strong and diversified economy, a large trading hinterland, and it was now served by three transcontinental railways. But Winnipeg was beginning to be rivalled by Calgary, Vancouver, and other new western cities. In the recession of 1913, and during the war that followed, its economy stalled and its rate of growth slowed down. While the previous half-century had brought about inconceivable changes, beyond the City of Winnipeg proper evidence remained of the old Red River Settlement: Scots- and English-Canadians inhabited the River Road towards Lower Fort Garry, French-speaking people dominated St Boniface, and some pockets of Métis lived to the south and west of the Forks.

This discussion has taken us into the railway age and the new economic and architectural orders it spawned—subjects that are properly treated in Chapters 9 and 10 in the second volume. Chapter 8 of this volume returns to the pre-railway era and looks at buildings on the West Coast.

CHAPTER 8

THE SETTLEMENT
OF THE WEST COAST

THE WEST coast of Canada is separated from the rest of the country by a series of high, rugged, north-south mountain ranges. Because of the difficult terrain, early approaches to the area were mostly by sea. The ancestors of the aboriginal inhabitants arrived by way of a land-bridge over the Bering Strait; the first Europeans, along with Russians and Americans, came by ship. Natives and Euro-Canadians alike found it easier to communicate and trade with people to the south rather than with those across the mountains.

The early architecture of the West Coast reflects this isolation from the rest of Canada. Native builders responded to their environmental needs, and the available materials, by creating dwellings that were very different from those to the east; and many early white settlers brought with them the architectural forms of California. Only the fur-traders, who arrived overland, clearly continued the building techniques that were used on the Prairies, and further east.

Native Building

Coastal tribes

The coast of British Columbia—and the entire northwest coast of North America—has been home to native peoples who produced a truly remarkable indigenous architecture. Built of massive posts, beams, and planks taken from the cedars that grow in the temperate rain forest, the houses of the coastal tribes employed a sophisticated and impressive building technology, while serving highly developed religious and social patterns of living.

Most of the native groups occupied permanent villages in winter and lived in either fixed or portable dwellings in the summer—sometimes taking the planks that covered the building-frames from the winter to the summer houses—as they moved about to harvest sea mammals, salmon, other fish, and berries. The social structure of the larger villages included a wealthy élite composed of chiefs or nobles, a body of commoners, and a class of slaves, who had been captured, purchased, or born into slavery. The chiefs handed down privileges through a formal gift-giving ceremony known as the potlatch. The plank-houses, as their buildings are called—erected in communities from Alaska to northern California—were essential expressions of a hierarchical culture.

The principal groups inhabiting today's British Columbia were the Haida and the Tsimshian in the north (the neighbouring Tlingit lived in what is now the Alaskan panhandle); the Kwakwaka'wakw (formerly known as Kwakiutl), Nuu-chah-multh (Nootka), and Nuxalk (Bella Coola) on the central coast; and the Coast Salish in the south. Each group developed a distinctive version of the plank-house. The few that survive are in ruins, but the records of early anthropologists and photographers, the work of contemporary archaeologists, and the traditional skills of Indian artisans have contributed a wealth of information about their construction, use, and appearance. Several reconstructed houses that represent the principal types stand in the Grand Hall of the Canadian Museum of Civilization in Hull.[1]

The North The remains of the Haida village of Ninstints on Anthony Island, one of the southern-most of the Queen Charlotte Islands, was among the first Canadian places to be accepted as a UNESCO World Heritage Site for its architectural and historical significance. When initial contact with Europeans was made in the late eighteenth century it was a thriving community of 300 Kunghit Haida; but the

8.1 Skidegate, Queen Charlotte Islands, British Columbia. Photograph by George M. Dawson, 1878. NAC/PA-037756.

ravages of smallpox took their toll, and the 30 people who survived abandoned the village in the 1880s. At its prime, Ninstints had seventeen or more large houses, averaging about 35 feet (10 m) square (the largest was 47 by 49 feet, or 14.3 by 14.9 m) and spaced only a few feet apart. All that stands above ground today is a large collection of carved poles, although archaeologists can read two millennia of history in the remains. Nevertheless, it is one of the best-preserved Haida villages.

The former appearance of the Haida villages is known through photography. A superb view of 1878 shows a part of **Skidegate [8.1]**, also on the Queen Charlotte Islands, to which the survivors of Ninstints moved. The two houses on the left were built in the 1860s and 1870s. The 'forest' of poles that so impresses visitors to Ninstints is evident here as well. They are family heraldic crests, depicted as stylized animal forms that are carved on poles to reflect the genealogical record of a family. Most of those seen in the picture are frontal poles,

fixed to the façades of the houses; some are corner house-posts with images at the top. At the left is a mortuary pole raised for Chief Skedans; the burial chamber on top bears an image of the moon with a thunderbird face, beneath which are a mountain goat (with two horns) and a grizzly bear. Dugout canoes line the shore. Skidegate has become a bustling modern community. None of the houses, and only one of the poles, survives.

Two kinds of houses were built at Ninstints, Skidegate, and other Haida villages. The more common type was the **six-beam house [8.2]**, so-called because the building was framed with six large longitudinal roof beams (whose projecting ends are clearly seen in the photograph); the other type had only two beams.

The magnificent six-beam house, unique among the Haida, was constructed with highly sophisticated joinery. Posts were raised at the four corners, and grooves at their bases received the ends of the wall plates. Massive sloping roof plates, made from cedar planks as large as 30 by 6 inches (75 by 15 cm), were inserted through slots in the corner posts and supported at the centre by pairs of posts,

366

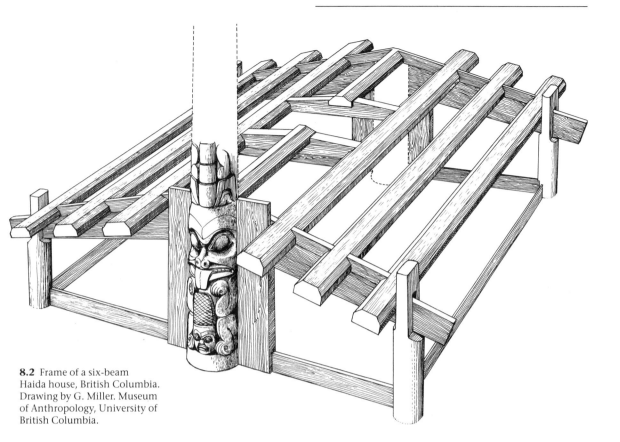

8.2 Frame of a six-beam Haida house, British Columbia. Drawing by G. Miller. Museum of Anthropology, University of British Columbia.

8.3 (*left*) 'House Where People Always Want to Go', Haina, Queen Charlotte Islands, British Columbia. Royal British Columbia Museum/PN 701.

against which the frontal pole was placed. Six large beams spanned the depth of the house and rested on the plates, while a seventh beam at the ridge was broken in the middle to allow an opening for the smoke hole. Vertical wall boards were set into grooves on the edges of the bottom and top plates, often with battens securing the joints, and planks or sheets of bark were laid loosely across the roof beams and held down with stones. The exterior walls were left unpainted.[2]

The structure of the Haida house is seen clearly at the **'House Where People Always Want to Go'** [**8.3**] at Haina. The six beam-ends project above the roof plate, and the corner posts rise above the roof line. Broad vertical planks form the wall. The original entrance was through the stomach of the thunderbird at the base of the frontal pole, which was a crest of the owner's wife. The owner's crest was the raven, seen near the top, with three watchmen above it.

367

The houses of the wealthier chiefs had a central pit, often reached by means of terraces. The house fire—used for heating, cooking, and drying clothing (and sometimes fish)—was set in the centre, and smoke escaped through the hole in the roof. Slaves slept in the pit, commoners on the intermediate tiers, and the people of the highest rank around the perimeter of the building, often within small sleeping compartments, with the chief's at the rear centre and others arranged by rank. The interior of the **house of Chief Wiah [8.4]** at Masset—built around 1850, and known as the 'big house' or the 'monster house'—is seen in a photograph taken about 1900. Said to have been the largest of the Haida houses, it measured nearly 55 feet (16.8 m) square, and the pit was about 8 feet (2.4 m) deep. It was so large that it was covered by eight rather than six roof beams.

George MacDonald has explained that the house functioned both in the secular realm as a dwelling and in the spiritual realm as a ceremonial centre. (Deceased ancestors resided in the house, as well as the living.) As in the buildings of many other native cultures, the house represented the cosmos, providing a symbolic (as well as a literal) structure that made the universe more readily comprehensible. Houses were all known by their names. Building a house was a significant event, and its dedication often occurred in conjunction with a potlatch.

It has been suggested that the six-beam house may have originated at Ninstints and developed only after contact with Europeans, when trade provided the Haida with metal tools and European techniques of joinery. If so, the house-form would have had a lifespan of only a century until its revival for community dwellings in the past generation. This theory remains inconclusive, however, as archaeologists have not yet fixed the dates of the earliest houses of the type.

Whatever the origin of the six-beam house, most scholars agree that the two-beam house was an earlier form. Two principal roof beams were supported on interior house posts (sometimes carved with crests), and the beam ends did not project through the sloping roof plates. Lighter beams set in the same longitudinal direction spanned the space between the corner posts. This type was used by other tribes in the region as well, including the Tsimshian, who lived on the mainland, near the mouths of the Nass and Skeena Rivers, and it was similar to the houses of the peoples of the central region.

8.4 Interior of Chief Wiah's house, Masset, Queen Charlotte Islands, British Columbia, *c.* 1850. Photograph *c.* 1900. University of Washington/Special Collections Division/NA701.

The central region The principal tribes of the central region—which includes central and northern Vancouver Island, the central mainland coast, and many islands between them—were the Kwakiutl, the Nootka, and the Bella Coola (who have recently chosen to be called, respectively, the Kwakwaka'wakw, Nuu-chah-nulth, and Nuxalk). Five houses in the Kwakwaka'wakw village of **Xumtaspi-Nawittl [8.5]** on Hope Island are seen in a photograph of the 1880s. The gable ends are similar in shape to those of the Haida houses, but there are no projecting beam ends or frontal poles, and family crests are painted on some façades. On the front of the house at the right are three crouched figures. The entrance is through the genital area of the middle one (passage through it symbolized death and rebirth). A sign over the door reads: 'BOSTON. He is true and honest. He don't

8.5 Xumtaspi-Nawittl, Hope Island, British Columbia. Photograph *c*. 1884. American Museum of Natural History/Department of Library Services/neg. 42298-Kwakiutl house.

8.6 Kwakwaka'wakw house-frame, Gwayasdums, British Columbia. Photograph 1955. Royal British Columbia Museum/(W. Duff) QPN 2429.

give no trouble to no white man.' It, and a similar sign next door, advertises the availability of village labour—revealing the immense transformation of native society from self-sufficiency to wage-earning.

Kwakwaka'wakw construction is evident in a **house-frame at Gwayasdums [8.6]**, photographed by anthropologist Wilson Duff in 1955. The two principal roof beams are supported by pairs of posts at the front and rear; the latter are carved. Two additional beams at the eaves connect the corner posts and also rest on an intermediate support. Rafters, and purlins fashioned from lighter members, are framed on the beams. The walls would have been made from vertical planks and the roof covered with loose planks. There was no fixed smoke hole: planks would be pushed aside to vent the smoke. Inside, a raised platform around the perimeter provided a base for sleeping compartments. Decorated interiors were often used as ceremonial spaces for elaborate ritual performances.[3]

The Nuu-chah-nulth, who lived on the west

8.7 *A View of the Habitation at Nootka Sound* at Yuquot, British Columbia. Engraving after a drawing by John Webber, April 1778. BCARS/PDP 237.

8.8 *(below) Inside of a House in Nootka Sound* at Yuquot, British Columbia. Engraving after a drawing by John Webber, April 1778. BCARS/PDP 235.

coast of Vancouver Island, built two types of houses: those in the north erected gabled structures with a single ridge beam, while those in the south built shed-roofed houses. These, too, were arranged along the beach. A group of **houses at Yuquot [8.7]** on Nootka Sound is seen in an engraving after a drawing of 1778 by John Webber, the artist on Captain Cook's third voyage, that shows members of the expedition meeting natives on the beach. The two rows of houses have gently sloped flat roofs. The racks fabricated from poles are for drying fish.

Webber also depicted the interior [8.8] of a house in the village. The massive roof beams overhead are supported by a cross-beam that rests on the two large carved posts. Low plank partitions at the right separate family units within the house. A woman is boiling water in the centre, and the smoke and steam escape through a hole that had been made by moving aside one of the roof planks. Fish and a blanket hang from the rafters to dry. The floor is partly covered with planks, and platforms around the edge are used for sitting, sleeping, and placing storage boxes.

A decade later, trader John Meares described a Nuu-chah-nulth house, just north of Yuquot:

> The door was the mouth of one of these huge images....We ascended by a few steps on the outside, and after passing this extraordinary kind of portal, descended down the chin into the house...The trees that supported the roof were of a size which would render the mast of a first rate man-of-war diminutive...three enormous trees, rudely carved and painted, formed the rafters, which were supported at the ends and in the middle by gigantic images, carved out of huge blocks of timber.[4]

Meares was amazed to find an estimated 800 people inside, awaiting a feast.

The south Shed-roofed longhouses—similar in construction to those at Yuquot, but often far greater in length—were the predominant type among the Salish-speaking groups of southwestern British Columbia. But gable-roofed houses with a single ridge pole were also built in the northern part of the region. Villages might consist of a single house or many houses: a Musqueam community near today's Vancouver, visited in 1876, had 76 houses arranged in a semicircle. In villages where the buildings were arranged in a row facing the shore, the roof would slope from front to rear.

Shed-roofed houses as long as 1500 feet (460 m) were observed in the Puget Sound area, in what is now the state of Washington. In 1808 explorer Simon Fraser saw a Musqueam house 800 feet (245 m) long near the mouth of the river that bears his name, and upriver he visited one nearly as large. He described the latter in his journal:

> The houses are built of cedar planks...the whole range, which is six hundred and fifty feet long by sixty broad, is under one roof; the front is eighteen feet high and the covering is slanting: all the appartements, which are separated by partitions, are square, except the chief's, which is ninety feet long.... Above, on the outside, are carved a human figure as large as life, with other figures in imitation of beast and birds.[5]

The horizontal planks that formed the walls were tied between pairs of poles and were easily removable. The Coast Salish would lash them and the roof planks between their canoes and re-erect them on house-frames set up at the summer camps. Captain George Vancouver observed the 'skeletons of houses', at first believing that they were abandoned villages, but then recognizing their role in the annual migration.

The lower Fraser valley has been inhabited for many millennia. A large house, which radio-carbon dating has established was built between 5200 and 5700 BP (i.e. 3200-3700 BC), was uncovered in 1990-1 near Mission, 50 miles (80 km) east of Vancouver. It was part of a community adjacent to Hatzic Rock—a sacred 'ancestor stone' or 'transformer site' with strong spiritual values—that was acquired by the British Columbia Heritage Trust in 1993. Other archaeological deposits on the site date back 9,000 years.[6]

Interior tribes

The principal tribes that inhabited the interior plateau of south and central British Columbia were the interior Salish, whose economy was based on the yearly runs of Pacific salmon, and the Kutenai, who were primarily hunters; both also gathered fruits and berries. Adapting their way of life and technology to changing climatic and environmental conditions, the natives were able to survive periods of deprivation.[7]

Most of the Plateau tribes on both sides of the present international border occupied semi-subterranean dwellings known as **pit houses [8.9, 10]** as their permanent winter residences. In the 1890s James Teit, an ethnographer from the Shetland Islands, visited the Thompson Indians of the Nicola Valley—an interior Salish tribal group— and, after mastering the Salish language and earning their trust, was able to learn the techniques and the beliefs associated with the pit house. The natives showed him their campsites in the sheltered river valleys and Teit watched with interest as they built a new pit house, recording his observations:

> When a new house was needed, the Thompson would begin to measure the floor excavation around mid-November. First they crossed two bark ropes the length of the proposed pit at right angles, pointing their ends in the semicardinal directions. Stakes marked the centre and quarter midpoints; then quarter circles were scored in the ground to complete the circumference. Using sharpened sticks and flat-bladed wooden scrapers, the women broke up the earth and hauled it to the side in baskets until they had a hole 3 to 4 feet deep, with sloping sides. Freshly cut logs were dragged to the site and stripped of bark. Four served as main house-posts and were planted in holes in the floor at an angle roughly parallel to the excavation walls (in treeless regions driftwood was saved for this purpose). Their tops were notched to support the four main roof beams, whose butt ends were sunk 2 feet into the topsoil at steep angles. Supple willows fastened these beams, which almost converged at the smoke hole, and also secured pairs of struts that braced them.

A webbing of spaced rafters was lashed in concentric circles from pit to smoke hole. This supported a snug layer of poles that was thickly padded with pine needles or grass. In the upper Plateau, where rainfall was heavy, cedar bark with the curved side up was laid at this stage. Finally, earth from the original pit was spread over the roof and stamped down, and a notched-log ladder was lowered through the smoke hole. With twenty to thirty people co-operating on the building, a pit house could be finished in a day. The following spring grass sprouted on the roof and, but for the ladder, the dwelling seemed to be a living part of the landscape.[8]

The pit-house ladder was once the object of artistic attention. Its top might be carved into the head of a bird or animal and painted to represent the guardian spirit of the head of the household. A hearth was located near the foot of the ladder—

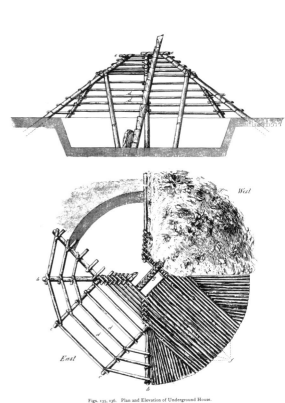

Figs. 135, 136.   Plan and Elevation of Underground House.

8.9 Plan and section of an Interior Salish pit house, British Columbia. Drawing by James Teit. From Teit and Boas, 'The Thompson Indians of British Columbia', *Memoirs of the American Museum of Natural History*, 2:4, 1900.

usually on its north side—and a stone slab protected the ladder from burning. The hearth was surrounded by an earthen platform, on which people probably sat and slept. Each of the areas in the pit house marked by one of the four main posts was known as a room, even though no partition separated it from the other rooms. This division was related to the natives' cosmological beliefs: they saw the world as being a huge, circular lodge that was divided into four compartments; after death, the soul crossed a river to the afterworld, which was also conceived as a large, round dwelling, although made of granite.

The communities visited by Teit typically had three or four pit houses, with between fifteen and thirty people occupying each one. Some late prehistoric communities, also located along rivers or streams, contained many more houses: at Lillooet there were about 100 pit houses, including one 20 metres in diameter, and another location had 180. Since many of the sites have been re-occupied over the centuries (and even over millennia) it is difficult to interpret the remains. The average pit house observed by Teit was about 25 to 30 feet (8-10 m) in diameter and 5 feet (1.5 m) deep. The oldest pit houses in British Columbia that have been dated positively are about 3,500 to 4,000 years old, and some in northern California and on the Columbia Plateau have been fixed at between 5,000 and 6,000 years old.[9]

The pit house has certain similarities with the Thule whale-bone house [13.1] in its technique of building. Some ethnologists have suggested that the prototype for a semi-subterranean dwelling insulated with earth originated in northeastern Asia and was transferred to America during the migrations across the Bering Strait—first appearing in the Arctic, then on the plateau, and subsequently revealing itself as the earth lodge of the American

Plains and the pit house of the American Southwest.[10] This may well have been stimulated, in part, by environmental factors: particularly in the semiarid climates, which produced trees of only small or moderate size, making wood-houses less practicable than in the Pacific rain forest or other climate zones.

During the historical period, British Columbia pit houses were built in a wide range of sizes, shapes, and construction techniques; they included circular, square, and elongated ground plans, and some had entrances in the side of the roof in addition to the ladder through the smoke hole. The Shuswap, who lived farther north, near today's Kamloops, sometimes used six principal posts and beams rather than four, producing a more conical profile.

8.10 Pit house, Nicola Valley, British Columbia. American Museum of Natural History/Department of Library Services/neg. no. 42776.

At about the time of initial contact with Europeans, many Plateau Indians discontinued using pit houses and began to build mat houses—lodges built of poles and covered with mats of tule (bulrushes) or with bark or grass. These multi-family dwellings were rectangular, with flat or rounded ends, typically 25 to 60 feet long 12 to 15 feet wide, and 10 to 14 high (7.6 to 18.3 m, 3.7 to 4.6 m, and 3.1 to 4.3 m respectively). The house was heated by one or more fires, and a long, narrow smoke hole was left open at the ridge. It was excavated slightly, and dirt and snow were banked against the base for insulation in winter.[11]

Fur-trader Alexander Ross visited a mat house and wrote: '. . . the fires are made in the centre, directly under the ridge pole, and about six or eight feet apart and are in proportion to the number of families who live under the same roof.'[12] The American explorers Lewis and Clark observed a Nez Percé village on the lower Columbia River that consisted of a single structure, 150 feet (45 m) long, with 24 fires and twice that number of families.

The third house-type found among the Plateau Indians was the tipi [7.2]. The Kutenai tipi had a four-pole foundation, with about 15 supplementary poles. The Upper Kutenai covered their tipis with buffalo hides, similar to those of the Plains Indians, while the Lower Kutenai made their covers by braiding and sewing the stalks of Indian hemp or dogbane.[13]

The reasons the pit house was abandoned by the early years of the present century are obscure, but they may have been related to changes in social organization caused by contact, European diseases, or environmental factors. It has been suggested that the Indians suffered ridicule from non-natives, who apparently compared pit houses to the dens of animals; this is corroborated by the fact that several groups denied that the pit house was a part of their past. A few families, however, retained memories of the technique. Mary Thomas and her sons of Salmon Arm, British Columbia, built a pit house at the Kelowna Museum in 1974, and five years later they reconstructed one at the Festival of American Folklife in Washington, DC. Federal-government archaeologist Roscoe Wilmeth excavated a pit house at Anahim Lake, BC, and then reconstructed one on its site with the help of the local band of Chilcotin Indians [8.11].[14] Activities such as these help to perpetuate the memory of an indigenous house-form that, for more than 5,000 years, provided an appropriate response to the lifeways and environment of the Plateau Indians.

8.11 Reconstructed pit house, Anahim Lake, British Columbia. Photograph by Roscoe Wilmeth, 1971. Canadian Museum of Civilization/s72-2021.

Contact and Early European Settlement

The natives on the West Coast did not encounter substantial European contact until the second half of the eighteenth century, somewhat later than on the rest of the continent. The Europeans' motivation for coming to this land was once again commercial: the profits to be reaped from the fur trade and the search for a trade route from Europe to the Orient, the so-called Northwest Passage (which was first entered from the Pacific in 1850 by Robert McClure).

Russia, Spain, and the fur trade

In the 1760s Russian fur-traders (*promyshlenniki*), in a pair of scientific expeditions, discovered the wealth of resources that lay east of the Bering Sea, and developed permanent posts on the northwest coast as early as the 1770s, long before any other nation. The Russian American Company, chartered in 1799, developed a string of trading posts down the Pacific coast, from the Aleutian Islands and the Alaskan mainland as far south as the present Fort Ross (founded 1812; the name was derived from the Spanish *Fuerto de los Rusos*), some 70 miles (110 km) north of San Francisco. The principal Russian settlement was at Sitka (established as New Archangel in 1799), near present-day Juneau in the

Alaska panhandle. Although they did not establish any posts on Canadian soil, the Russian traders stimulated events that affected Canada and Canadian architecture.[15]

Nootka Spain already had a firm grip on the Pacific coast from Mexico up to the present northern California and felt threatened by the Russian encroachments. Expeditions were sent north to explore the coast and assert Spain's claim to the territory. The first one, led by Juan Pérez Hernández aboard the *Santiago* in 1774, anchored at a place that Pérez Hernández called San Lorenzo, on the west coast of what is now Vancouver Island, and he traded with the natives for furs. This, and a second expedition the following year, missed the passage that had reportedly been discovered nearly two centuries earlier by Juan de Fuca, a Greek pilot in Spanish service, and which, it was believed, might have led to an inland sea.[16]

Captain James Cook, who explored the Pacific coast of North America for Britain on his third voyage in 1778, anchored near the spot that had been called San Lorenzo on 29 March. He named the inlet King George Sound and then renamed it Nootka Sound—likely a misnomer for the Indian village of Yuquot. The protected bay at the entrance to the sound came to be known as Friendly Cove. Cook found the Indians as friendly as the harbour, and he stayed until 26 April, repairing one of his two ships (the *Resolution*) and trading for 1,500 sea-otter furs. John Webber, the official artist on the expedition, took the opportunity to produce a series of detailed drawings of native houses at Yuquot [8.7, 8] that provide the best documentation of Nootkan building at the time of contact.[17]

News of the furs whetted the insatiable appetites of English merchants in Britain and the Far East, and before long Nootka Sound was receiving regular visits from British traders, as well as from American- and Portuguese-flag ships, while the Russians looked after their own interests as well. In 1788 English trader John Meares acquired a 'spot of ground' from Chief Maquinna at Friendly Cove and built a house from lumber that he had brought with him. From Meares' own description it would appear that this, the first building erected by Europeans in today's British Columbia, was a substantial dwelling:

The house was sufficiently spacious to contain all the party intended to be left in the Sound. On the ground floor there was ample room for the coop-

ers, sail makers and other artisans to work in bad weather: a large room was also set aside for the stores and provisions, and the armorers shop was attached to one end of the building and communicated with it. The upper story was divided into an eating room and chambers for the party. On the whole, our house, although it was not built to satisfy a lover of architectural beauty, was admirably well calculated for the purpose to which it was designed....

A strong breastwork was thrown up around the house, enclosing a considerable area of ground, which, with one piece of cannon, placed in such a manner as to command the cove and village of Nootka, formed a fortification sufficient to secure the party from any intrusion.[18]

Other Europeans who were at Nootka at the time remembered the house as being far less magnificent. The American trader Joseph Ingraham described it as 'a house, or rather a hut, consisting of rough posts covered with boards, made by Indians.' Portuguese Captain Francis Joseph Viana also called it small, and Chief Maquinna even denied that he had ever sold any land to Meares.[19]

Spain could not tolerate all this activity in territory it considered its own. In 1789 Esteban José Martínez was dispatched to Nootka (which the Spaniards called San Lorenzo de Nutka) to build a military and trading post. He arrived to find three ships in the harbour, and soon learned that the British were about to build their own permanent trading post. In the weeks that followed, Martínez seized two British ships and erected a small fortified battery on an island at the entrance to the harbour. Martínez's men, and those on a follow-up expedition the next year, set up an *establecimiento* at Nootka—forming the first European settlement on the west coast of today's Canada. For five years a Spanish governor and a company of the Volunteers of Catalonia occupied a small naval base at Nootka Sound, living in harmony with the natives in a land of abundance.

The Spanish settlement, consisting of more than twenty buildings, was commanded in the summer of 1792 by Juan Francisco de la Bodega y Quadra, a genial man who was respected by the British and American fur traders, as well as by the Nuu-chah-multh. A description by Archibald Menzies, the chief botanist on Captain George Vancouver's expedition of that year, offers an impression:

After dinner I accompanied Captain Vancouver with some of the Officers to pay our respects to

Don Quadra, Governor and Commandant of the Settlement. We found him on shore at a decent house two storey high, built of Planks with a Balcony in the front of the Upper Storey after the manner of the Spanish Houses. One end of the ground floor was occupied as a Guard Room, and the other as a Kitchen and Servants' Hall, while the Upper Storey was divided into small apartments and occupied by the Governor and his Officers, who were separated by a large Hall in the middle where they commonly dined. On our landing the Guard was turned out in honour to Captain Vancouver, and the Governor and his Officers received us at the door, and conducted us with great attention and civility up Stairs to the Great Hall. . . .

After leaving the Governor's we took a walk round the place and found several other Houses erected there by the Spaniards as Barracks, Store Houses and an Hospital on the Site of the Old Village formerly occupied by Maquinna the Chief of the District and his Tribe; there were also several spots fenced in, well cropped with the different European Garden stuffs, which grew here very luxuriantly. . . .

There was a well-stocked poultry yard, and Goats, Sheep and Black Cattle were feeding round the Village. Blacksmiths were seen busily engaged

8.12 Spanish settlement, Nootka Sound, British Columbia, begun 1789. Engraving from a drawing by Henry Humphrys, 1792. BCARS/PDP 236.

in one place and Carpenters in another, so that the different occupations of Building and repairing Vessels and Houses were at once going forward. In short the Spaniards seem to go on here with greater activity and industry than we are led to believe of them at any of their other remote infant Settlements.[20]

An engraving [8.12], after a drawing made by the Vancouver expedition's artist Henry Humphrys, shows the Spanish settlement at Nootka, crowded into a clearing by the shore, with the tall coniferous forest behind. Quadra's house is the two-storey building with the low gabled roof near the left; its second-floor balcony is evident and its wood walls are painted white. The building just to its left, with a steep roof and a covered porch, is the hospital, which outbreaks of scurvy, cholera, and a number of other diseases kept busy. To the right of Quadra's house we see a tall cross in front of a large fenced-in area; further right, behind a smaller fenced area, is a steep-roofed building that may have been the church. The covered shed still further along, seen over the sails of the vessel, was used for boat repairs. The little cove at the extreme right of the picture is the site of John Meares' house, which had been demolished; the small building seen there is probably his former boat shed. At the entrance to Friendly Cove, beyond the left edge of the picture, is the small island on which stood Nootka's small fortress of San Miguel, armed with cannon.

The more substantial buildings seem to be constructed of large logs or planks, and several are covered with plank roofs. Menzies noted that Quadra's house was built of planks. Since the natives split logs into planks for their own houses, this technology was available to the Spanish community. Some of the structures in the picture have thatched roofs, and the sheds are supported on poles. More information is becoming available as archaeologists begin to excavate the Nootka site.[21]

Hostile feelings ran high between long-time rivals Spain and Britain. The Nootka Sound Controversy, as the dispute became known, was settled by agreements that allowed both countries to trade in the area and established Nootka Sound as a free port. As finally resolved in 1795, the land became a British possession; Britain and Spain might both erect buildings, but only temporary ones. In a small but significant ceremony, the Spanish flag was lowered, the Union Jack raised, and the fort dismantled. The sea otter of Nootka Sound were soon all taken, ending fur-trading activity there, and it would be more than a generation before the coastal area would see new permanent construction by Europeans.[22]

During the five years of Spanish occupancy of Nootka, Spanish and British naval forces found the Strait of Juan de Fuca and charted the British Columbia coast. The Spanish efforts were led by Dionisio Alcalá-Galiano, Cayetano Valdéz y Floras Bazán, and Quadra, all of whose names are remembered in the gulf islands of the Strait of Georgia; the British initiative was by Vancouver, whose name became that of the area's largest city, and of the island itself. In names, as well as in diplomacy, the British remained dominant.

Interior trading posts During these same years the fur-traders of the North West Company were crossing the Rocky Mountains and entering today's British Columbia by overland routes. From his base at Fort Chipewyan, Alexander Mackenzie explored the basins of the Peace and Upper Fraser Rivers— venturing, in the summer of 1793, as far as the inlets of the central coast (eleven years before the American expedition led by Lewis and Clark reached the Pacific Ocean). John Finlay may have built the first fort in the Peace River area of today's British Columbia in 1794; but his journals have been lost, so this cannot be confirmed. It is certain, however, that a North West Company post called Rocky Mountain Fort was in operation near present-day Fort St John by 1798.[23]

Simon Fraser and David Thompson returned to this area in the following decade. In 1805 Fraser established the first post west of the Rocky Mountains at Fort McLeod, 90 miles (145 km) north of today's Prince George (not to be confused with Fort Macleod, Alberta). A year later Fraser established Fort St James—at the southern end of Stuart Lake, a short distance to the southwest—which became a major point of contact with the Carrier Indians and an administrative centre of the immense fur-trading district that Fraser called New Caledonia. It is the oldest continuously inhabited non-native community in British Columbia.

Between Fraser's time and the 1880s, Fort St James went through four separate building phases. Like most fur-trade posts, it consisted of a palisade, fortified at the corners by bastions, that enclosed a number of free-standing buildings, many of them hip-roofed and built in the *poteaux en coulisse* (grooved-post) technique that came west with the fur trade. An unusual building was a **fish cache** [8.13], which stored the salmon and sturgeon that formed the community's staple food (even Fraser had complained that he grew tired of dried fish). The building was raised off the ground on a dozen heavy posts to protect the fish from rodents and damp. The stilts—which were under the vertical posts of the wall system—transferred the structural load directly into the ground. The bottom of the fish cache was later closed in by skirting, which unfortunately concealed its unique design. To the left of the photograph, taken in the 1880s, is the general warehouse, a two-storey grooved-post structure. Parks Canada restored several buildings at Fort St James to their appearance in the 1890s, and opened them to the public in 1977 as a national historic park.[24]

In 1808 Fraser led a daring descent of the river that now bears his name, through its formidable canyon—the Carrier Indians had warned 'that in three places it was altogether impassable'[25]—and came to within a few miles of open water, in sight of the mountains of Vancouver Island. He and his men disembarked to inspect a large Musqueam house (page 371). When they returned to their canoes, a group of hostile Indians drove them back upriver. Fraser retreated in disappointment, having failed to reach the open sea.

The Fraser River became a major route for the fur trade, and subsequently for settlement, particularly after the North West Company became a part of the larger Hudson's Bay Company. **Fort Langley** was established about 30 miles (50 km) from the river's

8.13 General warehouse and fish cache, Fort St James, British Columbia, *c*. 1880s. Photograph *c*. 1971. PC.

mouth, at the head of navigation for sea-going vessels. Newly appointed chief factor James McMillan, and his party of twenty-four men, arrived at the site of the future fort on 29 July 1827. They immediately began work on building the post; but the enormous size of the trees, the heavy undergrowth, and the curiosity of local tribes made the task very difficult. 'The country here is very unfavorable for hurry in building Forts,' McMillan noted wryly. Nevertheless, work progressed well. By 8 September the pickets of the stockade were completed, the gates were hung, and two 12-foot-square (3.7 m) bastions were ready for the 'artillery'. The palisade measured 135 feet (41.2 m) by 120 feet (36.6 m), its walls 15 feet (4.6 m) high and 4 to 5 inches (about 9 cm) thick. McMillan boasted that 'the Tout ensemble made a formidable enough appearance', especially in the eyes of the natives.[26]

Within the palisade stood a number of log buildings in which the men lived and worked. As there were no white women at the post, several men married aboriginal women. The employees developed a small farm a short distance away and supplemented the produce with berries, deer, sturgeon, and especially salmon—which became their staple. Salmon were so abundant that the traders cured and sold the fish (initiating the west-coast salmon-packing industry, as well as creating a thriving barrel-making industry within the fort), and the proceeds maintained the post. Farming

and stock-raising also grew in importance, particularly after 1833 under the management of James Murray Yale, when Fort Langley began to provide food for the Company's other Pacific posts and for general export. This activity ensured its survival, since the yield of furs fell below expectations. By 1838 Fort Langley was supplying all the salmon and butter required by the Hudson's Bay Company west of the Rockies. Two decades later it was shipping salmon and cranberries (the latter traded from the natives) to San Francisco, Hawaii, and Australia.

This supply role led to the rebuilding of Fort Langley some 3 miles (5 km) further upriver, closer to the farm. James Douglas, the dynamic chief factor (who would later become governor of British Columbia), wrote in October 1839:

> We have abandoned the old Langley establishment which was in a delapidated state, as well as inconvenient in some respects for the business, and removed all effects, into a new fort built a few miles higher up on the banks of Fraser's River, the stockades of which, four block houses, and nearly all the necessary buildings are now erected. It is fully as convenient for the fur and Salmon trade, as the former site and, moreover, possesses the important and desireable advantage of being much nearer the farm.[27]

A year later the new fort was destroyed by fire, but it was immediately rebuilt. About a dozen buildings were erected within the stockade, three of which are seen in the 1858 drawing by architect Edward

Interior of Fort Langley, Yard, Looking S. showing the Hall

Mallandaine [**8.14**]. The most prominent was the 'Big House', at the right, which was the residence of the chief factor and the administrative and social centre of the post. Other buildings served as residences, storehouses, and artisans' workshops. The main structures were built in the post-and-groove technique that was standard for the buildings of the fur trade.

Fort Langley became an increasingly important commercial and communications centre, adopting such new industries as boat-building and ironwork. It nearly became the capital of British Columbia in 1858, but was passed over for New Westminster

8.14 Interior of the yard, Fort Langley, British Columbia, begun 1840. Drawing by E. Mallandaine, 1858. BCARS/PDP 3395.

(see below). Its economic roles subsequently became increasingly redundant and its prosperity waned. Chief trader Ovid Allard began the process of demolishing deteriorating structures and consolidating the operation within an ever-shrinking site. The farm and the livestock were sold in the 1870s and 1880s, and the post was closed by the Hudson's Bay Company in 1896.

8.15 Storehouse, Fort Langley, British Columbia, 1840. PC.

Fort Langley was commemorated as a national historic site in 1923. Only one building—a **storehouse** [8.15], used for a period as the cooperage—has survived into modern times, although somewhat altered. Built in 1840, it holds the distinction of being the oldest non-native building in British Columbia. In the 1930s it was rehabilitated to prevent it from collapsing, and beginning in 1956 other buildings were reconstructed. Fort Langley is now operated as a heritage attraction that interprets the heyday of the post in 1858.

Victoria

The Hudson's Bay Company moved its headquarters from Fort Vancouver on the Columbia River (in present-day Vancouver, Washington)—which became American territory under the Oregon Treaty of 1846—to Fort Victoria, situated on secure British territory at the southern tip of Vancouver Island, and selected by chief factor James Douglas in 1842. When he first viewed Victoria, he rhapsodized about the site:

> The place itself appears a perfect 'Eden', in the midst of the dreary wilderness of the North west coast, and so different is its general aspect, from

the wooded, rugged regions around, that one might be pardoned for supposing it had been dropped from the clouds into its present position.[28]

The local harbours were excellent and the land was suitable for farming, making the site ideal.

Construction of **Fort Victoria** began in 1843 under the direction of Douglas and chief trader Charles Ross. Douglas explained that they had formed a quadrangle 330 feet (100 m) by 300 feet (92 m), intended to contain eight buildings, each 60 feet (18 m) in length, with the outbuildings and workshops placed at their rear, 'so as not to disturb the symmetry of the principal square.'[29] Ross provided a few more details, noting that the quadrangle was

> surrounded by stoccades, eighteen feet high—one Octangular Bastion of three stories erected—also two men's houses, and one Store each measuring 60 by 30 ft. with 17 ft. Posts & Pavilion roofs. These have been thoroughly completed, and an Officers' & main house of 60 by 40 ft. are rapidly advancing to the same end.[30]

8.16 Fort Victoria, British Columbia, begun 1843. Photograph by Richard Maynard, *c.* 1862. BCARS/HP10601.

The work-force consisted of 53 Company men, most of them French Canadians who had served elsewhere in the Pacific Northwest, and the pickets for the palisade were cut by Songhees. As at Forts St James and Langley, the buildings were constructed in the post-and-groove technique. The eight-sided bastion was defended with 'Blunderbusses, muskets &c'.[31]

The fort revealed Douglas's penchant for symmetry—a declaration of imperial power, like the gridiron colonial town plans of a century earlier—although the harbour side was left open. In 1846-7 three additional 'stores' (warehouses) were built, one on stone piles in the harbour, all of them 100 feet (30.5 m) by 40 feet (12.2 m) and two storeys high, and a large cow barn was raised on the agricultural land near the fort. The stockade was enlarged in 1847, and again in 1849, at which time a second bastion was erected, destroying the original symmetry. The painter Paul Kane visited the fort in 1847 and noted that the Company 'had ten white men and forty Indians engaged in building new stores and warehouses.'[32]

Although Fort Victoria was demolished between 1860 and 1864 (it is remembered in the City of

8.17 Nanaimo Bastion, Nanaimo, British Columbia, 1852-3. Photograph by Harold Kalman, 1979.

Victoria's Fort Street and Bastion Square, which defined one corner), its appearance is known through drawings and a few photographs. The photograph [**8.16**] shows two of the original 'pavilion-' (hipped-) roofed buildings described by Ross, used as living quarters, with the main gate beyond them and a belltower at the left. The ground floors of the two buildings have been raised off the ground and provided with verandas in the manner of Quebec farmhouses, showing the persistence of French-Canadian architecture in the buildings erected for the fur trade. The appearance and scale of the bastions can be appreciated by looking at the **Nanaimo Bastion [8.17]**, a surviving Hudson's Bay Company defensive work built on the waterfront in that Vancouver Island community in 1852-3, and now used as a museum.[33]

Dr John Sebastian Helmcken, the first surgeon at Fort Victoria, described its appearance on his arrival in 1850:

> The Fort was nearly a quadrangle, about one hundred yards long and wide, with bastions at two corners containing cannon. The whole was stockaded with cedar posts about six or eight inches in diameter, and about fifteen feet in length . . . . There were inside about a dozen large block storey and a half buildings, say 60 x 40, roofed with long and wide strips of cedar bark. The buildings were for the storage of goods, Indian trading shop, and a large shop for general trade. It contained everything required. . . . A belfry stood in the middle of the yard and its bell tolled for meals, for deaths, for weddings, for church service, for fires, and sometimes for warnings.[34]

Vancouver Island became a Crown colony in 1849 and was leased to the Hudson's Bay Company on the condition that it undertake settlement. Douglas abandoned Fort Vancouver in that year and made Victoria his headquarters, and two years later he was appointed governor. The townsite of Victoria began to be surveyed in 1851 on the familiar imperial gridiron plan, and a roadway with the authoritarian name of Government Street—the first street in British North America west of the Rockies—was created.[35]

A number of company officials built themselves houses outside the stockade. One of the first houses in town, and the oldest surviving building in Victoria, was the **Helmcken house [8.18]**, built by Dr Helmcken in 1852 in preparation for his marriage to Cecilia Douglas, the daughter of his neighbour Governor James Douglas.[36] Helmcken later turned

8.18 Helmcken house, Victoria, British Columbia, 1852. Photograph by Harold Kalman, 1990.

8.19 Ground-floor plan of the Helmcken house, Victoria, British Columbia, 1852. Drawing by David Byrnes.

to politics and became the first Speaker (1856-66) of the first Legislative Assembly of Vancouver Island and participated in the negotiations that led to British Columbia's joining Confederation.

Helmcken's house is a rectangular one-storey building with a gable roof and flaring bellcast eaves. The entrance is on the broad south elevation, which is four bays wide. Its plan [**8.19**] is that of the vernacular double-house, with a partition and a triangular chimney dividing the building down the centre. The front door opens into a small entry about 6'-10" (2.1 m) by 8'-6" (2.6 m), which at the left leads to a staircase providing access to the low attic and to the adjacent wing (a later addition). Straight ahead is the largest room, likely the kitchen, and to the right are two smaller rooms, the one at the back opening onto the grounds at the rear. The post-and-groove technique was used in its construction, as in the buildings of Fort Victoria. (This is probably what Helmcken meant by 'block' buildings in his description of Fort Victoria.) The logs were covered with cladding of shingles.

Helmcken described at length its construction and the labour force he used, and also the difficulty he had in obtaining materials—providing valuable and interesting information on how a house was built:

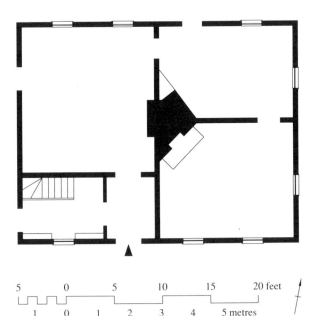

The piece of land was of course very rough and cost a good deal of time and money to clear it—this being done by Indians, chiefly from the north.

To build a house now [1892] is a very easy matter—but a very different matter then. How we studied over the design, i.e. interior divisions of the building 30 x 25 [actually 33 by 25 feet]!! Then to get it done—for there were no contractors, everything had to be done piecemeal. There being no lumber, it had to be built with logs squared on two sides and six inches thick. The sill and uprights were very heavy and morticed—the supports of the floor likewise—the logs had to be let into grooves in the uprights.

Well the timber had to be taken from the forest—squared there and brought down by water. All this had to be contracted for by French Canadians, then when brought to the beach—I had [to] beg oxen of the Company to haul it to the site. Then other Canadians took the job of putting the building up as far as the logs were concerned—and then shingling—the Indians at this time made shingles—all split. All this was very heavy, very expensive and very slow work, for the men were by no means in a hurry. Among the names I find Maurice—Peltier—Dubois—all dead now. They chiefly took their pay in blankets and provisions and other iktas—the balance in coin.

Well the shell is up—now to get it finished—lumber very scarce and a favor to get any at forty dollars per thousand in the rough—so it all had to be planed and grooved &c. by hand! Much of it was cut by Kanakas in a saw pit—so it was not very regular in thickness. I wrote to Blenkinsop at Fort Rupert [near today's Port Hardy] for plank—he sent me some and also at my wish some of yellow cedar, with these latter the door, windows and skirting boards were made.

It so happened that Gideon Halcro[w] a crofter—a mechanic of all work was here—he could do carpentering, plastering and everything connected with a house, so I got him to go on with the work, but oh, the grumbling about the irregular wood—so much planing down—besides the flooring was 8 or ten inches wide—no narrow plank then. Fortunately I had bought the two lots next mine—a house stood on it, put there by the man who built Mr. Douglas' house—at least who finished the inside. Here Halcrow worked and I think lived—but oh, how slowly—for I wanted the house to be finished by the springtime.

Then to get lime—this came from Langford's and McKenzie's [identified below]—who burned lime occasionally for their own use—after time and trouble I got this and Indians split cedar laths—a work pretty new to them—so the laths were too thin and springy. The expense and annoyance of all this was very great, in fact the house cost more than treble of a good house now.[37]

8.20 Tod house, Oak Bay, British Columbia, 1850-1. City of Victoria Archives.

The house stands on its original site, directly behind the Royal British Columbia Museum, with two later and taller additions (built by Helmcken in 1856 and 1883) abutting its west side. It is now owned and managed as a historic site by the provincial government. Next to it is the relocated St Ann's Schoolhouse, the first residence and school of the Sisters of St Ann, a small structure built in 1848 in the post-and-groove manner and later covered with clapboard. (The much larger St Ann's Academy on Humboldt Street was begun in 1871, in the manner of a Quebec convent, with many later additions.)

A form similar to that of the Helmcken house—the basic house-type of the establishment on the mid-century frontier—had been adopted two years earlier at the **Tod house** [8.20] at Oak Bay, 3 miles (5 km) east of Victoria. It was built as a retirement home by John Tod, who had been in charge of the

Hudson's Bay Company post at Kamloops. He accepted a claim of 200 acres (80 hectares) of waterfront land (he soon doubled his holding) and built his house in 1850-1. It too was built of logs—believed, but not confirmed, to be *poteaux-en-coulisse*—and was clad in horizontal siding. Photographs taken in the 1890s, when it was owned by Fred Pauline, a member of the Legislative Assembly, show the flaring eave covering a veranda and supported by a series of square posts with bracketed capitals. The veranda, front door, and other features were later altered, but the house survives—likely the oldest house in western Canada—as a private residence, owned jointly by the municipality of Oak Bay and the province of British Columbia.[38]

The Hudson's Bay Company required food and feed to maintain Fort Victoria and, as at Fort Langley, hoped to be able to raise cash by selling products, so Governor Douglas undertook a program of developing the hinterland for these purposes. In 1848 he built a flour mill and a sawmill at Esquimalt. He considered importing prefabricated houses (made in the eastern United States) that were available in California, but decided they were inadequate for the Canadian climate and that only windows should be ordered from abroad.[39]

The principal initiative for development and settlement was made through the Puget's Sound Agricultural Company, a Hudson's Bay Company subsidiary that had been established in the heyday of Fort Vancouver and had set up four farms on Vancouver Island. Each was under the supervision of a 'bailiff', with the work carried out by indentured labourers. The general supervisor of farming operations and the bailiff of Craigflower Farm—1,000 acres on the Gorge, an inlet a short distance west of Fort Victoria and north of the Royal Navy's base at Esquimalt—was Kenneth McKenzie, who had been recruited in East Lothian, Scotland, and arrived in Victoria in January 1853 with a party of sixty labourers, artisans, and family members. McKenzie tried to impress the other bailiffs with the need to operate their farms on a sound financial basis, but they seemed more determined to live like gentlemen rather than working farmers. Captain Edward Edwards Langford, the bailiff of Colwood Farm (named after his Sussex estate), was very much the English country squire. He erected eleven buildings for the use of the farm and his servants, and among the 'groceries' he charged to the Company in one year were 70 gallons of rum, sherry, and brandy.[40] McKenzie admonished Langford: 'Building new

Barns for every additional few acres that may be brought into cultivation will not do. It is profits we want at as little outlay as possible.'[41] Historian Margaret Ormsby notes that 'the bailiffs were to introduce the outlook, the pleasures and the customs of the English gentry and, with complete indifference to profit-making, live a life of comparative ease.'[42] In this respect they set the tone—one that is still maintained—of Victoria as a refined imperial outpost determined to maintain British customs, a city that was as Victorian as its name implied.

The aspirations and way of life of the bailiffs are revealed architecturally at **Craigflower Farmhouse** (or manor) on Craigflower Farm [8.21]. It has been generally understood to have been built in 1856 under the direction of Kenneth McKenzie, who was known as 'the Laird'. Evidence recently discovered by historian J.D. McDonald, however, suggests that it may have been built in 1852, before McKenzie's arrival. She found a map of Fort Victoria and environs allegedly showing the farmhouse as having been built before January 1853, and has cited a letter of 12 March 1852 from Company directors Eden Colville and John Pelly to James Douglas instructing that 'the Dwelling houses [at the farms] should be two stories high and arranged so as to admit of being easily enlarged and extended without having to make alterations in the passages and staircases'—that is, recommending a two-storey, centre-hall plan.[43]

Craigflower is a full-blown Georgian house—an architectural era away from the contemporaneous Helmcken house—with the same formal and symmetrical five-bay, two-storey façade that was seen in the residences of the British establishment in early-nineteenth-century Nova Scotia, New Brunswick, and Ontario. The Helmcken house represents the Quebec/fur-trade vernacular, whereas Craigflower Farmhouse is elegant Georgian high architecture. The latter measures about 50 by 25 feet (15.3 by 7.6 m) and places the staircase at the rear of the central hall [8.22]. The ground floor has one large room to the left, heated by a fireplace on the side (end) wall, and two interconnected rooms to the right—probably a parlour and a bedroom—each with a corner fireplace whose flues share a single chimney. The second floor contains six bedrooms, two on one side of the hall and four on the other. The building curiously combines two structural systems, reflecting the melding of European and American cultures in early Victoria. The ground floor is framed in the Hudson's Bay Company's post-and-groove manner, whereas the

8.21 Craigflower Farmhouse, near Victoria, British Columbia, *c*. 1852. Photograph by Douglas Franklin.

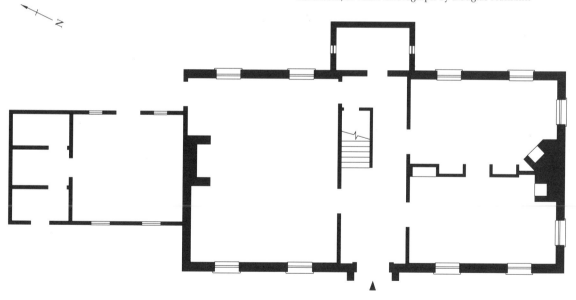

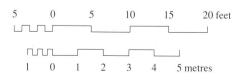

5   0   5   10   15   20 feet

1   0   1   2   3   4   5 metres

8.22 Plan of Craigflower Farmhouse, near Victoria, British Columbia, *c*. 1852. Drawing by David Byrnes after Peter Cotton.

8.23 Government Street, Victoria, British Columbia. Photograph early 1860s. BCARS/7893.

second floor has a timber frame of heavy vertical studs mortised and tenoned into horizontal plates, a technique that would have been familiar to McKenzie (or his predecessor) from his Scottish experience. The walls are covered externally with rough-sawn horizontal clapboard exposing 6 inches (15 cm) to the weather, and the original foundation was made of stone. The interior walls were all finished with lath and plaster—McKenzie noted getting 'hair for plaster from Nisqually'— and many rooms were originally wallpapered.[44]

A classical pediment and pilasters provide a dignified surround for the front door (whose fanlight has a pointed Gothic shape—a form in fashion at the time). Moulded window heads project atop the elegant 12/12 sash of the ground floor, and small pediments cap the upper-storey windows, making the house even more classical than its Georgian models. A note in the McKenzie papers suggests that some or all of the window sashes were imported from San Francisco, consistent with Douglas's decision to acquire windows from California.

The farm at Craigflower also had a steam-powered sawmill, built in 1853 (McKenzie had brought the equipment with him from Britain), and a number of cottages and workshops.

McKenzie arranged for the education of the settlers' children by recruiting a schoolmaster in England and building a schoolhouse. Craigflower School is also a clapboard-clad Georgian building, but simpler in design, lacking the decorative window heads. The schoolroom is on the ground floor; the schoolmaster's quarters are located at one end, on both floors; and three boarders' rooms are in the second storey. It opened in March 1855 with an enrolment of eight boys and six girls. Abandoned for a new school in 1911, the building—the oldest surviving school in Western Canada—was preserved in the 1920s through the intervention of the British Columbia Historical Society and the Native Sons and Daughters of British Columbia. It has been commemorated as a national historic site and, together with Craigflower Farmhouse, is operated as a museum by the provincial government.[45]

The settlement around Fort Victoria would have continued to grow at a gentle pace were it not for a momentous event: gold was discovered in the sand and gravel bars of the lower Fraser River. Rumours of finds were heard as early as 1855, and in 1858 hordes of fortune-hunters, many of them veterans of the California gold fields, created the Fraser River Gold Rush. Prospectors spread out through the territory looking for more of the precious metal, and their finds brought about a second, larger, stampede—the Cariboo Gold Rush of 1860-6.

The boats that carried the gold-seekers north from San Francisco put in at Victoria, as the town

386

around the fort was becoming known, and in 1858 an estimated 20,000 to 30,000 persons landed there. The boats brought miners, merchants, and 'an indescribable array of Polish Jews, Italian fishermen, French cooks, jobbers, speculators of every kind, land agents, auctioneers, hangers on at auctions, bummers, bankrupts and brokers of every description'. It was at Victoria that would-be prospectors were outfitted, received their permits, and transferred to the mainland. Many others stayed in the island community. Virtually overnight the quiet village became a bustling commercial city. Within six weeks some 225 buildings, 200 of them stores, sprang up in the newly laid-out downtown. Some were built permanently of brick, but many had wooden fronts and canvas sides. The surrounding countryside was covered with tents, 'resembling the encampments of an army.'[46]

A view of **Government Street [8.23]** at the intersection of Fort Street in the early 1860s shows the remarkable effects of this rapid change. A few years earlier this had been the east gate to Fort Victoria, which was located just to the left, and one of the bastions protruded into the roadway; but the bastion and this portion of the palisade were removed in 1860 and the street is now a built-up urban thoroughfare. The one-storey building at the extreme right is the popular Brown Jug Saloon. Further north, across Fort Street, stands the two-storey Alhambra Block, with a drugstore on the ground floor and a dancehall above. Beyond it is the Hotel de France and a number of business blocks, many with white blinds shielding produce from the sun. Most are built of brick, with round- and segmental-headed arched windows separated by vertical pilaster-like strips, and with a horizontal cornice capped by a parapet or balustrade along the flat roofline. These characteristics identify the Victorian Italianate style.

Between the Hotel de France and the next brick building, and also across Government Street at the left, are one- and two-storey wooden buildings with gabled roofs disguised from the street by flat-topped 'boom-town' fronts. These less-substantial buildings were typical of the first wave of gold-rush buildings, some of which had already been demolished after only a few years of service to make way for the brick structures, and many of which were still being erected at this time on cheaper properties along Victoria's less-prestigious streets. The horse-drawn barrel cart in front of the Brown Jug Saloon provided the town's water supply (the Victoria Waterworks Company began to construct its

system only in 1873). Between the Alhambra Block and the Hotel de France stands a gaslight, indicating that the picture was taken after the Victoria Gas Company began to illuminate the streets in 1862.[47]

The covered porches on both sides of the unpaved roadway sheltered the board sidewalks and pedestrians—many of whom are lingering in the shade by the Alhambra—and gave the street very much the look of a western frontier town. Something of Victoria's scale, look, and buildings at that time can be seen by visiting Old Sacramento State Historic Park in the California capital of Sacramento—the staging point for the California gold rush and the transcontinental railway—where a historic district features several blocks of restored and reconstructed commercial buildings of the 1860s.

The first brick building in Victoria was the Victoria Hotel (later called the Windsor Hotel), built in 1858 at the northeast corner of Government and Courtney Streets (behind the photographer's right shoulder).[48] The $2\frac{1}{2}$-storey building survives, although its brick exterior has been covered with wood-and-stucco mock half-timbering in the Tudor Revival mode that is so important a part of the mythical British colonial image of present-day Victoria. Such British imagery is largely a twentieth-century fabrication. In the gold-rush days and the period that followed, Victoria was architecturally far more a colony of California than of Britain.

Brick quickly became a popular building material. It was admired because it had a finished look, bestowed status on a building (and its owner), and was more fire-resistant than wood. Imported bricks—certainly from England and possibly also from Fort Vancouver—had been used for chimneys at Fort Victoria; but at Governor Douglas's instigation brickmaker George Mason came to Victoria from England in 1851 and established a brickyard southeast of the fort. 'Soft' firebricks were also being made at Colwood and Craigflower Farms by 1853 in sufficient quantities that by 1857 some were exported to Washington Territory and Russian America, and possibly also to Hawaii. At the same time 'hard' exterior bricks continued to be imported from England and the US (mostly California). With the 1858 boom a number of brickyards went into operation in and near Victoria, several of them just north of town on the Saanich Road, where large deposits of clay were discovered. The industry grew quickly and acquired increasingly sophisticated technology. In 1875 a brickmaking machine capable of producing 26,000 bricks a day was imported from Montreal, and a steam moulding machine was installed at Kempster Brothers' brickyard in 1885, raising the yard's capacity to 60,000 bricks a day. In the 1890s there were at least five brickyards in Saanich, with annual productions in excess of one million bricks.[49]

A few commercial buildings from the gold-rush era, other than the Victoria Hotel, are still standing. One of the most attractive is the **Rithet Building** (1861-88) on Wharf Street, which has been restored and is now used for provincial government offices [**8.24**]. Merchant Robert Paterson Rithet, who later served terms as mayor of Victoria and as a member of the Legislative Assembly, arrived in 1862 and quickly prospered in the shipping, insurance, salmon-canning, lumber, and sugar industries. He built a number of wharves and acquired several warehouses around Victoria harbour—shipping became a very profitable business after Victoria was proclaimed a free port in 1860. The three-storey Rithet Building is one of those warehouses; the two-storey building at the left (1129 Wharf Street), built in 1861, was also owned by Rithet. The cast-iron columns on the ground floor of the two-storey

building and on the left-hand (northern) portion of the taller building bear the name of the foundry, Peter Donahue's Union Ironworks in San Francisco, as well as the year, 1861. Those on the (later) right-hand bays are inscribed with the name of Victoria's Albion Ironworks—the city soon developed an iron industry—and are dated 1888. The two upper floors of the façade (the top storey is a slightly later addition) and the other walls are constructed of brick. The windows of each storey are treated in a distinct manner: those on the ground floor, between the iron columns, have low segmental arches; the second-storey windows have rectangular arches, with their bracketed projecting heads alternating in detail; and the top floor reverts to the segmental arch, but encases the window in a moulded frame. Pilaster strips divide the façade into three. Decorative horizontal architraves separate the floors.[50]

The Rithet Building and its neighbour are good examples of the Victorian Italianate style, the most popular vernacular commercial style of the day in the United States, which made its entry into Canadian cities at this time. It was not a direct revival of a past architectural style, as were the Gothic and Greek Revivals, but rather a reworking of conventional compositions with an emphasis on the decorative treatment of windows, rooflines, and other

8.24 1129 Wharf Street (left, 1861) and Rithet Building (right, 1861-88), Victoria, British Columbia. Photograph by Harold Kalman, 1991.

features, whose details are only loosely derived from Italian Renaissance and post-Renaissance sources. Most Italianate structures were the work of commercial builders; architects have seldom been identified with buildings in this manner. Although the style was gaining favour in the East as well as the West, it—like the iron columns—came to Victoria from San Francisco.

At the onset of Victoria's boom, with the arrival of so many rough-and-ready transients, the maintenance of law and order became a prime consideration for the authorities, and colonial interests took precedence over those of the Hudson's Bay Company. The government decided not to renew the Company's lease and moved quickly to declare its own authority. In 1858 the mainland from the Rocky Mountains to the coast became the colony of British Columbia, and it and the older colony of Vancouver Island both came under the administration of Governor James Douglas, who severed all his ties with the Hudson's Bay Company. Eight years later the two colonies were amalgamated as British Columbia, and the larger colony joined Confederation in 1871. Victoria, the capital of Vancouver Island, became the capital of British Columbia.

The first public architectural requirement was for new **Colonial Administration Buildings** [8.25], so that the government would no longer have to work out of Fort Victoria but could have its own identifiable presence. The initial intention was to build on Government Street, but in 1858 that property was subdivided into 37 lots and sold for

$27,500, taking advantage of the real estate boom, and a larger site was chosen on the south side of James Bay, near Douglas's and Helmcken's houses. Douglas rationalized its distance from downtown, in a speech to the Assembly, by noting that the site was 'dry, airy and spacious . . . being a public reserve, is acquired without expense...[and] by isolation from the town...[is] in a great measure secured against conflagration'; and he told the Colonial Secretary, the Duke of Newcastle, that the property was 'sufficiently near to the Town, while removed from its noise and confusion.'[51] A bridge 800 feet (nearly 250 m) long was built across James Bay on the alignment of Government Street in 1859, reducing the distance. Douglas's choice of site proved to be inspired, as it provided a memorable focus for the government buildings and the later development of Victoria's Inner Harbour.

The design of the new administration buildings was entrusted to Hermann Otto Tiedemann (1821-91), an assistant in the office of Surveyor General J.W. Pemberton. A native of Berlin who trained in Germany as a civil engineer, he arrived in Victoria in 1858, and may be credited with having been Victoria's first architect. Tiedemann created a symmetrical complex of five separate buildings—perhaps to reduce the risk of the spread of fire, as Douglas declared. In the centre stood the two-storey Administration Building (or Colonial Office, and known by a number of other names as well), 83

8.26 (*above*) Colonial Office, Victoria, British Columbia, *c*. 1860. BCARS/1790.

8.27 (*below*) Legislative Assembly Building, Victoria, British Columbia, 1859. BCARS/11372.

feet by 43 feet (25.3 by 13.1 m), containing twenty rooms and with a clock tower rising out of the centre of its hipped roof [8.26]. Flanking the Administration Building and slightly behind it were the Legislative Assembly Building [8.27] and the Supreme Court, each of them two storeys high in the centre with a one-storey wing projecting forward at either side and connected by an entrance porch. Further out at each side of the site were the Land Office and the Treasury, smaller one-storey buildings surrounded by verandas. A sixth building, the Guard House and Barracks (manned by a detachment of Royal Marines), stood at the rear. Contracts for the six buildings were drawn up in July 1859; the Legislative Assembly Building was completed in November of that year and the last portions of the complex were opened in 1864. The structures were replaced by the present Parliament Buildings in 1898, but one survived until 1957, when it was destroyed by fire.[52]

The most noticeable features of the buildings are their hipped roofs with flaring bracketed eaves; the prominent balconies and verandas; and the distinctive exterior treatment in which the red brick walls were overlaid by cream-coloured wood strips arranged in diagonal and perpendicular crossed patterns. The other surfaces were 'fancifully painted in various shades of red'. The press had a field day, describing the main building as 'something between a Dutch Toy and a Chinese Pagoda', 'a pagoda wigwam', and—closer to the mark— explaining that 'the style of architecture is that of the Elizabethan period'.[53] The buildings soon became known as 'The Birdcages', probably because of the cage-like appearance of the wood appliqué.

Several distinct architectural sources can be identified. The massing is derived from the 'colonial bungalow', an established Anglo-Indian building-form with strong imperialist roots characterized by low profiles and the use of pagoda-like broad hipped roofs and verandas. The wooden brackets and wall strips reveal a familiarity with the kind of woodwork popularized for cottages in picturesque rural landscapes by A.J. Downing (1815-52), and other American architectural writers in the 1840s and 1850s; they also hark back to the Elizabethan Tudor tradition of half-timbering, which would become a Victoria architectural cliché a half-century later (see Chapter 11 for bungalows, cottages, and the Tudor Revival). The symmetrical arrangement of the five principal buildings on either side of a central axis reflects a mode of planning public buildings that was then growing in popularity (and

which had been anticipated at Fort Victoria)—it is seen in the contemporaneous Parliament Buildings in Ottawa—and is later associated with the École des Beaux-Arts in Paris. The synthesis of these various sources identifies The Birdcages as British colonial public buildings set in the picturesque western Canadian landscape. Tiedemann made it easy to read the colonial meaning into his design; whether or not he did it consciously is immaterial, since the various sources and their connotations were familiar to all proficient architects of the time. The practice of combining metaphors drawn from a variety of historical precedents has been revived by the Post-Modern architects of our own day (see Chapter 15).

Other public structures served communications and defence. Fisgard Lighthouse [5.5], the first permanent light on Canada's Pacific coast, was built in 1860 at the entrance to Esquimalt Harbour. Architects H.O. Tiedemann and John Wright were both retained to provide components of the design. In 1878 a system of defences known as Fort Rodd Hill began to be constructed adjacent to the lighthouse to protect Victoria. The British garrison withdrew in 1906, but Fort Rodd Hill remained an active military station under Canadian command until 1956. It and Fisgard Lighthouse—which is still in service—are operated as a national historic park by Parks Canada.[54]

Fort Rodd Hill was also one of several installations intended to defend the large naval base at Esquimalt. The core of the base is the dockyard, which was officially created in 1865 (although it had already operated for a decade) as the headquarters of the Royal Navy's Pacific Station. In 1905 the Navy abandoned the base and turned it over to the Canadian government, who maintain it as Canadian Forces Base (CFB) **Esquimalt**. Many late-nineteenth-century masonry buildings, which replaced earlier wood-frame ones, remain in use. They form an impressive ensemble that still provides a superb impression of an imperial naval station.

The most impressive—and most characteristic— structures are the stores, workshops, and other industrial buildings that accommodated the work of the dockyard. These include the **Main Warehouse** [8.28], built in 1898, the 'factory' or principal industrial shop complex (1889-1903), the rum stores (1896), the salt meat stores (1895), the cordage and furniture stores, and the ordnance stores. Most are brick buildings articulated with brick pilasters and stone trim, with timber supports and roof trusses, medium-pitch gable roofs, and regular patterns of small, segmental-headed windows. Their design was descended from a long heritage of British industrial architecture originating in the late eighteenth century. Engineers have been identified with the construction of some of them; the Main Warehouse was likely designed by Thomas Woodgate, the rum stores by A.C.E. Perkins, and the salt meat stores by H.C. Reid.[55]

At the other end of the spectrum is the domestic elegance of the former **Naval Storekeeper's House** [8.29], now the official residence of the rear-admiral. It was built in 1885 to plans by Victoria architect John Teague (1833-1902), who also designed the former Royal Naval Hospital complex (1887-94) nearby. A formal two-storey house with Italianate window treatment, roof brackets, and quoins, it is built of brick with stone trim and is capped by a hipped roof and a widow's walk. A columned porch protects the entrance. Although the house has been altered somewhat, it retains

8.28 Main Warehouse, Dockyard, CFB Esquimalt, British Columbia, 1898. Photograph 1941. Canada. Department of National Defence/NAC/PA-176321.

8.29 (*below*) Naval Storekeeper's House, Dockyard, CFB **Esquimalt**, British Columbia, 1885. BCARS/7856.

392

most of its interior wood- and plaster-work, fire-places, and its fine staircase. In the early photograph the house is seen at the right. At the left is one of three 'Crimean Huts' built in 1855 for the Royal Navy by the Hudson's Bay Company as hospital units, anticipating casualties from a possible attack on Russia during the Crimean War. Artillery shells are seen piled in the foreground and at the left. In the rear, between the house and the Crimean hut, are a wash house and, above it, a water tank. Of this group, only the house is still standing.

The religious needs of the growing new community of Victoria had to be served, as well as its governmental and military ones. The Right Reverend George Hills—the first Anglican Bishop of Columbia, who arrived in Victoria in January 1860—found a willing benefactor in the Baroness Angela Burdett-Coutts, a wealthy London banking heiress who took an active interest in supporting the Church of England in distant colonies and had endowed bishoprics in Adelaide and Capetown. She never visited Victoria, but donated £25,000 to the diocese, consulted with Bishop Hills on its

8.30 Church of St John the Divine (the Iron Church), Victoria, British Columbia, 1860. BCARS/41221.

development, and organized boatloads of young women to provide brides for the settlers (not unlike the *filles du roi* of New France). She is remembered by Angela College [**6.46**] on Burdett Avenue (it and Coutts Way were named after her), Victoria's first collegiate school for girls, which was founded by the diocese at her request. This red-brick Gothic Revival school was built in 1866 to designs by Wright and Sanders, the leading Victoria architects of the day. The better-known John Wright (1830-1915), who was Scottish-born, came to Victoria in 1859; his partner George Sanders was an Englishman. (Other of their buildings will be discussed shortly.) In 1867 they both moved to San Francisco, where they designed more than 100 buildings in fewer than 30 years, including the offices of the Central Pacific Railroad and the Nob Hill mansion of railway baron Mark Hopkins. They are poorly remembered in that city, however, since virtually all their work was lost in the earthquake of 1906.[56]

The Baroness's generosity provided Victoria with a new Anglican church, the **Church of St John the Divine [8.30]**, known as the 'Iron Church'. The corrugated iron sections, cast-iron fittings, and wood frame were pre-assembled in London during the summer of 1859 by contractor Samuel Hemming. Bishop Hills visited it at Hemming's yard in Bow to give his approval, and the church was then dismantled and shipped round the Horn to Victoria, accompanied by two workmen from London: John Hemming, the son of the builder, and John Sharp. The church was erected the following summer on a brick-and-stone foundation, on its site on Douglas Street, under the direction of Victoria builder John G. Cochrane. It was consecrated in September 1860.[57]

The Iron Church was a surprisingly imposing building, with a high nave, lower side aisles, and square corner tower with a tall, pyramidal spire (added later). Its massing, the pointed-arched windows, and the half-timbering effect of the wood frame clearly placed the church within the Gothic Revival tradition. Inside, wood panelling and the timber trusses of the roof were more evident than the metal, but the sound of the British Columbia rain on the iron roof constantly reminded parishioners of the building material. The church was described in the local newspaper:

> It is wood, cased with corrugated iron plates, lined and panelled inside with Oregon red pine-wood.... The interior, which is stained very dark,

with the fittings, is extremely tasteful. There is a beautiful carved stone font, given by a late parishioner of the Bishop at Great Yarmouth [Hills' former parish in England]. A fine organ, also a gift, and other gifts are also on their way to the colony: a bell, altar-cloth, and east light of stained glass.[58]

In 1912 St John's was replaced by a stone church on a different site, and the Iron Church was demolished the following year.

Prefabricated buildings provided a convenient means of transferring building-types, values, and technology to the colonies. Victoria Bridge [5.17] at Montreal, another iron structure that was manufactured in England, was inaugurated in the same year as St John's. Metal structures had been popularized by the Crystal Palace (by horticulturalist and greenhouse-builder Joseph Paxton, 1803-65), which was erected in London's Hyde Park as the centrepiece of the Great Exhibition of 1851. English architect William Slater (1819-72) subsequently published a design for an iron church whose 'external walls are a framework of cast-iron, so arranged as to have the interstices faced internally and externally with corrugated plates, and packed between these plates with felt and sand.' The Ecclesiological Society promoted Slater's church for the colonies; whether or not Victoria's Iron Church used his system is not known.[59]

Other Christian denominations built houses of worship at this time, as did Victoria's small but secure Jewish community. The first Jews who arrived with the gold-seekers—most came from the United States and England, some from as far away as Germany and Australia—organized High Holy Day services in the fall of 1858 and soon determined to build a synagogue. Wright and Sanders were selected as the architects. The cornerstone of **Temple Emanuel** [8.31, 32] was laid on 2 June 1863 by a contingent of seventy local Freemasons as the climax of a gala procession, which was led by a band from the British warship HMS *Topaze* and included participants from the French Benevolent Society, the German Choral Society, and the St Andrew's Society, as well as the Mayor of Victoria and the Chief Justice of Vancouver Island. The *British Colonist* reported the multi-cultural ceremony in considerable detail and concluded:

Thus terminated an eventful day in the history of the Jews in Vancouver Island, and it must be a source of infinite gratification to that body, that the ceremonies of this day, partaking as they did

8.31 Temple Emanuel, Victoria, British Columbia, 1863. Photograph by Harold Kalman, 1993.

8.32 Interior of Temple Emanuel, Victoria, British Columbia, 1863. Photograph *c*. 1900. Collection of Cyril Leonoff.

8.33 Tong Ork On Hing block (1882) and the Chinese Consolidated Benevolent Association building (1885), Fisgard Street, Victoria, British Columbia. BCARS/67633.

of a purely denominational character, were participated in by all classes of our community with a hearty goodwill and brotherly feeling, evidencing in acts more powerful than words the high esteem in which they are held by the fellow townsmen of the City of Victoria.[60]

The brick synagogue, which was completed in November 1863, is treated as having two storeys, corresponding to the ground floor and the women's gallery that runs round three sides of the sanctuary. The windows contain stained glass in simple geometric patterns and the vaulted ceiling has a skylight. Three arched portals form the entrance to the building. The round-arched theme is continued in the heads of the windows on both levels; they, the central rose window, and the arched 'corbels' (the decorative band beneath the eaves and the gable) are characteristic of the Romanesque Revival style. The mode was popular for synagogues because the Romanesque style provided the precedent for the Gothic—the standard for Christian architecture—just as Judaism formed the foundation of Christianity. Evidently appreciating this, the building committee reported that the plan 'was very excellent and beautiful and in every [way] suitable for our purposes.'[61]

In 1948 Temple Emanuel suffered insensitive renovations inside and out, but they were removed and the original appearance was restored in 1982 by architect Nicholas Bawlf (b. 1938). The completion was celebrated by re-enacting the dedication

ceremony of 119 years earlier. Led by the Shriners' band, the parade included representatives of Victoria's ethnic communities in traditional costumes and 700 Masons in full regalia. Temple Emanuel takes pride in being the oldest standing synagogue in Canada (the first Canadian synagogue was built by Montreal's Shearith Israel Congregation in 1777),[62] and the oldest house of worship of any denomination in continuous use in British Columbia.

Many other ethnic groups—the most visible of whom were the Chinese—found security in Victoria. The first Chinese in Victoria—and, indeed, in Canada—arrived with other gold-seekers from San Francisco in the summer of 1858. While most went to the Fraser River goldfields, a number established businesses in Victoria, opening branches of the large San Francisco companies; but before long independent merchants began to set up shop. A distinct Chinatown develped a few blocks north of the fort, on the far side of the Johnson Street ravine. Between 1881 and 1884 many thousands more Chinese arrived—from China as well as the US—to work on the British Columbia section of the Canadian Pacific Railway. Once again many stayed behind in Victoria, and by 1886 most of the city's 3,000 Chinese lived in the four-block Chinatown.

Buildings erected in Chinatown between the 1860s and 1890s were characterized by a multiplicity of projecting wooden balconies, often multi-tiered verandas that were far more elaborate than the simple sidewalk shelters we saw along Government Street. A **view of Fisgard Street [8.33]**, taken in the late 1880s, shows two structures: at the left is a two-storey wood building, likely erected in the 1860s or 1870s, with a boom-town stepped parapet façade and a broad veranda accessed from the second floor. In the centre is the Tong Ork On Hing block, a three-storey brick building with a similar projecting veranda. It was built in 1882 by the Chan brothers of On Hing and Brothers Co., one of Victoria's largest import-and-export companies. The ground floor was a cigar factory, and the upper floors were residential. Seen at the right is the Chinese Consolidated Benevolent Association (Zhonghua Huiguan), a powerful umbrella agency that operated a school and temple and also functioned as a consulate; its directors represented the many 'tongs', or voluntary associations, that formed the community structure of Chinatown society. The CCBA building, built in 1885 to designs by John Teague, would be indistinguishable from other three-storey Victorian Italianate blocks were it not for the elaborate three-tiered balconies. Behind was a maze of narrow alleys. The Fook Yuen

8.34 Richard Carr house, Victoria, British Columbia, 1863. Photograph by Kate Williams. Heritage Properties Branch/ Ministry of Tourism and Ministry Responsible for Culture (British Columbia).

Opium Factory (one of ten in the city) operated behind the On Hing building.[63] Opium manufacture (but not consumption) was permitted in Canada until 1907, when a young Deputy Minister of Labour named William Lyon Mackenzie King convinced the federal government to prohibit the industry.

Balconies formed a prominent feature of the architecture of southern China, and were transferred from there to the buildings of San Francisco's and Victoria's Chinatowns. In the late 1890s Victoria declared the wood balconies a fire hazard and banned them. The CCBA building survives, but its ornate balconies were replaced by banal iron fire escapes. The Tong Ork On Hing block was rebuilt to double its width in 1912, replacing the wood structure and probably enveloping the 1882 block within a broad, buff brick building; it too still stands, accommodating a large restaurant. Since the balconies provided a vital social function, Chinatown's builders responded to their prohibition by recessing balconies within masonry façades. But by the early 1900s Vancouver's Chinatown was surpassing Victoria's in vitality, and it is in that city that the new architectural form is best seen [**9.66**].

Victoria's burgeoning population required housing, and the real-estate and construction industries prospered during the 1860s. Many of the new residents built houses in the James Bay area, behind (south of) the new Colonial Administration Buildings and not far from the pre-Gold Rush homes of Dr Helmcken and Governor Douglas. A rare survivor of this era is the **Richard Carr house [8.34]** on Government Street, built in 1863 by an English-born entrepreneur who had made some money in San Francisco, returned home in 1861, and soon resolved to go back to 'California or...a British Colony.' Richard Carr and his family chose the latter. They arrived at Esquimalt in July 1863, having spent a month en route visiting friends in San Francisco. Carr purchased four acres of land in James Bay for his home (he also bought other prop-

8.35 A Summer Seat and a Wayside Cottage. From Samuel Sloan, *The Model Architect* (1852).

erties for speculative purposes) and commissioned designs from Wright and Sanders.[64]

The Carr house is significant not only because of its age and its design, but also because Richard Carr's famous daughter, Emily, was born here in 1871 and grew up in it. The renowned painter wrote fondly of the family home in *The Book of Small*. Among her recollections, we find a passage that emphasizes the split in the allegiance of early Victorians to both California and Britain:

> [Father] built what was considered in 1863 a big fine house. It was all made of California redwood. The chimneys were of California brick and the mantelpieces of black marble. Every material used in the building of Father's house was the very best, because he never bought anything cheap or shoddy. He had to send far away for most of it...
>
> Father wanted his place to look exactly like England. He planted cowslips and primroses and hawthorn hedges and all the Englishy flowers. He had stiles and meadows and took away all the wild Canadian-ness and made it as meek and English as he could.[65]

Emily Carr was born eight years after the house was built, so she may have erred in some of the details of its construction. Recent analysis suggests, for example, that the structural members are fir and not redwood.[66] The house is a frame structure, with studs and plates spiked together to form a skeleton. The exterior walls are sheathed in horizontal wood siding. This structural system is typical of Victoria's wood buildings of the 1860s, in contrast to the grooved-post technique used by the Hudson's Bay Company in the previous decade and seen in the Helmcken house. The easy availability of sawn lumber, a result of the opening of numerous sawmills, made this lighter and more efficient method of construction standard.

The house is two storeys high, with a ground-floor veranda and a smaller porch off the second floor, in front of the projecting and gabled central bay. Its design, like that of the Rithet Building, is in the Victorian Italianate style. It is essentially American in its inspiration, with a general similarity to the cottages of the popular American architect and author A.J. Downing; its plan and elevation bear a resemblance to designs for a Summer Seat (in its composition and windows) and a Wayside Cottage (in the veranda) published by Philadelphia architect Samuel Sloan (1815-84) on a single page of *The Model Architect* (1852); **8.35**.[67]

The frame construction of the Carr house allows the walls to be opened up by large windows, with those on the upper floor having Italianate round arches. Decorative woodwork—such as the posts and fascia on the central part of the porch, the balustrades beside and above, the rafter ends that appear beneath the eaves, and the corbel-like serrations and finial of the gables—have been executed with evident joy. The symmetry, and the emphasis on the centre, are clearly reminiscent of Georgian houses of a half-century or more earlier; but the generally dour appearance of the earlier dwellings is replaced here by the lighter, more graceful, and more ornamental manner typical of the Victorian age.

The front portion of the interior is as symmetrical as the façade, with a central hall containing the staircase and flanked by two large rooms, probably a living-room and a parlour. Both have bay windows that project from the side elevations; the one on the left (north) is original, that on the right is a later addition. The rooms at the rear of the house, mostly the result of alterations, are arranged less formally. The house has been in public use since 1964 and was partially restored in 1967 by Victoria architect Peter Cotton (1918-78). (The gardens admired by Emily Carr have been reasonably well maintained.) The house is now owned by the provincial government.

Through the 1870s Victoria continued to establish its role as the principal supply and service centre on the Canadian west coast, as well as consolidating its status as the capital of British Columbia. Development was steady, and a number of substantial and significant buildings were erected. Among the institutions, the most important were the Custom House on Wharf Street (1873-5; **10.9**), designed by the Department of Public Works under the direction of Chief Architect Thomas S. Scott (1826-95), a mansard-roofed brick building that acknowledges the Second Empire Style; and Victoria City Hall (1878, with later additions), a Victorian Italianate building with an entrance tower, designed by architect John Teague. Commercial and residential building kept pace with the increase in population and trade.

A second wave of building began in the late 1880s, reflecting the new prosperity brought to the province by the completion of the Canadian Pacific Railway. But Victoria's pre-eminent position was soon challenged by booming Vancouver, the terminus of the railway. By the beginning of the new century the mainland city surpassed the island capital in size and economic importance.

The Settlement of the Interior

With the exception of the network of posts built by the overland fur-traders, early European settlement in British Columbia had been restricted to the coastal area. The Fraser River and Cariboo gold rushes of the late 1850s and early 1860s changed everything. Thousands of would-be prospectors who led the way into the rugged interior were soon accompanied by land agents, shopkeepers, missionaries, engineers, and others. Before long communications and architecture had developed sufficiently to allow and encourage permanent inland settlement.

The Royal Engineers

The colonial and imperial governments orchestrated development carefully and effectively, determined to maintain law and order as well as allegiance to the British Crown. Governor Douglas wrote to Westminster in August 1858 asking for help—'even a single company of infantry.' The Colonial Secretary, Sir Edward Bulwer-Lytton, had anticipated Douglas's request and dispatched a company of more than 150 Royal Engineers, intending that they would not only serve as a peacekeeping force but would help lay the foundations of a great colony. Bulwer-Lytton explained:

> It will devolve upon them to survey those parts of the country which may be considered most suitable for settlement, to mark out allotments of land for public purposes, to suggest a site for the seat of government, to point out where roads should be made, and to render you such assistance as may be in their power...[68]

The Columbia Detachment of the Royal Engineers arrived in 1858-9, under the command of Lt.-Col. Richard Clement Moody (1813-87). A seasoned veteran who had previously served as the first governor of the Falkland Islands, Moody was given a 'dormant' commission as Lieutenant-Governor of British Columbia in the event that Douglas became incapacitated.[69] In the few years before the detachment disbanded in 1863, the Royal Engineers had an immense impact on the development of the colony. Besides building their own camp, they surveyed townsites in order to accommodate settlers and sell land (the proceeds from the sales financed the Royal Engineers' expenses), constructed roads to the interior, and laid out the site for a new colonial capital.[70]

New Westminster and Sapperton Governor Douglas wanted the capital of the colony to be at Derby, the name that had been given to the site of Old Fort Langley, but Colonel Moody felt that its location was so close to the American border as to be vulnerable; he argued that 'at any moment the Americans could and would have their grip on the very throat of British Columbia.'[71] Moody chose a site closer to the mouth of the Fraser River, on its north shore. He called the future capital Queenborough (or Queensborough), in honour of the monarch; but he received a dispatch in May 1859 announcing that 'Her Majesty has been graciously pleased to decide that the Capital of British Columbia shall be called "New Westminster".'[72]

The site for the capital was a thick tangle of enormous trees. The Reverend John Sheepshanks, temporary chaplain to the Royal Engineers, reported in mid-summer 1859 on the progress of clearing:

> On turning a corner of the river, after an hour or two of steady steaming up stream, at about fifteen miles from the mouth of the river, the captain, who was standing by my side, said, 'There, sir, that is your place.' I looked up a long stretch of the river and there on the left hand side I saw a bit of a clearing in the dense forest. Mighty trees were lying about in confusion, as though a giant with one sweep of his mighty arm had mown them down. Many of the trunks had been consumed by fire. Their charred remains were seen here and there. The huge stumps of the trees were still standing in most places...and between the prostrate trees and stumps there were a few huts, one small collection of wooden stores, some sheds and tents, giving signs of a population of perhaps 250 people. This clearing continued up river to the extent of somewhat more than a quarter of a mile...this was New Westminster.[73]

Colonel Moody devised an ambitious plan for New Westminster, embellishing the familiar imperial gridiron with many subtleties. Drawn by Lance-Corporal James Conroy of the Royal Engineers, the plan attempted to capture the spirit of

8.36 Royal Engineers' plan of New Westminster, British Columbia. Lithograph of map drawn by Lance-Corporal James Conroy, 1861. BCARS/Map Collection/neg. no. 358553.

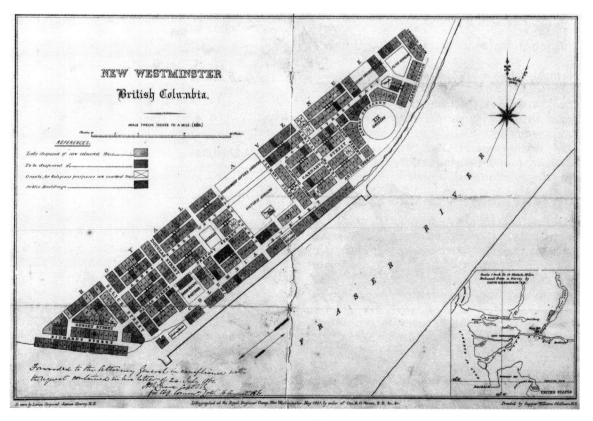

8.37 Government Assay Office and Mint, New Westminster, British Columbia, *c.* 1861. BCARS/31139.

a mature British Georgian town, such as Bath or Edinburgh New Town—which combine straight streets with squares, circles, and crescents, all lined with elegant and uniform 'terraces' (row-houses). The **plan for New Westminster [8.36]** proposed a linear development, defined by the Fraser River on one side and Royal Avenue on the other. The principal streets were oriented east-west (actually northeast-southwest, the direction of the river), with the main thoroughfare being Columbia Street (now Columbia Avenue), just above the waterfront and running between the Custom House on the west and Arthur Terrace and Albert Crescent—a curved street of houses opposite a circular park—on the east. Two squares occur along its route. Lytton Square, midway along Douglas Street, is aligned with the principal north-south axis, which is established by a government reserve and the large public Victoria Gardens, in the centre of which is the Anglican Church of the Holy Trinity. Several other north-south accents vary the plan, including a third square and a government reserve, on which the city hall and courthouse were subsequently built. Eight other church reserves are indicated as well.[74]

The government and public buildings erected in the early years of New Westminster had few architectural pretensions. As Governor Douglas noted in 1860:

> The public offices [of New Westminster] are plain, substantial buildings devoid of ornament and constructed on a scale adapted to our limited means; they are nevertheless roomy and commodious and on the whole, not unsuited to the present business of the colony.[75]

A temporary courthouse was built in 1859, followed by a separate Supreme Court building in 1860—an austere frame structure 40 feet (12.2 m) by 20 feet (6.1 m) that the newspaper dismissed as 'a disgrace to the town', and that was replaced in 1872, and again in 1891.[76] The Engineers also completed plans for gold assay offices, a church, a jail, barracks and officers' quarters, a customs house, a hospital, a pier, and a number of bridges. Their character is indicated by the **Assay Office and Mint [8.37]**, at the principal intersection of Main

400

and Columbia Streets, which also served as a land-registry office and post office: a series of three frame buildings, the scale of ordinary houses, linked by a one-storey passage. The front elevation of the left-hand block attempted an air of classical dignity by suggesting classical columns and a pediment; but the columns are merely open iron posts and the pediment an unornamented gable. The foreground is littered with stumps. Holy Trinity, an attractive frame Gothic Revival church, stood nearby only until its premature destruction by fire in 1865. It was designed by Lieutenant A.R. Lemprière, likely with assistance from the more talented Corporal John C. White (1835-1907), who subsequently left the Royal Engineers and went into private architectural practice in Victoria and San Francisco.[77]

As a result of the shallow public purse, and because New Westminster ceased to be the colonial capital in 1868, Moody's vision of a great city could not be sustained. Victoria Gardens and several of the proposed squares were never built, although Albert Crescent was developed as planned. A photograph taken about 1863 [8.38] from the far side of the river (the district south of the Fraser was named 'Surrey', after the English county located across the Thames from London and Westminster) shows that a fair amount of construction had taken

place, but with little apparent order or grace. A row of one- and two-storey frame buildings with boom-town fronts stand near the water, and many buildings, dominated by one three-storey brick block, rise behind them on Columbia Avenue. Holy Trinity Church can be seen (above and just to the left of the berthed steamship), with its gable roof parallel to the river. Despite the number of buildings, however, there is little overall to reveal Moody's grand intentions.

The Royal Engineers built their own camp, which came to be known as Sapperton (the Royal Engineers were often referred to as 'sappers' after they absorbed the Royal Sappers and Miners in 1856), a mile upriver (northeast) from New Westminster and separated from it by a large park reserve. By early 1859 they had built a temporary log house for the engineers and a shingled dwelling for the Colonel.[78] Moody's house was inadequate for his family, who came to New Westminster in May, and he informed Douglas of his intention to improve his living situation:

> I propose to construct what in England would be considered a cottage with Bedrooms in the roof

8.38 New Westminster, British Columbia. Photograph by F.G. Claudet, *c*. 1863. BCARS/9326.

401

8.39 Sapperton, New Westminster, British Columbia. Photograph by F.G. Claudet, *c*. 1862-4. BCARS/9324.

and which could be erected there for a small sum—a House *not* appropriate to my position in a Colony of such consequence...I will take care to design it however in such a manner that it can be further improved and added to some future day.'[79]

Moody built his 'cottage' during the summer of 1859—Admiral R.L. Baynes wrote to his wife that 'Col. M has built himself an excellent house, one, if it were of Brick instead of wood, I should have no objection to in England.'[80]

Even this, however, did not satisfy Moody, and so a year later he began work on a larger Government House (1861-3) on the edge of Sapperton, facing the river and the New Westminster townsite across the park reserve. Corporal White provided a design for a rectangular building 90 feet (27.5 m) wide and about 30 feet (9.2 m) deep, with three large rooms distributed across the ground floor, and on the second floor beneath the eaves of the roof; the staircase was at the rear, behind the central space, and a servants' wing was also built there. The steep roof, second-storey dormers, and full-width veranda on the main façade gave Government House the appearance of a Quebec farmhouse of a century earlier—a somewhat surprising situation, in that the designer was an English officer and not a

French Canadian employed by the Hudson's Bay Company.[81]

Moody moved into Government House shortly before he left British Columbia in November 1863, and then Douglas resided there for a month until Frederick Seymour arrived, in April 1864, to replace him as Governor of British Columbia. Seymour considered Government House to be too small. He made it 'tolerably habitable' by adding a ballroom wing with a tower, also designed by White, making the building decidedly asymmetrical. The newspaper account expressed the new picturesque sensibilities of the Victorian age when it noted that the 'ornamental tower...will much improve the appearance of the Vice-Regal residence from the river.'[82]

Government House (before the construction of Seymour's ballroom wing) is seen at the left in an early photograph of **Sapperton [8.39]**. The officers' quarters are in the verandahed building to the right of it; the sappers' barracks and dwellings rise up the hillside at the centre; and the hospital is the gable-roof building with two dormers to their right, just in front of the forest. Stores and boathouses stand along the river, at the right. The tallest building, behind them, is the gabled church of St Mary the Virgin, designed by White and built in 1865 to serve the sappers and the Governor. Its frame of eight-by-eight timbers is sheathed in horizontal

402

clapboard, over which is applied a pattern of crossed boards, not unlike the exterior treatment of The Birdcages in Victoria (where the wood was applied to a brick wall). A.W. Sillitoe, the newly appointed Bishop of New Westminster, noted in 1879 that 'St Mary's Church . . . is a model of what all wooden churches might be and ought to be.' The church stands today, although it has been much altered; most of the other buildings in the picture have gone; Government House was demolished in 1888.[83]

When British Columbia united with Vancouver Island in 1866, Victoria was named the capital city and New Westminster lost its privileged status. But it remained the most important city on the mainland until the late 1880s, when nearby Vancouver became the terminus of the Canadian Pacific Railway. The city maintained much of its prosperity for a decade, but on the night of 10 September 1898 a devastating fire destroyed virtually all the downtown. New Westminster was rebuilt, but it never recovered. It evolved a dual identity: as a small self-sufficient city, and as a dormitory suburb of Vancouver—a role that was accentuated in the 1980s with the construction of a rapid-transit line between the two centres.

From the Fraser Canyon north to the Cariboo The development of transportation routes was a particularly important activity in the isolated mountainous colony, even more so than in the rest of Canada; the firm imposition of imperial power, on the other hand, made itself felt in all of early Canada.[84] These two elements—roads and imperial

dominance—came together in the work of the Royal Engineers. Much of their activity in British Columbia was dedicated to providing roads, townsites, and public buildings along the way to the gold fields of the Fraser River, and subsequently further north in the Cariboo region.

In 1859, above the Fraser River from New Westminster, the Engineers laid out the townsites of Hope and Yale (previously minor fur-brigade outposts known as Fort Hope and Fort Yale), the latter being as far as a traveller could penetrate before reaching the nearly impassable walls of the Fraser Canyon. The sternwheelers that used to turn round at Fort Langley were now able to ascend a further 80 miles (125 km) upriver to Hope, a situation that contributed to the decline of Fort Langley. Although most of the early buildings at Hope and Yale have gone, the gridiron arrangement of streets remains. A year later the Engineers surveyed a townsite at Douglas (better known as Port Douglas) at the head of Harrison Lake.[85]

The Royal Engineers built churches in all three towns: Christ Church at Hope, St John the Divine at Yale, and St Mark's at Port Douglas. The designs of all three have been attributed to Captain Grant, although Colonel Moody was known on occasion to have asked for architectural assistance from John Wright in Victoria, and Wright and Sanders almost certainly participated in the designs. The first of the three to be built, and the best preserved today, was **Christ Church [8.40]** in Hope. Bishop Hills and Colonel Moody collaborated on the selection of the site in the summer of 1860. The church was built by contractors White and Manson of New

8.40 Christ Church, Hope, British Columbia, 1860-1. BCARS/9605.

8.41 Interior of Christ Church, Hope, British Columbia, 1860-1. Photograph by Barry Downs.

Westminster; their bill was paid in part by subscriptions from Governor Douglas, Judge Matthew Baillie Begbie, Dr Helmcken, Colonel Moody, and merchant David Oppenheimer—'together with many little-known citizens, Friends from England; and, two Chinamen'. It was consecrated in November 1861 to a full congregation, consisting of residents of Hope, native converts, and a company of Royal Engineers—as the Reverend William Burton Crickmer, the first Anglican missionary in Hope, played the harmonium.[86]

Archdeacon Wright called Christ Church 'a neat wooden structure, ecclesiastical in character, externally and internally.'[87] It is simple and stunning. What is particularly memorable is the directness of its design—a happy instance of the convergence of engineering and architecture—seen in the lack of historical references and the practical yet beautiful use of materials. Although the plan and profile clearly refer to Gothic Revival precedents, there are no overt stylistic allusions other than the abstracted pointed arches and quatrefoils of the hand-cut communion rail, which the *British Columbian* of New Westminster referred to as 'open gothic work'.[88] The implicit revivalism must have been what the newspaper report called 'Elizabethan' (it will be recalled that the same term was used to describe The Birdcages in Victoria, built at the same time). The direct use of wood is particularly memorable: in the horizontal siding on the outside, the vertical board-and-batten treatment inside [8.41], the chamfered members of the roof truss (painted white, in contrast to the stain used elsewhere), and the panelled pews. Other materials include handmade glass panes, in which air bubbles are apparent; the flags of the Royal Engineers that hang at the end of the nave; and the needlework carpet in the chancel, a gift of the Baroness Burdett-Coutts. The loving use of wood in a simply composed village church recalls the contemporaneous St Mary the Virgin in New Maryland, NB (1863-4; 6.40), although the eastern church offered a more committed rendition of the Gothic Revival.

The most extraordinary achievement of the Royal Engineers was the construction of the first portion of the Cariboo Wagon Road, a route that eventually led 400 miles (640 km) northwards from Yale to Quesnel. The idea of allowing wagons and coaches to drive through an impenetrable canyon, where trekkers dared not pass, must have seemed inconceivable; yet the Engineers turned their talents to doing just that. In 1862 a force of 53 sappers, under the direction of Captain Grant, built

the first, and most difficult, six miles (10 km) of roadway north of Yale to Chapman's Bar. Much of the road was blasted through solid rock, or built out over the canyon on wooden 'cribs'—log structures that were fitted together by partially notching their ends.[89]

The partially constructed road was extremely dangerous. Bishop Hills made the mistake of trying to use it in June 1862; upon missing a turn, he found that

> . . .we were in most imminent danger. The narrow pathway, on which ten horses (seven of them bearing packs) and six men were now standing, had not in some portions of it ten inches of footing. Above was the perpendicular mountain and below was a chasm down to the torrent, some 800 feet. What was to be done?. . .By God's great mercy, we succeeded in turning each horse, and after considerable anxiety and exertion regained the right path and continued our journey till dark, when we camped at a sweet spot.[90]

Only months later long wagon trains were passing through the canyon with little difficulty; and less than two dozen years later the trains of the Canadian Pacific Railway would steam through tunnels, and on trestles and bridges, that dwarfed the Royal Engineers' achievement.

Except for a 9-mile (15-km) section further north that was built by the sappers, the rest of the Cariboo Wagon Road, and most of the other new roads, were surveyed by the Royal Engineers and then let out to private contractors for construction. One such contractor was Joseph William Trutch (1826-1904), who also built the spectacular Alexandra Suspension Bridge [5.20] as part of the Cariboo Road; another was Edgar Dewdney (1835-1916), who created the Dewdney Trail that stretched some 250 miles (400 km) eastward from Hope to Galbraith's Ferry (later Fort Steele) on the Kootenay River, a route whose political purpose was to maintain British control over the increasing gold-mining activity in the southeastern part of the province. Trutch and Dewdney had subsequent political careers that both culminated in appointments as Lieutenant-Governor of British Columbia—indicating the high esteem that was placed on the people who opened the province to development.

The completion in 1863 of the Cariboo Wagon Road from Yale to Soda Creek, where travellers could board a steamship to Quesnel, provided relatively easy travel from Victoria to the heart of the

Cariboo gold fields, which had replaced the lower Fraser River as the focus of mining activity in the province.

The spectacular achievement of the Royal Engineers was recognized in a surprisingly unappreciative manner when the Colonial Office decided that the cost of maintaining the Engineers was too high and consequently disbanded the Columbia detachment in July 1863. Most of the sappers and non-commissioned officers chose to take their discharge in British Columbia, and accept a land grant of 150 acres (60 hectares). Some homesteaded, some succumbed to gold fever, and a number—including John C. White—went on to develop successful private careers as architects and engineers in the colony.[91]

The Cariboo Gold Rush

Once the Royal Engineers had provided the infrastructure for interior development, hordes of miners, followed closely by entrepreneurs in secondary industries, rushed to the gold fields of the Cariboo—the region of the Fraser Plateau north of Lytton and extending nearly to Prince George. John Rose and three partners made the first strike in the fall of 1860, and the word quickly spread. By the following spring miners were coming into the area by the hundreds, and with the completion of the Cariboo Wagon Road they flocked in by the

tens of thousands. The miners staked their claims, giving them a host of quaint names. Mucho Oro, Forest Rose, Prairie Flower, Ne'er Do Well, and Neversweat were but a few; others were named after the persons who discovered them.[92]

Most of the metal was found as 'placer' gold, occurring in a free state in the gravel beds of streams and recovered by panning, or by elaborate hydraulic works involving waterwheels, sluices, and flumes. When the shallow creek beds were exhausted, it became necessary to dig into the ground and use dredges, pumps, and other expensive machinery. This capital-intensive phase saw control shift from small groups of miners to large companies—and marked the end of the 'rush'.

A building was usually erected to support the hydraulic works and shelter the shafts and the workers. Three claims on or near Williams Creek reveal the variety: the structure might be as simple as a small dam, as at the Sheepshead Claim; a shed consisting of a roof supported by poles, as at the Cameron and Waittie Claim; or it might be an enclosed building, as at the **Mucho Oro Claim** [8.42] on Stout's Gulch, a gable-roofed frame structure with a lean-to shed covered by rough-sawn boards laid horizontally on the gable end and vertically beside the entrance. A large overshot waterwheel stood at the side. It would have powered a winch to raise the ore buckets, and a pump to keep the underground workings from flooding. This

8.42 Mucho Oro Claim, Stout's Gulch, British Columbia, 1860s. Vancouver Public Library/photograph no. 8640.

was a straightforward industrial structure, built to do a job—the industrial vernacular of the western frontier.[93]

The miners often camped in tents. Those who stayed longer than a single season required a more permanent residence for comfort, and as a place to leave their supplies between seasons, since most spent the winter in Victoria or San Francisco. Log cabins prevailed [8.43]. Most were built with round logs with saddle notches at the corners [2.24], the simplest and quickest of cabin forms, and one requiring relatively little carpentry skill. The spaces between the logs were chinked with moss or clay. The fireplace and chimney were built with clay and boulders. Roofs might be covered with boards, or with split poles similar to, but smaller than, the scoops of the eastern Ontario shanty. The cost and time required for a more elaborate dwelling could seldom be justified for so insecure an existence in a gold rush.[94]

James Anderson, who came to the Cariboo from Scotland in 1863, described a characteristic miner's cabin in verse, in his Scottish dialect:

> See yonder shanty on the hill,
> 'Tis but an humble biggin',
> Some ten by six within the wa's—
> Your head may touch the riggin'—
>
> The door stands open to the south,
> The fire, outside the door;
> The logs are chinket close wi' fog—
> And nocht but mud the floor—[95]

Few materials were used other than wood and stone found on the site. Bricks were used primarily for boilers for deep-lead mines and not for buildings. They were made at Beaver Pass, east of Quesnel, where clay was found.[96]

Barkerville The largest and most important of the gold towns—and the end of the gold trail (and the Cariboo Wagon Road)—was Barkerville, about 56 miles (90 km) east of Quesnel. Cornish sailor Billy Barker heard about the gold rush, jumped ship in Victoria, and headed for Richfield, a town on Williams Creek. He dug down into the ground nearby while others worked the surface gravel bars, and in August 1862, at a considerable depth—most say 52 feet (16 m)—he made the richest strike in British Columbia. Bishop Hills reported that 'all went on a spree for several days, except one Englishman, well brought up.' Barker was not that Englishman! When the party was over, he worked

8.43 Miner's cabin, Williams Creek, British Columbia. Photograph 1868. BCARS/766.

his mine; and the town that sprang up around his claim was called Barkerville, after him. He extracted a great deal of gold and spent a great deal of money, though he died penniless in 1894 in the Victoria Old Men's Home.[97]

The summer after Barker found gold, an estimated 10,000 people were living in **Barkerville**. Before long residents bragged that it was the largest city west of Chicago and north of San Francisco. A main street [8.44] quickly developed, lined with small, cheaply built wood-frame commercial buildings covered with steep gabled roofs and sporting large signboards. Some buildings had log sides and more elegant clapboard façades. A boardwalk was built high above the roadway that was barely wide enough for two carts to pass. Because the town was located in a narrow, steep valley—with water seeping from the hillsides and a creek and mine-waste running through its centre—the buildings and sidewalks were built on stilt-like pilings that could be jacked up every few months to stay above the gravel refuse. Here was classic gold-rush architecture: an instant town, built with high energy but little capital. The Royal Engineers arrived in the summer of 1863 to survey the townsite, but so

8.44 (*top*) Main Street (before the fire), Barkerville, British Columbia. Photograph by Frederick Dally, 1867. Vancouver Public Library/photograph no. 8637.

8.45 Main Street (after the fire), with St Saviour's Anglican Church (1869-70) in the distance, Barkerville, British Columbia. Photograph *c*. 1870s. BCARS/10110.

much had already been built that the best they could do was try to fit the random sites of existing buildings into some semblance of regular lots. 'Downtown' Barkerville already had 40 buildings, and nearby Richfield and Camerontown—a short distance up and down Williams Creek—were about the same size.[98]

Conditions became increasingly crowded each year, until the inevitable finally happened on 16 September 1868. A miner, it was said, leaned over to kiss a 'hurdy-gurdy' girl who was ironing her dress at the back of Barry and Adler's Saloon, knocked over a stovepipe, setting fire to the canvas ceiling. Within eighty minutes Barkerville had burned to the ground. Photographer Frederick Dally, who documented the fire, reported that 116 houses were destroyed.

Barkerville was immediately rebuilt with building more substantial than their predecessors—but things had changed. Merchants and miners, who had been there only for a quick profit, lost their money and could not afford to re-establish themselves. On the other hand, banks, churches, the library, and all the institutions and serious investors with a commitment to their community, stayed. They rebuilt in a more substantial and orderly manner. (The Royal Engineers' survey had an effect—though not until five years later.) Only six days after the fire, the *Sentinel* described the situation:

> Already are there over thirty houses standing in symmetrical order on the old site, and the foundation of several others laid; and many more would yet have been in the course of erection were it possible to obtain carpenters and tools.... The town when rebuilt will present a much more uniform and pleasant appearance. By the regulations of the local authorities, in concurrence with the people, the main street has been increased in width fifteen feet and the sidewalks fixed at a regular and uniform grade. Vacancies which were originally intended for cross streets but occupied by sufferance, are now to be left open, and altogether the new town will be much more convenient for business, and will be a decided improvement on the old.[99]

Wood frame was again the prevalent building technique, but many structures were larger and higher, the lumber was better, and the roofs were properly shingled [8.45]. Although professional architects were not involved, many buildings were designed with models in mind. The east end of Main Street was again Chinatown; and even though the Cariboo Gold Rush had ended, gold remained for any mining companies prepared to invest capital in recovering it. This time the town lasted.

St Saviour's Anglican Church, built in 1869-70, can be seen in the centre distance of the photograph [8.45], at the far west end of Main Street, as a herd of cattle is driven to slaughter. The Reverend James Reynard contributed his money and time to its construction and is credited with much of the finished carpentry; one chair, beautifully constructed with dowels and no nails, is attributed entirely to him. The *Sentinel* reported the construction of the church, revealing a fair understanding of the Gothic Revival and ecclesiological principles:

> The new church now building promises to be an elegant structure.... The style is 'Early English' in which architectural effect is attained by due proportion of parts, bold and simple forms, rather than by elaborate ornament. The church will consist of—nave, 30 ft. x 20 ft., and apsidal chancel, 16 ft. x 12 ft. Height of walls, 18 feet; of ceiling, from floor, 23 feet. A schoolroom and vestry complete the building. We congratulate the friends of the Anglican Church on possessing a church so appropriate to their worship. Certainly those who wish to pray, as their fathers prayed, may do so here, in a church which in form, if not in material, will remind them of the village churches of the 'fatherland.'[100]

The pointed arches of the windows, door, and belfry are explicit Gothic features; other connections with the historic style—such as the uplifting vertical proportions of the nave, the elegant chancel, and the board-and-batten siding—are Gothic by association only (as they were at Christ Church in Hope).

The rebuilt Barkerville had, perhaps belatedly, a **Firehall** (1868-9) on Main Street, for the Williams Creek Fire Brigade ('WCFB' is inscribed in the gable); the upper floor was an auditorium used as the **Theatre Royal** [8.46]. The tall frame building, with a gable facing the street and two large windows illuminating the auditorium, was described by the *Sentinel* as 'a very handsome and imposing structure—quite an ornament to the town.' It is seen in the photograph decorated with wreaths and garlands for the visit of Lieutenant Governor Anthony Musgrave in 1869. The last professional company to perform in the Theatre Royal at Barkerville came

8.46 Firehall (and Theatre Royal), Barkerville, British Columbia, 1868-9. Vancouver Public Library/photograph no. 8640.

in the summer of 1871. The lower storey become silted up, and so in 1872 the entire floor was removed and the structure lowered—eliminating the firehall—and seven years later it was raised on posts to protect it against further silting.[101]

Whereas other Cariboo towns disappeared overnight, Barkerville was sustained by the high level of capital investment in its mining and service facilities. But it faded slowly, and by the end of the nineteenth century it had lost its vigour. In the 1930s the town had about 500 people and saw some renewed mining activity—a result of President Roosevelt's raising the price of gold. Barkerville had become a satellite of nearby Wells, a town that was sustained by the Cariboo Gold Quartz Mining Company, which mined ore in 1926-7.

In the 1950s a group of local residents determined that what was left of Barkerville should be preserved. Their petitions to the provincial government succeeded, and in 1959 the town was declared a provincial park. Only 15 of the former 120-odd post-fire buildings still stood, most of them in poor condition. But some have been restored, and many others reconstructed. Barkerville has become

a popular historic townsite that allows visitors to re-live the days of the gold rush. Tourists can eat at Wake-Up-Jake Coffee Saloon and Lung Duck Tong Chinese Restaurant, buy sourdough bread at the Bakery, watch productions at the Theatre Royal, and pan for gold in the creek.[102]

Roadhouses and ranches Mining fostered the development of spin-off industries, including the hospitality business and ranching. Barkerville and the other Cariboo gold towns were a good distance from Victoria and New Westminster, and travel to them required considerable time and effort, so along the Cariboo Wagon Road a number of roadhouses—often at 10- to 15-mile intervals (16 to 24 km)—functioned as hotels, restaurants, and liveries. Some of these 'stopping-places' were also working farms or ranches that supplied provisions to their patrons and to the region. Roadhouses also provided depots for the express companies that hauled freight along the road. The leading express firm was the F.J. Barnard Company, better known as the 'BX', founded in 1862 as the British Columbia and Victoria Express Company. It inaugurated service along the Cariboo Wagon Road in 1864, was renamed the British Columbia Express Company in 1872, and survived well into the gasoline age.[103] Many roadhouses were simply identified by their mileage along the road: thus there were 47-Mile House (subsequently Clinton), 70-Mile House, 150-Mile House (like a number of others, it was also an active ranch)—and others similarly named.[104]

One of the quality stopping-places was **Cottonwood House [8.47]**, a day's travel east of Quesnel on the road to Barkerville. It served variously as a roadhouse, ranch, trading post, liquor outlet, telegraph station, post office, and, after the coming of the automobile, gasoline station. Built in 1864 by Allen Smith, the roadhouse was operated for nearly three-quarters of a century by Irish trader John Boyd and his descendants. Cottonwood is a two-storey log building that was built much more permanently than the cabins of the miners. The logs are squared and dovetailed, and the windows are well-fabricated double-hung sashes with broad sawn casings. The door leads into a large lounge, two-thirds the width of the building; the dining-room and the Boyds' suite are on the left, and a room containing six beds and the kitchen are at the rear. Four large sleeping-rooms, and some smaller rooms, occupy the upper floor. Cottonwood House has been restored by the provincial government and is open as an interpreted historic site.[105]

8.47 Cottonwood House, near Quesnel, British Columbia, 1864. BCARS/57396.

8.48 Hat Creek House, near Cache Creek, British Columbia, begun 1860. Photograph by Jim Weston. Courtesy British Columbia Heritage Trust.

Another important surviving roadhouse is **Hat Creek House** [8.48], much further south on the Cariboo Wagon Road, between Cache Creek and Clinton. Donald McLean, a retired trader with the Hudson's Bay Company, settled at Hat Creek in 1860 and began to operate a ranch and roadhouse in a group of log buildings. McLean's 'restaurant', as it was sometimes called, provided only the most basic kind of accommodation, as we learn from the Reverend Ebenezer Robson, a Methodist preacher who did not enjoy his stay in 1862:

> I was interested in Mr. McLean and so decided to put up at his wayside house, in the Bonaparte Valley, that night. But when I arrived at the sprawling groups of cabins, I felt disappointed. Such a bunch of men, women, children, cattle, horses, doop, and insects I had not often come in contact with....I waited long for my supper, which was being prepared by a chinaman....I did not take a bed, for the bunks were hard as a board the pillows seemed to be flour sacks filled with grass, and the dark looking blankets had unwrapped too many sweaty, dusty travellers since last washed, if indeed, they had ever been washed, so placing my Mexican saddle against the wall and spreading the saddle cloth in front of it, I pulled off my shoes, said my prayers, and using my coat for a covering slept the sleep of the weary.[106]

Hat Creek House gained in importance, and comforts, with the completion of the Cariboo Wagon Road and the initiation of service by the BX. After McLean died in 1864 (the victim of a shot in the back) a number of subsequent proprietors enlarged and improved the buildings. As it stands today, restored by the British Columbia government, the main house is a two-storey structure distinguished by its double veranda, which is protected by the broad flaring eave of the gabled roof. It achieved its present appearance in 1901, when the *Ashcroft Journal* noted:

> Hat Creek House...has been thoroughly fitted up within the past 2 months by R. Stoddard and assistants, and it is safe to say no better or more convenient house can now be found north of Ashcroft. A large addition has been built on, the sitting room changed to the south end of the house, and numerous new sleeping rooms added.[107]

The core of the building is a one-storey log structure that is likely the 1860s roadhouse of Donald McLean, or his successor George Dunne (this has been concealed by later additions and veneers). A cabin of squared logs with dovetail joints that stands behind the roadhouse, known as the McLean Cabin, certainly dates from McLean's days, as may some of the twenty other outbuildings, barns, and sheds that occupy the property.

While making their way to the Cariboo goldfields the miners not only required food and accommodation, they also needed an ongoing supply of meat. Cattle-ranching therefore became an important economic activity in the southern and central interior of British Columbia. Hat Creek House, for example, closed its doors to travellers about 1910 and became dedicated to ranching, when it was known as Hat Creek Ranch (the names 'Ranch' and 'House' were usually interchangeable).

When gold was discovered in British Columbia, the ranching frontier extended northward from the Oregon Territory to serve the new mining communities, encouraged by government policy with respect to pre-emption of land and the granting of pasturing leases. Brothers Jerome and Thaddeus Harper were among the earliest entrepreneurs to see profit in the business. Owners of gold claims and a large sawmill at Quesnel, they began in 1863 to spend the winters in Washington and Oregon buying cattle; then in May they would drive the cattle north to Barkerville. The herd would spend the summer on Bald Mountain, two miles from town, and be led to the slaughterhouse as needed. In a typical season some 1,400 head would be slaughtered in the town. (See the procession of cattle in **8.45**.)[108]

Another important cattle-drover, and one who left a significant architectural legacy, was the Ottawa-born Cornelius O'Keefe. In 1862 he built the original 104 Mile House on the Cariboo Road, then turned his interest to livestock. In 1867 he and two partners drove a herd of Oregon cattle to the west side of Okanagan Lake, along an old fur-trade route, stopping at the head of the lake to fatten the cattle on bunchgrass. They liked what they saw and never left. Each of the three men pre-empted land—O'Keefe's 162-acre (65-hectare) tract was the first to be granted in the region—and settled down fo raise cattle. O'Keefe continued to acquire land, and what began as a modest homestead grew by the 1890s to become the prosperous 15,000-acre (6,000-hectare) O'Keefe Ranch, with more than 1,000 head of cattle. Located near today's city of Vernon, it is the only early British Columbia ranch to retain a group of original buildings and preserve its general nineteenth-century appearance. The

8.49 Aerial view, O'Keefe Ranch, including the original O'Keefe log house (1868) and the O'Keefe frame house (1880), near Vernon, British Columbia. O'Keefe Ranch and Interior Heritage Society.

photograph [**8.49**], taken around 1952, shows the disorganization that is characteristic of a working ranch. In the 1960s the O'Keefe family rehabilitated the surviving buildings, reconstructed some demolished ones, tidied things up, and opened the ranch as a tourist attraction.[109]

One survivor is the original **O'Keefe log house**, built in 1868 (and seen, in the photograph in the middle right). Its timbers, according to local tradition, were 'hand hewn and whip sawn and all corners dovetailed.' The $1\frac{1}{2}$-storey structure has a lean-to wing along one side and a doorway in the gable end, like St Saviour's Church at Barkerville. If this is the original location of the door, rather than on the long side of the house, it would mark a transition to the gable-front house that would soon dominate domestic architecture (see **11.32**). The exterior was sheathed with sawn clapboard siding

(probably in the 1870s), as were Hat Creek House and many other log buildings of the day.

Comfortable though the house may have been, it was inadequate for the socially mobile O'Keefe and his wife Mary Ann, whom he married in Ottawa in 1877. In 1880 the O'Keefes built a large new **frame house**, seen at the left in the photograph. It was probably designed by architect Robert Brown Bell (1850-1940), who had recently come to Vernon from New Westminster. The house has since been enlarged and covered with stucco. The asymmetrical cross-gabled building would not have been out of place in Ontario (had it been built of brick). Although unremarkable now, it must have made eyes turn a century ago. The Okanagan correspondent to the *Colonist* reported that 'the residence of Mr O'Keefe is one of the finest in the country, and is furnished regardless of expense.'[110] It was evidently considered elegant enough to accommodate the Governor General, the Marquess of Lorne, who stayed there for two nights when he visited the Okanagan in October 1882.[111]

The O'Keefe Ranch became the service centre for the area. It was designated as the Okanagan post office in 1872, one of the first four post offices in the interior, and O'Keefe opened a small general store (which accommodated the post office) and blacksmith shop. Both have been reconstructed.

In 1886 the Roman Catholic **Church of St Ann's** [8.50] was built on the ranch, under O'Keefe's initiative, by local subscription. The proportions of the attractive little church—as well as its steep gabled roof, belltower, and small circular window over the door—recall the early parish churches and chapels of Quebec. The Gothic Revival windows and door and the clapboard siding (cut at the ranch's sawmill) make St Ann's very much a product of its own time and place, but O'Keefe succeeded in recreating the spirit of the kind of Catholic church that he would have grown up with back east. The church never had a resident priest, but it was frequented by travelling clergymen, particularly the Oblate missionaries of the Okanagan.[112]

The British Columbia ranching industry peaked in the 1890s, when the newly built railway provided easy access to Chicago and other distant cattle markets and more than compensated for the decline of the Cariboo trade. The largest land holdings were assembled by the Douglas Lake Cattle

Company in the Nicola Valley, midway between the Okanagan and Fraser valleys, a concern to which Cornelius O'Keefe regularly sold stock. Preempted as a homestead by John Douglas in 1872, the operation grew steadily. After 1959, under the ownership of department store magnate C.N.W. (Chunky) Woodward, it became Canada's largest cattle ranch, carrying a wintering herd of 11,000 head of Herefords. Douglas's original log cabin and most of the other original buildings have gone, but a number of early-twentieth-century structures spread over a large area tell the ranch's earlier history.[113]

The first ranch in the Okanagan had been started by Oblate missionaries in 1859 at L'Anse au Sable (today's Kelowna).[114] By then missionaries had been active in British Columbia for two decades. This chapter concludes with a consideration of some of the missions and mission churches they built. Many of the missions formed the basis for subsequent settlement by both natives and whites.

Missions

The first Canadian missionaries on the west coast were Fathers Modeste Demers and François Blanchet, French-Canadian Roman Catholic priests who were sent west because their archbishop considered all the territory as far west as the Pacific Ocean to be a part of the Diocese of Quebec. In 1838 they travelled with the fur brigade from the Red River to Fort Vancouver, intending to convert the natives to Christianity as well as to serve the needs of the white Catholic settlers in the Oregon territory. They, and most other missionaries, hoped to convince the aboriginal peoples to give up their traditional nomadic way of life and take up agriculture, while also helping them to lead Christian lives.[115]

Father Demers (who in 1846 would be named Bishop of Vancouver Island and New Caledonia) travelled north in 1842 through the Okanagan to Fort St James. He was the first Christian missionary to contact the natives of the northern interior, and along the way he baptized more than 400 white and native children. In that year he directed the construction (by Indians) of small chapels in the Cariboo at Fort Alexandria—the first church in mainland British Columbia—and Williams Lake, where the first mass was celebrated on Epiphany, 4 December 1842. The little building at Williams Lake (presumably built of logs) was warmed by a fireplace at one end and had skins stretched over

8.50 Church of St Ann's, O'Keefe Ranch, near Vernon, British Columbia, 1886. Photograph by Barry Downs.

the window sashes to keep out the cold, until they began to be eaten by starving dogs. It no longer survives, nor does the church (or any of the buildings) at Fort Alexandria. The present church of St Paul at Alexandria, built in 1906, stands near the site of Father Demers's first chapel.[116]

The French-Canadian priests were soon succeeded by the Oblates, whose accomplishments on the Prairies, beginning in the 1840s, were introduced in Chapter 7. The dedicated and hard-working Oblate missionaries, most of them from France, first went to the Oregon territory in 1847, and eleven years later they established themselves at Esquimalt. In October 1859 Father Charles-Marie Pandosy arrived in the Okanagan to found the first Oblate mission in the British Columbia interior. He and his colleagues established the **Mission of the Immaculate Conception** [8.51]—known today as the Father Pandosy Mission—just south of today's city of Kelowna. They built their residence, a small

8.51 Mission of the Immaculate Conception (Father Pandosy Mission), Kelowna, British Columbia, begun 1859. Photograph by Barry Downs.

church, a school (the latter two a modest 12 by 14 feet—3.7 by 4.3 m—in size, smaller than the average Ontario log cabin), and several utility buildings. The work was undertaken by Brother Philippe Surel—a lay brother who was a skilled carpenter—and his helpers, including Louis Falardeaux, a seventeen-year-old employee of the Hudson's Bay Company. The buildings were constructed of logs that were squared and dovetailed, and chinked with moss and clay. The roofs were covered with wood shakes fastened by wooden pegs. Three structures were restored in 1958, a year before their centenary, although a stable was demolished at that time. The mission is now run as a historic site.[117]

The missionaries had to set up an entirely self-sufficient community in virtually unsettled land. They developed a farm, including an orchard and a vineyard—following their lead, the Okanagan valley is now a major fruit- and wine-producing area—and, as mentioned above, they established a herd of cattle (their brand was OM, a shortened version of OMI—Oblates of Mary Immaculate). A report written in 1863 by Provincial Constable William C. Young noted their early progress:

The Catholic Mission buildings are new and very neat. All crops have been very good this past season and that without any aid from irrigation. I saw some very good tobacco of their own growing and was told by Fr. Richard that the total produce this year is not less than—wheat 1,000 bushels; barley 200 bushels; and potatoes 2,900 bushels.[118]

The most celebrated Oblate mission in its time was the **St Joseph's Mission** (called the Cariboo Mission) in the San José Valley near Williams Lake. It was founded by Father James Maria McGuckin in 1866-7 to serve nearby Carrier, Chilcotin, and Shuswap villages, as well as white people from the mining camps. The first mission building was a dilapidated house that came with the property and served for a while as residence, chapel, school-room, kitchen, refectory, and dormitory; but many more buildings followed. A log chapel, residence, and school were quickly built with the help of Brother Surel. A school for white boys was opened in 1871, a convent school for girls in 1876, and a federally assisted Indian Industrial School in 1891. The Cariboo chiefs balked at handing children over entirely to the care of the Church to be taught 'the new mysteries', and the anticipated enrolment did not materialize.[119]

A photograph [8.52] taken around 1910 indicates the extent of St Joseph's Mission. At the right

8.52 St Joseph's Mission (Cariboo Mission), near Williams Lake, British Columbia, begun 1866. Photograph *c.* 1910. Vancouver Public Library/photograph no. 3578.

is one side of the convent, a large three-storey frame building (110 by 30 feet—33.6 by 9.2 m) whose façade is nine bays wide and is accented by three gables and a cupola; it was augmented by an addition at the far end. To the immediate left is the log chapel, built in 1867; further left still are the three-gabled priests' and boys' residence (1885) and the industrial school. The other structures are mostly farm buildings that supported the mission's large cattle ranch. The cemetery is in the foreground. The buildings were poorly maintained and most of the farm structures were destroyed by fire or demolished in 1954 and replaced by fewer and smaller buildings. The Oblates operated the school until 1964, when the federal government took control of it.

Many other Oblate missions were built on Vancouver Island, in the Lower Mainland, the British Columbia interior, and the North. The two best known today are St Paul's, North Vancouver (formerly Ustlawn), and St Eugene's, on the present St Mary's Reserve near Cranbrook and Fort Steele. The former, a mission church to the Squamish Indians, began as a small chapel built in 1866 or 1868; a

8.53 View of Metlakatla, British Columbia. Photograph 1870s. BCARS/20388.

frame church constructed in 1884 was enlarged in 1909 to become the present St Paul's, whose twin towers used to serve as the official landmark for ships entering Vancouver harbour.[120] St Eugene's (1897) was built by the energetic and talented church-builder Father Nicholas Coccola, mainly from funds earned when the natives sold a silver, lead, and zinc mine they had discovered to the company that later became Cominco.[121] Both are superb Gothic Revival churches with fine wood detail and decorated interiors, and both have recently been restored.

The Roman Catholic Church was not alone in working with the Indians of British Columbia. All the principal Christian denominations sent missionaries west. The Anglican Church, for one, undertook an ambitious mission to the natives. Although most of Bishop Hills' churches primarily served whites, other Anglican missionaries focused their attention on natives. The most zealous was

William Duncan (1832-1918), a teacher, lay minister, and evangelical Protestant who was sent from England in 1856 by the Church Missionary Society. Expecting to be posted to Africa, Duncan found himself instead in Fort Simpson (now Port Simpson), a coastal community close to today's border with Alaska and the centre of the Pacific fur trade. Duncan quickly became upset watching native life being destroyed by contact with white traders. In 1862, in the midst of a devastating smallpox epidemic, he led a group of fifty Tsimshian followers 15 miles (24 km) south to the historic village site of Metlakatla, just north of today's city of Prince Rupert. There Duncan directed the natives in building a utopian community that was based on the enlightened industrial new towns of Victorian Britain—ironically using European models and customs in an effort to steer the natives away from negative European influences. Law and order were maintained by uniformed Indian police and a brass band welcomed visitors by playing 'God Save the Queen'. In order to help the town achieve industrial self-sufficiency, Duncan established a sawmill, a blacksmith's shop, a soap factory, and a furniture factory.[122]

Duncan assumed the role of planner and architect as he laid out a radial town plan for **Metlakatla** [8.53] whose focus, sited on a slight rise of land, was the church and community building. The streets were planted with rows of poplars and lined with neat rows of frame houses. The $1\frac{1}{2}$-storey dwellings, 18 by 34 feet (5.5 by 10.4 m), were based on workers' housing in England, but were modified for native use by placing apartments for multiple families at each end of a central common room.

The magnificent **Church of St Paul's [8.54]**, dedicated in 1874, seated 1,200 people and was claimed to be the largest church north of San Francisco and west of Chicago. Its heavy timber frame (sawn at the local mill) was sheathed in horizontal shiplap siding, and it had a steep roof, corner tower, and triple-gabled entrance. Buttresses along the sides (required to stabilize the structure), battlements on the tower, and iron cresting along the ridge of the roof recalled Gothic precedents. Duncan paid no attention to attempting to reproduce Gothic details, as the windows were headed by round arches and the nave was separated from the side aisles by massive square posts between which triangular spandrels formed high arches. The interior had no ornament, since Duncan believed that the Indians' emotions should not be aroused by objects or rituals. He even refused to offer Holy Communion, and the pulpit overshadowed the altar—an indication of his belief in teaching's being more important than ritual.

Metlakatla attracted a large influx of Tsimshian people. Bishop Hills visited the community in the late 1870s and marvelled at Duncan's remarkable progress:

> The new settlement has now grown to one thousand people, forming the healthiest and strongest settlement on the coast. Rules have been laid down for the regulation of the community, to which all residents are obliged to conform, and the use of spirituous liquors strictly prohibited. All are required to keep the Sabbath, attend church, and send their children to school. Industrious habits are diligently encouraged, and the people educated as farmers, blacksmiths, carpenters, merchants, etc. They live in well-built cottages, and have a beautiful Gothic church capable of seating one thousand persons. It is modelled after the old English cathedral, and was built by the Indian mechanics of that village.... They have also a school building that will accommodate seven hundred pupils. Besides these they have carpenter and blacksmith shops, store-

8.54 Church of St Paul's, Metlakatla, British Columbia, 1874. BCARS/33589.

house, saw-mill, etc., all owned and managed by the Indians; while all around the bay are well cultivated gardens and potato patches. The main street of the village along the beach is lighted with street lamps. . . . The village has a brass band of twenty-four instruments, a public reading-room and public guest-house for the lodging of strange Indians. Fifty two-storey dwelling houses were in process of erection at the time of my visit.[123]

Bishop Hills may have been impressed, but the authorities were not amused by Duncan's departures from Anglican practice, and he was dismissed from the Church Missionary Society. In 1887 Duncan and 600 natives moved 70 miles (110 km) north to Annette Island, Alaska, where they built a second utopian community called New Metlakatla. Bishop William Ridley was posted to Metlakatla in Duncan's stead. In July 1901, when the men were away fishing for salmon, a fire destroyed St Paul's and most of the other buildings in the village. A new, smaller church was built two years later, but it too burned down. Only a few vestiges of William Duncan's Metlakatla remain, and it is now a quiet community whose religious services are held in the Church Army Hall.

Methodists were also active among the Indians of British Columbia. The Reverend Thomas Crosby came to Victoria from Ontario in 1862 and was responsible for a number of missions on the North Coast. He created a Methodist village at Fort Simpson in the 1870s, shortly after Duncan's departure for Metlakatla. Crosby's achievement mirrored Duncan's in many respects, including the building of 60 houses and an impressive church 50 by 80 feet (15.3 by 24.4 m) in plan, with a tower 140 feet

(42.7 m) high that was designed by Thomas Trounce (1813-1900) of Victoria.[124]

When the Governor General, Lord Dufferin, visited British Columbia in 1876, his itinerary took him to both Metlakatla and Fort Simpson. He seems to have been less interested in the missionaries' construction programs than in the indigenous buildings and totem poles, remarking on the 'curious poles with strange, goggle-eyed crests in them' that he saw in front of the houses of chiefs at Fort Simpson.[125] Even now, more than a century after Lord Dufferin's visit—and two centuries after Captain Cook's—the remarkable wood architecture of the coastal Indians continues to impress observers with its design, scale, and fine construction.

The forms of aboriginal architecture remained distinct, just as the buildings of the various European-Canadian communities retained their individual characteristics. In the years leading up to Confederation, Canada was a series of regions, each with its own government, economy, culture—and, to a large extent, architecture. As we have seen, the Maritimes looked largely to New England for inspiration, Newfoundland to England and Ireland, Quebec to France, Ontario to the northeastern US and Britain, the Prairies to Ontario, and British Columbia to California (as well as Britain and the East). The fur trade was one of the few forces that worked towards standardizing building across the land, since the Hudson's Bay Company built in a consistent manner from Manitoba to Vancouver Island.

It would be left to the next generation to try to unify the country's architectural mannerisms, along with its political structure.

NOTES

CHAPTER 1 The First Buildings

1 Three accessible summaries of current knowledge are R. Cole Harris and Geoffrey J. Matthews, *Historical Atlas of Canada*, I, Toronto: University of Toronto Press, [1987,] pp. 1-6 and pl. 1-18; Robert McGhee, 'Prehistory', *Canadian Encyclopedia (CE)*, 2nd ed., Edmonton: Hurtig, 1988, III, pp. 1737-40; J.V. Wright, *Six Chapters of Canada's Prehistory*, Toronto: Van Nostrand Reinhold, 1976. See also George F. MacDonald, 'An Overview of Canadian Prehistory for the Last Decade', *Canadian Journal of Archaeology*, 6, 1982, pp. 47-54.

2 Jacques Cinq-Mars, 'Bluefish Cave I: A Late Pleistocene Cave Deposit', *Canadian Journal of Archaeology*, 3, 1979, pp. 2-32; Knut Fladmark, *British Columbia Prehistory*, Canadian Prehistory Series, Ottawa: Archaeological Survey of Canada, 1986, pp. 21-3. Further information was kindly provided by Professor J. Driver, Department of Archaeology, Simon Fraser University.

3 Conrad Heidenreich, *Huronia: A History and Geography of the Huron Indians, 1600-1650*, Toronto: McClelland and Stewart, 1971, pp. 115-47; Peter Nabokov and Robert Easton, *Native American Architecture*, New York: Oxford University Press, 1989. pp. 76-91; James A. Tuck, 'Northern Iroquoian Prehistory' and Conrad E. Heidenreich, 'Huron', in Bruce G. Trigger, ed., *Handbook of North American Indians*, 15: 'Northeast', Washington: Smithsonian Institution, 1978, pp. 322-33 and 368-88, respectively; Gary A. Warrick, 'Reconstructing Ontario Iroquoian Village Organization' and Christine F. Dodd, 'Ontario Iroquois Tradition Longhouses', both in Archaeological Survey of Canada, Paper No. 124, Ottawa: National Museum of Man, 1984; J.V. Wright, *Ontario Prehistory: An Eleven-Thousand-Year Archaeological Outline*, Canadian Prehistory Series, Ottawa: National Museums of Canada, 1972; Harris and Matthews, *Historical Atlas*, I, p. 5 and pl. 12, pp. 33-5; Robert McGhee, 'In the Longhouses of Ontario', *Canadian Heritage*, 10, October-November 1984, pp. 13-17. Additional publications, and references to the reports of excavations at individual sites, are found in the bibliographies of the above studies.

4 J.V. Wright, 'The Nodwell Site', Archaeological Survey of Canada, Paper No. 22, Mercury Series, Ottawa: National Museum of Man, 1974; see also the Ontario Pre-history Gallery, Royal Ontario Museum, curated by Peter Stock, 1977, 1981.

5 Harris and Matthews, *Historical Atlas*, I, pl. 12.

6 Quoted in Nabokov and Easton, *Architecture*, p. 82.

7 Kenneth E. Kidd, *The Excavation of Ste Marie I*, Toronto: University of Toronto Press, 1949; Wilfrid Jury and Elsie McLeod Jury, *Sainte-Marie Among the Hurons*, Toronto: Oxford University Press, 1954; John F. Hayes, *Wilderness Mission: The Story of Sainte-Marie-among-the-Hurons*, Toronto: Ryerson, 1969; Barbara McConnell and Michael Odesse, *Sainte-Marie Among the Hurons*, Toronto: Oxford

University Press, 1980. The reconstruction has been criticized for having failed to take Kidd's archaeological work fully into account, and for obscuring the archaeological evidence (a valid criticism of all *in situ* reconstructions); see C.E. Hedenreich, *The Huron: A Brief Ethnography*, Discussion Paper No. 6, Toronto: York University, 1972, p. 12; Martha A. Latta, 'Identification of the 17th Century French Missions in Eastern Huronia', *Canadian Journal of Archaeology*, 9:2, 1985, p. 165.

8 Rueben Gold Thwaites, ed., *The Jesuit Relations and Allied Documents*, Cleveland: Burrows Bros, 1896-1901, XVII (1639-1640), pp. 13-15.

9 Nabokov and Easton, *Architecture*, pp. 90-1.

10 Nabokov and Easton, *Architecture*, p. 63; Bock, 'Micmac', in Trigger, ed., *Handbook*, 15, pp. 109-22; Wilson D. Wallis and Ruth Sawtell Wallis, *The Micmac Indians of Eastern Canada*, Minneapolis: University of Minnesota Press, 1955. The National Anthropological Archives of the Smithsonian Institution, which holds the original photograph, notes that the location may be Tub Island, Labrador, and not Dartmouth, Nova Scotia.

11 Cited in Nabokov and Easton, *Architecture*, p. 63.

12 Bock, 'Micmac', p. 112.

13 Barrie Reynolds, 'Beothuk', in Trigger, ed., *Handbook*, 15, pp. 102-3. The sketches of *mamateeks* were published in James P. Howley, *The Beothucks, or Red Indians: The Aboriginal Inhabitants of Newfoundland*, Cambridge: Cambridge University Press, 1915 (reprinted Toronto: Coles, 1974); they are reproduced and discussed in Peter Such, *Vanished Peoples*, Toronto: NC Press, 1978; and in Reynolds, 'Beothuk', p. 102.

14 Father Chrestien Le Clercq, *New Relation of Gaspesia*, trans. and ed. by W.F. Ganong, Toronto: Champlain Society, 1910, p. 100; cited in Harold Franklin McGee, Jr, ed., *The Native Peoples of Atlantic Canada: A History of Ethnic Interaction*, Carleton Library, No. 72, Toronto: McClelland and Stewart, 1974, p. 44.

15 Nabakov and Easton, *Architecture*, pp. 52, 62; David I. Bushnell, Jr, 'Ojibway Habitations and Other Structures', Smithsonian Institution, *Annual Report of the Board of Regents*, 1917, Washington: Government Publications Office, 1919, pp. 609-17; Hugh Morrison, *Early American Architecture: From the First Colonial Settlements to the National Period*, New York: Oxford University Press, 1952, pp. 9-10.

16 Jack H. Steinbring, 'Saulteaux of Lake Winnipeg', in June Helm, ed., *Handbook of North American Indians*, 6: Subarctic, Washington: Smithsonian Institution, 1981, pp. 251-2; Ritzenthaler, 'Southwestern Chippewa', in Helm, *Handbook*, 6, pp. 748-9; Nabokov and Easton, *Architecture*, pp. 68-9. See also Werner Muller, *Die Blaue Hutte*, Wiesbaden: Franz Steiner Verlag, 1954; Basil Johnston, *Ojibway Heritage*, Toronto: McClelland and Stewart, 1976; Frances Densmore, *Chippewa Customs* (1929), reprint, n.p: Minnesota Historical Solciety Press, 1979, pp. 86-95.

17 A. Irving Hallowell, *The Role of Conjuring in Saulteaux Society*, Publications of the Philadelphia Anthropological Society, 2, 1942; cited in Nabokov and Easton, *Architecture*, p. 70; see also Steinbring, 'Saulteaux', p. 251; Sylvie Vincent, 'Structure de rituel: le tente tremblante et le concept de Mista'pe'w', *Recherches Amérindiennes au Québec*, 3:11-12, 1973.

18 Helge Ingstad, *Westward to Vinland*, London: St Martin's Press, 1969; Ingstad, *The Norse Discovery of America*, 2 vols, Oslo: Norwegian University Press, 1985; Anne Stine Ingstad et al, *The Discovery of a Norse Settlement in America: Excavations at L'Anse aux Meadows, Newfoundland 1961-1968*, Oslo: Universitetsforlaget, 1977; Joan Horwood, *Viking Discovery: L'Anse aux Meadows*, St John's: Jesperson Press and Newfoundland Historic Parks Association, 1985; Kate Gordon and Robert McGhee, *The Vikings and their Predecessors*, Ottawa: National Museums of Canada, 1981; Charles Lindsay, 'Was L'Anse aux Meadows a Norse outpost?' *Canadian Geographical Journal*, 94:1, February-March 1977, pp. 36-43; Birgitta Wallace, 'The Norse in Newfoundland,' *Conservation Canada*, Summer 1977, pp. 3-7; James Tuck, 'The Norse in Newfoundland,' *Canadian Antiques Collector*, 10:2, March-April 1975, pp. 20-1; Harry Hill, 'Where Viking Sagas are Written in the Earth', *Atlantic Advocate*, 59:7, March 1969, pp. 36-9.

19 Brigitta Linderoth Wallace, 'The L'Anse aux Meadows Site', in Gwyn Jones, *The Norse Atlantic Saga*, Oxford: Oxford University Press, 1986, pp. 288, 296; Brigitta Linderoth Wallace, 'L'Anse Aux Meadows: Gateway to Vinland', in Gerald F. Bigelow, ed., *The Norse of the North Atlantic*, Acta Archaeologica, LXI, 1990, Copenhagen: Munsgaard, 1991, pp. 166-97.

20 Wallace, 'L'Anse aux Meadows', pp. 285-304. The excavations are reported in *Research Bulletin de recherches*, National Historic Parks and Sites Branch, Parks Canada, nos. 20 (December 1974), 33 (July 1976), 67 (November 1977), and 86 (April 1978).

21 Farley Mowat, *Westviking: The Ancient Norse in Greenland and North America*, Toronto: McClelland and Stewart, 1965; Wallace, 'L'Anse aux Meadows', pp. 297-8.

22 Selma Barkham, 'The Basques: Filling a Gap in Our History Between Jacques Cartier and Champlain', *Canadian Geographic*, 96:1, February-March 1978, pp. 8-19; Barkham, 'A Note on the Strait of Belle Isle During the Period of Basque Contact with Indians and Inuit', *Études Inuit Studies*, 4:1-2, 1980, pp. 51-8; James A. Tuck, 'The World's First Oil Boom', *Archaeology*, 40, January-February 1987, pp. 50-5; Tuck, 'A Sixteenth Century Whaling Station at Red Bay, Labrador', in G.M. Story, ed., *Early European Settlement and Exploitation in Atlantic Canada: Selected Papers*, St John's: Memorial University of Newfoundland, 1982, pp. 41-52; Tuck and Robert Grenier, 'A 16th-Century Basque Whaling Station in Labrador', *Scientific American*, 245:19, November 1981, pp. 180-90; Harry Thurston, 'The Basque Connection', *Equinox*, 2:12 November-December 1983.

23 In addition to the references in the previous note, see James A. Tuck, '1984 Excavations at Red Bay, Labrador', in Jane Sproull Thomson and Callum Thomson, eds, *Archaeology in Newfoundland and Labrador 1984*, St John's: Newfoundland Museum, 1985, pp. 224-47; Tuck, 'Excavations at Red Bay, Labrador 1985', in Thomson and Thomson, eds, *Archaeology in Newfoundland and Labrador 1985*, Annual Report No. 6, St John's: Newfoundland Museum, 1986, pp. 150-8; José Antonio Hernandez Vera et al., 'Basque Expedition to Labrador, 1985', in *idem*, pp. 81-98; Willis Stevens and Peter Waddell, 'Marine Archaeological Research at Red Bay, Labrador: A Summary of the 1985 Field Season', in *idem*, pp. 99-120.

24 Translated by Selma and Michael Barkham and cited in Tuck, 'Station' (1982), p. 47.

25 Marcel Trudel, *The Beginnings of New France, 1524-1663*, trans. by Patricia Claxton, Toronto: McClelland and Stewart, 1973, pp. 12-13; Michelle Guitard, *Jacques Cartier in Canada*, Ottawa: National Library of Canada, 1984.

26 Guitard, *Cartier*, p. 24.

27 The entry by Marcel Trudel on Samuel de Champlain in *Dictionary of Canadian Biography (DCB)* I, Toronto: University of Toronto Press, 1966, pp. 186-99.

28 W.L. Grant ed., *Voyages of Samuel de Champlain 1604-18*, New York: Charles Scribner's Sons, 1907, pp. 42-3. See also Bill Spray, 'History Still Being Made on St Croix Island', *Atlantic Advocate*, 72:4, December 1981, pp. 10-13; L.K. Ingersoll, 'Island of History and Friendship', *Atlantic Advocate*, 74:2, October 1983, pp. 34-7.

29 The map is reproduced in H.P. Biggar, ed., *The Works of Samuel de Champlain*, I, 1599-1607 [Part 3, Book 1, Acadia and New England, trans. and ed. by W.F. Ganong], Toronto: Champlain Society, 1922, pl. 71.

30 Marc Lescarbot, *History of New France*, ed. by W.L. Grant, Publications of the Champlain Society, No. 7, II, Toronto: Champlain Society, 1911, p. 255.

31 W.F. Ganong, *Dochet (St Croix) Island, A Monograph*. Transactions of the Royal Society of Canada, Section 2, 1902, p. 182.

32 Noted as 'I' on Champlain's map of the entire island; reproduced in Biggar, *Works of Champlain*, I, pl. 70.

33 Biggar, *Works of Champlain*, I, p. 276, n.1.

34 Spray, 'History', p. 11.

35 Biggar, *Works of Champlain*, I, p. 367.

36 Lescarbot, *History*, II, p. 280.

37 Biggar, *Works of Champlain*, I, p. 878.

38 Lescarbot, *History*, II, pp. 282, 319.

39 F. Fraser Bond, 'Her Dream Rebuilt the Past', *Atlantic Advocate*, 48:5, January 1958, p. 42.

40 Bond, 'Dream', pp. 41-6; Charles W. Jefferys, 'The Reconstruction of the Port Royal *Habitation* of 1603-13', *Canadian Historical Review*, 20:4, December 1939, pp. 369-77; C.J. Taylor, *Negotiating the Past: The Making of Canada's National Historic Parks and Sites*, Montreal: McGill-Queen's University Press, 1990, pp. 67-9, 115-19.

41 Jefferys, 'Reconstruction', p. 376; Marius Barbeau, 'Types des maisons canadiennes', *Le Canada Français*, 29:1, September 1941, p. 37. Two recent studies have stated that Port Royal was reconstructed incorrectly using *poteaux en coulisse*, contradicting both Jefferys and Barbeau, who 'were there': Mary Cullen, 'Pre-1755 Acadian Building Techniques', Agenda Paper, Historic Sites and Monuments Board of Canada, Ottawa, 1983, p. 492 (citing Jefferys and Barbeau); and Taylor, *Negotiating the Past*, p. 118 (citing Barbara Schmeisser, 'Port Royal Habitation, 1928-1939; A Case Study in the Preservation Movement', paper presented at the annual meeting of the Canadian Historical Association, Montreal, May 1985, p. 35).

42 Biggar, *Works of Champlain*, II: 1608-1613. Part 1, Book 2. Toronto, 1925, pp. 24-5.

43 Biggar, *Works of Champlain*, II, pp. 35-6. See also Marius Barbeau, 'Nos bâtisseurs', *Le Canada Français*, 29:3, November 1941, pp. 169-74.

44 Trudel, 'Champlain', *DCB*, I, pp. 194-5; Françoise Niellon and Marcel Moussette, *Le Site de l'Habitation de Champlain à Québec: Étude de la collection archéologique (1976-1980)*, Quebec: Ministère des Affaires culturelles, 1985 (with references to the excavation reports); Luc Noppen, Claude Paulette, and Michel Tremblay, *Québec: trois siècles d'architecture*, n.p.: Libre Expression, 1979, pp. 3-6; G.W. Leahy, *Regards sur l'architecture du Vieux-Québec*, Quebec: Ville de Québec, 1986, pp. 9-11; André Robitaille, 'Évolution de l'habitat au Canada français', *Architecture Bâtiment Construction*, 21:240, April 1966, p. 33.

45 Biggar, *Works of Champlain*, VI, Appendix, pp. 378-9. Translation.

46 The chapel appears on Jean Bourdon's map of 1640; see Noppen et al., *Québec*, pp. 7, 222; Alan Gowans, *Church Architecture in New France*, Toronto: University of Toronto Press, 1955, p. 14.

47 Luc Noppen, *Les Églises du Québec (1600-1850)*, Quebec: Éditeur officiel du Québec/Fides, 1977, p. 3.

48 Gowans, *Church Architecture*, p. 16; Noppen, *Églises*, p. 3 (translations mine).

49 Gowans, *Church Architecture*, p. 15.

50 Dennis Reid, *A Concise History of Canadian Painting*, 2nd ed., Toronto: Oxford University Press, 1988, pp. 3-5.

CHAPTER 2 New France

1 R. Cole Harris and John Warkentin, *Canada Before Confederation*, Toronto: Oxford University Press, 1974, p. 32 and Chapter 2, *passim*; J.M.S. Careless, *Canada: A Story of Challenge*, 3rd ed., Toronto: Macmillan, 1974, Chapter 4; entry by André Vachon on Talon in *Dictionary of Canadian Biography (DCB)* I, Toronto: University of Toronto Press, 1966, pp. 614-32; entry by Peter N. Moogk on Talon in *Canadian Encyclopedia (CE)* IV, 2nd ed., Edmonton: Hurtig, 1988, p. 2110.

2 Bourdon's map, drawn in 1640, is known only from a nineteenth-century copy by surveyor Pierre-Louis Morin (Montreal Public Library); illustrated and discussed in Luc Noppen, Claude Paulette, and Michel Tremblay, *Québec: trois siècles d'architecture*, n.p: Libre Expression, 1979, p. 7. See also George W. Leahy, *Regards sur l'architecture du Vieux-Québec*, Quebec: Ville de Québec, 1986; David T. Ruddel, *Québec City 1765-1832: The Evolution of a Colonial Town*, Mercury Series, Ottawa: Canadian Museum of Civilization, n.d.

3 Noppen et al., *Québec*, pp. 272-8; Ernest Gagnon, *Le Fort et le château Saint-Louis (Québec): Étude archéologique et historique*, rev. ed., Montreal: Beauchemin, 1908. For Lajoüe (also spelled la Joüe), see A.J.H. Richardson et al., *Quebec City: Architects, Artisans, and Builders*, Ottawa: National Museum of Man, 1984, pp. 204-6; and Pierre Mayrand's entry in *DCB* II, pp. 337-9.

4 Noppen et al., *Québec*, pp. 290-4.

5 Ramsay Traquair, *The Old Architecture of Quebec*, Toronto: Macmillan, 1947, pp. 18-29; Noppen et al., *Québec*, pp. 203-7; Richardson et al., *Quebec City*, pp. 386-8.

6 Noppen et al., *Québec*, pp. 226-34; Honorius Provost, 'Le Séminaire de Québec: Terrains et constructions (1663-1700)', *La Revue de l'Université Laval*, 20:1, September 1965, pp. 3-23.

7 Donn J. Durry, *Marie de l'Incarnation*, Quebec: Les Presses de l'Université Laval, 1973, 2, p. 344; cited in Noppen et al., *Québec*, p. 12.

8 Frontenac to the Minister, 2 November 1672; cited in Noppen et al., *Québec*, p. 16.

9 Frontenac to the Minister, 13 November 1673; cited in Noppen et al., *Québec*, p. 17.

10 Peter N. Moogk, *Building a House in New France: An Account of the Perplexities of Client and Craftsmen in Early Canada*, Toronto: McClelland and Stewart, 1977, pp. 14, 51.

11 Annals of the Hôtel-Dieu, cited in Michel Gaumond, *Place Royale: Its Houses and Their Occupants*, trans. by Ronald Sheen, Civilisation du Québec, no. 6, Quebec: Ministère des Affaires culturelles, 1971, p. 11.

12 André Charbonneau, Yvon Desloges, and Marc Lafrance, *Québec, The Fortified City: From the 17th to the 19th Century*, Ottawa: Parks Canada, 1982, pp. 362-4; Gaumond, *Place Royale*; Noppen et al., *Québec*, pp. 412-14 and *passim*; Pierre-Georges Roy, *La Ville de Québec sous le régime français*, 1, Quebec: Service des Archives du Gouvernement de la Province de Québec, 1930, pp. 443-4.

13 Gaumond, *Place Royale*, pp. 34-6. Building contracts (*marchés*) form a valuable resource for Quebec's architectural history. See Doris Dubé and Marthe Lacombe, 'Inventaire des marchés de construction des archives nationales à Québec, XVIIᵉ et XVIIIᵉ siècles', *History and Archaeology/Histoire et archéologie*, 17, Ottawa: Parks Canada, 1977; Geneviève G. Bastien, D. Dubé, and Christina [Cameron] Southam, 'Inventaire des marchés de construction des archives civiles de Québec, 1800-1870', *History and Archaeology/Histoire et archéologie*, 1, Ottawa: Parks Canada, 1975. See also A.J.H. Richardson, 'Notarial Documentary Sources on French Colonial Buildings in North America', *Architecture Canada*, 46:2, 1969, pp. 37-41.

14 Charbonneau et al., *Québec*, pp. 117-25.

15 Richardson, *Quebec City*, pp. 175-8; entry by F.J. Thorpe on Chaussegros in *DCB* III, pp. 116-19; Charbonneau et al., *Québec*, pp. 131-4.

16 Noppen et al., *Québec*, pp. 29, 116-17, 151.

17 Christina Cameron and Jean Trudel, *The Drawings of James Cockburn: A Visit Through Quebec's Past*, Toronto: Gage, 1976, pp. 123-4.

18 Eric R. Krause, 'Private Buildings in Louisbourg 1713-1758', *Canada: An Historical Magazine*, 1:4, June 1974, pp. 47-9. The word *piquet* came into English as 'picket', as in picket fence.

19 John Fortier and Owen Fitzgerald, *Fortress of Louisbourg*, Toronto: Oxford University Press, 1979; Margaret Fortier, 'The Development of the Fortifications at Louisbourg', *Canada: An Historical Magazine*, 1:4, June 1974, pp. 16-31; Edward McM. Larrabee, 'Archaeological Research at the Fortress of Louisbourg, 1961-1965', *Canadian Historic Sites: Occasional Papers in Archaeology and History*, No. 2, Ottawa: Department of Indian Affairs and Northern Development, 1971, pp. 8-15; Krause, 'Louisbourg', *passim*; Christopher Moore, 'Louisbourg', *CE* II, pp. 1245-6; John Fortier, 'The Fortress of Louisbourg and its Cartographic Evidence', *APT Bulletin*, 4:1-2, 1972, pp. 3-11; Bruce W. Fry, *'An Appearance of Strength': The Fortifications of Louisbourg*, 2 vols., Ottawa: Parks Canada, 1984; Frederick J. Thorpe, *Remparts lointains*, Ottawa: Éditions de

l'Université d'Ottawa, 1980; Claribel Gesner, 'Louisbourg: A Town Out of Time', *Atlantic Advocate*, 60:12, August 1970, pp. 37-45.

20 Entry by F.J. Thorpe on Verville in *CE* IV, p. 2255; entry by F.J. Thorpe on Verrier in *CE* IV, p. 2253. See also Thorpe's entries on Verville and Verrier in the *DCB*, vols II (pp. 648-50) and III (pp. 643-6) respectively.

21 Blaine Adams, 'The Construction and Occupation of the Barracks of the King's Bastion at Louisbourg', *Canadian Historic Sites: Occasional Papers in Archaeology and History*, No. 18, Ottawa: Department of Indian and Northern Affairs, 1978, pp. 59-147; Charles S. Lindsay, 'Louisbourg Guardhouses', *Canadian Historic Sites*, No. 12, 1975, pp. 47-100.

22 Margaret Fortier, 'Fortifications', pp. 20-1.

23 Anne O'Neill, 'The Gardens of 18th-Century Louisbourg', *Journal of Garden History*, 3:3, July-September 1983, pp. 176-8.

24 Margaret Fortier, 'Fortifications', p. 27.

25 Francis Parkman, *Montcalm and Wolfe: France and England in North America*, 2, Toronto: Morang, 1899, p. 56; cited in C.J. Taylor, *Negotiating the Past: The Making of Canada's National Historic Parks and Sites*, Montreal: McGill-Queen's University Press, 1990, p. 18; see also pp. 77-83, 107, 175-87.

26 Adams to Harkin, 11 June 1923, National Archives of Canada (NAC); cited in Taylor, *Negotiating the Past*, p. 66.

27 See Richard Colebrook Harris, *The Seigneurial System in Early Canada: A Geographical Study*, Madison: University of Wisconsin Press and Quebec: Les Presses de l'université Laval, 1968; Marcel Trudel, *Le Régime seigneurial*, Ottawa: La Société historique du Canada, 1956; André Bérubé et al., *Histoire du régime seigneurial dans la vallée du Saint-Laurent: Évaluation des ressources in situ*, Quebec: Service canadienne des parcs, Région du Québec, 1990.

28 Harris, *Seigneurial System*, p. 173; Peter N. Moogk, *Building a House*, p. 16.

29 Jacques Mathieu, 'Seigneurial System', *CE* III, p. 1975; Pierre Deffontaines, 'Le Rang, type de peuplement rural du Canada français', in Marcel Rioux and Yves Martin, eds, *La Société canadienne-française*, Montreal: Éditions Hurtubise, 1971, p. 20. The article is an abridgement of a book of the same name published by Les Presses Universitaires Laval, 1953; an earlier variant of this article is cited in note 31 below. See also R. Cole Harris and Geoffrey J. Matthews, *Historical Atlas of Canada*, I, Toronto: University of Toronto Press, [1987,] pl. 52.

30 Deffontaines, 'Le Rang', p. 23.

31 Pierre Deffontaines, 'Le Rang: type de peuplement rural du Canada français', in *Proceedings*, Eighth General Assembly and Seventeenth International Congress of the International Geographical Union, Washington, 1952, p. 723.

32 Yves Laframboise et al., *Calixa-Lavallée: Répertoire d'architecture traditionnelle*, Les Cahiers du patrimoines, no. 4, Quebec: Ministère des Affaires culturelles, 1977.

33 Harris, *Seigneurial System*, p. 192.

34 'Remarques sur ce qui paroit important au Service du Roy', cited in Harris, *Seigneurial System*, p. 180.

35 Johanne Lachance, 'Le Vieux-Charlesbourg', *Continuité* 54, Summer 1992, pp. 28-34; Harris, *Seigneurial System*, pp. 176-8; Luc Noppen and John R. Porter, *Les Églises de Charlesbourg et l'architecture religieuse du Québec*, Civilisation du Québec, Série architecture, no. 9, Quebec: Ministère des Affairs culturelles, 1972, pp. 13-15; Vachon, 'Talon', *DCB* I, p. 619.

36 Harris, *Seigneurial System*, pp. 176-9.

37 Deffontaines, 'Le Rang', pp. 29-31.

38 Pierre Boucher, *Histoire véritable et naturelle des moeurs et productions du pays de la Nouvelle France*, Paris, 1664 (reprinted Boucherville, 1964); trans. by E.L. Montizambert, *Canada in the XVII Century*, Montreal, 1883, p. 73; quoted in Ramsay Traquair, *The Old Architecture of Quebec*, Toronto: Macmillan, 1947, p. 11.

39 Traquair, *Old Architecture*, p. 12. This book served as a summary of the many articles and monographs on Quebec building that Traquair had written and co-authored in the 1920s and 1930s, most of them published by McGill University.

40 Georges Gauthier-Larouche, *Évolution de la maison rurale traditionnelle dans la région de Québec: Étude tethnographique*, Quebec: Les Presses de l'université Laval, 1974, pp. 23-32. His source of information and illustrations of La Mulotière was Madame Pierre Montagne, *Tourouvre et les Juchereau. Un Chapitre de l'immigration percheronne au Canada*, Quebec: Société canadienne de généalogie, 1965, pp. 96-104. Subsequent research has suggested that the Girardin house was built *c.* 1673 as a small one-storey, one-room house, and was enlarged *c.* 1727 and again *c.* 1735; Michael Dufresne, *Beauport, de la côte à l'arrière-pays*, Les Cahiers du patrimoine, no. 8, Quebec: Ministére des Affaires culturelles, 1977, pp. 19-21, cited in Luc Noppen, 'La Maison québécoise: un sujet à redécouvrir', *Questions de Culture*, 4, 1983, p. 75. The illustration of the Girardin house before the recent alterations was published in Pierre-Georges Roy, *Old Manors Old Houses*, Quebec: Historic Monuments Commissions, 1927, p. 266.

41 Traquair, *Old Architecture*, p. 59; Harris and Matthews, *Historical Atlas*, I, pl. 55; additional information from Yves Laframboise.

42 R.H. Hubbard, 'The European Backgrounds of Early Canadian Art', Art Quarterly, 27, 3 (1964), pp. 298-9, citing cottages in a village near Laon and others illustrated in J.-S. Gauthier, *Les Maisons paysannes des vieilles provinces de France*, Paris, 1951.

43 Mère Françoise Juchereau de Saint-Ignace, *Histoire de l'Hôtel-Dieu de Québec*, Montauban, 1750; cited in Pierre Deffontaines, 'Évolution du type d'habitation rurale au Canada français', *Cahiers de géographie de Québec*, 24, December 1967, p. 500. Geographer Deffontaines first argued that the evolution of the Quebec house was primarily a response to environmental factors in *L'Homme et l'hiver au Canada*, Quebec: Les Presses de l'université Laval, 1957.

44 Gérard Morisset, *L'Architecture en Nouvelle-France*, Quebec, 1949, reprinted Quebec: Pélican, 1980, pl. 1b; Morisset, 'Quebec--The Country House / Québec—La Maison Rurale', *Canadian Geographical Journal*, 57:6, December 1958, pp. 184-5; Sarah M. McKinnon, *Traditional Rural Architecture in Quebec; 1600-1800*, University of Toronto, Centre for Urban and Community Studies and Centre for Medieval Studies, Toronto, 1977, pp. 7-12. The biography of Morisset is taken from Jacques Robert's preface to the 1980 reprint of *L'Architecture en Nouvelle-France*.

45 Marc-Aimé Guérin, 'La Maison de chaume des basses-terres du Saint-Laurent', *Revue canadienne de géographie*, 11:1, 1957, pp. 17-50.

46 Inventory of the property of Charles Bélanger and Geneviève Gagnon, 6 April 1746, greffes notariaux C.-Hilarion Dulaurent, Archives nationales du Québec; cited in Gauthier-Larouche, *Évolution*, pp. 47-9. One French foot is the equivalent of 1.066 English feet.

47 Gauthier-Larouche, *Évolution*, pp. 52-3.

48 Roy, *Old Manors*, pp. 331-2; Traquair, *Old Architecture*, pp. 47-9; Morisset, *L'Architecture*, p. 35 and pl. 3a; Morisset, 'Country House', p. 184; McKinnon, *Rural Architecture*, pp. 40-3, where it is called the l'Heureux house, after the current (in 1977) owner. Christina Cameron, who calls it the Auclair house, also questions the seventeenth-century date and suggests a date in the middle of the eighteenth century, citing a notarial document: 'Housing in Quebec Before Confederation', *Journal of Canadian Art History* (*JCAH*), 6:1, 1982, pp. 17-19 and n. 28. Noppen suggests that many houses were built in phases in 'La Maison québécoise', p. 76.

49 The *pavillon* roof appeared in the grand buildings of the period of François I (e.g. the Château of Azay-le-Rideau, 1521) and continued in use into the seventeenth century, often on the flanking pavilions (hence its name) of larger residences (e.g. the Luxembourg Palace, 1614-24); see W.H. Ward, *The Architecture of the Renaissance in France*, 2nd ed., I, London: Batsford, 1926, pp. 62, 236, and *passim*.

50 Peter Collins, 'Clapboarded Masonry', *Canadian Architect*, 12:8, August 1967, pp. 62-4; Moogk accepts this interpretation (*Building a House*, p. 25). Walls that were boarded often used horizontal tongue-and-groove boards; Gauthier-Larouche, *Évolution*, p. 141.

51 Morriset, 'Country House', p. 180.

52 Morriset, 'Country House', p. 182; Roy, *Old Manors*, p. 50.

53 *La Maison Saint-Gabriel*, brochure, Montreal, 1977; Traquair, *Old Architecture*, pp. 38-42; Jean-Claude Marsan, *Montreal in Evolution*, Montreal: McGill-Queen's University Press, 1981, pp. 110-12; Rémillard and Merrett, *Montreal Architecture*, p. 27; entry by Hélène Bernier on Bourgeoys in *DCB* I, pp. 115-19; entry by Cornelius J. Jaenen on Bourgeoys in *CE* I, p. 261. Florence Bertrand, Archivist of the Soeurs de la Congrégation de Notre-Dame, kindly provided assistance.

54 Morriset, *L'Architecture*, p. 32. The respected anthropologist Marius Barbeau—in 'Types de maisons canadiennes', *Le Canada français*, 29:1, September 1941, pp. 41-2—related the Quebec type to Normandy and the Montreal type to the Loire valley. See also Ramsay Traquair, *The Cottages of Quebec*, McGill University publications, series 13 (Art and Architecture), no. 5, 1926.

55 Moogk, *Building a House*, p. 35; Deffontaines, 'Évolution', pp. 497-522; Robert-Lionel Séguin, *La Maison en Nouvelle-France*, Musée national du Canada, Bulletin 226, Ottawa, 1968; Séguin, 'L'Habitation traditionnelle au Québec', *Cahiers des Dix*, 37, 1972, pp. 191-222; William Sener Rusk, 'The Influence of Norman Architecture in French

Canada', *Bulletin de l'Institut-Français de Washington*, 13, December 1940, pp. 11-20.

56 Noppen, 'La Maison québécoise', pp. 76-81; Yves Laframboise, *L'Architecture traditionnelle au Québec*, Montreal: Les Éditions de l'homme, 1975, p. 40; Laframboise, 'La Maison en pierre de Neuville', *RACAR*, 2:1, 1975, pp. 15-22; Laframboise et al., *Neuville: Architecture traditionnelle*, Les Cahiers de la patrimoine, Quebec: Ministère des affaires culturelles, 1976.

57 Léonidoff's data are presented in graphic form in Harris and Matthews, *Historical Atlas*, I, pl. 55-6. See also Georges-Pierre Léonidoff, 'L'Habitat de bois en Nouvelle-France: son importance et ses techniques de construction', *Material History Bulletin/Bulletin d'histoire de la culture matérielle*, 14: 1982, pp. 19-35; Léonidoff, 'Origine et évolution des principaux types d'architecture rurale au Québec et le cas de Charlevoix', Ph.D. thesis, Université Laval, 1980.

58 The original French text reads *'une belle & artificielle charpenterie'*; see note 87, and also the discussion in A.J.H. Richardson, 'A Comparative Historical Study of Timber Building in Canada', *APT Bulletin*, 5:3, 1973, p. 78.

59 Translation in C.E. Peterson, 'The Houses of French St. Louis', in J.F. McDermott, ed., *The French in the Mississippi Valley*, Urbana, Ill.: University of Illinois Press, 1965, p. 35; cited in Richardson, 'Timber Building,' p. 78.

60 H.P. Biggar, ed., *The Works of Samuel de Champlain*, V, Toronto: Champlain Society, 1933, pp. 201-3; cited in Richardson, 'Timber Building', p. 78.

61 Joyce Marshall, ed. and trans., *Word from New France: The Selected Letters of Marie de L'Incarnation*, Toronto: Oxford University Press, 1967, p. 129; Traquair, *Old Architecture*, p. 10; Moogk, *Building a House*, pp. 24, 28.

62 See, for example, the illustrations of *colombage* in the houses of Rouen and Lisieux in Richardson, *Quebec City*, figs. xvii, xx.

63 Jean Palardy, 'Architecture in Early Canada: The French Influence', *Canadian Antiques Collector*, 9:1, January/February 1974, p. 31.

64 Michel Lessard and Huguette Marquis, *Encyclopédie de la maison québécoise*, Montreal: Éditions de l'homme, 1972, pp. 219-27; Diane Caron, 'La Maison de colombage. Recherche historique, analyse architecturale et évaluation patrimoniale de la maison Pichet, à Sainte-Famille, Île d'Orléans', unpublished paper, Ministère des affaires culturelles, Quebec, 1982; Pierre Bureau, 'Maison Lamontagne, Rimouski-Est', unpublished paper, Ministère des affaires culturelles, Quebec, 1973; Paul Gagnon, 'Maison Lamontagne', *Monuments et sites historiques du Québec*, 1, Quebec: Les Publications du Québec, 1990. p. 512; Richardson, 'Timber Building', p. 83; McKinnon, *Architecture*, pp. 27-34.

65 Séguin, *La Maison*, p. 36. Séguin studied Quebec barns extensively: see Robert-Lionel Séguin, *Les Granges du Québec du XVIIe au XIXe siècle*, Musée national du Canada, Bulletin no. 192, Ottawa, 1963 (reprinted Montreal: Les Éditions Quinze, 1976); Séguin, 'La Grange au Québec', *Cahier des Dix*, 1976, pp. 205-35.

66 Thomas Ritchie, 'Plankwall Framing', *JSAH*, 30:1, March 1971, pp. 66-70.

67 Pierre Gaudet, 'L'Arbre généalogique de la maison de pièce sur pièce', *Habitat*, 23:1, 1980, pp. 24-37; François Varin,

'Les Maisons en pièce sur pièce', *Continuité*, 54, Summer 1992, pp. 44-7.

68 'Un Vieux Bastiment de piece, de bois Sur piece, partye esquarrie et partye ronde, Menassant Ruyne', cited in Séguin, *La Maison*, p. 13.

69 P. Margry, *Découvertes et Établissements*, 3, Paris, 1879, p. 179; cited in Richardson, 'Timber Building', p. 79 (italics mine). If the difference between the two houses lay in the jointing, then Joutel would not necessarily have been thinking of the dovetail as a Canadian feature.

70 Harris and Matthews, *Historical Atlas*, I, p. 56; see also the remark by Peter Kalm, page 57.

71 Séguin, *La Maison*, p. 19; Morisset, 'Country House', p. 181; information from Yves Laframboise.

72 Traquair, *Old Architecture*, pp. 14, 85.

73 Hubbard, 'Backgrounds', p. 299, citing examples illustrated in J. Viérin, *L'Architecture régionale de la Flandre maritime*, Brussels, 1921.

74 Traquair, *Old Architecture*, pp. 60, 65, citing material provided by C.E. Peterson; see also Peterson, 'Early Ste. Genevieve and Its Architecture', *Missouri Historical Review*, 35, 1941, pp. 207-32; and Peterson, 'Colonial Saint Louis', *Bulletin of the Missouri Historical Society*, 30, 1946-7, and 31, 1947-8, *passim*.

75 Hubbard, 'Backgrounds', p. 299; Traquair, *Old Architecture*, pp. 67-8; Hugh Morrison, *Early American Architecture: From the First Colonial Settlements to the National Period*, New York: Oxford University Press, 1952, pp. 119-23.

76 Pierre Deffontaines, 'Évolution', pp. 497-522; Deffontaines, *L'Homme et l'hiver*; André Robitaille, 'Évolution de l'habitat au Canada français', *Architecture Bâtiment Construction*, 21:240 (April 1966), pp. 32-8; R.H. Hubbard, 'An Architecture for All Seasons', *Transactions of the Royal Society of Canada*, ser. 4, no. 8, 1970, pp. 44-8. For the development of heating systems, see Marcel Moussette, *Le Chauffage domestique au Canada des origines à l'industrialisation'*, Quebec: Les Presses de l'université Laval, 1983.

77 Laframboise, 'La Maison en pierre', p. 20. Nineteenth-century types are discussed in Cameron, 'Housing in Québec', pp. 23-5.

78 Gauthier-Larouche, *Évolution*, p. 204.

79 Roy, *Old Manors*, pp. 134-7; Raymonde Gauthier, *Les Manoirs du Québec*, Quebec: Éditeur officiel du Québec/Fides, 1976, p. 205.

80 Louis Lemoine, *Le Château fort de Longueuil (1698-1810)*, Longueuil: Société d'histoire de Longueuil, 1987; Palardy, 'Architecture', p. 30.

81 Gauthier, *Les Manoirs*, pp. 128-9, 233; Roy, *Old Manors*, pp. 279-80; Bérubé et al., *Histoire du régime seigneurial*, pp. 174-5; Thibault, *Monuments*, p. 207 (Bérubé et al. and Thibault say that Mauvide built the house *c.* 1734, before becoming a seigneur). For general accounts of the Île d'Orléans by pioneer scholars, see [Pierre-Georges Roy,] *L'Île d'Orléans*, Quebec: Historic Monuments Commission, 1928; Marius Barbeau, 'L'Île d'Orléans', *Queen's Quarterly*, 49, 1942, pp. 374-84.

82 Ramsay Traquair and G.A. Neilson, 'The Old Presbytery at Batiscan', *JRAIC*, 10:1, January 1933, pp. 13-20; Traquair, *Old Architecture*, pp. 42-6.

83 A.J.H. Richardson [and Alan Gowans], 'Guide to the architectural and historically most significant buildings in the old city of Quebec...,' *APT Bulletin*, 2:3-4, 1970, p. 13; Thibault, *Monuments*, p. 177; Cameron, 'Housing in Québec', pp. 2-4. For Jacquet, Ménard, and subsequent owner Lajoüe, see Richardson, *Quebec City*, pp. 402-4, 319, and 203-5 respectively.

84 Mireille D. Castelli, 'L'Habitation urbaine en Nouvelle-France', *Cahiers de Droit*, 16, 1975, p. 413.

85 Ramsay Traquair, 'No. 92 St. Peter Street, Quebec: A Merchant's House of the XVIII Century', *JRAIC*, 7:5, May 1930, pp. 166-72, and 7:7, July 1930, pp. 264-71; Noppen, 'La Maison québécoise', pp. 86-8; Richardson, 'Guide', pp. 20-1; Christina Cameron and Monique Trépanier, *Vieux Québec: son architecture intérieure*, National Museum of Man, Mercury Series, no. 40, Ottawa, 1986, pp. 321-4.

86 Peter Kalm, *The America of 1750: Peter Kalm's Travels in North America*, an English translation of the 1770-1 ed. by Adolph B. Benson, 2 vols, New York, 1927; reprinted New York: Dover, 1966, II, pp. 429-30.

87 Kalm, *America*, II, p. 412. See also note 70.

88 Marsan, *Montreal*, pp. 118-20; Guy Pinard, *Montréal: son histoire son architecture*, Montreal: La Presse, 1986, pp. 65-76; François Rémillard and Brian Merrett, *Montreal Architecture: A Guide to Styles and Buildings*, Montreal: Meridian Press, 1990, p. 29.

89 Marsan, *Montreal*, pp. 112-18; Joshua Wolfe and Cécile Grenier, *Montreal Guide: An Architectural and Historical Guide*, n.p: Libre Expression, 1983, pp. 66-7; Rémillard and Merrett, *Montreal Architecture*, p. 32; Clément Demers et al., *L'Architecture du Vieux Montréal*, n.p: CIDEM-Communications, 1981, p. 4.

90 Marsan, *Montreal*, pp. 113-15; Moogk, *Building a House*, pp 16-18, 50-9; Castelli, 'L'Habitation', pp. 413-26; Noppen et al., *Québec*, pp. 34, 37-8; Noppen, 'La Maison québécoise', pp. 81-7, crediting Chaussegros de Léry with many of the innovations.

91 Demers, *Montreal*, p. 4; it is attributed to masons Jacques Roy and Charles-Esprit Genest in Pinard, *Montréal*, p. 229.

92 Information kindly provided by Yves Laframboise.

93 Noppen et al., *Québec*, pp. 25, 102; Gauthier-Larouche, *Évolution*, pp. 15-16. Aubert de la Chesnaye also built a second luxurious house (1679) on the edge of town—a suburban villa, known as the 'Maison blanche', at 870 rue Saint-Vallier. Several architects and craftsmen, including Claude Baillif, were involved. See Richardson, 'Guide', p. 18.

94 John Bland, 'Château Vaudreuil and Its Architect Gaspard-Joseph Chaussegros de Léry', *SSAC Bulletin*, 13:3, Sept. 1988, pp. 5-8; Cameron, 'Housing in Québec', pp. 13-16; Marsan, *Montreal*, pp. 55-7; Alan Gowans, *Building Canada: An Architectural History of Canadian Life*, Toronto: Oxford University Press, 1966, p. 25. A plan of the grounds (and the château) is reproduced in John J. Stewart, 'Canada's Landscape Heritage', *Landscape Planning*, 6, 1979, p. 216.

95 Luc Noppen and Marc Grignon, *L'Art de l'architecte/Three Centuries of Architectural Drawing in Québec City*, Quebec: Musée du Québec and Université Laval, 1983, p. 49.

96 Alan Gowans, *Church Architecture in New France*, Toronto: University of Toronto Press, 1955, p. 18.

97 Entry by André Vachon on Laval in *DCB* II, pp. 358-72; entry by Peter N. Moogk on Laval in *CE* II, pp. 1184-5.

98 Gowans, *Church Architecture*, pp. 53-8; Luc Noppen, 'Évolution de l'architecture religieuse en Nouvelle-France: Le Rôle des modèles architecturaux', *JCAH*, 4:1, Spring 1977, pp. 47-9; Noppen et al., *Québec*, pp. 217-20. Richard Short was a naval officer who entered Quebec with Wolfe's forces and made two important series of drawings, of Halifax and Quebec, that were engraved and published in London in 1761.

99 F.-X. de Charlevoix, *Histoire et description générale de la Nouvelle-France*, III, Paris, 1744, p. 76; quoted and translated in Gowans, *Church Architecture*, pp. 53-4.

100 R.G. Thwaites, ed., *Lahontan's New Voyages to North-America*, 1, Chicago, 1905, p. 39; quoted in Gowans, *Church Architecture*, p. 53.

101 Gowans, *Church Architecture*, p. 53.

102 Kalm, *America*, p. 448.

103 A.J.H. Richardson, 'Stone Pre-Fab in Quebec City in the Middle of the Eighteenth Century', *APT Bulletin*, 5:4, 1973, pp. 73-5.

104 Gowans, *Church Architecture*, pp. 58-61; Noppen, 'Évolution', pp. 49-51; Noppen et al., *Québec*, pp. 222-5. The attribution to Drué is made by Gérard Morisset in *Coup d'oeil sur les arts en Nouvelle-France*, Quebec, 1941, p. 14.

105 Gowans, *Church Architecture*, pp. 112-13, 140-2; Marsan, *Montreal*, pp. 101-6; Louise Voyer, *Églises disparues*, Quebec: Libre Expression, 1981, pp. 102-4. Chaussegros de Léry's façade was modified in 1811, and the church was demolished in 1830.

106 Marsan, *Montreal*, pp. 106-9; *Repertoire d'Architecture traditionelle sur le territoire de la Communauté urbaine de Montréal* (CUM), *Les Couvents*, Montreal, 1984, pp. 364-9; Rémillard and Merrett, *Montreal Architecture*, p. 24; the date of the wings was provided by Yves Laframboise. For the garden, see Susan Buggey, 'For Use and Beauty', *Canadian Collector*, 20:1, January-February 1985, p. 28.

107 Traquair, *Old Architecture*, pp. 29-33; Noppen et al., *Québec*, pp. 241-51; Richardson, 'Guide', pp. 12-13.

108 Jean Trudel, *Un Chef-d'oeuvre de l'art ancien du Québec: La chapelle des Ursulines*, Quebec: Les Presses de l'université Laval, 1972. For the Levasseurs, see Richardson, *Quebec City*, pp. 355-68.

109 Luc Noppen, *Notre-Dame de Québec*, Quebec: Éditions du Pélican, 1974, pp. 23-8; Noppen, *Églises*, pp. 5-6.

110 The name, and even the very existence, of this school of arts—and of a related institution at Saint-Joachim—have recently been questioned. See, for example, François-Marc Gagnon, 'L'École des arts et métiers de Saint-Joachim: un anachronisme?', in *Premiers peintres de la Nouvelle-France*, II, Quebec: Ministère des affaires culturelles, 1976, pp. 133-46; Richardson, *Quebec City*, p. 345.

111 Noppen, *Notre-Dame*; Noppen, *Églises*, pp. 162-5; Noppen et al., *Québec*, pp. 156-61. For the Baillairgé family, see Richardson, *Quebec City*, pp. 82-7; Christina Cameron, 'Baillairgé Family', *CE* I, pp. 163-4; David Karel, Luc Noppen, and Claude Thibault, *François Baillairgé et son oeuvre (1759-1830)*, Quebec: Le Groupe de recherche en art du Québec de l'Université Laval et le Musée du

Québec, 1975. See also entries in Volumes V, VI, and VIII of the *DCB*.

112 H.A. Scott, *Bishop Laval*, London, 1926, p. 150; quoted in Gowans, *Church Architecture*, p. 36.

113 Noppen, *Églises*, p. 4; Réné Villeneuve, *Les Églises de Charlesbourg*, Quebec: Éditions du Pélican, 1986, pp. 14-15 (where it is suggested that the first chapel at Charlesbourg, begun *c*. 1660, was built in this manner). For Père Chauchetière, see Dennis Reid, *A Concise History of Canadian Painting*, 2nd ed., Toronto: Oxford University Press, 1988, pp. 5-6.

114 Caron, 'La Maison de colombage', pp. 24-5.

115 Marshall, *Word from New France*, p. 312.

116 Gowans, *Church Architecture*, pp. 44-5, 107, 116, 122-3; Noppen, *Églises*, p. 12. The first Basilica of Sainte-Anne-de-Beaupré, built 1872-6 and burned in 1922, was replaced by the present Basilica, built 1925-70, which can accommodate 2,000 worshippers seated and 8,000 standing, and receives more than one million visits every year. Baillif's supposed Norman origins are discussed in Gowans, *Church Architecture*, p. 47; and Richardson, *Quebec City*, p. 89.

117 Alan Gowans, 'From Baroque to Neo-Baroque in the Church Architecture of Quebec', *Culture*, 10, 1949, p. 144. Leblond de Latour is often credited with having started a school of arts and crafts at Saint-Joachim, but the existence of this school has been questioned; see above, note 110. The interior of Saint-Anne de Beaupré was photographed, although after the retable had been altered; see Noppen, *Églises*, p. 26.

118 Gérard Morisset, 'Old Churches of Quebec', *Canadian Geographical Journal*, 43:3, September 1951, p. 100; Morisset, *L'Architecture*, p. 48.

119 Gowans, *Church Architecture*, pp. 93-7.

120 Annals of the Hôtel-Dieu; quoted in Harold Kalman and John de Visser, *Pioneer Churches*, Toronto: McClelland and Stewart, 1976, p. 26.

121 Luc Noppen, *Notre-Dame-des-Victoires à la place Royale de Québec*, Quebec: Ministère des affaires culturelles, 1974; Noppen, *Églises*, pp. 178-81; Noppen et al., *Québec*, pp. 177-9; Gowans, *Church Architecture*, pp. 50-1; Pierre-Georges Roy, *Les vieilles églises de la province de Québec 1647-1800*, Quebec: Commission des monuments historiques de la province de Québec, 1925, pp. 47-53; Kalman and de Visser, *Pioneer Churches*, pp. 16-17, 26-7. For the development of design, see Noppen, 'L'Évolution de l'architecture religieuse en Nouvelle-France', *La Société canadienne d'histoire de l'église catholique: Sessions d'étude*, 43, 1976, pp. 69-78; Noppen, 'Évolution', pp. 45-60.

122 Noppen and Grignon, *L'Art de l'architecte*, pp. 126-7; Gowans, *Church Architecture*, pp. 66-7, 82-4; Noppen, 'Évolution', pp. 45-7; John Bland, 'La Chapelle du palais épiscopal de Québec', *Vie des Arts*, 19:76, Autumn 1974, pp. 52-4; 117-8. Bland suggests that the plan was drawn by Jean Maillou's brother Joseph (d. 1702), but Noppen refutes this idea.

123 Noppen et al., *Québec*, pp. 295-9.

124 Ramsay Traquair and C.M. Barbeau, *The Church of St. François de Sales, Island of Orleans, Quebec*, McGill University Publications, Series 13 (Art and Architecture), 14,

1926; Noppen, *Églises*, pp. 226-9; Roy, *Églises*, pp. 159-62.

125 Morisset, *L'Architecture*, p. 46; Morisset, 'Old Churches', p. 101.

126 Noppen, *Églises*, pp. 70-3.

127 For Paquet, see Richardson, *Quebec City*, pp. 443-4.

128 Luc Noppen, 'Le Rejet du plâtre dans l'étude de l'art ancien du Québec: un point de vue', *Revue d'ethnologie du Québec*, 1:1, 1975, pp. 25-48. A notable exception cited by Noppen is the plasterwork in the nave of Notre-Dame de Québec (1744), by Chaussegros de Léry, who was born and trained in France.

129 Alan Gowans, 'Clapboarding and Whitewash in the Church Architecture of New France', *Bulletin des Recherches Historiques*, 58, 1952, pp. 50-4.

130 Ramsay Traquair and Marius Barbeau, *The Church of Saint Famille, Island of Orleans, Que.*, McGill University Publications, Series 13 (Art and Architecture), Montreal, 1926; Noppen, *Églises*, pp. 218-21; Roy, *Églises*, pp. 171-3; Gowans, *Church Architecture*, pp. 86, 110, 149; J. Soucy, 'L'Église de la Sainte-Famille', *Bulletin du Musée du Québec*, 13, December 1969.

131 Noppen, 'Évolution', pp. 58; Noppen, 'L'Évolution', p. 73.

132 John R. Porter and Jean Trudel, *The Calvary at Oka*, Ottawa: National Gallery of Canada, 1974; John R. Porter, 'The Calvary at Oka', *Canadian Antiques Collector*, 10:1, January-February 1975, pp. 9-13.

133 Jean Daigle, 'Acadia, 1604-1763, An Historical Synthesis', in Jean Daigle, ed., *The Acadians of the Maritimes: Thematic Studies*, Moncton: Centre d'études acadiennes, 1982, pp. 17-46; Léon Thériault, 'Acadia, 1763-1978, An Historical Synthesis', in Daigle, ed., *Acadians*, pp. 47-86; Père Anselme Chiasson et al., 'Acadia', *CE* I, pp. 5-10. For the origins of the colonists in Poitou, see Rev. Fr. C.-J. d'Entremont, 'The Acadians and their Geneology', *French-Canadian and Acadian Geneological Review*, 5, Summer 1978, p. 71; cited in Peter Ennals, 'The Folk Legacy in Acadian Domestic Architecture: A Study in Mislaid Self Images', *Dimensions of Canadian Architecture*, SSAC Selected Papers, Shane O'Dea and Gerald L. Pocius, eds, 6, 1983, n. 1. See also Andrew Hill Clark, *Acadia: The Geography of Early Nova Scotia to 1760*, Madison: University of Wisconsin Press, 1968; Naomi Griffiths, *The Acadians: Creation of a People*, Toronto: McGraw-Hill Ryerson, 1973.

134 Daigle, 'Synthesis', p. 31; Muriel K.Roy, 'Settlement and Population Growth in Acadia', in Daigle, ed., *Acadians*, p. 134.

135 See Robert G. LeBlanc, 'The Acadian Migrations', *Canadian Geographical Journal*, 81:1 (July 1970), pp. 10-19.

136 Rameau de Saint-Père, *Une Colonie féodale en Amérique: L'Acadie (1604-1881)*, Paris: Librairie Plon and Montreal: Granger Frères, 1889, I, p. 82.

137 W.F. Ganong, *Historic Sites in the Province of New Brunswick*, 1899, reprinted St Stephen: Print 'n Press, 1983, pp. 54, 80, the latter quoting a description of 1688 by Saint-Vallier.

138 Nicolas Denys, *Description géographique de l'Amérique septentrionale*, Paris, 1672; quoted in Ganong, *Historic Sites*, p. 88.

139 J. Rodolphe Bourque, *Social and Architectural Aspects of Acadians in New Brunswick*, Fredericton: Historical Resources Administration, 1971, p. 23.

140 Eve Donelle, 'Mount House', *Atlantic Advocate*, 77:11, July 1987, pp. 23-4.

141 A plan of 1692 in the Archives de la Marine, Paris, is illustrated in Ganong, *Historic Sites*, p. 61; a bird's-eye view was illustrated in Dièreville, *Relation du voyage du Port-Royale de l'Acadie ou de la Nouvelle-France*, [1699], in *Cahiers de la Société historique acadienne*, 16:3-4, September-December 1985, p. 31. For Fort Saint-Jean, see Harold E. Wright and Byron E. O'Leary, *Fortress Saint John: An Illustrated Military History 1640-1985*, Saint John: Partridge Island Research Project, 1985, pp. 16-17; Ganong, *Historic Sites*, pp. 66-7.

142 Alaric Faulkner and Gretchen Faulkner, *The French at Pentagoet, 1635-1674: An Archaeological Portrait of the Acadian Frontier*, Augusta: Main Historic Preservation Commission and Saint John: New Brunswick Museum, 1987.

143 Pierre Nadon, *Historical Report on Fort Beauséjour*, Manuscript Report No. 250, Ottawa: Parks Canada. *Fort Beauséjour National Historic Park*, brochure, Ottawa: Parks Canada, n.d; Barbara Schmeisser, 'Time-Travelling at Beauséjour', *Canadian Collector*, 20:2, March-April 1985, pp. 51-3; Lloyd A. Machum, 'Digging for History in Fort Beauséjour near Chignecto', *Atlantic Advocate*, 60:5, January 1970, pp. 36-44.

144 Allen Penney cites much-altered Acadian houses in Belleisle and Weymouth, NS, and one that was excavated in the Annapolis Valley, in *Houses of Nova Scotia: An Illustrated Guide to Architectural Style Recognition*, Halifax: Formac and Nova Scotia Museum, 1989, pp. 50-1, but none of these have been substantiated as predating the Expulsion. Mary Cullen, of Parks Canada, believes—probably correctly—that no extant houses claimed as having been built before the Expulsion can conclusively be identified as such, in 'Pre-1755 Acadian Building Techniques', Agenda Paper, Historic Sites and Monuments Board of Canada, Ottawa, 1983, pp. 491-516. Architect Mark Laing, who has been involved in investigations of purportedly Acadian buildings, shares this cautious opinion (in conversation with the author).

145 'Mémoire de Menneval', quoted in Père Anselme Chiasson, 'Les vieilles maisons acadiennes', *Société Historique Acadienne: 25ᵉ Cahier*, October-December 1969, p. 184; this, and several of the quotations that follow, are also cited in Alphonse Deveau, 'L'Architecture acadienne avant l'Expulsion', *Revue de l'Université Sainte-Anne*, 1982, pp. 40-2.

146 Letter of Soeur Chausson, 27 October 1701, cited in Deveau, 'L'Architecture', p. 41; slightly differently in Rameau de Saint-Père, *Une Colonie féodale*, 2, p. 339.

147 John Clarence Webster, ed., *Relation of the Voyage to Port Royal in Acadia or New France, by the Sieur de Dièreville*, trans. by Mrs Clarence Webster, Publications of the Champlain Society, No. 20, Toronto, 1933, pp. 82-4; the *Relation* was first published in 1708. See also J. Brian Bird, 'Settlement Patterns in Maritime Canada, 1687-1786', *Canadian Geographical Journal*, 45, 1955, p. 389.

148 Baron (Louis-Armaud de Lom d'Arce) de Lahontan, *New Voyages to North America*, London, 1703, 1, pp. 224-5; cited in Bird, 'Patterns,' p. 389.

149 [Charles Morris,] 'A Brief Survey of Nova Scotia', manuscript in the library of the Royal Artillery Regiment, Woolwich, cap. 2, pp. 25-6; cited in Clark, *Acadia*, p. 217.

150 Bird, 'Patterns', p. 386, n. 3.

151 Brenda Dunn, 'Research on Fort Anne Fortifications and Buildings', unpublished paper, Halifax: Parks Canada, 1982; cited in Cullen, 'Acadian Building Techniques', pp. 493-4.

152 R.W. Brunskill, *Illustrated Handbook of Vernacular Architecture*, New York: Universe Books, 1970, pp. 56-7; Morrison, *Early American Architecture*, pp. 15-30; Abbott Lowell Cummings, *The Framed Houses of Massachusetts Bay, 1625-1725*, Cambridge: Harvard University Press, 1979, *passim*.

153 Deveau, 'L'Architecture', p. 41.

154 Gargas, *Mon Séjour de l'Acadie*, in William Inglis Morse, ed., *Acadiensia Nova*, London: Bernard Quaritch, 1935; cited in Deveau, 'L'Architecture,' p. 40.

155 W.F. Ganong, ed., *Gamaliel Smethurst's Narrative . . .*, Collections of the New Brunswick Historical Society, No. 6, p. 368; cited in Bourque, *Acadians*, p. 76.

156 David J. Christianson, *Belleisle 1983: Excavations at a Pre-Expulsion Acadian Site*, Curatorial Report No. 48, Halifax: Nova Scotia Museum, 1984. The house in Vendée is cited in Pierre Drobecq, *La Cheminée dans l'habitation*, Paris: Vincent et Fréals, 1942, p. 58; cited in Christianson, p. 69. See also Marc Charles Lavoie, *Belleisle Nova Scotia 1680-1755: Acadian Material Life and Economy*, Curatorial Report No. 65, Halifax: Nova Scotia Museum, 1987.

157 Bourque, *Acadians*, p. 34, citing Document A, Antoine Bourg Collection, Vienna. Similar conclusions have been suggested in Clarke, *Acadia*, p. 105; and in William C. Wonders, 'Log Dwellings in Canadian Folk Architecture', *Annals of the Association of Americal Geographers*, 69:2, June 1979, p. 194—both cited in Cullen, 'Acadian Building Techniques', n. 12.

158 Deveau, 'L'Architecture,' pp. 40-1.

159 Capt. John Knox, *An Historical Journal of the Campaigns in North America for the Years 1757, 1758, 1759, and 1760* (London, 1769), cited in Bourque, *Acadians*, p. 23.

160 Bourque, *Acadians*, p. 21.

161 Rameau de Saint-Père, *Colonie*, II, p. 333, 341.

162 Deveau, 'L'Architecture', p. 40.

163 National Map Collection, NAC, C-15620; redrawn in Harris and Matthews, *Historical Atlas*, I, plate 29.

164 Robert Hale, *Journal of a Voyage to Nova Scotia Made in 1731, by Robert Hale of Beverly*, in *Historical Collections of the Essex Institute*, 42:3, July 1903; cited in Chiasson, 'Maisons', p. 184.

165 Deveau, 'L'Architecture', p. 42; also quoted in Christianson, *Belleisle*, pp. 71-2, where the source is identified as NAC, MG 23, fo. 1-2, DesBarres papers Series 2: Captain John MacDonald's Report, 1795.

166 Clarence Lebreton, 'Material Culture in Acadia', in Daigle, ed., *Acadians*, p. 433.

167 Bourque, *Acadians*, pp. 67-71. Bourque uses the term *en torchis* to describe the technique. See also Robert Cun-

ningham and John B. Prince, *Tamped Clay and Saltmarsh Hay (Artifacts of New Brunswick)*, Fredericton: Brunswick Press, 1976, pp. 11-16.

168 Chiasson, 'Maisons', p. 183; he claimed (in 1969) that the house was 200 years old.

169 Régis Brun, Bernard leBlanc, and Armand Robichaud, *Les Bâtiments anciens de la Mer Rouge*, 2:2-3, 1987-8, pp. 99-106.

170 Clarence Lebreton, *Yesterday in Acadia: Scenes from the Acadian Historical Village*, 2nd ed., Barcelona: Editorial Escudo de Oro, 1987, p. 23.

171 Lebreton, 'Material Culture', pp. 436-40.

Chapter 3 British and American Architecture on the Atlantic Coast

1 Donald Creighton, *Canada: The Heroic Beginnings*, Toronto: Macmillan, 1974, p. 27. Relatively recent photographs of flakes appear in Angus J. Campbell, 'Architecture in Newfoundland and Labrador', in volume 4 of *The Book of Newfoundland*, edited by J.R. Smallwood, St John's: Newfoundland Book Publishers, 1967, p. 196. For recent literature, see 'Newfoundland Architecture: A Bibliography', *SSAC Bulletin*, 8:2, June 1983, p. 20.

2 Shane O'Dea, 'Simplicity and Survival: Vernacular Response in Newfoundland Architecture', *Newfoundland Quarterly*, 13:3 (December 1982), pp. 19-31; reprinted in *SSAC Bulletin*, 8:2 (June 1983), pp. 4-11; Shane O'Dea, 'The Tilt: Vertical-log Construction in Newfoundland', in Camille Wells, ed., *Perspectives in Vernacular Architecture*, 1, Columbia, Missouri: University of Missouri Press, 1987, pp. 55-64; D.C. Tibbetts, 'The Newfoundland Tilt', *Habitat*, 11:5 (1968), pp. 14-17; David B. Mills, 'The Development of Folk Architecture in Trinity Bay, Newfoundland', in John J. Mannion, ed., *The Peopling of Newfoundland: Essays in Historical Geography*, St. John's: Memorial University of Newfoundland, 1977, pp. 81-3; reprinted as *The Evolution of Folk House Forms in Trinity Bay, Newfoundland*, Technical Papers of the Newfoundland Museum, No. 3, St John's, 1982. The word 'tilt' was not used to describe a dwelling in the 17th century; it originally referred to a temporary covering for a stack of dry fish. Fishermen's residences were then called 'cabins', 'huts', or 'houses' (information from Peter Pope, Memorial University).

3 Bacqueville de la Potherie, *Histoire de l'Amérique septentrionale*, Paris, 1722, after p. 16.

4 Sir Richard Henry Bonnycastle, *Newfoundland in 1842; A Sequel to 'The Canadas in 1841'*, II, London: Henry Colburn, 1842, p. 124.

5 Edward Wix, *Six Months of a Newfoundland Missionary's Journal, from February to August, 1835*, London: Smith, Elder and Co., 1836, pp. 54, 63-5; Tibbetts, 'The Newfoundland Tilt', p. 15.

6 O'Dea, 'Vertical-log Construction', p. 57; Abbott Lowell Cummings, *The Framed Houses of Massachusetts Bay, 1625-1725*, Cambridge: Harvard University Press, 1979, p. 21; Hugh Morrison, *Early American Architecture: From the First Colonial Settlements to the National Period*, New York: Oxford University Press, 1952, p. 9; James Marston Fitch, *American Building. I: The Historical Forces That Shaped It*,

Cambridge, Mass.: Riverside Press, 1966, pp. 2-3; Charles E. Peterson, 'The Houses of French St Louis', in J.F. McDermott, ed., *The French in the Mississippi Valley*, Urbana: University of Illionois Press, 1965, pp. 26-35.

7 Information and photograph kindly provided by David Mills; O'Dea, 'Simplicity and Survival', p. 21.

8 J.W. Withers, 'St John's Over a Century Ago' (1907), cited in *When Was That*, edited by H.M. Mosdell, St John's, 1974, and quoted in R.R. Rostecki, 'Early Court Houses of Newfoundland', in *Early Canadian Court Houses*, compiled by Margaret Carter, Ottawa: Parks Canada, 1983, p. 22. The 1806 law did allow building by permit—a kind of precursor to the building permit system of today.

9 Reeves and Crofton are both quoted in C. Grant Head, *Eighteenth-Century Newfoundland: A Geographer's Perspective*, Carleton Library, No. 99, Toronto: McClelland and Stewart, 1976, p. 230.

10 Information on the 1824 decision was kindly provided by Shane O'Dea.

11 John Guy to Master Slaney, Counsel of the Newfoundland Plantation, 16 May 1611; quoted in D.W. Prowse, *A History of Newfoundland*, London, 1895, reprinted Belleville: Mika, 1972, p. 126. See also Gillian T. Cell, 'The Cupid's Cove Settlement: A Case Study of the Problems of Early Colonisation', in G.M. Story, ed., *Early European Settlement and Exploitation in Atlantic Canada: Selected Papers*, St John's: Memorial University of Newfoundland, 1982, pp. 97-114; Gillian T. Cell, *English Enterprise in Newfoundland, 1577-1660*, Toronto: University of Toronto Press, 1970, pp. 53-80; Gillian T. Cell, *Newfoundland Discovered: English Attempts at Colonisation 1610-1630*, London: Hakluyt Society, 1982, pp. 6-7, 60 ff.; Robert A. Barakat, 'Archaeological Excavations at the Site of the Guy Colony', Ph.D. thesis, Memorial University of Newfoundland, 1973; for Guy's instructions to provide wood, see A.J.H. Richardson, 'The Earliest Wood-processing Industry in North America, 1607-23', *APT Bulletin*, 5:4, 1973, p. 82.

12 Other buildings were constructed at Cupid's, including Governor Guy's mansion (called Sea Forest House), mills, and farm buildings. Archaeological excavations in the early 1970s were inconclusive.

13 Quoted in Prowse, *Newfoundland*, p. 129.

14 J.R. Harper, 'In Quest of Lord Baltimore's House at Ferryland', *Canadian Geographical Journal*, 61:3 (September 1960), pp. 106-13; Robert A. Barakat, 'Some Comments on Lord Baltimore's House at Ferryland, Newfoundland', *Newfoundland Quarterly*, 72:4 (1976), pp. 17-27 (including several hypothetical reconstructions); Paul O'Neill, 'Lord Baltimore and the Avalon Plantation', unpublished paper, Newfoundland Historical Society, 1977; Raymond Lahey, 'Avalon: Lord Baltimore's Colony in Newfoundland', in Storey, *Early European Settlement*, pp. 116-31. The recent excavations are described in James A. Tuck, 'Looking for the Colony of Avalon', *Archaeology in Newfoundland & Labrador*, edited by Jane Sproull Thomson and Callum Thomson, St John's: Newfoundland Museum, 1985, pp. 378-96; James A. Tuck and Douglas Robbins, 'A Glimpse at the Colony of Avalon', *Archaeology in Newfoundland & Labrador 1985*, St John's, 1986, pp. 237-49; and James A. Tuck, 'Excavations at Ferryland, Newfoundland—1986', *Archaeology in Newfoundland & Labrador 1986*, St John's, 1989, pp. 296-307. The Fitzhugh

map is reproduced in Prowse, *Newfoundland*, p. 111. The house is indicated as 'Lady Kirk's' on James Yonge's map of Ferryland of the 1660s, reprinted in *The Journal of James Younge (1647-1721)*, edited by F.N.L. Poynter, London: Longman's Green, 1963. Peter Pope provided information in correspondence with Fern M. Graham and the author.

15 Centre-hall plans appeared in the seventeenth-century plantation houses of tidewater Virginia, although without the second row of rooms at the rear. This alternative in the Mansion House is possible if we understand Wynne's overall dimensions of 44 by 15 feet (13.4 x 4.6 m) to have included the hall, the entry, and the intended parlour—but that only the cellar beneath the parlour was completed before Christmas, and the parlour itself was added later. Although this would give the Mansion House an unprecedented (and therefore unlikely) proto-Georgian plan, it would explain the recent discovery of foundations near the supposed site of the house measuring at least 50 by 20 feet (15.3 by 6.1 m). Excavations at Ferryland in 1986 uncovered the stone foundations of a large building, from the early years of the colony, that had been in domestic use and measured at least 50 by 20 feet, larger than the 44 by 15 feet that had previously been accepted as the overall dimensions of Lord Baltimore's house. The walls were constructed of locally available slate, carefully fitted together, and were about 2 feet thick. See Tuck, 'Excavations, 1986', pp. 297-9; Morrison, *Early American Architecture*, p. 141.

16 Colonial Office Records, quoted in Barakat, 'Comments', p. 19.

17 Paul O'Neill, *The Oldest City: The Story of St John's, Newfoundland*, I, Erin: Press Porcepic, 1975, p. 43; Shane O'Dea, *The Domestic Architecture of Old St John's*, Pamphlet No. 2, St John's: Newfoundland Historical Society, 1974; Keith Matthews, *Lectures on the History of Newfoundland 1500-1830*, St John's: Memorial University of Newfoundland, 1973, p. 121-4; Head, *Newfoundland*, p. 82; Michael Hugo-Brunt, 'Two Worlds Meet: A Survey of Newfoundland Settlement', *Plan*, 5:1, 1964, pp. 22-36; 5:2, 1964, pp. 59-83.

18 O'Neill, *Oldest City*, I, p. 50.

19 John Downing, *A Brief Narrative*, 1676, in Colonial Papers, Newfoundland; quoted in Prowse, *Newfoundland*, p. 206, and in O'Dea, *Domestic Architecture*, n.p.

20 The letter was discovered by Raymond Lahey and published in O'Dea, 'Vertical-log Construction', p. 57.

21 Olaf Uwe Janzen, 'New Light on the Origins of Fort William at St. John's, Newfoundland, 1693-1696', *Newfoundland Quarterly*, 83:2, Fall 1987, pp. 24-31; Head, *Newfoundland*, pp. 45-6.

22 Public Record Office, London, CO 194/6; cited in O'Dea, *Domestic Architecture*, p. [7].

23 Maps in the National Map Collection, National Archives of Canada, particularly H2/140/St John's/1751, H1/140/St John's/1762, and H3/140/St John's/1779; also Board of Ordinance, map of St John's Town, 1728, Public Archives of Newfoundland and Labrador, redrawn and described in R. Cole Harris and Geoffrey J. Matthews, *Historical Atlas of Canada*, I, Toronto: University of Toronto Press, [1987], pl. 27. Edward H. Dahl kindly provided copies of these and other maps.

24 Head, *Newfoundland*, pp. 230-1; original in the PRO London.

25 Ibid., p. 231; original in the PRO London.

26 *Evening Telegram*, St John's, 18 March 1881; cited in O'Dea, *Domestic Architecture*, p. [10].

27 1 George IV, ch 51; cited in Hugo-Brunt, 'Newfoundland Settlement', p. 62.

28 Harold Kalman, 'A Bright Light in Old St John's', *Canadian Heritage*, December 1993-January 1984, pp. 34-6; Jean M. Ball et al., *A Gift of Heritage: Historic Architecture of St John's*, St John's: Newfoundland Historic Trust, 1975, no. 35; Sheppard, Burt and Associates et al., *St John's: Heritage Conservation Area Study*, St John's, 1976, pp. 76-91; *Call for Proposals: The A.H. Murray Buildings, Beck's Cove, St John's*, St John's: St John's Heritage Foundation, 1977.

29 O'Dea, 'Simplicity and Survival', p. 21; Mills, 'Folk Architecture', p. 86; John J. Mannion, *Irish Settlements in Eastern Canada: A Study of Cultural Transfer and Adaptation*, Toronto: University of Toronto Press, 1974, p. 147. See also Gerald L. Pocius, 'Architecture on Newfoundland's Southern Shore: Diversity and the Emergence of New World Forms', *SSAC Bulletin*, 8:2 (June 1983), pp. 12-19 (reprinted from Camille Wells, ed., *Perspectives in Vernacular Architecture*, Williamsburg: Vernacular Architecture Forum, 1982, pp. 217-32).

30 Mills, 'Folk Architecture', p. 86; O'Dea, 'Simplicity and Survival,' p. 22. For Quebec parallels, O'Dea cites Georges Gauthier-Larouche, *Evolution de la Maison rurale traditionelle dans la Région du Québec*, Québec: Les Presses de l'Université Laval, 1974, p. 67.

31 Pocius, 'Architecture', p. 14.

32 Examples are illustrated in Pocius, 'Southern Shore', pp. 14-17; O'Dea, 'Simplicity and Survival', p. 25. Mannion, *Irish Settlements*, pp. 120-2, suggests the original use of the linhay for livestock. The house and the barn have been attached in other regions of North America, including Maine and other parts of northeastern New England.

33 Mills, 'Folk Architecture', pp. 81-8.

34 Lewis Anspach, *A History of the Island of Newfoundland*, London: T. and J. Allman, 1819, pp. 467-8; quoted in Mills, 'Folk Architecture', p. 88.

35 O'Dea, 'Simplicity and Survival', pp. 23-5.

36 Pocius, 'Southern Shore', pp. 14-15.

37 George Kapelos and Douglas Richardson, 'Townscape in a Tickle: Greenspond', *Canadian Antiques Collector*, 10:2, March-April 1975, pp. 24-9. The quotation is from Robert Lowell, *New Priest in Conception Bay*, 1858, and is cited on p. 25.

38 Ron Brown, *Ghost Towns of Canada*, Toronto: Cannonbooks, 1987, pp. 20-7.

39 J.T. Smith, 'The Eighteenth Century English Background to Newfoundland Houses', *Dimensions of Canadian Architecture*, SSAC Selected Papers, edited by Shane O'Dea and Gerald L. Pocius, 6, 1983, pp. 34-43.

40 O'Dea, 'Simplicity and Survival', p. 25; Jean M. Ball et al., *Ten Historic Towns: Heritage Architecture in Newfoundland*, St John's: Newfoundland Historic Trust, 1978, no. 7.

41 O'Dea, *Domestic Architecture*, p. [13].

42 Pocius, 'Southern Shore', p. 14, citing advertisements for imported house frames that appeared in St John's newspa-

pers between 1814 and 1830. Frames from New England were being shipped to Newfoundland in the 1770s: C. Grant Head, *Eighteenth Century Newfoundland: A Geographer's Perspective*, Toronto: McClelland and Stewart, 1976, p. 116.

43 Smith, 'Background', p. 41.

44 Pocius, 'Southern Shore', p. 13; Ball et al., *Ten Historic Towns*, no. 3.

45 Ball et al., *Ten Historic Towns*, no. 10.

46 Martin Bowe, 'Commissariat House', *Canadian Antiques Collector*, 10:2, March-April 1975, pp. 59-61; *Commissariat House*, brochure, St John's: Department of Culture, Recreation & Youth, n.d. The house, a provincial historic site, is open to the public.

47 F.A. O'Dea, 'Government House', *Canadian Antiques Collector*, 10:2, March-April 1975, pp. 48-51.

48 Bowe, 'Commissariat House', p. 59.

49 O'Dea, 'Simplicity and Survival', p. 31.

50 Rostecki, 'Court Houses', p. 21.

51 Ibid., p. 22.

52 Ibid., pp. 23-4. Kough is discussed in O'Dea, *Domestic Architecture*.

53 *The Story of the Colonial Building*, St John's: Government of Newfoundland and Labrador, 1972; *Gift of Heritage*, no. 22; *The Colonial Building*, brochure, St John's: Department of Culture, Recreation, and Youth, n.d. See also the entry by Shane O'Dea on Purcell in *DCB* VIII, pp. 725-6.

54 Rostecki, 'Court Houses', pp. 25-6 and fig. 3.

55 O'Dea, 'Simplicity and Survival', pp. 29-30.

56 George A. Rawlyk says that there were 17,000 to 20,000 inhabitants by 1776: *Nova Scotia's Massachusetts: A Study of Massachusetts-Nova Scotia Relations, 1630-1734*, Montreal: McGill-Queen's Press, 1973, p. 222. Esther Clark Wright maintains that the population was 21,000 and 24,000: *Planters and Pioneers*, Hantsport, NS: Lancelot Press, 1978, p. 27. The parallels between Nova Scotia and New England buildings is the theme of Alan Gowans, 'New England Architecture in Nova Scotia', *Art Quarterly*, 25:1, Spring 1962, pp. 6-33. The pre-Loyalist migrations are plotted in Harris and Matthews, *Historical Atlas*, I, pl. 31.

57 Elizabeth Pacey, *Georgian Halifax*, Hantsport, NS: Lancelot Press, 1987, p. 14. See also Elizabeth Pacey, *Historic Halifax*, Toronto: Hounslow Press, 1988; *Founded Upon a Rock: Historic Buildings of Halifax and Vicinity Standing in 1967*, 2nd edition, Halifax: Heritage Trust of Nova Scotia, 1971; Louis W. Collins, *In Halifax Town*, Halifax, privately published, 1975; D.C. Harvey, 'Halifax 1749-1949', *Canadian Geographical Journal*, 38:1, 1949, pp. 6-37; L.B. Jenson, *Vanishing Halifax*, [Halifax:] Petheric Press, 1968.

58 Pacey, *Georgian Halifax*, pp. 14-16.

59 Ibid., pp. 14-15 (written 27 July 1749).

60 Peter L. McCreath and John G. Leefe, *A History of Early Nova Scotia*, Tantallon: Four East Publications, 1982, p. 201; see also pp. 196-230.

61 Thomas B. Akins, ed., *Selections from the Public Documents of the Province of Nova Scotia*, Halifax, 1869, p. 586; quoted in Winthrop Pickard Bell, *The 'Foreign Protestants' and the Settlement of Nova Scotia*, Toronto: University of Toronto Press, 1961, p. 345, n. 8a.

62 Pacey, *Georgian Halifax*, p. 15; McCreath and Leefe, *Early Nova Scotia*, pp. 201, 206; Collins, *Halifax*, pp. xv-xvi.

63 Cummings, *Framed Houses*, p. 60.

64 *Gentleman's Magazine*, September 1749; cited in Douglas Richardson, 'Georgian and Victorian Churches', unpublished manuscript.

65 For other early views of Halifax, see Mary Sparling, *Great Expectation: The European Vision in Nova Scotia 1749-1848*, Halifax: Mount St Vincent University, 1980.

66 Philip McAleer, 'St Paul's, Halifax, Nova Scotia, and St Peter's, Vere Street, London, England', *JCAH*, 7:2 (1984), pp. 113-37; J. Philip McAleer, 'St Paul's Church, Halifax: The Contracts for Building the Addition and New Steeple, 1812-1813', *Nova Scotia Historical Review*, 9:2 (1989), pp. 89-105; J. Philip McAleer, 'The Chancel of St Paul's Anglican Church, Halifax, Nova Scotia: Form Follows Convenience?' *RACAR*, 17:1 (1990), pp. 46-53. Reginald V. Harris, *The Church of Saint Paul in Halifax, Nova Scotia: 1749-1949*, Toronto: Ryerson, 1949; Pacey, *Georgian Halifax*, pp. 72-5; Pacey, *Historic Halifax*, pp. 80-1; Allan Duffus et al., *Thy Dwellings Fair: Churches of Nova Scotia, 1750-1830*, Hantsport, NS: Lancelot Press, 1982, pp. 46-52; Nathalie Clerk, *Palladian Style in Canadian Architecture*, Ottawa: Parks Canada, 1984, pp. 62-4; *Founded Upon a Rock*, pp. 12-13.

67 Beckles Wilson, *Nova Scotia: The Province That Has Been Passed By*, rev. ed., London, 1912, p. 46; cited in McAleer, 'St Paul's', n. 39.

68 The quotations are all from letters written to the Society for the Propagation of the Gospel in Foreign Parts (SPG), and are included in Harris, *St Paul*, and in the other sources cited in the previous notes.

69 McAleer, 'St Paul's', pp. 125-7.

70 The church can be seen before some of these changes were made in Short's illustrations; in a watercolour of c. 1819 reproduced in McAleer, 'St Paul's', p. 117; and in a daguerreotype of 1853 by Daniel J. Smith, now in the Nova Scotia Museum, published in Jim Burant, 'Pre-Confederation Photography in Halifax, Nova Scotia', *JCAH*, 4:1 (Spring 1977), fig. 4.

71 Duffus et al., *Thy Dwellings Fair*, pp. 60-3; John de Visser and Harold Kalman, *Pioneer Churches*, Toronto: McClelland and Stewart, 1976, pp. 112-13; Pacey, *Georgian Halifax*, pp. 76-7; Pacey, *Historic Halifax*, pp. 138-9.

72 Bell, 'Foreign Protestants', pp. 95-102; see also William Plaskett, comp., *Lunenburg: An Inventory of Historic Buildings . . .*, Lunenburg: Town of Lunenburg, 1984; Lunenburg Heritage Society, *A Walk Through Old Lunenburg*, Lunenburg, 1979; Bill Plaskett, *Understanding Lunenburg's Architecture*, Lunenburg: Lunenburg Heritage Society, 1979.

73 Bell, 'Foreign Protestants', p. 437.

74 Mather Byles DesBrisay, *History of the County of Lunenburg*, Halifax: James Bowes, 1870, pp. 25-6; also Mather Byles DesBrisay, *Lunenburg*, 2nd ed., Toronto: William Briggs, 1895 (reprinted Belleville: Mika, 1972), p. 38; cited in Bell, 'Foreign Protestants', p. 437.

75 Bell, 'Foreign Protestants', p. 437 and p. 443, n. 8a.

76 Beamish Murdoch, *A History of Nova Scotia or Acadie*, Halifax: James Barnes, 1866, II, p. 145.

77 Plaskett, *Lunenburg*, p. 10; *South Shore: Seasoned Timbers*,

vol. II, Halifax: Heritage Trust of Nova Scotia, 1974, pp. 56-7. The origins of the Lunenberg bump—which usually projects over the entrance and sometimes extends to the ground floor as a projecting bay—may be either cultural or structural, and remain the subject of speculation; see H.W. Schade, 'The Lunenberg Hump,' *SSAC Bulletin*, 9:2, July 1984, pp. 10-11. Peter Ennals states that the walls of the Romkey house are constructed of logs; Ennals, 'The Yankee Origins of Bluenose Vernacular Architecture', *The American Review of Canadian Studies*, 12:2, Summer 1982, p. 21, n. 16.

78 Pictou Heritage Society, *Wood and Stone*, n.p: Petheric Press, 1972, n.p. See J.M. Bumsted, 'Scottish Emigration to the Maritimes 1770-1815: A New Look At an Old Theme', *Acadiensis*, 10:2, 1981, pp. 65-85.

79 Irene L. Rogers, *Charlottetown: The Life in Its Buildings*, Charlottetown: The Prince Edward Island Museum and Heritage Foundation, 1983, pp. 1-4, 211-19. See also Douglas Baldwin and Thomas Spira, *Gaslights and Vagabond Cows: Charlottetown in the Victorian Era*, Charlottetown: Ragweed Press, 1988. For Plaw, see Irene L. Rogers, 'John Plaw 1745-1820', *Society for the Study of Architecture in Canada: Selected Papers*, III, Ottawa, 1982, pp. 68-81; entry in Howard Colvin, *A Biographical Dictionary of British Architects 1600-1840*, London: John Murray, 1978, pp. 642-3.

80 J. David Wood, 'Grand Design on the Fringes of America: New Towns for British North America', *Canadian Geographer*, 26:3, Fall 1982, pp. 243-55; Gilbert Stelter, 'The Classical Ideal: Cultural and Urban Form in Eighteenth-Century Britain and America', *Journal of Urban History*, 10:4, August 1984, pp. 351-82; John Reps, *Town Planning in Frontier America*, Princeton: Princeton University Press, 1969, pp. 155-80.

81 Rawlyk, *Nova Scotia's Massachusetts*, p. 199. See also James E. Candow, *The New England Planters in Nova Scotia*, Ottawa: Environment Canada—Parks, 1986.

82 Rawlyk, *Nova Scotia's Massachusetts*, pp. 219-21.

83 Edwin Crowell, *History of Barrington Township*, Yarmouth: n.p., 1923, p. 105.

84 Heather Davidson, 'Private Lives from Public Artifacts: The Architectural Heritage of Kings County Planters', in Margaret Conrad, ed., *They Planted Well: New England Planters in Maritime Canada*, Fredericton: Acadiensis Press, 1988, pp. 250-3. The Stephen Loomer house (*c.* 1764) at Habitant, near Canning, is similar in its appearance, evolution, and social history; see Daniel E. Norris, 'An Examination of the Stephen Loomer House, Habitant, Kings County, Nova Scotia', in Conrad, *They Planted Well*, pp. 236-48.

85 Allen Penney, *The Simeon Perkins House: An Architectural Interpretation 1767-1987*, Curatorial Report No. 60, Halifax: Nova Scotia Museum, 1987; summarized in Penney, 'A Planter House: The Simeon Perkins House, 1766-7, Liverpool, Nova Scotia', in Conrad, *They Planted Well*, pp. 218-35. See also *South Shore*, pp. 86-7; *Simeon Perkins House*, brochure, Halifax: Nova Scotia Museum, n.d.

86 See the references in note 110 below.

87 Crowell, *Barrington*, pp. 79, 121. See also I.F. MacKinnon, *Settlement and Churches in Nova Scotia, 1749-1776*, Montreal, 1930.

88 The Crowe house is discussed in Crowell, *Barrington*,

p. 124; the Sargent house is illustrated there opposite p. 113.

89 Evelyn M. Richardson, *Barrington's Old Meeting Place*, n.p., 1986; John R. Stevens, 'The Old Meeting House, Barrington, Nova Scotia', report, National Historic Parks and Sites Service, 1966; Duffus et al., *Thy Dwellings Fair*, p. 67; *South Shore*, pp. 134-5; Crowell, *Barrington*, pp. 270-1; *The Old Meeting House 1765, Barrington, Nova Scotia*, brochure, Halifax: Nova Scotia Museum, n.d.

90 Elizabeth G. West, 'Every Day Life in Pre-Loyalist New Brunswick', *Collections of the New Brunswick Historical Society*, 18, 1963, p. 34; de Visser and Kalman, *Pioneer Churches*, pp. 82-3—the Sandown Meeting House is illustrated on pp. 76-8.

91 George B. MacBeath, 'New England Settlements in Pre-Loyalist New Brunswick', *Collections of the New Brunswick Historical Society*, 18, 1963, pp. 28-9; W. Gordon Ross, '1762 and Thereafter', *Collections of the New Brunswick Historical Society*, 18, 1963, pp. 40-2; W.O. Raymond, 'Colonel Alexander McNutt and the Pre-Loyalist Settlements of Nova Scotia', *Transactions of the Royal Society of Canada*, Section II, 1911, p. 83; James Hannay, 'The Maugerville Settlement, 1763-1824', *Collections of the New Brunswick Historical Society*, 1, Saint John, 1894; Frederic Addison McGrand, *Backward Glances at Sunbury and Queens*, Fredericton: New Brunswick Historical Society, 1967.

92 Gowans, 'New England Architecture', p. 8.

93 de Visser and Kalman, *Pioneer Churches*, pp. 94; James Hannay, 'The Maugerville Settlement, 1763-1824', *Collections of the New Brunswick Historical Society*, I, Saint John, 1894, pp. 127-35; McGrand, *Sunbury and Queens*, p. 56.

94 Neil MacKinnon, *This Not Unfriendly Soil: The Loyalist Experience in Nova Scotia, 1783-1791*, Montreal: McGill-Queen's University Press, 1986.

95 W.H. Nelson, 'The Loyalist Legacy', *Acadiensis*, 15:1, Autumn 1985, p. 141.

96 Richard J. Diubaldo, 'The Early History of St Andrews, New Brunswick, 1784-1814', Manuscript Report No. 134, Ottawa: Parks Canada, 1966, pp. 69-97; Roger Nason, 'St. Andrews', *Canadian Collector*, 10:3, May-June 1975, pp. 73-5; M. Aileen Smith and Phoebe Anne Magee, eds, *St Andrews Heritage Handbook*, St Andrews: St Andrews Heritage Trust, n.d.

97 Diubaldo, 'St Andrews', pp. 72-3, 82; Bill Spray, 'History Still Being Made on St Croix Island', *Atlantic Advocate*, 72:4, December 1981, p. 13.

98 The plan of St Andrews is reproduced in *St Andrews Heritage Handbook*, p. 3. Several New England towns with square blocks are illustrated in Reps, *Town Planning*, pp. 100-25.

99 W.O. Raymond, ed., *Winslow Papers, 1776-1826*, Saint John, 1911, p. 201; cited in Diubaldo, 'St Andrews', p. 78.

100 Ibid.

101 Nason, 'St. Andrews', p. 73. The Canadian Inventory of Historic Building estimated the construction date to be later, *c.* 1785, but the house has not yet been carefully investigated.

102 Stuart Smith, 'Architecture in New Brunswick', *Canadian Antiques Collector*, 10:3, May-June 1975, p. 38; Mary

Pacey, ed., *Walking Tours of Fredericton, the Colonial Capital*, Fredericton: Fredericton Heritage Trust, 1977, no. 9; Isabel Louise Hill, *Fredericton, New Brunswick, British North America*, Fredericton: York-Sunbury Historical Society, 1968, pp. 138-9, 144.

103 Hill, *Fredericton*, pp. 4, 39; W. Austin Squires, *History of Fredericton: The Last 200 Years*, Fredericton: City of Fredericton, 1980, p. 22; Pacey, *Walking Tours*, no. 39.

104 Marion Robertson, *King's Bounty: A History of Early Shelburne, Nova Scotia*, Halifax: Nova Scotia Museum, 1983, pp. 33-5, 51, and *passim*.

105 Ken Gilmour, 'Shelburne's Ross-Thomson House', *Canadian Collector*, 19:1, January/February 1984, pp. 13-15. See also Glen Hancock, 'How They Fared in Nova Scotia', *Atlantic Advocate*, April 1983, pp. 33-9.

106 Governor Parr to Lord Shelburne, 16 December 1783, in *Collections of the New Brunswick Historical Society*, 8, p. 254; cited in Robertson, *King's Bounty*, p. 117.

107 Marston to I. Maudiuit, September 1784, in *Collections of the New Brunswick Historical Society*, 8, p. 268; cited in Robertson, *King's Bounty*, p. 117.

108 Robertson, *King's Bounty*, p. 118-20, relying on a number of sources, including J.R. Campbell, *History of the County of Yarmouth, N.S.*, Saint John: J. & A. McMillan, 1876, p. 87; Colonel Robert Morse, 'Report, 1784', NAC; Charles Bruce Fergusson, *Clarkson's Mission to America, 1791-1792*, Public Archives of Nova Scotia, Publication No. 11, 1971, p. 50; J. Rippon, ed., *Baptist Annual Register*, 1, London, 1793, pp. 473-83.

109 Gilmour, 'Ross-Thomson House'; *Ross-Thomson House, Shelburne, Nova Scotia*, brochure, Halifax: Nova Scotia Museum, n.d.

110 Ennals, 'Yankee Origins', pp. 5-21, uses the terms 'Cape Cod Cottage' (or 'Cape Cod House') and 'Colonial Georgian House'; Allen Penney, 'Halifax and Nova Scotian Architecture', *Transactions of the Royal Society of Canada*, Series 4, Vol. 19, 1981, pp. 105-12, uses the terms 'single-storey house' and 'Neoclassical brick house'; and Peter Ennals and Deryck Holdsworth, 'Vernacular Architecture and the Cultural Landscape of the Maritime Provinces—A Reconnaisance', *Acadiensis*, 10:2, Spring 1981, pp. 86-106, introduce six types of houses: the others are the hall-and-parlour house, the Maritime vernacular house (a centre-gabled nineteenth-century form), the 'temple' or end-gable entry house, and the thatch-roofed house. Allen Penney, in his *Houses of Nova Scotia*, Halifax: Formac Publishing and the Nova Scotia Museum, 1989, pp. 52-9, changes his earlier terminology and uses 'Neo-Classical' as an umbrella term that includes both kinds of houses. Joann Latremouille, *Pride of Home: The Working Class Housing Tradition in Nova Scotia 1749-1949*, Hantsport: Lancelot Press, 1986, pp. 17, 27-9, describes the 'original Nova Scotia cottage' and the 'Georgian working-class house' that correspond to the Cape Cod cottage.

111 For the American origins of the Cape Cod cottage, see Ernest Allen Connolly, 'The Cape Cod House: An Introductory Study', *JSAH*, 19, 1960, pp. 47-56.

112 Ennals and Holdsworth, 'Vernacular Architecture', p. 90.

113 Ennals, 'Yankee Origins', fig. 3.

114 *Seasoned Timbers*, I: *A Sampling of Historic Buildings*

Unique to Western Nova Scotia, Halifax: Heritage Trust of Nova Scotia, 1972, pp. 114-15; *North Hills Museum*, pamphlet, Halifax: Nova Scotia Museum, n.d; also Alan Gowans, *Building Canada: An Architectural History of Canadian Life*, Toronto: Oxford University Press, plate 49.

115 See Alan Gowans, *Styles and Types of North American Architecture: Social Function and Cultural Expression*, New York: Icon Editions, 1992, pp. 19-21, 49-75. The Palladian and Georgian styles are described in Nathalie Clerk, *Palladian Style in Canadian Architecture*, Studies in Archaeology, Architecture and History, Ottawa: Parks Canada, 1984; and 'The Palladian Style' in Leslie Maitland, Jacqueline Hunter, and Shannon Ricketts, *A Guide to Canadian Architecture Styles*, Peterborough; Broadview Press, 1992, pp. 21-9. The best account of British eighteenth-century architecture remains John Summerson, *Architecture in Britain 1530 to 1830*, 6th ed., Harmondsworth: Penguin Books, 1977. A good account of the styles' entry into the US is in William H. Pierson and William H. Jordy, *American Buildings and Their Architects*, vol. 1, *The Colonial and Neo-Classical Styles*, New York: Oxford University Press, 1987.

116 *Seasoned Timbers*, pp. 65-7; Arthur W. Wallace, 'Acacia Grove: Colonial Architecture in the Maritimes, Part III', *JRAIC*, September 1932, pp. 208-12; Wallace, *Early Buildings in Nova Scotia*, plates 47-9; *Prescott House, Starr's Point, Nova Scotia*, brochure, Halifax: Nova Scotia Museum n.d.; Susan Buggey, 'Some Considerations Regarding the Prescott House, Starr's Point, Nova Scotia', report, National Historic Parks and Sites Branch, 1973; Clerk, *Palladian Style*, p. 137. See the entry on Prescott by Susan Buggey in *DCB* VIII, pp. 709-11.

117 'Emily', 'Prescott's Garden', *Novascotian*, 29 September 1845, p. 310; 'Editorial Journeyings', *Times*, 8 September 1846, p. 282; both kindly provided by Susan Buggey.

118 Robert Cunningham and John B. Prince, *Tamped Clay and Saltmarsh Hay: Artifacts of New Brunswick*, Fredericton: Brunswick Press, 1976, pp. 50-1; Smith and Magee, *St Andrews*, p. 20. Susan Buggey provided the reference to the Naval Commissioner's house.

119 David Goss, 'Saint John's Loyalist House', *Atlantic Advocate*, 75:2, October 1984, pp. 45-9; 'Loyalist House', *Collections of the New Brunswick Historical Society*, No. 17, 1961, pp. 6-7; 'Loyalist House', *The Loyalist Gazette*, Autumn 1968, p. 4; Margaret Coleman, 'Loyalist House...', Agenda paper, Historic Sites and Monuments Board of Canada, Ottawa, *c*. 1991; Clerk, *Palladian Style*, p. 140.

120 Irene L. Rogers, 'Heritage in Building', *Canadian Antiques Collector*, 8:1, March-April 1973, pp. 26, 29; H.M. Scott Smith, *The Historic Houses of Prince Edward Island*, Erin, Ontario: Boston Mills Press, 1990, p. 120.

121 Gowans, 'New England Architecture', p. 22.

122 Power, 'Some Historic Buildings', p. 52; Cunningham and Prince, *Tamped Clay*, pp. 52-3; Clerk, *Palladian Style*, p. 136. The house is now a museum owned by the province of New Brunswick and operated by the Westmorland Historical Society.

123 Cora Greenaway, 'The Black-Binney House', *Canadian Collector*, 14:3, May/June 1979, pp. 40-42; Pacey, *Georgian Halifax*, p. 113; Pacey, *Historic Halifax*, pp. 48-9;

Founded Upon a Rock, pp. 26-7; Wallace, *Early Buildings in Nova Scotia*, plate 36.

124 *Seasoned Timbers*, pp. 16-17; *Uniacke House*, brochure, Halifax: Nova Scotia Museum, n.d; Arthur W. Wallace, 'Mount Uniacke: Colonial Architecture in the Maritimes', *JRAIC*, 7:8, August 1930, pp. 277-82; Wallace, *Early Buildings*, plates 57-60; Will R. Bird, 'Some Historic Houses of Nova Scotia', *Canadian Geographical Journal*, 57:2, August 1958, pp. 62-3; Clerk, *Palladian Style*, p. 132. The reference to Keillor is in Cunningham and Prince, *Tamped Clay*, p. 52.

125 Pacey, *Georgian Halifax*, p. 137.

126 Pacey, *Georgian Halifax*, pp. 128-36; Pacey, *Historic Halifax*, pp. 4809; *Founded Upon a Rock*, pp. 26-7; Janet Wright, *Architecture of the Picturesque in Canada*, Studies in Archaeology, Architecture and History, Ottawa: Parks Canada, 1984, pp. 137-9; John Harris, *Sir William Chambers*, London: Zwemmer, 1970, pp. 36-7.

127 Pacey, *Georgian Halifax*, pp. 137-46; *Founded Upon a Rock*, pp. 16-17; Gowans, *Building Canada*, plate 90. The clock was heavily restored in the 1960s.

128 J.S. Martell, *The Romance of Government House*, Halifax: Provincial Secretary and Queen's Printer, reprinted 1965; J.S. Martell, *Government House*, Bulletin No. 4, Halifax: Public Archives of Nova Scotia; Pacey, *Georgian Halifax*, pp. 30-7; Pacey, *Historic Halifax*, pp. 46-7; *Founded Upon a Rock*, pp. 18-19; Wallace, *Early Buildings in Nova Scotia*, pl. 35; Clerk, *Palladian Style*, p. 89.

129 Charles Bruce Fergusson, 'Isaac Hildrith (c. 1741-1807): Architect of Government House, Halifax', *Dalhousie Review*, 51:4, Winter 1970-71, pp. 510-16; see also the entry on Hildrith by M. Susan Whiteside in *DCB* V, pp. 423-4.

130 Pacey, *Georgian Halifax*, p. 32.

131 Cited in ibid., p. 43.

132 Entry by Susan Buggey on Merrick in *DCB* XVI, pp. 500-1; Shirley B. Elliott, *A History of Province House*, Halifax: [Government of Nova Scotia], revised 1973; Pacey, *Georgian Halifax*, pp. 43-55; *Founded Upon a Rock*, pp. 22-3; Wallace, *Early Buildings*, plates 1-14; Clerk, *Palladian Style*, p. 84.

133 Mary Peck, 'Construction of the New Brunswick Legislative Building in Fredericton', *Selected Papers, SSAC*, Ottawa, 1981, pp. 82-94; Clerk, *Palladian Style*, pp. 85-6; entry on John Elliott Woolford by Donald C. Mackay in *DCB* IX, pp. 849-50; C.A. Hale, 'Early Court Houses of the Maritime Provinces', in Carter, *Early Canadian Court Houses*, pp. 37-77.

134 Mary K. Cullen, *A History of the Structure and Use of Province House, Prince Edward Island*, Manuscript Report No. 211, Ottawa: Parks Canada, 1977; Rogers, *Charlottetown*, pp. 3-4; Clerk, *Palladian Style*, p. 88, 90; Marianne Morrow, 'The Builder: Isaac Smith and Early Island Architecture', *Island Magazine*, 18, Fall-Winter 1985, pp. 17-23.

135 Duffus et al., *Thy Dwellings Fair*, pp. 81-6 (which cites Bishop Inglis); Wallace, *Early Buildings*, plates 32-4; *Seasoned Timbers*, pp. 74-5.

136 Duffus et al., *Thy Dwellings Fair*, pp. 91-7; Wallace, *Early Buildings*, plates 23-8.

137 Duffus et al., *Thy Dwellings Fair*, pp. 107-14, *Seasoned Timbers*, pp. 56-7; 'The Old Covenanters' Church, Grand Pré, Nova Scotia', Historic Sites and Monuments Board reports, Ottawa, *c.* 1969.

138 Duffus et al., *Thy Dwellings Fair*, pp. 145-9.

139 Ibid., pp. 99-106; *Founded Upon a Rock*, pp. 14-15.

CHAPTER 4 **Classicism in Upper and Lower Canada**

1 For early Loyalist settlement and ideology, see particularly Robert S. Allen, ed., *The Loyal Americans: The Military Role of the Loyalist Provincial Corps and their Settlement in British North America 1775-1784*, Ottawa: National Museums of Canada, 1983; Jane Errington, *The Lion, the Eagle, and Upper Canada*, Kingston: McGill-Queen's University Press, 1987; Gerald M. Craig, *Upper Canada: The Formative Years 1784-1841*, Toronto: McClelland and Stewart, 1963; Philip Dunning, 'Loyalists: The First Year', *Canadian Collector*, Sept.-Oct. 1984, pp. 25-8. The migration of one group is traced in Larry Turner, *Voyage of a Different Kind: The Associated Loyalists of Kingston and Adolphustown*, Belleville: Mika, 1984.

2 Craig, *Upper Canada*, p. 5; Bruce Wilson, *As She Began: An Illustrated Introduction to Loyalist Ontario*, Toronto: Dundurn Press, 1981, p. 75.

3 John van Nostrand, 'Roads and Planning: The Settlement of Ontario's Pickering Township, 1789-1975', *City Magazine*, 3:2, December 1977, p. 16; J. David Wood, 'Grand Design on the Fringe, of Empire: New Towns for North America, *Canadian Geographer*, 26:3, Fall 1982, pp. 244-5; Gilbert A. Stelter, 'Urban Planning and Development in Upper Canada', in Woodrow Borah, Jorge Hardoy, and Gilbert A. Stelter, eds, *Urbanization in the Americas: The Background in Comparative Perspective*, Ottawa: National Museum of Man, 1980, pp. 143-6. Lord Dorchester's models were published as *Additional Rules and Regulations for the Conduct of the Land Office Department*, Quebec, 25 August 1789.

4 Quoted in Craig, *Upper Canada*, p. 21.

5 Kent Gerecke, 'The History of Canadian City Planning', *City Magazine*, 2:3-4 (Summer 1976), p. 18; Craig, *Upper Canada*, pp. 27, 34-5.

6 Holland to Haldimand, 26 June 1783, cited in J. Douglas Stewart and Ian E. Wilson, *Heritage Kingston*, Kingston: Agnes Etherington Art Centre, 1973, p. 36. The buildings of Kingston are described in Margaret Angus, *The Old Stones of Kingston: Its Buildings Before 1867*, Toronto: University of Toronto Press, 1966; Architectural Review Committee, City of Kingston, *Buildings of Architectural and Historical Significance*, 7 vols, Kingston: City of Kingston, 1971-91.

7 Fern Mackenzie, 'Wooden Architecture in Kingston 1783-1900', unpublished paper, Queen's University, 1983; Angus, *Old Stones*, pp. 7, 37. The structure of the Coffin house is described in Dana Johnson, *Reports on Selected Buildings in Kingston, Ontario*, I, Ottawa: Parks Canada, 1977, p. 6; cited in Mackenzie, p. 4. The Cartwright watercolour (in which the house is seen at the left and is identified as that of Archdeacon George Okill Stuart, a later resident) is reproduced in Stewart and Wilson, *Heritage Kingston*, no. 112. The moving and destruction of the

Lines house are illustrated in Brian S. Osborne and Donald Swainson, *Kingston: Building on the Past*, Westport: Butternut Press, 1988, p. 333. Information on the Lines house, and the illustration, were kindly provided by Fern Mackenzie Graham.

8 The plan, drawn in 1815, is identified as depicting 'a house formerly belonging to the Honorable Richard Cartwright'; the house was demolished in 1820. It is reproduced in Stewart and Wilson, *Heritage Kingston*, pp. 44-5. Cartwright's reminiscences are from [Richard Cartwright,] *Letters of an American Loyalist in Upper Canada...*, Quebec, 1810; cited in Errington, *The Lion*, p. 3.

9 [François-Alexandre-Frédéric,] Duc de la Rochefoucauld-Liancourt, *Travels Through the United States of North America, the Country of the Iroquois, and Upper Canada in the Years 1795, 1796, and 1797*, I, London, 1799, pp. 275, 279, 286.

10 John Ross Robertson, ed., *The Diary of Mrs John Graves Simcoe*, Toronto, 1911, p. 110.

11 The building is discussed in Stewart and Wilson, *Heritage Kingston*, pp. 46-7. The presence of the tradesmen in Kingston is cited in Verschoyle Benson Blake and Ralph Greenhill, *Rural Ontario*, Toronto: University of Toronto Press, 1969, p. 18.

12 Rochefoucauld, *Travels*, I, p. 287 and R.A. Preston, *Kingston Before the War of 1812*, Toronto, 1959, p. xc, both cited in Stewart and Wilson, *Heritage Kingston*, p. 46; and petition of the parishioners to Lieut-Gov. Sir Peregrine Maitland, 31 May 1825, cited in Allan J. Anderson, *The Anglican Churches of Kingston*, Kingston: n.p., 1963, p. 20. For St George's, see Jennifer McKendry, 'The Architects of St George's Cathedral, Kingston', *Queen's Quarterly*, 95:3, Autumn 1988, pp. 699-713; J. Douglas Stewart, 'George Browne's Influence: The Architectural Heritage of St George's', in *St George's Cathedral: Two Hundred Years of Community*, ed. by Donald Swainson, Kingston: Quarry Press, 1991, pp. 29-63; Angus, *Old Stones*, pp. 24-5; Architectural Review Committee, *Buildings*, I, pp. 12-16.

13 McKendry, 'St George's', p. 701.

14 Buckingham, *Canada, Nova Scotia, New Brunswick . . .*, London, 1843, pp. 62-3; cited in Stewart and Wilson, *Heritage Kingston*, pp. 97-8. Stephen A. Otto kindly provided the attribution to Okill.

15 Kelly Crossman and Dana Johnson, 'Early Court Houses of Ontario', in Margaret Carter, comp., *Early Canadian Court Houses*, Studies in Archaeology, Architecture and History, Ottawa: Parks Canada, 1983, p. 106-7; Campbell's remark—in the *Kingston Chronicle*, 8 September 1826, p. 1—is cited on p. 106. See also Marion MacRae and Anthony Adamson, *Cornerstones of Order: Courthouses and Town Halls of Ontario, 1784-1914*, Toronto: Clarke, Irwin, 1983, p. 39.

16 Stewart and Wilson, *Heritage Kingston*, p. 98.

17 The entry by S.R. Mealing on Sir David William Smith (Smyth) in *DCB* VII, pp. 811-14. Smith returned to England in 1802 and subsequently resigned all his appointments.

18 Rochefoucauld, *Travels*, I, p. 254, quoted in Susan Algie, 'Reports on Selected Buildings in Ontario', Manuscript Report Series No. 390, Ottawa: Parks Canada, 1979, p. 68. The house was vacated when Smith moved to York in 1797-8. The 'Plans and Elevations of the House of the Hon. D.W. Smith by Robert Pilkington, 1798, reproduced

by W. Chewitt, York, 28 April 1802', are in the Baldwin Room of the Metropolitan Toronto Library. The caption on the drawings (which were copied in 1802) has wrongly been interpreted as meaning that Captain Pilkington designed the house at the later date.

19 Dana Johnson and Nathalie Clerk, 'Homewood, Maitland, Ontario', manuscript on file, Ottawa: Parks Canada, c. 1982; Nathalie Clerk, *Palladian Style in Canadian Architecture*, Studies in Archaeology, Architecture and History, Ottawa: Parks Canada, 1984, p. 111; Marion MacRae and Anthony Adamson, *The Ancestral Roof: Domestic Architecture of Upper Canada*, Toronto: Clarke, Irwin, 1963, pp. 9-10, 14; Stephen A. Otto and Richard M. Dumbrille, *Maitland: 'A Very Neat Village Indeed'*, Erin: Boston Mills Press, 1985, pp. 26-7; Elva R. McGaughey, 'A Report for the Heritage Trust: Homewood and the Jones Family', Toronto: Ontario Heritage Foundation, 1977. A number of Georgian houses are illustrated in John Blumenson, *Ontario Architecture: A Guide to Styles and Building Terms, 1784 to the Present*, Toronto: Fitzhenry & Whiteside, 1990, pp. 5-12.

20 Ralph Greenhill, Ken MacPherson, and Douglas Richardson, *Ontario Towns*, Ottawa: Oberon, 1974, no. 2; MacRae and Adamson, *Ancestral Roof*, pp. 16-17, 21-4. The upper windows were enlarged into French doors at a later date, and the sidelights by the door may have been inserted at the same time.

21 Clerk, *Palladian Style*, p. 108; MacRae and Adamson, *Ancestral Roof*, pp. 56-8; 'Fraserfield: A Brief History and Building Description', unpublished paper, Toronto: Ontario Heritage Foundation, n.d.

22 Clerk, *Palladian Style*, p. 114; Harold Kalman and John Roaf, *Exploring Ottawa*, Toronto: University of Toronto Press, 1983, p. 153; Michael Newton, 'Maplelawn 1831-1979', manuscript on file, Ottawa: National Capital Commission, 1979; Harry Walker and Olive Walker, *Carleton Saga*, Ottawa: Carleton County Council, 1968, pp. 13, 110-12.

23 Mendel Mesick Cohen, 'Fort Johnson: Historic Structures Report', Washington: US Department of the Interior, 1978; Lois M. Feister, New York State Office of Parks, Recreation and Historic Preservation, kindly provided information on the three Johnson houses; Clerk, *Palladian Style*, pp. 124-5.

24 G.P. deT. Glazebrook, *The Story of Toronto*, Toronto: University of Toronto Press, 1971, p. 16. Eric Wilfrid Hounsom, *Toronto in 1810*, Toronto: Ryerson Press, 1970, pp. 54 ff.

25 Eric Arthur, *Toronto: No Mean City*, third edition, revised by Stephen A. Otto, Toronto: University of Toronto Press, 1986, pp. 21, 22-3; Clerk, *Palladian Style*, p. 101.

26 Quotation from Dickson's land petition of 1796 cited in Algie, 'Reports', p. 60; the entry by Bruce G. Wilson on Dickson in *DCB* VII, pp. 250-2 (which establishes the date); Clerk, *Palladian Style*, p. 100; information kindly provided by Bruce Wilson.

27 Algie, 'Reports', p. 61. The claim is found in NAC, Government of Canada, Department of Finance, vol. 3740, file 1, claim 5, abstract no. 4: claim of William Dickson.

28 Arthur Oswald, 'Winslow Hall, Buckinghamshire', *Country Life*, 110:2849, 24 August 1951; pp. 572-6; Hugh Morrison, *Early American Architecture*, New York: Oxford University Press, 1952, pp. 305, 528-30.

29 T. Ritchie, *Canada Builds 1867-1967*, Toronto: University of Toronto Press, 1969, pp. 206-7.

30 Marilyn Litvak, *The Grange: A Gentleman's House in Upper Canada*, Toronto: Art Gallery of Ontario, 1988; William Dendy and William Kilbourn, *Toronto Observed: Its Architecture, Patrons, and History*, Toronto: Oxford University Press, 1986, pp. 22-4; Arthur/Otto, *No Mean City*, p. 54; the entry by John Lownsbrough on D'Arcy Boulton in *DCB* VI, pp. 78-80.

31 Eagle House is illustrated in Colin Amery, ed., *Three Centuries of Architectural Craftsmanship*, London: Architectural Press, 1977, pl. 24; Gibbs's house is illustrated in William H. Pierson and William H. Jordy, *American Buildings and Their Architects*, vol. 1, *The Colonial and Neoclassical Styles*, New York: Oxford University Press, 1987, p. 128. Marble Hill and Danson Hill are illustrated in John Summerson, *Architecture in Britain 1530 to 1830*, 6th ed., Harmondsworth: Penguin Books, 1977, plates 143(A) and 150(A).

32 William Dendy, *Lost Toronto: Images of the City's Past*, Toronto: McClelland and Stewart, 1993, p. 37; Arthur/Otto, *No Mean City*, p. 44; Clerk, *Palladian Style*, pp. 102-4; G.M. Craig's entry on Strachan in *DCB* IX, pp. 751-65.

33 Both are illustrated in Morrison, *Early American Architecture*, pp. 284, 424.

34 Dendy and Kilbourn, *Toronto Observed*, pp. 28-9; Arthur/Otto, *No Mean City*, pp. 44, 61; Clerk, *Palladian Style*, p. 104.

35 Larry Tuner with John J. Stewart, *Perth: Tradition and Style in Eastern Ontario*, Toronto: Natural Heritage/Natural History Inc., 1992, pp. 35, 49; James Kinloch, 'Perth—Solidity and Style', *Canadian Geographical Journal*, 79:2, August 1969, pp. 40-51. For the Matheson house, see Greenhill et al., *Ontario Towns*, no. 31.

36 Harold D. Kalman, John J. Stewart, and Denis St-Louis, *The Summit, Perth: Restoration Report*, Ottawa, 1980.

37 Greenhill et al., *Ontario Towns*, plate 30. Domestic architecture in the region is described in Barbara A. Humphreys, 'The Architectural Heritage of the Rideau Corridor', *Canadian Historic Sites*, Occasional Papers in Archaeology and History, no. 10, Ottawa: Parks Canada, 1974, pp. 11-71; and R.H. Hubbard, 'The Land of the Stone Gable', *RACAR*, 2:1, 1975, pp. 23-32.

38 [Stephen A. Otto,] 'Ontario Heritage Foundation: McMartin House, Perth, Restoration Report', No. 6, Toronto: Ontario Heritage Foundation, November 1974, pp. 3-5; MacRae and Adamson, *Ancestral Roof*, pp. 62-5.

39 W.R. Riddell, 'The Wilson-Lyon Duel', in Edward Shortt, ed., *Perth Remembered*, Perth: Perth Museum, 1967, pp. 56-9; Jean S. McGill, *A Pioneer History of the County of Lanark*, n.p: 1968, pp. 137-41; Turner, *Perth*, pp. 35-40.

40 Turner, *Perth*, p. 52.

41 Harold Shurtleff, *The Log Cabin Myth*, Cambridge: Harvard University Press, 1939; John I. Rempel, *Building with Wood and Other Aspects of Nineteenth-century Building in Central Canada*, 2nd ed., Toronto: University of Toronto Press, 1980, pp. 26-32; Rempel, 'The History and Development of Early Forms of Building Construction in Ontario', *Ontario History*, 52:4, 1960, pp. 235-44, and 53:1, 1961, pp. 1-35; George Richardson, 'The Loyalist Search for Shelter 1784-1824', *Historic Kingston*, 25, 1977, pp. 45-51. For log building in general, see William C. Wonders, 'Log

Dwellings in Canadian Folk Architecture', *Annals of the American Association of Geographers*, 69:2, June 1979, pp. 187-207.

42 The different kinds of notching are described and illustrated in Terry G. Jordan, *Texas Log Buildings: A Folk Architecture*, Austin: University of Texas Press, 1978. Dovetails are discussed in Rempel, *Wood*, p. 51, and in R.-L. Séguin, *La Maison en Nouvelle-France*, Bulletin no. 226, Ottawa: Musée nationale du Canada, 1968, p. 35.

43 Blake and Greenhill, *Rural Ontario*, p. 7.

44 Illustrated in Greenhill et al., *Ontario Towns*, figure 2.

45 Rempel, *Wood*, pp. 48-9; Commonwealth Historic Resource Management Limited, 'Frontier Home', research paper prepared for the History Hall, Canadian Museum of Civilization, 1988.

46 Mary Quayle Innis, ed., *Mrs Simcoe's Diary*, Toronto: Macmillan, 1965, p. 160 (23 January 1795).

47 Henry Scadding, *Toronto of Old: Collections and Recollections*, Toronto, 1873, p. 436; citation kindly provided by Stephen A. Otto.

48 Arthur/Otto, *No Mean City*, pp. 17-20; Janet Wright, *Architecture of the Picturesque in Canada*, Studies in Archaeology, Architecture and History, Ottawa: Parks Canada, 1984, pp. 45-6.

49 Alexander Jackson Davis, *Rural Residences...*, New York: New York University, 1837; reprinted New York, Da Capo Press, 1980, not paginated.

50 Illustration from Rosemary Neering and Stan Garrod, *Life of the Loyalists*, Growth of a Nation Series, Toronto: Fitzhenry & Whiteside, 1975, p. 29. Series of early farmsteads have been reconstructed at the Ontario Agricultural Museum, near Milton, and at Upper Canada Village, near Morristown.

51 Mary Lou Evans, ed., *Mississauga's Heritage: The Formative Years 1798-1879*, Mississauga: City of Mississauga, 1983, pp. 36-7, 44-5.

52 Humphreys, 'Rideau Corridor', p. 17.

53 Ian Bowering, *Inverarden Regency Cottage Museum: A History 1816-1984*, Cornwall: Stormont, Dundas and Glengarry Historical Society, 1984; Ian Bowering, 'Inverarden: a Nor'Wester's Country Estate', *Canadian Collector*, 17:3, May-June 1982, pp. 41-3; Robert J. Burns, 'Inverarden: Retirement Home of Fur Trader John McDonald of Garth', *History and Archaeology*, No. 25, Ottawa: Parks Canada, 1979; Wright, *Picturesque*, p. 50; MacRae and Adamson, *Ancestral Roof*, pp. 82-5. See also Steven Parissien, *Regency Style*, Washington: The Preservation Press, National Trust for Historical Preservation, 1992.

54 Commonwealth Historic Resource Management Limited, 'Riverest: Preservation Report', Perth, 1984; Wright, *Picturesque*, p. 66; MacRae and Adamson, *Ancestral Roof*, pp. 88-9, 94-5.

55 W. John McIntyre, 'Diffusion and Vision: A Case Study of the Ebenezer Doan House in Sharon, Ontario', *Material History Bulletin*, 22, Fall 1985, pp. 11-20.

56 Mary-Etta Macpherson, 'Re-birth of a Canadian Classic', *Canadian Homes and Gardens*, 17, September 1940, pp. 31-40; MacRae and Adamson, *Ancestral Roof*, pp. 45-8; Eric R. Arthur, *The Early Buildings of Ontario*, Toronto: University of Toronto, 1938, pp. 10-11; Eric R. Arthur, 'The Architectural Conservancy of Ontario and the Barnum House,

Grafton', unpublished paper, n.d; Margaret McBurney and Mary Byers, *Homesteads, Early Buildings and Families from Kingston to Toronto*, Toronto: University of Toronto Press, 1979, pp. 168-9; information was also provided by Herb Stovel, Richard Unterman, Gorman Young, and Stephen A. Otto.

57 Leslie Maitland, *Neoclassical Architecture in Canada*, Studies in Archaeology, Architecture and History, Ottawa: Parks Canada, 1984, p. 100; the date is given in McBurney and Byers, *Homesteads*, pp. 144-5.

58 John Mactaggart, *Three Years in Canada...*, I, London: Henry Colburn, 1829; quoted in MacRae and Adamson, *Ancestral Roof*, pp. 34-5.

59 Brian Coffey, 'Factors Affecting the Use of Construction Materials in Early Ontario', *Ontario History*, 77:4, December 1985, pp. 301-18. Census data are also analysed in W.R. Wightman, 'Construction Materials in Colonial Ontario 1831-61', in F.H. Armstrong et al., eds, *Aspects of Nineteenth-Century Ontario*, Toronto: University of Toronto Press, 1974, pp. 114-34.

60 Blake and Greenhill, *Rural Ontario*, pp. 24-5. The acts were 43 George III, c. 12 (1803); 47 George III, c. 7 (1807), and 51 George III, c. 8 (1811); *Revised Statutes of Upper Canada*, I, Toronto: Queen's Printer, 1849. See also Olga Bishop, ed., *Publications of the Province of Upper Canada...*, Toronto: Ontario Ministry of Citizenship and Culture, 1984, p. 160.

61 William Cattermole, *The Advantages of Emigration to Canada*, London: Simpkin and Marshall, 1831, p. 133; cited in Coffey, 'Factors', p. 312. The statistic that follows is also cited by Coffey.

62 An attempt to categorize Ontario house-types by form—'free of...preconceptions' such as 'period style or folk-cultural tradition'—is presented in Darrell A. Norris, 'Vetting the Vernacular: Local Varieties in Ontario's Housing', *Ontario History*, 74:2, June 1982, pp. 66-94. Similar efforts have been made in C.F.J. Whebell, 'A Typology of 19th Century Ontario Rural Vernacular Houses', unpublished paper, 1980.

63 Rempel, *Wood*, pp. 190-3; Eric Arthur and Dudley Witney, *The Barn: A Vanishing Landmark in North America*, Toronto: McClelland and Stewart, 1972, pp. 58-83.

64 Rempel, *Wood*, pp. 194-9 (including pre-restoration photographs); Arthur and Witney, *The Barn*, pp. 85-8; Blake and Greenhill, *Rural Ontario*, Plate 3.

65 Simcoe to the Duke of Portland, 27 February 1796; cited in Eric Arthur, *From Front Street to Queen's Park: The Story of Ontario's Parliament Buildings*, Toronto: McClelland and Stewart, 1979, p. 33; see also Arthur/Otto, *No Mean City*, pp. 27-30; Edith G. Firth, ed., *The Town of York, 1793-1815*, I, Toronto: Champlain Society, 1962, p. 24.

66 Cited in Arthur, *Front Street*, pp. 31-2.

67 Arthur, *Front Street*, p. 33.

68 The second Parliament Building is illustrated in Arthur, *Front Street*, p. 36. In 1818 John Soane sent designs from London for a 'Government House for Upper Canada', but they were not executed: Dorothy Stroud, *The Architecture of Sir John Soane*, London: Studio, 1961, p. 165.

69 Dendy and Kilbourn, *Toronto Observed*, pp. 25-7; Susan Wagg, 'A Critical Look at Bank Architecture', in *Money Matters: A Critical Look at Bank Architecture*, New York: McGraw-Hill, 1990, pp. 33-4; Arthur/Otto, *No Mean City*, p. 58.

70 Arthur, *Front Street*, pp. 39-47; Arthur/Otto, *No Mean City*, pp. 60-1; Dendy, *Lost Toronto*, pp. 52-5. See also Maitland, *Neoclassical Architecture*, p. 134, note 35. Additional information was provided by Stephen A. Otto, who will show that the wings were built in 1830-2 (to designs by James G. Chewett) in his forthcoming book on Ontario architecture to 1914.

71 Arthur/Otto, *No Mean City*, p. 64; Dendy, *Lost Toronto*, pp. 59-61; Clerk, *Palladian Style*, p. 91. This building, like the third Parliament Buildings, was also formerly attributed to J.G. Chewett.

72 Both are seen in a familiar 1835 lithograph of King Street by Thomas Young; illustrated in Arthur/Otto, *No Mean City*, p. 46.

73 E.R. Arthur, 'The History and Architecture of the Fabric', in C.H.A. Armstrong, *The Honourable Society of Osgoode Hall*, Toronto: Clarke, Irwin, 1952, pp. 49-60; Arthur/Otto, *No Mean City*, pp. 101-8 (Robertson is cited on p. 101); MacRae and Adamson, *Cornerstones of Order*, pp. 45-50, 120-8; Crossman and Johnson, 'Court Houses', pp. 109-10; Dana Johnson and Leslie Maitland, 'Osgoode Hall, 140 Quebec Street East, Toronto, Ontario', unpublished manuscript, Ottawa: Parks Canada, n.d.; Clerk, *Palladian Style*, p. 92; Dendy and Kilbourn, *Toronto Observed*, pp. 71-2.

74 The Herbert house, Wrotham Park, and Somerset House are illustrated in Summerson, *Architecture in Britain*, plates 134B, 151, 168; the buildings in Newport are illustrated in Terence Davis, *The Architecture of John Nash*, London: Studio, 1960, figs. 127, 138; Dendy and Kilbourn, *Toronto Observed*, pp. 72-7.

75 See the discussion by Douglas Richardson in Greenhill et al., *Ontario Towns*, n.p. (with figure 10).

76 MacRae and Adamson, *Cornerstones of Order*, pp. 59-62; Crossman and Johnson, 'Court Houses of Ontario', pp. 112-13; Kelly Crossman, *The Early Court Houses of Ontario*, Manuscript Report Series, No. 195, I, Ottawa: Parks Canada, 1978, pp. 179-92.

77 Douglas Richardson, 'The Original Building and Its Architect', in George Baird et al., '999 Queen: A Collective Failure of Imagination', *City Magazine*, 2:3-4, Summer 1976, pp. 45-9; Arthur/Otto, *No Mean City*, pp. 71, 91, 251.

78 See, for example, MacRae and Adamson, *Ancestral Roof*; Blumenson, *Ontario Architecture*; Clerk, *Palladian Style*; and Maitland, *Neoclassical Architecture*.

79 Douglas Stewart, 'Architecture for a Boom Town: The Primitive and the Neo-Baroque in George Browne's Kingston Buildings', in Gerald Tulchinsky, ed., *To Preserve and Defend: Essays on Kingston in the Nineteenth Century*, Montreal: McGill-Queen's University Press, 1976, pp. 37-61; Ian E. Wilson et al., *Kingston City Hall*, Kingston: City of Kingston, 1974; Angus, *Old Stones*, pp. 20-3; Kingston, *Buildings of Architectural Significance*, I, pp. 3-9; MacRae and Adamson, *Cornerstones of Order*, pp. 77-86; G.E. Mills, 'Monumental Town and City Halls in Canada', in Marc de Caraffe et al., *Town Halls of Canada*, Studies in Archaeology, Architecture and History, Ottawa: Environment Canada—Parks, 1987, pp. 46-50. A sketch by Howard is illus-

trated, and its progeny discussed, in Richardson, 'Original Building', p. 46.

80 Sir Richard Bonnycastle, *Canada and the Canadians*, London, 1846, II, pp. 280-1; cited in Stewart, 'Architecture for a Boom Town', p. 53.

81 'Proposal for the Rebuilding of Osgoode Hall', 1855, National Archives of Canada; cited in Maitland, *Neoclassical Architecture*, p. 51.

82 Johnson and Maitland, 'Osgoode Hall'; and the entry by Frederic H. Armstrong and Peter Baskerville on Cumberland, in *DCB* XI, pp. 225-9.

83 Stuart to the Society for the Propagation of the Gospel, 1788; cited in Marion MacRae and Anthony Adamson, *Hallowed Walls: Church Architecture of Upper Canada*, Toronto: Clarke, Irwin, 1975, pp. 9-15. Anthony Adamson kindly provided additional information on the church, including portions of an unpublished research paper by Verschoyle Benson Blake (Ontario Ministry of Culture and Communications, plaque files).

84 MacRae and Adamson, *Hallowed Walls*, pp. 41-7; Clerk, *Palladian Style*, p. 78; Greenhill et al., *Ontario Towns*, no. 27; John de Visser and Harold Kalman, *Pioneer Churches*, Toronto: McClelland and Stewart, 1976, pp. 120-1, 132-3. See also J.G. Harkness, *Stormont, Dundas and Glengarry: A History 1784-1945*, Oshawa: Mundy-Goodfellow, 1946, pp. 51-2, 120.

85 *Upper Canada Village: 'Ontario's Living Heritage'*, Morrisburg: St Lawrence Parks Commission, n.d., n.p.

86 Information from correspondence with Edwin McDonald of St Andrews West, 1974-5, cited in de Visser and Kalman, *Pioneer Churches*, pp. 133-4; MacRae and Adamson, *Hallowed Walls*, pp. 20-6.

87 MacRae and Adamson, *Hallowed Walls*, pp. 28-30.

88 Ibid., pp. 30-4; Greenhill et al., *Ontario Towns*, no. 4; de Visser and Kalman, *Pioneer Churches*, pp. 118-19, 132.

89 de Visser and Kalman, *Pioneer Churches*, pp. 125-7, 143-4; MacRae and Adamson, *Hallowed Walls*, pp. 184-9; James L. Hughes, *Sketches of the Sharon Temple and of Its Founder David Willson*, Toronto York Pioneer and Historical Society, *c.* 1918; *Children of Peace*, Toronto, York Pioneer and Historical Society, n.d.; Gilbert Jones Doane, comp., *The Ebenezer Doane Family*, privately printed, 1961 (kindly provided by G. Kit. Doan).

90 Illustrated in MacRae and Adamson, *Hallowed Walls*, p. 66.

91 For St Andrew's, see MacRae and Adamson, *Hallowed Walls*, pp. 85-7; Arthur/Otto, *No Mean City*, p. 47. The Hardenhuish church is illustrated in Marcus Whiffen, *Stuart and Georgian Churches: The Architecture of the Church of England outside London, 1603-1837*, London: Batsford, 1947-8, fig. 73.

92 MacRae and Adamson, *Hallowed Walls*, pp. 87-90; Maitland, *Neoclassical Architecture*, p. 109. Holy Trinity, Marylebone, is illustrated in Stroud, *Soane*, fig. 187.

93 *Journal* of François Baillairgé, Québec Inventaire des biens culturels, fonds Gérard Morisset, p. 179; cited in Luc Noppen, 'François Baillairgé, architecte', in David Karel, Luc Noppen, and Claude Thibault, *François Baillairgé et son oeuvre (1759-1830)*, Quebec: Groupe de recherche en art du Québec de l'Université Laval, 1975, p. 71; André Giroux, 'Early Court Houses of Quebec', in Carter, *Court*

Houses, p. 78 (which attributes the design to Hall); Clerk, *Palladian Style*, p. 79 (which cites the passage about the Tuscan order); Luc Noppen, Claude Paulette, Michel Tremblay, *Québec: trois siècles d'architecture*, n.p: Libre Expression, 1979, pp. 286-7. See also Gérard Morisset, 'François Baillairgé (1759-1830)', *Technique*, 23, 1948, pp. 89-94, 187-91.

94 Clerk, *Palladian Style*, p. 80; Giroux, 'Court Houses', p. 78; Nathalie Clerk, 'Le Style Palladien au Québec', *Vie des Arts*, 28:112, September-November 1983, pp. 84-5.

95 Edward Allen Talbot, *Five Years' Residence in the Canadas . . .*, 2 vols, London, 1824, I, p. 71, cited in Wagg, 'Critical Look', pp. 32-3; Jean-Claude Marsan, *Montreal in Evolution*, Montreal: McGill-Queen's University Press, 1981, pp. 150-1. The attribution to Andrew White was kindly provided by Stephen A. Otto.

96 Clerk, *Palladian Style*, p. 121; Noppen et al., *Québec*, pp. 60-1; Christina Cameron and Monique Trépanier, *Vieux Québec: son architecture intérieure*, Mercury Series, no. 40, Ottawa: National Museum of Man, 1986, pp. 301-2; the entry by F. Murray Greenwood and James H. Lambert on Jonathan Sewell in *DCB* VII, pp. 782-90; the entry by James H. Lambert on Sewell in *CE* III, p. 1985.

97 Anna Van Buskirk LeBaron and Judith LeBaron Kerr, 'Joshua Copp House', *Canadian Antiques and Art Review*, 1:1, September 1979, pp. 14-19.

98 Thomas R. Millman, *Jacob Mountain: First Lord Bishop of Quebec*, Toronto, 1947; cited in de Visser and Kalman, *Pioneer Churches*, p. 134. Basil Clarke, *Anglican Cathedrals Outside the British Isles*, London: SPCK, 1958, pp. 8, 52.

99 Robe's report is cited in A.H. Crowfoot, *A Perambulation of the English Cathedral, Quebec*, Quebec, 1947, pp. 7, 20; and also in Frederick C. Würtele, 'The English Cathedral of Quebec', *Transactions of the Literary and Historical Society of Quebec*, 20, 1889-91, pp. 76-84. See also Alan Gowans, *Building Canada: An Architectural History of Canadian Life*, Toronto: Oxford University Press, 1966, pp. 72-4, plates 81-2; Clerk, *Palladian Style*, p. 71; John Bland, 'The Architecture After the Middle of the 18th Century', in *Three Centuries of Architecture in Canada*, Montreal: Federal Publications Service—Georges Le Pape, 1971, pp. 81-3; Luc Noppen, *Les Églises du Québec (1600-1850)*, Quebec: Éditeur officiel du Québec/Fides, 1977, pp. 158-161; Noppen et al., *Québec*, pp. 162-3; A.J.H. Richardson, 'Guide to the Architecturally and Historically Most Significant Buildings in the Old City of Quebec . . .', *APT Bulletin*, 2:3-4, 1970, p. 35.

100 Pierson, *Colonial and Neoclassical Styles*, pp. 131-40.

101 Noppen et al., *Québec*, p. 275.

102 Joseph Bouchette, *The British Dominions in North America . . .*, I, London: Longman et al., 1832, p. 245.

103 Marsan, *Montreal*, pp. 131, 153-7; Clerk, *Palladian Style*, p. 72; Frank Dawson Adams, *A History of Christ Church Cathedral, Montreal*, Montreal: Burton's, 1941, pp. 46-74; John Andre, *William Berczy: Co-Founder of Toronto*, Toronto: Borough of York, 1967, pp. 71-4. Andre bases his attribution to Berczy on *Canadian Magazine*, 1825, p. 530; Adams bases his on Newton Bosworth, ed., *Hochelaga Depicta*, Montreal, 1839, whose description is taken from the one in *Canadian Magazine*. See the entry on Berczy by Ronald J. Stagg in *DCB* V, pp. 70-2.

104 Benjamin Silliman, *Remarks Made on a Short Tour Between Hartford and Quebec, in...1819*, 2nd ed., New Haven: Converse, 1824. p. 369; Talbot, *Five Years' Residence in the Canadas*, p. 69; Bouchette, *British Dominions*, I, p. 222; all cited in Marsan, *Montreal*, p. 153.

105 Clerk, *Palladian Style*, p. 76; Maitland, *Neoclassical Architecture*, pp. 110-1; Noppen et al., *Québec*, pp. 164, 166-7; Noppen, *Églises*, 166, 182.

106 C.P.C. Downman, ed., *A Concise, Chronological and Factual History of St Stephen's Anglican Church, Chambly, Que.*, privately published, 1970; Peter Noone, 'St Stephen's Anglican Church, Chambly, P.Q.—Historical Report', agenda paper, Historic Sites and Monuments Board of Canada, 1970; Clerk, *Palladian Style*, p. 73; de Visser and Kalman, *Pioneer Churches*, p. 135.

107 Noppen, *Églises*, pp. 29-40, 80-3, 114-17; Gérard Morisset, 'L'influence de l'abbé Conefroy sur notre architecture religieuse', *Architecture—Bâtiment—Construction*, 8:82, February 1953, pp. 36-9; Morisset, 'Old Churches of Quebec', *Canadian Geographical Journal*, 43:3, September 1951, pp. 104-12. Conefroy's specifications and plans were seen by Morisset at the diocesan archives in Quebec, but have since disappeared.

108 Noppen, *Églises*, pp. 40-3, 76-9, 136-9.

109 Luc Noppen, 'Le Rôle de l'Abbé Jérôme Demers dans l'élaboration d'une architecture néo-classique au Québec', *JCAH*, 2:1, Summer 1975, pp. 19-33 (with bibliography on Demers); Gowans, *Building Canada*, pp. 56-7; Gérard Morisset, 'Une Figure inconnue: Jérôme Demers', *La Patrie*, 22 March 1953, pp. 36-7.

110 See Alan Gowans, 'Thomas Baillairgé and the Québecois Tradition of Church Architecture', *Art Bulletin*, 34, 1952, pp. 117-37.

111 Noppen, *Églises*, pp. 94-7; Luc Noppen and John R. Porter, *Les Églises de Charlesbourg et l'architecture religieuse du Québec*, Civilization du Québec, no. 9, Quebec: Ministère des Affaires culturelles, 1972.

112 All are illustrated in Noppen, *Églises*. See also Gowans, 'Thomas Baillairgé'.

113 *Le Canadien*, 17 July 1843; cited in Gowans, 'Thomas Baillairgé', p. 134.

114 Luc Noppen, *Notre-Dame de Québec*, Quebec: Éditions du Pélican, 1974, pp. 205-34; Noppen, *Églises*, pp. 162-5.

115 Maitland, *Neoclassical Architecture*, p. 43; Noppen et al., *Québec*, pp. 262-6; Michel Desgagnés, *Les Édifices parlementaires depuis 1792*, 2nd ed., Québec: Les Publication du Québec, 1992, pp. 15-19.

CHAPTER 5 Building for Communications, Defence, and Commerce

1 See also Norman R. Ball, ed., *Building Canada: A History of Public Works*, Toronto: University of Toronto Press, 1988; Harold Kalman and Douglas Richardson, 'Building for Transportation in the Nineteenth Century', *JCAH*, 3:1-2, Fall 1976, pp. 21-43; George P. deT. Glazebrook, *A History of Transportation in Canada*, Toronto: Ryerson, 1938; Thomas F. McIlwraith, 'Transportation in Old Ontario: Some Themes', in McIlwraith, ed., *By River, Road and Rail: Transportation in Old Ontario*, Toronto: Ontario Museum Association, 1984, pp. 1-16.

2 Brian Hallett, 'Beacons on the Lakes', *The Archivist*, 13:3, May-June 1986, p. 18.

3 John Johnston, 'Canada's First Lighthouse', *The Atlantic Advocate*, 76:6, February 1986, pp. 26-7; Edward F. Bush, 'The Canadian Lighthouse', *Canadian Historic Sites: Occasional Papers in Archaeology and History*, No. 9, Ottawa: Parks Canada, 1974, p. 32-4; Edward F. Bush, 'Beacon Lights on Canadian Shores', *Canadian Geographical Journal*, 90:2, February 1975, pp. 22-9; Dudley Witney, *The Lighthouse*, Toronto: McClelland and Stewart, 1975, pp. 100-1; Marilyn Smith and Bonnie Robertson, 'Lighthouses', *Canadian Antiques Collector*, 10:2, March-April 1975, pp. 80-1. For lighthouses elsewhere, see F. Holland, *American Lighthouses: Their Illustrated History Since 1716*, Brattleboro, Vt, 1972; A.D. Stevenson, *The World's Lighthouses Before 1820*, London: Oxford University Press, 1959. David M. Baird kindly offered help with this section.

4 Bush, 'Lighthouse', pp. 34-6; Will R. Bird, in 'Nova Scotia Has Many Lights', *Canadian Geographical Journal*, 54:3, March 1957, pp. 94-7, states that 'much of the building material came from Boston'; Witney, *Lighthouse*, p. 102.

5 Margot Magee Sackett, 'Cape Spear', *Canadian Collector*, 17:5, September-October 1982, pp. 22-5; Bush, 'Lighthouse', p. 45; Witney, *Lighthouse*, pp. 76-7.

6 Donald Graham, *Keepers of the Light: A History of British Columbia's Lighthouses and Their Keepers*, Madeira Park, B.C: Harbour Publishing, 1985, pp. 12-34 and *passim* (quotation on p. 17); Bush, 'Lighthouse', pp. 76-7; Susan M. Lambeth and Susan L. Jeaune, *A History of Fisgard Lighthouse and the West Coast Lighthouse System*, Manuscript Report Series, No. 356, 2 vols, Ottawa: Parks Canada, 1980.

7 Graham, *Keepers of the Light*, pp. 226-42. See also Donald Graham, *Lights of the Inside Passage*, Madeira Park: Harbour Publishing, 1986.

8 See John P. Heisler, 'The Canals of Canada', *Canadian Historic Sites: Occasional Papers in Archaeology and History*, No. 8, Ottawa: Parks Canada, 1973; Robert F. Legget, *Canals of Canada*, Vancouver: Douglas, David and Charles, 1976; Robert Passfield, 'Waterways', in Ball, *Building Canada*, pp. 113-42.

9 Heisler, 'Canals', p. 14.

10 Ibid., pp. 17-19. See John C. Kendall, 'William Twiss, Royal Engineer, 1745-1827', Manuscript Report Series, No. 132, Ottawa: Parks Canada, *c.* 1966. Twiss was involved in a number of important construction projects, including the building of Fort Haldimand on Carleton Island, ten miles southeast of Kingston, in 1777; see C.C.J. Bond, 'The British Base at Carleton Island', *Ontario History*, 52:1, March 1960, pp. 1-16.

11 R.F. Legget's entry on the construction industry in *CE* I, p. 508; Frances M. Woodward, 'The Influence of the Royal Engineers on the Development of British Columbia', *BC Studies*, 24, Winter 1974-5, pp. 3-37; Beth Hill, *Sappers: The Royal Engineers in British Columbia*, Ganges, BC: Horsdal & Schubart, 1987; T.W.J. Connolly, *The History of the Corps of Royal Sappers and Miners*, 2 vols, London: Longman, Brown, Green and Longmans, 1855.

12 Heisler, 'Canals', pp. 26, 41; Legget, *Canals*, pp. 144-9; Passfield, 'Waterways', p. 115.

13 Robert F. Legget, *Rideau Waterway*, 2nd ed., Toronto: University of Toronto Press, 1986; Hamnett P. Hill, 'The Construction of the Rideau Canal, 1826-1832', *Ontario Historical Society, Papers and Records*, 22, 1925, pp. 117-24; Robert W. Passfield, *Building the Rideau Canal: A Pictorial History*, Toronto: Fitzhenry & Whiteside and Ottawa: Parks Canada, 1982.

14 Suzanne Plousos, 'Entrance to the Rideau', *Canadian Collector*, 20:4, July-August 1985, pp. 64-6; *Major's Hill and Nepean Point*, Ottawa: National Capital Commission, 1983.

15 See R.H. Hubbard, *Rideau Hall: An Illustrated History of Government House, Ottawa, from Victorian Times to the Present Day*, Montreal: McGill-Queen's University Press, 1977.

16 See R.H. Hubbard, 'The Land of the Stone Gable', *RACAR*, 2:1, 1975, pp. 23-32; Barbara A. Humphreys, 'The Architectural Heritage of the Rideau Corridor', *Canadian Historic Sites: Occasional Papers in Archaeology and History*, No. 10, Ottawa: Parks Canada, 1974, pp. 11-71.

17 Robert L. Fraser's entry on Merritt in *CE* II, p. 1338.

18 Legget, *Canals*, pp. 163-77; Heisler, 'Canals', pp. 32-6; Roberta M. Styran and Robert R. Taylor, 'The Welland Canal: Creator of a Landscape', *Ontario History*, 72:4, December 1980, pp. 210-29; Francis J. Petrie, 'First Welland Canal Opened Back in 1829', *Inland Seas*, 25:1, Spring 1969, pp. 62-3.

19 Passfield, 'Waterways', pp. 130-2; Robert Passfield, 'The Peterborough Lift Lock, Peterborough, Ontario', Historic Sites and Monuments Board of Canada, Agenda Paper 1979-28, pp. 579-601; Jean M. Cole, ed., *The Peterborough Hydraulic Lift Lock*, Peterborough, 1987; Norman R. Ball, 'Mind, Heart, and Vision', *Professional Engineering in Canada 1887 to 1987*, Ottawa: National Museum of Science and Technology, 1987.

20 Legget, *Canals*, pp. 30-3; Harry E. Chapman, 'The Shubenacadie Canal', *Atlantic Advocate*, 55:8, April 1965, pp. 45-8.

21 R. Cole Harris and John Warkentin, *Canada Before Confederation*, Toronto: Oxford University Press, 1974, p. 214. For road construction, see Larry McNally, 'Roads, Streets, and Highways', in Ball, *Building Canada*, pp. 30-58.

22 Don W. Thomson, *Men and Meridians: The History of Surveying and Mapping in Canada*, I, Ottawa: Queen's Printer, 1966, chapter 15; Thomas F. McIlwraith, 'The Adequacy of Rural Roads in the Era Before Railways: An Illustration from Upper Canada', *Canadian Geographer*, 14:4, 1970, pp. 344-60; Andrew F. Burghardt, 'The Origin and Development of the Road Network of the Niagara Peninsula, Ontario, 1770-1851', *Annals of the Association of American Geographers*, 59:3, September 1969, pp. 417-40; John van Nostrand, 'Roads and Planning: The Settlement of Ontario's Pickering Township, 1789-1975', *City Magazine*, 3:2, December 1977, p. 17; Jacob Spelt, *The Urban Development in South-Central Ontario*, Assen, The Netherlands: Van Gorcum, 1955; Edwin C. Guillet, *The Story of Canadian Roads*, Toronto: University of Toronto Press, 1966.

23 Cited in Guillet, *Roads*, p. 62; and McNally, 'Roads', p. 31.

24 McNally, 'Roads', p. 32.

25 Catharine Parr Traill, *The Backwoods of Canada* (1836), Toronto: McClelland and Stewart, 1966, pp. 46-7.

26 Anna E. Hoekstra and W. Gillies Ross, 'The Craig and Gosford Roads, Early Colonization Routes in the Eastern Townships of Quebec', *Canadian Geographical Journal*, 79:2, August 1969, pp. 52-7.

27 Anna Jameson, *Winter Studies and Summer Rambles in Canada*, II, London, 1838, p. 214; cited in Jeanne Hughes, ' "Barely Tolerable"—Travellers' Views of Ontario's Early Inns and Taverns', in McIlwraith, ed., *Transportation in Old Ontario*, p. 27.

28 Edward Allen Talbot, *Five Years Residence in the Canadas*, II, London, 1824, p. 10; cited in Hughes, '"Barely Tolerable"', p. 26.

29 Marilyn Miller, 'Straight Lines in Curved Space: Colonization Roads in Eastern Ontario', research paper, Toronto: Ministry of Culture and Recreation, 1978, p. 70.

30 James Marsh, 'Railway History', *CE* III, p. 1821; Christopher Andreae, 'Railways', in Ball, *Building Canada*, pp. 88-112.

31 Robert F. Legget, *Railroads of Canada*, Vancouver: Douglas, David & Charles, 1973; Nick Mika and Helma Mika with Donald M. Wilson, *Illustrated History of Canadian Railways*, Belleville: Mika, 1986; and *Rails Across Canada*, Montreal: VIA Rail Canada, 1986—all provide overview histories of Canadian railways, and the first two contain bibliographical references to studies of individual lines. For the Champlain and St Lawrence, see François Cinq-Mars, *L'Avènement du premier chemin de fer au Canada*, St-Jean-sur-Richelieu: Éditions Milles Roches, 1986. The station is discussed in John Thompson, 'Does the Original Champlain and St Lawrence Railway Station Still Exist?', *Canadian Rail*, 395, November-December 1986, pp. 199-201. Reference provided by Christopher Andreae.

32 The Longueuil station is illustrated, and the drawing discussed, in Omer Lavallée, 'Dundee-Built Locomotives on Canada's First Railways', *Railroad History*, 149, Autumn 1983, pp. 36-40; and Omer Lavallée, 'The Walker Engraving', *Canadian Rail*, 383, November-December 1984, pp. 188-94 (kindly pointed out by Christopher Andreae); a photograph of the painting of the Montreal Lachine Railroad station is in the collection of CN Public Affairs and Advertising and illustrated in *Rails Across Canada*, p. 28 (information was provided by Connie Romani); American and British stations of this type are discussed in Carroll L.V. Meeks, *The Railroad Station in Architectural History*, New Haven: Yale University Press, 1956, pp. 50-1, and figs. 25-8.

33 G.R. Stevens, *Canadian National Railways*, I, Toronto: Clarke, Irwin, 1960, p. 49.

34 Kalman and Richardson, 'Building for Transportation', p. 37; J. Knight, 'The Original Grand Trunk Railway Stations—Historical Report', and M. Brosseau, 'The Original Grand Trunk Stations of Canada—Architectural Report', Historic Sites and Monuments Board of Canada, Screening Papers, May 1973; Janet Wright, 'Thomas Seaton Scott: The Architect versus the Administration', *JCAH*, 6:2, 1982, pp. 202-19; James Marsh, 'Grand Trunk Railway of Canada', *CE* II, pp. 924-5.

35 Sandford Fleming, *The Intercolonial*, Montreal: Dawson Brothers, 1876, pp. 112-13. See also David McConnell, 'The Stations on the Intercolonial Railway, 1867-1914 (Historical Report)', Historic Sites and Monuments Board of Canada, Screening Paper, May 1974, Part 2, p. 3.

36 Mathilde Brosseau, 'Stations on the Intercolonial Railway—Architectural Report', Historic Sites and Monuments Board of Canada, Screening Paper, May 1974, p. 13; Lloyd A. Machum, *A History of Moncton Town and City, 1855-1965*, Moncton: City of Moncton, 1965, pp. 37-98.

37 The stations at Sherbrooke and High Falls are both illustrated in *Rails Across Canada*, p. 33.

38 Joseph Bouchette, *The British Dominions in North America*, I, London, 1831, p. 82.

39 John Mactaggart, *Three Years in Canada*, I, London, 1829, p. 345; Kalman and Richardson, 'Building for Transportation', pp. 25-6. See also Phyllis Rose, 'Bridges', in Ball, *Building Canada*, pp. 7-29; David Cuming, *Discovering Heritage Bridges on Ontario's Roads*, Erin, Ontario: Boston Mills Press, 1983; David Plowden, *Bridges: The Spans of North America*, New York: Viking Press, 1974.

40 Lyn Harrington and Richard Harrington, *Covered Bridges of Central and Eastern Canada*, Toronto: McGraw-Hill Ryerson, 1976; Jacques Coulon, 'Covered Bridges', *Canadian Geographical Journal*, 79:2, August 1969, pp. 58-63.

41 The bridges at Trois Pistoles, Quebec, and over the Miramichi River in New Brunswick are illustrated in Ball, *Professional Engineering in Canada*, pp. 14-15.

42 Kalman and Richardson, 'Building for Transportation', pp. 30-2; Charles Legge, *A Glance at the Victoria Bridge and the Men Who Built It*, Montreal: John Lovell, 1860; James Hodges, *Construction of the Great Victoria Bridge in Canada*, London: John Weale, 1860.

43 William Toye, *The St Lawrence*, Toronto: Oxford University Press, 1959, p. 260.

44 Kalman and Richardson, 'Building for Transportation', p. 30.

45 Ibid., p. 33.

46 Ibid., p. 32; Department of Railways and Canals, *The Quebec Bridge Over the St Lawrence River Near the City of Quebec...*, 2 vols, Ottawa, 1919.

47 Keefer's drawing, in the National Archives of Canada—titled 'Design for Egyptian-Towers, Bout de l'Ile Suspension Bridge'—is illustrated in Kalman and Richardson, 'Building for Transportation', Fig. 10.

48 Ralph Greenhill and Thomas D. Mahoney, *Niagara*, Toronto: University of Toronto Press, 1969, pp. 61-4.

49 Kalman and Richardson, 'Building for Transportation', pp. 27-8.

50 Ibid., p. 28.

51 Harold Kalman, Ron Phillips, and Robin Ward, *Exploring Vancouver*, Vancouver: University of British Columbia Press, 1993, p. 118; Rose, 'Bridges', pp. 26-7.

52 For the Citadel, see Elizabeth Pacey, *Halifax Citadel*, Halifax: Nimbus, 1985; and John Joseph Greenough, 'The Halifax Citadel, 1825-60: A Narrative and Structural History', *Canadian Historic Sites: Occasional Papers in Archaeology and History*, No. 17, Ottawa: Parks Canada, 1977.

53 Nicolls to British military engineer Gother Mann, 20 December 1825, cited in Greenough, 'Citadel', p. 26.

54 Many of these conclusions are also reached in Greenough, 'Citadel', pp. 127-9.

55 Marilyn Gurney Smith, *The King's Yard: An Illustrated History of the Halifax Dockyard*, Halifax: Nimbus, 1985.

56 André Charbonneau, Yvon Desloges, and Marc Lafrance, *Québec The Fortified City: From the 17th to the 19th Century*, Ottawa: Parks Canada, 1982, chap. 2 and *passim*. The economic considerations are discussed on p. 72.

57 Charbonneau et al., *Québec*, pp. 452-7; Luc Noppen, Claude Paulette, Michel Tremblay, *Québec: trois siècles d'architecture*, [n.p.,] Libre Expression, 1979, pp. 143-7.

58 The best general account is Robert D. Bradford, *Historic Forts of Ontario*, Belleville: Mika, 1988. See also Fritz G.M. Winter, *Old Forts in Upper Canada*, University of Toronto Bulletin No. 146, Toronto: School of Engineering Research, School of Architecture, 1935.

59 W.S. Lavell, 'The History of the Present Fortifications at Kingston', *Ontario History*, 31, 1936, pp. 155-77; George F.G. Stanley, 'Historic Kingston and Its Defences', *Ontario History*, 46, 1954, pp. 21-35; George F.G. Stanley, 'Kingston and the Defence of British North America', in Gerald Tulchinsky, ed., *Essays on Kingston in the Nineteenth Century*, Montreal: McGill-Queen's University Press, 1976, pp. 83-101; Bradford, *Forts*, chaps. 9-10.

60 Robert S. Allen, 'A History of Fort George, Upper Canada', *Canadian Historic Sites: Occasional Papers in Archaeology and History*, no. 11, Ottawa: Department of Indian Affairs and Northern Development, 1974. pp. 62-93; Yvon Desloges, 'Structural History of Fort George', *History and Archaeology*, no. 3, Ottawa: Parks Canada, 1980; Bradford, *Forts*, chap. 7.

61 Richard J. Young, 'Blockhouses in Canada, 1749-1841: A Comparative Report and Catalogue', *Canadian Historic Sites: Occasional Papers in Archaeology and History*, no. 23, Ottawa: Parks Canada, 1980, pp. 5-116.

62 Ivan J. Saunders, 'A History of Martello Towers in the Defence of British North America, 1796-1871', *Canadian Historic Sites: Occasional Papers in Archaeology and History*, no. 15, Ottawa: Parks Canada, 1976, pp. 5-169; Sheila Sutcliffe, *Martello Towers*, Newton Abbot: David & Charles, 1972; Willard B. Robinson, 'North American Martello Towers', *JSAH*, 33:2, May 1974, pp. 158-64. For individual installations, see Charles Bruce Fergusson, 'The Martello Tower at Halifax', *Dalhousie Review*, 43:2, Summer 1963, pp. 212-19; 'Lancaster Martello Tower', *New Brunswick Museum, History Bulletin*, Summer 1963; Pierre-Georges Roy, 'Les Tours Martello à Québec', *Bulletin des Recherches historiques*, 42, 1936, p. 566; and the works cited above with respect to fortifications.

63 Saunders, 'Towers', p. 64.

64 Canada, *Journals of Assembly*, 1847, quoted in Spragge, 'Colonization Roads', p. 2. The report was allegedly written by Thomas Keefer, then working for the Department of Works. See also Miller, 'Straight Lines', p. 18.

65 Commonwealth Historic Resource Management Limited, 'Building Summary: Module 11, The Camboose Shanty', research paper prepared for the History Hall, Canadian Museum of Civilization, Perth, 1989, including an extensive bibliography.

66 The most useful general studies of mills are Carol Priamo, *Mills of Canada*, Toronto: McGraw-Hill Ryerson, 1976; William Fox, Bill Brooks, and Janice Tyrwhitt, *The Mill*, Toronto: McClelland and Stewart, 1976; Felicity L. Leung, 'Grist and Flour Mills in Ontario: From Millstones to Rollers, 1780s-1880s', *History and Archaeology*, no. 53,

Ottawa: Parks Canada, 1981; Nick and Helma Mika with Larry Turner, *Historic Mills of Ontario*, Belleville: Mika, 1987; Pauline Reaburn, 'Power from the Old Mill Streams', *Canadian Geographical Journal*, 90:3, March 1975, pp. 22-7.

67 Fred Bruemmer, 'Historic Mills of Quebec', *Canadian Geographical Journal*, 74:4, April 1967, pp. 118-23; Gérard Morisset, *L'Architecture en Nouvelle-France*, Quebec, 1949, reprinted Quebec: Pélican, 1980, plate 7b; F. Adam-Villeneuve and C. Felteau, *Les Moulins à l'eau de la vallée du Saint-Laurent*, Montreal: Les Éditions de l'Homme, 1978.

68 Barbara R. Robertson, *Sawpower: Making Lumber in the Sawmills of Nova Scotia*, Halifax: Nimbus and the Nova Scotia Museum, 1986, pp. 15-16.

69 Leung, 'Grist and Flour Mills', pp. 12-16; Thomas W. Casey, 'Napanee's First Mills and Their Builder', *Ontario Historical Society Papers and Records*, 6, 1905, pp. 50-4; A.M. Going, 'Old Mills of the Loyalists', *Canadian Geographical Journal*, 10:1, January 1935, pp. 43-50.

70 Robert Legget, *Ottawa Waterway: Gateway to a Continent*, Toronto: University of Toronto Press, 1975, pp. 102-3; Harold Kalman and John Roaf, *Exploring Ottawa*, Toronto: University of Toronto Press, pp. 82-3, 91-2.

71 Thomas Need, *Six Years in the Bush*, London: Simpkin and Marshall, 1838, p. 96; cited in Brian Coffey, 'Factors Affecting the Use of Construction Materials in Early Ontario', *Ontario History*, 77:4, December 1985, p. 312.

72 Robertson, *Sawpower*, p. 37; Brenda Lee-Whiting, 'Saga of a Nineteenth Century Sawmill', *Canadian Geographical Journal*, 74:2, February 1967, p. 47.

73 Robert W. Frame, *McDonald Brothers' Mill, Sherbrooke Village, Nova Scotia*, Halifax: Nova Scotia Museum, 1974.

74 Mika, *Mills of Ontario*, pp. 80; W.D. Thomas, *Bobcaygeon: The Hub of the Kawarthas*, Lindsay: Deyell, 1980, pp. 53-6; Commonwealth Historic Resource Management Limited, 'Building Summary: Module 13, Sawmill', research paper prepared for the History Hall, Canadian Museum of Civilization, Perth, 1989. The mill has been demolished.

75 Priamo, *Mills*, pp. 146, 129.

76 Leung, 'Grist and Flour Mills', pp. 55-69.

77 Rideau Valley Conservation Authority, *Guide to Watson's Mill*, Manotick, n.d; Mika, *Mills of Ontario*, pp. 121-4. For a detailed account of gristmill technology, see Leung, 'Grist and Flour Mills'.

78 Carolyn Smyly, 'The Keremeos Grist Mill', *The Beaver*, 304:2, Autumn 1973, pp. 28-31; Patrick R. Frey and John Stephenson, *The Keremeos Grist Mill: A Research Report*, Victoria: Parks Branch, British Columbia Department of Recreation and Conservation, 1974; J. Stricker, *Keremeos Grist Mill*, Victoria: Heritage Conservation Branch, British Columbia Ministry of Provincial Secretary, 1980; Ken Scopick, 'Keremeos Grist Mill', *Datum*, 5:3, Summer 1980, pp. 13-15; Linda Eversole, 'Price's Mill, Keremeos, B.C.', *B.C. Historical News*, 18:4, 1985, pp. 10-11. See also W.E. Ireland and F.W. Laing, 'Early Flour-Mills in British Columbia', *British Columbia Historical Quarterly*, 5:2-3, 1941, pp. 89-109, 191-213.

79 Robertson, *Sawpower*, p. 58.

80 Commonwealth Historic Resource Management Limited, *A History of the Wood's Mill Complex*, 2 vols, Ottawa, 1988.

81 *Wile Carding Mill, Bridgewater, Nova Scotia*, brochure, Hali-

fax: Department of Education, n.d; *Upper Canada Village: 'Ontario's Living Heritage'*, Morrisburg: St Lawrence Parks Commission, n.d., no. 4.

82 Paul E. Rivard, *Samuel Slater*, Pawtucket: Slater Mill Historic Site, 1974. See also David J. Jeremy, *Transatlantic Industrial Revolution: The Diffusion of Textile Technologies Between Britain and America, 1790-1830s*, North Andover, Mass.: Merrimack Valley Textile Museum and Cambridge: MIT Press, 1981.

83 Douglas Daamon Pond, *The History of Marysville New Brunswick*, privately printed, 1983; Glen McIntyre et al., *'And What of All This?' Alexander Gibson's Marysville: A Walking Tour*, Fredericton: Fredericton Heritage Trust, 1983; 'Marysville Place: Restoration & Renovations For Provincial Government Offices and Auxiliary Services...' unpublished paper, Fredericton: New Brunswick Department of Tourism, Recreation and Heritage, [1984]; Marsha Hay Snider and Mary Cullen, 'The Marysville Cotton Mill', Historic Sites and Monuments Board of Canada Agenda Papers, 21, June 1984, pp. 319-48; Felicity L. Leung, 'Catalogue of Significant Extant Textile Mills Built in Canada Before 1940', and A.B. McCullough, 'A Preliminary Report on the Textile Industry in Canada', papers prepared for the Historic Sites and Monuments Board of Canada, Ottawa, 1986.

84 The buildings of Marysville are described in McIntyre, *'And What of All This?'*.

85 T. Ritchie, 'A History of Windmills and Their Place in Canadian Life', *Canadian Geographical Journal*, 78:3, March 1969, pp. 106-9.

86 Robertson, *Sawpower*, pp. 11-15.

87 Fox et al., *The Mill*, pp. 174-5; Ritchie, 'Windmills', p. 106.

88 David Butterfield, *Architectural Heritage: The Selkirk and District Planning Area*, Winnipeg: Manitoba Culture, Heritage and Recreation, 1988, pp. 25-6 and n. 18; Barry Kaye, 'Flour Milling at Red River: Wind, Water and Steam', *Manitoba History*, 2, 1981, pp. 12-20; Ritchie, 'Windmills', p. 107.

89 J.F. Galbraith, *The Mennonites in Manitoba*, Morden: Chronicle Press, 1900, p. 34; cited in Jake E. Peters, 'Windmills in Early Manitoba Communities, 1876-1924', *Mennonite Historian*, 12:2, June 1986, p. 1; Peter A. Braun, 'The Steam and Windmills of the East Reserve', in Abe Warkentin, ed., *Reflections on Our Heritage: A History of Steinbach and the R.M. of Hanover from 1874*, Steinbach: Derksen Printers, 1971, pp. 53-6.

90 Information on the reconstruction from Henry Van Der Putton, Parks Canada, 9 June 1986.

91 Réal Boissonnault, *Les Forges du Saint-Maurice 1729-1883: 150 Years of Occupation and Operation*, Ottawa: Parks Canada, 1983; David Lee, *A Short History of the St Maurice Forges*, Manuscript Report Series, No. 132, Ottawa: Parks Canada, 1975; Louise Trottier, *Les Forges: Historiographie des Forges du Saint-Maurice*, Montreal: Boréal Express, 1980; Albert Tessier, *Les Forges Saint-Maurice (1729-1887)*, reprint, Montreal: Boréal Express, 1974.

92 Jean-Marie Roy and Laurent Goulard, 'Les Forges du Saint-Maurice Blast Furnace Complex', *APT Bulletin*, 18:1-2, 1986, pp. 33-7; François Leblanc, 'Les Forges du Saint-Maurice', *idem*, pp. 13-14; 'Les Forges du Saint-Maurice, Trois-Rivières', *Section a*, 3:2, 1985, pp. 23-5;

Gauthier, Guité, Roy, 'L'Ensemble du haut-fourneau des Forges du Saint-Maurice', *ARQ: Architecture Québec*, 26, August 1985, pp. 13-15; 'Ensemble du Haut-Fourneau, Trois Rivières', Québec, *Canadian Architect*, 32:2, February 1987, pp. 36-40.

93 George B. MacBeath, 'New England Settlements in Pre-Loyalist New Brunswick', *Collections of the New Brunswick Historical Society*, 18, 1963, pp. 29-30; D.G. Bell, *Early Loyalist Saint John: The Origin of New Brunswick Politics 1783-1786*, Fredericton: New Ireland Press, 1983, p. 36; Elizabeth W. McGahan, *The Port of Saint John*, I, Saint John: National Harbours Board, 1982; George W. Schuyler, *Saint John: Two Hundred Years Proud*, Burlington, Ont.: Windsor Publications, 1984; George W. Schuyler, *Saint John: Scenes from a Popular History*, Halifax: Nimbus, 1984; Wayne Harrison and Ross Leavitt, *A Heritage Now: Saint John*, Saint John: Tyson, 1984.

94 T.W. Acheson, *Saint John: The Making of a Colonial Urban Community*, Toronto: University of Toronto Press, 1985, Introduction and pp. 13-18; C.M. Wallace, 'Saint John, New Brunswick (1800-1900)', *Urban History Review*, 1, June 1975, pp. 12-21.

95 R. Pepall, 'Painted Illusions', *Canadian Collector*, 20:2, March 1985, pp. 21-5.

96 Leslie Maitland, *Neoclassical Architecture in Canada*, Studies in Archaeology, Architecture and History, Ottawa: Parks Canada, 1984, pp. 112, 119; Nathalie Clerk, *Palladian Style in Canadian Architecture*, Studies in Archaeology, Architecture and History, Ottawa: Parks Canada, 1984, p. 87.

97 Acheson, *Saint John*, pp. 79-81; Maitland, *Neoclassical Architecture*, p. 69.

98 Entry by Mary Elizabeth Smith on the Academy of Music, Saint John, in Eugene Benson and L.W. Conolly, eds, *The Oxford Companion to Canadian Theatre*, Toronto: Oxford University Press, 1989, p. 2; Robert Hunter, 'Last Performance This Season: The Architectural Legacy of Canada's 18th and 19th Century Theatres', *SSAC Bulletin*, 14:2, June 1989, pp. 35-6.

99 Gilbert A. Stelter, 'The City-Building Process in Canada', in Stelter and Alan F.J. Artibise, eds, *Shaping the Urban Landscape: Aspects of the Canadian City-Building Process*, Ottawa: Carleton University Press, 1982, p. 14.

100 George Gilbert, 'The Great Saint John Fire', *Atlantic Advocate*, 47:6, March 1957, pp. 25-30; John W. James, 'The Great Fire of Saint John', *Atlantic Advocate*, 67:10, June 1977, pp. 12-19. Fairweather is identified as Joseph Fairweather in some sources.

101 T.W. Acheson, 'The National Policy and the Industrialization of the Maritimes, 1880-1910', *Acadiensis*, 1:2, Spring, 1972, pp. 3-28; C. Anne Hale, *The Rebuilding of Saint John, New Brunswick, 1887-1881*, Fredericton: Province of New Brunswick, 1990.

102 The plan, in the McGill University library, was drawn *c*. 1644 by Jean Bourdon and is illustrated in John W. Reps, *Town Planning in Frontier America*, Princeton: University Press, 1969, pp. 82-3.

103 Jean-Claude Marsan, *Montreal in Evolution*, Montreal: McGill-Queen's University Press, 1981, pp. 49, 70-7. The summary of Montreal's development that follows is based in part on Marsan and on Paul-André Linteau,

Montréal', *CE* III, pp. 1379-83. See also Luc d'Iberville-Moreau, *Lost Montreal*, Toronto: Oxford University Press, 1975; Aline Gubbay, *Le Fleuve et la montagne: Montréal: The Mountain and the River*, Montreal: Trillium Books, 1981.

104 Marie Morin, *Annales de l'Hôtel-Dieu de Montréal*, Montreal: L'Imprimerie des éditeurs, 1921, pp. 25-6; cited and translated in Marsan, *Montreal*, p. 77. See Phyllis Lambert et al., *Opening the Gate of Eighteenth-Century Montreal/Montréal: Ville fortiée du XVIIIe siècle*, Montreal: Canadian Centre for Architecture, 1992.

105 Marsan, *Montreal*, p. 82.

106 Ibid., pp. 126-65.

107 J.G. Lambton, First Earl of Durham, *Report on the Affairs of British North America*, London, 1839, p. 103; cited in Ellen James, 'A Vision for McGill College', *Section a*, 3:2, 1985, p. 33; Ellen James, *John Ostell: Architecte, Arpenteur/Architect, Surveyor*, Montreal: McCord Museum, McGill University, 1985, pp. 34-48. See also CUM, *Les Édifices scolaires*, 1980, p. 140-5.

108 Ostell to the Rev. Dr John Bethune and George Moffatt, 24 August 1840; cited in James, 'Vision', p. 34.

109 *Journal of the House of Assembly of Lower-Canada*, 39 George III (1799), pp. 188-90; cited in Marsan, *Montreal*, p. 134.

110 Linteau, 'Urban Mass Transit', p. 62.

111 Marsan, *Montreal*, pp. 265-75; David Hanna, 'Vernacular Housing in Montreal', Walking Tour, Society of Architectural Historians, Montreal, 15 April 1989; Thomas Ritchie, 'Plankwall Framing', *JSAH*, 30:1, March 1971, pp. 66-70.

112 d'Iberville-Moreau, *Lost Montreal*, pp. 104-5; Marsan, *Montreal*, p. 258, citing John Bland, 'Domestic Architecture in Montreal', *Culture*, 9:4, December 1948, p. 403. David B. Hanna, 'The New Town of Montreal', M.A. Thesis, University of Toronto, 1977.

113 Marsan, *Montreal*, p. 170.

114 CUM, *Architecture industrielle*, pp. 6-9.

115 Ibid., pp. 170-3.

116 Leung, 'Textile Mills', pp. 98-103; CUM, *Architecture industrielle*, pp. 146-9.

CHAPTER 6 **The Return to the Past: The Victorian Revivals**

1 J.F.C. Smith, 'Drawings from the Archives, Ottawa', *JRAIC*, 15:6, June 1938, pp. 132-5; Derek Linstrum, *Sir Jeffry Wyatville*, Oxford: Clarendon Press, 1972, pp. 108, 246-7; R.H. Hubbard, 'Canadian Gothic', *Architectural Review*, 106, 1954, pp. 103-4; Mathilde Brosseau, *Gothic Revival in Canadian Architecture*, Canadian Historic Sites: Occasional Papers in Archaeology and History, No 25, Ottawa: Parks Canada, 1980, pp. 32-3; Luc Noppen, Claude Paulette, and Michel Tremblay, *Québec: trois siècles d'architecture*, [n.p:] Libre Expression, 1979, p. 263. Morrison is identified in A.J.H. Richardson et al., *Quebec City: Architects, Artisans, and Builders*, Ottawa: National Museum of Man, 1984, pp. 415-16. The drawings by Wyatt and Gandy are in the National Archives of Canada; additional drawings by Wyatt are in the Collection of Mr and Mrs Paul Mellon.

2 NAC, RG 5, A 1, p. 141861; copy kindly provided by Patricia Kennedy.

3 Linstrum, *Wyatville*, p. 247; Kenneth Clark, *The Gothic Revival: An Essay in the History of Taste*, rev. ed., Harmondsworth: Penguin, 1964, pp. 93-9.

4 For romanticism in American building, see James Early, *Romanticism and American Architecture*, New York: A.S. Barnes, 1965; William H. Pierson and William H. Jordy, *American Buildings and Their Architects*: vol. 2, *Technology and the Picturesque*, New York: Oxford University Press, 1987.

5 A. Graves, *The Royal Academy of Arts*, London, 1906, III, p. 199, and VIII, p. 373; cited in Hubbard, 'Canadian Gothic', p. 103.

6 The view was both drawn (*c.* 1831) and engraved (*c.* 1850) by L.S. Punderson; see Pierson and Jordy, *American Buildings*, vol. 2, *Technology and the Picturesque*, pp. 124-9.

7 Allan Duffus et al., *Thy Dwellings Fair: Churches of Nova Scotia, 1750-1830*, Hantsport: Lancelot Press, 1982, pp. 88-90. Elizabeth Pacey, who did the research on this church for the book, recollects that the windows appeared to be original and the documentation unambiguous.

8 Duffus et al., *Thy Dwellings Fair*, pp. 121-5.

9 Archibald Lang Fleming, *A Book of Remembrance: or The History of St. John's Church, Saint John, New Brunswick*, Saint John, 1925; C.A. Hale, '85 Carleton Street, Saint John, N.B.', Historical Building Report, Parks Canada, 1973; Evelyn Ward, *The Story of Stone Church*, Saint John: Corporation of St. John's Church, 1975; Brosseau, *Gothic Revival*, pp. 40-1. Johnston—called 'Johnson'—is named as the architect in the Saint John *Courier*, 16 July 1825 (cited in Fleming, p. 22); his name appears on an 1823 advertisement soliciting building materials, and on a plan dated 1824 (Fleming, p. 18, and opposite p. 21). Crookshank is identified in Fleming as having made the plans for a fee of $30 (p. 17). Cunningham reportedly designed the 'turrets' for the tower; the mason for the turrets was Joseph Bell, a Scot from Dumfries (Fleming, p. 22). The illustrated photograph was kindly provided by Harold Wright. St John's underwent interior alterations in 1872 and 1895.

10 Pierson and Jordy, *American Buildings*, vol. 2, *Technology and the Picturesque*, pp. 129-34; All Saints is illustrated on p. 132.

11 Cited in ibid., pp. 132-3.

12 H.M. Scott Smith, *The Historic Churches of Prince Edward Island*, Erin: Boston Mills Press, 1986, pp. 63-6; Hubbard, 'Canadian Gothic', pp. 103, 105.

13 J. Philip McAleer, 'St Mary's (1820-1830), Halifax: An Early Example of the Use of Gothic Revival Forms in Canada', *JSAH*, 45:2, June 1986, pp. 134-47; J. Philip McAleer, *A Pictorial History of the Basilica of St Mary, Halifax, Nova Scotia*, Halifax: Tech-Press, 1984; Elizabeth Pacey, *Georgian Halifax*, Hantsport: Lancelot Press, pp. 82-3; Duffus et al., *Thy Dwellings Fair*, pp. 152-5.

14 Pacey, *Georgian Halifax*, p. 82; also W. Foley, *The Centenary of St Mary's Cathedral, Halifax, N.S., 1820-1920, A Souvenir Memorial*, Halifax, 1920, p. 17; cited in McAleer, 'St Mary's', p. 138.

15 McAleer, 'St Mary's', p. 138.

16 Franklin Toker, *The Church of Notre-Dame in Montreal: An Architectural History*, Montreal: McGill-Queen's University Press, 1970 (2nd edition, 1991); Olivier Maurault, *La Paroisse: Histoire de l'Église Notre-Dame de Montréal*, Montreal, 1929 (reprinted Montreal: Therrien Frères, 1975); Alan Gowans, 'Notre-Dame de Montréal', *JSAH*, 11:1, March 1952, pp. 20-6; Brosseau, *Gothic Revival*, pp. 34-5; Jean-Claude Marsan, *Montreal in Evolution*, Montreal: McGill-Queen's University Press, 1981, pp. 157-65; Luc Noppen, *Les Églises du Québec (1600-1850)*, Quebec: Éditeur officiel du Québec/Fides, 1977, pp. 144-7; *Repertoire d'Architecture traditionelle sur le territoire de la Communauté urbaine de Montréal* (CUM), *Les Églises*, Architecture Religieuse 1, 1981, pp. 94-105; André Laberge, 'Un nouveau regard sur l'ancienne chapelle Notre-Dame-du-Sacré-Coeur de la Basilique Notre-Dame de Montréal', *JCAH*, 8:1, 1984, pp. 26-49.

17 Minutes of the building committee, 24 August 1823, cited in Toker, *Notre-Dame*, p. 19; for the building committee and its mandate, see pp. 15-21 and Toker's preface to the 1991 edition. For O'Donnell, see Franklin Toker, 'James O'Donnell: An Irish Georgian in America', *JSAH*, 29:2, May 1970, pp. 132-43.

18 *Albion* (New York), 3 April 1824; cited in Toker, *Notre-Dame*, p. 31. See M.H. Port, *Six Hundred New Churches*, London: S.P.C.K., 1961. Toker proposes rather convincingly that O'Donnell composed the façade in a modular system (p. 40), a classical-Georgian approach.

19 Robert L. Alexander, *The Architecture of Maximilian Godefroy*, Baltimore: Johns Hopkins University Press, 1974, pp. 41-71.

20 Demers to the vestry, 22 April 1824; discussed in Toker, *Notre-Dame*, p. 77, and Brosseau, *Gothic Revival*, p. 34.

21 *La Minerve* (Montreal), 27 April 1866; translated and cited by Gowans in 'Notre-Dame', p. 24. See also Alan Gowans, 'Sainte-Croix d'Orléans: A Major Monument Too Long Neglected', *Gazette des Beaux-Arts*, ser. 6, 112, 1988, pp. 69-76; Toker, *Notre-Dame*, p. 74.

22 O'Donnell to François-Antoine LaRocque, 16 March 1824; in Toker, *Notre-Dame*, pp. 83-6.

23 Ibid., p. 17, and preface to the 1991 edition; see also Gerald J.J. Tulchinsky, *The River Barons: Montreal Businessmen and the Growth of Industry and Transportation, 1837-53*, Toronto: University of Toronto Press, 1977.

24 Toker, *Notre-Dame*, p. 79; Gérard Morisset, *L'Architecture en Nouvelle-France*, Quebec, 1949; reprinted Quebec: Pélican, 1980, p. 89.

25 Marion MacRae and Anthony Adamson, *Hallowed Walls: Church Architecture of Upper Canada*, Toronto: Clarke, Irwin, 1975, pp. 114-21; Stephen A. Otto, 'Arthur McClean: Builder Architect 1779-1864', *Society for the Study of Architecture in Canada: Selected Papers*, 3, Ottawa, 1982, pp. 24-42; Brosseau, *Gothic Revival*, pp. 48-9; Ralph Greenhill, Ken Macpherson, and Douglas Richardson, *Ontario Towns*, Ottawa: Oberon, 1974, Plate 23. The Church of St Mary Magdalene is now unused.

26 Further changes were made in 1844, and the church burned in 1925. See Godrey Spragge, *The History and Architecture of the Village of Bath*, Kingston: Queen's University, 1976, p. 122; W.S. Herrington, 'The Court of Requests', *Lennox and Addington Historical Society: Papers and Records*, 6, 1915, p. 48.

27 Minutes of the building committee (1829) and the reference to the Brockville Recorder, 10 November 1831, were kindly provided by Mrs T.C. Mills. See John de Visser and Harold Kalman, *Pioneer Churches*, Toronto: McClelland and Stewart, 1976, pp. 124, 140-1. The attribution to McClean is in MacRae and Adamson, *Hallowed Walls*, pp. 119-23; Otto, 'McClean', pp. 28-9.

28 Newton Bosworth, ed., *Hochelaga Depicta: The Early History and Present State of...Montreal*, Montreal: William Grieg, 1839, pp. 119-20.

29 *Seasoned Timbers: A Sampling of Historic Buildings Unique to Western Nova Scotia*, I, Halifax: Heritage Trust of Nova Scotia, 1972, pp. 68-9.

30 Christina Cameron and Jean Trudel, *The Drawings of James Cockburn: A Visit Through Quebec's Past*, Toronto: Gage, 1976, pp. 77-8; Noppen et al., *Québec*, p. 350; Marie-Thérèse Thibault, ed., *Monuments et sites historiques du Québec*, Les Cahiers du patrimoine, no. 10, Québec: Ministère des affaires culturelles, 1978, p. 164; Richardson et al, *Quebec City*, p. 110.

31 Marcus Whiffen, *American Architecture Since 1780: A Guide to the Styles*, Cambridge: MIT Press, 1969, p. 56.

32 Brosseau, *Gothic Revival*, pp. 116-17; D.C. Masters, *Bishop's University: The First Hundred Years*, Toronto: Clarke, Irwin, 1950.

33 William Dendy, *Lost Toronto: Images of the City's Past*, Toronto: McClelland and Stewart, 1993, pp. 158-63, citing T.A. Reid, *A History of Trinity College*, Toronto, 1952, pp. 37-42. See also Eric Arthur, *Toronto: No Mean City*, Third Edition revised by Stephen A. Otto, Toronto: University of Toronto Press, 1986, pp. 126-7, and Brosseau, *Gothic Revival*, pp. 114-15.

34 Anna Brownell Jameson, *Winter Studies and Summer Rambles in Canada*, ed. by Clara Thomas, Toronto: McClelland and Stewart, 1963, p. 83. See Kelly Crossman and Dana Johnson, 'Early Court Houses of Ontario', in Margaret Carter, comp., *Early Canadian Court Houses*, Studies in Archaeology, Architecture and History, Ottawa: Parks Canada, 1983, p. 111; Nancy Z. Tausky and Lynne D. DiStefano, *Victorian Architecture in London and Southwestern Ontario: Symbols of Aspiration*, Toronto: University of Toronto Press, 1986, pp. 3-55; Marion MacRae and Anthony Adamson *Cornerstones of Order: Courthouses and Town Halls of Ontario, 1784-1914*, Toronto: Clarke Irwin, 1983, pp. 93-9; Peter John Stokes, 'Middlesex County Court House, London, Ontario', unpublished manuscript, National Historic Parks and Sites Branch, Parks Canada, 1963.

35 The York courthouse of 1824 is illustrated in MacRae and Adamson, *Cornerstones of Order*, p. 40.

36 Talbot to George, Hillier, 24 April 1827, cited in Tausky and DiStefano, *Victorian Architecture*, p. 45.

37 MacRae and Adamson, *Cornerstones of Order*, pp. 103-10, 116-19; Brosseau, *Gothic Revival*, p. 66; Tausky and DiStefano, *Victorian Architecture*, pp. 114-15.

38 Arthur/Otto, *No Mean City*, p. 48; Janet Wright, *Architecture of the Picturesque in Canada*, Studies in Archaeololgy, Architecture, and History, Ottawa: Parks Canada, 1984, p. 88; Dendy, *Lost Toronto*, pp. 34-6. Holland House was demolished shortly after fire destroyed much of the area in 1904; its former site is now occupied by the Royal Bank Plaza.

39 Cited in Christopher Hussey, *English Country Houses: Late Georgian, 1800-1840*, London: Country Life, 1958, pp. 60-1. See also Terence Davis, *John Nash: The Prince Regent's Architect*, London: Country Life, 1966, p. 36. One published source that anticipates features of Holland House is the 'Villa in the Gothic Style' in Edward Gyfford, *Designs for Elegant Cottages and Small Villas...*, 1806, reproduced in Wright, *Architecture of the Picturesque*, p. 29.

40 See Wright, *Architecture of the Picturesque*, pp. 12-20; Christopher Hussey, *The Picturesque: Studies in a Point of View*, London: Putnam, 1927; Nikolaus Pevsner, 'The Genesis of the Picturesque', *Architectural Review*, 96:575, 1944, pp. 139-43.

41 Wright, *Architecture of the Picturesque*, pp. 86-7.

42 Margaret Angus, *The Old Stones of Kingston: Its Buildings Before 1867*, Toronto: University of Toronto Press, 1966, pp. 54-5; Architectural Review Committee, City of Kingston, *Buildings of Architectural and Historic Significance*, II, Kingston: City of Kingston, 1973, pp. 108-13. The stable wing was subsequently demolished and a large stuccoed red-brick wing was added by architect William Newlands.

43 Arthur/Otto, *No Mean City*, pp. 93-96, 261; T. Ritchie, 'The Architecture of William Thomas', *Architecture Canada*, 44:5, May 1967, pp. 41-5.

44 Ibid., pp. 94-5; Patricia McHugh, *Toronto Architecture: A City Guide*, Toronto, 1985, pp. 169-70.

45 Thomas Rickman, *An Attempt to Discriminate the Styles of English Architecture from the Conquest to the Reformation*, 1817. Rickman also maintained a full practice as an architect, and his work included several churches in the earlier manner of the Gothic Revival. For the Gothic Revival in Britain, see Kenneth Clark, *The Gothic Revival*, London: Constable, 1928; Georg Germann, *Gothic Revival in Europe and Britain: Sources, Influences and Ideas*, London: Lund Humphries, 1972; Stefan Muthesius, *The High Victorian Movement in Architecture 1850-1870*, London: Routledge and Kegan Paul, 1972; George L. Hersey, *High Victorian Gothic: A Study in Associationism*, Baltimore: Johns Hopkins University Press, 1972.

46 See Eugene R. Fairweather, ed., *The Oxford Movement*, New York: Oxford University Press, 1964; G.W.O. Addleshaw and Frederick Etchells, *The Architectural Setting of Anglican Worship*, London: Faber and Faber, 1948.

47 A.W.N. Pugin, *Contrasts*, London, 1836; A.W.N. Pugin, *The True Principles of Pointed or Christian Architecture*, London, 1841; A.W.N. Pugin, *The Present State of Ecclesiastical Architecture in England*, London, 1843.

48 Cited in Phoebe B. Stanton, *The Gothic Revival and American Church Architecture: An Episode in Taste, 1840-1856*, Baltimore: Johns Hopkins Press, 1968, p. 16; see also James F. White, *The Cambridge Movement, the Ecclesiologists, and the Gothic Revival*, Cambridge: Cambridge University Press, 1962.

49 J.M. Neale and B. Webb, *The Symbolism of Churches and Church Ornaments* [1843], 3rd ed., London: Gibbins, 1906, p. xxiv; cited in Stanton, *Gothic Revival*, p. 18.

50 'Oxford Architectural Society', *Ecclesiologist*, 5, September 1845, p. 219; cited in Stanton, *Gothic Revival*, p. 54.

51 'Ecclesiological Publications', *Ecclesiologist*, 1, November 1841, p. 15; cited in Stanton, *Gothic Revival*, p. 128.

52 *Ecclesiologist*, 5:30, June 1848, p. 361.

53 Frank Wills, *Ancient English Ecclesiastical Architecture and Its Principles Applied To the Wants of the Church at the Present Day*, New York: Stanford and Swords, 1850, pp. 109-11; Stanton, *Gothic Revival*, p. 130. See also Peter Malmberg, 'Saint Anne's Chapel, Fredericton, New Brunswick: A Living Exhibit of Material Culture', *Material History Bulletin*, 30, Fall 1989, pp. 51-8.

54 Wills, *Ecclesiastical Architecture*, p. 109.

55 Stanton, *Gothic Revival*, pp. 98-112. The contract to build St James the Less was signed in October 1846, and it was announced in *The Ecclesiologist* a month later.

56 Leon B. Litvack, 'An Auspicious Alliance: Pugin, Bloxam, and the Magdalen Commissions', *JSAH*, 49:2, June 1990, pp. 154-60.

57 Robert L. Watson, *Christ Church Cathedral, Fredericton: A History*, Fredericton: Bishop and Chapter of Christ Church Cathedral, 1984; Stanton, *Gothic Revival*, pp. 127-48; Douglas S. Richardson, 'Christ Church Cathedral, Fredericton, N.B.', MA Thesis, Yale University, 1966; Brosseau, *Gothic Revival*, pp. 68-9; Cynthia Wallace-Casey, 'Christ Church Cathedral, National Historic Site', *Material History Bulletin*, 26, Fall 1987, pp. 46-52.

58 *Ecclesiologist*, 5, February 1846, p. 81; cited in Stanton, *Gothic Revival*, p. 129. Wills' original 'Snettisham' design, dated 1845, is known from a lithograph in the Diocesan Archives. Butterfield's scheme was published in *The Ecclesiologist*, 8, June 1848, opp. p. 361; the twin-towered design ascribed to Wills was published in the *Illustrated London News*, 1 April 1849. Additional unsigned drawings—some of them likely by Wills, and others by Butterfield—are in the Diocesan Archives.

59 John Medley, *A Charge to the Clergy of the Diocese*, by John, Bishop of Fredericton, Fredericton: Royal Gazette Office, 1853, pp. 3-6, and Appendix, 'Account of Architecture', pp. 31-8. The praise for Exwick Chapel is from *The Ecclesiologist*, 2, October 1842, p. 23; cited in Douglas Scott Richardson, 'Hyperborean Gothic; or, Wilderness Ecclesiology and the Wood Churches of Edward Medley', *Architectura: Zeitschrift für Geschichte der Architektur*, 1, 1972, p. 48n.

60 The entry by Phoebe B. Stanton on Wills in the *Macmillan Encyclopedia of Architecture*, ed. by Adolf K. Placzek, IV, New York, 1982, pp. 404-5.

61 Frank Dawson Adams, *A History of Christ Church Cathedral, Montreal*, Montreal: Burton's, 1941; CUM, *Les Églises*, pp. 8-15; Brosseau, *Gothic Revival*, pp. 82-3; Marsan, *Montreal*, pp. 203-4; Phlip J. Turner, 'Christ Church Cathedral, Montreal', *Construction*, 20:11, November 1927, pp. 347-54 (also published in *McGill University Publications*, series 13, no. 17, Montreal, 1927); Franklin Morris, 'Christ Church Cathedral, Montreal', *Dalhousie Review*, 35:2, Summer 1955, pp. 176-8.

62 'The Montreal Cathedral', *Ecclesiologist*, n.s. 88:122 (December 1857).

63 Feild to Ernest Hawkins, secretary of the Society for the Propagation of the Gospel in Foreign Parts (SPG), 27 February 1844 (in the context of the cathedral's pews); cited in Frederick Jones, 'Bishop Feild, A Study in Politics and Religion in Nineteenth Century Newfoundland', Ph.D. dissertation, University of Cambridge, 1971, p. 31; second letter cited in William Scott, 'On Wooden Churches', *Ecclesiologist*, 9, August 1848, p. 21.

64 *A Gift of Heritage: Historic Architecture of St John's*, St John's: Newfoundland Historic Trust, 1975, no. 30; *Tour Guide to the Cathedral Church of St John the Baptist...*, St John's, n.d; *The Cathedral of St John the Baptist...*, pamphlet, St John's, n.d; C. Francis Rowe, *In Fields Afar: A Review of the Establishment of the Anglican Parish of St John's and Its Cathedral*, St John's: SeaWise Enterprise, 1980; Leslie Sternberg, 'Towards a History of St. John's Architecture', unpublished manuscript, Department of Anthropology, Memorial University of Newfoundland, 1972, pp. 7-8.

65 William Dendy and William Kilbourn, *Toronto Observed: Its Architecture, Patrons, and History*, Toronto: Oxford University Press, 1986, pp. 56-9; Shirley G. Morriss, 'The Nine-Year Odyssey of a High Victorian Goth: Three Churches by Fred Cumberland', *JCAH*, 2:1, Summer 1975, pp. 46-9; Arthur/Otto, *No Mean City*, pp. 128-9, 136-7; F.H. Armstrong, 'The Rebuilding of Toronto After the Great Fire of 1849', *Ontario History*, 53, December 1961, pp. 241-8.

66 Arthur/Otto, *No Mean City*, p. 135; MacRae and Adamson, *Hallowed Walls*, p. 159.

67 C.J. Taylor, et al., *Some Early Ottawa Buildings*, National Historic Parks and Sites Branch, Parks Canada, Manuscript Report No. 268, Ottawa, 1975, pp. 77-81; Harold Kalman and John Roaf, *Exploring Ottawa*, Toronto: University of Toronto Press, 1983, p. 67.

68 Brosseau, *Gothic Revival*, pp. 84-5.

69 Dendy and Kilbourn, *Toronto Observed*, pp. 81-3; Morriss, 'Odyssey', pp. 49-52; Arthur/Otto, *No Mean City*, p. 134; Brosseau, *Gothic Revival*, pp. 154-5.

70 *Ecclesiologist*, 8, June 1848, pp. 362-3; cited in Richardson, 'Hyperborean Gothic', p. 51.

71 Richardson, 'Hypoborean Gothic', pp. 62-6.

72 William Scott, 'On Wooden Churches', *Ecclesiologist*, 9 (August 1848), pp. 24-5. Scott is cited, and Medley's churches are discussed, in Richardson, 'Hyperborean Gothic', pp. 48-74.

73 Wills, *Ecclesiastical Architecture*, pl. 17; Richard Upjohn, *Upjohn's Rural Architecture*, New York, 1852; both are discussed in Stanton, *Gothic Revival*, pp. 259-68, 293. See also de Visser and Kalman, *Pioneer Churches*, pp. 141-4.

74 Donna McGee, 'St Patrick's Church, Montreal: Sorting Out the Beginnings', *SSAC Bulletin*, 12:1, 1987, pp. 7-9; CUM, *Les Églises*, pp. 340-7; Brosseau, *Gothic Revival*, pp. 80-1; Marsan, *Montreal*, pp. 200-3; François Rémillard and Brian Merrett, *Montreal Architecture: A Guide to Styles and Buildings*, Montreal: Meridian Press, 1990, p. 51.

75 Marsan, *Montreal*, pp. 209-10; CUM, *Les Églises*, pp. 360-7; Rémillard and Merrett, *Montreal Architecture*, p. 52. For Bourgeau, see Raymonde Gauthier, 'Une pratique architectuale aux XIXᵉ siècle: Victor Bourgeau 1809-1888', *ARQ: Architecture Quebec*, 41, February 1988, pp. 10-23; see also the entry on him by Luc Noppen in *DCB* XI, pp. 91-3.

76 CUM, *Les Églises*, pp. 282-5; Joshua Wolfe and Cécile Grenier, *Montreal Guide*, [Montreal:] Libre Expression, 1983, p. 275.

77 Gowans, 'Baroque Revival', p. 12.

78 Arthur/Otto, *No Mean City*, pp. 120-1, 250.

79 William Hay, 'The Late Mr Pugin and the Revival of Christian Architecture', *Anglo-American Magazine*, 2, 1853, p. 70; cited in William Westfall, *Two Worlds: The Protestant*

Culture of Nineteenth-Century Ontario, Kingston: McGill-Queen's University Press, 1989, pp. 134-5. The full article is contained in Geoffrey Simmins, ed., *Documents in Canadian Architecture*, Peterborough: Broadview Press, pp. 44-51.

80 Westfall, *Two Worlds*, p. 158, and Chapter 5, 'Epics in Stone: Placing the Sacred in a Secular World'. For the churches, see Arthur/Otto, *No Mean City, passim*.

81 Elizabeth Pacey *et al.*, *More Stately Mansions: Churches of Nova Scotia, 1830-1910*, Hantsport: Lancelot Press, 1983, pp. 75-80; Brosseau, *Gothic Revival*, pp. 90-1.

82 Norman J. Ronnenbert, 'The Bittersweet Life of John Wright', in *John Wright (1830-1915): Grandfather of West Coast Architecture*, Victoria: Maltwood Art Museum and Gallery, 1990, not paginated; Martin Segger and Douglas Franklin, *Victoria: A Primer for Regional History in Architecture, 1843-1929*, Watkins Glen, NY: American Life Foundation and Study Institute, 1979, pp. 214-15.

83 Brosseau, *Gothic Revival*, pp. 106-7, citing Suzanne Bernier-Héroux, 'Dossier sur le Manoir Rouville-Campbell', manuscript, Ministère des Affaires culturelles, Québec, 1977; Raymonde Gauthier, *Les Manoirs du Québec*, Québec: Fides/Éditeur officiel du Québec, 1976, pp. 74-5.

84 *Earnscliffe: Home of Canada's First Prime Minister and Since 1930 Residence of the High Commissioner for the United Kingdom in Canada*, London: Commonwealth Relations Office, 1984; Brosseau, *Gothic Revival*, pp. 146-7; Kalman and Roaf, *Exploring Ottawa*, p. 121.

85 Sandra Gwyn, *The Private Capital: Ambition and Love in the Age of Macdonald and Laurier*, Toronto: McClelland and Stewart, 1984, p. 201.

86 Laugier, *An Essay on Architecture...*, London: Osborne and Shipton, 1755; cited in John Summerson, *Architecture in Britain, 1530 to 1830*, 4th ed., Harmondsworth: Penguin Books, 1963, p. 247. See also Wolfgang Herrmann, *Laugier and Eighteenth Century French Theory*, London: Zwemmer, 1962.

87 Leslie Maitland, *Neoclassical Architecture in Canada*, Studies in Archaeology, Architecture and History, Ottawa: Parks Canada, 1984, p. 51 and *passim*. See also Leslie Maitland, 'Pillars, Pilasters and Porticoes', *Canadian Collector*, 17:2, March-April 1982, pp. 47-9.

88 T.W. Acheson, *Saint John: The Making of a Colonial Urban Community*, Toronto: University of Toronto Press, 1985, p. 19; Alix Granger, 'Banking', *CE* I, p. 172.

89 Fiske Kimball, 'The Bank of the United States 1818-1824', *Architectural Record*, 58, December 1925, p. 581; cited in Susan Wagg, 'A Critical Look at Bank Architecture', in *Money Matters: A Critical Look at Bank Architecture*, New York: McGraw Hill, 1990, p. 26.

90 Maitland, *Neoclassical Architecture*, p. 66.

91 Ibid., pp. 8-10; C.A. Hale, 'Early Court Houses of the Maritime Provinces', in Carter, *Early Canadian Court Houses*, pp. 51, 57; *South Shore: Seasoned Timbers*, II, Halifax: Heritage Trust of Nova Scotia, 1974, pp. 100-1.

92 Maitland, *Neoclassical Architecture*, p. 117.

93 Arthur/Otto, *No Mean City*, pp. 127, 131; Maitland, *Neoclassical Architecture*, p. 68.

94 Luc d'Iberville-Moreau, *Lost Montreal*, Toronto: Oxford University Press, 1975, p. 81; Maitland, *Neoclassical Architecture*, p. 96. For Biddle and his house, see Talbot

95 Maitland, *Neoclassical Architecture*, pp. 37-8; Elizabeth Collard, 'Nelson in Old Montreal', *Country Life*, 146:3777, 24 July 1969, pp. 210-11; Wolfe and Grenier, *Montreal Guide*, p. 69.

96 Nikolaus Pevsner, *A History of Building Types*, London: Thames and Hudson, 1976, p. 21.

97 Information and citations were kindly provided by Stephen A. Otto, who will describe the two Brock Monuments in his forthcoming book on Ontario architecture to 1914.

98 Bill Witcomb, 'The St Andrews Court House', *Atlantic Advocate*, 75:1, September 1984, pp. 29-31; Hale, 'Early Court Houses', pp. 51-3, illustrating the similar Queen's County Courthouse in Gagetown, NB (1836-7); Maitland, *Neoclassical Architecture*, pp. 48-50.

99 Kingston *Chronicle and Gazette*, 16 December 1843; cited in Maitland, *Neoclassical Architecture*, p. 8.

100 Maitland, *Neoclassical Architecture*, pp. 61-2, citing Bosworth, *Hochelaga Depicta*, p. 14; CUM, *Les Édifices publics*, 1981, pp. 146-51; Rémillard and Merrett, *Montreal Architecture*, p. 43.

101 *Seasoned Timbers*, pp. 40-1.

102 Douglas Richardson, 'Georgian and Victorian Churches', unpublished manuscript, c. 1975, pp. 17-18, citing the source in Benjamin and the note on the plans; Ralph Greenhill et al., *Ontario Towns*, Plate 14 and introduction (not paginated); E.R. Arthur, *St Andrew's Church, Niagara-on-the-Lake*, Bulletin 153, School of Engineering Research, University of Toronto, Toronto, 1938, which reproduces the original plans; MacRae and Adamson, *Hallowed Walls*, pp. 199-204; Maitland, *Neoclassical Architecture*, pp. 114-15.

103 The entry by Abbott Lowell Cummings on Benjamin in the *Macmillan Encyclopedia of Architects*, I, pp. 176-9; Richardson, 'Churches', p. 17.

104 Maitland, *Neoclassical Architecture*, p. 118.

105 Arthur/Otto, *No Mean City*, pp. 83-4; Arthur, ibid., 1st ed., Toronto, 1964, pp. 72-5; Dendy and Kilbourn, *Toronto Observed*, pp. 46-7.

106 Christina Cameron, *Charles Baillairgé: Architect & Engineer*, Montreal: McGill-Queen's University Press, 1989, pp. 40-5; Maitland, *Neoclassical Architecture*, p. 67.

107 Bosworth, *Hochelaga Depicta*, p. 112.

108 d'Iberville-Moreau, *Lost Montreal*, pp. 128-9.

109 W.A. Langton, ed., *Early Days in Upper Canada: Letters of John Langton*, 1926; cited in Dendy and Kilbourn, *Toronto Observed*, pp. 64-70; Douglas Richardson et al., *A Not Unsightly Building: University College and Its History*, Oakville: Mosaic Press, 1990. See also Arthur/Otto, *No Mean City*, pp. 138-45, 151.

110 Richardson, *University College*, pp. 73-4; Margaret E. McKelvey and Merilyn McKelvey, *Toronto: Carved in Stone*, Toronto: Fitzhenry and Whiteside, 1984, p. 17; Arthur/Otto, *No Mean City*, p. 271; Mary Willan Mason, 'Rossetti's Wombat?' *Canadian Collector*, 21:2 (March 1986), p. 27.

111 Alan Gowans, 'The Baroque Revival in Quebec', *JSAH*, 14:3, October 1955, pp. 8-14.

112 Gowans, 'Baroque Revival', pp. 8-9; Ellen James, *John Ostell: Architecte, Arpenteur/Architect, Surveyor*, Montreal: McCord Museum, 1985, pp. 60-1. CUM, *Les Églises*, 1981, pp. 112-17.

113 Olivier Maurault, *St-Jacques de Montréal*, Montreal, 1923, p. 8; cited in Gowans, 'Baroque Revival', p. 11.

114 *Courrier du Canada*, 20 February 1857; cited in Gowans, 'Baroque Revival', p. 11.

115 Gowans, 'Baroque Revival', pp. 13-14; CUM, *Les Églises*, pp. 232-9; Marsan, *Montreal*, pp. 210-12.

CHAPTER 7 Early Building on the Prairies

1 Ted J. Brasser, 'Home, House and Temple Among the Plains Indians', *Canadian Collector*, 11:1, January-February 1976, pp. 31-4; Ted J. Brasser, 'The Tipi as an Element in the Emergence of Historic Plains Indian Nomadism', *Plains Anthropologist*, 27:98, pt. 1, 1982; Peter Nabokov and Robert Easton, *Native American Architecture*, New York: Oxford University Press, 1989, pp. 150-67; John C. Ewers, *Blackfeet Indian Tipis: Design and Legend*, Bozeman: Museum of the Rockies, 1976; Reginald and Gladys Laubin, *The Indian Tipi: Its History, Construction and Use*, 2nd ed., Norman: University of Oklahoma Press, 1980; Walter McClintock, 'The Blackfoot Tipi', *Southwest Museum Leaflets*, No. 5, Los Angeles: Southwest Museum, n.d. For the Prairies generally, see Trevor Boddy, 'Introduction: Notes for a History of Prairie Architecture', *Prairie Forum*, 5:22, Fall 1980, pp. 123-41.

2 James T. Finnigan, *Tipi Rings and Plains Prehistory: A Reassessment of Their Archaeological Potential*, Mercury Series, Archaeological Survey of Canada, Paper No. 108, Ottawa: National Museums of Canada, 1982.

3 David G. Mandelbaum, *The Plains Cree: An Ethnographic, Historical, and Comparative Study*, Canadian Plains Studies, No. 9, Regina: Canadian Plains Research Centre, University of Regina, 1979, p. 90.

4 Claude E. Schaeffer, *Blackfoot Shaking Tent*, Occasional Paper No. 5, Calgary: Glenbow-Alberta Institute, 1969.

5 John H. Brumley, 'The Ellis Site (EcOp-4): A Late Prehistoric Burial Lodge/Medicine Wheel Site in Southeastern Alberta', in David Burley, ed., *Contributions to Plains Prehistory*, Archaeological Survey of Alberta, Occasional Paper No. 26, Edmonton: Alberta Culture, 1985, pp. 180-225. *Medicine Wheels in Alberta*, brochure, Edmonton: Alberta Culture and Multiculturalism, n.d.

6 Daniel Williams Harmon, *A Journal of Voyages and Travels...* (1820), cited in Rodger Guinn, *The Red-Assiniboine Junction: A Land Use and Structural History, 1770-1980*, Manuscript Report Series No. 355, Ottawa: Parks Canada, 1980, p. 13.

7 Guinn, op. cit., p. 40.

8 'Peter Fidler's Account of the Red River District: 1819', Hudson's Bay Company Archives; quoted in Guinn, *Junction*, p. 54.

9 Dale Miquelon, 'A Brief History of Lower Fort Garry', *Canadian Historic Sites: Occasional Papers in Archaeology and History*, No. 4, Ottawa: Department of Indian Affairs and Northern Development, 1970, pp. 9-41; Simpson's dispatch of 18 July 1831, Hudson's Bay Company Archives, is cited on p. 11. See also George Ingram, 'Industrial and Agricultural Activities at Lower Fort Garry', and Ingram, 'The Big House, Lower Fort Garry', *Canadian Historic Sites*, 4, pp. 43-92, 93-164, respectively; James V. Chism, 'Excavations at Lower Fort Garry, 1965-1967', *Canadian Historic Sites*, 5, 1972, pp. 7-96.

10 Gerald Friesen, *The Canadian Prairies: A History*, Toronto: University of Toronto Press, 1984, pp. 70-80; see also *Thomas Douglas, Fifth Earl of Selkirk*, Winnipeg: Manitoba Culture, Heritage and Recreation, 1984; *Red River Settlement*, Winnipeg: Manitoba Culture, Heritage and Recreation, 1988.

11 Marius Barbeau, 'The House that Mac Built', *The Beaver*, Outfit 276, December 1945, pp. 10-13; Jill Wade, 'Red River Architecture, 1812-1870', M.A. thesis, University of British Columbia, 1967; David Butterfield, *Architectural Heritage: The Selkirk and District Planning Area*, Winnipeg: Manitoba Culture, Heritage and Recreation, 1988, pp. 18-28.

12 Guinn, *Junction*, pp. 47-9; *Peter Fidler*, Winnipeg: Manitoba Culture, Heritage and Recreation, 1984.

13 Thomas Thomas to Lord Selkirk, 15 September 1815, in Selkirk Papers, Public Archives of Manitoba; quoted in Guinn, *Junction*, p. 49.

14 William Douglas, 'New Light on the Old Forts of Winnipeg', paper read before the Historical and Scientific Society of Manitoba, ser. 3, no. 11, edited by Paul Yuzyk, Winnipeg: Historical and Scientific Society of Manitoba, 1956, p. 7, citing an account by Peter Fidler, Selkirk Papers, 6 August 1814, p. 18432; cited in Wade, 'Red River Architecture', p. 9.

15 John West, *The Substance of a Journal During a Residence at the Red River Colony*, 1824; cited in John de Visser and Harold Kalman, *Pioneer Churches*, Toronto: McClelland and Stewart, 1976, pp. 149, 165; Kelly Crossman, *A Study of Anglican Church Buildings in Manitoba*, Winnipeg: Manitoba Culture, Heritage and Recreation, 1989, p. 9; Wade, 'Red River Architecture', p. 9.

16 *Kildonan Presbyterian Church*, Winnipeg: Manitoba Department of Cultural Affairs and Historical Resources, 1981; Neil R. Bingham, *A Study of the Church Buildings in Manitoba of the Congregational, Methodist, Presbyterian and United Churches of Canada*, Winnipeg: Manitoba Culture, Heritage and Recreation, 1986, pp. 14-15, 249.

17 *St Boniface*, Winnipeg: Manitoba Culture, Heritage and Recreation, 1988, pp. 4-5.

18 Martha McCarthy, *To Evangelize the Nations: Roman Catholic Missions in Manitoba, 1818-1870*, Papers in Manitoba History, Report No. 2, Winnipeg: Manitoba Culture, Heritage and Recreation, 1990, pp. 11-14

19 Antoine Lussier and D. Bruce Sealey, *The Other Natives: The/Les Métis, 1700-1885*, Winnipeg: Manitoba Métis Federation Press / Éditions Bois-Brûlés, 1978, pp. 6-7, 22.

20 *St Norbert Heritage Park*, Manitoba, Winnipeg: Department of Cultural Affairs and Historical Resources, 1983, p. 10.

21 J.C. Hamilton, *The Prairie Province*, Toronto: Belford Brothers, 1876, p. 225, cited in K. David McLeod, 'Archaeological Investigations at the Delorme House (DkLg-18), 1981', *Papers in Manitoba Archaeology*, Final Report No. 13, Winnipeg: Department of Cultural Affairs and Historical Resources, 1982, p. 8 (see pp. 5-15 and *passim*); and *St Norbert Heritage Park*, p. 14.

22 Ken L. Elder, 'Riel House, St. Vital, Manitoba: Architectural Analysis and Conservation Concept Report' (1976) and 'Riel House, St. Vital Manitoba: Architectural Investigation Report' (1973) manuscripts on file, Restoration Services Division, Parks Canada, Ottawa. See also Robert Gosman, *Riel House, St. Vital, Manitoba* (1975) and *The Riel and Lagimodière Families in Métis Society, 1840-1860* (1977), Manuscript Report Series No. 171, Ottawa: Parks Canada.

23 Guillaume Charette, *Vanishing Spaces: Memoirs of Louis Goulet*, Winnipeg: Éditions Bois-Brûlés, 1980, pp. 3-6, 14.

24 Jean Friesen, 'The Heritage of the River Road, Manitoba', *SSAC Bulletin*, 12:3, September 1987, pp. 14-19.

25 *Seven Oaks House*, Winnipeg: Department of Cultural Affairs and Historical Resources, 1983. Neil Einarson kindly provided additional information.

26 *St. James Church*, Winnipeg: Manitoba Culture, Heritage and Recreation, rev. ed., 1985; Crossman, *Anglican Church Buildings*, pp. 12-13, 154; de Visser and Kalman, *Pioneer Churches*, pp. 165-7.

27 Taylor to SPG, cited in *St James Church*, p. 2.

28 Cited in Crossman, *Anglican Church Buildings*, p. 13.

29 Wade, 'Red River Architecture', p. 9; D.W. Buchanan, 'Lumbering in Manitoba', *Manitoba Colonist*, 3:8, January 1889, p. 366.

30 Robert Coatts, *St Andrew's Church, Red River: An Historical and Architectural Survey*, Research Bulletin No. 289, [Ottawa:] Environment Canada—Parks Service, 1991; Colin Inkster, 'William Cochran', in W.B. Heeney, ed., *Leaders of the Canadian Church*, II, Toronto, 1920, pp. 39-61; Hal Guest, 'The Historic Landscape of the Parsonage at St Andrew's', report, National Historic Parks and Sites Branch, Ottawa, 1981; Crossman, *Anglican Church Buildings*, pp. 9-10, 125; de Visser and Kalman, *Pioneer Churches*, pp. 148, 165; Butterfield, *Selkirk and District*, pp. 44-5; M.L. Kennedy, 'The Mission at the Rapids', *The Beaver*, Outfit 264:2, September 1933, pp. 52-4.

31 *Duncan McRae*, Winnipeg: Manitoba Culture, Heritage and Recreation, 1984; Butterfield, *Selkirk and District*, p. 4.

32 *Duncan McRae*, pp. 44-8.

33 Butterfield, *Selkirk and District*, pp. 38-9.

34 Frederick Jackson Turner, 'The Significance of the Frontier in American History' (1893), in Turner, *The Frontier in American History*, New York, 1920. The Canadian reaction to the frontier hypothesis is summarized in J.M.S. Careless, 'Frontierism, Metropolitanism, and Canadian History', *Canadian Historical Review*, 35:1, March 1954, pp. 1-21.

35 John Warkentin, *The Western Interior of Canada: A Record of Geographical Discovery 1612-1917*, Toronto: McClelland and Stewart, 1964; John Warkentin, 'Steppe, Desert and Empire', in A.W. Rasporich and H.C. Klassen, eds, *Prairie Perspectives*, 2, Toronto, 1973; Friesen, *Prairies*, pp. 107-10.

36 Ged Martin, 'British Attitudes to Prairie Settlement', *Alberta Historical Review*, 22:1, Winter 1974, pp. 1-11; Friesen, *Prairies*, p. 110; *Daily Telegraph* (London), 25 November 1864, cited in Martin, 'Attitudes', p. 2; *Edinburgh Review*, 119, 1864, quoted in Leslie J. Hurt, *The Victoria Settlement 1862-1922*, Historic Sites Service, Occasional Paper No. 7, Edmonton: Alberta Culture, 1979, p. 103.

37 Cited in Martin, 'Attitudes', p. 5

38 J.F. Klaus, 'Early Trails to Carlton House' and Russ Clarke, 'Carlton House Reconstruction', *The Beaver*, Outfit 297, Autumn 1966, pp. 32-9 and 40-1.

39 Friesen, *Prairies*, pp. 100-1.

40 Heinz W. Pyszczyk, 'The Architecture of the Western Canadian Fur Trade: A Cultural-Historical Perspective', *SSAC Bulletin*, 17:2, June 1992, pp. 32-41; Barbeau, 'The House that Mac Built'.

41 James G. MacGregor, *A History of Alberta*, rev. ed., Edmonton: Hurtig, 1977, pp. 77, 165; Howard Palmer with Tamara Palmer, *Alberta: A New History*, Edmonton: Hurtig, 1990. p. 25. See also Judy Larmour, 'Emile Grouard, Artist Bishop of the North: The Altar Paintings and Decoration of the Sanctuary in St Charles Church, Dunvegan', *SSAC Bulletin*, 17:4, December 1992, pp. 105-8.

42 Emeric Drouin, 'Saint Albert', *Canadian Collector*, 11:1, January-February 1976, pp. 20-2.

43 Doras C. Kirk, 'Church of the Pioneers', *The Beaver*, Outfit 282, December 1950, pp. 52-3; R.R. Rostecki and Janet Wright, 'Holy Trinity Church, Stanley Mission, Saskatchewan', Agenda Paper, Historic Sites and Monuments Board of Canada, Ottawa, n.d; Saskatchewan Association of Architects, *Historic Architecture of Saskatchewan*, Regina: Focus, 1986, pp. 115-17.

44 Church Mission Society, 'Journal of the Reverend Robert Hunt', Public Archives of Manitoba, 10 April 1854; cited in Rostecki and Wright, 'Holy Trinity Church', p. 2.

45 John McDougall, *Saddle, Sled and Snowshoe: Pioneering on the Saskatchewan in the Sixties*, Toronto, 1896, p. 54, cited in Hurt, *Victoria Settlement*; 'Victoria Settlement', *Alberta Past*, 3:2, December 1987, pp. 1-3.

46 Elizabeth McDougall, 'An Alberta Christmas', unpublished manuscript, Glenbow Archives, Calgary; John McDougall, *Saddle, Sled and Snowshoe*; both cited in Hurt, *Victoria Settlement*, p. 15 and n. 28; MacGregor, *Alberta*, p. 86.

47 Hurt, *Victoria Settlement*, p. 108 and n. 202, the latter citing Frank E. Mitchell, *A History of Pioneering in the Pakan District*, n.p., 1973, p. 6. Both Whitford and Turner are listed as having been resident in the Red River before 1870 in D.N. Sprague and R.P. Frye, *The Genealogy of the First Metis Nation*, Winnipeg: Pemmican, 1983.

48 George M. Grant, *Ocean to Ocean: Sandford Fleming's Expedition Through Canada in 1872*, Toronto, 1873 (fascimile reprint of second edition, with introduction by L.H. Thomas, Hurtig: Edmonton, 1967), p. 163.

49 de Visser and Kalman, *Pioneer Churches*, pp. 166-7; Hugh A. Dempsey, in 'The Last Letters of Rev. George McDougall' (unidentified periodical), illustrates a sketch of the towerless church, drawn by Dr Richard Nevitt of the NWMP in the late 1870s.

50 M.A. Kennedy and B.O.K. Reeves, 'An Inventory and Historical Description of Whiskey Posts in Southern Alberta', unpublished report, 2 vols, Edmonton: Alberta Culture, 1984.

51 *Globe*, Toronto, 30 December 1882; cited in Kennedy and Reeves, 'Whiskey Posts', I, plate 93.

52 Greg Thomas and Ian Clarke, 'The Garrison Mentality and the Canadian West', *Prairie Forum*, 4:1, Spring 1989, pp. 83-104.

53 Donna Coulter, 'North West Mounted Police', in *Fort Macleod: Our Colourful Past*, Fort Macleod, 1977, p. 18. See also E.J. Chambers, *The Royal North-West Mounted Police: A Corps History*, 1906, reprinted 1972; A.L. Haydon, *Riders of the Plains*, Toronto, 1911, reprinted Edmonton: Hurtig, 1971; Grace Lane, 'The Forts of the Mounties', *Imperial Oil Review*, 3, 1971, pp. 3-9; Harold Kalman, 'Homes of the Scarlet Serge', *Canadian Heritage*, 10:5, December 1984-January 1985, pp. 13-17.

54 Max Foran and Heather MacEwan Foran, *Calgary: Canada's Frontier Metropolis*, Calgary: Windsor Publications, 1982, pp. 34-63; Harold D. Kalman, Bailey Consulting Associates, and Keith H. Wagland, 'A Master Plan for Fort Calgary', [Ottawa] 1983, pp. 5-13.

55 James V. Sciscenti et al., *Archaeological Investigations at a Late Nineteenth Century Northwest Mounted Police Post, Fort Walsh, Saskatchewan: 1973-74 Field Seasons*, Manuscript Report Series No. 200, Ottawa: Parks Canada, 1976; Jeffrey S. Murray and James V. Sciscenti, *Archaeological Investigations at a Late Nineteenth Century N.W.M.P. Post, Fort Walsh, Saskatchewan: Preliminary Report on the 1975 Excavations*, and Jeffrey S. Murray, *Archaeological Investigations at a Late Nineteenth Century N.W.M.P. Post, Fort Walsh, Saskatchewan: Preliminary Report on the 1976 Excavations*, Manuscript Report Series No. 281, Ottawa: Parks Canada, 1977.

56 Canada. House of Commons, *Sessional Papers*, No. 23, Ottawa: Queen's Printer, 1883, pp. 19-20, which includes a description of the prefabricated systems; Canada. North-West Mounted Police, *Report of the Commissioner of the North-West Mounted Police Force*, 1883, Ottawa: Queen's Printer, 1884, n.p.

57 Chester Martin, *'Dominion Lands' Policy*, Toronto: Macmillan, 1938; J.G. MacGregor, *Vision of an Ordered Land: The Story of the Dominion Land Survey*, Saskatoon: Western Producer Prairie Books, 1981.

58 See Wilhelm Kristjanson, *The Icelandic People in Manitoba: A Manitoba Saga*, Winnipeg: Wallingford, [*c.* 1965]; Walter Jacobson Lindal, *The Icelanders in Canada*, Ottawa: National Publishers, 1967; also local histories of Gimli, Riverton, and Hecla.

59 Lyle Dick, *A History of Prairie Settlement Patterns, 1870-1930*, Microfiche Report Series No. 307, Ottawa: Canadian Parks Service, 1987, pp. 4-6, 68-71, 130-6; *Mennonite Settlement: The East and West Reserves*, Winnipeg: Historic Resources Branch, Department of Cultural Affairs and Historical Resources, 1981; David K. Butterfield and Edward M. Ledohowski, *Architectural Heritage: The MSTW Planning District*, Winnipeg: Historic Resources Branch, Department of Culture, Heritage and Recreation, 1984, pp. 78-128; John Warkentin, 'Mennonite Agricultural Settlements of Southern Manitoba', *Geographical Review*, 49:3, July 1959, pp. 342-68. See also E.K. Francis, *In Search of Utopia: The Mennonites of Manitoba*, Altona: Friesen, 1955; Frank H. Epp, *Mennonites in Canada, 1786-1920*, Toronto: Macmillan, 1974; *Mennonite Village Museum, Steinbach, Manitoba, Canada*, rev. ed., Steinbach: Mennonite Village Museum, 1984.

60 Cited in Warkentin, 'Settlements', p. 343.

61 Cited in Peter D. Zacharias, *Reinland: An Experience in Community*, Reinland: Reinland Centennial Committee, 1976, p. 86.

62 P.W. Toews, cited in E.K. Francis, 'The Mennonite Farmhouse in Manitoba', *Mennonite Quarterly Review*, 28:1, January 1954, p. 56.

63 Francis, 'Mennonite Farmhouse', p. 56. See also John C. Reimer and Julius G. Toews, 'Mennonite Buildings', in Lawrence Klippenstein and Julius G. Toews, eds, *Mennonite Memories: Settling in Western Canada*, Winnipeg: Centennial Publications, 1977, pp. 114-18; Rolf Wilh. Brednich, *Mennonite Folklife and Folklore: A Preliminary Report*, Canadian Centre for Folk Culture Studies, Paper No. 22, Ottawa: National Museums of Canada, 1977; Butterfield and Ledohowski, *Architectural Heritage: MSTW*, pp. 89-94; John C. Lehr, 'Folk Architecture in Manitoba: Mennonites and Ukrainians', *SSAC Bulletin*, 11:2, June 1986, pp. 3-5; Gwendolyn Dowsett, 'The Vernacular Architecture of Two Ethnic Groups in Manitoba: A Comparative Study', *SSAC Bulletin*, 12:3, September 1987, pp. 7-13.

64 Butterfield and Ledohowski, *Architectural Heritage: MSTW*, pp. 90-1. See also Jerry Dick, 'The Russian Mennonite House-barn of Manitoba: A Study in Cultural Transformations', unpublished BIS thesis, University of Waterloo, 1984.

65 John C. Reimer, 'The Mennonite House Plan', in Abe Warkentin, ed., *Reflections on Our Heritage: A History of Steinbach and the R.M. of Hanover from 1874*, Steinbach: Derksen Printers, 1971, pp. 29-32; Peter Goertzen, *Teichroeb: A Family History and Geneaology...*, Winnipeg: privately printed, 1979, pp. 58-9.

66 Butterfield and Ledohowski, *Architectural Heritage: MSTW*, pp. 131-2; Jake Peters, *Mennonite Private Schools in Manitoba and Saskatchewan 1874-1925*, Historical Series 11, Steinbach: Mennonite Village Museum, 1985.

67 Marcel Giraud, 'Métis Settlement in the North-west Territories', *Saskatchewan History*, 7, 1954, pp. 1-16.

68 Commonwealth Historic Resource Management Limited, *Historic Building Technology of Métis Communities*, Microfiche Report No. 213, Ottawa: Parks Canada, 1985; Donald G. Wetherell and Irene R.A. Kmet, *Homes in Alberta: Buildings, Trends, and Designs 1870-1967*, Edmonton: University of Alberta Press and Alberta Culture and Multiculturalism, 1991, pp. 13-15.

69 J.R. Stan Hambly, *The Battle River Country: An Historical Sketch of Duhamel and District*, New Norway, Alberta: Duhamel Historical Society, 1974, pp. 9-18; Commonwealth Historic Resource Management, *Métis Communities*, pp. 146-7.

70 Paul F. Donahue et al., *Batoche Archaeology Project: 1977 Structural and Survey Report* and David Burley, *Batoche Archaeological Research: A Report on the 1978 Field Programme*, Manuscript Report No. 359, Ottawa: Parks Canada, 1978; Diane Payment, *Structural and Settlement History of Batoche Village*, Manuscript Report No. 246, Ottawa: Parks Canada, 1977; Diane Payment, 'Monsieur Batoche', *Saskatchewan History*, 32:3, Autumn 1979, pp. 81-103; Diane Payment, *Batoche (1870-1910)*, St Boniface: Éditions du Blé, 1983; Diane Payment, 'Structural and Material Culture History of the Church at St Antoine-de-Padoue, Batoche', manuscript, Winnipeg: Parks Canada, Prairie Region, 1981.

71 Gary William David Abrams, *Prince Albert: The First Century 1866-1966*, Saskatoon: Modern Press, 1966.

72 Art Loucks, 'Prince Albert—Lumber Mills', unpublished manuscript, 4 parts, n.d; 'Transcript by J.W. Sanderson', unpublished manuscript, n.d; R. Mayson, 'Lumbering Industry of Early Prince Albert', Prince Albert Historical Society, No. 204b; 'Town of Prince Albert', pp. 31-40—all in the Prince Albert Historical Museum; see also 'Town of Prince Albert', *McPhillips's Saskatchewan Directory*, 1888, p. 32. The lumber industry after 1900 is described in James Shortt, *A Survey of the Human History of Prince Albert National Park*, 1887-1945, Manuscript Report Series No. 239, Ottawa: Parks Canada, 1977, pp. 13-14.

73 *Prince Albert Times and Saskatchewan Review*, 30 January 1885; Payment, 'Church at St. Antoine-de-Padoue', p. 32.

74 Art Loucks, 'Prince Albert—The Brick Yards', unpublished manuscript, n.d., Prince Albert Historical Museum.

75 Walter Hildebrandt, *Fort Battleford: A Structural History*, Manuscript Report No. 252, I, Ottawa: Parks Canada, 1978, pp. 1-17, 28-36; Walter Hildebrandt, 'Public Buildings in Battleford, 1876-1878', *Saskatchewan History*, 35:1, Winter 1982, pp. 17-24.

76 Effie Storer, 'John G. Oliver, Western Pioneer', *The Saskatchewan Farmer*, 3 January 1944, cited in Hildebrandt, 'Fort Battleford', I, p. 28.

77 Report, 20 September 1877, National Archives of Canada, cited in Hildebrandt, 'Fort Battleford', I, p. 31.

78 Report of the Commissioner, 1878, cited in ibid., I, p. 29.

79 Alan Artibise, *Winnipeg: An Illustrated History*, Toronto: James Lorimer, 1977, pp. 11-22; R.R. Rustecki, 'The Growth of Winnipeg, 1870-1886', M.A. thesis, University of Manitoba, 1980; Ivan J. Saunders, R.R. Rostecki, and Selwyn Carrington, *Early Buildings in Winnipeg*, Manuscript Report No. 389, 2 vols, Ottawa: Parks Canada, 1977.

80 George Young, *Manitoba Memories*, Toronto, 1897, pp. 63-4; cited in Artibise, *Winnipeg*, p. 16.

81 George B. Brooks, *Plain Facts About the New City Hall*, Winnipeg: Walker and May, 1884, cited in Marc de Caraffe et al., *Town Halls of Canada: A Collection of Essays on Pre-1930 Town Hall Buildings*, Studies in Archaeology, Architecture and History, Ottawa: Environment Canada—Parks, 1987, p. 232; Alec Clifton-Taylor in the *Winnipeg Free Press*, 15 September 1956, cited in William Paul Thompson, *Winnipeg Architecture: 100 Years*, Winnipeg: Queenston House, 1975, p. 69; Alan F.J. Artibise, 'Winnipeg's City Halls 1876-1965', *Manitoba Pageant*, 22:3, Spring 1977, pp. 5-10; R.R. Rostecki, 'Barber and Barber, Architects Extraordinaire', *SSAC Bulletin*, 7:3-4, December 1981, pp. 9-13.

82 *1979: The Year Past: Report of the City of Winnipeg Historical Buildings Committee*, Winnipeg: City of Winnipeg, 1979, p. 29; Thompson, *Winnipeg Architecture:*, p. 11.

83 *1979: The Year Past*, pp. 45-50; Harold Kalman, Keith Wagland, and Robert Bailey, *Encore: Recycling Public Buildings for the Arts*, Don Mills: Corpus, 1980, pp. 104-9.

84 Leonard K. Eaton, 'Winnipeg: The Northern Anchor of the Wholesale Trade', in *Gateway Cities and Other Essays*, Ames, Iowa: Iowa State University Press, 1989, pp. 84-112; *1985: The Year Past: Report of the City of Winnipeg Historical Buildings Committee*, Winnipeg: City of Winnipeg, 1985, pp. 23-6; Thompson, *Winnipeg Architecture*, p. 24; E.J Gaboury and Associates, *A Feasibility Study: Arts Accommodation in the Historic Winnipeg Area*, Stage 1, Winnipeg, 1983, Appendix, No. 49; Artibise, *Winnipeg*, p. 18. For the Exchange District generally, see M. Ross Waddell, *The Exchange District: An Illustrated Guide to Winnipeg's Historic Commercial District*, Winnipeg: Heritage Winnipeg Corporation, 1989; and William P. Thompson et al., *Winnipeg's Historic Warehouse Area: Its Revitalisation Through Conservation*, Winnipeg: Heritage Canada and the Manitoba Historical Society, 1976.

CHAPTER 8 The Settlement of the West Coast

1 Wayne Suttles, ed., *Handbook of North American Indians*, 7: *Northwest Coast*, Washington: Smithsonian Institution, 1990; Peter Nabokov and Robert Easton, *Native American Architecture*, New York: Oxford University Press, 1989, pp. 226-85; Joan Vastokas, *Architecture of the Northwest Coast Indians of America*, Ph.D. thesis, Columbia University, 1966, reprinted by University Microfilm International, Ann Arbor; George Woodcock, *Peoples of the Coast: The Indians of the Pacific Northwest*, Edmonton: Hurtig, 1977; Knut R. Fladmark, *British Columbia Prehistory*, Ottawa: Archaeological Survey of Canada, National Museum of Man, 1986; Robert McGhee, *Ancient Canada*, Ottawa: Canadian Museum of Civilization, *c*. 1989.

2 Nabokov and Easton, *Architecture*, pp. 270-1; Margaret B. Blackman, 'Haida: Traditional Culture', in Suttles, ed., *Handbook*, 7, pp. 242-4; George F. MacDonald, *Haida Monumental Art: The Villages of the Queen Charlotte Islands*, Vancouver: University of British Columbia Press, 1983, pp. 18-24; George F. MacDonald, *Ninstints: Haida World Heritage Site*, Museum Note No. 12, Vancouver: University of British Columbia Press and UBC Museum of Anthropology, 1983; Hilary Stewart, *Cedar: Tree of Life to the Northwest Coast Indians*, Vancouver: Douglas and McIntyre, 1984.

3 Helen Codere, 'Kwakiutl: Traditional Culture', in Suttles, ed., *Handbook*, 7, p. 365; Nobokov and Easton, *Architecture*, pp. 244-57.

4 Cited in Nabokov and Easton, *Architecture*, p. 243; see also Eugene Arima and John Dewhirst, 'Nootkans of Vancouver Island', in Suttles, ed., *Handbook*, 7, pp. 397-9.

5 Cited in Stewart, *Cedar*, p. 65; see also Dorothy I.D. Kennedy and Randall T. Bouchard, 'Northern Coast Salish', and Wayne Suttles, 'Central Coast Salish', in Suttles, ed., *Handbook*, 7, pp. 446, 462; Nabokov and Easton, *Architecture*, pp. 232-41; Homer G. Barnett, *The Coast Salish of British Columbia*, Eugene: University of Oregon Press, 1955.

6 Gordon Mohs, 'Spiritual Sites, Ethnic Significance and Native Spirituality: The Heritage and Heritage Sites of the Sto:lo Indians of British Columbia', M.A. Thesis, Simon Fraser University, 1985.

7 Fladmark, *British Columbia Prehistory*; J.V. Wright, *Six Chapters of Canada's Prehistory*, Ottawa: Archaeological Survey of Canada, National Museum of Man, 1976; Wayne Choquette, 'Prehistoric Native Occupation and Land Use', in Commonwealth Historic Resource Management Limited, *Kootenay Heritage Tourism Study*, prepared for the Heritage Conservation Branch, British Columbia Ministry of Municipal Affairs, Recreation and Culture, Vancouver, 1990, pp. 15-23.

8 James A. Teit, 'The Thompson Indians of British Columbia', *Memoirs of the American Museum of Natural History*, 2:4, 1900, pp. 163-392; cited in Nabakov and Easton, *Architecture*, pp. 177-9.

9 See also Marian W. Smith, 'House Types of the Middle Fraser River', *American Antiquity*, 12:4, 1947, pp. 255-67; James A. Teit, 'The Lillooet Indians', *Memoirs of the American Museum of Natural History*, 4:5, 1906, pp. 193-300; James A. Teit, 'The Salishan Tribes of the Western Plateau', Bureau of American Ethnology, Annual Report 45, 1930.

10 Nabokov and Easton, *Architecture*, pp. 174-6, citing the theories of T.T. Waterman and Ralph Linton.

11 Ibid., pp. 180-1.

12 Quoted in ibid., p. 180.

13 Ibid., p. 183; Dorothy Kennedy and Randy Bouchard, 'Native People', *CE* III, p. 1445.

14 Nabokov and Easton, *Architecture*, pp. 186-7; 'Building a Winter Dwelling', *Kelowna Centennial Museum Booklet*, II: 2, Kelowna: Lamong-Surtees, 1975.

15 Margaret A. Ormsby, *British Columbia: A History*, Toronto: Macmillan, 1958, pp. 6-7, 58; Jean Barman, *The West Beyond the West: A History of British Columbia*, Toronto: University of Toronto Press, 1991, pp. 28-9; James R. Gibson, 'The Russian Fur Trade', in Carol M. Judd and Arthur J. Ray, eds, *Old Trails and New Directions: Papers of the Third North American Fur Trade Conference*, Toronto: University of Toronto Press, 1978, pp. 218-30; Mary K. Cullen, 'The History of Fort Langley, 1827-96', *Canadian Historic Sites*, No. 20, Ottawa: Parks Canada, 1977, p. 9.

16 Christon I. Archer, 'Spanish Exploration and Settlement of the Northwest Coast in the 18th Century', in Barbara S. Efrat and W.J. Langlois, eds, *Nutka: Captain Cook and the Spanish Explorers on the Coast*, Sound Heritage, 7:1, 1978, pp. 33-53; Ormsby, *British Columbia*, p. 7; Michael E. Thurman, *The Naval Department of San Blas: New Spain's Bastion for Alta California and Nootka, 1768 to 1798*, Glendale, California: Arthur H. Clark, 1967; Iris H. Wilson, ed., *Noticias de Nutka: An Account of Nootka Sound in 1792 by José Mariano Mozino*, Seattle, 1970.

17 Barry M. Gough, 'Nootka Sound in James Cook's Pacific World', in Efrat and Langlois, *Nutka*, pp. 1-32.

18 John Meares, *Voyages Made in the Years 1788 and 1789...*, London: Logographic Press, 1790, pp. 115-16.

19 Derek Pethick, *The Nootka Conection: Europe and the Northwest Coast, 1790-1795*, Vancouver: Douglas and McIntyre, 1980, pp. 136-7.

20 Cited in Barry Downs, *Sacred Places: British Columbia's Early Churches*, Vancouver: Douglas and McIntyre, 1980, p. 27.

21 Archer, 'Spanish Exploration', pp. 41-6; John Kendrick, *The Men with Wooden Feet: The Spanish Exploration of the Pacific Northwest*, Toronto: NC Press, 1985, pp. 44-9; Downs, *Sacred Places*, pp. 27-8. A number of early views of Nootka are included in Thomas Vaughan and Bill Holm, *Soft Gold: The Fur Trade and Cultural Exchange on the Northwest Coast of America*, Portland: Oregon Historical Society, 1982, pp. 218-25.

22 Christon I. Archer, 'Retreat from the North: Spain's Withdrawal from Nootka Sound, 1793-1795', *BC Studies*, 37, Spring 1978, pp. 19-36; Ormsby, *British Columbia*, pp. 16-26; J. Lewis Robinson, 'British Columbia', *CE* I, p. 279.

23 K.R. Fladmark, 'Early Fur-trade Forts of the Peace River Area of British Columbia', *BC Studies*, 65, Spring 1985, pp. 48-65; Ormsby, *British Columbia*, pp. 29-48.

24 Ken Favrholdt, 'Fort St James', *Canadian Collector*, 11:3, May-June 1976, pp. 38-41; James McCook, 'Furs, Fish and Books at Old Fort St James', *Canadian Geographical Journal*, 99:1, 1979, pp. 64-7; Rosemary Neering, 'Fur Fort Revisited', *Beautiful British Columbia*, 21, Spring 1980, pp. 11-19; Thomas W. Tanner, 'Fort St. James', in *Miscellaneous Historical Papers: The Fur Trade*, Manuscript Report Series No. 131, Ottawa: Parks Canada, 1969, pp. 123-81; Teresa M. Homick, *A Social History of Fort St James, 1896*, Microfiche Report Series No. 144, Ottawa: Parks Canada, 1984.

25 Ormsby, *British Columbia*, p. 32.

26 Cullen, 'Fort Langley', pp. 17-19 and *passim*; J. Morton, *Fort Langley: An Overview of the Operations of a Diversified Fur Trade Post...*, Microfiche Report Series No. 340, Ottawa: Canadian Parks Service, [1987]; Jamie Morton, *Fort Langley: A Site History, 1886-1986*, Microfiche Report Series No. 329, Ottawa: Canadian Parks Service, n.d; B.A. McKelvie, *Fort Langley: Birthplace of British Columbia*, Victoria: Porcépic Books, 1991; Ormsby, *British Columbia*, pp. 61-2; Tom H. Inkster, 'Fort Langley: Mainland B.C.'s Big Town, 1827-58', *Canadian Geographical Journal*, 95:1, 1977, pp. 48-53; *Fort Langley National Historic Park, British Columbia*, brochure, Ottawa: Environment Canada—Parks, 1987.

27 Douglas to Governor (John McLoughlin) and Committee, 14 October 1839; cited in Cullen, 'Fort Langley', p. 32.

28 Douglas to James Hargrave, 5 February 1843, in G.P. deT. Glazebrook, ed., *The Hargrave Correspondence 1821-1843*, Toronto: Champlain Society, 1938, p. 420; quoted in Ormsby, *British Columbia*, p. 80.

29 Douglas to Sir George Simpson, 16 November 1843; cited in Derek Pethick, *Victoria: The Fort*, Vancouver: Mitchell Press, 1968, p. 54.

30 Ross to Simpson, January 1844; cited in Pethick, *Victoria*, p. 54.

31 Roderick Finlayson, 'History of Vancouver Island and the Northwest Coast', Public Archives of British Columbia, p. 18; quoted in Ormsby, *British Columbia*, p. 85. See also W. Kaye Lamb, 'The Founding of Fort Victoria', *British Columbia Historical Quarterly*, 7:2, April 1943, pp. 70-92; Kenneth Mackenzie, 'Fort Victoria: The Hudson's Bay Company's Centre on Vancouver Island', in Barry Gough, ed., *The Hudson's Bay Company in British Columbia: Fort Langley, Kamloops, Victoria and Simpson*, History Department, Simon Fraser University, 1983, p. 9. General studies of Victoria that include a discussion of Fort Victoria include Harry Gregson, *A History of Victoria 1842-1970*, Victoria: Victoria Observer, 1970; Michael Kluckner, *Victoria: The Way It Was*, North Vancouver: Whitecap Books, 1986; and Terry Reksten, *More English than the English: A Very Social History of Victoria*, Victoria: Orca, 1986.

32 Douglas and John Work to Governor Simpson, 7 December 1846 and 6 November 1847, cited in Hartwell Bowsfield, ed., *Fort Victoria Letters 1846-1851*, Winnipeg: Hudson's Bay Record Society, 1979, pp. 5, 16-17; Paul Kane, *Wanderings of an Artist Among the Indians of North America*, Toronto: Radisson Society, 1925, chap. 14, pp. 144-5; cited in Pethick, *Victoria*, p. 60.

33 J. Yardley, *Restoration Study: The Bastion, Nanaimo, B.C.*, Ganges, B.C., 1989.

34 *The Reminiscences of Doctor John Sebastian Helmcken*, edited by Dorothy Blakey Smith, Vancouver: University of British Columbia Press, 1975, p. 281.

35 Ingebourg Woodcock and George Woodcock, *Victoria*, Victoria: Morriss, 1971, n.p.

36 Douglas's two-storey house next door (built in 1851 and demolished in 1906) is described and illustrated in Peter Neive Cotton, *Vice-Regal Mansions of British Columbia*, Vancouver: Elgin Publications, 1981, pp. 17, 33; the Royal British Columbia Museum now occupies its site.

37 *Reminiscences of...Helmcken*, pp. 127-8. See also Martin Segger and Douglas Franklin, *Victoria: A Primer for Regional History in Architecture 1843-1929*, Watkins Glen, NY: American Life Foundation and Study Institute, 1979, pp. 187-8; G.E. Mills, *Architectural Trends in Victoria, British Columbia, 1850-1914*, Manuscript Report No. 354, I, Ottawa: Parks Canada, 1976, pp. 265-70. Floor plans, drawn by the provincial Department of Public Works in 1963, were kindly provided by the Heritage Properties Branch.

38 Stuart Stark, *Oak Bay's Heritage Buildings: More Than Just Bricks and Boards*, Oak Bay: Corporation of the District of Oak Bay, 1986, pp. 3-5.

39 Douglas and Work to Simpson, 5 December 1848; Douglas to Archibald Barclay, 16 November 1850; cited in Bowsfield, *Letters*, pp. 25, 135.

40 Gregson, *Victoria*, p. 8.

41 McKenzie to E.E. Langford, 6 March 1855, PABC; quoted in Ormsby, *British Columbia*, p. 103. See also Barry M. Gough, 'Corporate Farming on Vancouver Island: the Puget's Sound Agricultural Company, 1846-1857', *Canadian Papers in Rural History*, 4, 1984, pp. 72-82.

42 Ormsby, *British Columbia*, p. 102.

43 This map, in the Hudson's Bay Company Archives, has not yet been photographed. J.D. McDonald, 'Craigflower: Schoolhouse and Farmhouse', unpublished paper, Victoria: Heritage Properties Branch, 1990, pp. 2, 5.

44 Peter Cotton, *Craigflower Manor, Vol 1: The Structure*, report prepared for the Department of the Provincial Secretary, Victoria, 1970; Segger and Franklin, *Victoria*, pp. 324-7.

45 Segger and Franklin, *Victoria*, pp. 328-9.

46 Alfred Waddington, *The Fraser Mines Vindicated . . .*, Victoria, 1858, pp. 17-18, cited in Ormsby, *British Columbia*, pp. 140-1, and Pethick, *Victoria*, pp. 153-4; Gregson, *Victoria*, pp. 12-26; Gough, 'Farming', p. 80.

47 Gregson, *Victoria*, pp. 17-19; Cecil Clark, *The Best of Victoria Yesterday & Today*, Victoria: Victorian Weekly, 1973, n.p.; Pethick, *Victoria*, pp. 190, 209. A view of *c.* 1858 showing the same stretch of Government Street, looking south rather than north, is reproduced in Cotton, *Mansions*, p. 18. See also Edward Mills, '"Old Town" Commercial District, Victoria, British Columbia', Agenda Paper, Historic Sites and Monuments Board of Canada, Ottawa, 1987.

48 Clark, *Best of Victoria*, n.p; Gregson, *Victoria*, p. 17; Victoria *Gazette*, 1859, reproduced in Cotton, *Mansions*, p. 18; noted also by architect Edward Mallandaine in 1858, cited in John D. Adams, 'Bricks in Pre-1871 Victoria: Their

Manufacture, Trade and Use', *BC Studies*, 74, Autumn 1987, p. 16.

49 Adams, 'Bricks', pp. 3-20; Segger and Franklin, *Victoria*, pp. 36-7. For a general discussion on brickmaking in Canada, focusing on Ontario, see T. Ritchie, *Canada Builds 1867-1967*, Toronto: University of Toronto Press, 1967, pp. 205-27.

50 *This Old Town: City of Victoria Central Area Heritage Conservation Report*, rev. ed., Victoria: City of Victoria, 1983, pp. 62-3; Mark Bawtinheimer, 'Victoria's Rithet Building', *Heritage West*, 5:1, Spring 1981, pp. 12-13; Carolyn Smyly, 'The American Commercial Influence', *Western Living*, 7:11, November 1977, pp. 57-8.

51 Message to the Assembly, 12 May 1858, and Douglas to Newcastle, 12 September 1859; both cited in Martin Segger, ed., *The British Columbia Parliament Buildings*, Vancouver: Arcon, 1979, pp. 42-3.

52 Segger, *Parliament Buildings*; Segger and Franklin, *Victoria*, pp. 39, 348. Tiedemann is one of several architects whose careers are sketched in Madge Wolfenden, 'The Early Architects of British Columbia', *Western Homes and Living*, September 1958, pp. 17-19.

53 Victoria *Gazette*, 20 September 1859, cited in Ormsby, *British Columbia*, p. 130; Victoria *Colonist*, 26 August 1859 and 4 April 1864, Victoria *Gazette*, 20 September 1859, all cited in Pethick, *Victoria*, p. 195.

54 *Fort Rodd Hill National Historic Park, British Columbia*, brochure, Ottawa: Environment Canada—Parks, 1986.

55 Ian Doull, 'Dockyard, CFB Esquimalt...', Federal Heritage Buildings Review Office, Building Report 89-202, 2 vols, Ottawa, 1989 (with bibliography); Sally Coutts, 'Warehouse D85, Esquimalt Dockyard, Victoria, B.C.', Federal Heritage Buildings Review Office, Building Report 85-01, Ottawa, 1985; F.D.W. Nelson and N.E. Oliver, *CFB Esquimalt: Military Heritage*, n.p., 1982. Ian Doull kindly provided this material.

56 Norman J. Ronnenberg, 'The Bittersweet Life of John Wright', in *John Wright (1830-1915): Grandfather of West Coast Architecture*, Victoria: Maltwood Art Museum and Gallery, 1990; Segger and Franklin, *Victoria*, pp. 214-5; Gregson, *Victoria*, p. 37; Harold Kirker, *California's Architectural Frontier: Style and Tradition in the Nineteenth Century*, rev. ed., Santa Barbara: Peregrine Smith, 1973, p. 94.

57 Stuart Underhill, *The Iron Church: 1860-1985*, Victoria: Braemar Books, 1984, pp. 1-16; Segger and Franklin, *Victoria*, pp. 236-9.

58 Victoria *Union*, 7 December 1860; cited in Segger and Franklin, *Victoria*, p. 237.

59 Cited in Underhill, *Iron Church*, p. 4. Slater's design was published by the Ecclesiological Society in 1856 in *Instrumenta Ecclesiastica*; see George L. Hersey, *High Victorian Gothic: A Study in Associationism*, Baltimore: Johns Hopkins University Press, 1972, pp. 179-82; Stefan Muthesius, *The High Victorian Movement in Architecture 1850-1870*, London: Routledge and Kegan Paul, 1972, pp. 199-201.

60 *Planned Restoration of the Synagogue of Congregation Emanuel*, Victoria, n.d., [p. 1]. See also Martin Levin, 'The Founding and Restoration of Canada's Oldest Surviving Synagogue: A Different Jewish History', *Canadian Jewish Historical Society Journal*, 8:1, 1984, pp. 1-11; Edward Mills

and Leslie Maitland, 'Congregation Emanuel Temple, 1461 Blanshard Street, Victoria, British Columbia', Agenda paper, Historic Sites and Monuments Board of Canada, 1979; Cyril Edel Leonoff, 'Victoria, Vancouver Island: Birth of a Jewish Community and Erection of a Tabernacle of God', *Western States Jewish History*, 24:4, July 1992, pp. 324-43. Segger and Franklin, *Victoria*, pp. 226-7; Sheldon Levitt, Lynn Milstone, and Sidney T. Tenenbaum, *Treasures of a People: The Synagogues of Canada*, Toronto: Lester & Orpen Dennys, 1985, pp. 36-7.

61 *Minute Book 1862-1886*, Congregation Emanuel, Victoria, PABC, 11 January 1863, p. 9; cited in Leonoff, 'Birth of a Jewish Community', p. 331.

62 Stuart E. Rosenberg, *The Jewish Community in Canada. Volume I: A History*, Toronto: McClelland and Stewart, 1970, p. 42; cited in Mills and Maitland, 'Congregation Emanuel Temple', p. 19.

63 David Chuenyan Lai, *The Forbidden City Within Victoria*, Victoria: Orca, 1991, pp. 2-8, 119-22, 149-51; *This Old Town*, p. 73.

64 Judith Stricker, *Richard Carr House—A History*, Victoria: Heritage Conservation Branch, n.d., pp. 1-21; Robert W. Baxter and the Wade Williams Partnership, *Richard Carr Residence: Exterior Architectural Analysis*, Victoria, 1984; Segger and Franklin, *Victoria*, pp. 182-3; *This Old House: An Inventory of Residential Heritage*, Victoria: City of Victoria, n.d., p. 22; Mills, *Architectural Trends in Victoria*, I, pp. 135-41.

65 Emily Carr, *The Book of Small*, Toronto: Clarke Irwin, 1966, pp. 8, 10.

66 Stricker, *Carr House*, p. 23. The author of the study may also be in error—referring, perhaps, to Douglas fir.

67 Baxter et al., *Carr Residence*, p. 6.

68 Bulwer-Lytton to Douglas, 31 July 1858, cited in Frances M. Woodward, 'The Influence of the Royal Engineers on the Development of British Columbia', *BC Studies*, 24, Winter 1974-5, p. 14.

69 Entry by Dennis F.K. Madill on Moody in *Canadian Encyclopedia*, III, pp. 1385-6; Cotton, *Mansions*, p. 19.

70 For the work of the Royal Engineers, see Beth Hill, *Sappers: The Royal Engineers in British Columbia*, Ganges, B.C: Horsdal & Schubart, 1987; Woodward, 'Royal Engineers', pp. 3-37; Barry V. Downs, 'The Royal Engineers in British Columbia', *Canadian Collector*, 11:3, May-June 1976, pp. 42-6; Frederick William Howay, *The Work of the Royal Engineers in British Columbia*, Victoria: Wolfenden, 1910.

71 Moody to Arthur Blackwood, 1 February 1859; cited in Hill, *Sappers*, p. 43.

72 Jack David Scott, *Once in the Royal City: The Heritage of New Westminster*, North Vancouver: Whitecap Books, 1985, p. 9. See also Alan Woodland, *New Westminster: The Early Years 1858-1898*, New Westminster: Nunaga, 1973.

73 D. Wallace Duthie, *A Bishop in the Rough*, London: Smith, Elder & Co., 1909; cited in Hill, *Sappers*, p. 46.

74 Downs, 'Engineers', p. 46.

75 Downs, 'Engineers', p. 44.

76 G.E. Mills, 'Early Court Houses of British Columbia', in Margaret Carter, comp., *Early Canadian Court Houses*, Ottawa: Parks Canada, 1983, pp. 171, 174, 179; *The Court House of New Westminster*, New Westminster: Heritage

Preservation Foundation of New Westminster and the BC Heritage Trust, n.d.

77 Downs, 'Engineers', p. 44; Scott, *Royal City*, p. 50.

78 Cotton, *Mansions*, pp. 19-20.

79 Moody to Douglas, 18 May 1859; cited in Cotton, *Mansions*, p. 21.

80 Baynes to his wife, 6 October 1859, cited in Cotton, *Mansions*, p. 23.

81 Cotton, *Mansions*, pp. 19-29, 34-5.

82 Victoria *Colonist*, 11 November 1864; cited in Cotton, *Mansions*, p. 27.

83 Downs, *Sacred Places*, p. 88; Downs, 'Engineers', p. 43; Scott, *Royal City*, p. 25. See also *Sapperton, New Westminster: A Walking Tour Through History*, New Westminster: Heritage Preservation Society, n.d.

84 Barry M. Gough, 'The Character of the British Columbia Frontier', *BC Studies*, 32, Winter 1976-7, pp. 28-40.

85 *Forging a New Hope: Struggles and Dreams, 1848-1948 . . . A Pioneer Study of Hope, Flood, and Laidlaw*, Hope: Hope and District Historical Society, 1984; T.W. Paterson, *Fraser Canyon*, British Columbia Ghost Town Series, No. 3, Langley: Sunfire, 1985, pp. 52-76; Bruce Ramsey, *Ghost Towns of British Columbia*, Vancouver: Mitchell Press, 1963, pp. 6-10.

86 Downs, *Sacred Places*, pp. 144-7; Downs, 'Engineers', pp. 44-5; *Forging a New Hope*, p. 33; Hill, *Sappers*, p. 157; Ronnenberg, 'John Wright' (not paginated).

87 *Forging a New Hope*, p. 33.

88 Cited in Downs, *Sacred Places*, p. 144.

89 Harold Kalman and Douglas Richardson, 'Building for Transportation in the Nineteenth Century', *JCAH*, 3:1-2, Fall 1976, p. 28; Hill, *Sappers*, pp. 96-113; Ormsby, *British Columbia*, pp. 187-9.

90 Columbia Mission, *Annual Report*, 1862, p. 18; cited in Hill, *Sappers*, p. 101.

91 Hill, *Sappers*, pp. 114-44.

92 Art Downs, *Wagon Road North*, rev. ed., Surrey: Foremost Publishing, 1969; Gordon R. Elliott, *Barkerville, Quesnel and the Cariboo Gold Rush*, 2nd ed., Vancouver: Douglas and McIntyre, 1978; Robin Skelton, *They Call It the Cariboo*, Victoria: Sono Nis Press, 1980; Richard Wright and Rochelle Wright, *Cariboo Mileposts*, Vancouver: Mitchell Press, 1972.

93 All are illustrated in Skelton, *Cariboo*; for Mucho Oro see also Downs, *Wagon Road*, p. 16.

94 Downs, *Wagon Road*, p. 61; Fred W. Ludditt, *Barkerville Days*, Vancouver: Mitchell Press, 1969, p. 66.

95 Published in the *Cariboo Sentinel*; cited in Downs, *Wagon Road*, p. 61.

96 Ludditt, *Barkerville Days*, p. 102.

97 Skelton, *Cariboo*, p. 60. For Barkerville, see Ludditt, *Barkerville Days*; Bruce Ramsay, *Barkerville: A Guide to the Fabulous Cariboo Gold Camp*, 2nd ed., Vancouver: Mitchell Press, 1966; Richard Thomas Wright, *Discover Barkerville: A Gold Rush Adventure*, Vancouver: Special Interest Publications, 1984; Lorraine Harris, *Barkerville: The Town That Gold Built*, Surrey: Hancock House, 1984; Alastair W. Kerr, 'The Restoration of Historic Barkerville', *Canadian*

Collector, 11:3, May-June 1976, pp. 47-50; Louis LeBourdais, 'Billy Barker of Barkerville', *British Columbia Historical Quarterly*, 1:3, July 1937, pp. 165-70.

98 Wright, *Barkerville*, pp. 60-1.

99 *Cariboo Sentinel*, 22 September 1868; cited in Elliott, *Barkerville*, pp. 37-8.

100 Cited in Ramsey, *Barkerville*, p. 62; see also Joan Weir, *Canada's Gold Rush Church: A History of St Saviour's Church in Barkerville, British Columbia*: Anglican Diocese of Cariboo, 1986; Downs, *Sacred Places*, pp. 118-23; John de Visser and Harold Kalman, *Pioneer Churches*, Toronto: McClelland and Stewart, 1976, pp. 162-3, 179-81.

101 Michael R. Booth, 'Gold Rush Theatre: The Theatre Royal, Barkerville, British Columbia', *Northwest Pacific Quarterly*, 51:3, July 1960, pp. 97-102.

102 Kerr, 'Restoration'; *Barkerville Historic Town, British Columbia, Canada*, brochure, Victoria: Ministry of Municipal Affairs, Recreation and Cuture, n.d.

103 Wills J. West, 'Staging and Stage Hold-Ups in the Cariboo', *British Columbia Historical Quarterly*, 12, 1948, pp. 188-9.

104 Murphy Shewchuk, 'Roadhouses of the Cariboo', *Beautiful British Columbia*, 24, Spring 1983, pp. 2-15. Mile 0 changed, however, from Lillooet, to Yale, and then to Ashcroft and Cache Creek; see Wright, *Cariboo Mileposts*, pp. 10-11.

105 Judith Stricker, *Cottonwood House: A Documented History*, Victoria: Heritage Conservation Branch, 1982; Henry Pejril, 'Stabliization at Cottonwood House Historic Park', *Datum*, 5:4, 1980, pp. 3-4.

106 Ebenezer Robson, in *Western Methodist Recorder*, 6:6, December 1904; cited in Linda Eversole, 'Hat Creek Ranch', unpublished manuscript, Heritage Conservation Branch, 1981. See also Nicholas R. Bawlf and Harold Kalman, *Hat Creek Master Plan*, Victoria, 1982; Dorothy Blakey Smith, 'Hat Creek Ranch', unpublished manuscript, 1966, in Provincial Archives of British Columbia; Donald Tarasoff, 'Hat Creek House', Heritage Conservation Branch, 1979; Linda Parke, 'Hat Creek House... Cariboo Heritage', *Heritage West*, 4:1, Winter 1979-80, pp. 3-5.

107 Tarasoff, 'Hat Creek', p. 4.

108 Gregory E.G. Thomas, 'The British Columbia Ranching Frontier: 1858-1896', MA thesis, University of British Columbia, 1976; Skelton, *Cariboo*, pp. 176-7.

109 Ted Mills and B.A. Humphreys, 'O'Keefe Ranch, Vernon, British Columbia', Screening Paper, Historic Sites and Monuments Board of Canada, Ottawa, 1973; John Stephenson, 'O'Keefe Report', Historic Parks and Sites Branch, Victoria, 1974; Stan McClean, *The History of O'Keefe Ranch*, Vernon, 1984; Mary Moon, 'The O'Keefe Ranch', *BC Motorist*, 12:2, March-April 1973, pp. 46-6; *O'Keefe Ranch*, brochure, n.p., n.d.

110 Victoria *Colonist*, 11 August 1888, p. 4; cited in Stephenson, 'O'Keefe Report', p. 5.

111 Victoria *Colonist*, 22 October 1882; cited in Mills and Humphreys, 'O'Keefe Ranch', p. D.10.

112 de Visser and Kalman, *Pioneer Churches*, pp. 175-6, 179-81; Downs, *Sacred Places*, pp. 138, 143.

113 Nina G. Woolliams, *Cattle Ranch: The Story of the Douglas Lake Cattle Company*, Vancouver: Douglas and McIntyre, 1979.

114 Margaret A. Ormsby, 'A Study of the Okanagan Valley of British Columbia', MA Thesis, University of British Columbia, 1931, p. 49; cited in Mills, 'O'Keefe Ranch', p. D.1.

115 Margaret Whitehead, *The Cariboo Mission: A History of the Oblates*, Victoria: Sono Nis Press, 1981, pp. 13, 17.

116 Downs, *Sacred Places*, p. 30; John Veillette and Gary White, *Early Indian Village Churches: Wooden Frontier Architecture in British Columbia*, Vancouver: University of British Columbia Press, 1977, pp. 146-7; Fr. Modeste Demers and Fr. François Blanchet, *Notices and Voyages of the Famed Quebec Mission to the Pacific Northwest*, translated by Carl Landerholm, Portland: Oregon Historical Society, 1956.

117 F.M. Buckland, *Ogopogo's Vigil: A History of Kelowna and the Okanagan* (1946), reprinted Kelowna: Okanagan Historical Society, 1966; Primrose Upton, *The History of Okanagan Mission: A Centennial Retrospect*, Kelowna: Okanagan Mission Central Committee, 1958; H.C.S. Collett, 'The Restoration and Rededication of the Father Pandosy Mission', in *The 22nd Report of the Okanagan Historical Society*, 1958, pp. 9-14; de Visser and Kalman, *Pioneer Churches*, pp. 160-1, 177.

118 Buckland, *Ogopogo's Vigil*, p. 28; cited with variations in Upton, *Okanagan Mission*, p. 8.

119 Whitehead, *Cariboo Mission*; Downs, *Sacred Places*, pp. 148, 153.

120 Thomas A. Lascelles, OMI, *Mission on the Inlet: St Paul's Indian Catholic church, North Vancouver, B.C., 1863-1984*, privately printed, c. 1984; Veillette and White, *Churches*, pp. 37-9; Downs, *Sacred Places*, pp. 133, 136; Harold Kalman and John Roaf, *Exploring Vancouver 2*, Vancouver: University of British Columbia Press, 1978, p. 238.

121 Downs, *Sacred Places*, pp. 138-41; Veillette and White, *Churches*, pp. 90-4; Margaret Whitehead, ed., *They Call Me Father: Memoirs of Father Nicolas Coccola*, Vancouver: University of British Columbia Press, 1988.

122 Downs, *Sacred Places*, pp. 154, 158-9; Veillette and White, *Churches*, pp. 57-9; Jean Usher, *William Duncan of Metlakatla*, Publications in History, No. 5, Ottawa: National Museums of Canada, 1974.

123 Cited in Downs, *Sacred Places*, p. 158.

124 Downs, *Sacred Places*, pp. 158-62; Veillette and White, *Churches*, p. 60.

125 Ormsby, *British Columbia*, p. 274.

BIBLIOGRAPHIES
ON THE HISTORY OF
CANADIAN ARCHITECTURE

ALLAN, NORMAN R., 'Some Recent Notes on Manitoba Architectural Bibliography', *SSAC Bulletin* 11:2, June 1986, pp. 9-10.

Federal Heritage Buildings Review Office/Bureau d'examen des édificies fédéraux à valeur patrimoniale. Indexes to Reports. Ottawa.

KALMAN, HAROLD, 'Recent Literature on the History of Canadian Architecture', *Journal of the Society of Architectural Historians*, 31:4, December 1972, pp. 315-23.

KERR, ALASTAIR, 'The Growth of Architectural History in British Columbia', *SSAC Bulletin*, 10:1, March 1985, pp. 21-4.

LERNER, LOREN R., and MARY F. WILLIAMSON, *Art and Architecture in Canada: A Bibliography and Guide to the Literature to 1981/Art et architecture au Canada: Bibliographie et guide de la documentation jusqu'en 1981*, 2 vols, Toronto: University of Toronto Press, 1991.

'Newfoundland Architecture: A Bibliography', *SSAC Bulletin*, 8:2, June 1983, p. 20.

1993 Bibliography/Bibliographie 1993, Manuscripts and Publications, Research Divisions, National Historic Parks and Sites Branch, Parks Canada, Ottawa, 1993.

RICHARDSON, DOUGLAS, ed., *Architecture in Ontario: A Select Bibliography on Architectural Conservation and Architecture*, compiled by Patricia Crawford, Philip Monk, and Marianna Wood [Toronto: Ministry of Culture and Recreation,] 1976.

SIMMINS, GEOFFREY, *Bibliography of Canadian Architecture/Bibliographie d'architecture canadienne*, Ottawa: Society for the Study of Architecture in Canada, 1992.

WADE, JILL, *Manitoba Architecture to 1940: A Bibliography*, Winnipeg: University of Manitoba Press, 1978.

GLOSSARY

ACROTERION An ornamental projection at the corner, or peak, of a roof; or the base that supports the ornament.

ANTA, ANTAE, ANTIS In CLASSICAL architecture, an *anta* is the exposed end of a wall, usually decorated with a PILASTER; *antae* are two adjacent and aligned wall ends; and COLUMNS between the *antae* are described as being *in antis*.

ANTHEMION In CLASSICAL architecture, an ornamental form based on the honeysuckle or palmette.

APSE In a church, a semicircular or polygonal projection at the altar (usually east) end, beyond the SANCTUARY.

ARCADE A row of ARCHES.

ARCH A form of curved construction, usually made from MASONRY, that spans an opening in a wall and distributes the weight above it on the walls or PIERS at either side.

ARCH-AND-SPANDREL MOTIF A wall treatment similar to a PIER-AND-SPANDREL MOTIF, but in which the piers are joined at the top by ARCHES.

ARCHITRAVE A horizontal BEAM or LINTEL, that rests on COLUMNS or PIERS; or the lowest portion of an ENTABLATURE; or a decorative moulding around a door, a window, or an ARCH.

ARCHIVOLT One of several parallel curved, and often decorated, MOULDINGS on the inside of an ARCHED opening; a curved ARCHITRAVE.

ASHLAR Stone that has been cut square and DRESSED.

ATRIUM In CLASSICAL architecture, an interior courtyard that is open to the weather. In contemporary architecture, a significant interior space, often skylighted, used for circulation.

ATTIC The top floor of a building, often reduced in height and unfinished; in CLASSICAL architecture, a storey that is inserted within the ENTABLATURE.

BALDACHIN A canopy above a church altar, often supported on COLUMNS.

BALUSTRADE A railing composed of POSTS (balusters) and a handrail.

BARGEBOARD Boards or other decorative woodwork fixed to the edges or projecting rafters of a GABLED roof. Sometimes called gingerbread.

BARREL VAULT A MASONRY VAULT in the form of a semicircular ARCH.

BASTION In military architecture, an angular and pointed projection, often diamond-shaped and usually located at a corner, that enabled gunners to defend the ramparts and CURTAINS of a fortification.

BATTEN A narrow vertical strip of wood, placed over joints of wider boards to protect the joints from the weather; the combination is called board-and-batten construction. *See also* SIDING.

BATTLEMENT A notched PARAPET, originally intended for defence; the notches are called battlements or crenellations. Hence a battlemented parapet is also known as a crenellated parapet.

BAY A window, door, or other opening, comprising one visual division of an elevation or a façade.

BEAM A principal horizontal structural member.

BELLCAST An EAVE that curves, or flares, outward like the flanges of a bell.

BELT COURSE In a MASONRY wall, a distinctive COURSE that usually projects slightly and may be decorated, forming a distinct horizontal band; also called a string course.

BOARD AND BATTEN See SIDING.

BOSS In MASONRY construction, a projecting ornament, often located at the intersection of two components.

BROACH SPIRE A polygonal spire set on top of a square tower; the transitional elements are called broaches.

BRACKET A member, often triangular in form, that projects from a wall or other vertical surface and supports another component, such as an EAVE.

BUTTRESS A vertical strip of heavy masonry applied to the wall of a building to provide structural reinforcement against lateral forces (as from a VAULT or an ARCH). When the buttress is a free-standing PIER attached to the wall by one or more arches, it is called a flying buttress.

CAMPANIFORM In the shape of a bell.

CANOPY A horizontal, sloped, or arched surface that projects from a wall—usually over a door or a window—to provide shelter from the weather.

CANTILEVER A BEAM or other horizontal member that projects beyond a vertical support and is unsupported at one end.

CAPITAL The decorative head of a COLUMN, PILASTER, PIER, or other vertical support.

CAPONIER In military architecture, a relatively small projection that provides a firing position, similar to a DEMI-BASTION but covered.

CARTOUCHE A decorated panel, often curvilinear in form.

CASEMENT A window that opens by being hinged along one side.

CHAMFER A sloping or bevelled edge.

CHANCEL In a church, the SANCTUARY at the altar (usually east) end, used by the clergy.

CHANNEL A groove, often decorative.

CHOIR In a church, the portion between the NAVE and the CHANCEL, used by the choir for singing.

CHEVRON V-shaped decoration.

CLADDING The external, non-structural material that protects the structural wall or FRAME from the weather.

CLAPBOARD See SIDING.

CLASSICAL Derived from the architecture of ancient Greece or Rome.

CLERESTORY A row of windows located near the top of the wall of a NAVE or room or other space.

CLOCHER A belltower on a church (from the French *cloche*, or bell).

COFFER A recessed decorative panel in a ceiling, VAULT, or dome.

COLONETTE See POST.

COLUMN See POST.

CONCRETE A mixture of cement, aggregate (usually sand and gravel), and water that hardens and attains great compressive strength. When used structurally it is usually reinforced by being poured around steel rods or mesh to give it tensile strength as well. Concrete may be poured into forms (usually wood) directly in place in a structure, or it may be precast away from the site and then placed into position. Concrete blocks are precast and used as building blocks.

CORBEL A kind of BRACKET composed of a single projecting block, or of several graduated projecting courses of MASONRY, providing a ledge.

CORNICE The uppermost portion of an ENTABLATURE; often used to indicate the projecting horizontal element (to shed rainwater and for decoration) at the top of a building, or a similar feature (often in plaster) at the top of the wall of a room.

COUNTERSCARP In military architecture, the outer wall of a ditch.

COURSE A single horizontal row of brick, stone, or other walling material.

COVE A concave MOULDING or recess, usually where a ceiling adjoins a wall.

CRENELLATED See BATTLEMENT.

CRÉPI A lime plaster used as a coating on stone buildings, particularly in New France, to protect the wall and the mortar joints from the weather.

CRESTING A decorative rail, a row of FINIALS, or another feature at the top of a building, often along the RIDGE of the roof.

CROCKET An upwardly projecting repeated decorative element, often along spires and GABLES in Gothic Revival architecture.

CUPOLA A feature at the top of a roof, usually dome-shaped and opened up by windows or COLUMNS.

CURTAIN In military architecture, a wall.

CURTAIN WALL An exterior wall that is fastened to a FRAME and protects the building from the weather; it has no structural function, and supports only its own weight.

DADO Panelling, usually wood, that is applied to the lower portion of a wall, above a baseboard.

DEMI-BASTION In military architecture, a BASTION composed of only two angled faces.

DENTIL A small, tooth-like square block, used in a row as a decorative feature in a CORNICE.

DORMER A window that projects from a sloping roof, with a small roof of its own.

DOVETAIL A joint of two interlocking blocks that flare outwards in the shape of the tail of a dove.

DRESSED Of stone: cut square on all sides and smoothed on the face.

DRIP MOULDING A projecting MOULDING that is shaped to allow rainwater to drip off its edge, away from the wall below it.

DRUM A cylindrical MASONRY component that forms one unit of a COLUMN; also a cylindrical STAGE below a dome.

EARTHWORKS In military architecture, a defensive structure constructed of earth.

EAVE The projecting edge of a roof.

ECHINUS A convex projecting moulding near the top of a CAPITAL.

ENGAGED Of a COLUMN or PILASTER: attached to a wall.

ENTABLATURE The horizontal component, usually decorated, that lies directly above a COLUMN or other support; in CLASSICAL architecture, the entablature is composed of an ARCHITRAVE, a FRIEZE, and a CORNICE.

FASCIA A plain horizontal band (i.e. a vertical surface), as in a board below an EAVE.

FINIAL An ornamental projection at the top of a GABLE, roof, or other high component.

FLÈCHE A slender spire atop a tower; French for 'arrow'.

FLUTES Vertical grooves on the shaft of a COLUMN or other support.

FRAME The structural skeleton of a building; as an adjective, referring to timber structure.

FRIEZE The middle portion of an ENTABLATURE, or any decorated horizontal band.

FRONTISPIECE The central portion of the main façade.

GABLE The triangular portion of wall beneath the end of a GABLED ROOF.

GABLED ROOF A roof that slopes on two sides.

GAMBREL ROOF A roof that has a double slope, with the lower slope steeper and longer than the upper one; a MANSARD ROOF.

HALF-TIMBERED In early building, a wall constructed of timber with the spaces between the members filled with MASONRY (in French, *colombage pierroté*); since the late nineteenth century, a wall that imitates half-timbering, even if the timber members are not structural.

HAMMER-DRESSED Stone that is DRESSED with a lightly textured surface.

HIPPED ROOF A roof that slopes on four sides.

HOOD MOULDING A MOULDING located at the top of a window to deflect rainwater.

IMPOST A MOULDING, BRACKET, or MASONRY course in a wall that supports the end of an ARCH.

IN ANTIS See ANTA.

JOIST A secondary horizontal structural member, usually supported by a BEAM at each end, and itself supporting a floor, ceiling, or roof.

KEYSTONE The wedge-shaped central block, or VOUSSOIR, at the apex of an ARCH.

KING POST In a roof TRUSS, the vertical member that extends from the centre of the principal beam (called the TIE BEAM) to the underside of the RIDGE.

LANTERN A windowed superstructure at the top of a roof or dome; a small CUPOLA.

LINHAY In Newfoundland, a row of utility rooms across the rear of a house.

LINTEL The horizontal supporting member at the top of a door or window.

LOGGIA A gallery that is open on one or more sides, often with an ARCADE.

LOOPHOLE In military architecture, a narrow hole in a wall through which ordnance or arms can be fired.

LOZENGE Diamond-shaped ornament.

MANSARD ROOF A roof that has a double slope, with the lower slope steeper and longer than the upper one; a GAMBREL ROOF. Named after the seventeenth-century French architect François Mansart.

MASONRY Stone, brick, concrete, tile, or any other non-organic and non-metallic building material.

METOPE In CLASSICAL architecture, the panel between TRIGLYPHS in a Doric FRIEZE.

MORTISE In a timber connection, a slot into which a TENON is inserted.

MOULDING A shaped decorative element, usually a horizontal band, that projects slightly from the surface of a wall.

MULLION A thin upright member within a window or between adjacent windows.

MUTULE In CLASSICAL architecture, a block-like decorative element on the SOFFIT of a Doric CORNICE.

NAVE The principal room or space in a church, which accommodates the congregation.

OGEE A double curve, usually used to describe an ARCH or a MOULDING.

PALISADE A row of logs or poles inserted upright into the ground and used as a wall or fence.

PALLADIAN Related to the buildings of the sixteenth-century Italian architect Andrea Palladio, or to the eighteenth-century English revival of his style.

PARAPET A portion of wall that projects above a roof.

PARTERRE In landscape gardening, a formal area of planting, usually square or rectangular.

PAVILION An articulated portion of the façade of a building, often higher than, or projecting forward from, the rest. If it is in the centre, it is called a FRONTISPIECE.

PEDIMENT The triangular end of a GABLE, or a triangular ornamental element resembling it, defined by a MOULDING (or series of mouldings) along its three edges.

PENDENTIVE The curved and sloping surfaces beneath a dome that mark the transition from the circle of the dome (or its DRUM) to the square of the supports.

PIANO NOBILE In Italian, the principal storey, usually above the ground floor.

PIER See POST.

PIER-AND-SPANDREL MOTIF A wall treatment that emphasizes the play between vertical PIERS and horizontal SPANDRELS.

PILASTER See POST.

PILLAR See POST.

PLATE In wood FRAME construction, a horizontal component that connects the tops or bottoms of POSTS or BEAMS.

PLINTH A block used as the base of a COLUMN or other upright support.

PORTE-COCHÈRE A covered entrance porch for vehicles.

PORTICO A covered porch, often consisting of COLUMNS supporting a PEDIMENT.

POST A generic word for any upright support that has several variants. It is used either in a general sense (e.g. POST-AND-BEAM construction) or in specific reference to a timber support. Pillar is a somewhat archaic word synonymous with post. A pier is a post of square or rectangular section, usually of MASONRY. A column is a post of circular section; a steel or iron member used vertically is also called a column. A colonette is a small column. A pilaster is a shallow rectangular upright support set into a wall and used mainly as decoration.

POST-AND-BEAM A building system that emphasizes the regular use of vertical and horizontal (or slightly sloping) structural members.

PROSTYLE Characterized by free-standing columns that stand forward from a wall (contrasted with columns *in ANTIS*).

PURLIN In timber roof construction, a secondary horizontal component parallel to the RIDGE and supported at each end by a RAFTER.

QUATREFOIL A decorative form characterized by four lobes.

QUOIN One of a series of blocks or block-like components at the corner of a wall; in a MASONRY wall, its function is to reinforce the corner.

RAFTER In timber roof construction, a principal sloping component that runs from the wall PLATE to the RIDGE.

RAVELIN In military architecture, a freestanding triangular outwork.

RETABLE In a church, a decorative wall treatment or screen behind the altar; also called a reredos.

RETICULATED Patterned, often in a net-like design.

REVEAL The surface of a window or door opening; its width is usually the thickness of the wall.

RIDGE The apex of a roof, usually horizontal; or the structural component at the top of a roof.

ROUNDEL A circular panel or decorative component.

RUBBLE Rough, uncoursed stonework.

RUSTICATION Rough-surfaced or heavily textured stonework.

SACRISTY In a church, a room for the storage of sacred objects and for the carrying-out of certain church activities.

SANCTUARY In a church, the area around the principal altar. In a synagogue, the NAVE.

SASH In a window, the wood or metal frame that holds the glass.

SCOOP A hollowed-out half-log, used on a roof as a channel to carry away rainwater.

SEGMENTAL ARCH An ARCH whose profile comprises an arc smaller than a semicircle.

SHED ROOF A roof with only one slope; also used to describe the roof of a DORMER window if it has only one slope.

SHIPLAP See SIDING.

SIDELIGHT A window beside a door, forming part of the door unit.

SIDING A facing material, or CLADDING, applied to the outside of a wood-framed building to make it weatherproof. Sometimes called weatherboarding. Several kinds of wood siding are common in Canada. Shiplap (or drop siding) consists of horizontally laid boards with notched edges that make an overlapping joint; the face of each board is parallel to the plane of the wall. Clapboard (or bevelled siding) consists of bevelled boards laid horizontally and overlapping at the top and bottom; the face of each board is oblique to the wall. Board-and-batten siding is composed of vertically applied boards whose joints are covered by narrow strips (BATTENS). Shingles may also be used as siding, and materials other than wood are often employed. Composition siding is made of asphalt, asbestos, or synthetic materials, often imitating brick or shingle. Metal siding (usually composed of aluminum or galvanized steel) and vinyl siding are also used, often imitating wood.

SILL A horizontal member at the bottom of a wall (sometimes called a sill PLATE) or a window.

SOFFIT The underside of an EAVE, BEAM, or other component.

SPANDREL The portion of wall between the top of one window and the window SILL above it; or the roughly triangular surface between two adjacent arches.

STAGE One tier in a tower or other vertically composed structure.

STRING COURSE A BELT COURSE.

STRINGER A BEAM; also a sloping structural member that supports a staircase.

STUD In timber construction, one of a series of vertical supports, or POSTS.

TENON In a timber connection, a projecting tongue that is inserted into a MORTISE.

TERRA COTTA Fired clay (literally 'baked earth') commonly shaped in a mould and frequently glazed after firing.

TERREPLEIN In military architecture, the flat roof of a fortification, on which ordnance was mounted.

TIE BEAM In a roof TRUSS, a principal beam that spans from one wall to the other.

TRANSEPT In a church, a projecting space that is perpendicular to the NAVE; the nave and transepts intersect at the crossing to produce a cruciform plan.

TREFOIL A decorative form characterized by three lobes.

TRIFORIUM In a church, a passage or gallery above the NAVE arcade and below the CLERESTORY.

TRIGLYPH In CLASSICAL architecture, one of a series of raised ornamental panels in a Doric FRIEZE that consist of three vertical bands; triglyphs alternate with METOPES.

TRUSS A structural framework, made of either timber or metal, that is composed of individual members fastened together in a triangular arrangement.

TYMPANUM The panel, usually semicircular, located between the underside of an ARCH and the top of a doorway within the arch; also the triangular space enclosed by a PEDIMENT.

VAULT An arched ceiling constructed of MASONRY materials; the undersurface, or SOFFIT, is usually curved. If the vault is generated from a series of pointed, rather than round, arches, it is called a groin vault.

VOLUTE In CLASSICAL architecture, the spiral ornament on a CAPITAL.

VOUSSOIR One of the wedge-shaped masonry blocks out of which an ARCH or VAULT is composed. The central voussoir is the KEYSTONE.

INDEX
OF CANADIAN BUILDINGS

Saskatchewan

468